ISBN 978-1-61619-351-5

Lawbook Exchange edition 2013

The quality of this reprint is equivalent to the quality of the original work.

THE LAWBOOK EXCHANGE, LTD.
33 Terminal Avenue
Clark, New Jersey 07066-1321

Please see our website for a selection of our other publications and fine facsimile reprints of classic works of legal history:
www.lawbookexchange.com

Library of Congress Cataloging-in-Publication Data

Jameson, John Alexander, 1824-1890.
A treatise on constitutional conventions : their history, powers and modes of proceeding / by John Alexander Jameson ; With a new introduction by John R. Vile, Middle Tennessee State University. -- Lawbook exchange edition.
pages cm
Includes bibliographical references and index.
ISBN 978-1-61619-351-5 (hardcover : alk. paper) -- ISBN 1-61619-351-4 (hardcover : alk. paper)
1. Constitutional conventions--United States. 2. Constitutional conventions--United States--States. 3. Jameson, John Alexander, 1824-1890. I. Vile, John R. John Alexander Jameson's enduring constitutional legacy. II. Title.
KF4555.J3 2013
342.7302'92--dc23

2013007261

Printed in the United States of America on acid-free paper

A TREATISE

ON

CONSTITUTIONAL CONVENTIONS;

THEIR

HISTORY, POWERS, AND MODES OF PROCEEDING.

BY

JOHN ALEXANDER JAMESON, LL. D.
LATE JUDGE OF THE SUPERIOR COURT OF CHICAGO, ILLINOIS.

Respublica est res populi; populus autem non omnis hominum cœtus quoque modo congregatus, sed cœtus multitudinis juris consensu et utilitatis communione sociatus. — CICERO, *de Repub.*

They that go about by disobedience to do no more than reforme the commonwealth shall find that they do thereby destroy it. — HOBBES, *Leviathan.*

Fourth Edition,

REVISED, CORRECTED, AND ENLARGED.

With a new introduction by
John R. Vile
Middle Tennessee State University, Murfreesboro, TN

THE LAWBOOK EXCHANGE, LTD.
Clark, New Jersey

INTRODUCTION

JOHN ALEXANDER JAMESON'S ENDURING CONSTITUTIONAL LEGACY

It is perhaps significant that the fourth, and last, revision of John Alexander Jameson's editions of his monumental *Treatise on Constitutional Conventions* was issued in 1887, the year that marked the centennial of the writing of the U.S. Constitution by a Convention that had met in Philadelphia.[1] More than 125 years later, Jameson's work remains a legal landmark, notable not simply as the first treatise in this area but also for its continuing insights into issues of constitutional change at both the state and national levels. Although it no longer occupies the field as it once did,[2]

---

[1] The first edition of Jameson's work, *The Constitutional Convention Its History, Powers, and Modes of Proceedings*, was published by Scribner of New York in 1867. The second edition, published by E.B. Myers in Chicago in 1869, was titled *A Treatise on the Principles of American Constitutional Law and Legislation, The Constitutional Convention: Its History, Powers, and Modes of Proceeding*. The third edition published by Callaghan and Company in Chicago was titled *The Constitutional Convention: Its History, Powers and Modes of Proceedings*, and the fourth edition, reprinted here, was published by the same company in 1887 and had the same title.

On a personal note, Jameson's work was called to the author's attention early in his career by Professor Kermit L. Hall, a prolific author and gifted administrator, whose untimely death, remains a major loss for the study of the American judiciary and constitutional law.

[2] Subsequent works, none of which compares in length and scope to Jameson's include: Walter F. Dodd, *The Revision and Amendment of State Constitutions* (Baltimore, MD: Johns Hopkins Press, 1910); Roger Sherman Hoar, *Constitutional Conventions: Their Nature, Powers, and Limitations* (Boston: Little, Brown and Company, 1917); Elmer E. Cornwell, Jr., Jay S. Goodman, and Wayne R. Swanson, *Constitutional Conventions: The Politics of Revision* (New York: National Municipal League, 1974) and *State Constitutional Conventions: The Politics of the Revision Process in Seven States* (New York: Praeger, 1975), and G. Alan Tarr, Robert F. Williams (and for vol. 2, Frank P. Grad) *State Constitutions for the Twenty-first Century*, 3 vols. (Albany, NY: State University of New York Press, 2006).

Jameson's treatise remains the single most comprehensive work on the subject and a fertile source of insights and ideas.

Jameson, who wrote shortly after the ratification of three critical federal amendments from 1865 to 1870,[3] could not have known that 125 years after his death, the nation would have ratified only 12 additional amendments.[4] Nor could he have known that the provision within Article V of the Constitution requiring Congress to call a constitutional convention to propose amendments at the request of two-thirds of the state legislatures, would remain both highly contested and unused.[5]

Because of both these facts, however, his analysis remains more relevant than had it been overwhelmed by a surfeit of additional precedents. Moreover, as a careful writer, Jameson did not simply state conclusions (with which not all scholars agreed), but he carefully explained his rationale for them, thus leaving a

---

[3] The Thirteenth Amendment (1865) permanently eliminated involuntary servitude, except as punishment for a crime; the Fourteenth Amendment (1868) defined U.S. citizenship and guaranteed basic rights of due process, equal protection, and privileges and immunities to all, and the Fifteenth Amendment (1870) prohibited discrimination in voting on the basis of race.

[4] Excellent histories of the constitutional amending process include David E. Kyvig, *Explicit & Authentic Acts: Amending the U.S. Constitution, 1776-1995* (Lawrence, KS: University Press of Kansas, 1996), Richard B. Bernstein with Jerome Agel, *Amending America* (New York: Random House, 1993), Alan P. Grimes, *Democracy and the Amendments to the Constitution* (Lexington, MA: D.C. Heath and Company, 1978); and Kiris E. Palmer, ed, *Constitutional Amendments: 1789 to the Present* (Detroit: Gale Group, 2000). For a recent collection of original source materials see Mark Grossman, *Constitutional Amendments*, 2 vols. (Amemia, NY: Grey House, 2012).

[5] Article V states, in full:

> The Congress, whenever two thirds of both Houses shall deem it necessary, shall propose Amendments to this Constitution, or, on the Application of the Legislatures of two thirds of the several States, shall call a Convention for proposing Amendments, which, in either Case, shall be valid to all Intents and Purposes, as Part of this Constitution, when ratified by the Legislatures of three fourths of the several States, or by Conventions in three fourths thereof, as the one or the other Mode of Ratification may be proposed by the Congress; Provided that no Amendment which may be made prior to the Year One thousand eight hundred and eight shall in any Manner affect the first and fourth Clauses in the Ninth Section of the first Article; and that no State, without its Consent, shall be deprived of its equal Suffrage in the Senate.

virtual treasure trove for those who remain interested in issues of constitutional change.

JAMESON, THE MAN

Jameson was born in Irasburg, Vermont on January 25, 1824 to Thomas Jameson and Martha Gilchrist, but, in a day when individuals often expressed pride in their ethnic heritages, more than one biographer thought it important to emphasize that he came from hearty Scotch-Irish stock.[6] Jameson's father, who was the county's sheriff, subsequently acquired an iron foundry, and apprenticed his son to be an iron moulder. The son, who retained pride in his training, used the occasion of an injury to pursue an education first at an academy in Browington and then at the state University in Burlington where he enrolled in 1842, with the apparent intention of entering the ministry. Overcoming another injury in college, which apparently stimulated an interest in studying medicine, he graduated in 1846, after which he served for four years as director of an academy in Stanstead, Canada. After tutoring at his alma mater, he entered Harvard Law School in 1852, where he spent a year before he moved with a classmate to Chicago, where he was admitted to the bar and became active in establishing the state Republican Party.

Jameson married Eliza Denison, of Royalton, Vermont, in 1855, and they settled in the area of Chicago now known as Hyde Park. In 1865, Jameson was selected as a Judge of the Superior Court of Chicago. He served for three continuous terms from 1865 to 1883, specializing in chancery cases. During this time he issued more than 100 opinions some of which were regarded as landmarks with respect to issues of family law and church governance.[7]

---

[6] See especially Francis Newton Thorpe, *In Memoriam* (Philadelphia: American Academy of Political and Social Science, 1890), pp. 3–4, and J. [otherwise unidentified] "John Alexander Jameson," 1 *Law Mag. Law & Laymen.* (1889–1890) 1.303–304.

[7] Thorpe, p. 20, identifies his most important cases as *Roth v. Roth*, 104 Ill. 35, *Cheney v. Chase* (1888), and *Breit v. Yeaton* (1888).

In his memoriam to Jameson, Francis Newton Thorpe, a noted legal scholar at the University of Pennsylvania who, like him, was deeply interested in state constitutional development, noted that Jameson had a gift for linguistics and appears to have been assembling manuscripts for a book on trusts, which, however, remained unfinished at his death. Thorpe says that Jameson was also one of the founders of the American Academy of Political and Social Science and of the Literary Club of Chicago; the first President of the Prisoners' Aid Association of Illinois; a supporter of the Industrial Training School of Illinois; and president of the village of Hyde Park.[8] In addition, Jameson lectured to classes at the Union College of Law and edited *The American Law Register*.

In his research on constitutional conventions, Jameson collected numerous volumes on the history of various conventions in U.S. history, which he donated to the University of Pennsylvania, where his intention of lecturing was cut short by his unexpected death at home at the age of 67 on June 16, 1890. He was buried in Chicago's Oakwoods Cemetery. Thorpe says that Jameson was a gifted speaker and that his miscellaneous writing included about 500 titles, including an essay entitled "National Sovereignty" that was published by the *Political Science Quarterly* in June of 1890.[9] Among Jameson's most interesting works is a publication, the title of which accurately reflected its theme, called *Responsibilities of American Merchants for the Conversion of the World to Christ*.[10]

MOTIVATION FOR JAMESON'S TREATISE

Jameson helped found the Republican Party in opposition to the expansion of slavery, and he lived at a time of Civil War (1861-1865) during which the Union endured its greatest crisis. Although he typically identified the conventions that had crafted secession constitutions as rebellious bodies and favored Congressional

[8] Thorpe, p. 24.
[9] *Ibid.*, pp. 25–26.
[10] New York: I.W. Brinckerhoff, 1855.

Reconstruction,[11] in the Preface to his *Treatise*, Jameson identified the specific impetus for his own research as a convention (rumored to be influenced by the secessionist "Knights of the Golden Circle") within Illinois in 1862 that expressed the view that it was a sovereign body.[12] Whereas many would have been content to answer such arguments in a single speech or article, Jameson thought that it was important to commence "a study of the Convention as an American institution from its foundation and in all aspects and relations, with a view to ascertain whether the claim of power referred to was warranted either by history or by constitutional principles."[13]

KEY DISTINCTIONS IN JAMESON'S BOOK

One of the primary virtues of Jameson's study was its empirical quality. In the course of his treatise, Jameson examined 192 constitutional conventions that had occurred in American history.[14] Just as Herman Ames, a professor of the University of Pennsylvania (who likely drew from the manuscripts that Jameson had deposited there), would do in compiling the first list of proposed amendments to the U.S. Constitution,[15] so too, Jameson sought to examine each of these conventions for the light they shed

---

[11] Jameson, p. 249.
[12] Jameson, 1887, p. iii.
[13] Ibid., p. iii.
[14] Ibid, Appendix B, pp. 643–655, lists and describes each of these conventions in chronological order.
[15] *The Proposed Amendments to the Constitution of the United States During the First Century of its History*. This was first published in a two-volume report as part of the *Annual Report of the American Historical Association for the Year 1896* (Washington: Government Printing Office, 1897), and subsequently reprinted as a book. It and subsequent compilations of proposed amendments have been compiled in John R. Vile, ed, *Proposed Amendments to the U.S. Constitution, 1787–2001*, 4 vols., with the fourth being a supplement for the years 2001–2010, by The Lawbook Exchange (Clark, New Jersey, 2011). For an issue-by-issue discussion of proposed amendments, see John R. Vile, *Encyclopedia of Constitutional Amendments, Proposed Amendments, and Amending Issues, 1789–2010*, 3rd ed., 2 vols. (Santa Barbara, CA: ABC-CLIO, 2010). This Encyclopedia contains a brief essay on Jameson at 1:258–259.

on constitutional change. Long before historian Gordon Wood traced the evolution of the convention mechanism in his path-breaking work, which chronicled U.S. constitutional history from 1776 to 1789,[16] Jameson sensed that the theory and practice of conventions had undergone a change. At the outset of his book, Jameson accordingly divided conventions into four types. By his classification, the "spontaneous convention" was largely synonymous with a public meeting and the "legislative convention" with a general assembly.

His primary distinction, however, was between the "revolutionary convention" and the "constitutional Convention."[17] The former, sometimes necessary in tumultuous times, was designed to bridge the gap from one form of government to another. A revolutionary convention might thus be exercising ordinary (or extraordinary) legislative powers at the same time that it was crafting a new government. Such conventions had their origins in the English Revolutions of 1660 and 1689 and were adapted to the revolutionary situation that confronted the one-time American colonists when they decided to revolt against Great Britain. Whereas such conventions might of necessity exercise sovereign powers, Jameson thought it was essential to distinguish such bodies from "constitutional conventions," which were created by, and thus subservient, to legislative direction. In Jameson's words, such conventions were "subaltern." As he explained, such a convention "never supplants the existing organization. It never governs. Though called to look into and recommend improvements in the fundamental laws, it *enacts* neither them nor the statute law; and it performs no act of administration."[18]

Jameson's classification might face an immediate objection. As the colonists learned in disputing the powers of the English Parliament, that legislature, or more correctly, "The King (or Queen) in Parliament," claimed to be sovereign. Jameson

---

[16] *The Creation of the American Republic, 1776–1789* (New York: W.W. Norton, 1969). On p. 342, Wood classified the convention mechanism as "an extraordinary invention, the most distinctive institut8ional contribution, it has been said, the American Revolution made to Western politics."

[17] Jameson, pp. 1–12.

[18] Jameson, p. 10.

recognized these differences both in his second chapter on sovereignty and his third on constitutions. He thus distinguished in his third chapter between a constitution, like that in Britain, that was the growth of "organic growth" and one, like that of the U.S., which was what he called "an instrument of evidence."[19] Similarly, Jameson contrasted what he called "Cumulative Constitutions" and "Enacted Constitutions," and "Unwritten Constitutions" and "Written Constitutions."[20] Whereas subsequent critics of the U.S. Constitution have often identified it as too rigid[21] and compared it unfavorably to that of Britain,[22] Jameson distinguished what he regarded as what was better in theory from what he believed was better adapted to the American situation. He thus identified cumulative constitutions as appropriate for a nation where "an accurate understanding of their political rights and duties," was "general among the citizens" and where there was "sleepless vigilance to detect violations of the Constitution, and the utmost promptness and energy to resist and punish them."[23] By contrast, for communities, like those of the U.S. "whose training has been imperfect, or which is subject to fits of political apathy alternating with those of intense zeal for reform," he argued that "a written Constitution is doubtless the better one."[24] Similarly, later in the book, Jameson disputed Sidney George Fisher's assessment in his *Trial of the Constitution*, that a parliamentary system would have

---

[19] Jameson, p. 67.

[20] Jameson, pp. 75–76.

[21] See for example, James Bryce, "Flexible and Rigid Constitutions," in *Constitutions* (Germany: Scientia Verlag Aalen, 1905. Reprint of New York and London edition, 1980). Donald S. Lutz has demonstrated in "Toward a Theory of Constitutional Amendment," *American Political Science Review* 88 (June): 355–370, that the U.S. Constitution is one of the most difficult national constitutions to amend in the world.

[22] For a summary of such critiques, see John R. Vile, *Rewriting the United States Constitution: An Examination of Proposals from Reconstruction to the Present* (New York: Praeger, 1991), pp. 157–158. For a recent attack on the continuing viability of the written constitution, see Louis Michael Seidman, "Let's Give Up on the Constitution," *The New York Times*, December 30, 2012.

[23] Jameson, p. 81.

[24] *Ibid.*

had more success than the American system of separated powers in avoiding the Civil War.[25]

Undoubtedly with a view to the role of constitutional change to serve as a safety-value that could prevent violent revolution, Jameson observed that written constitutions could fail in either of two ways. One was "to idolize the letter of it," and the other was to "under-estimate its real sacredness, and so to degrade it to the level of ordinary laws."[26] In contrast to contemporary scholars — most notably Bruce Ackerman[27] — who stress the irregularity and unwritten quality of what Ackerman calls "constitutional moments" — Jameson thought it was important that: "When great historical movements, like those which have lately convulsed the United States, have resulted in important political changes, that are so consummated and settled as to indicate a solid foundation in the actual Constitution, they should be immediately registered by the proper authority among the fundamental laws."[28] Jameson further thought it was important to distinguish three different parts of written constitutions: The Bill of Rights, the Frame of Government, and the Schedule, or implementing provisions.[29]

Whereas Ackerman believes that the model of extralegal change has been normative in the periods of greatest change in American history, the beauty of Jameson's distinctions is that they largely allow him to distinguish proceedings of conventions that were called in revolutionary (or secessionist) circumstances from those that occurred in less troubling times. Although his primary focus is thus on *state* constitution-making, Jameson joins a host of modern writers in recognizing how important the early state

---

[25] Jameson, p. 567. For Fisher's work, see *The Trial of the Constitution* (New York: Da Capo Press, 1971; reprint of J.B. Lippincott & Co., 1862). For further analysis see John R. Vile, *The Constitutional Amending Process in American Political Thought* (New York: Praeger, 1992), pp. 95–102.

[26] Jameson, p. 82.

[27] See Ackerman's *We the People: Foundations* (Cambridge, MA: Belknap, 1991) and his *We the People: Transformations* (Cambridge, MA: Harvard University Press, 1996).

[28] Jameson, p. 83.

[29] Jameson, p. 92.

conventions and constitutions were in establishing precedents for the U.S. Constitutional Convention of 1787.[30]

Jameson believed that it was important to distinguish between conventions that were "illegitimate" from those that were "revolutionary." As he explained: "Illegitimacy refers to illegality of origin, and is pertinent rather to a person or body of persons than to an act. The term revolutionary, on the other hand, may be used to characterize indifferently a body or an act, and involves the idea . . . of illegality in general, that is, of either a want of express legal warrant, or a violation of positive law."[31] He further recognized that "A Convention justly stigmatized as illegitimate, may, notwithstanding its origin, become valid as fundamental law" either "by its adoption by the elected body, according to the forms of existing laws; or, by the mere acquiescence of the sovereign society."[32] Having offered such distinctions and rhetorically posed the question "why insist so strenuously upon the fact that the Conventions of the Revolutionary period were revolutionary bodies, if it be admitted that they were grounded upon an imperious necessity, and that from them, as from a fountain, has flowed the present order of things, confessed to be legitimate?" Jameson responded that "if they are truly revolutionary bodies, they must be set down as such, in order that their action may not be drawn into precedent, as that of normal Constitutional Conventions."[33]

Although Jameson dealt with a plethora of examples, he constantly sought to arrange and sort them into categories so that he

---

[30] I have attempted to stress these links in *The Writing and Ratification of the U.S. Constitution* (Lanham, MD: Rowman & Littlefield, 2012), pp. 6-8. For other treatments see, Willi Paul Adams, 2001, *The First American Constitutions: Republican Ideology and the Making of State Constitutions in the Revolutionary Era* (Lanham, MD: Rowman & Littlefield, 2001); *The Constitution and the States: The Role of the Original Thirteen in the Framing and Adoption of the Federal Constitution*, ed. Patrick T. Conley and John P. Kaminski (Madison (WI: Madison House, 1988); John J. Dinan, *The American State Constitutional Tradition* (Lawrence, KS: University Press of Kansas, 2006); and Sanford Levinson, *Framed: America's 51 Constitutions and the Crisis of Governance* (New York: Oxford University Press, 2012).

[31] Jameson, p. 104.

[32] Jameson, p. 112.

[33] Jameson, pp. 154–155.

would not draw false conclusions. Thus, in classifying conventions that had occurred since the implementation of the U.S. Constitution, he distinguished those conventions that were formed within preexisting states, those which were formed for states created within U.S. territories, and those which were called to revise existing state constitutions.[34] He further subdivided some of these divisions, as when, for example, distinguishing those that had been "regularly assembled" within territories according to prior enabling acts and those that had been convened in more irregular fashion.[35]

THE CONNECTION BETWEEN POPULAR SOVEREIGNTY AND CONVENTIONS

Like the American Framers, Jameson recognized that conventions could be legitimate expressions of popular will, but he drew a distinction between a convention (or even a popular majority) and the sovereign, which the author of this introduction believes is particularly salutary. In recent years, a number of scholars, most notably Akhil Reed Amar of Yale University, have argued that the mechanisms within Article V are not exclusive and that a majority of voters could therefore petition Congress to call a national constitutional convention or that Congress could submit amendments to a popular vote or referendum,[36] which would become part of the Constitution when so approved. Perhaps in part because he served as a judge who recognized that such results might be challenged in court, Jameson viewed such an approach as an invitation to anarchy. Were the U.S. ever to approach a revolutionary situation, it is possible that subsequent acquiescence in such amendments might ultimately give them legitimacy, but, in addition to recognizing the likelihood of creating constitutional mischief, Jameson would clearly recognize such amendments as the

---

[34] Jameson, pp. 155–156.

[35] Jameson, p. 173.

[36] Akhil Reed Amar," Philadelphia Revisited: Amending the Constitution outside Article V," *University of Chicago Law Review* 55 (Fall, 1988): 1:43–1104.

products of revolution rather than as the exercise of constitutional government.

In addressing the alleged right "for the people to establish and to change their governments at pleasure," Jameson thus responded:

> But who are the people? In the true sense of the term, it means the political society considered as a unit, comprising in one organization the entire population of the State, of all ages, sexes, and conditions. Unquestionably, it is the right of the people in this sense to found its institutions, and to determine how they shall and how they shall not be abolished or amended. Having ordained the mode, however, in which changes therein may, and in which they shall not, be made, clearly no mode can be *legal* which contravenes the express letter of that fundamental provision. [37]

The United States, of course, has faced such situations, not only in the period from 1776 to 1789, but in the notorious Dorr Rebellion within Rhode Island in 1842, which led to the historic decision in *Luther v. Borden*, in which the Court articulated the political questions doctrine.[38] Not surprisingly, Jameson classified as "heresy" the idea that "a mere majority in numbers of the adult male citizens, without regard to legal provisions, can at any time call a Convention to alter or abolish the Constitution."[39]

Jameson was, of course, writing before the adoption of women's suffrage[40] or the widespread adoption of constitutional initiatives and referenda,[41] both of which were largely Progressive Era reforms and the latter of which continue to be in tension with republican, or representative, democracy. Moreover, Jameson was

---

[37] Jameson, pp. 598–599.

[38] 48 U.S. (7 How.) 1 (1949). For Jameson's treatment, see pp. 222–234.

[39] Jameson, p. 309.

[40] Jameson, p. 329 thus observes that "In the cabin of the Mayflower it was the Pilgrim fathers, not the Pilgrim mothers, who framed the first Puritan Commonwealth." Although the Seneca Falls Convention had called for such suffrage in 1848, the Nineteenth Amendment to the U.S. Constitution, prohibiting national discrimination against women in voting, was ratified in 1920.

[41] Jameson, p. 398, did, however, take note of state legislative referenda "within the last twenty years" involving laws regulating the sale of alcohol.

writing at a time when he could still refer to suffrage not as a "right" but merely as "a duty, a trust, enjoined upon, or committed to, some citizens and not to others."[42] Still, he recognized that mere assemblages of voters did not, per se, constitute an official mechanism either to prescribe rules for government or to write new ones.

ORGANIZATIONAL STYLE

Jameson's tome is long enough, and intimidating enough, that it is never likely to become beach reading, and yet it profits from its logical format, and its clear system of classification. Jameson rarely made a general point without giving specific illustrations, and readers can often shorten their journey through his work by noting the time and place of the convention that he is describing, without reading the entire illustration — which remains available for those who need the details — that follows.

Jameson's writing also sparkles with occasional analogies and metaphors, which enliven the text. Attentive readers will undoubtedly want to compile their own lists, but this author's favorites include the following: his description of the Revolutionary Convention as a "bridge over a chasm between two orders of things: an order that has expired or been extinguished; and an order emerging, under the operation of existing social forces, to replace it";[43] his observation that "the state of nature for the bee is that of union in the swarm; and so the state of nature for mankind is that of association in political communities";[44] his notation that "the harvest of constitutional reforms has become ripe";[45] his question as to whether the president of a convention that claimed to have perpetual powers might "call the body together, as he might his hounds, for ordinary purposes of party or of administration";[46] his observation that the convention mechanism "is of revolutionary parentage; it was originally the child of

---

[42] Jameson, p. 330.
[43] Jameson, p. 6.
[44] Jameson, p. 71.
[45] Jameson, p. 422.
[46] Jameson, p. 487.

illegality, and has come into the constitutional household by adoption, and hence has been ever the subject, in all questions of power and competence, of fatal misconceptions";[47] and his analogy (not, however, original to him) to constitutional amending provisions as "safety-valves."[48]

THE MAIN POINT

The most remarkable aspect of Jameson's work is the manner in which it primarily addressed issues of *state* constitutional reform. His main aim was to establish that constitutional conventions, whose powers he feared more than that of ordinary state legislatures, did not exercise sovereignty but that they were recommendatory bodies that were bound to accept the constitutional metes and bounds that legislatures set out for them. The *Treatise*'s greatest weakness in this respect may, in fact, be that it focused almost exclusively on the convention mechanism, which Jameson himself recognized[49] was primarily suited for initiating new constitutions or radically altering them, rather than on the more mundane processes for enacting individual amendments. Jameson at one point acknowledged that "Doubtless as our Constitutions become riper and more perfect with time and experience, the necessity of employing the more expensive mode by Conventions will be found to be less and less."[50]

At a time when few, if any, scholars possessed Jameson's encyclopedic knowledge of convention history and procedures, his *Treatise* was a virtual guidebook for states seeking to institute constitutional conventions. Although these parts of the work do not make for particularly scintillating reading, they provided "nuts and

---

[47] Jameson, pp. 490–491.
[48] Jameson, p. 549.
[49] Jameson thus observed, p. 562, that legislative action was an appropriate way to initiate constitutional changes "which are few, simple, independent, and of comparatively small importance." By contrast, "For a general revision of a Constitution, or even for single propositions involving radical changes as to the policy of which the popular mind has not been informed by prior discussion, the employment of this mode is impracticable, or of doubtful expediency.
[50] Jameson, p. 552.

bolts" information for constitutional reformers at a time when model state constitutions and manuals were not as prevalent as they are today. Jameson thus addressed such questions as: who should preside (normally someone elected by the convention itself); whether conventions should be unicameral or bicameral (since the convention's work was subject to approval, he thought the former was preferable); who should pay delegates (the legislature); what powers they had over members (largely that of censure and expulsion), who should elect them (either all existing electors or an even more inclusive body of voters), how long they should last (largely determined by legislative enactment and by the nature of their tasks), and similar issues.

Although Jameson briefly addressed the development of the Constitutional Commission mechanism for proposing change,[51] his general guidelines for ordinary amendments went little beyond his statement that in adopting amendments "a majority is too small, and a unanimous vote too large, for either practicability or safety."[52] In a passage that appeared to reflect innate conservatism, Jameson further observed that the "three great evils of popular government" were "hasty legislation, excessive legislation, and partisan legislation."[53]

OTHER AMENDING ISSUES

Perhaps sensing that many readers might be more interested in, or familiar, with change at the national level than at the state level, Jameson addressed a host of amending issues in his final chapter, and his answers, while not beyond cavil, remain relevant to modern

---

[51] Jameson, p. 570.

[52] Jameson, p. 553. Perhaps practical wisdom requires a relatively high degree of generality in such an area. Defending the amending process in Federalist No. 43, James Madison thus praised Article V as guarding "equally against that extreme facility, which would render the Constitution too mutable; and that extreme difficulty, which might perpetuate its discovered faults." See Alexander Hamilton, James Madison, and John Jay, *The Federalist Papers* (New York: New American Library, 1961), p. 278.

[53] Jameson, p. 552.

disputes over the subject.[54] The most important issue he addressed was whether legislatures could limit the subject matter of conventions. Like modern writers who seek to limit the possibility of "runaway" conventions, Jameson clearly believed that legislatures had such power, and the weight of scholarly opinion arguably supports his view. Jameson did, of course, recognize that a revolutionary action might later be sufficiently accepted as to become part of the fundamental law. Although his focus was almost entirely legal, the stronger position, perhaps best articulated in more recent years by Weber and Perry, is that there are sufficient "political" controls on such a convention to make such concerns largely chimera.[55]

Citing both the precedent and the logic of the U.S. Supreme Court's decision in *Hollingsworth v. Virginia*,[56] Jameson argued that executive approval was not required for the legitimate ratification of amendments.[57] At the state level, Jameson wisely thought that legislatures could initiate amendments in the cases of constitutions that failed specifically to grant them that power, while arguing that where the Constitution did provide amending procedures, members of government should follow them. Although he followed available precedents, Jameson was not necessarily consistent in arguing that state legislatures should be able to ratify a federal amendment that they had previously rejected but that they should not be able (before ratification by the necessary three-

---

[54] This author has addressed many of these issues in his *Contemporary Questions Surrounding the Constitutional Amending Process* (Westport, CT: Praeger, 1993).
[55] See Paul J. Weber and Barbara A. Perry, *Unfounded Fears: Myths and Realities of a Constitutional Convention* (New York: Praeger, 1989), pp. 105–125. Also see Russell L. Caplan, *Constitutional Brinkmanship: Amending the Constitution by National Convention* (New York: Oxford University Press, 1988) and Wilbur Edel, *A Constitutional Convention: Threat or Challenge*? (New York, NY: Praeger, 1981). For contrasting views on the subject compare Walter Dellinger's "The Recurring Question of the 'Limited' Constitutional Convention," *Yale law Journal* 88 (1979): 1623–1540, denying congressional power to limit such conventions and William Van Alsytne's ,"Does Article V Restrict the States to Calling Unlimited Conventions Only?—A Letter to a Colleague," *Duke Law Journa*l 1978 (January): 1295–1306, arguing that it does have such authority.
[56] 3 U.S. (3 Dall.) 379 (1798).
[57] Jameson, pp. 586–592.

fourths majority) to rescind ratification of amendments they had previously approved.

Whereas some writers (perhaps fearing the kind of extra-constitutional additions that Jameson himself abhorred) have questioned the authority of Congress or a designated officer to "promulgate" an amendment by declaring it adopted,[58] Jameson regarded this action as largely unproblematic and little different from the recognition of ordinary laws.[59]

At a time before amendments fairly routinely include ratification deadlines within their texts (thus making them self-enforcing in a way in which the one in the accompanying authorizing resolution to the Equal Rights Amendment did not prove to be),[60] Jameson thought that an amendment "has relation to the sentiment and the felt needs of today, and that, if not ratified early while that sentiment may fairly be supposed to exist, it ought to be regarded as waived, and not again to be voted upon, unless a second time proposed by Congress."[61] Indeed, in the concluding sentence of his text, Jameson favored adoption of "a constitutional statute of limitations, prescribing the time within which proposed amendments shall be adopted or be treated as waived."[62] Jameson thus appeared to anticipate (if indeed he did not influence) the decision in *Dillon v. Gloss*, in which the U.S. Supreme Court decided that, in order to be valid, ratifications needed to reflect a contemporary consensus.[63]

---

[58] See Walter Dellinger, "The Legitimacy of Constitutional Change: Rethinking the Amending Process," *Harvard Law Review* (December 1983): 380–432.

[59] Jameson, p. 542.

[60] In a very controversial action, Congress thus extended the original designated time to ratify the amendment. See Brannon P. Denning and John R. Vile, "Necromancing the Equal Rights Amendment," *Constitutional Commentary* 17 (Winter 2000): 593–602.

[61] Jameson, p. 634.

[62] Jameson, p. 636.

[63] 256 U.S. 368 (1921). Writing for a unanimous Court, Justice Willis Van Devanter thus observed, at p. 375 of the decision, that "[A]s ratification is but the expression of the approbation of the people and is to be effective when had in three-fourths of the states, there is a fair implication that it must be sufficiently contemporaneous in that number of states to reflect the will of the people in all sections at relatively the same period, which, of course, ratification scattered through a long series of years would not do. "

AN ENDURING LEGACY

Jameson's *Treatise* remains a remarkable work that impresses both by the depth and breadth of its scholarship. It is a careful blend of empirical scholarship, thoughtful deduction, and passionate argument that has withstood the test of time. Like the records of the Federal Convention of 1787, which were first preserved by James Madison and other delegates and then collected by historian Max Farrand,[64] Jameson's work did not simply record what he believed but the arguments for (and against) his beliefs. His wide-ranging coverage of conventions, his presentation of his own beliefs, and his judicious explication of them remain surprisingly relevant to a number of contemporary issues.

John R. Vile
Middle Tennessee State University
2013

The practical force of this opinion was undercut by the decision in *Coleman v. Miller*, 307 U.S. 433 (1939), in which the U.S. Supreme Court decided that the decision of how long was too long was a "political question" for the elected branches, and not the judiciary, to decide.

This precedent has arguably been undercut by a district court decision in *Idaho v. Freeman*, 529 F. Supp. 1107 (1981), relative to ratification of the proposed Equal Rights Amendment, and by the belated and putative ratification of the Twenty-seventh Amendment relative to the timing of congressional pay raises, in 1992 (it has originally been proposed in 1789 as part of the Bill of Rights) – on p. 635, Jameson had denied that Ohio had the power to add its ratification to the amendment in 1873.

For further information on the Twenty-seventh Amendment, see Richard B. Bernstein, "The Sleeper Wakes: The History and Legacy of the Twenty-seventh Amendment," *Fordham Law Review* 56 (December, 1992): 497–557.

[64] Max Farrand, *The Records of the Federal Convention of 1787*, 4 vols. (New Haven, CT: Yale University Press, 1966).

A TREATISE

ON

CONSTITUTIONAL CONVENTIONS;

THEIR

HISTORY, POWERS, AND MODES OF PROCEEDING.

BY

JOHN ALEXANDER JAMESON, LL. D.
LATE JUDGE OF THE SUPERIOR COURT OF CHICAGO, ILLINOIS.

Respublica est res populi; populus autem non omnis hominum cœtus quoque modo congregatus, sed cœtus multitudinis juris consensu et utilitatis communione sociatus. — CICERO, *de Repub.*

They that go about by disobedience to do no more than reforme the commonwealth shall find that they do thereby destroy it. — HOBBES, *Leviathan.*

Fourth Edition,

REVISED, CORRECTED, AND ENLARGED.

CHICAGO:
CALLAGHAN AND COMPANY.
1887.

The Riverside Press, Cambridge:
Electrotyped and Printed by H. O. Houghton & Co.

PREFACE.

In 1862, certain influential members of the Illinois Constitutional Convention, then in session, set up for that body, in debate, a claim of inherent powers amounting almost to absolute sovereignty, — maintaining, for instance, that though the Act of the General Assembly under which the Convention had met required it to submit the fruit of its labors to the people, for ratification or rejection, it might lawfully refuse to do so and put the Constitution it should frame in operation without any reference whatever to the people. At the same time rumors were current throughout the State that there were in that body, seeking to control it, many members of a secret organization supposed to be disloyal to the Union, called the "Knights of the Golden Circle." Alarmed by this claim of power, which he deemed excessive, as well as by these sinister rumors, the author commenced a study of the Convention as an American institution from its foundation and in all its aspects and relations, with a view to ascertain whether the claim of power referred to was warranted either by history or by constitutional principles. The result was the text of the first edition of this work. Because, in the course of his examination of the Convention system, the author found reason to believe, as he thought, that the origin, functions, and powers of the institution had been widely misapprehended, and that, as conceived by the "natural man," without knowledge or experience, jumping to conclusions respecting it hastily, it had been and was a source of extreme danger to the republic, the work was published by him in the autumn of 1866. The same considerations, strengthened by subsequent reflection and research, and by the change of sentiment in regard to the subject, which he could not but observe after the first edition of his work was published, a change as apparent as it was gratifying, not only in the press and in the debates of our

Conventions and legislatures, but in the courts, have impelled the author to issue subsequent editions of the work until this, the fourth edition, now appears. His object in writing it having been simply to throw light upon a part of our constitutional apparatus which had not previously attracted the attention of lawyers and publicists, should the work have effected this, whatever the result otherwise may have been, the author will regard the many years of labor devoted by him to its preparation as not spent in vain.

In reference to the execution of the work a word of explanation may, perhaps, be necessary. In the citation of parts of Constitutions and statutes the figures denoting the articles or sections referred to have been generally, with a view to economy of space, omitted, seeing that the constitutional clauses cited have been those relating to the amendment of Constitutions, or to the calling of Conventions, both of which are always embraced in an article of one, or at most two, sections placed near the end of the respective instruments. So, in regard to parts of statutes, when not otherwise specified, they have always been cited from Acts calling Conventions, which are short, and found in the volumes of laws published by the several States in the year in which the respective Conventions met, or in the year preceding. They are, therefore, referred to as the Convention Acts of such or such a Convention, giving the year in which it met. On the other hand, Acts of Congress have been generally cited by naming the volume and page of the United States Statutes at Large in which they are to be found.

To name all the gentlemen throughout the Union who have kindly aided the author in the collection of materials for the work would be hardly possible. Special reference ought, however, to be made to the following persons, to whom the author is indebted for important information or documents relating to Conventions in the various States of the Union: —

Ex-Senators Charles Sumner, deceased, of Massachusetts; and Lyman Trumbull, of Illinois. Ex-Governors, Henry C. Warmoth, of New Orleans; F. H. Pierpoint, and Gilbert C. Walker, deceased, of Virginia; Robert McClelland, deceased, of Michigan; and D. H. Chamberlain, of South Carolina. Judges, John G. Rogers, deceased, of Chicago, Ill.; John G. Speer, Oakland, Fla.; Willard Hall, deceased, of Wilmington, Del.; James T.

Mitchell, of Philadelphia, Pa.; C. I. Bradley, of Rhode Island; John W. May, deceased, of Boston, Mass.; James McM. Shafter, of California; Hugh Buchanan, of Newnan, Ga.; Hiram A. Gillett, of Valparaiso, Ind.; Matthew Hale, of Albany, N. Y.; George Denison, of St. Louis, Mo.; L. Crounse, Nebraska. College Presidents, Sidney H. Marsh, deceased, of Salem, Or.; Israel W. Andrews, of Marietta, Ohio. Professors, Dr. Francis Lieber, deceased, of New York; and James Denison, of the National Deaf Mute College, Washington, D. C. The Hon. John C. Hurd, New York; Francis L. Barlow, New York; W. G. De Saussure, Charleston, S. C.; James M. Barrett, Cincinnati, Ohio; Edward Cantwell, Wilmington, N. C.; Edward I. Golladay, Nashville, Tenn.; W. O. Tuggle, Georgia; B. D. Silliman, New York; William P. Wells, Detroit, Mich.; Edward Russell, Leavenworth, Kan.; R. D. Benedict, New York; H. F. Prentiss, deceased, Milwaukee, Wis.; J. Hammond Trumbull, Hartford, Conn.; H. B. Dawson, New York; Charles E. Gorman, Providence, R. I.; George S. Denison, deceased, New Orleans; John H. Sahler, Omaha, Neb.; W. P. Ballinger, Austin, Tex.; W. W. Wilshire, Little Rock, Ark.; R. N. Ely, Atlanta, Ga.; S. B. McCracken, Detroit, Mich.; and R. T. Merrick, deceased, Washington, D. C., Esquires. Charles Reed, late State Librarian of Vermont, and John Langdon Sibley, deceased, late Librarian of Harvard College, Cambridge, Mass., and the Secretaries of State of nearly all the States in the Union. To those gentlemen the thanks of the author are due for many and valued courtesies in supplying him with detailed information and often with important documents.

JOHN A. JAMESON.

CHICAGO, *May*, 1887.

TABLE OF CONTENTS.

CHAPTER I.

OF THE VARIOUS KINDS OF CONVENTIONS.

CHAPTER II.

OF SOVEREIGNTY.

CHAPTER III.

OF CONSTITUTIONS.

CHAPTER IV.

OF THE REQUISITES TO THE LEGITIMACY OF CONVENTIONS, AND OF THEIR HISTORY.

CHAPTER V.

OF THE ORGANIZATION AND MODES OF PROCEEDING OF CONVENTIONS.

CHAPTER VI.

OF THE POWERS OF CONVENTIONS.

CHAPTER VII.

OF THE SUBMISSION OF CONSTITUTIONS TO THE PEOPLE.

CHAPTER VIII.

OF THE AMENDMENT OF CONSTITUTIONS.

APPENDIX.

TABLE OF CASES CITED.

CONSTITUTIONAL CONVENTIONS.

CHAPTER I.

OF THE VARIOUS KINDS OF CONVENTIONS.

§ 1. It is my purpose, in the following pages, to inquire into the history, powers, and modes of proceeding of the Constitutional Convention, one of the most important and most characteristic of the political institutions of the United States. Of the American system of government, the two leading principles are, first, that laws and Constitutions can be rightfully formed and established only by the people over whom they are to be put in force; and, secondly, that the people being a corporate unit, comprising all the citizens of the state, and, therefore, too unwieldy to do this important work directly, agents or representatives must be employed to do it, and that, in such numbers, so selected, and charged respectively with such functions, as to make it reasonably certain that the will of the people will be not only adequately but speedily executed.[1]

The function of framing and enacting the statute law is commonly, by the practice of all representative governments, intrusted to a numerous body, called a legislature. Constitutions, on the other hand, considered as written instruments, are the work of various agencies, according to the genius or special circumstances of the states concerned, some being formed by the executive branch of the government, some by the legislature, and some by a body for that purpose specially chosen and commissioned. Thus, in England, this duty is exclusively committed to King, Lords, and Commons in Parliament assembled. Under the imperial *régimes* of the first and the third Napoleons, in France, the *plebiscites*, determining the form and powers of the government, though nominally the work of the Senate, were and are really dictated by those monarchs. With us, in Amer-

[1] See *Works of Daniel Webster*, Vol. VI. pp. 221-224.

ica, there is set apart a special agency, to which is confided wholly, or mainly, the business of fundamental legislation, — the Constitutional Convention. It is this agency which frames our Constitutions, and which, generally, as changes in them become necessary, is charged with maturing the needed amendments. In some cases, under authority for that purpose expressly given, it both forms and establishes our fundamental codes, but commonly it acts in conjunction with some other department of the existing government; the one presenting, after mature deliberation, in the form of proposals, a connected scheme, and the other by its sanction imparting to that scheme the force and vigor of law.

§ 2. To any society, far enough advanced in civilization to demand as well the ascertainment as the protection of its civil and political rights, no institution could be of more interest than one charged thus with the *rôle* of both founder and restorer of its social machinery. Is this institution, it might be asked, subject to any law, to any restriction? What claims does it itself put forth, and what do the precedents teach, in relation to its nature and powers? When called into existence, is it the servant, or the master, of the people, by whom it was spoken into being? Whatever be its relations to the general source of political power, whether those of subordination or of independence, what is the place in our system, what are the relations to other governmental agencies, the normal functions and powers, of an institution, that, however hedged about by legal restraints, obviously exhibits more features that are menacing to republican liberty than any other in our whole political structure.

§ 3. To the interest attaching to the Convention, thus, from abstract considerations, has been added a greater, resulting from the connection of that institution with recent political events. The desolating war of secession, which closed, in 1865, could hardly have been inaugurated but for the use made by the revolting faction of that institution. For reasons, which will be more fully explained hereafter, it had come to be a maxim in the practical jurisprudence of the United States, at least in some of the States, that whatever had been done by a Constitutional Convention, had been done by the people, "in their primary and sovereign capacity," and was therefore absolutely unquestionable, on legal or constitutional grounds; and there were not wanting those who arrogated to that ill-defined assembly, as by an extension to it of the absurd maxim, that "the voice of the people is the voice of God," an omnipotence transcending that higher law, to which ordinary legislative assemblies acknowledge themselves at all times subject. When to this, which is deemed one of the most impudent heresies of our times, was added its fellow, the dogma of State sovereignty, with its corollary, the duty of State allegiance, the transformation of a loyal community into a band of parricides seeking to pull down the edifice of our liberties, need be but the work of a day. To effect it, there was needed but a vote of a few conspirators, sitting as a Constitutional Convention, pretending to utter the voice of the people, and refusing to submit their ordinances to the test of a popular vote, under the false plea that neither the theory of the Convention system nor the practice of the fathers made such a submission necessary.

This picture of treachery and cunning, playing upon popular ignorance for their country's ruin, describes with precision the historical drama that culminated in the secession of the States of the South, in 1860–1. For, surely, it is not too much to say that without the moral effect of those disorganizing maxims, which impressed upon Southern consciences the duty of "going with one's State," there could have been no victories won by the armies of treason, even had an outbreak of hostilities been possible.

Of an institution to which are conceded a position so important and influence so decisive, but of which the true character and relations are so ill understood as to give rise to wide-spread misapprehensions, no apology is needed for an attempt to develop the history and illustrate the true nature and principles.

§ 4. Before entering upon the task indicated, it is important to clear the way by carefully discriminating the institution in question from others known under the same general designation of *Conventions*, but differing from it in their essential principles and functions. To do this, will be the principal object of this chapter.

There are known to the social life of our times, in America four species of *Conventions*, namely: —

I. The Spontaneous Convention, or Public Meeting.

II. The Ordinary Legislative Convention, or General Assembly.

III. The Revolutionary Convention.

IV. The Constitutional Convention.

These will now be considered in their order.

§ 5. I. By Spontaneous Conventions, I mean those voluntary assemblages of citizens, which characterize free communities in advanced stages of civilization, having for their purpose agitation or conference in respect of their industrial, religious, political, or other social interests. These gatherings are at once the effects and the causes of social life and activity, doing for the state what the waves do for the sea: they prevent stagnation, the precursor of decay and death. They are among the most efficient manufactories of public opinion; or, rather, they are public opinion in the making, — public opinion fit to be the basis of political action, because sound and wise, and not a mere echo of party cries and platforms. Spontaneous assemblages, for such purposes, of the masses of a people, betoken a very high state of civilization, or instincts that are sure to develop into it. To be possible, in perfection, as we see them amongst us, freedom must be ripe and well-nigh universal. But when rulers and social institutions do not favor them, to their occurrence at all would be necessary a native passion for liberty strong enough to break all chains, and which could be daunted by no perils. We are prepared, therefore, to believe that it is only our own race, here and in England, that has thus far successfully vindicated the right of freely assembling. This right was asserted in England as early as the twelfth century,[1] history telling us of the "*conventus publicos propria authoritate*,"[2] or voluntary meetings of the people, under the protection of the common law. With some fluctuations, as the work of social development proceeded, this right became more firmly rooted in the parent soil, and from it a vigorous scion was planted in America, which has exhibited a still stronger vitality, and now overspreads the land.[3] A common and most invaluable provision of our constitutions, State and Federal, guarantees to the people the right "peaceably to assemble and petition the government for a redress of grievances." The right, thus expressed,

[1] For a most excellent view of the vicissitudes of this right under the English Constitution, see May's *Constitutional History of England*, Vol. II. ch. ix.

[2] Hinton's *Hist. United States*, Vol. II. pp. 324, 325.

[3] May's *Const. Hist. Eng.*, Vol. II. ch. ix.

involves those of discussing all measures of the government; of embodying in resolutions or remonstrances the general sentiment in regard to the policy and the acts of the public authorities; and, in general, of exercising the privilege, without which freedom is impossible, of saying and hearing whatsoever one pleases, being at the same time responsible for abuses of that privilege.[1] Such is the Spontaneous Convention: a body which meets upon the call of any individual; adjourns when it pleases; is wholly unofficial; whose determinations have no efficacy whatever, except as expressions of matured or maturing opinion; which is subject to no laws but the *lex parliamentaria*, — common sense applied to the action of numerous assemblies, — and the law which enjoins upon all men to keep the peace; and yet a body which is quite as important to the continued healthy life of a commonwealth as either of the four species of Conventions mentioned.[2]

§ 6. II. The second species of Conventions, consisting of our General Assemblies, is so well known, that I need not dwell upon it. A General Assembly is, in our American system, a collection of representatives of the people, freely elected in pursuance of the Constitution, and empowered to enact the ordinary statute law. Deriving its existence and powers from the people, through the Constitution, it can do nothing except by the authority contained in that instrument, and is, therefore, official, or vicarious, but at the same time subaltern, — the people being the principal and paramount source of power. Yet, as we shall have occasion to note hereafter, though subordinate in relation to the people, considered as the creator of the government and Constitution, the legislature is nevertheless *prima inter pares*, when compared with other departments of the government; or, as it has been expressed by speculative writers, is more nearly sovereign than any of the departments which are ordinarily regarded as coördinate with it.

[1] "This is true liberty, when free-born men
Having to advise the public may speak free,
Which he who can, and will, deserves high praise;
Who neither can nor will may hold his peace.
What can be juster in a state than this?"

MILTON, *Areopagitica*, from EURIPIDES.

[2] See remarks of Dr. Lieber on this class of Conventions, *Political Ethics*, Part II. p. 467.

§ 7. III. The third species of Conventions, as its name implies, is a part of the apparatus of revolution. It consists of those bodies of men who, in times of political crisis, assume, or have cast upon them, provisionally, *the function of government.* They either supplant or supplement the existing governmental organization. The principal characteristics of this species are, that they are *dehors* the law; that they derive their powers, if justifiable, from necessity, — the necessity, in default of the regular authorities, of protection and guidance to the Commonwealth, — or, if not justifiable, from revolutionary force and violence; that they are possessed, accordingly, to an indeterminate extent, depending on the circumstances of each case, *of governmental powers;* finally, *that they are not subaltern or ancillary to any other institution whatever, but lords paramount of the entire political domain.* To this may be added, that they are of no definite numbers or organization, comprising sometimes one and sometimes several chambers, and composed indifferently of ex-officers of the government that was, of persons possessing neither office nor the qualifications requisite for it, nor even for the elective franchise, or of a mixture of all of these together, as chance may have tossed them to the surface. The general purpose of the Revolutionary Convention, moreover, is to bridge over a chasm between two orders of things: an order that has expired or been extinguished; and an order emerging, under the operation of existing social forces, to replace it. In short, a Revolutionary Convention is simply a PROVISIONAL GOVERNMENT.

§ 8. Examples of the Revolutionary Convention have been numerous in the political history of the world, and they are becoming daily more so. Among the most famous and, for our purpose, the most important, are those held in England in 1660 and in 1689.

In those cases the ruling dynasty having abdicated the throne, or been expelled from it, there was in the kingdom not only no organized government, but no central authority legally competent to institute one. There was, it is true, the people of England, but they could not so assemble as to act as a unit. The parliament had ceased, in law, to exist with the reign of the monarch by whose writ it had been summoned, and no new parliament could be legally called, because for that the royal writ was absolutely necessary. In these alarming crises, and as the last and only resource for temporary government, as well as for providing the initial points of new organizations, Conventions were summoned. That called in 1660 consisted of persons elected by the several constituencies of the realm, as for a lawful parliament, but elected illegally, on the recommendation of a rump of the old Parliament, which had been dispersed by the army under Richard Cromwell, and, for that reason, as Macaulay observes, more accurately described as a *Convention*, as having been called without the royal writ.[1] The Convention of 1689, summoned by the Prince of Orange, afterwards William III., on his accession by force to the throne left vacant by James II., consisted of persons elected in a similar manner, on the call of the usurping prince, issued at the recommendation of the lords spiritual and temporal at the time in London, forming a *quasi* House of Lords, and of old members of the House of Commons, together with the magistrates of the city of London, acting as a House of Commons. This Convention, also, though made up of members chosen by the electors for members of Parliament, in their several districts, was not styled or considered a Parliament, because called by a person not constitutionally authorized, acting on the advice of an assembly, which, though regarded by the nation with a large measure of the respect due to a Parliament, on account of the eminence and former official station of its members, was yet without a shadow of legal authority. The proceeding was revolutionary, and so universally admitted to be. Such were the two great English Conventions, the models after which most subsequent bodies of the same class have been formed or organized, both in this country and in Europe, and of which, as we shall see, our Constitutional Conventions are special adaptations or modifications. They were Provisional Governments, — the only governments England had during the periods of their existence. And for our purpose it will be interesting to note further, that the English Convention of 1689, having taken steps, as a revolutionary body, to settle the succession to the throne, passed a bill declaring itself to be a parliament, and from that time acted as such in conjunction with the king it had itself called to the throne.[2]

[1] Macaulay, *Hist. Eng.*, Vol. I. ch. i.

[2] Id. Vol. II. ch. xi.

§ 9. Interesting examples of the Revolutionary Convention are found in our own history. The first occurred in New England simultaneously with the English Convention of 1689, its assembling being the result, in part, of the same causes which led to that, but, in part, of causes local to New England. Both, however, were called and composed in a similar manner, and organized after the same model, that of 1660, convened at the time of the Restoration.[1]

The leading facts in the history of that held in New England are as follows: —

Whilst the tyrannical acts of James II. were, in England, exciting the discontents which finally led to his abdication, those of Sir Edmond Andros, the Governor of Massachusetts, were arousing the fiercest opposition in New England, against both the colonial and the imperial administrations. It is believed that as early as January, 1689, before the news of the landing of the Prince of Orange in England had reached the colony, arrangements had been made in the latter to rise against the unpopular governor. So soon as that news arrived an outbreak occurred. On the 18th of April, a "Declaration of the Gentlemen, Merchants, and Inhabitants of Boston and the country adjacent," was published, recounting their oppressions, and announcing their purpose to "seize upon the persons of those few ill men which have been (next to our sins) the grand authors of our miseries." The governor and the magistrates and crown officers adhering to him, were accordingly thrown into prison; the castle was occupied by colonial militia, and an English frigate, lying in the harbor, was forced to surrender.[2] On the day following this revolutionary outbreak, the leaders in the movement with twenty-two others, whom they now associated, formed themselves into a Provisional Government, under the name of a "Council for the Safety of the People and Conservation of the Peace." Feeling the weakness of their position, since they "held their place neither by deputation from the sovereign nor by election of the people," and hesitating to set up again the charter, "formally condemned by the King's courts," "they decided to call a *Convention*, to consist of two delegates from each town in the jurisdiction, except Boston, which was to send four." This Convention met on the 9th of May, and attempted to put

[1] See § 133, *post*.

[2] Palfrey's *Hist. New Eng.*, Vol. III. pp. 574–587.

the charter in force, but meeting with opposition from the magistrates, steps were taken to call a second Convention with "express instructions from their towns." Fifty-four towns sent delegates to this latter Convention, the large majority of them with instructions to insist on the resumption of the charter. After two days' debate, the governor and magistrates, chosen at the last election under the charter, were prevailed upon "to assume the trusts committed to them, and, in concert with the delegates recently elected, to form a General Court," or Legislature, "and administer the colony, for the present, according to the ancient forms." [1]

Two days after this revolutionary government was established, a ship arrived from England with the news that the revolution there had succeeded, and bringing orders to the authorities to proclaim King William and Queen Mary.

The Convention, organized as above stated, by which this revolution was effected, was evidently of the species I have denominated Revolutionary Conventions. It rested for its warrant upon necessity, and sought its ends through force. It was a *government*, intended to supplant another government, and not merely a political institution designed to be subservient to a government conceived of as existing in full activity.

§ 10. Thus the *Revolutionary Convention* became domesticated in America. Since this first appearance, there have been numerous others, a few during the colonial condition, but most of them in the course of our two great civil revolutions, those of 1776 and 1861. As we shall see in a subsequent chapter, most of the organizations, by which, under the names of "Provincial Conventions," or "Provincial Congresses," the first of those revolutions was consummated, and all of those by which the late secession movement was carried through, were strictly Revolutionary Conventions.

One of the best known examples of the Revolutionary Convention is the National Convention, by which was effected the bloody overthrow of the old feudal monarchy of France at the close of the last century. Enough has been said, however, to show the characteristic features of an institution, too often, as we shall see, confounded with the Constitutional Convention, to which I now pass.

[1] Palfrey's *Hist. New Eng.*, Vol. III. pp. 587–589.

§ 11. IV. The last species of the Convention is the CONSTITUTIONAL CONVENTION. It differs from the last preceding, in being, as its name implies, *constitutional;* not simply as having for its object the framing or amending of Constitutions, but as being within, rather than without, the pale of the fundamental law; as ancillary and subservient and not hostile and paramount to it. This species of Convention sustains an official relation to the state, considered as a political organization. It is charged with a definite, and not a discretionary and indeterminate, function. It always acts under a commission, for a purpose ascertained and limited by law or by custom. Its principal feature, as contradistinguished from the Revolutionary Convention, is, that at every step and moment of its existence, it is subaltern, — it is evoked by the side and at the call of a government preëxisting and intended to survive it, for the purpose of administering to its special needs. It never supplants the existing organization. It never governs. Though called to look into and recommend improvements in the fundamental laws, it *enacts* neither them nor the statute law; and it performs no act of administration. As John Randolph said in the Virginia Convention of 1829, it is called as counsel to the people, "as a state physician, to propose remedies for the state's diseases." But it is a physician whose ministrations are confined to the extraordinary maladies requiring a fundamental change in the Constitution, not to those constantly recurring but petty disorders which demand the interposition of the ordinary legislature.

§ 12. It is apparent that institutions, whose definitions thus mutually exclude each other, cannot be the same, however similar the names by which they are popularly known.[1]

But it may happen, (instances will be hereafter mentioned in which it has happened,) that the Constitutional Convention may, by usurpation, assume one or more of the powers of the Revolutionary Convention; or that the latter may exercise those of the former. How, in such a case, is the usurping body to be classed? This question is one of great importance, but is susceptible of a ready answer.

[1] I am gratified to be able to fortify myself in the distinctions here made between Constitutional and Revolutionary Conventions by the authority of a judge of the South Carolina Court of Appeals, in an opinion delivered upon the hearing of the so-called allegiance cases. See the opinion of Mr. Justice O'Neall, 2 Hill's S. C. R., 222.

A Revolutionary Convention, because it is, *ex vi termini*, unlimited, in respect of both the kind and the degree of its powers, may take upon itself the functions of either of the three lower species of conventions, under the same warrant by which it justifies the assumption of revolutionary powers. A body which can, violently and without law, uproot all existing institutions, can clearly do the lesser act of digesting, or even of enacting, amendments to the Constitution. But, in doing so, it does not change its original character; it is still a Revolutionary Convention, and all its acts must stand on the footing of those which involve the widest stretch of power.

But the converse of this proposition does not hold true. If a Constitutional Convention step outside the circle of the law, it does not continue to be a Constitutional Convention, but, so far, becomes that whose powers or methods it assumes, — a Revolutionary Convention. It leaves the domain of law, which is one of specified and restricted powers, and enters upon that of arbitrary discretion, within which law is silent, and where he is master who wields the greater force.

Whenever, therefore, a Constitutional Convention, appointed, as we shall see it usually is, for a specific duty under the Constitution, presumes to overpass the limits imposed by its commission, by custom, or by the maxims of political prudence, and to do acts requiring the exercise of a *revolutionary discretion*, it ceases to be a Constitutional, and becomes, in the eye of the law, *ab initio*, a Revolutionary Convention.

§ 13. If I mistake not, in the confounding of the distinctions noted in the preceding sections between the Constitutional and the Revolutionary Convention, will be found the origin of the most fatal misconceptions attaching to any part of our political system. To show how those misconceptions arise, as well as to obviate their effects by bringing into as clear a light as possible the distinctions indicated, it is necessary to inquire into the genesis and historical development of the Constitutional Convention.

The history of that institution may be summed up in a few words; it is an adaptation to the exigencies of constitutional life and government, in the United States, of the Revolutionary Convention, as derived from our English ancestors of 1660 and 1689. How the transformation occurred, by which the wild scion from the woods was domesticated in the garden of the Constitution and made to subserve the purposes of regulated life, will now be shown.

When the American colonies assumed the position of *independent States*, the revolt, by which the change in their political relations was accomplished, was conducted by revolutionary conventions in the several States, patterned after those described in the previous sections of this chapter. In other words, our fathers borrowed the revolutionary machinery which history showed to have been so efficacious in the time of Charles II. and James II., as they also, in general, inherited the political principles and the forms of administration of the mother-country. Thus, the institution was planted upon American soil.

The next step, if less obvious, was not less important. The Revolution accomplished, when our fathers came to embody the rights achieved by it in institutions independent of the crown, two circumstances led them to establish governments limited to the exercise of granted powers. The first of these was affection for their charters, so long, in many of the colonies, the most effective barriers against parliamentary oppression; the second, apprehension of an American monarchy, — a mere phantom, as we now know, but a phantom which, at that time, to many imaginations, threatened immediate and serious evils. However this may be, the tendency indicated was universal, and has given character to our political institutions to this day.

But it was not forgotten that the colonial charters were mere royal grants, and that the tenures by which they were held had sometimes been very insecure. Here, it is true, there was no sovereign authority but the people, represented chiefly by the General Assemblies, a circumstance which might be thought to render the wrongful abrogation of their charters improbable, if not impossible. But as the worst oppressions, experienced by them as colonies, had been at the hands of Parliament, — a popular assembly, in theory, if not in fact, representing the Commons of the whole empire, — might not their own assemblies in time become their oppressors, especially if allowed to retain not only the power of ordinary legislation, but that transcendent one exercised by the English Parliament, of framing the organic law?

This apprehension, nearly universal at the time of our separation, led the statesmen of the Revolution to seek some other depositary of the latter power. This they found in Conventions, called by the governments in force in the several colonies, modelled, in point of structure and organization, after the Revolutionary Conventions, with which they were so familiar, but charged with the single function of maturing the charters, or Constitutions, rendered necessary by the altered condition of their affairs. As thus used, the Convention ceased to be the revolutionary body which had alone been known by that name in former times. But it was the same institution, for our fathers knew no other, but the same with important differences. Brought into operation as a regular constitutional agency, in aid of a system established, it was shorn of the extraordinary powers possessed by it when it was itself the government; the government, too, of a state in a time of social upheaval and transition, in which the laws were silent, and those intrusted with the public administration were restrained by no law but that of the strongest.

§ 14. It is not my purpose here to trace at any great length the limits of this new development. It is enough to observe, that the change began with the Revolution, of the fruits of which it constituted so valuable and characteristic a part. It was not accomplished, however, in a moment, nor can it be said to be even yet completely consummated, since there are doubts and misconceptions widely prevalent regarding it, which are inconsistent with the idea of a perfect development of the new institution. An important step in that development has only lately been taking, in the case of the Lecompton Convention, so-called, of the Territory of Kansas. In the discussion of that case, in 1857–9, the question, whether or not a Constitutional Convention has power either to refuse to submit the fruit of its deliberations to those who are to be governed by it, or to submit it to them in such a way as to deprive them substantially of a voice in determining its form and character, was for the first time definitively settled. The same process will doubtless continue in the future.

When the first Constitutions were framed for the colonies, in 1776, the limits and distinctions, above explained, were far less understood than they have since become. In a subsequent chapter it will be seen that the most important principle in the Convention system — that which requires the Constitutional Convention to be kept totally disconnected, as well in theory as in practice, from the Revolutionary Convention — was sometimes, in those early days, disregarded. The statesmen of the Revolutionary period, though familiar with the principles and, to some extent, with the administration of the English government, were necessarily less so with those that were springing up about them; and of the features indispensable to be impressed upon an old institution coming now to be employed for a new constitutional purpose, so as to render **its** working easy and safe, they were wholly ignorant. Accordingly, in their first essays at constitution making, partly from this ignorance and partly from the urgent needs of the time, they allowed the functions of the Constitutional Convention, in some cases, to be exercised by its revolutionary prototype, — the Revolutionary Conventions assuming the duty, with others, of framing their first constitutions.

But, if the necessity of keeping the two institutions distinct was not at first generally apparent, it required but little experience of actual administration to convince men as intelligent and jealous of their liberties as our fathers, that if, to the function of suggesting, the Constitutional Conventions, becoming so common amongst them, should join that of establishing, their Constitutions of government, and not only so, but of framing and administering the ordinary laws of their respective States, as being but the less involved in the greater power, there would be practically no security at all for their liberties. Accordingly, we find that the cases in which the incompatible functions indicated were actually accumulated in the same hands were confined to the first years of the war, when the idea had not been dissipated that a satisfactory peace with England would soon make unnecessary the continuance of the State organizations, thus far regarded as temporary establishments for the government of the colonies, whilst the contest with England should continue.

§ 15. We are to conceive of the Constitutional Convention, then, as an adaptation to constitutional uses of an institution originally revolutionary; that is, whose methods and principles of action, as well as whose purposes, were alien and hostile to established laws and Constitutions. And this is the real occasion of most of the misconceptions prevalent as to its true character. Thus, the notion has been common among even the well-informed, that the Constitutional Convention is above the law, the Constitution, and the government, all of which it may, therefore, it is conceived, respect and obey or not at its discretion; that it is possessed, in short, of the powers of its revolutionary namesake.

The origin of this misconception is ignorance of the simple facts of our constitutional history above detailed, and of the principles of our political system. To determine the rightful powers of the institution as adapted to our constitutional uses, men point to the English Conventions of 1660 and 1689, to that of the latter year in Massachusetts, to those by which our first Revolution was, in the various American colonies, begun and consummated. Those bodies, which, unquestionably, in many cases, framed Constitutions, were known to be possessed of other and extraordinary powers. They were called by high-sounding titles: "The Estates of the Realm;" "The People in their Primary and Sovereign Capacity;" — phrases, in whose indefiniteness could be discovered, or concealed, all possible attributions of power. The error has received additional currency from the extraordinary proceedings of the Conventions held in France, particularly that which piloted her upon the breakers in the closing years of the last century.[1] Was not the Convention of our first ally, it is asked, which uprooted the monarchy and laid the foundations of the French Republic, an institution borrowed from us, — an institution, therefore, which has not here developed the extraordinary powers, exhibited by it in France, only because our occasions have never called them forth? The upshot of this reasoning is, the establishment of the axiom, that a Constitutional Convention wields all the powers, which, by the law of nature or of nations, are conceded to exist in the sovereign for which it acts — a degree of omnipotence to which, in a government of law, there can be found no parallel, and which is inconsistent with the fundamental principles of American liberty.

§ 16. The Constitutional Convention, then, I consider as an exotic, domesticated in our political system, but in the process so transformed as to have become an essentially different institution from what it was as a Revolutionary Convention. In

[1] See Appendix A, *post.*

the following pages an attempt will be made to vindicate the accuracy of that view by inquiring into the institution in all its relations, as well to the people as to the government in its various departments, connecting with the theoretical considerations necessarily involved in the discussion, historical sketches of such Conventions as have thus far been held in the United States.

§ 17. Before proceeding to this inquiry, it will be useful to develop, with such completeness as space will allow, two fundamental conceptions, to which reference will be constantly made in the following pages, — that of *Sovereignty*, or of a *sovereign Body;* and that of a *Constitution*, or *Law fundamental*, as distinguished from an ordinary municipal law.

Without an accurate comprehension of these two subjects, it will be impossible to arrive at the truth in relation to the institution we are considering, since the first, being the source and foundation of all just authority in the state,[1] determines its powers; and the second, being the object, to create which or to aid in creating which that institution is employed, ascertains the field of its operations. To these conceptions, therefore, will be devoted the two following chapters.

[1] The word *state* is used in this treatise, first, generally, to denote any organized political community; that is, synonymously with commonwealth; and, secondly, in a limited sense, to designate a member of the American Union. When employed in the former sense, it begins with a small letter, and when in the latter, with a capital.

CHAPTER II.

OF SOVEREIGNTY.

§ 18. By the term *sovereign* is meant the person or body of persons in a state, to whom there is, politically, no superior.[1] Sovereignty is the state or condition of being a sovereign — the possession of sovereign powers.[2]

§ 19. The marks by which the possession of sovereignty may be determined, in particular cases, have been thus described by Mr. John Austin, one of the most eminent authorities upon the philosophy of jurisprudence: —

"The superiority," says he, "which is styled sovereignty, and the independent political society which sovereignty implies, is distinguished from other superiority, and from other society, by the following marks or characters: —

1 The term *sovereign* is derived from a low-Latin word, *supranus*, formed from *supra*, by the following transformations: *soprano*, *sovrano*, *souverain*, *sovereign*. Du Cange, *in verb.* Milton spells the word *sovran*. Richardson's *Dictionary*, *in verb.*

The meaning of the term sovereignty, then, is simply superiority; but it is, humanly speaking, an absolute superiority. Rutherforth, in his *Institutes of Natural Law*, contends, not without reason, that when we speak of relative superiority, we use the word supremacy. He says: — "Whenever we speak of sovereign power or of supreme power, we are led into some mistakes by using these words indiscriminately. When we call any power supreme, the expression seems to be relative to some other subordinate powers; to call any power the highest of all is not very intelligible, if there are no other powers below it. Sovereign power is also a relative term; but then it has not a necessary relation to subordinate powers. To call any power by the name of sovereign power, does not necessarily imply that there are any other powers in subordination to it. Whatever power is independent, so as not to be subject to any other power, though it has in the mean time no other power subject to itself, may with propriety enough be called by this name. In short, that power may well be called sovereign to which none is superior; whereas none can be called supreme, unless there are others inferior to it." Book II. ch. iv. pp. 75, 76.

2 Dr. Lieber, in his *Political Ethics*, defines sovereignty from the point of view of its moral limitations, thus: "The necessary existence of the state, and that right and power which necessarily flow from it, is sovereignty."

"1. The *bulk* of the given society are in a habit of obedience or submission to a *determinate* and *common* superior, let that common superior be a certain individual person, or a certain body or aggregate of individual persons.

"2. That certain individual, or that certain body of individuals, is *not* in a habit of obedience to a determinate human superior. . . . . .

"Or, the notions of sovereignty and independent political society may be expressed concisely thus: If a *determinate* human superior, not in a habit of obedience to a like superior, receive *habitual* obedience from the *bulk* of a given society, that determinate superior is sovereign in that society, and the society (including the superior) is a society political and independent."[1]

§ 20. It is impossible to describe sovereignty with greater completeness or felicity, but I shall venture to add to the marks given by Mr. Austin two not unrelated to them, expressed in terms more familiar to the jurisprudence of the United States. They are these: —

1. Whenever, within the same territorial limits, there exist two political organizations, or two political entities, so related to each other that one determines its own powers and jurisdiction, and, in so doing, limits, enlarges, or abolishes those of the other, being at the same time itself, not only subject to no reciprocal modification, but independent of all the world, the former is a sovereign organization or entity, and the latter is not.

2. Whatever, historically considered, may have been the original relations of two political bodies at present distinguished from each other by the mark indicated, the powers wielded by the inferior must be conceived as delegated by the superior, since at no moment would its possession of them continue without the consent of that superior.[2]

This follows from the definition of sovereignty, and will aid us further on, when we come to consider the question of sovereignty in the United States.

§ 21. With the abstract question of the ground upon which the right of sovereignty rests, I shall not concern myself.[3]

[1] Austin, *The Province of Jurisprudence Determined,* Vol. I. p. 170.

[2] Id. p. 337.

[3] The principal theories as to the ground of sovereignty, and, consequently, as to the ultimate foundation of civil government, are, that it rests, first, *upon*

A question of less difficulty, and, for my purpose, of greater practical importance, is, where — theoretically considered, and without reference to particular states — does sovereignty reside, and what are its attributes?

To the first branch of the question, the answer is: sovereignty resides in the *society* or *body politic;* in the corporate unit resulting from the organization of many into one, and not in

Divine appointment; secondly, *upon compact,* and, thirdly, *upon the development of natural forces, according to natural laws.*

In reference to these theories, I shall only observe, that, rightly considered, they and the numerous modifications of them, which figure in the books, seem to me to be expressions of the same truth, seen from different points of view, and naturally seen with different degrees of clearness and completeness. Thus, if the phenomena of civil society be viewed with particular reference to Divine Providence, whose interposition, whether special or general, through the operation of natural laws, is unquestionably a principal, if not the exclusive component of the forces whose resultant is the state, the ground of those phenomena might, not without apparent reason, be regarded as the Divine will. Let the attention, on the other hand, be directed chiefly to the fact, apparent in any political society during even the stormiest periods of its history, that the bulk, the majority in weight and influence, if not in numbers, of its members, acquiesce in, (see *post,* § 65,) perhaps have formally assented to, the forms of its social and political organization. and it would seem proper to refer those forms to a compact between the individuals composing it. But if, beside the Divine will, and beside the apparent consent or agreement of those who constitute the bulk of a society, account be taken, as it certainly ought, of the will of men, often perverse, always unstable, and which, if a will at all, whatever theologians may say, is not determined by the Divine will, but is independent of it; the will of men, too, not comprised in that bulk of the society which seems to organize political institutions by compact, but constituting a protesting or rebellious minority, by whose hostile pressure or assault those institutions are modified, though not determined; and if, further, account be taken of the natural or historical conditions of soil, climate, laws, degree of civilization, habits, passions, aversions, religion, and race, all of which are constantly appearing elements of the social problem in every state, whatever its rank in the scale of civilization; it would seem reasonable to ground sovereignty and civil government upon the development of natural forces, according to natural laws. By this view, the problems of political philosophy are problems of vital dynamics; the state is an object of natural history, like a coral reef, a swarm of bees, or a family of beavers; a composite animal, a union of many persons into one, but a vital union, not a mere aggregation by accident or choice of individuals by nature independent of each other; a union dating from the creation of the parts, and, therefore, under some form and conditions, a necessary union. The *way* in which such a composite being achieves what measure it does of social life and development, under the combined operation of all the social forces indicated, together with the modes of operation of these forces, are the constitution and laws of that being.

the individuals constituting such unit, nor in any number of them as such, nor even in all of them, except as organized into a body politic and acting as such. Thus, Justice Iredell, in a case in the Supreme Court of the United States, decided in 1795, after describing the formation of our governments, said: "In such governments, the sovereignty resides in the great body of the people, but it resides in them not as so many distinct individuals, but in their political capacity only."[1]

§ 22. As to the second branch of the question, relating to the *attributes* of sovereignty, little need be said. The attributes of sovereignty, mentioning such only as tend to throw light upon the problems discussed in this work, are as follows:—

1. A true sovereign can never voluntarily abdicate or divest itself of the sovereignty. A sovereign political society may cease longer to exist as such, — may become merged in another society, and so lose its sovereignty; but so long as it remains an independent political society, it must possess and exercise sovereign powers.

2. Sovereignty is indivisible. To establish this, we need but to try to conceive of the contrary. If the sovereignty of a state were divided among its citizens, whether a few or all of them, the recipients of it would each be possessed of equal sovereign power, and, there being no common superior, government would be impossible.[2]

3. Sovereignty is indefeasible; that is, it is incapable, by any juggle based upon legal analogies, of being defeated or abrogated. As expressed by James Wilson, in the Convention of Pennsylvania to adopt the Federal Constitution, "sovereignty is and *remains* in the people."

4. Sovereignty is inalienable; that is, "society never can delegate or pledge away sovereignty."[3] "Being inherent, naturally

[1] Penhallow *v.* Doane's Admrs., 3 *Dallas'* R. 54. See, also, to the same point, the testimony of Judge Tucker, in Tuck. *Blackst. Com.*, Vol. I. Appendix, p. 9, ed. 1803.

So, also, Dr. Brownson: "The political sovereignty, under the law of nature, attaches to the people, not individually, but collectively, as civil and political society. It is vested in the political community or nation, not in an individual or family, or a class." — *The Amer. Republic*, p. 135.

[2] For a statement of the absurd consequences of a divisible sovereignty, see Lieber's *Political Ethics*, Vol. I. p. 252. See also Brownson's *American Republic*, pp. 192–196.

[3] Lieber's *Polit. Ethics*, Vol. I. p. 251.

and necessarily, in the state, it cannot pass from it so long as the latter exists." [1]

By this is not meant that the *exercise* of sovereignty may not be delegated. Such a delegation is of the essence of government. But to delegate to another the exercise of a power within prescribed limits, or for a determinate time or purpose, is no alienation of it, but supposes it to be still virtually in the original hand.

5. Sovereignty, as we have said, is indivisible, but the sovereign body itself is not. The latter may be divided into several sovereigns, each distinct and independent. To be convinced of this, we have but to imagine a body politic split by overwhelming force into several parts. The fragments survive the shock, become new independent societies, and run separate careers. Each is a sovereign society. An instance of such a disruption occurred in the British empire at the time of the American Revolution. Previously to our Declaration of Independence, England was, as she has ever since continued to be, a sovereign society, but of that England the colonies formed a part. When the connection was severed, the "United Colonies," by which the separation was effected, became a new political society, independent of the crown, and, as such, invested with all sovereign rights.

6. Finally, two or more sovereign bodies may by force or by consent become united and form a new political society. In such a case, sovereignty forsakes the composing units and becomes inherent in the resulting aggregate. To have that effect, however, it is doubtless necessary that the union should not be a mere juxtaposition, but a fusion, of the constituent elements.

§ 23. The characteristic marks and attributes of sovereignty being comprehended, it is important to ascertain the various modes of its manifestation.

Sovereignty manifests itself in two ways: first, *indirectly*, through individuals, acting as the agents or representatives of the sovereign, and constituting the civil government; and, secondly, *directly*, by organic movements of the political society itself, without the ministry of agents; the movements referred to exhibiting themselves either in those social agitations, of which the resultant is known as *public opinion*, that *vis a tergo*

[1] Lieber's *Polit. Ethics*, Vol. I. p. 250.

in all free commonwealths, by which the machinery of government is put and kept in orderly motion; or in manifestations of *original power*, by which political or social changes are achieved irregularly, under the operation of forces wielded by the body politic itself immediately.[1]

Of the two direct manifestations of sovereignty indicated, *public opinion* is by far the most important, the most constant, and the least dangerous. By it is meant, not the opinion of this or that man or class, but the opinion of the body politic, which is the resultant of the concurring, divergent, and clashing opinions of the whole body of the citizens. The object upon which this important social force expends itself is either the government, considered as the servant of the sovereign, or the society employing it, which is the sovereign itself. But the peculiarity of it is, that while constitutions and laws make no allusion to public opinion as a legitimate political force, all administrative agencies bow before it as though it were true, as is often affirmed, that "the voice of the people is the voice of God."

The other direct manifestation of sovereignty, the irregular exhibition of power, is witnessed when society, by a general and irresistible impulse, does an act because it *will* do it, taking less account of its lawfulness than of its necessity or desirableness, though often, for example's sake, covering its contempt of legal forms with a thin varnish of fiction or sophistry. In plain language, such an exhibition of original power is in the nature of a *coup d'état*, an act of force originating in lawlessness, but, because done by a body whose power is overwhelming, an act which it were folly to impeach. A striking instance of this sort of original manifestation of sovereignty occurred in England in consummating the Reform movement in 1832. The English people had been excited to the verge of revolution by the agitators for reform in the electoral system. A reform bill, passed by the Commons, had been twice thrown out by the Lords. Neither house giving way, and an outbreak of violence seeming inevitable, the prime minister, Lord Grey, took measures forcibly to carry the bill, when the Lords yielded and allowed it to pass. Here, the organic pressure of the nation, culminating in the ministerial project of deluging the House of Lords with new peers, who would vote for the Reform Bill, consummated a

[1] Lieber's *Polit. Ethics*, Vol. I. p. 256.

change in the constitution of Parliament upon which the hearts of the people had become fixed. It was a revolution effected by the direct action of the body politic, and not by the vulgar usurpation of a prince or military leader, so common in the history of political revolutions.

§ 24. With the indirect manifestations of sovereignty, through the intermediation of agents, all are familiar. Save in the exceptional modes just described, the sovereign exercises the right of sovereignty in no other way than by procuration. It cannot meet to deliberate, as it must do to engage directly in legislation. When laws are established, it cannot in person expound or apply them ; nor, when expounded or applied, can it superintend their execution. It is a society sovereign as a totality, but, as such, so unwieldy, that a direct exercise of its functions, save in miniature states, like the ancient democracies, or the city commonwealths of the Middle Ages, is wholly impracticable. For this reason it organizes systems of agencies, to which it delegates the right to exercise such powers as it chooses to grant. The agents holding these delegated powers, collectively considered, constitute the civil government of the society.

In most modern governments, including our own, there are four distinct branches or departments, to which are confided the powers delegated by the sovereign. Of these, the first is the *Electors*, whose function is that of choosing out of their own number the functionaries employed in the other departments, to which in the United States is added that of enacting the fundamental laws. The electoral body is the most numerous in the state, charged with an official function. It comprises the suffrage-holders, or voters, or, in a qualified sense, *the people*, and differs from the other three departments in that it constitutes a body which never assembles, but acts in segments of such convenient size as not to render conference and coöperation impracticable.

The other three departments are familiar under the names of legislative, executive, and judicial departments, charged with the duties indicated by those terms respectively.

To these four systems of agencies, common to the best governments of both Europe and America, those of the United States have added a fifth, unknown abroad,— the Constitutional Convention,—whose functions, as we have already seen, are such as to rank it as a legislature, but a special legislature, whose duty it is to participate in the framing or amending of Constitutions.

Of these five departments, the last four represent the sovereign only mediately, — those who fill them being either elected, in accordance with legal provisions, by the first, the electors, or appointed by some coördinate department. The electors, on the other hand, represent the sovereign immediately, being designated by the latter in the original act constituting the government, the Constitution.

It is evident that neither of the five systems of agencies named is possessed of sovereignty, though by delegation, mediate or immediate, they all exercise more or less of its powers. There is observable amongst them, moreover, a gradation : first, with respect to the extent to which they are vested with sovereign powers; and, secondly, with respect to the nearness of their relations to their head, the sovereign. Thus, in both particulars, the electoral body ranks high, since it stands, as we have seen, nearest to the sovereign, and its functions, though limited, are extremely important. The two legislative departments are vested with powers more extensive than any others: the convention, with power to frame the fundamental laws, to be passed upon by the electors; and the legislature, with the broad powers of remedial and punitory legislation. After these follow the executive and judiciary, charged severally with functions more limited, though of vast importance to the state.

On the whole, if required to marshal the five systems of agencies according to their relative rank, to be determined by the degree in which, in the various respects indicated, they represent the sovereign power, I should place them thus: 1, the Electors; 2, the Legislature; 3, the Convention; 4, the Executive; and 5, the Judiciary.

§ 25. Before proceeding further with the discussion of sovereignty, I desire to draw from what has preceded one or two corollaries having a direct practical bearing on the main subject of this treatise, the Constitutional Convention, its powers and functions. These corollaries are deducible from the principles enunciated above, by the aid of what I may call *the doctrine of constitutional presumptions*, which may be explained as follows:

The sovereign, having once established agencies for the government of the state, retires from view, and, except by the pressure of opinion, or by power from time to time irregularly applied, ceases to interfere in the conduct of affairs; in this respect, dealing with the system established by it as the Deity dealt with the universe, when, having created it, He left it, as it were, "wound up," to run according to the laws He had ordained, and interfered with it only by affecting the consciences of men, or occasionally, perhaps, by special providences, when some crisis demanded it. In the act of retiring thus the sovereign virtually says: "These are my agents. What this proclaims, in the forms prescribed, you shall consider as law. To this, I have given power to expound and apply the law, and to this, power to carry the law into effect, using, if needful, the entire public force. When the system I have established needs reparation or renewal, let this body propose, and this other ratify, the needed changes. Here is the commission by whose letter or spirit all are to be guided — the Constitution."

Now, respecting a system thus established, what presumptions arise as against any other system or institution springing up by its side, unknown or hostile to it?

They are two:—

1. That, at any given time, the sovereign body is content with the establishment now existing, created by its own act — a presumption arising from the very fact that that establishment exists.

2. That if the sovereign body desired a change in the structure or functions of the government founded by itself, it would prefer to indicate that desire through its own agents, and not through strangers or persons standing to it in no official relation; and that it would choose to effect such change by some authorized organic action of the system itself, whereby harmony between governors and governed would be assured, rather than by irregular methods, as by exhibitions of original power by itself, or by usurpations on the part of individuals or public bodies, savoring of revolution, and rendering such harmony impossible.

These, I apprehend, are the presumptions warranted by the relations indicated. Applying these as a test to the case of political action, the following corollaries are justified:—

1. That all interference with the frame or working of a government established, by persons *ab extra*, that is, not commis-

sioned for that purpose by the government itself, is usurpation, though participated in by every citizen in the Commonwealth, and is therefore illegal and revolutionary.[1]

2. That whenever a public body, belonging to the governmental system established by the sovereign, assumes, without an express warrant in the Constitution, laws, or approved customs of the country, to meddle with that Constitution, with the laws, or with the public administration, it is guilty of usurpation, and its acts are null and void.

§ 26. In the general discussion of sovereignty, in the preceding sections, that power has been supposed to reside in the body politic, comprising the whole population of the Commonwealth, without distinction of age or sex. This presents the theoretical view of the question. It is important for my purpose to go beyond this, and ascertain how far the theoretical view corresponds with historical or existing facts, and if discrepancies should appear, to explain their causes and character.

The question may be considered with reference, — I., to Foreign States; and II., to the United States of America.

I. In most civilized states abroad, there is much confusion of ideas in regard to the location of the sovereign power. In some, it is placed in the monarch or chief executive officer, who, in fact, exercises wide, and often unlimited, powers. In others, it is located in a close corporation of nobles, wielding similar powers. In a third class, comprising governments of a mixed character, with a monarch, a privileged nobility, and a commonalty representing the nation at large, the latter is practically recognized as the true sovereign. But while in this case there is a real conformity to principles, the fiction is entertained that the monarch is the fountain of all power, the sovereign in fact, as in name. In the other two varieties, the existence of the nation as a power distinct from the court, is ignored in law, and appears as a fact only in those terrible moments when the giant, overthrown and trodden under foot of his servants, heaves beneath them, crumbling to pieces the structures founded upon the theory of his permanent subjection. The course of history demonstrates that the power of the nation is always in the long run superior to that of any fraction of it, and needs but to

[1] For an exposition of the import of the terms *revolution* and *revolutionary*, as used in this treatise, see ch. iv. §§ 109–113.

be called out. What Sully has said of the populace, is true of nations: "They never rebel from a desire of attacking, but from an impatience of suffering." When the limit of endurance has been reached, governments and dynasties are in their presence but as flax before the fire. If the body politic, like Gulliver among the Lilliputians, is bound by the pigmy tribe intrusted with its protection, it is not because it has lost either its power or its right, nor because in its betrayers there exists that irresistible potency which is everywhere recognized as the basis of dominion. The despotism practised by them is a permissive one, founded on the good nature, the inertness or the temporary distraction of its victims. Let the step too far be taken, and it springs up sovereign by a title as indisputable as a decree of fate — that of superior force.

In the states in question, then, the real sovereign is the body politic, as theory requires. But in most of them, the true sovereign has allowed itself to be stripped of its robes of state by usurping servants. Its very existence as a fountain of authority is denied, the relations of superior and inferior being, practically, through the supineness of the former, reversed.

§ 27. II. I come now to the most important question of all, namely, —

Where lies the sovereignty in the United States, and how does it exist in the person or body ascertained to be the depositary thereof?

1. The first branch of this question may be considered from two points of view, in the main independent of each other, namely: (*a*), from that of the elementary principles of sovereignty, developed in the foregoing sections; and (*b*), from that of historical facts and principles evolved in the life of this and other peoples, and having a tendency to determine the question of *American nationality.*

A short space will be devoted to this question from each of these points of view.

(*a*). Distinguishing the territory and people of the United States from the residue of the territory and peoples of the earth, and considering the same as forming an independent society, it is evident that the right of sovereignty resides somewhere within it in as ample a measure as in any other political society.

The difficulty is, in the jumble of National and State organizations, to locate it.

Recurring now to the definition and marks or tests of sovereignty laid down in this chapter, let us see if it be possible to find, with their help, where that power probably resides in the United States.

A sovereign person or body, as we have seen, is one to whom there is, politically, no superior.

Contrasting the State governments, as political organizations, with the Federal government as a political organization, it is evident that the former cannot be said to be sovereign, or by consequence to be possessed of sovereignty, either collectively or individually, since if their *equality* with the Federal government were conceded, they certainly are not its *superior*. But their equality cannot be conceded. By the Constitution of the United States, that instrument and the laws of the United States, made in pursuance thereof, are declared to be the supreme law of the land, and the judges in every State are to be bound thereby, and all State officials, legislative, executive, and judicial, are to be bound by oath to support that Constitution. If, therefore, it might seem from the fact that a separate and independent jurisdiction is apportioned to the several States on the one hand, and to the general government on the other, that they are equal to each other, these clauses of the Constitution show that such is not the case, but that, in all that wide field, where the powers of both are concurrent, or where it is doubtful with which the power is lodged, and collisions occur or impend, the latter is to be taken as supreme. If either of the two, therefore, the States or the general government, is sovereign, it is not the former but the latter.

But is it true, that sovereignty is lodged with the general government?

Applying the same principles, and, in their light, contrasting the federal government with the people of the United States, — the only other imaginable depositary of sovereign powers, — it is clear that those powers must belong to the latter and not to the former, for two reasons. 1. The people of the United States "ordained and established" the Federal government, — created it. As between creator and creature, the former must be the political superior of the latter. 2. Governments are always secondary and vicarious. They are agencies, and to suppose them possessed of sovereign powers, is to make those powers alienable beyond redemption, which is opposed to the true conception of sovereignty. It is rather the people of the United States, who, having created, may be presumed competent to alter or abolish, their government, that is the true sovereign.

So much for the inferences to be drawn from the definition of sovereignty.

§ 28. Let us now subject the three political bodies or entities specified to a rigid scrutiny, to see if in either of them there can be discovered the distinguishing marks of sovereignty above described.

"If a determinate human superior," says Mr. Austin,[1] "not in a habit of obedience to a like superior, receive *habitual* obedience from the *bulk* of a given society, that determinate superior is sovereign in that society."

What political body, institution, or entity is there, in the United States, not in a habit of obedience to any other body, etc., which receives *habitual* obedience from the *bulk* of the Union, but the people of the United States? It certainly is not the States, for they have habitually obeyed, each and all of them, the people of the United States ever since the latter entered into a union as one people.[2] The people of the United States, in 1788, threw the existing Constitutions of the several States into hotchpotch, and repartitioned amongst those bodies the powers they were thenceforth to exercise, giving a portion thereof to the States, a portion to the general government, and reserving the residue to themselves. And the States have *habitually* conformed to the edict which thus curtailed and ascertained their powers.

Not only this: the States, since the foundation of the Union, have not received "habitual obedience from the *bulk*" of the Union; certainly not, severally considered; for while the respective States have received habitual obedience, each from the bulk of its own people, they have not received it severally from the peoples of the other States; that is, the State of Virginia has

[1] See *ante*, § 19.

[2] The word *habitually* is inserted by Mr. Austin in this test of sovereignty to cover the very case lately presented by the United States; that is, the case in which a part of the society should be for a time in revolt against the sovereign whole. It is the *general habit* of all the parts to obey, that is to determine where the sovereignty resides.

received habitual obedience from the bulk of the Virginians, but not from that of the people of the whole Union.

If it be urged that the States collectively have received obedience from the bulk of the Union, and therefore fulfil the conditions necessary to make them sovereign organizations, the reply is, that the term "States" is ambiguous, meaning either the citizens of the United States, comprised within the State lines respectively, or the governments established by them within the same lines. In the latter sense, it is not true that the States, considered either severally or collectively, have ever received obedience from the bulk of the society forming the Union. The State governments have no extra-territorial operation, and, of course, receive no extra-territorial obedience. In the former sense, by the "States," collectively considered, would be meant the entire people of the United States, and the hypothesis in question would attribute sovereignty to that people, acting in groups by States — a view of the subject whose correctness I shall have occasion to examine when I come to consider *how* sovereignty exists in the people of the United States. For the present, I shall only observe, that if the case last supposed were conceded to express the real fact, it would not make the States, as such, sovereign, either individually or collectively, but the people of the United States, acting in a particular way or under particular conditions, as in groups, discriminated from each other by State boundaries.

§ 29. Tested by the concluding mark above described,[1] the result is the same.

Whenever, it was said, there exist, within the same territorial limits, two political organizations so related to each other that one determines its own powers and, in so doing, limits, enlarges, or abolishes those of the other, being itself at the same time not only subject to no reciprocal modification, but independent of all the world, the former is a sovereign organization, and the latter is not.

Seeking amongst the political entities of the United States one which answers to these conditions, it is plain that no one of them does so, unless it be the people of the United States. Neither the *government* of the United States, nor the *people* nor *government* of the several States, answers either of those conditions, being each of them subject to the modifying influence of a

[1] *Ante*, § 20.

power underlying them all, from which they received either their origin or those structural changes by which their present form and scope were determined. That underlying power is the people of the United States.[1] To attribute sovereignty to the former, therefore, would be an abuse of terms.

On the other hand, the conditions of sovereignty required are all fulfilled by the people of the United States. Neither their powers nor their modes of administration are determined by the States, severally considered, whether as peoples or governments, nor by the government of the Union, but by themselves alone in some mode selected by themselves. It rests with them, moreover, to remodel or to abolish the governments both of the States and of the Union, and, if they choose, to wipe out the States themselves as political organizations. Under what conditions this may be done, will be the subject of future consideration. For my present purpose, it is enough that the thing may be done under some conditions. This fact alone indicates that the people of the United States are the only sovereign. If it turn out, as it will, that the conditions prescribed under which alone they can do this, are prescribed by themselves, and, therefore, are enforcible only by moral sanctions, that they are the sovereign will become perfectly certain.

§ 30. (*b*). I pass now to consider briefly a few historical facts and principles tending to determine the mooted question of *American nationality*, with a view to furnishing other if not more solid grounds of inference as to the location of sovereignty in the United States. For, if the latter, as a political society, constitute a NATION, there is an end of all question, — the sovereignty dwells in the people of the United States, considered as a body politic and corporate.[2]

Do the United States, then, constitute a Nation?

Before attempting to answer this question, let us determine what it is, and what it is not, to be a nation.

A nation is defined to be "a race of men; a people born[3] in

[1] For a more complete exhibition of this relation of the people of the United States to the people and government of the States respectively, see *post*, §§ 58 and 62.

[2] "Now, an independent nation is, *ex vi termini*, a sovereign." — Grimke, *arguendo*, 2 Hill's S. C. Rep. 58. Vattel, bk. 1, ch. 1, sec. 12.

[3] "*Nascor*," "*natus*," "*natio*," — *to be born.*

the same country, and living under the same government, a people distinct from others."[1]

In this definition is evidently involved the idea of descent from a common stock. This, though substantially correct, would exclude those cases in which different races are mingled in a lasting political union; as when, to a central stock, there are accreted foreign elements by adoption.

A nation, then, in its largest sense, is analogous to, but not identical with, the family. It is a distinct, independent people; consisting of men of one blood, with such accretions from alien races as, resulting from common affinities, are destined to be permanent; occupying a determinate territory, within whose limits it maintains its own forms of social organization; possessing the same language, laws, religion, and civilization, the same political principles and traditions, the same general interests, attachments, and antipathies; in short, a people bound together, by common attractions and repulsions, into a living organism, possessed of a common pulse, a common intelligence and aspirations, and destined apparently to have a common history and a common fate.

So far of the affirmative definition of a nation.

§ 31. The negative may be given in equally few words.

1. To be a nation is not to be, literally, of one blood or race, but, as we have seen, to be mainly of one blood or race, but with permanent accretions from other races, undergoing, consciously or otherwise, the process of assimilation to the prevailing type.

2. To be a nation, it is not necessary that all its constituent members should be continuously, and under all circumstances, willing or even acquiescent participators in the common national life. Civil wars and dissensions, though facts tending to disprove the existence of nationality in a particular case, are far from decisive of that question, being as inconclusive evidence of its non-existence as a strong and enduring friendship between two contiguous nations would be that they constituted but a single nation. Wars arise as often, perhaps, between factions of the same blood and race, impelled by political animosity or ambition, but confessedly forming a single nation, as between parties of diverse descent, scrambling for ascendency in a con-

[1] Worcester's *Dictionary*, *in verb.*

federation, possessing no distinctive national features. If civil commotions, however extensive, were proof that a people did not constitute a nation, what nation has ever existed?

§ 32. Proceeding, now, in the light of these definitions, it may be inferred that the United States constitute a nation, —

1. From the fact that, in their development from sparse settlements into a compact and powerful state — *e pluribus unum* — there is observable *a perfect conformity to the method of nature in the genesis of nations.*

Let us see what that method is: —

Nations do not spring into life, in full bloom of population, wealth, and culture. They are developed from rude beginnings, by a process of assimilation and growth analogous to that in organic life. In their origin, they commonly form a chaos of heterogeneous materials. These, Nature subjects to her kindly influences of warmth and pressure, till they assume a character homogeneous, and, because formed under new conditions, distinctive.

There are two modes in which the diversified materials that ultimately fuse into nations are brought into the contact necessary to a vital union. They may be superimposed, like geological strata; as, where a race comes in by conquest over another, whose polity it subverts, and which it keeps beneath itself as subjects or vassals; or those materials, being dropped apart, like chance seeds, in a wide territory, may take root and spread, each from its little centre, and come in turn to press upon each other laterally.

Whichever of these modes obtains, the constant phenomena are at first estrangements, swelling into wars by reason of collisions of interests, or differences of character and habit. Time, however, kneads the colliding elements gradually into consistency. From being like, they soon come to like, each other. Perhaps the process by which their fusion is completed is, that they suffer some common affliction, or wage together some great war, in which every drop of blood cements them into a firmer union.

§ 33. Of the first mode, most European nations furnish examples. From the earliest historical dates have been witnessed in them wave after wave of conquering races rolling from the east and north, and dashing one upon the other as they went westward and southward, but never returning. Out of these diverse and hostile alluviums Nature has built the great races that we have seen in modern times in Europe.

Of the other mode, early Rome was an example. In the first years of her history, Italy was filled with petty states, among which Rome was but *prima inter pares*. As they grew, jealousies led to border wars, in which that single city long maintained a doubtful conflict with neighbors too nearly her equals to be completely subdued. As Rome waxed great, and the privileges of her citizenship became more and more highly prized, what her arms alone had failed to accomplish, she did by her policy; she absorbed the neighboring tribes into her own organization, and thus, from one of the loosest, became one of the compactest and most enduring nationalities that the world has ever seen.

Such is the method of Nature in the genesis of nations; beginning with elements diverse and discordant, she ends by kneading them into likeness and unity.

It should be noted, too, that whether this process be slow or rapid, the nature of the result is the same. Thus, what Rome was many centuries in accomplishing, under the circumstances that surrounded her — barbaric populations on all sides, want of roads, of facilities for education, of a sufficient public revenue, of nearly every thing that gives impulse to national growth, — a people, however heterogeneous, endowed with steam, in its thousand applications, with the telegraph, the printing-press, and, above all, with that modern spirit, which is fruitful of great enterprises, in all departments of human endeavor, under circumstances the most adverse, would be able to achieve in a few decades of years.[1]

Now, the conditions presented by the United States were, in our early history, similar to those of Rome. Our land was dotted over with isolated communities, that had sprung up here and there sporadically, as chance had led to settlement. Growing from remote and too frequently hostile societies, out into the presence of each other, what affinities they had, from identity of race, laws, literature, and religion, and from similarity of circumstances and condition with respect to European nations, were set actively at work, as also their mutual repulsions.

But there was this difference between America and Rome, —

[1] Mommsen, *Hist. Rome*, Vol. I. pp. 68, 69.

the latter arose slowly, and with struggles tedious and endless, ages before the birth of Christ; the former sprang up two thousand years later, after the life and teachings of that Divine personage had fruited into the institutions of our time, when, as compared with that of Rome, a day, in its actual achievement, is as a thousand years.

In this manner and under these influences, the United States have become what we see. Whether the result has been to make of them a nation, is the question. So far as the *method* of their development is concerned, there are furnished, I think, affirmative indications.

§ 34. When we look closely at the successive steps by which we came to be what we are, the probability that we have ripened into a nation is much increased.

The most prominent characteristic of American constitutional history, is *a constant and irrepressible tendency toward union.*

Including the crowning act, by which the people of the United States crushed the attempt at disunion in 1861–5, there have been taken in our history eight capital steps toward the consummation of a complete national union. These occurred in 1643, in 1754, in 1765, in 1774, in 1775, in 1781, in 1788, and 1861–5. Comparing these steps with one another, there is visible in them a steady progress in two particulars: first, in the number of the colonies or States participating in them; and, secondly, in the scope of the successive schemes of union, the establishment of which was sought or accomplished by them respectively.

1. Thus, a scheme of union was formed in 1643 by four colonies; in 1754, by seven; in 1765, by nine; in 1774, by twelve; in 1775, by thirteen, — the last two resulting in the revolutionary congresses preceding the confederation; in 1781, by thirteen, with great reluctance establishing the confederation; in 1788, by thirteen, still with reluctance, but driven to it by financial necessities, founding the present establishment; and in 1861–5, by twenty-five loyal, and a loyal minority in each of eleven disloyal States, by force of arms crushing the power of a faction seeking to destroy the Union.

2. Without particularizing the scope of each of these eight efforts at the consolidation of a union, with which all readers of our history are familiar, it is enough to observe, that the first

was a simple league of four New England colonies against the Indians, and their hostile neighbors, the Dutch; the two following were similar in their general purpose, but broader in intent and compass; the next two, as explained above, were broader still, embracing practically the entire continent, and being designed to conduct the contest with Great Britain; the sixth was the first formal and regular attempt to establish a government for united America, but undertaken with such fear and jealousy, that the system established stood only so long as it was held together by pressure from without; the seventh was an abandonment of the idea of confederation, and the introduction of the conception of a national government, framed by the people of the United States, the several State governments being at the same time shorn of much of their former power, and relegated to the secondary position held by them as colonies under the Crown. The last, supreme step was that in which two million men in arms have, in our day, stamped with condemnation the heresy of secession, and denied the rightfulness of disunion either as fact or as theory; thus giving to that series of acts and charters by which the rights of the colonies were defined and guaranteed, a practical construction, and justifying the inference, *that union — the consolidation of the various communities forming the United Colonies into one people, one nation — was at once the purpose of God, and the design, sometimes consciously and sometimes unconsciously entertained, of the men of all times in America.*

§ 35. Every step of our progress from 1643 to 1865 being upon convergent lines, of which the point of meeting would be a perfected union, in my judgment, when the Constitution of 1788 was ratified, if not before, we *became* that which, on the 4th of July, 1776, we had *declared* ourselves to be, "one people" or nation, free and independent. Then, at the latest, the bundle of States, loosely bound together by the Articles of Confederation, emerged into view as a political society, and, as such, assumed the power of ordaining a government for itself, as well as for its members, before that claiming to be sovereign. Certainly, if the process of fusion, which a century and a half had been carrying on, had not then become complete, the conditions necessary for its ultimate completion had been supplied, the collective society having been placed in such bonds and subjected to such influences that the process must go on, and that rapidly. These bonds, every year of the union has seen growing stronger and stronger. Beginning, as we have seen, with the same blood, language, religion, and civilization, with a love of the same liberties, with a unanimous voice for the same republican forms, with a compact territory, and a recognized name abroad only as a Union, to these there have been added the bonds of nearly a century of associated life, to say nothing of wars prosecuted together and shedding a common glory over that Union, for whose defence or enlargement they have been waged. All these, it seems, whatever we may have been when we started in the race, ought to have left us a *nation*, in heart and affection, as they have in fact and in law.

§ 36. The next fact to which I shall advert, as furnishing a ground of inference that we are a nation, is, that the Constitution of 1788 *was ratified by the people of the United States;* in this respect violating the law and departing from the precedents previously in force.

By the thirteenth of the Articles of Confederation, it had been provided, that *no alteration of said articles should at any time thereafter be made, unless such alteration should be agreed to in a Congress of the United States, and "be afterwards confirmed by the legislature of every State."* That is, by the Federal Constitution, in force when the present one was formed, no change could be made in the provisions of the former, but by the action of the *State governments*, that is, of the States, considered as political organizations. This important constitutional interdict the Convention of 1787, for reasons deemed adequate, disregarded. It provided for the ratification of the proposed Constitution *by Conventions of the people to be called in the several States by the legislatures thereof;* that is, for its ratification by the people of the United States, acting, as was alone possible, in groups of such size as to be not inconvenient, and so arranged that advantage could be taken of the existing electoral machinery, which belonged exclusively to the States. This method was wholly new, and involving, as it clearly did, a violation of the Articles of Confederation, must have been adopted, because it was thought absolutely necessary to bring forward the Constitution just matured under wholly new conditions; to base it, not upon the States, but upon the broader and more solid foundation of the people of the United States, conceived of no longer as a cluster of badly cohering populations, but as a majestic unit, which, having emerged into existence, had at last compelled its own general and public recognition. Such is the lesson to be learned from the mode of ratification of the present Constitution.

§ 37. It must be admitted, that a different view has been taken of the bearing of the mode of ratifying the Federal Constitution on the question of our nationality. The political school, of which Mr. Jefferson was the founder, and Mr. Calhoun the great apostle and expositor, known as the "States Rights School," have deduced their favorite dogma of the sovereignty of the States, from the alleged ratification of the Constitution by the States; the argument being, that what the States formed and established they may, for reasons deemed to be sufficient, abrogate and annul. This school, admitting that the Constitution was required by its terms to be ratified by Conventions of delegates "chosen in each State by the people thereof," that is, by the people of the United States, considered as gathered into groups, by States, nevertheless maintain that, as a majority of the voices in each group or State was made requisite to its adoption, and not simply a majority of the aggregate of all the groups, the ratification must be considered substantially as pronounced by the States.

The reply is, that a majority of each State's electors, rather than of the aggregate of the electors of the Union, was required, not out of respect for the rights of the States, or with a view to found the new system upon the States, but to conform, as nearly as might be, to the positive requirements of the existing Constitution. The thirteenth of the Articles of Confederation required all alterations therein to be recommended by Congress and to be confirmed by the *legislature of each State*. Now, two difficulties were apprehended in attempting to conform strictly to this requirement. First, it was doubted whether a unanimous vote of all the States could be secured for the proposed plan. Hence it was provided by the Convention — Article VII. of the new Constitution — that the ratification of the Constitution *by nine States* should be sufficient for the establishment thereof between the States so ratifying the same. Secondly, it was feared that reluctance to surrender the reins of power, now in their hands, might lead the majority in the several *State legislatures*, if the question of ratifying the Constitution were left to those bodies, to reject it, even in States, whose citizens would be disposed to ratify it. Hence the Convention wisely determined to disregard the thirteenth article requiring a ratification in that manner, and to commit the fate of the instrument to Conventions specially chosen by the people for the very purpose of passing upon it.

But, while the Convention resolved to disobey the letter of the Constitution in allowing the system to be established on the ratification of nine States, and in substituting Conventions for legislatures as the ratifying bodies, they departed from the requirements of the Constitution no farther than was deemed necessary. The principle of unanimity was preserved by requiring the consent of each State which should be comprised in the new system to be given to its provisions; that is, no State was to be compelled to adopt the proposed Constitution, or, without adoption by its own citizens, to be governed by it. So, also, the old principle of independent State action was made to coexist and harmonize with the new principle of founding the political structure upon the basis of the people of the United States, by requiring the vote upon its establishment to be taken in the several States, but by the people thereof in their elementary character as citizens, and not as forming the governments of the States respectively. This, indeed, as already stated, was the only way in which a vote could have been taken at all, under any effective safeguards to secure its authenticity and purity. Except in the States, there was a total lack of the machinery necessary to inaugurate Conventions to adopt or reject the proposed Constitution.

§ 38. But, even if it were admitted that the present Constitution was ratified by the States, in the manner and in the capacity claimed by the politicians of the States Rights School, it would not follow that the separate communities brought thereby into a closer union did not, by the federal act, become a nation; nor, if they be conceded to have been sovereign societies under the Confederation, that they did not merge, each its separate sovereignty, in that of the Union. We have seen that two or more sovereign societies may become united into one, and that upon such union sovereignty becomes inherent in the resultant society. Whether it does so or not, however, depends upon the closeness of the union, to be ascertained from all the facts of the case, among the most important of which is doubtless the intent of the uniting peoples, as determined by the phraseology of the instrument embodying the conditions of the union. If, by the true construction of that instrument, the States, theretofore supposed to be sovereign, were intentionally shorn of their sovereignty and subordinated to a new organization, by its terms declared to be supreme, and especially if, by it, there were recognized as existing in the United States, — whether then for the first time or not, matters not, — a power competent to control, alter, or annul both the States and the general government, thus declared to be supreme, it could not be denied, that such power, the people of the United States, was the sovereign power of the Union, from the time such instrument was ratified. Indeed, if it be assumed, that the purpose of the people in forming the present Constitution was to merge in the single sovereignty of the Union the sovereignties of thirteen independent sovereign States, no mode of ratifying the instrument was possible, but that by the action of the States themselves, substantially like that which actually took place.

§ 39. One of the most valuable indications from which to determine whether or not we became a nation by the establishment of either of our two Constitutions, is derived from the expressed opinions of contemporary statesmen, friends as well as enemies of the systems thereby founded.

Respecting the effect of the first Federal Constitution, called the Articles of Confederation, some doubt has been not unnaturally entertained. It did not *make* of us a nation, for that is what no Constitution could do. Nor did it, in explicit terms, *declare* us to have become, or to be, a nation. And, yet, in my judgment, at the time the Confederation was formed, we were in fact a nation, though the process of fusion had not been completed. The insane passion for state autonomy, rife during the early years of the Revolutionary war, had not subsided. Because the war had proved successful, notwithstanding the imperfection of the Union, men gave to the sleazy fabric, under which it had been carried on, more credit for that result than it deserved. It took six years of peace, crowded with inter-state bickerings, and with constant exhibitions of imbecility by a government, which, whatever else it could do, could not govern, to teach our fathers, that, if their union still subsisted, it was in spite of their government, and that if they did not desire, within the borders of each State, to see a repetition of the rebellion kindled by Shay in Massachusetts, ending, perhaps, in a general civil war, they must substitute for the rotten structure of the Confederation a Constitution which should confirm and not undermine and break up their actual union. Under these impulses, the Constitution was framed. But the circumstances I have mentioned led to the formation of two parties, one strenuous for its adoption and the other bent, by any and all means, upon defeating it. The charges and admissions of the two disputants discussing its provisions, furnish valuable indications as to the nature of the Union and of its connecting bond, as viewed by men then living. The citations I shall make will be such as bear especially on the present Constitution.

§ 40. In the Convention which framed the Federal Constitution, the opposing views indicated were brought into prominence by a question of power, early raised by the partisans of a confederate government. Mr. Randolph of Virginia having introduced what is known as the Virginia plan, which formed the basis of the Constitution finally established, it was assailed by the friends of a Confederation on the ground that it was a scheme of national government, and that, as their credentials restricted them to the proposing of amendments to the system then in force, it was beyond their powers to form such a government. To the answer made to this objection, that the government then in force, however improved and strengthened, would be, as it had been, utterly insufficient to secure the declared objects thereof, it was replied, that that might be true, but that if so, it furnished a reason rather for adjourning and seeking further powers than for usurping such as were confessedly not vested in them.[1] The

[1] The first resolution of Mr. Randolph was as follows: — "*Resolved*, That a union of the States, merely federal, will not accomplish the objects proposed by the Articles of Confederation, namely, common defence, security of liberty, and general welfare." Mr. Charles Pinckney observed, that "if the Convention agreed to it, it appeared to him, that their business was at an end; for, as the powers of the house, in general, were to revise the present confederation, and to alter or amend it, as the case might require, to determine its insufficiency or incapability of amendment or improvement, must end in the dissolution of the powers."—Yates' *Minutes*, (1 Ell. *Deb.*) pp. 391, 392.

force of this argument was felt, but the Convention relieved itself from the dilemma, by recalling the fact that its duty was not to conclude but to recommend, and that where such was the case, particularly under the circumstances of the country, they must recommend measures that promised to be adequate to the exigencies of the occasion; and that to adjourn without doing so, because they found the defects of the old system more radical than had been supposed, would be to plunge into anarchy and civil war. Mr. Randolph, as reported by Mr. Madison, said, — "When the salvation of the Republic was at stake, it would be treason to our trust not to propose what we found necessary."[1] Mr. Hamilton said, — "He agreed with the honorable gentleman from Virginia (Mr. Randolph) that we owed it to our country to do on this emergency whatever we should deem essential to its happiness. The States sent us here to provide for the exigencies of the Union. To rely on and propose any plan not adequate to these exigencies, merely because it was not clearly within our powers, would be to sacrifice the end to the means."[2]

Mr. Madison took a similar view. He said, — "A new government must be made. Our all is depending on it; and if we have but a clause that the people will adopt, there is then a chance for our preservation."[3] Mr. Mason said, — "The principal objections against that" (the plan) "of Mr. Randolph, were the want of power and the want of practicability. There can be no weight in the first, as the *fiat* is not to be here but in the people. He thought with his colleague (Mr. Randolph) that there were, besides, certain crises in which all the ordinary cautions yielded to public necessity. He gave as an example the eventual treaty with Great Britain, in forming which the commissioners of the United States had wholly disregarded the improvident shackles of Congress; had given to their country an honorable and happy peace, and instead of being censured for the transgression of their powers, had raised to themselves a monument more durable than brass."[4] Mr. C. C. Pinckney "thought the Convention authorized to go any length in recom-

1 Elliott's *Deb.*, Vol. V. p. 197.

2 Id. p. 199.

3 Yates' *Minutes*, in Vol. I. Ell. *Deb.* p. 423.

4 Ell. *Deb.*, Vol. V. p. 216.

mending, which they found necessary to remedy the evils which produced this Convention."[1]

§ 41. From these extracts two things are evident, — first, that a change from the Confederation was deemed by the Convention absolutely necessary for the preservation of the States, for that body acquiesced in the reasonings contained in them and acted upon them;[2] and, secondly, that the national plan of Mr. Randolph, or some approach to it, was what was demanded by the exigencies of the Union.

§ 42. Thus it was that the new Constitution was viewed and characterized in the Federal Convention. Another indication may be drawn from the arguments used by its enemies in the several State Conventions, called to pass upon it. To those State conventions the Constitution was submitted as a project of a complete system, to take the place and supply the deficiencies

[1] Ell. *Deb.*, Vol. V. p. 197. See also Yates' *Minutes*, in Vol. I. Ell. *Deb.* pp. 414, 415, 417, 418, 428, 492–5.

[2] How urgent the necessity for a government of large powers was thought to be, may be inferred from the intimations, several times thrown out during and after the Convention, that it might become necessary to compel a union under the proposed Constitution, if not accepted voluntarily. Thus Gouverneur Morris said in the Convention: — "This country must be united. If persuasion does not unite it the sword will. He begged this consideration might have its due weight." (Ell. *Deb.*, Vol. V. p. 276.) Madison, in a letter to Washington, written while the question of adopting the Constitution was pending in New York, said: — "There is at present a very strong probability that nine States at least will pretty speedily concur in establishing it" (the Constitution). "What will become of the tardy remainder? They must be either left, as outcasts from the society, to shift for themselves, or be compelled to come in, or come in of themselves when they will be allowed no credit for it." Id. p. 568. Two days afterwards, October 30, 1787, Gouverneur Morris, writing also to Washington of the prospect of adopting the Constitution in New York, and of the condition of things in case she were to reject it, said: — "Jersey is so near unanimity in her favorable opinion that we may count with certainty on something more than votes should the state of affairs hereafter require the application of more pointed arguments. New York, hemmed in between the warm friends of the Constitution, will not easily, unless supported by powerful States, make any important struggle, even though her citizens were unanimous, which is by no means the case. Parties there are nearly balanced." (Ell. *Deb.*, Vol. I. p. 505.) In the Massachusetts Convention, Colonel Thompson spoke of force as contemplated, after nine States should have adopted the Constitution, to compel the remaining four to come in. He said: — "Suppose nine States adopt this Constitution, who shall touch the other four? Some cry out, Force them. I say, Draw them." — Ell. *Deb.*, Vol. II. p. 61.

of the old Confederation. Admitting, as did both the friends and the enemies of the Constitution, the absolute necessity of a change, how far did the latter regard the change proposed by it as extending? It is perhaps not fair to take the charges, often mere calumnies, of its enemies, as decisive of its character and powers. But the charges made were made by the States Rights party of that day, and there seems a sort of justice in quoting that party against itself, when its arguments against the Constitution are at different times mutually destructive. Besides, if a presumption is to be indulged, it is, that there was greater honesty in the party when in the early days of our political history it charged that the proposed Constitution formed a national or a consolidated government, than when at a later day, and still in the interest of State autonomy, it charged that it founded a government not differing in principle from that of the Confederation.

The ablest opponent of the new Constitution was doubtless Patrick Henry of Virginia, and the main ground of his opposition was, that it was a scheme of a consolidated government. In the Convention of that State, he said, —

"And here I would make this inquiry of those worthy characters who composed a part of the late Federal Convention. I am sure they were fully impressed with the necessity of forming a great consolidated government, instead of a confederation. That this is a consolidated government is demonstrably clear; and the danger of such a government is, to my mind, very striking. I have the highest veneration for those gentlemen; but, sir, give me leave to demand, what right they had to say, *We the people?* My political curiosity, exclusive of my anxious solicitude for the public welfare, leads me to ask, who authorized them to speak the language of, *We the people,* instead of, *We the States?* States are the characteristics and the soul of a confederation. If the States be not the agents of this compact, it must be one great consolidated national government of the people of all the States."

So, in the North Carolina Convention, Mr. Taylor said: — "This is a consolidation of all the States. Had it said, *We the States*, there would have been a federal intention in it. But, sir, it is clear that a consolidation is intended. Will any gentleman say, that a consolidated government will answer this country? . . . I am astonished, that the servants of the legislature of North Carolina should go to Philadelphia and, instead of speaking of the State of North Carolina, should speak of the people. I wish to stop power as soon as possible, for they may carry their assumption of power to a more dangerous length. I wish to know where they found the power of saying, *We the people*, and consolidating the States." [1]

A similar charge was made in perhaps every one of the State Conventions called to pass upon the Constitution.

§ 43. Now, it is not pretended, nor was it ever admitted by the friends of the Constitution, that that instrument in fact proposed a consolidated government. A consolidated government was defined by those who considered ours to be such, to be either, first, one "which puts the thirteen States into one," [2] or, secondly, "one that will transfer the sovereignty from the State governments to the general government." [3] It is preposterous to apply either of those definitions to the system contained in the Constitution. The first does not apply, because, as stated by Mr. Wilson, in the Pennsylvania Convention, the proposed government "instead of placing the State governments in jeopardy, is founded on their existence. On this principle its organization depends; it must stand or fall, as the State governments are secured or ruined." [4] The second definition applies no better, because the Constitution, whatever else it does, clearly does not transfer the sovereignty to the general government. Nobody, so far as I am aware, ever supposed the source of all power in the United States to be the general government. But the friends of the Constitution did not and could not deny, that it comprised the outlines of a firm national government of extensive powers. The scheme it presented, however, had other than national features. It was, in a word, a project of a mixed character, partly federal, as not annihilating, but on the contrary weaving into its texture as an essential part, the States, shorn doubtless of much of their powers, but still powerful and dignified organizations; and partly national, as founding the whole system, in all its features, both federal and national, on *the peo-*

[1] Ell. *Deb.*, Vol. III. pp. 22, 23.
[2] Ell. *Deb.*, Vol. II. pp. 503–504.
[3] Ibid.
[4] Ibid.

ple of the United States, then first emerging from the chaos of political elements into distinct and unmistakable prominence as a society, to be, according to that Constitution, one and indivisible forever.[1]

§ 44. Such was the character of the Constitution as viewed by its earliest enemies and its earliest friends; it was partly federal and partly national. Though it was the original purpose, unquestionably, of some of the most important States, to found a government possessed of more national features than the one proposed, that purpose had been frustrated by the determined opposition of the smaller States in the Convention, and a compromise had been made by which the government was to be, in its foundation and in its principal features, national, but, so far as the continued existence of the States was concerned, federal, — a most happy compromise, and perhaps the only one ever made in America, which, on the whole, sound statesmanship not only ought not to regret, but ought to regard as the most valuable and admirable feature in our whole system.

§ 45. As bearing on the question whether we are a nation or not, the facts stated above justify the following observations: —

1. The fact that the *government* under which we live, founded by the existing Constitution, is national only in part, does not prove that we are not now, or were not, at and before the time of its formation, a nation. It is evidence merely that, if we had been a nation before we formed it, it had not been deemed expedient to establish a government in which the principle of our nationality should be prominently asserted; but, on the contrary, that the nation should forego its right to found a single establishment by which to govern itself as a whole, and should permit the peoples of the several States to exercise in ample measure, but still in subordination to it, self-government, so far as concerned their local affairs.

2. The fact, on the other hand, that the general government was, in its inception, national to any extent, is conclusive evidence that there was a nation back of it as its founder. It is impossible to escape from this conclusion. It is only a nation that can found a national government, or a government of which substantive features are national, to continue forever, for it is

[1] See the masterly exposition of the mixed character of the government founded by the Constitution, made by Madison, in the *Federalist*, No. 39.

incredible that many distinct communities, not become one in sentiment, opinion, and physical circumstances, to such an extent as to render an entirely separate existence impossible, should ever consent to such a government. The leading points in the definition of a nation are, first, that there is such a unity of blood, of interest, and of feeling, in its component parts, that they fly together by a force of attraction that is practically irresistible, — they *must* live a common life; and, secondly, that there is such an identity in their situation, in relation to other communities, and consequently in the estimation in which they are held and in the dangers which threaten them, that they cannot live asunder. Both of these points concurred in the system founded by the Constitution of 1787. Our fathers must, as they expressed it, "join or die;" that is, they were impelled by every consideration that can draw men together, — the ties of blood, language, religion, common interest, and common glory, — to live together; and it was impossible, on account of inevitable border wars, carried on from ambition or revenge, and of the greed of foreign nations, that they should live apart.

§ 46. There remains still another source of evidence bearing on the question of our nationality, namely, judicial decisions and the opinions of statesmen and publicists subsequent to the formation of the existing Constitution. From the multitude of authorities of the kind referred to, I shall select but a few, and those mainly of an early date, bearing, some on the question of our nationality and some directly on the question of the location of the powers of sovereignty in the United States.

In 1793, during Washington's administration, the question arose in the Supreme Court of the United States, directly and unequivocally, where rests the sovereignty in the United States? Does it reside in the States or in the government of the United States, or, finally, is it lodged in the people of the United States?

The question arose thus: In the case of Chisholm, executor, a citizen of South Carolina, *v.* The State of Georgia, a motion was made by the Attorney-General, of counsel for the plaintiff in that court, requiring the State of Georgia to cause an appearance to be entered therein, in her behalf, on or before a day named, or, in default thereof, that judgment go against the State by default. The State refused to appear formally, but counsel represented her informally, and protested against the jurisdiction of the court to require the State to appear before it, *on the ground, with others, that she was a sovereign State, and so, not suable by a citizen of another State in the courts of the Union, or elsewhere, except in her own courts, without her own consent.* The nearly unanimous decision of the five judges then composing the court was against the State of Georgia on all the points raised. I shall cite mainly from the opinion delivered by Mr. Justice Wilson, one of the profoundest constitutional judges that ever graced the bench in the United States, not inferior, in my judgment, to Chief Justice Marshall himself. Justice Wilson said: "This is a case of uncommon magnitude. One of the parties to it is a STATE, certainly respectable, claiming to be *sovereign.* The question to be determined is, whether this State, so respectable, and whose claim soars so high, is amenable to the jurisdiction of the Supreme Court of the United States. This question, important in itself, will depend on others more important still; and may, perhaps, be ultimately resolved into one no less *radical* than this: 'Do the people of the United States form a NATION?'"[1] After a luminous exposition of the various meanings of the term state, he defines sovereignty, and proceeds: "As a citizen, I know the government of that State (Georgia) to be republican; and my short definition of such a government is, one constructed on this principle, — that the supreme power resides in the body of the people. As a judge of this court, I know, and can decide upon the knowledge, that the citizens of Georgia, when they acted upon the large scale of the Union, as a part of the 'people of the United States,' did not surrender the supreme or sovereign power to that State; but, *as to the purposes of the Union, retained it to themselves. As to the purposes of the Union, therefore, Georgia is* NOT *a sovereign State.*"[2] In another part of the same opinion, the learned judge makes the following important observation: "To the Constitution of the United States the term sovereign is totally unknown. There is but one place where it could have been used with propriety. But, even in that place, it would not, perhaps, have comported with the delicacy of those who *ordained* and *established* that Constitution. They might have announced themselves "SOVEREIGN" people of the United States. But,

[1] Chisholm, Ex'r, *v.* State of Georgia, 2 Dall. 453.
[2] Id. 457.

serenely conscious of the *fact*, they avoided the ostentatious declaration."[1] Concluding an exhaustive examination of the Constitution, Justice Wilson thus announces his opinion on the ultimate question with which he began, Are we a nation? "Whoever considers, in a combined and comprehensive view, the general texture of the Constitution, will be satisfied that the people of the United States intended to form themselves into a nation for national purposes. They instituted for such purposes a national government, complete in all its parts, with powers legislative, executive, and judiciary; and, in all those powers, extending over the whole nation."[2]

§ 47. It would be easy to fill these pages with judicial opinions confirmatory of these views, but space will not permit.[3] I confine myself to such as were delivered before the heresies of the Kentucky and Virginia resolutions were broached, — while the government of the Union was running under its original impulse, and before the party platform had been elevated into an ulterior constitution, assuming to control the exposition of that which the fathers had formed.

A few citations will now be made of the opinions of statesmen, historians, and publicists, of a later period, to whom has been accorded authority on constitutional questions. Thus, Washington, in a letter of June 8, 1783, said: "It is *only* in our *united* character that we are known as an empire, that our independence is acknowledged, that our power can be regarded, or our credit supported abroad."[4] So, still more explicitly, in his first inaugural address of April 6, 1789, he said: "Every step by which they" (the United States) "have advanced to the character of an independent nation, seems to have been distinguished by some token of providential agency."[5] In his history of the American Revolution, published in 1789, and afterwards in his history of the United States, Dr. Ramsay says: "The act of independence did not hold out to the world thir-

1 Chisholm, Ex'r, *v.* State of Georgia, 2 Dall. 454.

2 Id. 465. See also the opinions in the same case of Justices Cushing and Blair, and of Chief Justice Jay.

3 See, on the whole subject, Martin *v.* Hunter, 1 Wheat. 304 (324); McCullough *v.* The State of Maryland, 4 Wheat. 316.

4 5 Marsh. *Washington*, p. 48.

5 *Presidential Speeches*, p. 31.

teen sovereign States, but a common sovereignty of the whole in their united capacity."[1] So, General C. C. Pinckney, in a debate in the South Carolina House of Representatives, in 1788, speaking of the Declaration of Independence, said: "This admirable manifesto sufficiently refutes the doctrine of the individual sovereignty and independence of the several States. In that declaration the several States are not even enumerated, but after reciting, in nervous language, and with convincing arguments, our right to independence, and the tyranny which compelled us to assert it, the declaration is made in the following words. . . . . The separate independence and individual sovereignty of the several States were never thought of by the enlightened band of patriots who framed this declaration. The several States are not even mentioned by name in any part, as if it was intended to impress the maxim on America, that our freedom and independence arose from our union, and that, without it, we never could be free or independent. Let us, then, consider all attempts to weaken this Union, by maintaining that each State is separately and individually independent, as a species of political heresy, which can never benefit us, but may bring on us the most serious distresses."[2] Charles Pinckney, also, in his observations on the plan of government submitted by the Federal Convention, said: "The idea, which has been falsely entertained, of each being a sovereign State, must be given up, for it is absurd to suppose that there can be more than one sovereignty within a government."[3]

§ 48. Coming down to later times, I shall first cite the opinion of Mr. Grimke, a South Carolinian without guile and of eminence not inferior to that of the great names of the Revolution. Commenting on the opinions of the two Pinckneys, given in the last section, in the celebrated "allegiance cases," argued before the Court of Appeals of South Carolina, in 1834, Mr. Grimke said: "I do not fully agree with either of the Pinckneys, but certainly the truth that the United States constitute *one nation*, and that the States are *not nations*, is found in various forms scattered all along the highway which our country has been travelling since 1776. It would be difficult to find his-

[1] Ramsay's *Hist. U. S.* Vol. III. pp. 174, 175.

[2] 4 Ell. *Deb.* p. 301.

[3] Quoted by Mr. Grimke, *arguendo*, in 2 Hill's S. C. R. 57.

torical evidence on any point more full, particular, and various." To the same effect, Chancellor Kent, speaking of the colonies in 1776, in his Commentaries, says: "Gradually assuming all the powers of national sovereignty, they at last, on the 4th of July, 1776, took a separate and equal station among the nations of the earth, by declaring the united colonies to be free and independent States."[1] So, John Quincy Adams, referring to the same declaration, in 1831, said: "By the Declaration of Independence, the people of the United States had assumed and announced to the world their united personality as a nation, consisting of thirteen independent States. They had thereby assumed the exercise of primitive sovereign power; that is to say, the sovereignty of the people."[2] Justice Story makes a similar observation. "From the moment," he says, "of the declaration of independence, if not for most purposes at an antecedent period, the united colonies must be considered as being a nation *de facto*, having a general government over it created, and acting by the general consent of the people of all the colonies."[3] These authorities are of great interest, as indicating that the point of time when we first announced ourselves to be a nation, preceded the establishment of the present Constitution by about thirteen years. We were, then, a nation during all the long eclipse of the Confederation, whilst unwise jealousy was preventing the constituent peoples of the Union from admitting in their government the most salient and the most salutary fact of their history, namely, that they were one people forever, until driven to do so by the overwhelming pressure of events.

§ 49. So far, then, as the question, Where does the sovereign power in the United States reside? depends upon the other question, Are we a nation? we are entitled to affirm that that power resides in the people of the United States constituting the American nation. Before formally drawing that conclusion, however, I desire to refer to a few authorities, from which it may be gathered that there has never been a time in our history when the States were sovereign; and I shall do so at some length, because, it is obvious that if the States were not sovereign at any time before the establishment of the present govern-

[1] 1 Kent's *Com.* 208.

[2] Eulogy on Monroe, in *Lives of Madison and Monroe*, p. 236.

[3] Story's *Com. on Const.* § 215.

ment, they cannot be so now, after having been shorn of many powers before that undoubtedly exercised by them, and at the same time not reinforced by a concession of new ones.

In the Federal Convention, in 1787, Mr. Madison, as reported by Mr. Yates, delegate from New York, said: "There is a gradation of power in all societies, from the lowest corporation to the highest sovereign. The States never possessed the essential rights of sovereignty. These were always vested in Congress. Their voting, as States, in Congress, is no evidence of sovereignty. The State of Maryland voted by counties. Did this make the counties sovereign? The States at present are only great corporations, having the power of making laws, and these are effectual only if they are not contradictory to the general Confederation. The States ought to be placed under control of the general government, at least as much so as they formerly were under the King and British Parliament." [1]

§ 50. The opinion expressed thus in the Convention, that the States had never been sovereign, was in effect confirmed by the Supreme Court of the United States in 1795, in a case of prize, occurring under resolutions of the old Congress of the Confederation, passed in 1775. One question made in the case was, whether that body had power to authorize the taking of prizes, which properly belongs to the sovereign power. It was decided that it had. Justice Paterson said: "The question first in order is, whether Congress, before the ratification of the Articles of Confederation, had authority to institute such a tribunal," ("Commissioners for Appeals," for prize cases,) "with appellate jurisdiction in cases of prize? Much has been said respecting the powers of Congress. . . . . The powers of Congress were revolutionary in their nature, arising out of events, adequate to every national emergency, and coextensive with the object to be attained. Congress was the general, supreme, and controling council of the nation, the centre of union, the centre of force, and the sun of the political system. To determine what their powers were, we must inquire what powers they exercised. Congress raised armies, fitted out a navy, and prescribed rules for their government. Congress conducted all

[1] Yates' *Minutes*, in Vol. I. of Elliott's *Deb.* pp. 461, 462. I do not use Madison's report of the same debate in this case, because, though not contradictory of Yates, it is very brief.

military operations, both by land and sea. Congress emitted bills of credit, received and sent ambassadors, and made treaties; Congress commissioned privateers. . . . . These high acts of sovereignty were submitted to, acquiesced in, and approved of by the people of America. In Congress were vested, because by Congress were exercised, with the approbation of the people, the rights and powers of war and peace. In every government, whether it consists of many states or of a few, or whether it be of a federal or consolidated nature, there must be a supreme power or will; the rights of war and peace are component parts of this supremacy, and incidental thereto is the question of prize. The question of prize grows out of the nature of the thing. If it be asked, in whom, during our Revolutionary war, was lodged, and by whom was exercised, this supreme authority? no one will hesitate for an answer. It was lodged in, and exercised by, Congress; it was there or nowhere; the States individually did not, and with safety could not, exercise it."[1] So Chief Justice Jay, in a case in the same court, before referred to,[2] said: "The Revolution, or rather the Declaration of Independence, found the people *already* united for general purposes, and at the same time providing for their more domestic concerns by State Conventions, and other temporary arrangements. From the crown of *Great Britain* the sovereignty of their own country passed to the people of it. . . . The people . . . continued to consider themselves, in a national point of view, as one people; and they continued without interruption to manage their national concerns accordingly. Afterwards, in the hurry of the war and in the warmth of mutual confidence, they made a confederation of the States the basis of a general government. Experience disappointed the expectations they had formed from it, and then the people, in their collective and

[1] Penhallow *v.* Doane's Administrators, 3 Dall. 54 (80). As the learned judge founds what he calls the sovereignty of Congress upon the acquiescence or approbation of the people, and implies that, without it, the power would not have belonged to that body, it is evident that he is in error in lodging sovereignty with Congress at all. The *exercise* of sovereign powers was permitted to that body by the people of the United Colonies, who were the true sovereign; (see *post*, §§ 55, 56.) This error, however, does not affect the general soundness of his argument, which in effect lodges the power of sovereignty with some other than the States.

[2] Chisholm, Ex'r, *v.* State of Georgia, 2 Dall. 419 (470).

national capacity, established the present Constitution. It is remarkable that, in establishing it, the people exercised their own rights and their own proper sovereignty; and, conscious of the plenitude of it, they declared with becoming dignity, 'We the *people of the United States* do ordain and establish this Constitution.' Here we see the people acting as sovereigns of the whole country, and, in the language of sovereignty, establishing a Constitution by which it was their will that the State governments should be bound, and to which the State constitutions should be made to conform." [1]

§ 51. Conceding, then, that we are a nation, the answer to the question with which we started some pages back — Where resides the sovereignty in the United States? — is ready to our hand. It resides, and must reside, in the nation, considered as a political society or body corporate. Back of all the States and of all *forms of government* for either the States or the Union, we are to conceive of the NATION, a political body, one and indivisible, made up of the citizens of the United States, without distinction of age, sex, color, or condition in life. In this vast body, as a corporate unit, dwells the ultimate power denominated sovereignty. It is this body which declared itself, by the Continental Congress, and under the name of the "United Colonies," to be free and independent: "We, therefore, the representatives of the United States of America, . . . do, *in the name and by the authority of the good people of these Colonies*, declare that *these United Colonies* are . . . free and independent States," — independent, that is, of the crown of Great Britain, not of each other. This body it is which formed the government of the Confederation, granting to it, indeed, few powers, and still leaving many and important ones to the peoples of the several States; and it is this which afterwards, as we have seen, "ordained and established" the present Constitution, parcelling out anew and in different measure, the powers it saw fit to grant at all; giving to the government of the Union broad national powers, making its laws and Constitution supreme, and leaving to the peoples of the States other powers for local purposes, but stamping them with the mark of inferiority, as the parts are severally inferior to the whole.

§ 52. If I am right in lodging the sovereign power in the

[1] See further on this subject, Story's *Com. on Const* §§ 210–216.

nation, the perplexing question of allegiance is easily determined.

Allegiance (*alligo*) is for the citizen, with respect to the state or sovereign society, what religion (*religo*) is for man, with respect to God, a dutiful recognition of the bond which connects them, in their relations as subject and sovereign. Allegiance relates to a temporal, as religion does to a spiritual or Divine, sovereign. Accordingly, as it would be sacrilege for a man to recognize as his spiritual sovereign or to acknowledge the bond implied in the term religion as uniting him with any being but God, so it would be an act of treason, in morals if not in law, for a citizen to recognize as entitled to sovereign rights — that is, to render allegiance to — any person or body, but the true sovereign, the nation.

But although the nation is the only real sovereign, the States are often, by a misuse of language, called sovereign. This arises partly from reasoning upon the supposed condition of the original colonies at the moment of their separation from the mother country, and still more from confusion of ideas in regard to the relations of the States to the people of the Union, as established by the Articles of Confederation. Even if it were conceded that the original thirteen colonies were sovereign communities at the time of their separation from England, and in some way managed to retain their sovereign powers after joining the Union, the same would not be true of the twenty-five or more Territories, or inchoate States, which have been admitted into the Union since 1789. With the possible exception of Vermont, not one of these was a sovereign community before it became a State, and it will not be claimed that they became such by virtue of the act of admission. And yet they possess, in the Union, to its full extent, every power belonging to the original thirteen States. Nevertheless, it is true — and here is the source of the confusion of ideas referred to — that the States have always, under the Federal and State Constitutions, been entrusted with the *exercise* of powers of government within their respective boundaries. These powers are sovereign powers. But, as we have seen, not every person or body of persons permitted to exercise sovereign powers is a sovereign, else were the governor, each legislator, each functionary of the State, a sovereign, since each, by virtue of the Constitution, exercises some sovereign powers.[1] It is unfortunate for the interests of constitutional government that our courts, and many of our writers on constitutional law, have not always distinguished this permissive exercise from the original possession of sovereign powers, and that they have spoken of the States accordingly as sovereign communities,—a character which can be attributed neither to the States, whether in the capacity of peoples or of governments, nor to the general government of the Union itself.

§ 53. As allegiance is due only to the sovereign, there can be no such thing in law as allegiance to one's State. The same confusion of ideas, however, referred to in the last section, has led to the conception of State allegiance, and from it have resulted, in the past history of the Union, the most disastrous consequences. The war of secession was begun and prosecuted in the main under the inspiration of that dogma, and with a view to carry it into practical effect. Some writers, recognizing the impropriety of applying the term *allegiance* to the obedience one owes to the government of his State, have denominated it a "qualified allegiance," a thing as absurd as a qualified omnipotence, unless by it be meant an allegiance which is not real but seeming; that is, an act of obedience which would be one of allegiance were the body to which it is paid a sovereign body. Thus, in a late case decided by the Supreme Court of the United States, Justice Grier said: "Under the very peculiar Constitution of this government, although the citizens owe supreme allegiance to the federal government, they owe also a qualified allegiance to the State in which they are domiciled." [2] Treason is a crime against sovereignty, a violation of one's allegiance. Hence, there is really no such thing as treason against any political body in the Union but the United States. If a State, by its courts, punishes treason, it must be not as treason against itself, but as treason against the Union; and, in this view, the propriety of that State legislation which defines treason against the State and affixes to it particular penalties, is doubtful. It would seem that the only principle on which such legislation can be sustained is, that a State has a right, under its general power of regulating its own internal police, to punish acts dangerous to

[1] See *ante*, § 22.

[2] Claimants of the Schooner Brilliant, &c., Appellants, *v.* The United States, Am. Law Register, Vol. II. (new series) 334.

the peace and safety of its citizens, giving to them such names as it pleases, although the same acts may constitute treason against the United States, and as such be punishable under the laws of the latter. On that principle, State laws have been sustained by the Supreme Court of the United States, affixing penalties to the act of counterfeiting the coin of the United States and other offences against the laws of the Union; the same acts being declared, upon different grounds, having respect to the interests of each, to be crimes against both jurisdictions.[1]

§ 54. 2. I come now to consider the second branch of the question stated, namely, *How* does sovereignty inhere in the people of the United States?

To this question two answers may be given: —

(*a*). That sovereignty inheres in the people considered simply that is, as a unit, without conditions, or State or other internal discriminations.

(*b*). That it inheres in the people only as discriminated into and acting in groups by States.

To determine which of these answers is the correct one, in my judgment, we need but consider what is involved in the conception of sovereignty inhering in a society under conditions, as where the sovereign body is regarded as capable of acting as such only when discriminated into groups, by States, or otherwise.

It is evident, that any particular mode of existence exhibited by sovereignty, except that of inhering in the political body as a unit, must be the result of voluntary regulation by the sover-

[1] See Fox *v.* State of Ohio, 5 How. 432. Also, Moore *v.* The People of Illinois, 14 How. R 13. Upon the whole doctrine of allegiance, in relation to both the States and the United States, see The State *ex rel.* M'Cready *v.* Hunt, and The State *ex rel.* M'Daniel *v.* M'Meekin, (the so-called "allegiance cases,") 2 Hill's S. C. R. 1–282. These cases arose in South Carolina, in 1834, in connection with the nullification ordinances of the convention of that State, and involved the whole subject of sovereignty, allegiance, the relation of the States to the Union, and kindred questions. The majority of the court held, that the oath of allegiance prescribed to officers of the militia by the Act of 1833, "to provide for the military organization of this State," was "unconstitutional and void." No constitutional question has ever been discussed with greater ability and learning in the United States, than were those raised in these cases. They were argued for the relators by Mr. Grimke and Mr. Petigru, each *clarum et venerabile nomen.*

eign itself; be, in other words, a self-imposed limitation, enforcible only by moral sanctions. For, to suppose that sovereignty so inheres in the political body that it can manifest itself only through some particular instrument, or in some particular mode, is to rob the sovereign of its essential attribute, that of perfect freedom, or the power of absolute self-determination. The fact that a particular instrument or mode has become established, may furnish a weighty moral reason why it should be used or followed; but to suppose a power anywhere existing of compelling the employment of either, would be to subject the sovereign to some extrinsic human superior, that is, to make, not it, but another, the real sovereign.

§ 55. Again: the terms *modes* and *instruments*, when used in relation to the manifestation of sovereignty, merely indicate how sovereignty is *exercised; refer*, in short, *to systems of government established by the sovereign, or conceived to be within its competence to establish.*

To contend, therefore, that sovereignty so exists in the sovereign body that it is exercisible only in some particular mode, or through some particular instrument, is to say, that when government has been once ordained by sovereign authority, the latter ceases, with respect to that government, to be any longer sovereign; in other words, that, in the act of creation, sovereignty leaves the creator, and takes up its abode with the creature.

The error upon which such an hypothesis rests, is that of taking the secondary forms into which the sovereign body resolves itself as being severally the primary, substantial, and necessary form of sovereignty itself. On the contrary, that only can be the ultimate and essential form, which precedes the establishment and survives the dissolution of all those special adjustments needed to bring into regular exercise the powers of sovereignty, which constitute government.

§ 56. To a full comprehension of the analysis exhibited in the last two sections, it is necessary to consider further, with reference to some particular form of government, as that of the United States, what is signified by the terms, *the exercise of sovereign powers.*

By the *exercise* of sovereign powers is meant either, 1. The *regular*, which, historically considered, is commonly, also, in constitutional governments, the *actual* exercise of it; and, 2.

The *irregular*, though *possible*, exercise of it, — a field of indefinite extent, commensurate with the needs of the sovereign body, as determined by itself.

To be *regular*, unquestionably, the exercise of sovereignty must be conformable to established *rule* (*regula*); that is, to the Constitution and laws at the time in force. This is true by whomsoever it be exercised; that is, whether by the sovereign body, acting as an organic whole, directly, — if that be possible, — or by functionaries, by itself charged with governmental duties.

The *irregular* exercise of sovereignty, on the other hand, as contradistinguished from the *regular* exercise of it, is that which, conforming to no rule, would be exhibited were the sovereign body to manifest its powers of sovereignty independently, or in violation, of an established rule, following, instead, its own arbitrary will. This exercise of sovereignty is to be characterized simply as *irregular*, or as *revolutionary*, according to the extent of the irregularity.

But by the word *possible*, as applicable to this exercise of sovereignty, is meant *possible* only *in fact*, not *legally possible*. The possibility in fact of such an exercise of sovereignty, however, is a circumstance of vast significance, under all forms of government — which it would be well if statesmen kept more constantly in mind. In the United States, doubtless, if there is anywhere in it lodged a truly sovereign power, there lies, outside the narrow limits which bound the regular exercise of it, a wide space, in which the sovereign may expatiate in the exercise of all possible sovereign powers, as freely as in any government under the sun. For, in a word, to the sovereign all things are in fact possible; all things may, according to circumstances, become rightful or justifiable; though many things, which under the circumstances are rightful or justifiable on moral grounds, may be irregular or revolutionary. The wider field, moreover, is to be trodden only by the sovereign body itself, or under its immediate command: the narrower field — that of established rules of action — is that of government, which is but one phase of existence voluntarily assumed by the sovereign body, and which, however solemnly it may have bound itself to maintain it, it may, in fact, discontinue at will.

§ 57. Applying these principles to the United States, with a view to ascertain whether sovereignty inheres in the people of the United States considered simply as a corporate unit, or only as discriminated into the subordinate groups, known as States, the problem seems to be of easy solution.

Judging by the *regular* exercise of sovereign powers in the United States, — that is, by the Constitution of government now established, — sovereignty would seem, as a practical power, to reside in the people, as discriminated into the groups known as States. Of the numerous circumstances indicating this I shall mention but two. The first is, that by the Constitution of 1788 the electoral function for the Union is performed, not by the electors acting as a single body, under regulations established by the legislature of the Union, the total result to be determined by a simple majority of all the votes cast, but by the electors discriminated into groups conterminous with the States, voting in accordance with State laws, the total result to be determined by grouping the several State majorities, sometimes giving them a weight proportionate to their respective numbers, and sometimes an equal weight, without regard to their numbers.

The second circumstance is, that by the same Constitution, the power, *par excellence* a sovereign power, of amending that instrument, instead of being confided to the people or to a Convention of the people of the Union, acting directly, as a sovereign unit, is given to them acting indirectly, either through Congress, or through a national Convention, called by Congress at the instance of the State legislatures, and that, by way of recommendation merely, such action to be followed, in either case, by the ratification of the State legislatures or of Conventions called in the several States, as Congress may have determined. Thus the States seem to be inextricably interwoven with the machinery provided for the exercise of the most fundamental right of sovereignty, that of forming the organic law. But it is to be noted that it is with the *regular* exercise of that power that they are thus interwoven. The American nation, by which that system was established, can undo the work of 1788, if not in pursuance of its own provisions, then irregularly, being still, as before the formation of the Constitution, a sovereign political unit, the product of vital forces which had been active and accumulating long before it deemed it expedient to form that instrument. Although, in a moment of weakness, it saw fit to curtail its own powers, in relation especially to the sovereign act of amending the Constitution,[1] still, if in fact the nation should outgrow the system thus established, and should by a general movement institute a change which should not only violate the provisions of that instrument, in reference to State equality in the Senate, but abolish the States entirely, it would be within its actual competence as a sovereign body so to do, though, from a constitutional point of view, it would be, perhaps, a revolutionary act. The point, in a word, to be kept in mind, is, that the present Constitution, determining the exercise of sovereign power by the servants of the sovereign, is not a finality for any body but those servants,—certainly not for the people of the United States, however they may have fettered themselves by the fundamental act of 1788. As the Constitution, as an organic growth, develops with the growth of the nation, the Constitution, as an instrument of evidence of that growth, must develop correspondingly. If by its terms it cannot do so, shall the nation be bound by it? In law, yes. As a matter of practical statesmanship, no.

§ 58. Assuming, then, that by the present Constitution of the United States, sovereignty, so far as relates to its regular exercise, inheres in the people of the United States, *as discriminated into groups by States*, a word is necessary as to the CAPACITY in which those groups act in performing the function indicated, when proceeding regularly.

We have seen in a former section that the States participate in the act of amending the fundamental law in a double capacity: first, as State governments — the State legislatures applying to Congress to call a Convention for proposing amendments, or ratifying such as have been proposed; and, secondly, as subordinate peoples, together composing the people of the United States, — as, in case of Conventions meeting in the several States to ratify proposed amendments. In this last case, however, the two capacities would be blended, as the call of such Conventions would probably issue from the respective State legislatures, and not from Congress.

The same distinctions run through the whole Constitution. Thus a large part of the legislative, and a corresponding part of the executive and judicial functions required in the United

[1] See the concluding part of Article V of the Constitution, relating to equality of representation of States in the United States Senate.

States, have been committed by the sovereign body of the Union, the nation, to the States, as governments organized in subordination to the Union; I refer to the powers of local legislation and administration, sometimes erroneously regarded as belonging originally, and as of sovereign right, to the States. Properly considered, these are a branch of the sovereign powers of the Nation, of which, by the present Constitution, the exercise has been delegated to the State governments.

In like manner, the State governments are charged with the exercise of sovereign powers, with reference to the Union, in the election of senators through the State legislatures;[1] in the issuance of writs of election to fill vacancies in Congress, by the State executives;[2] in the appointment of officers for the national militia, given in general terms "to the States;" and in giving their consent to the building of forts and arsenals, and the erection of new States, by Congress, within the jurisdiction of existing States.[3]

On the other hand, in several particulars contained in the Constitution, the States, as subordinate peoples, without immediate reference to their organization into State governments, have been charged with the exercise of sovereign powers for the Union; as in choosing the President of the United States, through electors chosen by such peoples directly,[4] and in electing the members of the national House of Representatives, a duty committed to "the people of the several States."[5]

§ 59. In all these cases, however. the circumstance already mentioned is to be noted, that the States, considered either as parts of the national people or as State governments, in no case act in either of those capacities purely and simply; the framers of the Constitution seeming carefully to have connected the exercise of sovereign powers by them in one capacity with their exercise of them in the other capacity, as if to make them, as parts of the national people, checks upon themselves when acting as State governments. Without stopping to cite instances

1 Art. I. sec. 3, cl. 1, Const. U. S.

2 Art. I. sec. 2, cl. 4, Const. U. S.

3 Art. I. sec. 8, cl. 17, and Art. IV. sec. 3, cl. 1, Const. U. S.

4 Art. II. sec. 1, Const. U. S.

5 Art. I. sec. 2, cl. 1, Const. U. S. On the whole subject discussed in the foregoing sections, see *Federalist*, No. 39.

of this system of internal checks, I observe that the States, in both capacities, are, by the Constitution, subjected to checks in the form of direct prohibitions emanating from a source external to themselves as States, being limitations upon their exercise of sovereign powers, imposed by the people of the United States.[1] Admitting, then, that the powers of sovereignty, under the present Constitution, are exercisible only by the people as discriminated into States, and, as such, acting in the two capacities of State peoples and State governments, the fact that such limitations have been imposed is a further and an incontestable proof that the States are not themselves in any capacity, either separate or united, *the sovereign* power in the Union, but only the depositaries for the time being of such sovereign powers as the sovereign has chosen to have exercised.

§ 60. The theory, nevertheless, that sovereignty inheres in the people of the United States, not simply, or as a political unit, but as discriminated into States, has the sanction of high authority. Although I believe this to be an error, arising from not distinguishing the sovereign body from the system of functionaries in whom is temporarily vested by the sovereign the *exercise* of sovereign powers, I shall give extracts from the writings of one or two publicists who hold the view indicated.

Mr. John Austin, in his work, "The Province of Jurisprudence Determined," contrasting what he calls *supreme federal governments* with *permanent confederacies of supreme governments*, says of the government of the United States: —

"The supreme government of the United States of America agrees (I believe) with the foregoing general description of a supreme federal government. I believe that the common government, consisting of the Congress and the President of the United States, is merely a subject minister of the United States governments. I believe that none of the latter is properly sovereign or supreme, even in the state or political society of which it is the immediate chief. And lastly, I believe that the sovereignty of each of the states, and also of the larger state arising from the Federal Union, resides in the states' governments, *as forming one aggregate body;* meaning by a state's government, not its ordinary legislature, but the body of its citizens which appoints its ordinary legislature, and which, the Union apart, is

[1] See Art. I. secs. 8, 9, and 10, Const. U. S.

properly sovereign therein. If the several immediate chiefs of the several United States were respectively single individuals, or were respectively narrow oligarchies, the sovereignty of each of the states, and also of the larger state arising from the Federal Union, would reside in those several individuals, or would reside in those several oligarchies, as forming a collective whole." [1]

There is, perhaps, some ambiguity in this passage, as it is not clear whether, by the body of the citizens of a State "which appoints its ordinary legislature," the author means the totality of its citizens, forming a corporate unit, which, "the union apart," *virtually* appoints the legislature, or the body of the electors, which immediately and formally appoints it. If the former was intended, his theory was clearly what I have supposed above; if the latter, it was the wholly untenable one, that sovereignty in the United States inheres in the electors or voting people of the respective States, considered "as forming a collective whole," — a theory which has the sanction of so eminent an authority as Mr. Hurd.[2]

§ 61. A similar view of the mode in which sovereignty inheres in the people of the United States has been lately propounded by Mr. Brownson, with his characteristic force and ingenuity, in his work, "The American Republic." Having located political sovereignty, in general, in the people, "not individually, but collectively, as civil and political society," he proceeds to determine how it exists in the people of the United States. Commenting upon the opening words of the preamble of the Federal Constitution, "We, the people of the United States," he says: "Who are this people? How are they constituted, or what the mode and conditions of their political existence? Are they the people of the States severally? No; for they call themselves the people of the *United* States. Are they a national people, really existing outside and independently of their organization into distinct and mutually independent States? No; for they define themselves to be the people of the United *States*. If they had considered themselves existing as States only, they would have said, 'We, the States;' and if independently of State

[1] John Austin, *The Province of Jurisprudence Determined*, Vol. I. p. 222.

[2] Hurd, *Law of Freedom and Bondage*, Vol. I. § 343, note 2; *The Theory of National Existence*, pp. 127, 144, and 147.

organization, they would have said, 'We, the people, do ordain,' &c.

"The key to the mystery," he continues, "is precisely in this appellation, *United States*, which is not the name of the country, for its distinctive name is America, but a name expressive of its political organization. In it there are no sovereign people without States, and no States without union, or that are not *united* States. The term *united* is not part of a proper name, but is simply an adjective qualifying *States*, and has its full and proper sense. Hence, while the sovereignty is and must be in the States, it is in the States united, not in the States severally, precisely as we have found the sovereignty of the people is in the people collectively, or as society, not in the people individually. The life is in the body, not in the members, though the body could not exist if it had no members; so the sovereignty is in the Union, not in the States severally; but there could be no sovereign union without the States, for there is no union where there is nothing united."[1]

§ 62. In concluding this discussion of sovereignty in the United States, it should be stated that whenever, in judicial decisions or in common parlance, the term *sovereign* is applied to a State or to its people, it must be taken to signify the possession by such State or people of the right to exercise sovereign powers in subordination to the people of the Union, from whom it has received such powers by delegation. Under the Constitution of the nation, comprising the Federal and all the State Constitutions, each State is permitted by the sovereign to frame for its own people its local Constitution, subject always to the guaranty of the national government. In performing that work, State Conventions and legislatures often assume the airs and the language of representatives of real sovereigns. In truth, however, a State is not a sovereign. In passing upon a local Constitution, the people of a State are performing a delegated function, — exercising, by permission, and in behalf of the people of the United States, a sovereign power belonging only to the latter. That this is the most characteristic, and by far the most valuable, of all the features of the national Constitution, is undeniable, but that fact does not at all affect its intrinsic character as above explained. With a proper defini-

1 *The American Republic*, pp. 220, 221.

tion of "States Rights," then, every lover of his country, and every friend of its liberties, must be a "States Rights man"; but that definition must be such as to leave a country to love, — a thing possible only when the States are regarded as expedients subordinate to the nation, subservient in all respects to its interests, and therefore, if the nation so will, temporary.[1]

[1] Upon the whole question of sovereignty, its location and its exercise by the extensive hierarchy of representatives of the sovereign, state and national, see Webster's speech in the case of Luther *v.* Borden, 7 How. R. 1, in *Great Speeches of Daniel Webster*, by E. P. Whipple (Little, Brown & Co., 1879), p. 538.

CHAPTER III.

OF CONSTITUTIONS.

§ 63. THE function of the Constitutional Convention being, as we have seen, to participate in the framing or amending of Constitutions, before attempting to ascertain the extent of its powers in that regard, it is necessary to form an accurate conception of what a Constitution is.

By the Constitution of a commonwealth is meant, primarily, its make-up as a political organism; that special adjustment of instrumentalities, powers, and functions, by which its form and operation are determined.

This is a Constitution, *considered as the outcome of social and political forces in history, as an organic growth*, or, as I shall sometimes describe it, *as a fact*.

Beside this, the term "Constitution" has a secondary meaning, which is, perhaps, more common than the one given, involving equally the conception of a system of political instrumentalities, powers, and functions, specially adjusted for the purposes of government; but conceived of, not as an organic growth, but as a systematic description of such a growth, in the shape of *formulæ* addressed to the understanding. In other words, a Constitution, in this secondary sense, is the result of an attempt to represent in technical language some particular constitution. existing as an organic growth. This is a Constitution *considered as an instrument of evidence*.[1]

[1] Since this part of the text was written, I have been pleased to find that substantially the same distinction here noted, between *Constitutions as organic growths* and *Constitutions as instruments of evidence*, has been taken in two works lately published; that of Mr. Hurd, *On the Law of Freedom and Bondage*, and that of Dr. Brownson, *The American Republic*. The latter author says: —

"The Constitution of the United States is twofold, — written and unwritten, — the constitution of the people, and the constitution of the government. The written constitution is simply a law ordained by the nation or people instituting and organizing the government; the unwritten constitution is the real or actual constitution of the people as a state or sovereign community, and constituting them such or such a state. It is providential, not made by the nation, but born

§ 64. A third variety of Constitutions, so-called, may be noted, but only to exclude them from the list of legitimate Constitutions, that is, *Constitutions "as they ought to be."* These must be carefully distinguished from Constitutions considered as organic growths. They are Constitutions framed in the closet, according to abstract ideas of moral perfection, for imaginary commonwealths. Of this class are the instruments thrown off in such numbers by the constitution-mongers of France, during her great democratic revolutions, and those hardly more unsubstantial ones framed by Plato, More, Bacon, and Harrington for their ideal republics.

As contrasted with these, the Constitution considered as an organic growth, is that Constitution which has actually, under the operation of social and political forces, evolved itself in a State. This Constitution may differ much from that inscribed in the volume of the laws. Thus, there may have been wrought out fundamental changes in the structure of a government by the usurpations of its functionaries, followed by the acquiescence of the sovereign society; in which case, those changes would become a part of the Constitution as a fact. The usurpations, having this effect, might or might not have been intentional. The purchase of Louisiana, admitted by Mr. Jefferson, who effected it, to have been an unconstitutional act, may be cited as an instance of an usurpation resulting in important constitutional modifications, which was committed intentionally, because of its supposed great benefit to the country.[1] It is the opinion of many lawyers, that State banks of issue are unconstitutional. Admitting that they are so, but that, when first authorized, they were believed to be within the scope of State legislative power, and conceding that they are now so firmly established as to be practically irrepealable, they would present an illustration of an unintended usurpation, ripening by long acquiescence into a change of the Constitution as a fact. Similar changes might arise, in the course of the national progress, from the growth of opinion, or from some general but gradual organic movement of the society at large, of importance so fundamental that they must be set down as modifications of the

with it. The written constitution is made and ordained by the sovereign power, and presupposes that power as already existing and constituted." — *The American Republic*, p. 218.

[1] See *Jefferson's Works*, Vol. IV. pp. 504–506.

Constitution as a fact. The eradication of domestic slavery from a nation whose fundamental code in its letter permitted it, as a result of civil war, would be such a change.

§ 65. I pass now to consider *the nature* and *specific varieties* of Constitutions of the first two kinds, that is, of Constitutions considered, —

First, as organic growths; and

Secondly, as instruments of evidence.

I. Adverting to the first of the proposed subjects of inquiry, what I have to say upon the *nature* of Constitutions considered as organic growths, will be confined to this central question: Are Constitutions founded upon compact?

When it is affirmed that a Constitution is founded upon compact, what is meant? Obviously, either that, at the opening of its historical development, it became what it did by virtue of an actual agreement between the individuals then composing the state, to which agreement all subsequently born individuals became, from time to time, parties; or, that while there was never, probably, an agreement between such individuals in fact, their relations to each other and to the state, and their consequent rights and duties, are what they would be, had there in fact been such an agreement; in other words, that if there was no agreement in fact, one may be supposed, to account for facts not otherwise so easily explained. That is, the doctrine of compact, as the foundation of Constitutions, must be asserted either *as a fact* or *as an hypothesis*. Considered as a fact, it is sufficient to deny that a Constitution ever thus originated, in a proper sense of those terms. All Constitutions, and, of course, all governments, are growths, the products of social and political forces; among these reckoning as well the traditions, and the physical, intellectual, and moral conditions of the society, as its relations to other political societies. It is doubtless true, that, whilst one effect of these forces is, in the domain of fact, to evolve the actual Constitution, another is, in the domain of opinion, to evolve what is called the consent of the governed. The two effects are, indeed, necessary concomitants, being the different results of the same causes operating in the diverse spheres specified. But to say that the Constitution is based upon that consent is, in my view, as absurd as to attribute to the consent of its component particles the structure and functions of a plant.

Doubtless those particles acquiesce, and if they were sentient beings, with conscience and will, that acquiescence, without ceasing to be determined by natural laws and forces, might be denominated consent. So the acquiescence of great societies or races in the founding of governments and dynasties is only by a figure of speech to be called their consent; it is rather resignation to the action of forces which they have neither ability nor desire to countervail. The human race have always acquiesced in the revolution of the earth about the sun; they have sat down to study its causes, and recognized with thankfulness its accruing advantages, no faction, so far as history shows, — the church, perhaps, in Galileo's time excepted, — ever even protesting against it; but it does not follow, therefore, that the system of planetary motion, of which that revolution is a part, was founded on the consent of the earth or its inhabitants, or on a compact between them and the residue of the universe.

§ 66. If, on the other hand, the doctrine that Constitutions, considered as facts, are founded upon compact, is put forth as an hypothesis merely, for purposes of illustration, and if its hypothetical character is kept constantly in the foreground, it may be viewed with more indulgence. The true office of an hypothesis is to provide a theory of causation adequate to account for known facts, and yet without vouching for its absolute verity. It *supposes* the theory *may be true*. It also equally supposes it *may be false*, admitting readily, indeed, that the next fact discovered is nearly as likely to prove it false as true. But, whether in fact false or true, its usefulness for scientific purposes is the same. It serves as a lay figure, on which to exhibit to advantage in all their relations truths that are connected but obscure. But the danger is that that which is *supposed* will insensibly lose its hypothetical character and come to rank as a truth, and so be made the basis of reasoning to other truths as unsubstantial as itself, but ignorantly, on account of the regularity of their deduction, accepted as undoubted. An instance of such a perversion of hypothesis into political axiom is seen in the history of the *dictum* of the Roman jurisconsults, based on the fiction of a "Law of Nature," namely, that "all men *are* by nature equal;"[1] which, revived by the French lawyers and by

[1] "*Omnes homines naturâ æquales sunt*," the maxim of the Roman lawyers of the Antonine era. — Maine, *Ancient Law*, p. 89.

Rousseau, passed from them, through Jefferson, into the American Declaration of Independence. Mr. Maine, in his late profound work on "Ancient Law," has demonstrated, that in its inception, this doctrine was propounded merely to express the relations of the various peoples of Rome to one another, *under an hypothetical law of nature*. According to that supposed law, he says, "there was no difference in the contemplation of the Roman tribunals between citizen and foreigner, between freeman and slave, agnate and cognate." In those tribunals, then, the maxim as to the equality of all men meant, that in the eye of an *imaginary law*, derived from a *supposed* "*state of nature*," all the inhabitants of Rome were equal. But, when taken up by the writers of later times, the doctrine that all men are by nature equal was used in a different sense, no longer bearing on merely civil, but also on political relations, namely, to signify that "all men *ought to be* equal." [1] Thus, what was originally a particular statement relative merely to an hypothetical code of civil law for the "Latin name," has come to be propounded as a political axiom of general application.[2]

§ 67. Conceding, then, that the doctrine of compact we are considering was propounded by its authors as an hypothesis merely, the danger was that men should come to look upon it as the expression of a fact, and thereupon spin from it conclusions that would be disastrous to society. Precisely such has been the fortune of this famous doctrine during the last hundred years. It has been received as a political axiom of general application and of absolute truthfulness. The fact, however, is, that it is a fallacy, or, at least, a fancy, which is dignified beyond its deserts when it is ranked as an hypothesis. History records no instance in which such a compact as the theory supposes was ever made; and to imagine it, except for the purpose of exposition or illustration, is as puerile as to trace the social union of a swarm of bees to a compact made at some imaginary congress, when each bee was in a "state of nature." The state of nature for the bee is that of union in the swarm; and so the state of nature for mankind is that of association in political communities, patriarchal or other. The rights and obligations growing out of the social state are as old as the absolute rights of indi-

[1] Maine, *Ancient Law*, pp. 70–92.

[2] Ibid.

viduals. They are not the results of compact, but are parts of the system of human society, devised by the Creator "in the beginning."

§ 68. It may be well in this place to complete our view of the theory of compact, as the basis of Constitutions, by considering its application to the second class of Constitutions noted, namely, Constitutions considered as instruments of evidence. Of these, compacts, in a proper sense of the term, often form parts. To explain my meaning, it is necessary to consider how Constitutions of that kind arise. It will be seen in subsequent sections that some are merely collections of customs, statutes, and judicial decisions, published by unofficial persons, that is, persons without authority to pronounce definitively upon their letter or import; whilst others are simply statutes enacted by sovereign authority. Of the former kind, the English Constitution is an example, and of the latter, that of the United States. Now, when a people frame a Constitution in the second sense, or make a law or a treaty, which becomes a part of such a Constitution, what is the nature of their act? It is a translating into appropriate legal language, and a formal registering amongst the archives of the nation, stamped with the *fiat* which marks the national acquiescence and gives to it authenticity, of the Constitution, or part of a Constitution, which has, in the progress of the nation and under the operation of all its social forces, actually evolved itself as a fact.

Such a work evidently requires the highest powers, and is not likely to be executed with unanimity. Where the details of the Constitution as a fact are so apparent that the people are of one mind as to the legal *formulæ* requisite to embody them, there would be no compact; for, to produce that, there must be divergence of opinions, resulting finally in agreement. Where, however, a divergence had arisen, but had finally ended in a compromise, involving, not a conviction in the minds of one party that the views of its opponents were correct, but a surrender of its own, that results might be achieved, there would be a compact. Thus, to illustrate, there arose in the Federal Convention two parties on this question: Given the absolute necessity of a closer union of the States, for their prosperity and safety, and the necessity, on the other hand, equally absolute, for the conservation of our liberties, that the States should be retained as political organizations, what is the representation in the national Congress that is alone consistent with the attainment of both those objects? One party said, it must be that of representation proportioned to population. This party was composed of the large States. The other party, made up of the small States, replied: "No; such a rule would place our fate in your hands; you would combine and wipe out State lines, and thus bring shipwreck upon our liberties. The Constitution of the United States, as a fact, as it has evolved itself under the operation of existing forces, and for which we are seeking an adequate expression, involves State equality, because, without it the system cannot stand. The representation must be set down by us as equal from all the States, great and small." This divergence of opinion was radical, and, as is well known, came near frustrating the efforts at a closer union. Happily, however, a compromise was effected. A middle course was found, which fully satisfied neither, namely, to declare that the representation sought for — the unknown quantity in the problem — was, in the House, a representation proportioned to population, in the Senate, equal. This was a compact. But it is important to note, that it was a compact, to use a common phrase, but "skin deep." It was a compact which settled, not that the Constitution, as a fact, was as laid down in the instrument then framed, but that it should for the nonce be so declared and considered; each party retaining still its opinion as to the fact, and the right, in the way pointed out in the instrument itself, to cause that opinion ultimately to prevail. Whether the *formulæ* agreed upon did in truth embody the then existing Constitution as an objective fact, is a wholly different question, which I do not decide.[1]

§ 69. It is evident that, if the views presented in the foregoing sections be sound, a very important question may arise, namely. admitting the possibility of discrepancies between the Constitution of a state, as a fact, and its constitution as an instrument of evidence, which has the superior validity? In answering this question, it would be easy — and to some minds the temptation would be strong — to propound doctrines subversive of all regulated liberty. The reply seems reasonable, that the Constitution, as an organic growth, the Constitution, as it ought to be written out, to harmonize with the results of existing social

[1] See Commonwealth *v.* Aves, 18 Pick. R. 193, per Shaw, Ch. J.

forces, ought to prevail, rather than any empirical transcript of it made by fallible men, and therefore inadequate at the start, or become so by the progress of society. But such a doctrine would be anarchical — one according to which no government of laws could long exist. The Constitution as it has been solemnly declared to be, with as well its compacts as its bare transcriptions, must be the sole guide, as to all matters and persons within its proper cognizance.

But, at this point, a distinction should be made. The people of a commonwealth sustain to its Constitution a double relation, — first, that of its enactors; and, secondly, that of citizens amenable to its provisions. In the first relation, they make up the political society of which it is the Constitution. In the second, they are simply individuals, being either private citizens or persons charged for the time being with public functions under the Constitution; in both of which predicaments they are absolutely subject to every provision of the Constitution, to which, while it exists, there is for them nothing in the shape of law superior. But, for the people considered in the first relation, as the enactors of Constitutions, provisions of the written Constitution not according with the Constitution as a fact, are in general of no binding force whatever: not only may the people, but, if they would insure peace with progress, they must by amendments cause the former to conform substantially to the latter. I say "in general," because two cases may be exceptions: first, that of compacts, of which the occasions — divergence of views or of interests, resulting in compromise — still subsist in substance unchanged; and, secondly, that of constitutional interdicts, couched in negative terms, and having practically the same effect as compacts. In both these cases the constitutional provisions referred to operate, through their effect on the subordinate agents, by whom alone the sovereign can act, as a limitation upon the sovereign itself; it cannot, without a violation of morals or of the fundamental law, or of both, disregard what it has, under such circumstances or in such terms, ordained and established.

§ 70. II. Constitutions considered as facts, may be discriminated, with reference to the participation of the citizens in the exercise of the powers granted by them, into several species.

1. Of these, the first comprises those Constitutions in which a

single citizen monopolizes the entire powers of the government. These are the Constitutions of what are called absolute monarchies, or autocracies, and the peculiar arrangement of powers by which they are characterized is the result of usurpation on the part of the servants of the true sovereign, the state, followed by the acquiescence of the latter.

2. The next species embraces Constitutions in which a few citizens, instead of one, monopolize all the powers of government. These are styled aristocracies, and the same remark respecting their origin is applicable, just made with reference to that of monarchies. The term "few," as denoting the number who participate in the functions of government, is, of course, indefinite, but it is intended to designate by that term a very small minority of the citizens forming generally a close corporation, to which admission is practically denied.

3. The third species is made up of Constitutions which recognize a single monarch, theoretically the fountain of honor and authority, but in which considerable numbers of the citizens, or certain favored classes of them, participate in the government by representation. Governments controlled by such Constitutions are called limited monarchies, a good example of which is that of England.

4. The fourth species comprises Constitutions, in which, while there is no monarch, and the people are recognized as the fountain of all law and authority, a large proportion of the citizens, determined by the sovereign body, exercise the powers of government by representation. Of this species are the Constitution of the United States, and those of the several States of the Union.

5. The last species I shall mention consists of Constitutions in which all the citizens participate, or may participate, in the government directly, without representation — as the Constitutions of some of the Swiss Cantons. This kind of Constitutions is obviously practicable only in states of small territorial extent.

§ 71. Constitutions, considered in their evidentiary character, that is, as evidence of what some particular Constitutions are as organic growths, may be discriminated, first, with reference to the mode in which they originate, into two classes, namely: —

1. Cumulative Constitutions.
2. Enacted Constitutions.

Secondly, with reference to their general characteristics as sources of evidence, into two others, closely allied to the former, namely: —

3. Unwritten Constitutions.

4. Written Constitutions.

§ 72. 1. By a cumulative Constitution, is meant one made up gradually of accumulated usages and common-law principles, decisions of the courts, spontaneous and enacted institutions, compacts and statutes, of fundamental importance or embodying principles of political magnitude.[1] The leading idea in this variety is, that they are evolved gradually, as the exigencies of the national life require. Whenever a weak spot in the political fabric is discovered, the law or institution extemporised to supply the defect becomes a part of the Constitution. Two things, consequently, are essential to their successful operation: first, an alert and well-instructed public opinion, prepared at a moment's warning, to provide the constitutional device necessary to the exigency; and, secondly, public servants trained to a thorough knowledge of the institutions intrusted to their management, to a love and reverence for them, and with a disposition to obey with equal alacrity its new and its old provisions. Of this peculiar kind of Constitutions, those of ancient Rome and of England are conspicuous examples.

§ 73. 2. Enacted Constitutions, as the name implies, are such as are positive enactments, made commonly at one time, though sometimes at different times, by the appropriate legislative authority. From Constitutions of this kind, customs, compacts, decisions of courts and ordinary statutes, except to aid in construing doubtful clauses, are excluded. The Constitutions established in the United States, and such as have been modelled after them abroad, are examples of enacted Constitutions.

§ 74. 3 and 4. The two remaining varieties of Constitutions, the written and unwritten, embrace respectively the same Constitutions as the two above described, but viewed in a different relation. In those they were considered with reference to their origin or mode of development; in these they will be considered with reference to their characteristic qualities as sources or instruments of evidence. When a Constitution is spoken of

[1] Adapted from Dr. Lieber, *Civil Liberty*, p. 166, note 1.

as *written* or *unwritten*, those words are used in a sense analogous to that in which the terms *lex scripta*, and *lex non scripta* are employed in treatises on municipal law, referring, not to the present, but to the original character of the laws in question, as written or unwritten. It is well known that the common law, which is strictly *lex non scripta*, is embodied in writing as fully as the statute law, which is properly styled *lex scripta*; but in its inceptive stages the case was different. Precisely the same distinction exists between written and unwritten Constitutions. But the principal analogy between the two great classes of laws thus characterized, the constitutional and the municipal, is in the rules of construction and the evidentiary effect of the written or *scripta*, on the one hand, and the unwritten or *non scripta*, on the other. In illustrating this analogy, I shall confine my observations to the construction and effect, as evidence, of Constitutions. An unwritten Constitution is made up largely of customs and judicial decisions, the former more or less evanescent and intangible, since in a written form they exist only in the unofficial collections or commentaries of publicists and lawyers; and the latter composing a vast body of isolated cases, having no connecting bond but the slender thread of principle running through them, a thread often broken, sometimes recurrent, and never to be estimated as a whole but by tracing it through its entire course in the thousand volumes of law reports. The result is, that what the custom or what the course of judicial decisions may be upon any point of fundamental law, is a most complicated question, the answer to which can at best be but an inference from many disconnected facts.

§ 75. Not so with written Constitutions. As I have said, customs, decisions of courts, and institutions growing up spontaneously, have no place in them. Such Constitutions are statutes merely, covering the whole ground and, so far as the purpose of their framers is answered, precluding the possibility of construction. It is only when human skill in the expression of ideas is baffled, that a case can arise in which a court must pronounce what the Constitution is. The field thus provided for construction, though infinitely narrower than in unwritten Constitutions, is still ample, for a Constitution can only deal in generalities, whereas its application to particular cases is precisely that which must daily be determined. The crowning difference between the two species of Constitutions lies in this: that the duty of those who construe a written Constitution is merely, first, to ascertain the meaning of the general clause of it covering the case; and, secondly, to determine its application to the particular facts in question; the duty, on the other hand, of those who construe an unwritten Constitution is, first, to enter upon an exhaustive search after the repositories or memorials in which the Constitution lies enshrined; secondly, having gotten together these, to interpret them, and finally to settle by construction, if necessary, the application of their general provisions to the particular facts of the case. In other words, the scope of construction in a written Constitution is principally to ascertain what particular clauses of a determinate instrument mean; whilst in an unwritten Constitution this inquiry must be prefaced by another still more difficult, as to the contents or tenor of the Constitution to be construed. In the former case, construction is confined — that is, it operates only upon the Constitution itself considered as an instrument which is already determined; in the latter, it is at large; it first inquires what the terms of the law are and then proceeds to determine their meaning and application.

§ 76. It is obvious, that out of the distinction just announced must grow important consequences. One of these is that unwritten Constitutions are the playthings of judicial tribunals. They are flexible, because in the vast store-house of heterogeneous matter, out of which their provisions are to be gathered, it is easy to find or not to find, that which one will. A prejudice or a prepossession may readily give shape to the results of the most honest researches. So, the pressure of opinion, or of some great public necessity, may warp the judgment and lead the judicial mind to see what it is desirable should be seen. The same may doubtless happen to some extent in case of a written Constitution. Doubtful clauses are fields in which passion or prejudice have play, but that is an evil inseparable from the nature of mankind. It is probable that written Constitutions reduce the power of judicial legislation by construction to its *minimum*. Here is the text; what does it mean. taking its language, not in a strained sense, or *diverso intuitu*, but in its ordinary signification at the time the instrument was indited? What is the precise meaning intended by its authors?

If judicial legislation is an evil, written Constitutions are clearly barriers in the way of its progress. How far they are advantageous on the whole is yet an unsettled question. A short statement of the comparative advantages and disadvantages of written and unwritten Constitutions, may be useful before leaving this branch of the subject.

§ 77. The advantages of written Constitutions are chiefly the following: —

1. "When the political life of a people has been unpropitious for the foundation and growth of civil institutions, they are frequently the only possible starting point, and however slow, superficial, or deficient their action may be for a long time, still they form often the first available means to give civic dignity and political consciousness to a people, as well as the beginning of distinct delineation of power."[1] 2. They "form, in times of political apathy, if not too great, a passage, a bridge to pass over to better times."[2] Had the United States had an unwritten Constitution during the last thirty years, would the battle with slavery have been fought with such persistency and success as we have witnessed, amid the general and increasing political ignorance and moral depravation of our people? 3. "It gives a strong feeling of right, and a powerful impulse of action, to have the written law clearly on one's side, and though power, if it comes to the last, will disregard the written law as well as the customary, yet it must come to the last before it dares to pass the Rubicon, and to declare revolution."[3] 4. A written Constitution has the peculiar advantage of serving as a beacon to apprise the people when their rights and liberties are invaded or in danger.[4] 5. Though written Constitutions may be violated in moments of passion or delusion, yet they furnish a text to which those who are watchful may again rally and recall the people; they fix too for the people the principles of their political creed."[5]

§ 78. Against these advantages must be set down certain drawbacks.

[1] Lieber, *Polit. Ethics*, Pt. I. p. 394.

[2] Id. p. 395.

[3] Ibid.

[4] Tucker's *Black. Com.*, Appendix to Vol. I. p. 20.

[5] Jefferson, in a letter to Dr. Priestley, *Works*, Vol. IV. p. 441.

1. Written Constitutions are liable, if not frequently amended, to become inadequate, — an evil inseparable from all attempts to define the powers of that which is in a state of transition or growth. 2. If facility exist for producing amendments, there is danger that constitutional changes may be made the objects of party warfare for party purposes. Changes might thus be forced into the written instrument before they had wrought themselves out in the Constitution as a fact. 3. Written Constitutions, whatever may be the facilities afforded for amending them, are too inflexible. In a nation of the magnitude of ours, the process of changing its Constitution is, at best, slow. In the mean time, its rulers may be tempted, under the influence of great national interests, or under the pressure of threatening calamities, to violate it; the danger of doing which is much greater where its provisions are generally understood, than under an unwritten Constitution, most of whose provisions are doubtful or unfamiliar.[1]

§ 79. The advantages of unwritten Constitutions may be embraced in a single proposition: they are likely at all times to be more correct expressions than any others of the corresponding Constitutions, considered as objective facts. This follows from the process of their development. An unwritten Constitution is a record, by more or less competent observers, of fundamental changes which have occurred in the structure, principles, or guaranties of the Constitution considered as a fact. These changes are not made, but work themselves out under the operation of determinate social and political forces. They do not evolve themselves *per saltum*, as in written Constitutions, but gradually and continuously. They who transcribe such a Constitution, merely watch, pen in hand, the play of the producing forces and note results as they are achieved. These results become parts of the Constitution as a fact, and the delineation of

[1] De Maistre thus sums up his opinion of written Constitutions: He maintains, "1. That the foundations of political Constitutions exist in advance of all written law. 2. That a Constitution is and can be but the development of a preexisting unwritten law. 3. That that part of a Constitution which is most essential, most intrinsically constitutional, in short, which is truly fundamental, never is, and without imperiling the whole political system, never can be, reduced to writing. 4. That the weakness of a Constitution, and consequently its liability to infraction, are directly proportioned to the multiplicity of its written articles." — *Works*, Tom. I. p. 12.

them, made by the observer, a part of the unwritten Constitution considered as an instrument of evidence.

§ 80. It is obvious that if Constitutions, considered as facts, could develop into institutions as conspicuously and as perfectly as does the tree into fruit, the unwritten would be by far the most perfect of Constitutions, since then the text of it would immediately reflect actual fundamental changes. This, however, is not the fact. Excepting occasionally when a change is wrought out by a charter or by a statute, whose terms of course would be certain, unwritten Constitutions are determined by the growth of customs or of institutions, emerging often so imperceptibly as to elude common observation. And wherever there is obscurity or doubt, there are the conditions of conflict. Hence, though it is probable fundamental changes will be sooner registered in an unwritten Constitution, they are no more likely to have developed themselves peacefully than when they occur under a written Constitution. The truth is, that conflict is the condition of such changes everywhere. It is, however, less likely to be prolonged when, as soon as it is ended and the victory announced, the battle-cry of the victorious party is inscribed in the Constitution, as a part thereof, than when it must still be embodied in it by a formal vote of the electors.

§ 81. Considering the excellencies and defects of the two varieties of Constitutions, it is not easy to strike a balance between them. For a community whose political training has been carried to a high degree of perfection, in my view, an unwritten Constitution would, on the whole, be preferable. In that training two elements would be of vital consequence to the safety of the system: 1. An accurate understanding of their political rights and duties, general among the citizens. 2. Sleepless vigilance to detect violations of the Constitution, and the utmost promptness and energy to resist and punish them. Without either of these elements, the usurpations of public functionaries must bring the system to speedy ruin. But for a community whose training has been imperfect, or which is subject to fits of political apathy alternating with those of intense zeal for reform, a written Constitution is doubtless the better one. While less flexible to the pressure of the national will, and therefore liable, in many of its provisions to become obsolete and oppressive, it is a formidable barrier against usurpation. Its provisions are so plain that he who transgresses them must generally do so intentionally, and that fact must be so apparent that usurpation would in most cases not be ventured upon, as likely to rouse a dangerous opposition. The superiority of such a Constitution in the circumstances supposed, follows from the fact that immobility, with its train of possible evils, is less dangerous than movement that is ill-judged or unconstitutional.

§ 82. To render a written Constitution safe, however, under the most favorable conditions, it must embrace efficient machinery for its own amendment, and that machinery must be so devised as neither to operate with too great facility, nor to require to set it in motion an accumulation of force sufficient to explode the system. Two tendencies are observable in reference to the way in which a Constitution is regarded by the citizens of a state, both equally reprehensible: the tendency to idolize the letter of it, or, on the contrary, to under-estimate its real sacredness, and so to degrade it to the level of ordinary laws. The latter leads to undue tampering with constitutional provisions for purposes of selfish or partisan ambition. The former begets that foolish kind of conservatism which clings to its worn-out garments until the body is ready to perish with cold. Mr. Jefferson insisted that no Constitution ought to go longer than twenty years without an opportunity being given to the citizens to amend it. This opinion he based upon the consideration that, by the European tables of mortality, it appeared that a generation of men lasted, on an average, about that number of years, and that every succeeding generation, like its predecessor, had "a right to choose for itself the form of government it believed most promotive of its own happiness; consequently, to accommodate to the circumstances in which it finds itself, that received from its predecessors." [1] If to this there be appended the provisos, that amendments shall only then be attempted if they are pronounced necessary by the representatives of the people, and that they may be made at any time when so pronounced by a vote cast under circumstances making it probable that it reflects the settled will of the people, the opinion is doubtless a sound one.

§ 83. But it is not enough that a Constitution provide a mode for effecting its own amendment; it is necessary that

[1] Letter to Samuel Kercheval, of July 12, 1816. Jefferson's *Works*, Vol. VII. pp. 9–17.

there should be developed a political conscience impelling to make amendments in the written Constitution when such as are really important have evolved themselves in the Constitution as a fact. Our courts can, in general, recognize no law as fundamental which has not been transcribed into the book of the Constitution. When great historical movements, like those which have lately convulsed the United States, have resulted in important political changes, that are so consummated and settled as to indicate a solid foundation in the actual Constitution, they should be immediately registered by the proper authority among the fundamental laws. Why embarrass the courts and fly in the face of destiny by refusing to recognize accomplished facts? A point of honor should in such cases be cultivated, compelling the citizen to acquiesce in the decrees of the Almighty as written in events, similar to that which forces an English minister, on an adverse division upon an important measure, to resign his office. If political self-abnegation cannot, under written Constitutions, be developed to the extent indicated, it may be laid down as certain, that no commonwealth, governed by such a Constitution, can long survive.[1]

§ 84. In the United States, all Constitutions, considered in their evidentiary character, with two exceptions, have been written Constitutions. The peculiar circumstances of our political situation which occasioned this uniformity have been explained in the first chapter. And the exceptions alluded to are as significant of the principles which determined the rule as the cases strictly comprised within it. Connecticut and Rhode Island had unwritten Constitutions at the time of the Revolution, modelled in general after that of England, which continued in force until 1818 and 1842 respectively. The democratic character of those Constitutions had so satisfied the people of those colonies, and their experiences under them of parliamentary oppression had been so slight, that there seemed no need of a change when the yoke of England was cast off. As their rulers had not been able to oppress them under the old order of things, it was believed they would be unable to do so under the new; hence their polity was left unchanged. In the other colonies, the principle of express

[1] For a vigorous discussion of the article of the Federal Constitution pertaining to amendments, in which the position is taken that that article is wholly inadequate, see Fisher's *Trial of the Constitution*, ch. i.

limitation of powers was universally adopted. The result has been the formation of a hundred or more Constitutions, conforming strictly to the character of written Constitutions above presented. Throughout all these, a family likeness is observable in every feature, internal and external. It will be the object of the remaining sections of this chapter to point out the varieties, the mutual relations, and the internal structure in general of these Constitutions, so far at least as the exposition may tend to aid us in determining the powers and duties of *conventions*, whose function it is to frame them — the real purpose of this work.

§ 85. Before proceeding to the task indicated, however, it may be useful to ascertain with precision the distinction between a *Constitution* or *fundamental ordinance*, and an *ordinary municipal law*. Both must be denominated laws, since they are equally "rules of action laid down or prescribed by a superior."[1] Ordinary laws are enactments and rules for the government of civil conduct, promulgated by the legislative authority of a state, or deduced from long-established usage. It is an important characteristic of such laws that they are tentatory, occasional, and in the nature of temporary expedients. Fundamental laws, on the other hand, in politics, are expressions of the sovereign will in relation to the structure of the government, the extent and distribution of its powers, the modes and principles of its operation, and the apparatus of checks and balances proper to insure its integrity and continued existence. Fundamental laws are primary, being the commands of the sovereign establishing the governmental machine, and the most general rules for its operation. Ordinary laws are secondary, being commands of the sovereign, having reference to the exigencies of time and place resulting from the ordinary working of the machine. Fundamental laws precede ordinary laws in point of time, and embrace the settled policy of the state. Ordinary laws, are the creatures of the sovereign, acting through a body of functionaries existing only by virtue of the fundamental laws and express, as we have said, the expedient, or the right viewed as the expedient, under the varying circumstances of time and place.

§ 86. It is perhaps possible best to illustrate the distinction

[1] Worcester's *Dictionary*, *in verb.*

between fundamental and ordinary laws, by considering the case of a ship dispatched by its owner upon a distant voyage.

It would obviously be in the power of the owner to prescribe in advance as well the particular duties of the captain and crew from day to day, as the general nature and purpose of the adventure. But, how would a prudent owner manage in such a case? He would content himself with dictating the *termini* and object of the voyage, the rank and pay of the various officers, to which he might add general directions for the safety of the freight and the health and comfort of the crew. Beyond this, every thing relating to the voyage would be left to the officers. They would make rules for particular exigencies, as they should arise, direct when to tack, when to furl and when to unfurl the sails to conform to the variations of the weather, and prescribe the particular course in which to steer from day to day, to avoid rocks and shoals, keeping constantly in view, nevertheless, and, as far as practicable, acting in literal conformity to the owner's instructions. Now, such general directions relating to the objects of the voyage, the equipment of the ship, and the number and duties of those to whom her management should be intrusted, as it would be practicable to lay down in advance, as being not only thoroughly settled in the owner's mind, but as applicable under all circumstances of wind and weather, and in any probable condition of the ship, might be considered as fundamental to the adventure, and as proper for a prudent owner to prescribe. All such regulations, on the other hand, and all such devices and arrangements as would show themselves to be necessary only from time to time as the voyage should progress to protect the ship, freight, or crew, in special emergencies, or to advance the general purposes of the voyage, would not be fundamental, because not only would they be of less general consequence, but they would depend on circumstances that would be casual, and, therefore, not to be foreseen; and hence they would properly be left to the discretion of the master on the spot.

§ 87. The comparison of a commonwealth to a ship has been a favorite conception of poets and philosophers in all ages, but I doubt if in any respect the parallelism between them is so complete as in that specified above. I shall not occupy further space by pointing out minutely wherein that parallelism consists, but observe simply that the important points are, first, that fundamental laws are either structural, or expressive of the *settled policy* of the state; and second, that they may, consequently, be, as they theoretically are, laid down in advance, for ages to come; whilst, on the contrary, ordinary laws are merely temporary expedients or adjustments, and cannot be allowed to stiffen into constitutional provisions without extreme danger to the commonwealth; that, in other words, they have no place in a Constitution, and, therefore, as will be more fully shown in a subsequent chapter, are not proper subjects for the action of bodies charged with framing Constitutions.

§ 88. The Constitutions framed for the United States, and for its several component States, have all, save two,[1] been written Constitutions; and, in the two States whose Constitutions, as already explained, were originally unwritten, written Constitutions have lately been adopted. Of the whole number of Constitutions thus far framed in the United States, there have been two distinct varieties, namely, those framed for the general government, and those framed for the several States. The characteristic differences between these varieties depend upon the extent of the grants of power to them respectively, and upon the modes in which the limits of the several grants are determined. In the two Constitutions of the Union, the Articles of Confederation and the existing federal charter, the sum of the powers granted was comprised in several particular grants, and it was declared that the governments thereby established were confined to the exercise, the former, of powers "*expressly delegated*," and the latter, of powers "*delegated*," by that term designating, as it has been construed, express powers, and such as are necessary to carry into effect express powers. In these Constitutions, limitations of the grants of power are involved in the very terms in which they are made, the clear import of the instruments being, without an express declaration to that effect, that no power not affirmatively authorized by them can be exercised. In other words, the governments of the United States delineated in those Constitutions were governments of limited powers, but of powers ranking highest in the political scale, and within the scope of those powers, they were supreme. This is more particularly true of the Federal government than of the Confederation, though substantially so of that also.

§ 89. To the State governments, on the contrary, were appor-

[1] See § 84, *ante*.

tioned the residuary powers, or most of them, not comprised in the federal grants. Thus, under the Confederation, according to the articles establishing it, each State retained every power, jurisdiction, and right not expressly delegated to the United States; that is, retained the sum total of the residuary powers. When the new Constitution, however, went into effect in 1789, the State governments were vested by the people of the Union with such of the residuary powers only as were not reserved to the latter;[1] which reserved powers were, first, such sovereign powers as are not delegated to the ordinary departments of our governments, as that of amendment; and, secondly, such as, not being delegated to the Federal government, were prohibited to those of the States. Conceiving of the State governments, as we must, whatever the historical fact may be, as erected subsequently to that of the Union, they took all such powers as the people had to give except where the contrary was expressed or from the nature of the case implied. In other words, the State governments were made governments of general powers, except when limited by the principles of morality or by the terms of the Federal Constitution.

§ 90. The Federal Constitution being designed particularly to delineate the structure and powers of the Federal government, it touches upon those of the States only so far as they are related to that of the Union, and that with a view to prevent collisions. It therefore deals in this respect only in prohibitions to the States. The State constitutions, on the other hand, contain affirmative grants of power, and the mode of making them is to give to their governments powers, as of legislation, in general terms, and afterwards to limit those powers, if deemed desirable, by express provisions. Within the general domain allotted to the States, then, whatever any government can of right do, a State government can do. The government of the Union, on the other hand, though permitted a discretion as to modes of carrying into effect its granted powers, can do only what it is affirmatively authorized to do — finding itself hedged in from the general mass of governmental powers, while those of the States are free to

[1] The words of the 10th amendment are: "The powers not delegated to the United States by the Constitution, nor prohibited by it to the States, are reserved to the States respectively, or to the people," — not to the people of the States, but to the people of the Union, who make the grant.

expatiate at large, save where powers are hedged in from them.

§ 91. These peculiarities of structure and function give rise to special rules of construction, depending on the differences mentioned. Thus, although within the sphere of its acknowledged powers, the general government is entitled to all liberal intendments, still, in determining that sphere, it is a presumption of law that a power does not belong to it, unless it be expressly granted, or be necessary, in a legal sense, to carry into effect some power expressly granted. This follows from the fact that it is a government of enumerated powers. Within the sphere of their powers, on the other hand, while the States are entitled to liberal intendments and to complete dominion, save where some of their powers are concurrent with those of the government of the Union, the presumption, in determining that sphere, is, that a power belongs to them if the contrary do not appear by a fair construction of their own Constitutions and that of the United States. This results from the fact that they are vested with all the powers which are neither granted to the general government, reserved to the people, nor prohibited to the States.

§ 92. And here I may remark that the Constitution of the United States is a part of the Constitution of each State, whether referred to in it or not, and that the Constitutions of all the States form a part of the Constitution of the United States. An aggregation of all these constitutional instruments would be precisely the same in principle as a single Constitution, which, framed by the people of the Union, should define the powers of the general government, and then by specific provisions erect the separate governments of the States, with all their existing attributions and limitations of power. There is not a particle of question that the people of the United States could have thus framed their Constitution, had it been thought advisable, or that they could still — whether regularly or not is another question — melt the thirty odd Constitutions into a single one. To do the latter, undoubtedly they must first recall the power, conceded by the existing Constitution to the people of the several States, to frame, each in a *quasi* sovereign capacity, its own Constitution. But this, if they are the sovereign, they unquestionably have, if not the legal competence, at least the physical ability to do; or they may even, as we have seen, under like conditions, abolish the States, as distinct political organizations.[1]

§ 93. It follows from the principles above announced, regulating the distribution of powers to the Federal and State governments, that they are both really governments of limited jurisdiction; and that they are equally required to confine themselves to the exercise of granted powers. Hence it would seem to follow that they are equal to each other. If it were objected to this conclusion, that the rules of construction just explained indicate a superiority of the powers appropriated to the States, in point of breadth or scope, it may be replied, that, while that is true, those powers are of a grade far less exalted than those apportioned to the general government. On the whole, laying out of view all positive provisions subordinating either to the other, the two systems of government, State and Federal, save, perhaps, in notoriety or *éclat* abroad, must be pronounced equal. But, when reference is made to the Federal Constitution, it is found that a subordination is established by positive regulation. Article VI. declares that "this Constitution and the laws made in pursuance thereof, and all treaties made, or which shall be made, under the authority of the United States, *shall be the supreme law of the land;*" to which is added a provision that all legislative, executive, and judicial officers of both Federal and State governments "shall be bound by oath or affirmation to support this Constitution." From these clauses, it is evident the government of the Union is made, in some of its operations, to be supreme over those of the States. As each of the two is of course absolute within the field appropriated to itself, the supremacy referred to must relate to the exercise of powers not recognized as absolutely belonging to either, but such as are denominated concurrent, or as lie on the boundary between the two, and respecting which there may be doubts to which government they belong. Thus, it would be wrong to say that the Federal government is supreme over those of the States in the matter of declaring war, for that power belongs exclusively to the general government. So it would be improper to say of a State that it is supreme over the general government, in the exercise of a power to which the latter can make no pretence, but

[1] See *ante*, §§ 56-58.

which certainly belongs to the former.[1] Supreme implies a comparison of power, and in these cases there could be no comparison, because one has all the power and the other has none.

§ 94. It is, therefore, only on those points where the regulations of the two governments, in the shape of State laws or Constitutions on the one hand, and the Constitution, laws, or treaties of the Union, on the other, come in conflict, that the conditions of supremacy can exist. If a power is concurrent in the two, its exercise by the States must be subordinated to its exercise by the general government, where both cannot exercise it fully without collision. So, where a power may fairly be claimed to belong to both jurisdictions, if it be asserted by the general government, it becomes *pro tanto*, on account of its supremacy, rightful to it alone. That is the supremacy meant by the constitutional provision. As the authors of the "Federalist" have shown, it expresses but the condition on which alone a complex system of government by means of distinct and yet not wholly independent political organizations, like ours, can exist. Either the States must be subordinated to the Union, or the Union must be subordinated to the States; in which latter case, as they well observed, "the world would have seen for the first time a system of government founded on an inversion of the fundamental principles of all government; it would have seen the authority of the whole society everywhere subordinate to the authority of the parts; it would have seen a monster, in which the head was under the direction of the members." [2]

§ 95. While considering the relations of the two varieties of Constitutions in the United States, namely, that of the Union and those of the States, it may be well to remark, that, although they together form the Constitution of the Union, yet, as in theory their spheres of operation are distinct, so, in practice, they should be kept disconnected in respect of the rights and duties apportioned to each. They ought not, in other words, to make themselves ancillary to each other's operations. This remark is applicable more particularly to the Constitutions of the States in

[1] See Rutherforth's definition of the word "supreme" as distinguished from the word "sovereign," *ante*, § 18, note.

[2] *Federalist*, No. 44, by Madison. See, also, 2 Peters' R. 449; 4 Wheaton's R. 122.

relation to that of the United States. Thus, as the right to coin money is given exclusively to the general government, counterfeiting the national coin is properly, as such, an offence only against the United States, and ought to be punished by it alone. For a State, either in its Constitution or laws, to make provision for punishing it, would be inexpedient, if not a breach of constitutional duty. If the governments founded by the people of the United States, and charged with distinct and independent functions, are unable to sustain themselves without extra-constitutional aid from each other, that would be a reason for applying to the original fountain of authority for an increase of their powers, not for exceeding their respective jurisdictions, with a view to effect what can only be properly done by the people themselves. Such an assumption of power would be for our legislative bodies to make, not to administer, the fundamental laws.

This idea was admirably enforced by Mr. Webster in the Massachusetts Convention of 1820. He said: It was inexpedient to connect "the State Constitution with provisions of the National Constitution. He thought it tended to no good consequence to undertake to regulate or enforce rights and duties arising under the general government, by other means than the powers of that government itself. He would wish that the Constitution of the State should have as little connection with the Constitution of the United States as possible. Some of the States have sometimes endeavored to come in aid of the general government, and to enforce its laws, by their own laws. State statutes had been passed to compel compliance with statutes of Congress, and imposing penalties for transgressing those statutes. This had been found very embarrassing, and, as he thought, mischievous, because its tendency was to mix up the two governments, and to destroy the real essential distinction which exists between them. The true constitutional, harmonious movement of the two governments was as much interrupted by their *alliance* as by their *hostility*. They were ordained to move in different spheres, and when they came together, be it for the purpose of mutual harm or mutual help, the system is deranged. Whatsoever was enjoined on the legislature by the Constitution of the United States, the legislature was bound to perform; and he thought it would not be well by a provision of *this* Constitution to regulate the mode in which the legislature should exercise a power conferred on it by another Constitution."[1]

§ 96. I pass now to consider briefly the internal structure of written Constitutions, as they exist in the United States.

The American Constitutions commonly consist of three distinct parts: 1. The Bill of Rights. 2. The Frame of Government. 3. The Schedule. Of these, the first two are generally present, though often blended together, and not in separate parts. The third, especially in the earlier Constitutions, is not always found.

1. A Bill of Rights consists of solemn declarations of abstract principles, relating to the origin, ground, and purposes of government, and practical injunctions and prohibitions, promulgated with a view to its safe and equitable administration, digested out of the experience of the free peoples of England and America during six hundred years of struggle for constitutional liberty, and intended as at once a guide and a limitation to the government in the exercise of power. I call the principles embodied in a Bill of Rights abstract, but only in deference to the common forms of speech, which thus characterize whatever is viewed as disconnected from the circumstances of time and place. Properly considered, however, those principles are the most concrete of all, as being such, not simply under certain conditions, but irrespective of all conditions.

In the progress of English liberty during the period mentioned, there have been taken these cardinal steps: 1. The Magna Charta, with its thirty confirmations by the Plantagenets and Tudors; 2. The Petition of Right, addressed by the Parliament to the second of the Stuarts; 3. The Declaration of Right, made by the Convention Parliament on the restoration of Charles II.; 4. The Habeas Corpus Act, passed in the thirty-first year of his reign; and, 5. The Act of Settlement by which the crown was settled upon William and Mary in 1689, upon terms and conditions imposed by a second Convention Parliament, being the crowning stone in the arch of English freedom. The liberties wrought out or secured by these famous Acts, were as much

[1] *Deb. Mass. Conv.*, 1820, p. 112. It has even been made a question whether a State Constitution ought to provide for taking an oath to support the Constitution of the United States. See *Deb. Penn. Conv.*, 1837, Vol. I. pp. 195–215. See, also, on the general question discussed in the text, *Deb. Ohio Conv.*, 1850, pp. 233–236.

those of English freemen living in America as of those dwelling in England. They were perhaps even more fondly cherished by the former than by the latter, since circumstances taught them more clearly their great value, and the precarious tenure by which they were held. Accordingly, in all the public papers emitted by the colonies during their struggle with England, they grounded themselves distinctly on these great constitutional acts. Indeed, it is now admitted by the political writers of England, that it was our fathers alone who held aloft the liberties of England for Englishmen themselves in that struggle, and that the triumph of the crown would probably have been the downfall of the entire Constitution, built up with such infinite toil and blood.[1]

§ 97. When it became apparent, accordingly, in the course of our Revolutionary struggle, that independence was inevitable, and the colonies came to provide regular governments based on the authority of the people, they sought to erect at the same time a system of guaranties of their old-time liberties. To this end, in imitation of their ancestors, they engraved the maxims and principles forming the most valued portions of those acts — all of them, indeed, that were deemed applicable to their condition and circumstances — upon the front of their constitutional charters, as if for a perpetual *caveat* to their rulers. To realize the great value of these principles, I have but to refer to a few of the most important and well known of them. They were: That no freeman ought to be taken, imprisoned, or disseized of his freehold, liberties, or privileges, or outlawed or exiled, or in any manner destroyed or deprived of his life, liberty, or property but by the law of the land: That the people ought not to be taxed, or made subject to the payment of any impost or duty, without the consent of themselves, or their representatives in General Assembly, freely given: That no freeman should be convicted of any crime but by the unanimous verdict of a jury of good and lawful men, in open court, as theretofore used: That excessive bail should not be required, nor excessive fines imposed, nor cruel or unusual punishments inflicted: That the freedom of the press was one of the great bulwarks of liberty, and therefore ought never to be restrained: That for redress of grievances, and for amending and strength-

[1] May's *Const. Hist. of England*, Vol. II. pp. 28–30.

ening the laws, elections ought to be often held: That perpetuities and monopolies were contrary to the genius of a free state, and ought not to be allowed. To these were added prohibitions against general warrants, standing armies, *ex post facto* laws, the suspension of laws or the granting of hereditary emoluments or privileges, and injunctions designed to secure the privilege of the writ of *Habeas Corpus*, the right of petition and of freely assembling, the freedom of worship and of the press, and the establishment of a militia for the public defence.

§ 98. As is generally the case with constitutional provisions, these principles are not couched in the technical language of laws, nor are they coupled with sanctions. But it is, nevertheless, impossible to overstate their importance as guides to the departments of government in the exercise of their functions.[1] From their nature this is especially true of the State governments. To a government like the Federal, whose powers are such only as have been expressly granted, or as are necessary to carry into effect such as are expressly granted, the range for aberrations from constitutional paths, and therefore the need of cautionary or restrictive maxims, are much less than in governments constructed like those of the States. Accordingly there was no Bill of Rights in the Federal Constitution as originally framed, nor properly afterwards, though the amendments carried soon after its establishment consisted almost exclusively of principles usually embodied in Bills of Rights. The reason for enacting these amendments was, that the people of the United States were not content to rest their liberties upon any constitutional inability of the Federal government to infringe them. Such a security was a negative one, at best, and subject always to be neutralized by construction in the wide field of incidental powers. They insisted upon positive landmarks, and not only that, but upon the erection of such a barrier of principles and asserted rights as should deter any but the intentional usurper from passing the line of permitted powers. Without a tacit understanding that such a barrier should be provided, it is beyond question that the system would not have been ratified. The case was different with regard to the State Constitutions. They contained grants of power so extensive and so undefined, that the propriety of prefacing them by declarations of rights

[1] Hamilton *v.* St. Louis County Court. 15 Mo. R. 1, (23).

was never denied or even doubted; and, as we have seen, though there have been exceptions, in general all Constitutions of that class have contained Bills of Rights.

§ 99. The chief practical advantage of Bills of Rights, as above intimated, is that they furnish a guide to the departments of the government in the exercise of their powers and duties in cases of doubt. They are for them what prudential maxims resulting from individual experience are for men in the ordinary concerns of life. But the experience from which the former are drawn is that of society, accumulated in the course of many centuries, and so, not likely to be that also of the individuals who administer the government, nor to be known to them unless specially inculcated in some conspicuous manner. It is upon the determinations of courts of justice that they have the most direct and beneficial effect. In questions of constitutional power or duty, in their bearing upon private rights, they are an invaluable guide, and our books of reports are filled with cases, the decisions of which turned upon the principles embodied in them. These principles, indeed, may be distinguished from the provisions of that part of the Constitution denominated the Frame of Government, as embracing, the former, guaranties for private rights, and the latter provisions relating to the policy of the State and to its political power and organization.[1] It being impossible in general language to lay down rules for the determination of particular cases, our courts would, on very many questions of construction, be wholly afloat, without the fixed principles of public policy and private right laid down in our Bills of Rights.

§ 100. 2. The Frame of Government is that part of a written Constitution in which are described the structure and functions of the government; that is, the distribution of political power, the particular agencies which are to wield it, the extent and duration of their authority, their emoluments, modes of appointment or election, and the apparatus designed for amending or reproducing the system. Though in general all official persons and duties are delineated in this part of the Constitution, there are some exceptions, as in case of sheriffs, whose election merely is regulated, without specifying their duties or powers. They being officers well known at common law, a description of those

1 Sedgwick on *Stat. and Const. Law*, pp. 475–6.

particulars is deemed unnecessary, as being involved, to the common apprehension, in the name of the office. The same is true of some other functionaries, as coroners, the higher military officers, judges of the courts, and others.

§ 101. In the Frame of Government are often, especially in the later Constitutions, included also positive provisions relating rather to the general policy of the State than to its political power or organization. Thus, many contain clauses designed to promote education, to encourage charitable institutions, to determine the *status* of the citizens of the State, as slave or free, or to regulate corporate rights, as of banks or of railroad companies, or the privileges of particular classes of citizens, such as homestead exemption, rights of married women, and the like. Indeed, as Constitutions embody settled policy, as well as the general features of the political organization, so fast as measures of policy become really settled, that is, removed from the arena of party conflict, they are commonly enshrined in the Constitution, so that every generation, in communities like ours open to progress, witnesses an extension of these provisions in our fundamental charters. Beside these provisions, State Constitutions usually contain others defining the boundaries of the territory claimed as within their jurisdiction ; and, in close relation thereto, announcing the State policy with reference to the management and disposition of the public domain, or to internal improvements.

§ 102. 3. The Schedule is that part of a written Constitution in which are comprised provisions deemed necessary — 1, to ascertain the will of the people with respect to the adoption of the instrument, matured by a Convention, as the Constitution of the State ; 2, to effect, without inconvenience or embarrassment, the transition from the old to the new order of things, and to save rights, acquired under existing laws, from lapsing by their repeal; 3, to set up and put in operation the institutions and agencies described in the Constitution, so far as not already in operation. These provisions are mostly temporary in purpose and effect ; and although they are, some of them, of a character more or less fundamental, they seem incongruous with the permanent provisions of the Constitution, properly so called, and with the Bill of Rights. Beside these, which are the usual and proper contents of a Schedule, are sometimes found others, whose true place is in the Frame of Government, or whose character is such that they cannot rightfully find any place in a Constitution. Of the former, sections relating to subjects treated of in the body of the instrument, but bearing upon points which have apparently been forgotten, or which are mere after-thoughts, are instances. It is, perhaps, rather a sense of logical completeness and order than substantial propriety which is offended by such provisions; but if a Schedule is a proper subdivision of a Constitution, it should be, not in the nature of a labor-saving postscript, made at the expense of clearness and finish, but of an appendix, in which to gather provisions of a temporary and miscellaneous character, related to the instrument in the main only as subservient to its general objects. Among provisions which ought to find no place in a Constitution at all, but which are, nevertheless, occasionally placed in a Schedule, may be mentioned laws or ordinances relating to the submission of the Constitution to the people, to take effect at once, in cases where power to make such laws or ordinances has been expressly withheld by the legislature calling the Convention, or where different directions have already been given to that end by the legislature itself, and, perhaps, where the legislature has been altogether silent on the subject of submission. The objection to such provisions is, that they are exercises of a legislative discretion not belonging to a Convention; and as, from the nature of the case, the action of such a body, in placing them in the Schedule as rules of conduct, cannot be revised, but is definitive, it is an excess of authority to assume to enact them. Whether or not it might be allowable to make such provisions in the case last supposed, where the legislature has been silent on the subject of submission, or of the time and mode in which it shall be made, is a fair subject for argument, which will be considered in a subsequent chapter.[1]

§ 103. It should be noted that the Schedule did not make its appearance until after the first batch of Constitutions, including those of the Union, had been framed and put in operation. The first Constitutions in which it was used were those of South Carolina and Pennsylvania, framed in 1790. Of the Constitutions now in force, only about two in three have them, though in a

[1] See §§ 480, 481, 497–499, *post*.

few instances a separate article containing similar provisions is embraced in the Constitution, without special designation, or under the title of General Provisions.

§ 103 *a*. Beside schedules, there are appended to many Constitutions acts adopted by Conventions, called ordinances. Not all ordinances, however, are so appended, or have any direct relation to Constitutions. They are in their nature resolutions of the bodies adopting them, but taking the name, ordinances, to distinguish them from the similar acts of legislative bodies, denominated resolutions, which may be adopted by the Houses severally or jointly. Within the scope of the powers of a Convention, ordinances may be valid and effectual according to their terms and purpose. If they are employed to provide for temporary emergencies of the Convention, and do not transcend the limits of its powers as defined or implied in the act calling it, they are valid. If they are appended to the Constitution, and with it are submitted to the people for adoption or rejection, when submission is not dispensed with, and with it adopted, they are as valid as any part of the Constitution, and are equally binding upon the various departments of the Government.[1]

Before leaving the subject of Constitutions, it is proper to observe, that, wherever in this work the term "Constitution" is used, a written Constitution will be intended, unless the contrary is intended.

[1] Stewart *v.* Crosby, 15 Texas R., 546 ; 13 Am. Law Reg. (O. S.), 716.

CHAPTER IV.

OF THE REQUISITES TO THE LEGITIMACY OF CONVENTIONS, AND OF THEIR HISTORY.

§ 104. HAVING, in the two preceding chapters, considered the doctrine of *sovereignty*, by which are mainly to be determined the powers of the *Constitutional Convention*, and defined what is meant by a *Constitution*, to frame which is the business of that body, I pass now to a series of inquiries having for their purpose to determine the requisites to the legitimacy of Constitutional Conventions, namely, first, *What is the proper mode of initiating or calling a Convention?* and, secondly, *By whom should Conventions be elected?*

These questions will form the subject of the present chapter, and will be considered from two separate points of view; 1, from that of theoretical principles; and, 2, from that of historical precedents.

§ 105. Before entering upon the wide field thus brought to view, it will be useful to ascertain the import of two terms, which will be very frequently used in the course of the discussion, namely, *legitimacy* and *revolution*, with their derivatives.

The primary signification of the term *legitimacy* is accordance with the law, and it is most commonly employed with reference to the birth of children, to characterize it as lawful. In European governments, sovereignty being generally ascribed to the reigning monarch, from whom it descends to his offspring, according to certain rules, the legitimacy of a government follows from the personal legitimacy of the occupant of the throne, and *vice versa;* hence the term has there come to bear very commonly a merely political signification to characterize governments deemed to be regular and lawful, because, in the devolution of the rights of sovereignty from one incumbent of the throne to another, the established rules of legitimate succession have been observed.

§ 106. To the legitimacy of a prince of the blood, it is essential that he should be the offspring of the reigning monarch and his wife, begotten and born in lawful wedlock and during their joint occupancy of the throne, or the legitimate offspring of parents sustaining that relation. This rule, though apparently arbitrary, is based on the experienced necessities of state for many ages in the European monarchies; and, if exceptions to it have occurred, they have been rather acquiesced in than commended, and that from the same considerations of expediency that gave rise to the rule. To render a government legitimate, then, the rule requires the exclusion from the succession of all persons not the offspring of the royal pair; the exclusion of all the issue of them or either of them begotten, or conceived, out of the sovereign condition, or in a morganatic union of sovereign and subject; and, especially, of their bastard issue. To realize the importance of this rule, one needs but to call to mind the wars of succession that devastated the European monarchies, before it was established or because its application was disputed.

§ 107. Now, with the exception of royal titles and the physical circumstances of marriage and birth of children, which give a local coloring to the doctrine of legitimacy in Europe, it is applicable, in similar terms and for the same reasons, in the United States. It is true here, as there, that, to be lawful or legitimate, successive forms of government must be the offspring, regularly and lawfully begotten, the later of the earlier. They must be developed, one out of the other, after the order of Nature in the genesis and growth of her organic products. A system of government, in other words, having been established, it must itself govern, as well in the matter of reproducing or repairing itself as in that of protecting itself and its subordinate members from the operation of harmful agencies without. A government, once founded, *is* the people, as organized for the attainment of the ends of government. Neither a part nor all of that people, in their individual capacity, or acting as a dissociated, non-organized mass, are legally competent to change their political structure. If that is to be done at all, consistently with the integrity of the government, or with the safety or happiness of the citizens, it must be done through the people themselves, as organized for the purposes of government. In a word, it is a right of the governed to know where to look for lawful successors to the institutions and magistrates under which they now live — a thing impossible except when the succession takes place according to law.

The rules and legal principles by which this right is secured and rendered effectual, limit and explain the doctrine of legitimacy under our system of government.

§ 108. To determine whether an institution or a public body, claiming to exercise any of the powers of sovereignty, is legitimate, in a political sense, it is necessary to ask two questions:

1. Has it, in its inception, the stamp of legality — of conformity to the law of the land?

2. Do the law itself and the proceedings in which it originated conform to the fundamental principles of the Constitution, and to those prudential maxims which define the limits and conditions of a safe constitutional rule, from the point of view of the existing government?

Whatever can answer these questions in the affirmative is legitimate. Whatever, on the other hand, is *extra legem*, that is, established without law, and from a point of view external to the existing order; and whatever, more especially, is adverse in its methods or influences, though not, perhaps, in its intent, to the government in being, or violates the principles necessary to its conservation, is illegitimate.[1]

Thus far of the term legitimacy.

§ 109. The term *revolution* (*revolvo*, *to roll* or *turn over*,) was used originally to signify, in a political sense, an uprising of ambitious or discontented subjects, with a view to subvert the existing social order. From this has been derived the meaning, most common nowadays, with which I use the term, namely, to denote a political act or acts done in violation of law, or without law. The act must be a political one, since it would be an abuse of the term "revolution" to apply it to ordinary misdemeanors or felonies, which, though infractions of the municipal law, have neither in intent nor effect a political bearing. A political act is one done either in the exercise or in derogation or subversion of political rights, as defined and guaranteed by the government established. Such an act, to be revolutionary, accordingly, must be done either, first, in violation of law; that is, of the Constitution, or of the customary or statute law, including in the term law, the letter, with its necessary implications; or, secondly, without law; by which is meant, that the act must rest, for its warrant, on abstract considerations, such as physical power, necessity, or natural equity, and not upon the authority of the existing social order, to which it is extrinsic or hostile.

From these definitions it follows, that it is erroneous to impute to all revolutions, what are unhappily the concomitants of some, bloodshed and violence. Revolutions are of various kinds: —

[1] Compare Guizot, *Hist. Civilization in Europe*, Vol. I. Lect. III.

First, such as manifest themselves in desolating wars, as that of the Roses, in England, or that which has just deluged our own land with blood.

Second, such as run their course without bloodshed, but are attended by angry collisions of parties, threatening an outbreak of violence.

Third, such as are consummated quietly, without a breach of the peace, or even excitement, — often without a distinct perception, on the part of the people, of their occurrence.

§ 110. Of each of the kinds of revolution enumerated, the consequences may be varied, wholly without relation to the apparent magnitude of the forces at work in them. They may, indifferently, result in great and permanent changes in the Constitution of the society in which they occur, or in its laws or social condition, whether pronounced successful or not. Or, on the other hand, though they may seem to involve colossal forces and to be producing great transformations, the resulting changes may be slight and temporary.

Strictly speaking, it is erroneous to distinguish revolutions as small or great. It is the want of legality in what is done that constitutes the revolution; and when a thing is done for which there is no law, or which is in violation of law, there are no degrees in the illegality, — one thing is as legal as another, when both are illegal. It is only of the concomitants or effects of revolutions that magnitude can be predicated.

§ 111. A single further remark is necessary to explain the import of the term revolution. In what has preceded, revolutionary acts have been conceived of as done, not by the government, but by persons without it, though subject to it. But the term revolutionary is often applicable to acts done by the functionaries of a state, whilst pursuing its enemies, to defeat them and to preserve the state. There is a homely maxim, according to which it is proper "to fight the devil with fire," which applies well to counter-revolutionary acts. On principle, as being done without law or against law, though with the patriotic purpose of saving that for which all laws are made, such acts must nevertheless be classed as revolutionary. The moral character to be affixed to them, however, is to be determined by the degree of their necessity. So far as they are necessary to save the existing order, they are for it proper weapons of defence, and their inherent illegality is to be laid to the account of those who necessitated their use. So far, on the other hand, as they are unnecessary, they are to be stigmatized not only as illegal, but as morally indefensible, because stepping farther outside the circle of the law than is necessary to grasp and destroy its enemy.

§ 112. The importance of defining the term revolution, and of characterizing as revolutionary whatever, by its lack of legality, deserves the name, arises from the consideration, that, co-extensive with the domain of law, is that of precedents. A precedent has been defined to be "something to show that, because a thing has been done before, therefore it may be done again."[1] Being always relative to some rule, it is in the nature of a practical construction put upon it by the public authorities, from which it is fair to presume they will not depart in similar cases. Now, when, in treating of constitutional or political questions, it has been determined that an act or thing is without the domain of law, having no relations to it except those of hostility, that is, is revolutionary, it is also shown to be beyond the domain of precedents; it is, in short, incapable of being drawn into precedent. In this respect a revolutionary act is like one of theft or of homicide. While it is impossible to call either of the latter legal, it cannot be denied that both may, under some circumstances, be necessary and justifiable, as to preserve life. But such cases are extreme ones, and rest on their own circumstances. Because a man yesterday took life justifiably, under circumstances specified, it does not follow that I may take life to-day, though the same circumstances may exist, as, in my case, from a thousand causes, there may be no necessity for taking life. I may be stronger, or my antagonist weaker, than in the case cited as a precedent, and the particular of relative strength may not have been adverted to in that precedent. If, judging by my case alone, it is absolutely necessary for me to take life, I am justifiable in doing so, otherwise not. So, with every act that can be characterized as revolutionary. If it be done at all, it must be because the doer deems it absolutely indispensable. Moreover, it must be done at the doer's risk. If it result successfully, it so far lays the foundation for a new order of things. If it fail,

[1] Judge Joel Parker, in the Massachusetts Convention of 1853. *Debates Mass. Conv.* 1853, Vol. I. p. 83.

he who did it is liable to the penalties of treason under the old. But — and this is the important point — in no event can such an act be drawn into precedent, because not done in pursuance of any accredited rule or law, of which it can be regarded as a practical construction.

§ 113. A single remark further as to the terms illegitimate and revolutionary. These terms are, to a certain extent, convertible, but the latter is of a wider signification than the former. Illegitimacy refers to illegality of origin, and is pertinent rather to a person or body of persons than to an act. The term revolutionary, on the other hand, may be used to characterize indifferently a body or an act, and involves the idea, as we have seen, of illegality in general, that is, of either a want of express legal warrant, or a violation of positive law.

§ 114. To revert now to the subjects proposed for discussion in this chapter: —

I. What is the proper mode of initiating a Convention, looking at the question from the point of view of theoretical principles?

There are but two modes in which a Convention can be initiated. First, it may be done through the intervention of unofficial persons; that is, by persons acting as private citizens, but giving expression, perhaps, to a general desire; or, secondly, by the intervention of persons belonging to some branch of the existing government, acting in their official capacity, and by that government's desire.

1. A Convention called in the first mode would obviously be nothing more than the "Spontaneous Convention" or public meeting explained in the first chapter. Lacking official character and relations, the extent to which such a body would express the public will, would be simply a matter of conjecture. As no legal provision could be appealed to to guide it in determining whether all parts of the political body were proportionately represented in it, or whether they, who claimed to sit as delegates, were entitled to do so, it would be impossible for such an assembly to vindicate its legal character or its exclusive jurisdiction for any purpose whatever. And yet, regarded as a collection of persons interested in effecting constitutional changes, that is, as a mere public meeting, such a body would be obnoxious to no exception. But those who maintain the propriety and legal-

ity of that mode go farther. They claim for a Convention thus assembled, if deputed by a majority of the adult male citizens of the State, an official representative character, in virtue of which its action is to some extent legally binding on the whole State.

§ 115. How this may be, upon judicial authority, will be the subject of future examination. Considered upon principle, it is sufficient to remark: —

First, that, if the proposition announced in a former chapter, as involved in the definition of sovereignty, be a sound one, that sovereignty inheres, in no sense, and to no degree, in the citizen as an individual, nor in any number of citizens as individuals, but in the society considered as a corporate unit; then, any aggregation of individuals, not exhibiting a warrant from the sovereign, through some one of its recognized ordinary agents, for assembling and acting in its name, is a mere spontaneous assembly or *caucus*. It has nothing official in it, and can bind no one by its proceedings. If it affect to frame a law or a Constitution, and to put it in force, its action is revolutionary. As a body, it is neither the sovereign nor any body sprung from it, and so known to the law, but is unknown and hostile to both. It is, therefore, illegitimate.

Secondly. The hypothesis that a Convention, called by unofficial persons, should express the general desire, is the most favorable one that could be made for those who ascribe legal validity to the acts of such a spontaneous assembly. In actual experience, insurmountable difficulties would attend the authentic ascertainment of that fact. How could it be made known, without legal direction and scrutiny, who participated in that expression, or whether the returns were correct of those who opposed, as well as of those who favored, the call? Probably, as a fact, few meetings, thus originated, would represent more than a clique. To those interested in securing the objects of the Convention, the attendance of such as were not, would be undesirable, and either the latter, therefore, would receive no notice of the election of delegates, or the result of it would be falsified. Opposing interests would have each its primary meeting and its delegates. Where all was loose and spontaneous, whose duty should it be to determine, among the adverse claimants to whom the seats in the Convention should be awarded?

The rejected delegations might really represent the majority. At any rate, believing themselves to do so, or pushed on by passion to pretend it, rival Conventions, each announcing itself as "the people in their sovereign capacity," might assemble, and harass the State by conflicting ordinances, heralded as supreme laws for its citizens. In all this, there would be, at bottom, no legality, because done without law, in the face of the existing government. One of the most important ends of government, is to ascertain, for the citizen, who are the magistrates, and what are the laws. Under its ægis, he can never be embarrassed by two sets of functionaries asserting validity for two rival sets of laws or two opposing Constitutions. Looking at those whom he knows to represent the sovereign, the officers of the existing order, he can rest satisfied, that what they recognize as legal is so, and what they denounce as illegal, is illegal. The mode of calling Conventions now in question would render this impossible. No citizen could know either the magistrate, the Constitution or the laws he was bound to obey. A Convention, then, called in such a mode, it would be a perversion of language to style legitimate.[1]

§ 116. 2. The other mode of calling Conventions is by an authentic act of the sovereign body acting through some branch of the existing government representing it, as the electors, or one of the three departments — legislative, executive, and judicial.

The propriety of this mode is inferrible from considerations, already presented, of the embarrassments resulting from any other possible mode. But it is easy to demonstrate the absolute impropriety of any other mode. In a former chapter, we have seen, that any body of men claiming to act in the name of the sovereign, in the discharge of any political function, must be presumed to be impostors or usurpers, unless exhibiting a warrant so to do from the sovereign, in the shape of some law or constitutional provision.[2] If it have no official character whatever, its individual members are impostors. If, having a quasi-official character from that of its individual members, as belonging to the system of agencies established by the body politic and constituting the government, it nevertheless assume a function not intrusted to

[1] See *Webster's Works*, Vol. VI. pp. 224–229.

[2] See § 25, *ante*. Also *Webster's Works*, *ubi sup.*

it, — its members are usurpers. The philosophy of the whole subject may be summed up thus: The State has a clear right to reproduce itself, as an animal does, at its own will and by its own appropriate organs. Only by the exercise of that right can its reputed offspring or successor be legitimate, or, what is of perhaps equal importance to the citizen, escape the reputation of illegitimacy.

§ 117. Conceding that the principle just stated, as a general one, is true, it remains to inquire into the particulars comprised in the term mode; that is, to determine with reference to all the pertinent categories, how a Convention ought to be called to be at once legitimate and safe. Taking the word in its broadest sense, there must be included in the *mode* of calling a Convention a description, first, of the agencies through which the call is to be effected; and, secondly, of the manner in which it is to be done. These will be considered in their order.

§ 118. 1. As we have seen, the agency through which a Convention ought to be called, is some branch of the existing government, that is, either the electors or one of the three ordinary departments indicated. To select out of these that one which is best fitted for such a trust, though a work of some difficulty, is one which can be done with considerable exactitude.

(*a*). Should it be committed to the electors, independently of other departments of the government?

The electoral body, though less numerous than the sovereign body which it represents, is yet so organized as to incapacitate it for assembling or acting together. It has no ministers through whom either its functions can be performed or its will in relation to them be ascertained. If charged with the duty of deliberating upon the call of Conventions, it would act under disadvantages precisely the same as would attend the call of such bodies spontaneously by the entire people, or by a majority of the adult male citizens. There could be no certitude as to results. To produce that, there must be legal provisions, prescribing time and mode of passing upon the question of calling such Conventions. With such a guide, however, the electors would not act independently, in the sense intended, but in subordination to the legislature.

§ 119. (*b*). Should the power of calling Conventions be left to the judicial department? It is very doubtful whether the judiciary are adapted to perform this function. However extensive the State may be, that department is never, in point of numbers, large, and it is commonly less numerous relatively in large than in small communities. It is intended, moreover, for a definite and limited function — that of expounding and applying the laws. Whenever the judiciary confines itself to its proper sphere of action, which is to determine what the law is, it is, by that circumstance, unfitted to pronounce what, in a complicated maze of facts constituting, at any time, the actual situation, the law ought to be. It is therefore observable that great judges, like Mansfield, often fail as legislators. By training and habits of mind they are retrospective, and distinguish themselves more often by obstinate conservatism than by those broad practical views, "looking before and after," which constitute statesmanship. Such idiosyncracies disqualify those who possess them for the leadership in reformatory movements, and often blind them to their necessity. Being, moreover, a body small in numbers, and, for that reason, not likely adequately to represent the prevalent wishes or opinions of the people, the judicial body ought not to wield the power of calling or refusing to call Conventions by which propositions of reform are to be digested.

§ 120. (*c*). Somewhat similar objections exist to the executive as a depositary of the power in question. That department consists of a single individual, noted, often, rather for political tact than for wisdom or statesmanship. But, if it were conceded that our governors were always what, happily, they very generally are, wise men and statesmen, and if they could be presumed fairly to represent the nation in reference to questions of reform, grave objection would still exist against lodging the power I am considering in their hands. In our system of popular government, it is the executive in whom has been discovered the greatest centrifugal tendency, and who is, therefore, most likely to break through the restraints of law. If our system ever perish, it will probably do so, not from legislative or judicial, but from executive, usurpation. And though this remark seems applicable rather to the Federal executive than to those of the States, it is pertinent, also, to the latter. Within the sphere of the States, executive usurpation is quite as likely to arise on the part of their governors as in the wider sphere of the nation on the part of the President. Which of the two it is from whom most danger is to be apprehended, need not now be determined. Until the late war, the executive authority in the States seemed most to threaten our integrity. Perhaps, now, the danger may be reversed. But this is clear: a power from which usurpation and overthrow may be apprehended, is not the power to be invested with the high sovereign function of summoning and commissioning the body by whom constitutional changes are to be initiated or made.

§ 121. (*d*). The alternative, therefore, as our governments are constituted, is, that the function of calling Conventions shall be committed to the legislature, under such restrictions as the sovereign body shall prescribe, or as shall accord with the maxims of political prudence.

The legislature is the fittest body to act upon the question of calling a Convention, because, of all questions, that is most dependent, for a proper decision, on a wise balancing of expediencies. If the question of making or not making constitutional changes were one of abstract principles, the opinion of a single publicist might outweigh that of the nation. But such is not the case; it is a mixed question of principles and of facts, and the task of those who frame Constitutions is, to cause the two, however repugnant they may be, as far as possible to harmonize in the system established. To accomplish this, the principles underlying all government, and particularly that to be reformed, as well as the circumstances, interests, prepossessions, and aversions of the people, are to be weighed and allowed for. A government built up on any other plan would be a machine constructed on the hypothesis that there were no such forces as inertia and gravity, and no such drawback as friction. In this respect, the legislature is, of all public bodies, that which is best adapted to this particular work. It is its prime function to determine the expedient. Besides, of all representative bodies, excepting only the electors, it is, under all forms of government, the most numerous. In the United States it is more so than elsewhere. The United Kingdom of Great Britain and Ireland, with a population of about thirty millions, is represented in Parliament by about eleven hundred members, including both Lords and Commons. The United States, with a population of thirty-four millions, has, in the National and State governments, whose combined jurisdictions correspond to that of the Parliament in England, five thousand two hundred and fifty representatives. In this number I do not reckon the city, town, and county boards for local self-government, which, in the two countries, may be considered as offsetting each other. These representatives are, moreover, subject to frequent elections. No change of opinion can be permanent or widespread, without soon making itself felt and respected in the legislative body. Practically, the interests of our commonwealths, therefore, are nearly as safe in the hands of our legislatures as in those of the electors, whom we ordinarily designate by the term people; the difference being only that a less numerous body is proportionately more accessible to corrupting influences.

§ 122. 2. The question next in order is, in what manner shall a legislature call a Convention? The general answer is, by some legislative act. As the objects of intrusting the call to that body are, first, to insure the assembling of a Convention whenever, within constitutional or reasonable limits, public opinion should have settled upon its necessity, and, secondly, to throw around the body, coming comet-like into the system, all the legal restraints of which it is susceptible, some act of legislation would be requisite to accomplish either object. A simple resolution or vote, would commonly give expression to the general desire, but were that all, there would be danger that party spirit might avail itself of majorities to call Conventions for partisan purposes. This danger being far from unreal, doubtless the wiser course would be for the legislature so to act as to forestall it. A check ought to be found by which the probability of its occurrence would be reduced to a *minimum*. An expedient has been adopted in many States, as we shall see more fully in a subsequent chapter, by which this is effected. It has been provided, in their Constitutions that, whenever, in the opinion of the legislature, a Convention is desirable to revise the fundamental law, that body shall so declare, by vote or resolution; that thereupon, after a prescribed notice by publication, the sense of the people shall be taken on the question of calling a Convention; and that the legislature shall thereupon call one, or not, according to the result of the popular vote. This mode was much commended, in 1820, by the eminent persons then composing the

New York Council of Revision,[1] by whom it was declared to be most consonant to the principles of our government and to the practice in other States, and they accordingly vetoed a bill for an act to call a Convention to assemble in the following year, on the ground that it did not propose to submit the question to the people. There can be no doubt, that this decision was a sound one, on constitutional principles. The intervention of the legislature is necessary to give a legal starting-point to a Convention, and to hedge it about by such restraints as shall ensure obedience to the law; but as a Convention ought to be called only when demanded by the public necessities, and then to be as nearly as possible the act of the sovereign body itself, it would seem proper to leave the matter to the decision of the electoral body, which stands nearest to the sovereign, and best represents its opinion. Such seems to be the prevailing sentiment in most of the States which have revised their Constitutions since the date of the decision referred to.

§ 123. There may, then, be two cases: first, where the legislature itself passes upon the question of calling a Convention, without the intervention of the electoral body; and, secondly, where the legislature first recommends a call, then refers the question to a vote of the electors, and, finally, on an affirmative vote by the latter, issues the call.

In the first case, the act of the legislature calling the Convention is an act of legislation, strictly so called. It prescribes a rule of action for the electors, fixing the time, place, and manner of the election to be held by them, and commonly provides penalties for misconduct either in the officers conducting the election or making the returns thereof, or in the electors voting thereat. Such a rule of action is a law.[2] In the second case, so much of the original act of the legislature as merely recommends a Convention, cannot be said to be a law. It is, rather, an expression of opinion, intended to preface a reference of the question to the people, by whom it is to be decided. The subsequent act, or other sections of the same act, however, by which a legislature refers the question to the people, must be conceded to be a law, since it has always the force as well as the form

[1] Kent and Spencer, Justices, and Governor Clinton. For the whole opinion of the Council, see Appendix, F., *post*.

[2] 1 Blackstone's *Commentaries*, 44.

of a law, being in all particulars similar to that by which it finally calls the Convention, if ordered by the people.[1]

§ 124. Before closing the discussion of the principles regulating the legitimate call of Constitutional Conventions, one remark is necessary to guard against misconstruction. A Constitution, or an amendment to a Constitution, originating in a Convention justly stigmatized as illegitimate, may, notwithstanding its origin, become valid as a fundamental law. This may happen in two ways: namely, first, by its adoption by the electoral body, according to the forms of existing laws; or, secondly, by the mere acquiescence of the sovereign society. Such a ratification of the supposed Constitution or amendment would not, however, legitimate the body from whom the Constitution or amendment proceeded. That no power human or divine could do, because, by the hypothesis, such body was in its origin illegitimate, that is, as shown in previous sections, convened either against law or without law, which in a government of laws, is one and the same thing. The ratification by the acquiescence of the sovereign, would be a direct exercise of sovereign power, illegal doubtless, but yet standing out prominently as a fact, and as such finding in the original overwhelming power of the sovereign a practical justification, which it would be folly to gainsay.[2]

§ 125. Let us now see to what extent the practice, under the political system of the United States, has conformed to the theoretical principles thus developed.

The Constitutional Conventions thus far held — by those terms designating, for the purposes of this chapter, all such bodies, legitimate and illegitimate, as have framed Constitutions or parts of Constitutions, either for the United States or for States, members of the Union — may be divided, primarily, with reference partly to convenience and partly to their most general characteristics, into two great classes:[3]

(*a*). The first class comprises such Conventions as were held during the *Revolutionary period*, extending from 1775 down to the establishment of the Federal Constitution in 1789.

(*b*). The second class comprises the Conventions of the *post-*

[1] For a more full discussion of the distinctions here indicated, which are not without important practical bearings, see ch. viii., *post*.

[2] See § 23, *ante*.

[3] For a complete list of these bodies, with the dates of their assembling and adjournment, so far as can be ascertained, see Appendix, B., *post*.

Revolutionary period — that is, such as have been held since the 4th of March, 1789.

These two classes will now be considered at length, and in their order.

§ 126. (*a*). To understand, and therefore properly to characterize, the Conventions embraced in the first class, it will be necessary to look into the history of the times in which they were convened, and to elucidate the general causes and the particular acts by which their legal character was determined.

When the colonies entered upon that course of opposition to the crown which ripened into the Revolution, it was neither their intention nor their desire to effect a separation from Great Britain. To bring them to favor such a measure, there were necessary the thirteen following years of agitation, crowded with distress and humiliation on the part of the colonists, and with contemptuous denials of redress and contumelious reproaches on that of the imperial authorities. As the contest thickened, however, and blood began to flow, the colonial establishments one by one succumbed or were suppressed, the royal governors fleeing from their enraged subjects, or being arrested by them and thrown into prison. To maintain order and tranquillity, while the contest with the mother country should continue, it became necessary, therefore, to establish new political organizations in the several colonies. But, because the necessity for them was thought to be temporary, the arrangement at first made was merely provisional. The organizations provided were of the simplest character, consisting of *Provincial Conventions* or *Congresses*, modelled on the same plan as the general Congress at Philadelphia, comprising a single chamber, in which was vested all the powers of government. These bodies, found in all the colonies, save Connecticut and Rhode Island, whose Assemblies, fairly chosen by the people, it was not found necessary to supersede, were made up of deputies elected by the constituencies established under the crown, or appointed by meetings of the principal citizens or by the municipal authorities of the chief towns and cities. All legislative authority was exercised by those bodies directly. Their executive functions were intrusted to Committees of Correspondence, of Public Safety, and the like, appointed by themselves, and during the sittings of the Conventions or Congresses, were discharged under their own supervision.

In the *interims* between their sessions, however, the powers of those committees were substantially absolute.

§ 127. Under organizations thus loose and unrestricted, government was carried on in the colonies for many months, and that without protest or discontent, so long as the general expectation of a return to allegiance, following upon a redress of grievances, continued to exist. As time advanced, however, and it became evident, on the one hand, that the mother country would not purchase the submission of her revolted subjects by compromise or even by conciliation, and, on the other, that the work of subduing them, if possible at all, could be accomplished only by a long and bloody contest, there arose a general desire for the establishment of more regular governments than those by Congresses and committees.[1] Thus, in May, 1775, the Provincial Convention of Massachusetts, charged with the government of the colony, applied to the Congress at Philadelphia for explicit advice respecting the proper exercise of the powers of government. In reply, after declaring that no obedience was due to the act of Parliament lately passed for altering her charter, that body recommended that the Convention should write letters to the several towns entitled to representation in the Assembly, requesting them to choose representatives to form an Assembly, and to instruct the latter, when convened, to elect counsellors; adding their wish, that the bodies thus formed should exercise the powers of government until a governor of the king's appointment would consent to govern the colony

[1] This is apparent from the preamble to the resolutions of the New York Congress on the subject of forming for that State its first Constitution. It runs as follows:—

"*Whereas*, the present government of this colony, by Congress and committees, was instituted while the former government, under the Crown of Great Britain, existed in full force; and was established for the sole purpose of opposing the usurpation of the British Parliament, and was intended to expire on a reconciliation with Great Britain, which it was then apprehended would soon take place, but is now considered as remote and uncertain. And *whereas*, many and great inconveniences attend the said mode of government by Congress and committees, as of necessity, in many instances, legislative, judicial, and executive powers have been vested therein, especially since the dissolution of the former government by the abdication of the late governor, and the exclusion of this colony from the protection of the King of Great Britain." . . . .

See New York Constitution of 1777, in the preamble to which these resolutions are embodied.

according to its charter.[1] This answer was made in June, 1775, and the advice given was followed, and the government thus constituted was the only one Massachusetts had until the establishment of her first Constitution in 1780. In October, 1775, the delegates to the Continental Congress from New Hampshire laid before that body instructions, received by them from the New Hampshire Convention, to obtain the advice and direction of Congress in relation to the establishment of civil government in that colony. Similar requests were, about the same time, sent up from the Provincial Conventions of Virginia and South Carolina. At length, on the 3d and 4th of November, 1775, Congress agreed upon a reply to these applications, in which those bodies were advised "to call a full and free representation of the people, in order to form such a form of government as, in their judgment, would best promote the happiness of the people, and most effectually secure peace and good order in their provinces during the continuance of the dispute with Great Britain."[2]

§ 128. These important recommendations were extorted from Congress by the importunity of colonies whose situation was critical, that body being reluctant to inaugurate a general reconstruction of government upon a permanent basis, so long as there was a possibility of an accommodation with Great Britain. Accordingly, as we see, the most that could be wrung from it was a recommendation to establish temporary governments, without any specification as to the form they should assume, or the distribution of their powers. But in this, Congress lingered far behind some of its leading members. Ever since the previous May, John Adams had exerted all his eloquence to induce Congress to lead off in the work of founding permanent organizations in the States independent of Great Britain. In his own language, he urged "the necessity of realizing the theories of the wisest writers, and of inviting the people to erect the whole building with their own hands, upon the broadest foundation." He declared "that this could be done only by Conventions of representatives, chosen by the people in the several colonies, in the most exact proportions . . . . and that Congress ought now to recommend to the people of every colony to call

[1] Curtis' *Hist. Const. U. S.*, Vol. I. pp. 36, 37.

[2] *Jour. Cont. Cong.*, Vol. I. p. 219.

such Conventions immediately, and set up governments of their own authority." [1]

At length, one after another of the Provincial Conventions signifying the readiness of the people to support a declaration of independence of Great Britain, and it becoming apparent to the least far-sighted that such a measure could not long be delayed, as a preparation for it, or rather as the first and not the least important step in its consummation, definite action was taken on the subject of permanent governments in the States. On the 10th of May, 1776, Congress adopted the decisive resolution, and on the 15th prefixed to it the preamble, which follow:—

"*Whereas*, his Britannic Majesty, in conjunction with the Lords and Commons of Great Britain, has, by a late act of Parliament, excluded the inhabitants of these united colonies from the protection of his crown; and, *whereas*, no answer whatever to the humble petitions of the colonies for redress of grievances and reconciliation with Great Britain has been or is likely to be given; but the whole force of that kingdom, aided by foreign mercenaries, is to be exercised for the destruction of the good people of these colonies; and, *whereas*, it appears absolutely irreconcilable to reason and good conscience, for the people of these colonies now to take the oaths and affirmations necessary for the support of any government under the crown of Great Britain, and it is necessary that the exercise of every kind of authority under the said crown should be totally suppressed, and all the powers of government exerted, under the authority of the people of the colonies, for the preservation of internal peace, virtue, and good order, as well as for the defence of their lives, liberties, and properties, against the hostile invasions and cruel depredations of their enemies, therefore,—

"*Resolved*, That it be recommended to the several Assemblies and Conventions of the united colonies, where no government, sufficient to the exigencies of their affairs, hath been hitherto established, to adopt such government as shall, in the opinion of the representatives of the people, best conduce to the happiness and safety of their constituents in particular, and America in general." [2]

§ 129. This resolution was the turning-point in the Revolu-

[1] *Works of J. Adams*, Vol. III. pp. 13–16.

[2] *Journal of Continental Congress*, Vol. II. pp. 158, 166.

tion, since it foreshadowed and necessitated that of July 4th, 1776, declaring the independence of the colonies. So well was this understood, that, in the debate upon it those delegates who opposed its passage did so on the ground that it was the first step, to which, if taken, independence must succeed. Mr. Duane stigmatized the resolution, to Mr. Adams, as "a machine for the fabrication of independence;" to which the latter, characterizing it with still greater accuracy, truthfully replied, that "it was independence itself."[1]

The intention of Congress in passing this resolution probably was, to recommend that the work of erecting governments in the several colonies should be undertaken by the *legislative authorities* thereof; that is, by the Assemblies, in such colonies as possessed them, and by the Conventions or Congresses in such as had no Assemblies. If this be so, the measure came far short of the wise recommendations of Mr. Adams, as well as of the requirements of principle. What should have been done was, to propose the calling of Conventions for the specific and only purpose of framing Constitutions for the colonies, — the calls for them to issue from the legislative departments of the existing establishments, whatever those establishments might be. It is true, on examining the language of the resolution another construction suggests itself as the one possibly intended by Congress, namely, one which should require the calling in each State, of a body of representatives of the people, to frame and propose a Constitution, to be afterwards submitted to and adopted by the Assembly or Convention calling it. The phraseology is: "That it be recommended *to the several Assemblies and Conventions* of the united colonies . . . to adopt such government as shall, *in the opinion of the representatives of the people, best conduce*," &c. Had "the representatives of the people," intended by Congress, been those constituting "the several Assemblies and Conventions," it might seem more natural, after referring to the latter, to use the terms, "to adopt such government as shall in *their* opinion best conduce," &c. But such a construction is, I think, strained. It certainly, as will be found hereafter, was not the one adopted in the contemporary expositions made of the resolution in the several States. Assuming that the true construction devolved

[1] *Works of J. Adams*, Vol. III. p. 46.

upon the "Assemblies and Conventions" the whole duty of framing and putting in operation Constitutions for their respective colonies, the resolution was less conformable to principle than that of the November preceding, containing advice to the conventions of New Hampshire and South Carolina. The latter recommended to those bodies "to call a full and free representation of the people, in order to form such a government as in their judgment would best promote," &c. It is fair to remark, however, that the science of Constitution-making was then in its infancy. Our fathers had not yet, from actual administration, learned the dangers that attend fundamental legislation, nor discovered the safeguards against them which experience alone can reveal. Even what seem now to be steps taken with a view to conformity to principle, and, therefore, to be strictly regular, were not unfrequently the results of chance or of considerations of temporary convenience, and so, deserving of little weight as indicating the degree of knowledge existing on the subject among the statesmen of the day.

§ 130. Upon these recommendations, special or general, the several colonies embraced in the first class acted, in framing their earliest Constitutions.

Before proceeding to describe the separate action of each colony, with a view to determine whether or not, and how far, that action was conformable to principles or otherwise, it will be useful to state as concisely as may be, first, the conditions of the problem our fathers were required to solve in establishing permanent republican institutions in place of the make-shifts which sprung up with the Revolution; and, secondly, the elements presented by the actual historical situation, for its solution.

1. The conditions of the problem were simple. The political society, known, since the Declaration of Independence, as "the United States of America," was called upon to erect for itself an independent government, suitable to its needs. This important work must be done, so far as possible, regularly and peacefully, and, therefore, with the approval and through the ministry of the political organizations, or fragments of political organizations, then existing, however imperfect they might be, and whatever might have been their origin. Of these several organizations, wherever there was a subdivision into legislative, executive, and judicial departments, use must be made, to initiate the work,

of the legislative department, as by its character and functions alone fitted to undertake it safely or successfully. Finally, no action of any department of the existing organization was, unless absolutely necessary, to be taken as definitive, but the people, or electoral body, in which the powers of sovereignty were practically lodged, must be appealed to to pronounce the *fiat* by which the proposition of the legislature or Convention was to be ripened into law. Such were the conditions of the problem.

2. The elements given for its solution were hardly more complex. There were the indeterminate provisional organizations by which whatever of government the several colonies possessed was conducted, being in most of them the irregular and revolutionary Conventions or Congresses, and in a few the still subsisting Assemblies, established under the crown, to which reference has been made. There was then the equally indeterminate government of the Union, whose powers were lodged in the single chamber known as the Continental Congress; a body in every respect conforming to our definition of a Revolutionary Convention. To these organizations, local and general, must be added those which, during the revolutionary period, were in a few cases constructed to succeed them. And, lastly, there was the people of the United States, considered, first, as the political unit, by which independence was declared, and, secondly, as the subordinate groups constituting the States either as peoples or as political organizations. Amongst these three orders of political entities, in a manner explained in the second chapter, was distributed the exercise of sovereign powers, on the breaking out of the Revolution, and, therefore, by them, in their several spheres and in a mode conformable to their respective powers in the general system, was the work in question to be effected.

§ 131. The first colony to act upon the recommendations of Congress was New Hampshire. In less than a fortnight after the passage by Congress of the resolutions of November 3d, 1775, the Provincial Convention of that colony took into consideration the mode in which "a full and free representation" for the purpose indicated by Congress should be constituted.[1] It was finally determined that it should take the form of a new Convention, to be summoned by the Provincial Convention, and that for the purpose of apportioning fairly the delegates to be

[1] Belknap, *Hist. N. H.*, Vol. II. p. 305.

chosen to it, a census of the inhabitants should be taken. It was moreover recommended, that the representatives chosen "should be empowered by their constituents to assume government, as recommended by the general Congress, and to continue for one whole year from the time of such assumption."[1] Having recommended this plan, and "sent copies of it to the several towns, the Convention dissolved."[2] In pursuance of the recommendations accompanying the plan, a new Convention was chosen, and assembled on the 21st of December following, by which the first Constitution of New Hampshire was framed, and her first formal government, independent of the crown, established.[3] According to Dr. Belknap, the historian of the State, "as soon as the new Convention came together, they drew up a temporary form of government; and, agreeably to the trust reposed in them by their constituents, having assumed the name and authority of a House of Representatives, they proceeded to choose twelve persons, to be a distinct branch of the legislature, by the name of a Council."[4] This form of government was practically limited to a single year by an ordinance providing "that the present Assembly should subsist one year, and if the dispute with Great Britain should continue longer, and the General Congress should give no directions to the contrary, that precepts should be issued annually" for the return of "new Counsellors and Representatives." By the Convention thus called and organized were assumed all the powers of government. In a word, it was a Revolutionary Convention. As distinguished from the body itself, there was no judiciary, and no executive. The only feature in which it resembled a regularly constituted government, was in its division into two chambers. But even this resemblance vanishes, when it is considered that it was a

[1] Belknap, *Hist. N. H.*, Vol. II. p. 305.

[2] Nov. 16, 1775; Id. p. 305.

[3] Jan. 5, 1776.

[4] Belknap, *Hist. N. H.*, Vol. II. pp. 305, 306. The idea of thus transforming the Convention into a legislative assembly with two chambers, was doubtless borrowed from the Convention called by King William in 1689, which, illegally called and constituted, changed itself into a parliament, since known as the Convention Parliament. Though unquestionably a revolutionary body, this parliament became the basis on which the English government, as then reconstructed, rested and still rests. See remarks of Mr. Webster on this subject, *Works*, Vol. VI. pp. 225, 226.

voluntary division, the Council being its own creation, and, of course, as little independent of the main body as any one of its committees. All the powers of the State were concentrated in that single body, which was revolutionary not only in its proceedings, but in its origin, as called by one revolutionary Convention at the instance of another, and as exercising, when assembled, the functions of a government, provisionally, in place of that by which it was convened.

§ 132. The people of New Hampshire, however, becoming dissatisfied with the temporary Constitution of 1776, an attempt was made three years later to frame a new one. A Convention of delegates, chosen for that purpose, under the direction of the existing government, drew up and presented to the people a form of a Constitution, but so deficient in its principles and so inadequate in its provisions, that, being proposed to the people in their town-meetings, it was rejected.[1] On the failure to adopt this, a new Convention was elected for the same purpose, and commenced its sessions in 1781. The year before, Massachusetts had adopted a Constitution, in the main from a draft prepared by John Adams, which was supposed to be an improvement on all that had been framed in America. Having the advantage of this, the New Hampshire Convention digested a plan and submitted it to the people in their town-meetings, with a request that they should state their objections distinctly to any particular part, and return them to the Convention at a fixed time. The objections were so many and various, that it became necessary to alter the form and send it out a second time.[2] The second plan was generally approved by the people, and thus, finally, after nine sessions of the Convention, running through more than two years, a Constitution was adopted and put in operation, — the instrument being completed October 31, 1783, and established with religious solemnities June 2, 1784.

Of these two last Conventions, it is to be noted, that, unlike the first, they were, in the strict sense of the term, Constitutional Conventions. They were initiated by the existing government of the State, which, whatever may be thought of its legitimacy or regularity, was a *de facto* government, by revolution placed in power, and made the basis on which the political structure of the State has ever since rested; the people were fairly repre-

[1] Belknap, *Hist. N. H.*, Vol. II. p. 333. [2] Id. pp. 335, 336

sented in them; they confined themselves strictly to their constitutional duty, that of proposing a code of organic laws, abstaining from all usurpation of governmental powers; and, finally, they severally submitted their projected Constitutions to a vote of the electors of the State, in their town meetings — an act which, as we shall see, constitutes the best guaranty of the sovereign right of the people over the form of their government that has ever been devised.[1]

§ 133. The next colony to act on the recommendations of Congress was South Carolina. Like the other colonies whose legislatures had been dissolved, South Carolina had governed herself, since the rupture with Great Britain, by Provincial Conventions or Congresses, constituting provisional governments, founded upon the right of revolution. The first of these had been summoned November 9, 1774, by what was styled "the general committee" of the colony.[2] This body was organized similarly to those in the other colonies, and, after the flight of the royal governor in September, 1775, centred in itself, or in its committees, all the powers of government not vested, by the nature of the case, in the Continental Congress. Toward the close of the latter year, the necessity for a more stable, as well as a more responsible government, made itself felt, and the Convention applying to Congress, as we have seen, for advice as to the formation of such a government, had been recommended, in the same terms as New Hampshire, "to call a full and free representation of the people, to establish such a form of government as in their judgment will best promote the happiness of the people."[3] Acting upon this advice, and following, though not perfectly, the example of New Hampshire, the South Carolina Congress, in conformity to the course of the Convention of 1689, in England, and to that of their ancestors in 1719, "voted themselves to be the General Assembly of South Carolina," and framed a Constitution, March 26, 1776, to exist "till a reconciliation between the colonies and Great Britain should take place." This Constitution was modelled after that of Great

[1] See *post*, ch. VII.

[2] This general committee consisted of ninety-nine members, and was appointed by resolution of a public meeting held at Charleston July 6, 1774. Hild. *Hist. U. S.*, (1st series,) Vol. III. p. 40.

[3] Resolution of the Continental Congress of Nov. 3, 1775, *ante*, § 127.

Britain, and consisted of three branches: the Congress electing thirteen of its most respectable members to be a legislative council; a president and vice-president; a chief-justice and three assistant judges, an attorney-general, secretary, ordinary, and judge of the admiralty.[1] The instrument embodying this plan of government was put in force as the Constitution of South Carolina, and was recognized as such for over two years, when it was superseded by a new one.

§ 134. It is obvious that the mode of proceeding of which the result was the establishment of the first Constitution of South Carolina, was extremely irregular. The people of the State were in no manner consulted in relation to its formation. The body by whom that important business was done, was an extraordinary assembly, "appointed," as the historian Ramsay says, "without the authority of any written law or any definite specification of powers." To the function of a Constitutional, it added those of a Revolutionary, Convention; its character as the latter being in nowise affected by the change in its organization, by which it assumed the form of a regular government. The only element of legitimacy possessed by it was, that the action taken by it was based upon a recommendation of the Continental Congress, in whom was vested for general purposes the exercise of the national sovereignty.

§ 135. A Constitution thus constructed was not likely to be long-lived. A second, but hardly more successful, effort was made in 1778. In this case it was not an unauthorized and revolutionary Convention, but an usurping legislature, which undertook the task. In the autumn of 1776, the elections throughout the State, says the historian Ramsay, "were conducted on the idea that the members chosen, over and above the ordinary powers of legislators, should have the power to frame a new Constitution, suited to the declared independence of the State." "Authorized in this manner," he continues, "the legislature in January, 1777, began the important business of framing a permanent form of government. The generous confidence reposed in the elected by the electors met with a suitable return of fidelity on their part. Instead of increasing their own powers, as legislators, they diminished those of which they were in possession by the temporary Constitution, and extended the privileges

[1] Ramsay, *Hist. S. C.*, Vol. I. p. 263.

of their constituents; nor did they proceed to give a final sanction to their deliberations on the subject of the Constitution till they had submitted them for the space of a year to the consideration of the people at large. From the general approbation of the inhabitants, the new Constitution received all the authority which could have been conferred on the proceedings of a Convention expressly delegated for the express purpose of framing a form of government."[1]

§ 136. It would be easy to demonstrate that the Constitution of 1778, thus framed, was wholly invalid as an act of fundamental legislation. Without stopping to do this, I shall merely cite authority establishing the fact that it was so regarded by leading minds at the time of its formation.

"This temporary Constitution" (that of 1776), says the same historian, Ramsay, in his history of South Carolina, "in a little more than two years gave place to a new one formed on the idea of independence, which in the mean time had been declared. The distinction between a Constitution and an act of the legislature was not at this period so well understood as it has been since. The legislature elected under the Constitution of 1776, with the acquiescence of the people, undertook to form a new Constitution, and to give it activity under the forms and with the name of an "Act of Assembly!" The doubt thus implied was entertained by other eminent South Carolinians. President Rutledge refused his assent to the new Constitution, on the ground, with others, that the legislative authority, being fixed and limited, could not change or destroy itself without subverting the Constitution from which it was derived. He finally, however, so far yielded to the pressure for a change as to resign his office, whereupon his successor, Rawlins Lowndes, signed the Constitution, and it went into operation.[2]

§ 137. As to the character of the body by which the Constitution was framed, on the other hand, there can be no doubt whatever. As a Constitutional Convention, it lacked all the elements needed to give it legitimacy. It was elected and assembled as

[1] Ramsay's *History of the Revolution in South Carolina*, pp. 128, 129.

[2] That the first two South Carolina Constitutions were merely ordinary statutes, repealable by the General Assembly, was distinctly affirmed by the Supreme Court of that State, in the case of Thomas *v.* Chesley Daniel, 2 McCord's R. 354, (359, 360).

a legislature, and as nothing else. Notwithstanding the loose assertion of Dr. Ramsay, that that body had been elected "*on the idea*" that, "over and above the ordinary powers of legislators," it should have power to frame a new Constitution, whatever it did beyond the scope of ordinary legislation must be set down, in the absence of any regular expression to that effect of the public will, as mere usurpation. How general was that *idea?* What mode was taken to ascertain its existence, and, much more, to ascertain the extent to which it was not entertained? Not only did the legislature undertake, without legal warrant, to frame a code of organic laws, but it practically ignored the existence of the people, putting its work into operation without a submission to them that was at all effectual. It thus became guilty of acts of revolution, for which ignorance of "the distinction between a Constitution and an act of legislation" only can be received as an excuse.

§ 138. Next in order after South Carolina, in the work of erecting a government, followed Virginia.[1] This she did, as New Hampshire and South Carolina had done, in pursuance of the resolutions of the Continental Congress of the 3d and 4th of November, 1775, referred to, advising those colonies "to call a full and free representation of the people" for that purpose. The mode adopted by Virginia was similar to that followed in those colonies. The Provincial Convention elected in April, 1776, to continue in office one year, met at Williamsburg on the 6th of May thereafter, and on the 29th of June following framed and established the first Constitution of Virginia.[2] This Convention was elected as a revolutionary assembly, to carry on, as Mr. Jefferson expresses it, "the ordinary business of the gov-

[1] It has been usual to concede to Virginia the honor of having framed the first American Constitution. If by that be meant the first which was complete according to later ideas of what a Constitution should be, the concession is just. The first Constitutions of New Hampshire and South Carolina, which were several months earlier in date than that of Virginia, were very imperfect, while the latter was so skilfully framed that it was not found necessary to change it until 1830, nearly three quarters of a century after its formation. In this statement I leave out of the account altogether the instruments of government drawn up by the early Puritan settlers of Massachusetts and Connecticut. If those instruments are to be called Constitutions, the earliest American Constitution was that framed on board of the Mayflower, before the landing at Plymouth.

[2] *Journal of Virginia Convention*, 1776, pp. 15, 16, 150.

ernment," in default of the House of Burgesses, and to "call forth the powers of the State for the maintenance of the opposition to Great Britain."[1] It was not pretended, if the same authority is to be credited, that, in assuming to frame a Constitution, the Convention had any warrant or authority whatever, except such as enured to it by virtue of its revolutionary character. In so doing, then, it is to be regarded, not as a Constitutional, but as a Revolutionary Convention. It was not empowered to discharge the special and high function of enacting a fundamental code, by any law or by the express desire of the people, but acted on its own authority; and it did not deign to take upon its work the sense of the people whom it pretended to represent.[2]

§ 139. Very similar to that just described was the course of events in New Jersey. Like most of the colonies, at the time the resolution of Congress of May 10, 1776, passed that body, New Jersey was under the government of a Provincial Congress and committees. The Congress being in session directly after the resolution was published, prompt action was taken to carry out its recommendations. A resolution was adopted for the election of a new Congress, to be held on the 4th Monday of May, 1776. Representatives were accordingly chosen at that time in all the counties, and the delegates elected, sixty-five in number, being five from each county, convened at Burlington, on the 10th of June, 1776.[3] It does not appear, that this Congress or Convention (for, elected by the former name, it formally changed its title from "Congress" to "Convention" in the course of the session at which the Constitution was framed) was elected for the sole purpose of framing a Constitution, but rather as the successor of that Congress by whose resolution it had been constituted. Nevertheless, it is probable, that the purpose of electing new delegates was understood by the people to be to take action upon the two momentous questions of independence and of the formation of a government suitable to the altered condi-

[1] Jefferson, *Notes on Virginia*, *Works*, Vol. VIII. p. 363.

[2] Ibid. As to the invalidity of the first Virginia Constitution, as an act of organic legislation, and therefore as to its repealability by the General Assembly in consequence of the irregular character of the Convention of 1776, see Jefferson's *Notes on Virginia*, *Works*, Vol. VIII. pp. 363–367. For an opposite view, see Tucker's *Black. Com.*, Vol. I. Pt. 1, Appendix, pp. 85, 86, and Kamper *v.* Hawkins, 1 Virg. Crim. Cases, 20.

[3] Mulford, *Hist. N. J.*, p. 415.

tion of affairs. However that may be, when the Congress met at Burlington, petitions were received from the inhabitants in different parts of the province, praying that a new form of government might be established.[1] On the 21st of June, therefore, a resolution was adopted by a vote of 54 to 3, "that a government be formed for regulating the internal police of this colony, pursuant to the recommendation of the Continental Congress of the 15th of May last."[2] On the 24th, a committee of ten persons was appointed to draft a Constitution, by whom a report was made on the 26th of the same month, and the draft reported, after discussion in the committee of the whole, was, on the 2d of July, adopted as the Constitution of the State, and put in operation.

§ 140. It is not surprising that doubts have existed as to the precise character of the first New Jersey Convention. It was not the Assembly of the colony, established under the crown, but a Provincial Congress, convened to direct the Revolution, which called the body together. It was, therefore, probably, a revolutionary assembly. This becomes certain, when it is seen that the body "had not been chosen for the particular purpose of forming a Constitution," but that it had "entered upon it in pursuance of the recommendation of the General Congress, and in compliance with petitions from the people, together with the sense of the body itself, as to the necessity of the measure,"[3] this function being added, without legal warrant, to the mass of powers claimed and exercised by it in virtue of its revolutionary character. As a Constitutional Convention, then, the body was irregular and illegitimate. It was a provisional revolutionary government, resting on force, and invested with such powers as it chose to assume.[4] Though mention is made of petitions of the people, they were obviously of no validity as forming a basis for fundamental legislation. What the Convention did,

[1] Mulford, *Hist. N. J.*, pp. 415–418; *Journal of N. J. Conv.*, 1776, pp. 9, 14, 23.

[2] Mulford, *Hist. N. J.*, pp. 415–418; *Journal of N. J. Conv.*, 1776, p. 23.

[3] Mulford, *Hist. N. J*, p. 415, n. (24).

[4] The journal of this Convention, like those of most of the Conventions of the Revolutionary period, was largely made up of legislative and executive details, covering the whole ground of a government for the colony in civil as well as in military affairs. It *administered* — a function, as we have seen in the first chapter, never properly belonging to a Constitutional Convention. See Journal, *passim*.

was done by virtue of its own arbitrary discretion, and no reference was made, in any stage of the proceedings, to the people, to ascertain their sense, much less to derive from their ratifying voice the *fiat* which should give to the Constitution the form as well as the effect of law. The first New Jersey Convention was legitimate as a Constitutional Convention only as any self-elected junto would be so, which had the physical power to give to its ordinances the force of law.

§ 141. Of the proceedings of the Convention which framed the first Constitution of Delaware, few traces have been preserved. That that body itself, however, was, for the time when it was held, exceptionally regular, may be inferred from the few records relating to its origin which remain.

In July, 1776, the Delaware House of Assembly passed the following preamble and resolutions, to wit: —

"The House, taking into consideration the resolution of Congress of the 15th of May last for suppressing all authority derived from the Crown of Great Britain, and for establishing a government upon the authority of the people, and the resolution of the House of the 15th of June last, in consequence of the said resolution of Congress, directing all persons holding offices, civil or military, to execute the same in the name of this government until a new one should be formed; and also the declaration of the United States of America, absolving from all allegiance to the British Crown, and dissolving all political connection between themselves and Great Britain, lately published and adopted by this government, as one of those States, are of opinion that some speedy measures should be taken to form a regular mode of civil polity, and this House, not thinking themselves authorized by their constituents to execute this important work —

"Do *resolve* —

"That it be recommended to the good people of the several counties in this government to choose a suitable number of deputies, to meet in Convention, there to organize and declare the future form of government for this State.

"*Resolved*, also —

"That it is the opinion of this House, that the said Convention should consist of thirty persons, that is to say, ten for the County of New Castle, ten for the County of Kent, and ten for the County of Sussex; and that the freemen of the counties respectively do meet on Monday, the 19th day of August next, at the usual places of election for the county, and then and there proceed to elect the number of deputies aforesaid, according to the direction of the several laws of this government for regulating elections of the members of Assembly, except as to the choice of inspectors, which shall be made on the morning of the day of election by the electors, inhabitants of the respective Hundreds in each county. . . . .

" *Resolved*, also —

" That it is the opinion of this House that the deputies, when chosen as aforesaid, shall meet in Convention in the town of New Castle, on Tuesday, the twenty-seventh day of the same month, (August,) and immediately proceed to form a government on the authority of the people of this State, in such sort as may be best adapted for their preservation and happiness." [1]

§ 142. In pursuance of the recommendations contained in these resolutions, a Convention was elected on the 19th of August, 1776, which met at the town of New Castle on Tuesday, the 27th of August, and, after a session of twenty-eight days, adopted the first Constitution of Delaware.

If, to the particulars given in the foregoing resolutions, there be added the caption to the new Constitution, the perfect regularity and legitimacy of the Convention thus called, from the point of view of the new State of Delaware, will become apparent. That caption is as follows: " The Constitution or system of government agreed to and resolved upon by the representatives in full Convention, of the Delaware State, formerly styled," &c., " *the said representatives being chosen by the freemen of the said State, for that express purpose.*"

Here was a Convention called by the legislative Assembly of the existing government, by an Act making careful provisions for a fair election, and, as may be inferred, elected for the express and only purpose of framing a Constitution. Confining itself

[1] *Journal of Del. Conv. of* 1776. For the foregoing extract I am indebted to William T. Read, Esq., of New Castle, Del., who has in his possession a manuscript copy of the journal, the only one known to be in existence. It was procured from Mr. Read through the kindness of the Hon. Willard Hall, of Wilmington, Del., to whom I am indebted for valuable information respecting the various Conventions of that State.

probably to this limited function, it was strictly a Constitutional Convention.

§ 143. In Pennsylvania, the last Assembly elected under the proprietary government continued to meet down almost to the Declaration of Independence, but often without a quorum. At length, in July, 1776, it was superseded by a Provincial Convention, which, based on revolutionary principles, took the government into its own hands. The mode of calling that body was as follows: On the 18th of June, 1776, a number of gentlemen met at Carpenter's Hall, in Philadelphia, being deputed by the committees of several of the counties of the province, to join in conference, in pursuance of a circular letter from the committee of Philadelphia, inclosing the resolution of the Continental Congress of May 10th, 1776.[1] After a vote approving of that resolution, it was unanimously resolved by the conference, that it was necessary that a Provincial Convention should be called by them, "for the express purpose of forming a new government for this province, on the authority of the people only."[2] The conference then proceeded to fix the qualifications of electors of deputies to the Convention, giving a vote to all "associators" in the province, of the age of twenty-one years, who had lived one year in the province, and paid or been assessed toward any provincial or county tax, and also to every person qualified by the laws of the province to vote for representatives in Assembly, upon their taking a prescribed oath. A committee, appointed to apportion the representation in the Convention amongst the several districts of the province, recommended, and the conference voted, that eight representatives should be sent by the City of Philadelphia, and eight by each county in the province. The electors were then required to meet on the 8th of July following, to elect the members of the Convention, and the latter, to meet on the 15th of the same month. On the day appointed the Convention met at Philadelphia, and continued in session until the 28th of September following, when it adopted and put into operation the first Constitution of Pennsylvania.

§ 144. Although the resolution of the conference calling this Convention "for the express purpose of forming a new government," &c., might be construed to limit that body to that par-

[1] *Conventions of Pennsylvania*, p. 35.

[2] Id. p. 38.

ticular business, yet it did not in fact so restrict itself, and it is doubtful if the conference intended so to restrict it, for, by subsequent resolution, passed on the 23d of June, the latter recommended to the Convention to choose delegates to the Continental Congress, and also a Council of Safety to exercise the whole executive powers of government, so far as related to the military defense of the province, and to make such allowance for their services as should be reasonable. Thus the Convention received from the body calling it, so far, at least, as the latter could give it, authority to exercise both legislative and executive functions, in addition to those enuring to it by virtue of its special commission; and the journal of that body shows, that much of its time was occupied, from day to day, while framing the Constitution, in business of an ordinary legislative or executive character. Of the illegitimacy, therefore, of this Convention, considered as a Constitutional Convention, there is no doubt. Based upon necessity, in times of revolution, while that body became the foundation of a new order of things, to which must be conceded, especially after it received the acquiescence of the people, a relative legality or legitimacy, yet it was itself, both in its origin and in its essential character, a revolutionary assembly. It was not only that, it was for a revolutionary assembly formed less regularly, that is, with a greater divergence from safe constitutional precedents, than was really necessary. It was called by a self-constituted conference of committees, themselves appointed without legal sanction; and the question of its assembling, or of ratifying the fruit of its labors, was not submitted to a vote of the people, though it is true the delegates of which it was composed were chosen by the electors under the old establishment, but by them together with *others named by the conference.* This latter circumstance, instead of adding to its regularity, was a wider departure from safe precedents than any other that occurred, since the power of election was given to persons by existing laws not authorized to vote at general elections. From all this it is clear, that, however perfectly the body may have reflected the public will, the first Pennsylvania convention was a Revolutionary and not a Constitutional Convention. It was itself, for the term of its existence, the government of Pennsylvania, not a mere auxiliary or adviser to the government.

§ 145. Substantially the same observations may be made respecting the Convention which framed the first Constitution of Maryland. For over two years prior to the assembling of that body, the colony of Maryland had been governed by a provisional organization of revolutionary origin, her Provincial Congress, which, like most of its fellows in the sister colonies, wielded all the powers of government — legislative, executive, and judicial. This body, having early received a copy of the resolution of the Congress of May 10th, 1776, after much reluctance and hesitancy, on the 3d of July, 1776, resolved, "That a new Convention be elected for the express purpose of forming a new government, by the authority of the people only, and enacting and ordering all things for the preservation, safety, and general weal of this colony." It then proceeded to apportion the representation in the Convention, determine the qualifications of voters, and the mode of conducting the elections, and to appoint judges thereof. The city of Annapolis, the town of Baltimore, and the several districts of the county of Frederick, were to have two representatives each, and the remaining counties four each. Every freeman above twenty-one years of age, possessed of the freehold or other property qualification specified in the resolutions, was entitled to vote at the election of representatives in the Convention. The members elected were to meet in Convention on Monday, the 12th of August, 1776, and were to continue in session not beyond the first day of December, 1776.[1] The Convention met in accordance with these resolutions, framed and adopted a Constitution November 8th, 1776, and, on the 11th of the same month, after a session of eighty-nine days, adjourned.

As in the case of the Pennsylvania Convention, a very large proportion of all the time occupied in the session of that of Maryland, was taken up in ordinary legislative and executive business, or, in the language of the resolutions under which it assembled, in "enacting and ordering all things for the preservation, safety, and general weal" of the colony. It was, in a word, the only government that colony had during the *interim* between the adjournment of the old Provincial Convention and the establishment of the State government under the first Constitution. It was, therefore, not a Constitutional Convention, but

[1] *Conventions of Md.*, pp. 184–189.

a provisional government, or Revolutionary Convention. Or, if the circumstance that the body assumed no powers not specifically granted by the Provincial Congress, be urged as indicating that it was not a revolutionary body, it was at least an abnormal assembly wielding the combined powers of government, and, besides, exercising the incompatible power of remolding the political society from which all its ordinary powers were derived. Considering its origin, however, and the fact that the structure founded by it was established by the sole authority of the Convention itself, that body was clearly, as a Constitutional Convention, irregular and revolutionary.

§ 146. In North Carolina an early but unsuccessful effort was made to establish a civil government independent of the crown. At its session at Halifax, in April, 1776, the Provincial Convention of North Carolina appointed a committee of its ablest men to prepare a draft of a Constitution. This committee being unable to agree upon any form, after much debate and frequent postponements, the question was adjourned, and a committee appointed to propose a temporary form of government until the next session. The system adopted was that of a Council of Safety, which body recommended to the people to elect, on the 15th of October, delegates to a Congress, to assemble at Halifax on the 12th of November following, "which was not only to make laws but also to frame a Constitution, which was to be the corner-stone of the law."[1] The Convention met at the time and place appointed, and, on the 18th of December, adopted the first Constitution and Bill of Rights of North Carolina.[2] As recommended by the Council of Safety, this Convention did not confine itself to the business of framing a Constitution, but "performed the functions of an ordinary legislature."[3]

If it were conceded, then, that that body was legitimate in its origin, as having been called by the *de facto* government of North Carolina, the Council of Safety, it ceased to be legitimate as a Constitutional Convention the moment it assumed general powers of legislation and government. It then became a Revolutionary Convention, with independent powers, whose extent was limited only by its own discretion. But it was not legiti-

[1] Wheeler's *Hist. N. C.*, p. 84.

[2] Id. p. 86.

[3] *Rev. Code of N. C.*, (1845,) p. 5.

mate even in its origin. It was at once the appointee and the successor of the Council of Safety, a revolutionary tribunal, in whose single hands was massed the whole power of the State, which it passed over to the Convention called by itself.

§ 147. The first independent government of Georgia consisted of a Provincial Congress, organized in January, 1775.

Feeling the need, however, of some broader basis of action, the Provincial Congress itself, on the 15th of April, 1776, adopted a preamble and resolutions as the groundwork of a more stable and formal government, the result of which was the establishment of a system similar to that adopted in New Hampshire and other colonies, under the recommendations of Congress of November 3 and 4, 1775; that is, the Provincial Congress resolved itself into a legislature, and appointed a President, a Council of Safety of thirteen members, and judicial and executive officers,[1] — an evident imitation of the action of the English convention of 1689 in voting itself to be a Parliament. By the terms of the resolutions, however, the system was to be a temporary one, to continue only "for the present, and until the further order of the Continental Congress, or of this or any future Provincial Congress."

Accordingly, when, in July, 1776, the Declaration of Independence was adopted, it was deemed necessary "to take down the old civil and political superstructures and erect new establishments in their places." In the words of the historian of the State, "to meet the exigency arising from this new attitude of the Continental Congress, in declaring the American colonies free and independent, President Bullock issued a proclamation, based on a recommendation of the general Congress, ordering the several parishes and districts within this State to proceed to the election of delegates, between the 1st and 10th days of September next, to form and sit in Convention; and the delegates so elected are directed to convene at Savannah on the first Tuesday in October following, when business of the highest consequence to the government and welfare of the State will be opened for their consideration."[2]

"The deputies," he continues, "met in Convention at the time appointed, and took up the important subject before them.

[1] Stevens' *Hist. of Geo.*, Vol. II. pp. 291, 292.

[2] Id. pp. 296, 297.

Much other business, however, pressed upon them, consequent on putting the State in a proper posture of defence; but, after one or two adjournments, they accomplished their work, and on the 5th of February, 1777, ratified in convention the first Constitution of the State of Georgia."[1]

From this account of the first Georgia Convention, it is evident the body was a Revolutionary Convention. It was called in an irregular manner, by proclamation of the executive head of the temporary establishment, and, when assembled, it entered upon the discharge of the general duties of a government, concerning itself with the measures necessary for "putting the State in a proper posture of defence." In this course of administration it was guided only by its own discretion, having neither law nor Constitution to fetter it. A body thus assembled, and thus charged with discretionary powers, cannot be a Constitutional Convention, strictly so called.

§ 148. The second attempt of Georgia to supply herself with a Constitution was made with greater regularity.

The Federal Convention, having submitted to the States the project of a new Constitution, and the prospect seeming fair that it would be adopted, in order to bring the State government into harmonious action with that instrument, as well as to remedy certain defects experienced in the practical working of the State Constitution, under which the government of Georgia had been working since 1777, it was found necessary to revise the latter, or construct a new one. Accordingly, on the 30th of January, 1788, the legislature resolved, "that they would proceed to name three fit and discreet persons from each county, to be convened at Augusta by the executive, as soon as may be after official information is received that nine States have adopted the Federal Constitution; and a majority of them shall proceed to take under their consideration the alterations and amendments that are necessary to be made in the Constitution of this State, and to arrange, digest, and alter the same in such manner as, in their judgment, will be most consistent with the interest and safety, and best secure the rights and liberties to the citizens thereof."[2]

On the 6th of October, 1788, the official letter of the secre-

[1] Stevens' *Hist. of Geo.*, Vol. II. pp. 297, 298.
[2] Id. p. 388.

tary of Congress, stating that nine States had accepted the Constitution, was laid before the executive council; and, accordingly, Governor Handley called the members nominated and appointed by the legislature to meet at Augusta on the 4th of November, "in order to carry the aforesaid resolutions of the General Assembly into execution."[1]

The Convention met accordingly, and on the 24th of November agreed to and signed a Constitution to be proposed for adoption to another body, created by a resolution of the General Assembly, composed of three persons from each county, chosen by the inhabitants thereof on the first Tuesday in December, and who were to meet at Augusta on the 4th of January, 1789, "vested with full power, and for the sole purpose of adopting and ratifying or rejecting" the Constitution.[2]

This second Convention met in January, and proposed certain alterations of the form laid before them. These, by direction of the General Assembly, were also made known to the people; and Governor Walton was directed to call a third Convention "to adopt the said original plan or form of government, with or without all or any of the alterations contained and expressed in the after-plan of January last."

This Convention met on the 4th of May, 1789, considered the several articles and plans before them, and on the 6th of the same month adopted that portion of them known as the second Constitution of Georgia.[3]

§ 149. Though the series of acts resulting in the establishment of the second Georgia Constitution, on the whole, gives evidence of an anxious desire on the part of the public authorities to found that Constitution on the people, still there were anomalies in the mode of calling the Convention which framed it, that indicate great ignorance or great disregard of sound principles, and tend to throw doubt on the legitimacy of that body. The deputies to form the Convention were, in effect, but a committee of the legislature, since, at the time of calling that body, the latter proceeded "to name three fit and discreet persons from each county" to constitute the Convention. In substance, then, it was the legislature, taking upon itself the work of remodeling the Constitution, from which it derived its exist-

1 Stevens' *Hist. of Geo.*, Vol. II. pp. 388, 389.

2 Id. p. 390.

3 Ibid.

ence and its powers — a blending of functions which is never permissible under our Constitutions, and which has the sanction of no respectable authority. The body was, therefore, not legitimate as a Constitutional Convention.

§ 150. Close in the wake of Georgia in the work of adopting a Constitution, followed New York. The party of the Revolution meeting in New York with much greater opposition than elsewhere, that colony was comparatively tardy in adopting either a provisional government or a Constitution. The legislature, from a variety of causes, refusing, in the spring of 1776, to elect delegates to the second Congress at Philadelphia, a vote was taken throughout the city of New York, on the question of sending representatives to that body, when there appeared 825 votes for, and 163 against it. After this indication of public sentiment, the rural counties coöperating with the city, a Provincial Congress of forty-one delegates met on the 20th of April, 1776, and reëlected the members of the Continental Congress. Other Congresses or Conventions of a similar character succeeded, and took upon themselves the government of the colony. At length, on the 31st of May, 1776, the one then in session, after premising, in terms already referred to, that the government by Congress and committees then prevailing in the colony, had originally been designed to continue only until a reconciliation with Great Britain, of which no hope any longer existed; that "many and great inconveniences" attended "the said mode of government by Congress and committees, as, of necessity, in many instances, legislative, judicial, and executive powers" had been "vested therein, especially since the dissolution of the former government;" that doubts had arisen that Congress were invested with sufficient power and authority to deliberate and determine on so important a subject as the necessity of erecting and constituting a new form of government and internal police, to the exclusion of all foreign jurisdiction, dominion, and control whatever; and, finally, declaring that it belonged of right solely to the people of the colony to determine the said doubts,

"*Resolved*, That it be recommended to the electors in the several counties in this colony, by election in the manner and form prescribed for the election of the present Congress, either to authorize (in addition to the power vested in this Congress)

their present deputies, or others in the stead of their present deputies, or either of them, to take into consideration the necessity and propriety of instituting such new government as, in and by the said resolution of the Continental Congress is described and recommended; and if the majorities of the counties, by their deputies in Provincial Congress, shall be of opinion that such new government ought to be instituted and established, then to institute and establish such a government as they shall deem best calculated to secure the rights, liberties, and happiness of the good people of this colony, and to continue in force until a future peace with Great Britain shall render the same unnecessary." [1] By another resolution, the Congress recommended the mode in which the election should be conducted, and that the Convention so elected should assemble on the second Monday in July, 1776.

§ 151. In pursuance of these resolutions, a Convention [2] was elected, which met at White Plains on the 9th of July, 1776. The first action of this body was upon the Declaration of Independence, a copy of which had been received. It expressed its concurrence in the reasons set forth in the recital of said declaration, and, adopting that instrument, instructed its delegates in Congress to use their best efforts to obtain the objects of said declaration. Soon after the time of its assembling, the condition of affairs in the State became so perilous, on account of the advance of the enemy, and the time of the Convention was so much taken up with the transaction of legislative and executive business, that it made but little progress in framing a Constitution. At length, however, a draft of a Constitution was presented, in the handwriting of Mr. Jay, on the 12th of March, 1777. It was under discussion from that day until the 20th of April, 1777, when it was adopted with but one dissenting voice. After its adoption, the Convention continued in session until the 8th of May, 1777, engaged in business as a Council of Safety, and adopting ordinances necessary to put the new government in operation.

§ 152. The instrument thus framed was at that time generally regarded as the most excellent of all the American Constitutions.

[1] Preamble to the N. Y. Const. of 1777.

[2] When this body first convened, it was denominated a Congress, but it afterwards adopted the title of Convention.

Mr. Jay took a leading part in its formation, having, it is said, left Congress to attend the Convention for that purpose. The proceedings, moreover, which resulted in its adoption, seem, considering the circumstances of the time, to have been so ordered as to make it substantially the work of the people. But the Convention by which that instrument was framed, was tainted by the vice inherent in most of those held during the Revolutionary period; it exercised, by usurpation or by the pretended grant of the Provincial Congress, governmental powers. While occupied in framing the Constitution, it spent much of its time in administrative business, and, after its completion, it continued to act, as above stated, as a Council of Safety, adopting the ordinances necessary to put the new government in operation. It was, therefore, a Revolutionary Convention.[1]

§ 153. The position of the State of Vermont, during the period we are now considering, was peculiar. Engaged, like the thirteen colonies forming the Union, in a war with Great Britain, in behalf of "the continent," she maintained, at the same time, a spirited contest, on her own account, with her powerful neighbor, New York, to repel what she deemed unjust territorial aggressions. The particulars of this double contest it is unnecessary to rehearse. It is sufficient to say that at the end of the war with Great Britain, Vermont had succeeded in establishing her independence, not only of Great Britain, but of New York, under a Constitution, which, in most of its important features, has remained unchanged to this day. The first step in this course was to call a Convention to pass upon the question of Independence, in imitation of the Continental Congress acting for the thirteen colonies. Circular letters were addressed by some of the most influential persons to the different towns, in pursuance of which delegates were appointed to a Convention, which met at Dorset, on the 24th of July, 1776. By different adjournments, a decision of the question was postponed until January, 1777, when the Convention again assembled at Westminster, and declared the New Hampshire Grants, for thus was Vermont then styled, a free and independent State. The Convention then adjourned, to meet again at Windsor, in the following June. The little State, thus boldly claiming for herself

[1] For an account of the proceedings of the first New York Convention, see *Deb. of the N. Y. Conv.*, 1821, Appendix, pp. 691–696.

a position among the nations of the earth, at once became an object of general attention. That New York would not readily acquiesce in her pretensions was certain, and it was very doubtful whether the Congress would recognize her independent character, much less admit her into the Union. At this juncture, a citizen of Philadelphia, Thomas Young, a prominent Democrat, and an experienced Constitution-maker,[1] published an address, urging the people of Vermont to maintain the ground they had taken, assuring them that he had taken the minds of the leading members of Congress, and that all they had to do was to "send attested copies of the recommendation" of the Congress, "to take up government, to every township . . . . and invite all freeholders and inhabitants to meet in their respective townships and choose members for a general Convention, to meet at an early day, to choose delegates for the general Congress, a Committee of Safety, and to form a Constitution."[2] This address was dated the 11th of April, 1777. At the adjourned session of the Convention, therefore, in June, 1777, in pursuance of this advice and of the recommendation of the Congress, that body appointed a committee to draft a Constitution, and then, by resolution, recommended the people to elect delegates, in their several towns, to meet in convention, at Windsor, on the 2d of July following, to pass upon the draft prepared by the committee. Delegates were accordingly elected, who met on the day named, and afterwards adjourning, and coming together in December, adopted and put in operation the first Vermont Constitution.[3]

§ 154. For a Convention called by a people in a condition so thoroughly revolutionary as that of Vermont, it is doubtful whether more of the elements of regularity could be expected than are here exhibited. Still, it was a Revolutionary Convention, that is, one exercising, beside the special function of a Constitutional Convention, the high powers of a Council of Safety, which were thoroughly despotic and of every variety wielded by any government whatever, so far as deemed by itself to be necessary. Moreover, the Constitution framed by the Convention was not submitted to the people for ratification. Though

[1] The marked similarity of the first Vermont Constitution to the first Constitution of Pennsylvania, was doubtless owing to him.

[2] Williams' *Hist. Vt*, p. 75.

[3] Id. p. 79.

the necessity of submitting it for that purpose was not denied, it was deemed unsafe to do so, on account of the perils then surrounding the State, as well from foreign as domestic enemies. But the failure to base the new government on the people, awakened a general distrust as to its validity. Objection was made to it, that the credentials of the delegates to the Convention authorized them to form a Constitution, but were silent as to its ratification by them, and that it never was submitted to the people for ratification or rejection.[1] Attempts were made, on several occasions, to remedy this defect, and the mode in which this was sought to be done, marks the immaturity of the views prevalent at that time in regard to the proper method of effecting constitutional changes. The legislature of the State, at its session in February, 1779, passed an Act declaring, that the Constitution, "as established by general Convention, held at Windsor in July and December, 1777, together with and agreeable to such alterations and additions," as should be made in pursuance of its provisions, should "be forever considered, held, and maintained, as part of the laws of the State."[2] Not content with this, the same body, at a subsequent session, held in 1782, passed another Act in similar terms, for the same purpose, which, by the preamble, was declared to be "to prevent disputes respecting the legal force of the Constitution of this State."[3]

§ 155. In 1786, a revision was made of the first Vermont Constitution, by a Convention called for that express and only purpose. By the 44th section of that instrument, provision had been made for the appointment, in 1785, and at the end of every seven years thereafter, of a Council of Censors, whose duty it should be, with other things, to call, by a vote of two-thirds of its members, a Convention to amend the Constitution, "if there should appear to them an absolute necessity of so doing." By a subsequent clause, all amendments were to be proposed by the Council of Censors, and the Convention were merely to pass upon them; and, to make it certain that the changes, if any, should be substantially the work of the people, the Council were required to publish the articles to be amended, and the proposed amendments thereto, at least six months before the

1 Slade's *State Papers*, p. 240, *note*, referring to Allen's *Hist. Vt.*

2 Act of February 11, 1779. See Slade's *State Papers*, p. 288, *note*.

3 Act passed in June, 1782. See Slade's *State Papers*, p. 449.

day appointed for the election of the Convention, "for the consideration of the people, that they may have an opportunity of instructing their delegates on the subject."

Under this system, copied from that of Pennsylvania, Councils of Censors were chosen every seven years down to the year 1869. That Council which held its session in 1785–86, called a Convention, to meet in June of the latter year, by which the Constitution was revised and published as the Constitution of 1786. Though differing from the Conventions of any other State in the Union, as to the extent and nature of their functions, those of Vermont, excepting her first, must be conceded to be, in their origin, at least, legitimate. Whether the facts, that they have received the amendments, upon which they have deliberated, from the Councils which called them, and that they have been required by the Constitution to pass upon those amendments definitively, distinguish them essentially from Constitutional Conventions, may be the subject of some doubt. Probably, the correct view to take of them is to regard them as Constitutional Conventions, exercising extraordinary powers, not by usurpation, as did their prototype, the Revolutionary Convention of 1777, but by virtue of special constitutional provision — in which view it would be impossible to deny to them regularity and legality.[1]

§ 156. The latest of all the original States of the Union to frame a Constitution, was Massachusetts. We have seen, that as early as May, 1775, the Provincial Convention of that State, on the withdrawal of her charter, had applied to the Congress at Philadelphia, for advice respecting the proper exercise of the powers of government in that colony.[2] In answer, the Congress had recommended the election of representatives by the several towns, to form a General Court, which was to meet and choose councilors, and had added the wish that those bodies should exercise the powers of government until a governor of the King's appointment would consent to govern the colony according to its charter. The arrangement thus recommended, which was provisional and temporary, was made, but no written Constitution was drawn up. For reasons set forth in the cases of the other colonies, this establishment proving unsatisfactory, in September, 1776, the Massachusetts Assembly voted to take steps

[1] See *post*, § 220, and *note*.

[2] See § 127, *ante*.

toward "the framing of a form of government." Accordingly, on the 5th of May following, the same body recommended to the people to authorize their representatives to the General Assembly next to be chosen, to form a Constitution, to be submitted to them for adoption or rejection, and, if approved by a two-thirds vote of the people, to be put in force by the General Assembly. On the 28th of February, 1778, the succeeding General Assembly, sitting as a Convention, agreed upon a Constitution, in the preamble to which, referring to the resolution of the 5th of May preceding, they recited that their constituents had instructed them "in one body with the Council," to form such a Constitution as they should judge best calculated to promote the happiness of the State. This Constitution, being submitted to the people at town-meetings held throughout the State, was, by the large majority of five to one, rejected. The reasons for this rejection were twofold: first, what were thought to be defects in the instrument itself; and, secondly, dissatisfaction on account of "the anomalous nature of the body by which it had been framed."[1] The anomaly, doubtless, consisted in its double character of Assembly and Convention, which the people had the good sense to recognize as of dangerous tendency. It must, moreover, have been doubtful whether it was the sense of the people that the Assembly should assume to meddle with the fundamental law, since it does not appear that a regular vote was taken throughout the State, by the returns of which it could have been determined, with certainty, on which side of the question was cast a majority of votes.

§ 157. The next attempt to frame a Constitution for the State was more successful. The General Court, as the legislature was called, on the 20th of February, 1779, directed the selectmen of the several towns to cause the freeholders and other inhabitants in their respective towns, duly qualified to vote for representatives, to be lawfully warned to meet together in some convenient place therein, on or before the last Wednesday of May following, to consider of and determine upon the following questions: — first, whether they chose, at that time, to have a Constitution, or form of government made; secondly, whether they would empower their representatives for the next year to vote for the calling a State Convention, for the sole purpose

[1] *Proceedings of the Mass. Conv. of* 1820, p. vi., *note.*

of forming a Constitution, provided it should appear to them, on examination, that a major part of the people, present and voting at the meetings called in the manner and for the purpose aforesaid, should have answered the first question in the affirmative.[1]

The people assented to both of these propositions by large majorities. Accordingly, the General Court, by a resolution passed June 17, 1779, provided for the election of delegates to a Convention, to meet on the first of September following.[2] The delegates elected under this resolution, assembled on the day appointed, and chose a committee of thirty to prepare a Constitution and Declaration of Rights, and adjourned over to the 28th of October. The committee delegated to John Adams, one of their number, the task of preparing the Declaration of Rights, and to him, with James Bowdoin and Samuel Adams, that of drafting the Constitution. At the adjourned session commencing October 28th, the Committee presented their draft, which, after full discussion, and several adjournments for the purpose of securing a full attendance of the members, was adopted by the Convention, March 2, 1780. The Convention then adjourned again to the first Wednesday of June, 1780, having first made provision for taking the sense of the people upon the Constitution, and adopted an address to them explaining the principles of that instrument. On the 7th of June, 1780, the Convention reassembled, and, it appearing that the whole Constitution had been approved by the people, by more than a two-thirds vote, declared, June 16, 1780, "the said form to be the Constitution established by and for the inhabitants of the State of Massachusetts Bay."

§ 158. Such was the jealousy exhibited by the people of Massachusetts, of the unauthorized interference of any body of men with their appropriate function of establishing the fundamental law. Being the latest of all the original thirteen States to engage in the work of Constitution-making, Massachusetts possessed the great advantage of being able to profit by the example of her sister-colonies, to adopt their improvements, and avoid their mistakes. She had also the benefit of the enlightened counsels of John and Samuel Adams, the former of whom is

[1] *Journal of the Mass. Conv. of* 1779–80, Appendix, No. 1.

[2] *Proceedings of Mass. Conv. of* 1820, p. vi., *note.*

entitled to rank as the father of the American system of governments, considering as well their peculiar adjustments of power, as the modes and processes by which they are built up. From the first essay, made by New Hampshire, in January, 1776, it is evident a great advance had been made in all respects during the four years ending with the adoption of the first Constitution of Massachusetts. At first, the people had very inadequate notions of the true methods of fundamental legislation. Having only the examples of their forefathers in England, in 1660 and 1688, with a few contemporaneous imitations in the colonies, they were convinced the work, in their then revolutionary condition, must be initiated by Conventions, but under what conditions and limitations, they seem to have been wholly ignorant. By degrees, however, they came to realize what John Adams had taught them in May, 1775, that it was necessary "that the people should erect the whole building with their own hands," and to that end, that the Conventions called by them should be limited to the single function of proposing constitutional enactments, leaving it to the electors by their *fiat*, pronounced through the ballot-box, to give to them the force and vigor of law. It is hardly necessary to observe, that the proceedings by which the Massachusetts Convention of 1779 was called, and by which its work was matured and confirmed by the final vote of the people, were strictly regular, and that, therefore, the body was legitimate as a Constitutional Convention.[1]

§ 159. There remain now to be considered those conventions of the revolutionary period, by which were framed and ratified the two Constitutions of the United States.

We have seen that, upon the breaking out of hostilities with Great Britain, the several colonies, except Connecticut and Rhode Island, established temporary governments, by means of Provincial Conventions or Congresses, operating in the main through committees, and exercising unlimited powers. In taking this step, they imitated the example set them by United America, in establishing a government for the continent by the Congress at Philadelphia. The contest with Great Britain had been opened, and, so long as the body existed, was conducted

[1] For a full and most excellent account of the proceedings resulting in the framing of the first Massachusetts Constitution, see *Works of John Adams*, Vol. IV. pp. 213-218.

by the Revolutionary Congress, which met at Philadelphia on the 5th of September, 1774. When that body expired, there succeeded to its place and office the Congress which met at the same city on the 10th of May, 1775. To the revolutionary government administered by these two bodies, belonged all the powers needed for the successful prosecution of the war. As those powers, however, grew out of necessity, and not out of an express grant, it was found difficult to secure acquiescence in their exercise, except when the separate colonies were made tractable by imminent public dangers. To remedy this evil, it was early proposed to frame articles which should not only make the union of the colonies perpetual, but so ascertain the powers intrusted to the central government by written memorials, that cavil and disobedience should be prevented. According to Mr. Madison, there remains on the files of Congress, in the handwriting of Dr. Franklin, a sketch of such articles, submitted by him to that body, as early as the 21st of August, 1775, entitled, "Articles of Confederation and Perpetual Union of the Colonies." But this attempt was premature, and nothing came of it. When Congress, in 1776, appointed a committee to draft a Declaration of Independence, it appointed at the same time another to prepare a plan of a confederation for the Colonies. The committee reported a plan, on the 12th of July, 1776, based on that sketched by Dr. Franklin, which was debated and amended from time to time until the 15th of November, 1777, when the Congress passed it and agreed to propose it to the States. This plan, entitled "Articles of Confederation and Perpetual Union between the States of New Hampshire," &c., &c., was finally ratified by the legislatures of the several States, but only after long delay, the date of the earliest ratification being the 9th of July, 1778, and that of the latest, the 1st of March, 1781.

§ 160. Thus was effected, for the United States, the transition from a revolutionary condition, under a provisional government, to one that was, in idea, at least, fixed and permanent, under a written Constitution. The body by which this Constitution was framed, the Continental Congress, I have classed with Constitutional Conventions, but in strictness that classification is incorrect. That Congress was a revolutionary government, charged by the patriotic majority in the several colonies to see to it that the interests of United America received no detriment. For that purpose its powers were undoubtedly ample, but they did not extend to the framing of a fundamental law; at least, the credentials of its members contemplated — and, considering the time when they were drawn up, could have contemplated — no such special function for that body, unless the framing of a Constitution should be thought to be among the proper means of discharging adequately the trust committed to it. Whatever force or validity those articles derived from the Congress, sprang solely from their excellence as propositions to be acted on by the several States, or from the force wielded by their proposers as a revolutionary government. They were obligatory upon no one, and, in fact, it was less the weight of the Congress than the urgent perils of the times that led to their final adoption by the States. Their real validity, as a Constitution for America, depended solely upon the ratification so tardily given by the constituent commonwealths.

§ 161. The mode in which the ratification of the Articles of Confederation was effected, is deserving of notice, as bearing on the question of the legitimacy of that Constitution. It was ratified by the States, and not by the citizens of the several States or of the Union. It was by the States, speaking through their respective legislative assemblies. In one aspect of the case, this mode of ratifying those articles was the proper one, for the Confederation was a league of distinct commonwealths, struck by their ambassadors, and, therefore, to derive its force only from those whom the ambassadors represented. These being States, it was they alone that could dictate the terms upon which their union should subsist. The Constitution of the Confederation, therefore, when ratified in the manner explained, was an entirely legitimate one; that is, it was proposed to the constituent bodies to be governed by it, and by the latter ratified and confirmed by an express vote; but it was legitimate only for what it purported to be — a league between States, and not a national Constitution, in the proper sense of the term. Tested by the principles that should preside over the formation of a *Constitution*, it was, in its inception, not legitimate, for it wanted the sanction of the people, who, as distinct from their governments, are alone the constituents, or have power to ratify a Constitution.

The Congress, on the other hand, considered as a Constitutional Convention, possessed not a single one of the elements necessary to give it legitimacy. The people had no direct agency in calling it, no voice in prescribing its duties or ascertaining its powers, and were not directly consulted in the act of putting the fruit of its deliberations in force.

§ 162. Such was the first essay of our fathers in framing a government for United America. The system resulting from it, the joint product of inexperience and State jealousy, came soon to merit the general contempt from its weakness. The government of the Confederation, from its peculiar character as a league between States, needed, more than one which should deal immediately with individuals, to be strong enough to make itself either respected or feared. But it failed to secure either fear or respect. With considerable legislative power, it had no distinctively judicial, and next to no executive, power. It presented the anomaly of a government for an immense expanse of country, empowered to enact laws, but invested with scarcely any power of enforcing them. The disordered state of the finances, which it was utterly unable to remedy, was the proximate cause of its collapse. The requisitions for the support of the government were first paid by a few of the States, the rest contributing nothing, and then disregarded by all alike.[1] But, had it been the destiny of the United States to tide over the financial difficulties growing out of the war, a state of peace and prosperity would have demonstrated, more strikingly than one of financial distress, the utter inadequacy of its Constitution of government. There is scarcely a function of a good government in which it would not have proved itself altogether wanting.

§ 163. The immediate occasion of the steps which finally led to the supersession of this worthless fabric by a real Constitution, grew out of the absolute necessity of filling the national coffers. In 1781, and on several subsequent occasions, serious efforts had been made to induce the States to vest in Congress power to levy imposts on imported goods, for the purpose of raising the necessary public revenue. But they had all been vain. At

[1] Attorney-General Randolph, in arguing before the Supreme Court of the United States the case of Chisholm's Executors *vs.* The State of Georgia, wittily characterized the Confederation, in view of the facts stated in the text, as "a government of supplication." 2 Dall. R. 419.

length, on the 21st of January, 1786, the House of Delegates of Virginia appointed eight commissioners, to meet such others as might be appointed by the other States, at a time and place to be agreed upon, with instructions "to take into consideration the trade of the United States . . . . to consider how far a uniform system in their commercial regulations may be necessary; and to report to the several States such an Act relative to this great subject, as, when unanimously ratified by them, will enable the United States in Congress assembled effectually to provide for the same; that the said commissioners shall immediately transmit to the several States copies of the preceding resolution, with a circular letter requesting their concurrence therein, and proposing a time and place for the meeting aforesaid."[1]

This resolution was the origin of what is known as the Annapolis Convention; the instructions to the Virginia commissioners being carried out by them and delegates, according to their invitation, assembling from several of the States at Annapolis, the place named for the purpose by the commissioners. Toward the object for which it was assembled, the Annapolis Convention did nothing directly, only five of the States responding to the call; but it gave expression to its "unanimous wish, that speedy measures may be taken to effect a general meeting of the States in a future Convention, for the same and such other purposes as the situation of public affairs may be found to require." The delegates then stated that, in their opinion, "the idea of extending the powers of their deputies to other objects than those of commerce, which has been adopted by the State of New Jersey,[2] was an improvement on the original plan, and will deserve to be incorporated into that of a future Convention." They further recommended "a Convention of deputies from the different States, for the special and sole purpose of entering into this inquiry, and digesting a plan for supplying such defects as may be discovered to exist;" and that the Convention meet on the 2d Monday in May, 1787, at Philadelphia, "to take into consideration the situation of the United States, to devise such further provisions as shall appear to them necessary to render the Con-

[1] Ell. *Deb.*, Vol. I. pp. 93-100.

[2] New Jersey had instructed her delegates to the Annapolis Convention "to consider how far a uniform system in their commercial regulations *and other important matters* might be necessary."

stitution of the Federal government adequate to the exigencies of the Union, and to report such an act for that purpose to the United States in Congress assembled, as, when agreed to by them, and afterwards confirmed by the legislatures of every State, will effectually provide for the same."

Having published the above recommendations, the Convention adjourned, September 14, 1786.

§ 164. The two documents mentioned in the last section — the instructions to the Virginia delegates and the recommendations of the Annapolis Convention—evidently contemplated nothing more than an amendment of the Articles of Confederation, in the main according to the mode pointed out by the thirteenth of those Articles. The course of action recommended by the first, however, involved a variation from that mode in one particular not contained in the second, namely, in that it required the act relative to trade regulations, which the commissioners might mature, to be reported "to the several States," and to take effect "when unanimously ratified by them." The Annapolis Convention, on the other hand, recommended that the Convention to meet at Philadelphia in May following, should "report such an Act" in regard to the interests of the Union, therein mentioned, "to the United States, in Congress assembled, as, when agreed to by them and afterwards confirmed by the legislatures of every State," would "effectually provide for the same." In other words, the Virginia instructions proposed to amend the Articles of Confederation by referring the new or additional Articles to only one of the sources of authority prescribed by the Articles themselves, that is, to the States, omitting "the Congress of the United States," which body, by the 13th Article, was first to agree upon them. In this respect, the recommendations of the Annapolis Convention are free from objection, since the course pointed out by that body for securing amendments to the Articles was in scrupulous conformity to the 13th Article, except that they went further than the latter in proposing to call *a Convention* to frame such amendments in the first instance — a step not provided for in the 13th Article. Indeed, that Article contained no indication of the persons by whom amendments to the Articles should or should not be suggested or proposed, but required only that they should be agreed to and confirmed in a particular manner, that is, first, by the Congress, and then by the State legislatures.

§ 165. From these seeds sprang the Federal Convention of 1787, by which was framed the present Constitution of the United States.

The recommendations of the Annapolis Convention having been communicated by letter to Congress, that body, on the 21st of February, 1787, passed the following preamble and resolution: —

"*Whereas*, there is provision in the Articles of Confederation and Perpetual Union for making alterations therein, by the assent of a Congress of the United States and of the legislatures of the several States; and, *whereas*, experience hath evinced that there are defects in the present Confederation, as a means to remedy which several of the States, and particularly the State of New York, by express instructions to their delegates in Congress, have suggested a Convention for the purposes expressed in the following resolution; and such Convention appearing to be the most probable means of establishing in these States a firm national government, —

"*Resolved*, That, in the opinion of Congress, it is expedient that, on the 2d Monday in May next, a Convention of delegates, who shall have been appointed by the several States, be held at Philadelphia, for the sole and express purpose of revising the Articles of Confederation, and reporting to Congress and the several legislatures such alterations and provisions therein as shall, when agreed to in Congress and confirmed by the States, render the Federal Constitution adequate to the exigencies of government and the preservation of the Union."[1]

In pursuance of this resolution, delegates were chosen and met at Philadelphia on the day appointed, and by them was matured, in a session of something over four months, the present Constitution of the United States. The first State to act upon the resolution was Virginia, whom all the other twelve States followed in the course of a few months, and before the assembling of the Convention, except New Hampshire, Connecticut, and Maryland, whose delegates were appointed and accredited after that body had been organized at Philadelphia.

§ 166. The question as to the legitimacy of the Federal Convention, in the sense in which I have defined that term,[2] is not a difficult one to answer.

[1] Ell. *Deb.*, Vol. I. pp. 119, 120.

[2] See §§ 105–108, *ante*.

There being, as I have shown, in the Articles of Confederation, no specification of the persons by whom, or of the mode in which, alterations of those Articles *should be proposed*, but only of the manner in which they *should be ratified and established*, some range was left to the people of the Union for a choice both of persons and mode. The only limitation, indeed, upon their action, was, that whatever mode and whatever persons should be employed, there should be a substantial conformity to the principles presiding over the genesis of Constitutions, described in a former chapter, of which the most important are, first, that the work shall be committed to persons duly commissioned by the existing government, for the sole and express purpose of accomplishing that work; and, secondly, that to the sovereign body shall be accorded an opportunity fully and freely to express its will in relation to the call of such Convention.

That the Federal Convention conformed to the first of these principles, in all essential particulars, is beyond question. It was made up of delegates appointed by the legislatures of the several States, assembling, on the basis of federal equality, for the sole and express purpose of proposing such alterations of the existing Constitution as should make it adequate to the exigencies of government and the preservation of the Union.

It, also, in my judgment, conformed substantially to the second. The sovereignty of the Union, as then constituted, resided in the people of the United States, either as a unit or as distinguished into groups under the name of States. Hence, it is evident that when the Congress, which represented the sovereign as a unit, recommended and called the Convention, and the State legislatures, which collectively represented that sovereign as distinguished into the groups known as States, acceded to that recommendation and appointed delegates to the Convention, nothing more could be needed to show that the call of that body was made with the assent, if it was not directly the act, of the sovereign authority of the Union.

Whether or not, in any of its acts, that Convention exceeded its jurisdiction, assumed revolutionary powers, and thus, so far, divested itself of its original character as a Constitutional Convention; whether or not, in other words, the Constitution proposed by it was the fruit of a fair exercise of the powers intrusted to it, or, on the other hand, was the offspring of violated instructions, of usurpation, is a different question, which will be considered further on.[1]

§ 167. The Conventions of the eleven States which ratified the Federal Constitution, previously to its establishment in March, 1789, — the only remaining ones held during the Revolutionary period, — were all regularly called by the legislatures of their respective States.[2] The same may be said of the two Conventions which ratified that Constitution subsequently to its establishment — those of North Carolina and Rhode Island — as well as of the Convention of the independent republic, Vermont, whose ratification was dated January 10th, 1791.

The only observation I deem necessary respecting these Conventions is, that they differ from the great bulk of the Conventions held in the United States, in that their function was, not to mature, but to adopt and establish, a code of organic law. Doing this, however, under special instructions, I have considered those bodies as belonging to the class of Constitutional Conventions. This mode of enacting Constitutions has been practiced by several of the States. Under the first Constitution of Pennsylvania, and under all those of Vermont, constitutional changes have been recommended by bodies called Councils of Censors, and then passed upon by Conventions called for that express and only purpose. What has in those States been a matter of Constitutional regulation, has in several instances occurred in other States, generally, and perhaps always, without special authorization in the fundamental law. Thus, the second Constitution of the State of Georgia was framed by a Convention which assembled in 1788, and was submitted for adoption to two Conventions held in 1789, by one of which certain amendments to the plan were proposed, and by the other were ratified and established.[3] In a few cases a similar use has been made of Conventions in new States, to give the sanction of such States, in a solemn and authentic form, to amendments to their Constitutions demanded by Congress as conditions of their admission into the Union. Such Conventions were those of

1 See §§ 383–386, *post.*

2 See Appendix B, for a list of these bodies.

3 See § 148, *ante.*

Michigan, of 1836, (two Conventions,[1]) of Iowa, of 1846, of West Virginia, of 1861–3, (final session,) and others; some of which, however, were not newly-elected Conventions, but those previously in session for the usual purpose, but subsequently reassembled to give the sanction of the State to the conditions indicated. In regard to these latter instances, the only question as to the regularity of the Conventions depends on the power of the legislative bodies calling them to give them the right of definitive legislation, involved in the act of passing thus upon a fundamental law, — a subject which will be considered in another part of this work.[2]

§ 168. Respecting the principal Conventions of the Revolutionary period, two or three observations should be made, to prevent misconceptions.

1. Considerable stress has been laid, in the preceding sections, upon the fact, that most of the Conventions of that class were revolutionary, either in their origin or in their methods of procedure, or in both. This imputation against the character of those bodies, however, is not intended as an impeachment of them as having no basis in political necessity, but only as a denial to them of regularity and legality as Constitutional Conventions. Those bodies were irregular, from the nature of the case, for they came in to supply the *hiatus* caused by the subsidence of regular governments in the several colonies. The old organizations being broken up, the elements were forced to seek new combinations, and, to that end, to find somewhere new centres about which to arrange themselves according to their several affinities. The Conventions, originating in popular movements, semi-official, semi-spontaneous, were those centres. The wonder is, not that there were irregularities, judging by the standards of peace and established order, but that the aberrations were not greater and more numerous.

2. But, it may be asked, why insist so strenuously upon the fact that the Conventions of the Revolutionary period were revolutionary bodies, if it be admitted that they were grounded upon an imperious necessity, and that from them, as from a fountain, has flowed the present order of things, confessed to be legitimate? The answer is, because, if they are truly revolutionary

[1] See §§ 202–204, *post.*
[2] See §§ 480–486, *post.*

bodies, they must be set down as such, in order that their action may not be drawn into precedent, as that of normal Constitutional Conventions. If, with reference to the colonial establishments founded by the crown, those Conventions and the proceedings of those Conventions were not revolutionary, then, neither would similar Conventions and proceedings, antagonistic to the now existing order, be revolutionary with respect to that order.

§ 169. 3. If, in any particular, relating to their initiation or to their procedure, the Conventions of the revolutionary period should seem to be more irregular than was necessary, it should be remembered that much of their irregularity was due to the dangers of the times, and much to the ignorance and inexperience of those who managed them. While the foundations of our civil polity were being laid, our fathers were staggering under the burdens of a long war, replete with public and private disasters. For the public safety, it was often found necessary to omit some of those forms by which regular governments, in times of peace and order, are accustomed to ascertain the public will. Moreover, the process by which the purely Revolutionary Conventions, theretofore known, were gradually adapted to a defined constitutional purpose, was then just commencing. The absolute necessity, afterwards so well understood, of limiting the Constitutional Convention to its special function, in subordination to the government to which it is ancillary, was very imperfectly recognized. Hence, as we have seen, the Conventions generally throughout the War of Independence united in themselves functions proper only for bodies vested temporarily with dictatorial powers — for those provisional organizations, which, in times of crisis, are, for the public safety, or to forward the purposes of ambition, intrusted with a revolutionary discretion, incompatible with the existence of any other government.

§ 170. (*b*). The second and most numerous class of Conventions consists of such as have been assembled since the Federal Constitution went into operation, on the 4th of March, 1789, and they may be divided into these three principal varieties: —

1. Such as have been convened for the purpose of framing Constitutions for new States to be formed within the territorial jurisdiction of States already members of the Union.

2. Such as have been called to frame Constitutions for new

States to be formed out of territory of the United States, organized under its authority, or acquired in an organized condition from foreign States.

3. Such as have been assembled for the revision of the Constitutions of States, members of the Union.

It will be the chief purpose of what remains of this chapter to bring into view these several varieties of Conventions, in order to ascertain how far the modes in which they were called or initiated conform to the principles enunciated in the opening sections of this chapter.

§ 171. 1. Of the first variety of Conventions enumerated, there have been held, up to the present time, reckoning the first Convention of Vermont, which may with propriety be classed with them, though held previously to 1789, four Conventions:[1] those which framed the first Constitutions of Vermont, Kentucky, Maine, and West Virginia.

The first clause of the 3d section of the 4th Article of the Federal Constitution provides, that "no new State shall be formed or erected within the jurisdiction of any other State, nor any State be formed by the junction of two or more States or parts of States, without the consent of the legislatures of the States concerned, as well as of the Congress." To render a Convention legitimate, therefore, for the purpose of erecting a new State within the jurisdiction of any other State or States, under this clause, three things must concur: first, the prior consent of the legislature of the State or States out of which the new one is to be carved; second, that of the Congress of the United States; and, third, that of the inhabitants or people of

[1] The territory now comprised in the State of Vermont was, at the time she declared her independence, claimed by the State of New York. It was not until October 17th, 1790, after the formation of the present Constitution of the United States, that New York consented to her erection into a new State. She was admitted into the Union in 1791, after she had maintained her independence against the State of New York and the United States for fourteen years. As Vermont was erected into an independent State and admitted into the Union, therefore, with the consent of New York, and, of course, of Congress, the conditions required by the Federal Constitution seem to have been fulfilled. For the details of the action of Vermont herself, see *ante*, §§ 154, 155. The consent of New York was given through commissioners appointed by that State, on the 17th of October, 1790, Vermont paying to New York for a relinquishment of all claim, as well of soil as of jurisdiction, the sum of thirty thousand dollars.

the proposed State. The first and second of these requisites follow from the terms of the constitutional provision, and the third, I think, from the reciprocity of right and obligation subsisting between the several portions of a State. Each of these owes obedience, or a *quasi* allegiance to the parent State, and, in return, is entitled to protection, which excludes the idea that the State, as a whole, can rightfully sever from connection with itself a part thereof, without its consent.

§ 172. Before the adoption of the Federal Constitution, no rule upon this subject existed, and an attempt to dismember a State, however conducted, would have been revolutionary. The case of Vermont, before referred to, exhibits the embarrassments to which such a condition of things was likely to give rise. There were many years during which the troubles between that State and New York threatened to breed a civil war, not between those States alone, but between those States and such allies as they might respectively secure.[1] The clause of the Federal Constitution, above cited, was intended to obviate the dangers foreseen, if a system were established, permitting no changes in the territorial extent of the States, or allowing them to be consummated without the consent of Congress. And yet, as was perhaps to be expected, not a single instance of the dismemberment of a State has ever occurred, under the clause quoted, without proceedings more or less irregular or revolutionary. By this is not meant, that the final Acts by which the new States have been erected, have in any case come short of conforming substantially to the constitutional provision, but, either that the consent of the parent States has been wrung from them by the pressure of events — perhaps, secured by political advantages accepted as the price of that which must be yielded at all events — or the Conventions, by which the initiatory movements have been conducted, have been illegally called, and so have been, in character, revolutionary.

[1] No native of Vermont would willingly charge the revolutionary leaders of that State with entertaining seriously the project of forming an alliance with Great Britain against New York and the other twelve colonies. But it cannot be denied, that they at least coquetted, in a very imprudent manner, with the British generals; and, had the policy, so long pursued by Congress under the inspiration of New York, of practical hostility to Vermont, been continued, that little Commonwealth might have been driven to seek, in a detested alliance with a common enemy, that freedom which was denied her by those of her own household.

§ 173. After Vermont, the first State erected within the jurisdiction of another State, was Kentucky. As this case occurred after the Federal Constitution had gone into operation, it is worthy of attentive consideration, as the earliest in which an application could be made of the constitutional provision in question.

That part of Virginia, now composing the State of Kentucky, was separated from the older portions of the State by intervening mountains. When the war of the Revolution was concluded, the financial distresses common to Virginia and to all the States of the Union caused the infant settlements west of the mountains to be neglected. The hostile tribes of Indians on their southern and western frontiers, took advantage of their defenceless condition, and were repressed by the settlers only with great difficulty, and at their own cost. In the fall of 1784, the exigencies of the public defense called together an assemblage of citizens at Danville, Kentucky, the danger to be guarded against being an attack by the Cherokee Indians. On consultation, it was found that they had no power to raise forces, or to do any thing to protect themselves, and it was therefore resolved to call a Convention of the entire Kentucky district. To constitute that body, the assemblage addressed the people in a circular letter, in which it was recommended to each militia company in the district to elect, on a day named by the assemblage, one representative, to meet in Danville, on the 27th of December, 1784, to take into consideration the important subject of self-defense. The Convention met at the time appointed, and then, the subject of a separation from Virginia being broached, they voted in favor of it by a large majority. Another Convention followed in May, 1785, at which a similar expression of opinion was made, and resulted in a petition to the Assembly of Virginia for liberty to form a new State.[1] A third Convention, which met in August of the same year, having commenced its proceedings by a unanimous vote in favor of the project of separation, the Assembly of Virginia, at its session in November, 1785, passed an Act, authorizing the election of five delegates from each of the seven counties of Kentucky, to take into consideration the forming an independent government. Should the Convention determine upon it, separation was assented to

[1] Hildreth, *Hist. U. S.*, Vol. III., 1st Series, p. 457.

provided Congress, before the first of June, 1787, would admit the new State into the Union; and provided further, that Kentucky would agree to assume her proportion of the Virginia debt.[1]

§ 174. The Convention thus authorized by the Virginia Assembly, was prevented by an expedition against the Indians north of the Ohio, from meeting, except in numbers less than a quorum; but an application to Virginia, on the part of such members of the Convention as had met at the time appointed (September 17, 1786), resulted in a new Act of the Virginia Assembly, authorizing a new Convention, to be held the following year.[2] Accordingly, on the 17th of September, 1787 — the very day on which the Federal Convention closed its labors at Philadelphia — a fifth Convention met at Danville, Kentucky, resolved unanimously in favor of separation from Virginia, adopted an address asking admission into the Union, and, in conformity to the provisions of the Act under which they met, directed the election of a new Convention to frame a State Constitution.[3]

These Acts and proceedings seem to have been attended by no results; for, on the 18th of December, 1789, another Act was passed by Virginia, proposing terms of separation, which were accepted by a Convention, which met on the 26th of July, 1790, the separation to take effect on the 1st of June, 1792. Finally, this Convention resolved, that in December, 1791, an election should be held for forty-five representatives to form a Constitutional Convention, to be elected under certain restrictions as to residence, by the free male inhabitants of each county, above the age of twenty-one years, the Convention to be held at Danville on the first Monday in April, 1792. At the time and place appointed this Convention met, and by it was framed the first Constitution of Kentucky, to take effect, as above stated, on the 1st day of June, 1792. In the mean time, on the 4th of February, 1791, an Act had been passed by Congress, declaring the consent of that body, that a new State, by the name of Kentucky, might be formed within the jurisdiction of the Commonwealth of Virginia,[4] and admitting the same into the Union, the Act to

1 Hildreth, *Hist. U. S.*, Vol. III., 1st Series, p. 470.

2 Id. pp. 470–1.

3 Id. p. 529.

4 1 *U. S. Stat. at Large*, p. 189.

take effect on the same day as the Constitution. Thus Kentucky became, from a district of the State of Virginia, a State in the Union, and that with substantial regularity.

§ 175. The next example of the dismemberment of a State was that of Maine, formed from a portion of the State of Massachusetts.

As early as 1786, before the adoption of the Federal Constitution, the project of erecting the District of Maine into a separate State had been entertained, and a Convention had at one time met at Portland to consider the subject.[1] It was not, however, until after the second war with England that the project assumed definite proportions. The stand taken by the Federal party during that war had reflected great odium upon Massachusetts, which had been controlled by it, and in which it had been more offensively conspicuous than in any State in the Union. As in most new and sparsely settled districts, the Democratic or war party was in a majority in the District of Maine, and it was natural that its leaders should chafe under the sway of the Federalists in the older part of the State. Nothing, indeed, stood in the way of a separation but the political ambition of the parent State, it being evident that to part with that District would reduce Massachusetts to a second-rate position in national affairs, in which she would be forced to yield the leadership of the North, hitherto held by her, to the rising State of New York. The weight of her unpopularity, however, was so great, after the war, that she despaired of longer retaining her primacy in the Union, and her federal politicians were not unwilling to strengthen themselves for a while at home by letting Maine go. The Federalists of Maine protested against this desertion, but the people of that District, after two or three trials, having pronounced decidedly in favor of separation, a Convention was called, under the authority of an Act of the legislature of Massachusetts, to form a State Constitution. By this body, as we shall see, was framed the first Constitution of Maine.

§ 176. The earliest official action relating to the proposed separation was the Act of the Massachusetts legislature referred to, entitled, "An Act relating to the Separation of the District of Maine from Massachusetts proper, and forming the same into a separate and independent State," passed June 19, 1819.

[1] Hildreth, *Hist. U. S.*, Vol. III. 1st series, p. 472.

The parts of this Act important for my purpose were as follows: —

"*Whereas*, it has been represented to this legislature, that a majority of the people of the District of Maine are desirous of establishing a separate and independent government within the said District, therefore be it enacted," &c.

"That the consent of this commonwealth be, and the same is, hereby given, that the District of Maine may be formed and erected into a separate and independent State, if the people of the said District shall, in the manner, and by the majority hereinafter mentioned, express their consent and agreement thereto, upon the terms and conditions: and provided the Congress of the United States shall give its consent thereto, before the fourth day of March next, which terms and conditions are as follows": — (the terms and conditions relate to the public property and the guaranty of existing rights) "subject, however, to be modified or annulled by the agreement of the legislatures of both of said States, but by no other power or body whatsoever."

§ 177. The requisites, as to manner and majority, of the assent and agreement to be given by the people of the District of Maine, prescribed in the second section, were, "that the inhabitants of the several towns, districts, and plantations in the District of Maine, qualified to vote for Governor or Senators," should "assemble in regular meeting, to be notified by warrants of the proper officers, on the fourth Monday of July next, and" should "in open meeting, give in their votes on this question: 'Is it expedient that the District of Maine shall become a separate and independent State, upon the terms and conditions provided in an Act entitled,'" &c. The Act then proceeded to give minute regulations for conducting the election, the return and canvassing of the votes, and the proclamation of the result to the people. It finally provided, that, in case there should have been cast in favor of such separation a majority of fifteen hundred votes, "then and not otherwise the people of said District" should "be deemed to have expressed their consent and agreement that the said District" should "become a separate and independent State, upon the terms and conditions above stated." In which case it required the Governor, in his proclamation, to "call upon the people of said

District to choose delegates to meet in Convention for the purpose" of framing a Constitution for the proposed State.

In pursuance of this Act, a Convention was elected, and met at Portland on the 11th of October, 1819, and, after a session of eighteen days, adopted and submitted to the people of the District a Constitution, which the latter, on the 6th of December, 1819, in their town-meetings, ratified and confirmed. This Constitution having been presented to Congress, with a petition for the admission of the State into the Union, an Act was passed for that purpose on the 3d of March, 1820, which, after reciting the Act of Massachusetts, and that, in pursuance thereof, "the people of that part of Massachusetts heretofore known as the District of Maine, did, with the consent of the legislature of said State of Massachusetts, form themselves into an independent State, and did establish a Constitution for the government of the same, agreeably to the provisions of said Act," enacted, "that from and after the 15th of March, 1820, the State of Maine be and be declared to be one of the United States of America."

Respecting the legitimacy of the Convention thus called, no extended observations are necessary. That body undoubtedly possessed, in full measure, each of the requisites to give it a legitimate character as a Constitutional Convention, — viz., the consent of the people of the State of Massachusetts, expressed, as the Constitution of the United States requires, by the legislature of the State; that of the inhabitants of the district, and that of Congress.

§ 178. The only remaining instance of the formation of a State by the dismemberment of another State, is that of West Virginia.

The official proceedings culminating in the establishment of this new State, were as follows: —

On the 17th of April, 1861, a body of men, assembled by the legislature of Virginia, on the 13th of February preceding, and styling themselves "the Convention of Virginia," passed a pretended ordinance of secession from the United States, and, so far as they had power to do so, carried the State, as a political organization, out of the Union. The officers of the State, with great unanimity, joined the rebel cause, carrying with them the public funds, the archives of the State, and such of the national forts and arsenals within the limits of Virginia, as they had the physical ability to seize and maintain. The insurgents not actually withdrawing from the State, the situation was as follows: There was the State of Virginia, considered territorially as a portion of the national domain; there were the rebel forces, government, and population in hostile possession of that part of the State occupied by their camps (for they could be recognized by the United States and its adherents as only temporarily encamped upon a portion of the territory of the Union); and there were the loyal Virginians settled, in an unorganized condition, upon the residue. In these circumstances, and at this stage of events, it is evident that the people of the State of Virginia, so far as the Constitution or Government of the United States could recognize a people at all, consisted only of its loyal inhabitants; and they were left, as by some great calamity, wholly destitute of a government, except, for national purposes, that of the Union, — reduced, so far as their internal administration was concerned, to a state of nature. In other words, so far as related to their local institutions, they were in a condition analogous to that in which their fathers were, when, upon the suppression of the royal government in 1774, they were compelled themselves, in their original capacity, to gather up the ravelled threads of government and weave them anew into a system for their defence. In 1774, there had existed a colonial establishment, but organized under the crown, and therefore hostile to their liberties, for which reason it had been repudiated by the people of Virginia; so, in 1861, there was a State organization, which, having ceased to be loyal to the Union, for which the Virginians, not seduced by the treason of their seceding rulers, still retained their affection, and to which they deemed allegiance still due, they ceased to follow in its eccentric course, or to obey. They, therefore, under the protection and with the countenance of the United States Government, commenced, as with a *tabula rasa*, the reconstruction of society from its foundations. This was possible only by employing the methods of revolution. The initiative must be taken by some body of persons having rights of jurisdiction within the limits of Virginia. No such body existed. It could not regularly be done by the citizens of Virginia still remaining loyal, because they were mere private individuals. It could not be regularly done by the people or Government of the Union, for, by the Federal Constitution, the right of founding and amending Constitutions for the State of Virginia had been delegated to the people of that State, acting by and through their State organization, subject merely to the federal guaranty that such Constitutions should be republican — which State organization had ceased to exist. The work of reconstruction, therefore, must be inaugurated irregularly, since a government must be forthwith established. Of the only two modes of effecting this work, at that time practicable, namely, that by a spontaneous movement of the loyal citizens of Virginia, and that by an enabling Act to be passed by the Congress of the United States, both irregular, the former was adopted, as I have said, with the countenance and under the protection of the United States.[1] The steps taken to this end were as follows: —

§ 179. On the 11th of June, 1861, a Convention of loyal Virginians met at Wheeling upon the call of influential persons in different parts of the State, with a view to reconstruct the State government. Taking their stand upon the Virginia Bill of Rights, framed in 1776, and reaffirmed in 1830 and 1851, they assumed to themselves the powers of government, forfeited by the treason of their rulers, and pronounced the Act of the General Assembly calling the Convention of February, 1861, without the previously expressed consent of the people, to be an act of usurpation. After denouncing the acts of that Convention as abuses of the powers intrusted to it, stigmatizing especially its attempt "to bring the allegiance of the people of the United States into direct conflict with their subordinate allegiance to the State; thereby making obedience to their pretended ordinances treason against the former," they solemnly declared, "in the name and on behalf of the good people of Virginia, that the preservation of their dearest rights and liberties, and their security in person and property, imperatively" demanded "the reorganization of the government of the Commonwealth, and that all acts of said Convention . . . . tending to separate this Commonwealth from the United States, or to levy and carry on war against them," were "without authority and void; and that the offices of all who" adhered to "the said Convention . . . . whether legislative, executive, or judicial," were "vacated." The Convention then, by an Ordinance, passed

[1] See §§ 251–253, *post*.

on the 19th of June, 1861, provided for the appointment of a governor, and other State officers, to continue in office six months, or until their successors were elected and qualified, and for a General Assembly, to consist of the members elected in May preceding, and such as might be elected under the Ordinances of the Convention, and to hold their offices until the end of the terms for which they should be elected. The General Assembly was required to meet on the 1st of July, 1861, and to proceed to organize themselves, as prescribed by existing laws, in the respective branches.

§ 180. Thus far the proceedings of the Convention related to the reconstruction of the State government. Now commenced those having for their object the dismemberment of the State. On the 20th of August, 1861, the Virginia Convention passed an Ordinance, entitled, "An Ordinance to provide for the formation of a new State out of a portion of the territory of this State." The material portions are as follows: —

"*Whereas*, it is represented to be the desire of the people inhabiting the counties hereinafter mentioned, to be separated from this commonwealth, and to be erected into a separate State, and admitted into the Union of States; . . . . The people of Virginia, by their delegates assembled in Convention at Wheeling, do ordain that a new State, to be called the State of Kanawha, be formed and erected out of the territory included within the following limits" (describing the territory in the main afterwards embraced in the State of West Virginia); that "all persons qualified to vote within the boundaries aforesaid, and who shall present themselves at the several places of voting within their respective counties, on the fourth Thursday in October next, shall be allowed to vote on the question of the formation of a new State;" and that the commissioners conducting the election at the several places of voting shall "cause polls to be taken for the election of delegates to a Convention to form a Constitution for the government of the proposed State." The Ordinance further provided (sec. 6) that it should be the duty of the Governor, "on or before the 15th day of November next, to ascertain and by proclamation make known the result of the said vote; and, if a majority of the votes given within the boundaries" prescribed, "shall be in favor of the formation of a new State, he shall so state in his said proclamation, and shall call upon the said delegates to meet in the city of Wheeling on the 26th day of November next, and organize themselves into a Convention; and the said Convention shall submit, for ratification or rejection, the Constitution that may be agreed upon by it, to the qualified voters within the proposed State, to be voted upon by the said voters, on the fourth Thursday in December next." By sections 8 and 10 it was required of the Governor to lay before the General Assembly, at its next meeting, "for their consent, according to the Constitution of the United States, the result of said vote," if a majority should appear to have voted in favor of a new State, and of the proposed Constitution; and that, when the General Assembly should have given its consent to the formation of such new State, it should forward to the Congress of the United States such consent, together with an official copy of such Constitution, with the urgent request that the new State might be admitted into the Union.

§ 181. In pursuance of this ordinance, a vote of the people within the territory mentioned was taken on the question of forming a new State and for delegates to a Constitutional Convention, should the vote favor the formation of such State. The election was held on the fourth Thursday in October, 1861, as prescribed in the ordinance, and resulted largely in favor of forming a new State. The delegates elected on the same day, accordingly, on the proclamation of the Governor, convened at Wheeling on the 26th of November, 1861, the day fixed by the ordinance, and during their session framed a Constitution, which was adopted by the people at a general election held on the 3d day of April, 1862.[1] A few days thereafter, on the 6th of May, 1862, an extra session of the legislature of the State of Virginia, as reconstituted by the Convention, was held at Wheeling. Its first Act, passed on the 13th of May, was entitled "an Act giving the consent of the legislature of Virginia to the forma-

[1] Such is the date contained in the preamble to the Act of Congress admitting the State conditionally into the Union. The day required by the ordinance of the Convention for the vote on the Constitution was the fourth Thursday in December, 1861. The address, to their constituents, of the delegates composing the Convention, called in 1863 to consider and pass upon the amendment to the Constitution of the new State, required by Congress to be made before the State should be admitted into the Union, on the other hand, speaks of the ratification of the Constitution as having been made in April, 1862. For a more detailed statement of the facts, see Preface to 1 W. Va. R., 72-78.

tion of a new State within the jurisdiction of this State." It purported to give the consent of the State to the erection of certain counties, named in the Ordinance above referred to, into a new State, to be called West Virginia instead of Kanawha, and that to them might be added four other counties specified in the Act, whenever the voters thereof should ratify and consent to the Constitution, at an election held for that purpose. It also required the Act, together with the Constitution, to be transmitted to the Senators and Representatives of Virginia in Congress, and requested those officers to use their endeavors to obtain the consent of Congress to the admission of the State of West Virginia into the Union.

Here, then, after a sort, were two of the three requisites to the legitimacy of the new State; the consent of the people to be embraced within its jurisdiction and that of the parent State, given first by its Convention and then by its so-called legislature, in apparent conformity to the letter of the Federal Constitution.

§ 182. Copies of the Act of the Virginia legislature and of the proposed Constitution of the new State having been transmitted to the Virginia delegation in Congress, a bill was introduced into that body giving its assent to the separation. Objections were entertained, however, to one provision of the Constitution, — that relating to slavery. The Convention which had framed that instrument had been about equally divided as to the propriety of inserting in the Constitution a clause providing for gradual emancipation. Some desired to avoid the contention the agitation of the subject would inevitably engender, while others thought that without the insertion of such a clause the consent of Congress would not be given to the separation from the parent State. Under these circumstances a compromise clause had been agreed on, which had received the unanimous vote of the Convention and been inserted in the Constitution. It provided simply that no slave should be brought, nor free person of color be permitted to come, into the State for permanent residence. This Constitution, as we have seen, was ratified by the people. This is the clause to which, when the Constitution was considered in Congress, exception was taken, and the result of the action of that body was, that the proposed State was constrained to substitute for the clause in question another, providing for gradual emancipation. On the 31st of December, 1862, an Act was passed by Congress entitled, "An Act for the Admission of West Virginia into the Union, and for other purposes," which, after reciting the proceedings I have before considered, and that both the Convention and the legislature of Virginia had requested that the new State should be admitted into the Union, declared the consent of Congress, that the forty-eight counties named in the Act should be formed into a separate and independent State, and admitted as such into the Union, provided, that said Act should not take effect until after a proclamation of the President of the United States should be issued, stating the fulfilment of the following condition, viz., — the people of the proposed State, by their Convention, were to insert in the Constitution, in lieu of the compromise clause, the following section: —

"The children of slaves, born within the limits of the State after the fourth of July, eighteen hundred and sixty-three, shall be free; and all the slaves within the said State, who shall, at the time aforesaid, be under the age of ten years, shall be free when they arrive at the age of twenty-one years; and all slaves over ten and under twenty-one years shall be free when they arrive at the age of twenty-five years; and no slave shall be permitted to come into the State for permanent residence therein."

This provision was, by the Convention, on the 18th of February, 1863, substituted for the one objected to by Congress, and the Constitution, as thus amended, was thereupon submitted a second time to the people for ratification or rejection. The election for that purpose was held on the 26th of March, 1863, and the result was that it was ratified by a very large majority.

As required by the Act of Congress, this result having been certified, under the hand of the President of the Convention, to the President of the United States, the latter issued his proclamation announcing the fact, and West Virginia, sixty days thereafter, is supposed, according to the terms of the Act, to have become a State in the Union.

§ 183. Whether the erection of West Virginia into a separate State was a constitutional act or not, depends on the question whether the so-called legislature of Virginia, which met at Wheeling on the 6th of May, 1862, and passed the Act purporting to give the consent of Virginia to its own dismemberment, was, in law, the legislature of the State of Virginia. If it was such, obviously the three conditions required by the Federal Constitution, and by the principles of our political system, for the valid dismemberment of a State, namely, the consent of the legislature of the State concerned, of the Congress, and of the inhabitants of the proposed new State, were all fulfilled.

That that legislature was the lawful legislature of Virginia is, in my judgment, beyond question.

1. It should be observed, that the legal character of that body is not to be determined by that of the Convention which called it together or constituted it. In the initiation and in the proceedings of that Convention there was doubtless, if not a revolutionary taint, at least an irregularity. But it is clear that an institution or a form of government, ordained by a Revolutionary Convention, may, by a formal ratification, or even by the acquiescence of the proper authority, become legal and valid.[1] Were not the General Assemblies established in the original thirteen States, by their first Constitutions, regarded from the point of view of "United America," legal Assemblies?

§ 184. 2. Properly considered, then, even if judged by the principles of public law alone, the question of the legality of the Virginia legislature is *one of general and continuous recognition as such.* Under the Federal Constitution, while the question is of the same nature, the scope of the recognition required to stamp that legislature as legal is narrowed to that of the United States. It is not necessary, in other words, that, to be legal and valid, that legislature should present itself backed by a major part of the citizens of the State. It is enough if it show itself to be a branch of a *de facto* government, in force in Virginia, and have upon its front the stamp of Federal recognition.

That this is a correct view of the case, follows from the decision of the Supreme Court of the United States in the case of Luther *v.* Borden, involving the legality of the so-called "People's Constitution" and government of Rhode Island.[2]

The fourth section of the fourth Article of the Constitution of the United States provides, that "the United States shall

[1] See § 179, *ante.* See also *Am. Law Reg.*, Vol. I. new series, pp. 651–660, case of Williamson *v.* Jones.

[2] 7 How. (U. S.) R. 1. For a full account of the proceedings from which this case arose, see *post*, §§ 226–228.

guarantee to every State in this Union a republican form of government, and shall protect each of them against invasion; and, on application of the legislature, or of the executive (when the legislature cannot be convened), against domestic violence."

The "people's party," constituting, as it was claimed, the majority of all the adult male citizens of Rhode Island, having, in defiance of the Charter government of that State, framed and adopted a Constitution and form of government, and attempted forcibly to put the same in operation, the question of the legality of that Constitution and government, as against that existing under the Charter of Charles II., came finally to be passed upon by the Supreme Court of the United States, in the case referred to. It appearing to the court, as a part of the history of the case, that the Governor of Rhode Island, under the Charter government, had applied to the President of the United States for the protection guaranteed in the section specified, and that the President had promised the same, and made arrangements to call out the militia to sustain the Charter government, should it become necessary — thus, by an authentic act, recognizing such government as lawful and valid — it was held, Judge Taney delivering the opinion of the court, that this act of federal recognition, done in pursuance of the Constitution and laws of the United States, was decisive as to the legality of the Charter government, and as to the illegality of that of the "people's party."

The court say: —

"Under this article of the Constitution" (Art. IV. Sec. 4), "it rests with Congress to decide what government is the established one in a State; for, as the United States guarantees to each State a republican government, Congress must decide what government is established in the State before it can determine whether it is republican or not; and when the senators and representatives of a State are admitted into the councils of the Union, the authority of the government under which they are appointed, as well as its republican character, is recognized by the proper constitutional authority, and its decision is binding on every other department of the government, and could not be questioned in a judicial tribunal.

"So, too, as relates to the clause of the Constitution, providing for cases of domestic violence, it rested with Congress to determine upon the means proper to be adopted to fulfil this guarantee. They might, if they had deemed it most advisable to do so, have placed it in the power of a court to decide when the contingency had happened which required the Federal Government to interfere. But Congress thought otherwise; and by the Act of February 28, 1795, provided that, in case of an insurrection in any State against the government thereof, it shall be lawful for the President of the United States, on application of the legislature of such State, or of the executive (when the legislature cannot be convened), to call forth such numbers of the militia of any other State or States, as may be applied for, as he may judge sufficient to suppress such insurrection. This power, conferred upon the President by the Constitution and laws of the United States, belongs to him exclusively. The President has acted in the case of Rhode Island; not, it is true, by actually calling out the militia, on the application of the Governor of Rhode Island, under the Charter government, but by recognizing him as the executive of the State, by taking measures to call out the militia to support his authority, if it should be found necessary for the general government to interfere. This interference by the President, by announcing his determination, was as efficient as if the militia had been assembled under his orders; it ought to be equally authoritative; and no court of the United States would, knowing this decision, be justified in recognizing the opposing party as the lawful government."[1]

§ 185. Under whichever clause of the constitutional provision the case of Virginia should be thought to come,[2] the conditions necessary to bring it within the principles of this decision, were fulfilled.

1. By the first clause, the United States are required to guarantee to every State in the Union a Republican form of government. Such a guarantee involves an undertaking, first, that some government, acting in harmony with that of the Union,

1 Luther *v.* Borden, 7 How. (U. S.) R. 44.

2 Virginia, through her Governor, elected in pursuance of an Ordinance of the Wheeling Convention, of June 11, 1861, formally demanded of the *President* the fulfilment of the Constitutional guarantee in her favor, and the President admitted the obligation, and promised his best efforts to fulfil it. See the *Ann. Cyclop.* for 1861, Art. "*Virginia, Western*," citing a letter of Attorney-General Bates. The call upon the President, instead of upon Congress, would indicate that Virginia placed her case under the second clause of the Constitutional guarantee. See § 184, *ante*, opinion of Judge Taney.

shall be established in each State thereof; and, secondly, that the government so established, shall conform to our general republican scheme.

If, then, previously to the time when Congress passed the Act admitting West Virginia into the Union, Virginia be regarded either as having no legitimate government at all, or as having one or more whose conformity to republican standards was denied, Congress, by the very act of admitting into the Union a new State, whose formation was necessarily based on the consent of some Virginia legislature, recognized the consenting legislature as part of a legal and valid government. Such a recognition would be implied in that act. But it is not necessary to rest the case upon an implied recognition. The Act admitting West Virginia into the Union expressly refers to, and recognizes as a lawful body, the legislature of Virginia in question. In the preamble, there appears the following recital:— "And whereas, the *legislature of Virginia*, by an Act passed on the 13th day of May, 1862, did give its consent to the formation of a new State within the jurisdiction of the said State of Virginia," &c.

2. If, on the other hand, the case of Virginia be brought within the latter clause of the constitutional provision, requiring the United States to guarantee the States against domestic violence, or against invasion, the repeated acts of the United States in all its departments, recognizing the loyal government of Virginia of which the legislature in question was a part, as an existing State government, stamped that government and legislature as legal and valid. For over four years after the establishment of the loyal government of Virginia, the President of the United States was engaged, in concert with that government, in expelling from her borders the rebel invaders — during two years of that time, the senators and representatives of the new State of West Virginia, founded upon its consent, as upon that of a valid government, actually sitting in Congress.

For these reasons it is impossible to deny that the legislature of Virginia in question was a lawful legislature. What has been uniformly recognized as legal by the legislative and executive branches of the United States government, by the Constitution and laws made the exclusive judges of that fact, and to whose decision on the question, the Supreme Court of the United

States admits itself bound to conform, must be set down as legal.

§ 186. 2. The second variety of Conventions assembled since the establishment of the Federal Constitution, consists of such Conventions as have been called to frame Constitutions for new States, to be formed out of territory of the United States, organized under its authority, or acquired in an organized condition from foreign states.

For convenience, this variety may be subdivided into two others, comprising —

(*a*). Such Conventions as have been assembled regularly, in pursuance of enabling Acts of Congress; and

(*b*). Such as have been convened by the inhabitants, or the temporary governments of organized Territories, irregularly, without enabling Acts of Congress.

These will be considered in their order.

§ 187. (*a*.) Since the establishment of the Federal Constitution, in March, 1789, twenty-two new States have been formed out of Federal territory, and admitted into the Union. Conventions, concerned in framing Constitutions for fourteen of these States, have been regularly assembled under the authority of prior enabling Acts. These are those of Ohio, Louisiana, Indiana, Mississippi, Illinois, Alabama, Missouri, Texas, the first of the two Conventions of Wisconsin, that of Minnesota, the third of the four Conventions of Kansas, the second of the two Conventions of Nevada, the first of the three Conventions of Nebraska, and the first of the three Conventions of Colorado.

Respecting these Conventions, a detailed statement of facts is deemed unnecessary. I shall, therefore, confine myself to a brief reference to the principles by which their regularity is to be determined, and to a survey, equally brief, of the most general facts that preceded their call and assembling.

According to the principles developed in the second chapter of this treatise, the sovereign authority over the Territories, whether organized or unorganized, resides in the people of the United States; but while that is true, the exercise of this sovereign authority has, by the Constitution of the Union, been committed to the Congress of the United States. To these principles, universally recognized, add this other, that it is only the sovereign political body, acting through its representatives, by whom the Constitution of government existing in any State or Territory, can be changed or abolished, or the rights of territory or of jurisdiction belonging to such sovereign body, modified or abridged, and we have the key to the whole subject of Conventions in the Territories of the United States. To be legitimate, a Convention, called to erect a State out of Federal territory, or to frame for it a Constitution, must have been assembled with the knowledge and consent of Congress; to be regular, it must have been called by a formal Act of that body; and to give to the fruit of its labors any force or vigor whatever as law, it must submit it to the same assembly, as the principal depositary of the sovereign rights of the Union, for ratification or rejection.

Tested by these principles, the Conventions that framed the Constitutions under which the States above named were admitted into the Union, are believed to have been strictly regular and legitimate.

The course of proceeding uniformly pursued in such cases has been for the inhabitants of the Territory desiring to be transformed into a State, or for some branch of the Territorial government, to move the matter in Congress by petitions or memorials, and then for Congress, if the erection of a State be deemed proper and expedient, to pass an Act expressly authorizing the assembling of a Convention of delegates to pass upon the question of State organization, and, if that should be desired, to frame a Constitution.

In all the Acts of this kind, commonly known as "enabling Acts," conditions are imposed, upon compliance with which either the proposed State is in advance declared to be admitted into the Union, or the President is authorized to issue his proclamation announcing such compliance, and declaring the State thereupon to be admitted into the Union.

In nearly all the States embraced in this class, the final act, following after the formation of the Constitution according to the enabling Act, and the submission of the same to the judgment of Congress, has been the passage by the latter of a formal Act or resolution, reciting the proceedings of the Convention, and declaring, first, that the Constitution framed for the proposed State is republican in form; and, secondly, that the State is thereby admitted into the Union on a footing of equality with the original States. In Missouri and Nevada, the final act was a proclamation by the President of the United States, made in pursuance of a previous Act or resolution of Congress.[1]

§ 188. (*b*.) Belonging to the remaining variety of Conventions concerned in framing Constitutions for new States to be formed out of Federal territory, comprising such as have been called irregularly, without enabling Acts of Congress, there have been thirteen, assembled in twelve different States, namely, — the Convention of Tennessee, held in 1796, the three Conventions of Michigan, held in 1835 and 1836, those of Arkansas and Florida, held respectively in 1836 and 1838, the two of Iowa of 1844 and 1846, that of Wisconsin of 1847,[2] that of California of 1849, those of Kansas of 1855, 1857, and 1859, that of Oregon, the first of the two Conventions of Nevada, and the second, so-called, Convention of Nebraska, and the second and third Convention of Colorado.

These various Conventions will be considered with some particularity, beginning with that of Tennessee, the first in point of time.

Before entering, however, upon this examination, it will be useful to bring into view certain deeds, Acts of Congress, and treaties, whose provisions have been supposed to establish, if not the regularity of those Conventions, at least the essential rightfulness of their proceedings, in attempting without the formal consent of Congress, to erect their several Territories into States.

The Ordinance of 1787 for the government of the territory lying northwest of the river Ohio, the most important of these acts, provided substantially as follows: —

[1] For the several enabling Acts in these cases, see 2 *U. S. Stat. at Large*, 173–175 ; id. 641–643 ; 3 do. 289–291 ; id. 428–430 ; id. 489–492; id. 546–548; 5 do. 797 ; 9 do. 56–58 ; 11 do. 166 ; id. 269–272; 13 do. 30 ; id. 32 ; id. 47 ; 18 do. 474 ; 19 do. 5.

[2] The first Convention of Wisconsin, held in 1846, met in pursuance of an enabling Act of Congress ; the Convention framed a Constitution, which, being submitted to the people in April, 1847, was rejected. In the mean time, probably expecting that the people would adopt the Constitution, Congress, on the 3d of March, 1847, passed an Act admitting the State into the Union, upon condition that the Constitution should be ratified by the people. The rejection by the people left the Territory without a Constitution, and outside the Union. Whether it left it with an enabling Act for a second Convention is, in my judgment, doubtful. I have accordingly classed the second Convention, called by the Legislative Assembly of Wisconsin in October, 1847, to meet in the following December, by which the present Constitution of the State was framed, with those called without enabling Acts.

After dividing the territory northwest of the Ohio, now constituting the five States of Ohio, Indiana, Illinois, Michigan, and Wisconsin, into three prospective States, by lines corresponding in the main with the east and west boundaries of Ohio, Indiana, and Illinois, but extending to the Canadian frontier, with a proviso that they might, if Congress should deem it expedient, be made into five States, the Ordinance proceeds: — "And whenever any of the said States shall have sixty thousand free inhabitants therein, such State shall be admitted, by its delegates, into the Congress of the United States, on an equal footing with the original States in all respects whatever, and shall be at liberty to form a permanent Constitution and State government: *Provided*, The Constitution and government so to be formed shall be republican, and in conformity to the principles contained in these articles, and so far as it can be consistent with the general interest of the Confederacy, such admission shall be allowed at an earlier period, and when there may be a less number of free inhabitants in the State than sixty thousand."

The provisions of this Ordinance, framed under the Confederation, were continued in force after the adoption of the present Constitution of the United States, by an Act of the first Congress, that met under the latter.

Whatever rights, therefore, were secured by this Ordinance, belonged equally to the three States, or the five States, as the case might be, into which the territory covered by it should be divided.

The territory now known as the State of Tennessee was ceded to the United States by the State of North Carolina, of whose territory it had previously formed a part. The cession was not absolute, but was made upon certain conditions, afterward accepted by the United States, as will be more fully explained hereafter,[1] the purpose of which was to guarantee to the inhabitants of the ceded district the same rights secured by the Ordinance of 1787 to the inhabitants of the territory northwest of the river Ohio.

§ 189. The States of Arkansas, Iowa, Kansas, and Nebraska were framed out of territory acquired by the United States from France by the treaty of April 30, 1803, the third article of which contained the following provision: —

[1] See § 191, *post.*

"The inhabitants of the ceded territory shall be incorporated in the Union of the United States, and admitted as soon as possible, according to the principles of the Federal Constitution, to the enjoyment of all the rights, advantages, and immunities of citizens of the United States."[1]

In like manner, by the treaty of February 22, 1819, between the United States and his Catholic Majesty, the King of Spain, by which the territory known as East and West Florida was ceded by the latter to the former, it was provided as follows: —

"Article VI. The inhabitants of the territory which his Catholic Majesty cedes to the United States by this treaty, shall be incorporated in the Union of the United States, as soon as may be consistent with the principles of the Federal Constitution, and admitted to the enjoyment of all the privileges, rights, and immunities of citizens of the United States."[2]

Finally, by the treaty between the United States and Mexico of February 2, 1848, by which the former acquired California and New Mexico, it was stipulated on behalf of the inhabitants of the ceded territories, Article IX., as follows: —

"Mexicans who, in the territories aforesaid, shall not preserve the character of citizens of the Mexican Republic, conformably with what is stipulated in the preceding article, shall be incorporated into the Union of the United States, and be admitted at the proper time (to be judged of by the Congress of the United States) to the enjoyment of all the rights of citizens of the United States, according to the principles of the Constitution," &c.[3]

Covered by the provisions of this treaty were the States of California, Nevada, and Colorado, not to mention the Territories carved out of the ceded Mexican territory, but not yet admitted into the Union, — Utah, New Mexico, and Arizona.

The title of the United States to the original territory of Oregon having accrued to it by virtue of prior discovery and settlement, no conditions of any kind were attached to it.[4]

Thus, of the Territories comprised in the list now under consideration, which have proceeded irregularly to form themselves

[1] *U. S. Stat. at Large*, Vol. VIII. pp. 200–202.

[2] Id. pp. 252–258.

[3] Do. Vol. IX. pp. 922–930.

[4] See *Jefferson's Works*, ed. of 1854, Vol. VII. p. 51, letter from Jefferson to Mr Mellish.

into States, all, except Oregon, were acquired by the United States under deeds or treaties of cession containing stipulations binding the latter to admit them sooner or later into the Union, either when they should have come to have a population of sixty thousand free inhabitants, or as soon as it should be consistent with the principles of the Federal Constitution. The handle made of these stipulations will be seen when we come to consider the Conventions of the States named, separately, to which I now pass, beginning with that of the State of Tennessee.

§ 190. The early history of Tennessee was, in many respects, similar to that of Kentucky, detailed in previous sections.[1] Originally a part of North Carolina, the difficulties experienced by the latter in defending her, or even in administering government over her, led to such neglect, that early in the course of the war with England, Tennessee had set up an independent government, in defiance of the parent State, called herself the State of Frankland, elected a governor and other State officers, and prepared by arms to maintain her independent position. This rebellion was quelled, but the causes of it still operated, and finally resulted, after a series of transitions, about to be explained, in the admission of the district into the Union as the State of Tennessee.

The first act of importance in her history, after the suppression of the State of Frankland, was the passage by the legislature of North Carolina of an Act proposing, upon certain conditions, the cession to the United States of her western territory, now known as Tennessee — the motives leading to the cession being in the preamble declared to be, the repeated and earnest recommendation of Congress, made with a view to the payment of the public debts and to the establishing of the harmony of the United States, and the desire of the inhabitants of such Western territory, that the cession should be made, "in order to obtain a more ample protection than they have heretofore received." Amongst the conditions of this proposed cession, the fourth, and, for our purpose, the most important, was as follows: — *Provided*, "That the territory so ceded shall be laid out and formed into *a State or States, containing a suitable extent of territory*, the inhabitants of which shall enjoy all the privileges, benefits, and advantages set forth in the Ordinance of the late Congress for the government of the western territory of the United States."[2]

[1] See *ante*, §§ 173, 174.

[2] *U. S. Stat. at Large*, Vol. I. pp. 106–109.

By the same Act, the senators of the State of North Carolina, in Congress, were required to execute a deed of cession of the said territory, upon the conditions therein expressed, which was done, by a deed bearing date the 25th of February, 1790.

§ 191. A few days after the execution of the deed of cession, an Act was passed by Congress, approved April 2d, 1790, accepting the cession upon the conditions imposed.[1] In May of the same year, Congress passed a second Act, for the government of the ceded territory, providing, that it should constitute a single district; that the inhabitants should enjoy all the privileges, benefits, and advantages set forth in the Ordinance of the late Congress for the government of the territory northwest of the Ohio; and that the government of said territory should be similar to that which was then exercised," &c., &c.[2]

It is important now to note the provisions of the "Ordinance of the late Congress," thus variously designated as passed for the government of "the Western territory of the United States," and of "the territory Northwest of the Ohio," commonly known as "the Ordinance of 1787," so far as those provisions have a bearing on the construction of the deed of cession. That Ordinance, in the 5th Article of the part of it styled "the Compact," after providing for the division of the territory, covered by it, into not less than three nor more than five States, prescribes, that "Whenever any of the said States shall have *sixty thousand free inhabitants therein*, such State shall be admitted, by its delegates, into the Congress of the United States, on an equal footing with the original States in all respects whatever, and shall be at liberty to form a permanent Constitution and State government; *provided*, the Constitution and government, so to be formed, shall be republican; and in conformity to the principles contained in these articles, and, so far as it can be consistent with the general interest of the Confederacy, such admission shall be allowed at an earlier period, and when there may be a less number of free inhabitants in the State than sixty thousand."

This Ordinance, though adopted before the establishment of the Federal Constitution, and so, perhaps, in effect, repealed by that Act, was afterwards expressly revived by the Congress under the new Constitution, without any changes, except merely

[1] *U. S. Stat. at Large*, Vol. I. pp. 106–109. [2] Id. p. 123.

such as were necessary to adapt it to the altered state of things.[1] The right of admission into the Union, therefore, guaranteed by this Ordinance to the inhabitants of the territory northwest of the Ohio, was, by the effect of the deed of cession and of the Act of Congress accepting the same, incorporated into that deed, and became the right of the inhabitants of the Tennessee territory.

§ 192. The question whether the territory, thus ceded, should form one or more than one State, being left undecided, so that it could not be known when the contingency of there being sixty thousand free inhabitants, within the meaning of Congress, had happened, there was evidently room for a disagreement between that body and the Territory, or some portion of it, claiming admission into the Union as its right under the deed of cession. Such a disagreement actually arose, and was followed by a protracted and angry controversy, of which the effects are not entirely unfelt to this day.

§ 193. In July, 1795, the Territorial legislature of Tennessee ordered a census of the whole Territory to be taken, for the purpose of ascertaining whether there was the requisite number of inhabitants to entitle her to admission into the Union, according to the Ordinance of 1787 and the deed of cession. The Act for this purpose provided, that "if it should appear that there were sixty thousand inhabitants, counting the whole of the free persons, including those bound to service for a term of years, and excluding Indians not taxed, and adding three-fifths of all other persons, the Governor be authorized and requested to recommend to the people of the respective counties, to elect five persons for each county to represent them in Convention, to meet at Knoxville, at such time as he shall judge proper, for the purpose of forming a Constitution or permanent form of government."[2]

The census was taken in the autumn of 1795, and the result was, that there were declared to be 77,262 inhabitants, of whom 10,613 were slaves. In November, 1795, the Governor announced this result, and, in pursuance of the Act for that purpose, called on the people to elect delegates to a Convention to frame a Con-

[1] 1 *U. S. Stat. at Large*, p. 50. That the adoption of the present Constitution did repeal the Ordinance, has been expressly held by the Supreme Court of the United States. Strader *v.* Graham, 10 How. (U. S.) R. 82.

[2] Parton's *Life of Andrew Jackson*, Vol. I. pp. 169, 170.

stitution, to meet at Knoxville on the 11th of January, 1796. Accordingly, a Convention was elected, and met there on that day, consisting of fifty-five members, five from each of the eleven counties, and, on the 6th of February following, adopted the first Constitution of Tennessee. A copy of this Constitution was, on the 19th of the same month, forwarded by the Governor of the Territory to the President of the United States, with a notification that on the 28th of March, at which time the General Assembly of the State of Tennessee would meet to act on the Constitution, the temporary government established by the Congress would cease. This copy and notification, with accompanying documents, were received by President Washington on the 28th of February, and by him were, on the 8th of April, communicated to Congress. The claim of Tennessee to admission, based upon the provisions of the Ordinance of 1787, did not receive from that body a ready or an unquestioned assent. After an energetic discussion, however, an Act for the admission of the State was, on the 6th of May, 1796, passed by a vote of 43 to 30, and was approved by the President on the first of June following, to take effect immediately.

§ 194. The grounds of the opposition, which, in the Senate especially, was strenuous, were briefly as follows: That the compact, under which admission was claimed, was capable of two constructions: one, that so soon as sixty thousand free inhabitants should be collected within the Territory, they should be entitled to a place in the Union as an independent State; the other, that Congress must first lay off the territory into one or more States, according to a just discretion, defining the same by bounds and limits; and that the admission of the States thus defined should take place as their population respectively amounted to the number of free inhabitants mentioned; that is, that the sixty thousand could not claim admission into the Union, unless they were comprised within a State whose territorial limits had been previously ascertained by an Act of Congress; that the latter construction was the preferable one, because it was conformable not only to the spirit, but to the letter of the Ordinance and deed of cession, which contemplated the erection of Tennessee into "one or more States," as Congress might determine; that the Territory of Tennessee had no other or greater rights than had the Territories northwest of the Ohio, for whom the ordinance had been expressly enacted; and it could not be pretended that the latter would be entitled to admission into the Union as one State so soon as their population should amount to sixty thousand, because the Ordinance itself divided that country into three separate and distinct States, each of which must contain sixty thousand free inhabitants before it could claim to be received; that the action of Congress upon the question now would be regarded and followed hereafter as a precedent, and hence it was of the utmost importance that no sanction should be given to any proposition which expressly or even impliedly admitted that the people inhabiting either of the territories of the United States could, at their own mere will and pleasure, and without the declared consent of Congress, erect themselves into a separate and independent State; that the provision of the Ordinance relating to the admission of new States, when there should be sixty thousand free inhabitants within their respective limits, evidently contemplated the taking of a census, and as Congress were to act upon the result of such census, it was more proper that it should be taken in pursuance of its own order than by that of a community whom interest might lead to exaggerate its numbers, and whose report, therefore, if accurate, would be received with distrust; and, finally, that there was reason to doubt the accuracy of the count taken by the territorial government, since its orders required the sheriffs of the several counties to include in their enumeration all persons within their respective limits within the period allowed for making it, which was two months; hence, that the same men might have been counted in several counties, nay, in every county in the Territory, and that without any intentional fraud.[1]

§ 195. On the other hand, the friends of the bill contended, that the people of Tennessee became, *ipso facto*, a State, the moment they numbered sixty thousand free inhabitants, and that it became the duty of Congress, as part of the original compact, made at the time the Territory was ceded to the United States, to recognize them as such, and to admit them into the Union, whenever satisfactory proof was furnished to them of that fact; that, to the objections, that, previously to the proof of that fact being given, it was necessary that Congress should

[1] Benton's *Abr. Deb. in Cong.*, Vol. I. pp. 754–759; Id. Vol. XII. p. 751. See also Scott *v.* Jones, 5 How. (U. S.) R. 373.

have laid out and formed that territory into "one or more States," and that the proof of their number should have been given under direction and by order of Congress, the people being incompetent to give that proof themselves, it was a sufficient answer that both those objections supposed a construction of the Ordinance of 1787 and of the deed of cession, which was inadmissible, since it rendered that compact binding upon one party and not upon the other; that it was absurd to suppose that that Ordinance, whose object it was to establish the principles of a free government, and to determine with certainty the conditions of the admission of new States into the Union, had made the time when those people were to enjoy that government and be admitted as a member of the Union depend, not on the contingency of their having sixty thousand free inhabitants, but on certain Acts of Congress; in other words, on the sole will of Congress; that either it must be conceded that their admission depended solely on the condition of the compact being fulfilled, to wit, their having the population required, or it must be declared that it rested on another act, which might be done or refused by the other party; that, as to the return of the number of inhabitants, no mode had been fixed by the compact how that number should be determined, but, as by the Acts of Congress establishing temporary governments in the territory affected by the Ordinance of 1787, whenever they should have respectively five thousand inhabitants, the governors of the Territories were especially authorized to cause the enumeration to be made, there could be no doubt the same course was to be pursued with respect to their qualifications for becoming members of the Union; that, at most, it was merely a question of evidence; and, if no mode had been presented for taking the enumeration. it only made it more difficult for Congress or the territory to be satisfied of the fact of their having the requisite number, but that it could not affect the right; that, instead of caviling at the mode of proof, Congress ought to address itself to the task of weighing the evidence which the parties interested had collected and brought forward; that it would be well to consider the consequences of refusing, at that time and under those circumstances, to receive Tennessee into the Union; that, if it was desired to establish a temporary government there, it was doubtful whether that could be accomplished for the people believed that in changing their government they only exercised a right which had been secured to them by a sacred compact, and, under that belief, they would be disposed to defend it.[1]

§ 196. Respecting the illegitimacy of the first Tennessee Convention, there can be, in my judgment, no doubt. Saying nothing of the possible inaccuracy or falsification of the census, in fact, the cardinal objection remains, that one of the two parties expected to act officially upon the result of it, could not know that it was not fraudulent. It was taken by that one of the two parties which was alone interested to make the enumeration as great as possible. The probability of an honest count would have been much greater had it been made under the direction and superintendence of Congress.

Again: The Convention was called without an enabling Act of the body in whom was lodged, practically, the sovereignty of the Union, so far as relates to the Territories, — the Congress of the United States. The purpose of that Convention was to initiate a change in the mode and instrumentalities in and through which the sovereign body of the Union should exercise over the Territory of Tennessee its rights of sovereignty; that is, a change which should divest Congress of its jurisdiction to make local laws for the Territory, and give that power to a political organization, to be erected within the latter by the people thereof. Such a change involved the exercise of sovereignty, and could be effected only by the interposition of the sovereign body acting through some one of its recognized agents, forming the government of the Union.[2]

§ 197. Moreover, the argument of those who favored the admission of Tennessee, to the effect that, the right *at some time* to be admitted into the Union being conceded, the Territory would be legally justifiable in forcing her way into the Union, if Congress should neglect to take steps to admit her, whenever the right should have in fact accrued, is wholly unfounded. Undoubtedly, if Congress were, without good cause, to refuse, upon any conditions, to admit a Territory entitled to admission, such refusal would be an abuse of power, and if persevered in to a sufficient length, might justify or necessitate a revolution. But

[1] Benton's *Abr. Deb. in Cong.*, Vol. 1. pp. 754–759.

[2] See opinion of McLean, J., in Scott *v.* Jones, Lessee, &c., 5 How. (U. S.) R. 380–382.

the right to admit involves the right to refuse to admit, at least, within certain limits, as, until prescribed conditions are not only in fact fulfilled, but can be ascertained to have been fulfilled. Whether a Territory shall be admitted or not, is largely a question of expediency with reference to the national interests, and of that expediency the national legislature is, by the Federal Constitution, made the exclusive judge. In exercising its discretion, that body might act ignorantly or factiously, but it could hardly be said to act unconstitutionally; and no Territory could be justified, on constitutional grounds, in resorting to force, or to methods that involve it, to accelerate or reverse its decision. If, in the face of the dissent, or without the express initiative, of the Congress of the United States, a Territory were to proceed to frame — much more to establish — a State government, it would place itself outside the pale of the law, and invoke the methods and the forces of revolution.

For these reasons, I deem the first Convention of Tennessee legally without warrant or justification, and therefore revolutionary. And the argument is not affected by the fact that the action of that body was finally acquiesced in by Congress. The acquiescence of Congress might legitimate the *Constitution*, but could not remove from the body which framed it the revolutionary taint imparted to it in its inception. The only conclusion properly deducible from the acquiescence of Congress would be that, having the right to strangle the child, as illegitimate, it had seen fit to forego the exercise of that right, preferring, rather, on the whole, to receive it into the household, and confer upon it the privileges of offspring lawfully begotten.

§ 198. The people of the Territory of Michigan having, in 1832, by a vote of a decided majority, determined to apply for admission into the Union, the Legislative Council of the Territory, at their next succeeding session, memorialized Congress on the subject. A bill was accordingly reported, in February, 1833, for an enabling Act for that purpose; but, owing to the opposition of Ohio, growing out of disputes about boundaries, the bill was not passed. On the 6th of September, 1834, the Legislative Council of Michigan passed an Act, on the suggestion of the acting Governor of the Territory, Stevens L. Mason, providing for taking "a census of the inhabitants of the Peninsula, as well as of those west of Lake Michigan," with a view, if the population should be found sufficient, to take steps for the erection of a State out of said Territory. The result of the census was, that there were found to be within the limits of the Territory, eighty-seven thousand two hundred and seventy-three free inhabitants. Thereupon, the same body, on the 26th of January, 1835, passed an Act, entitled, " An Act to enable the People of Michigan to form a Constitution and State Government," in pursuance of which delegates were elected, and met in Convention at Detroit on the 11th of May, 1835. By this Convention a Constitution was framed and submitted to the people for adoption or rejection, at an election held on the 5th of October following, when it was ratified by a decisive vote of over five to one, and thereupon a State government in all its departments was organized.

By section 10 of the Schedule appended to the Constitution, it was made the duty of the President of the Convention, in case of its ratification, to transmit a copy of it, together with copies of the Act of the Legislative Council calling the Convention, and of so much of the census of the Territory as should exhibit the number of free inhabitants in the portion thereof comprised within the limits of the proposed State, to the President of the United States, with a request for admission into the Union. The limits of the State, as prescribed by the Legislative Council in its Act calling the Convention, as well as by the Convention, embraced a strip of territory now belonging to the State of Ohio, being so much of that State as lies between its north line, as at present established, and an east and west line, running through the southerly point of Lake Michigan. It should be also noted that the proposed State did not embrace the whole of the Territory of Michigan, as established by the Acts of Congress of January 11, 1805, and April 18, 1818, but only that part of the Territory lying between the Lakes Michigan and Huron, extending south as far as to an east and west line running through the southerly point of Lake Michigan — thus cutting off that large tract forming a part of the Michigan Territory, which afterwards constituted the Wisconsin Territory.

§ 199. On the 9th of December, 1835, in the first week of the session, President Jackson called the attention of Congress to the application of Michigan for admission, in a special message, in which, without expressing any opinion on its merits, he based the claim of that State upon the provision of the Ordinance of 1787, above referred to. The matter coming up for consideration, objection was made to the admission with the boundaries specified in the Constitution, and exception was taken to the irregular proceedings of the Legislative Council in calling the Convention without the authorization of Congress.[1] A bill, however, was finally carried, admitting the State into the Union, but requiring a modification of its boundaries. By this Act, entitled, "An Act to establish the Northern Boundary Line of the State of Ohio, and to provide for the admission of the State of Michigan into the Union, upon the conditions therein expressed," approved June 15, 1836, it was provided, as follows: —

"That the Constitution and State government which the people of Michigan have formed for themselves be, and the same is hereby, accepted, ratified, and confirmed, and that the State of Michigan is hereby admitted into the Union. . . . *Provided always*, and this admission is upon the express condition, that the said State shall consist of, and have jurisdiction over, all the territory included within the following boundaries, and over none other, to wit" (setting forth the boundaries). The Act then provided as follows: —

[1] The subject was specially called to the attention of the Senate by a memorial from "the Senate and House of Representatives of the State of Michigan," relating to the right to be admitted into the Union. On motion of Mr. Hendricks, of Indiana, this memorial was refused, accompanied by a declaration "that the Senate regard the same in no other light than as the voluntary act of private individuals." Mr. Ruggles, of Maine, moved to strike out this declaration; and, on the yeas and nays, his motion was rejected by a vote of 30 to 12. Thus the Senate solemnly determined that the so-called "Legislature of Michigan" was a mere assembly of private individuals. Again, the bill for the admission of Michigan into the Union, when first reported by the committee, provided, that the assent to the boundaries of the State, required by the third section, should be given by their senators and representatives in Congress, and by the legislature of the State. Senator Wright, of New York, moved to strike out this provision, and to insert in its stead, that the assent required should be given by "a Convention of delegates elected by the people of the said State for the sole purpose of giving the assent herein required." This motion was carried by an unanimous vote of the Senate, — again indicating the opinion of that body, that the so-called State organization was a nullity, and its supposed officers and representatives entitled to no consideration. See Speech of James Buchanan, in Benton's *Abr. Deb. in Cong.*, Vol. XIII. p. 80.

"Sec. 3. And be it further enacted, that, as a compliance with the fundamental condition of admission contained in the last preceding section of this Act, the boundaries of the said State of Michigan, as in that section described, declared and established, shall receive the assent of a Convention of delegates elected by the people of the said State, for the sole purpose of giving the assent herein required." [1]

It then made it the duty of the President of the United States, as soon as such assent should have been given, to announce the same by proclamation, whereupon the admission of the State into the Union was to be complete.

By this Act, it will be observed, no mode was specified in which the Convention to pass upon the condition should be called. One, however, was elected, in pursuance of an Act passed July 25, 1836, by the State legislature, as organized under the Constitution. This Convention met on the 26th of September following, and rejected the condition imposed by Congress, on the ground that that body had no right to annex such a condition to the admission of the State into the Union, according to the terms of the Ordinance of 1787, and communicated its dissent to the President of the United States.

Public opinion, however, being much divided upon the question, subsequently a new Convention,[2] composed of delegates elected by a spontaneous movement of those who favored admission on the terms proposed by Congress, was called on the 14th of December, 1836, by which the condition was declared accepted. By information gathered subsequently to its adjournment, it was made to appear probable that from 5000 to 6000 votes for members of this latter Convention had been cast at the first election for those who had opposed the acceptance of the condition in the former Convention, and from 8000 to 9000 in favor of those who urged the acceptance of the same. Such was the evidence that Michigan had complied with the fundamental condition imposed by Congress.

§ 200. The action of this Convention having been immediately communicated to the President of the United States, that officer, on the 26th of the same month — December, 1836 — sent a message, with accompanying documents, to the Senate, em-

[1] *U. S. Stat. at Large*, Vol. V. pp. 49, 50.

[2] Derisively called "the frost-bitten convention."

bodying the request of Michigan for admission into the Union, and committing the whole matter to the judgment of Congress; the President at the same time stating, that had the information communicated arrived during the recess of Congress, he would have issued his proclamation declaring the State admitted into the Union, since, in his opinion, she had complied with the requisite terms of admission. This message being referred to the Committee on the Judiciary, a bill was reported to the Senate for the admission of the State into the Union, of which the preamble was as follows: —

"*Whereas*, in pursuance of the Act of Congress of June the fifteenth, eighteen hundred and thirty-six, entitled 'An Act to establish the Northern Boundary Line of the State of Ohio, and to provide for the Admission of the State of Michigan into the Union,' a Convention of delegates, elected by the people of the said State of Michigan for the sole purpose of giving their assent to the boundaries of the said State of Michigan, as described, declared, and established in and by the said Act, did, on the fifteenth of December, eighteen hundred and thirty-six, assent to the provisions of said Act," enacts that said State be admitted, &c.

As a prelude to the discussion of this bill, Mr. Morris, Senator from Ohio, moved to strike out this preamble, as asserting what was not the fact, namely, that the Convention, which undertook to assent to the change of boundaries required by Congress, was a legal Convention; which motion he afterwards varied by moving an amendment to the preamble, recapitulating the proceedings in Michigan under the Act of June 15, 1836, but expressing or implying no opinion as to the validity of the Convention. The result of the discussion was, that the bill, as modified by him, was finally passed and approved January 26, 1837, and the State thereby admitted into the Union.[1]

§ 201. Tested by the canons laid down in previous sections of this chapter, it is easy to see that neither of the three Conventions concerned in the formation of Michigan into a State was regular, or, strictly speaking, legitimate. But there was, nevertheless, a difference between them in respect of the degrees of their irregularity, the first and third being far more obnoxious to exception than the second.

[1] *U. S. Stat. at Large*, Vol. V. p. 144.

The first Michigan Convention — that by which the Constitution under which the State finally became a member of the Union was in the main framed — was an illegitimate body, because called by the Territorial legislature, not only without the authorization of Congress, but implicitly, at least, against its will.[1] As we have seen, the people of the Territory had for several years been endeavoring, unsuccessfully, to procure the passage by Congress of an enabling Act, permitting the erection of the Territory into a State. What Congress, which alone had jurisdiction to act in the matter, had refused to permit, obviously could not be done but in derogation and defiance of its authority.

§ 202. The second Convention, assembled under the Act of Congress of June 15, 1836, was irregular, as having been called, not without an apparent authorization of Congress, but by an unauthorized and unconstitutional body within the Territory, the so-called State legislature. The Act of January 15, 1836, as we have seen, admitted the Territory into the Union, " on condition that a Convention, specially called for the purpose," should assent to the boundaries thereby prescribed. There being no specification of the body by which the Convention should be called, the question as to the body intended, or most proper, to perform the duty, was one of presumptions. There were in the Territory two bodies which might be conceived to be authorized to perform it: first, the Legislative Council, the proper law-making power of the Territory, elected under the authority of Congress; the body by which the Convention had been called that had framed the State Constitution, referred to in the Act; and, secondly, the body elected under the new Constitution, and denominated the State legislature — an assemblage of men unknown to the only laws in force in the Territory, those of Congress; and not only so, but so far antagonistic to Congress itself, that if the former had any validity whatever, as a local legislature for the Territory, the latter had absolutely none; the jurisdictions of the two being exclusive of each other. Under these circumstances, it is clear, that when Congress prescribed the calling of a Convention to do an act which was to impart its first and only vitality to the State organization, it did not intend

[1] See *post*, § 209, note, Opinion of Attorney-General of the United States.

to call upon a member of that embryo organization to initiate such Convention; but rather upon the legislative branch of the Territorial government, created by itself, in the enjoyment of all its functions, and in every way qualified to perform the duty.

§ 203. The third Convention, got together by a spontaneous movement of the people, to reverse the action of the second, was, if possible, the least regular, the most distinctly illegitimate, of the three. It was a body resting on the authority neither of Congress, the Legislative Council of the Territory, nor the supposed State legislature, but on that of individuals only, acting outside of the law. Under an established Territorial government, such a body would be revolutionary, even if resting on the vote of every inhabitant of the Territory, since no assemblage of citizens could have power to speak in the name of such government, much less in that of Congress, unless specifically authorized by law. The Act of July 15, 1836, requiring a Convention to be called, furnished no such authorization. That it did not, was implicitly admitted by the public men and citizens generally of Michigan, since, in pursuance of it, they first proceeded to call such Convention through the State legislature, and only had recourse to the action of irresponsible caucuses, when the Convention called by the legislature had refused its assent to the condition of admission imposed by Congress.

§ 204. Enough has, perhaps, been said to show the true character of the third Michigan Convention, but the question of its regularity is so important, that I venture to borrow somewhat freely from the speeches of senators of the United States, made in the course of the discussion of the final bill for the admission of Michigan into the Union.

After rehearsing the facts relating to the three Conventions, substantially as detailed above, the Hon. John C. Calhoun said:—

"Such are the facts out of which grows the important question,—Had this self-constituted assembly" (the third Convention) "the authority to assent for the State? Had they the authority to do what is implied in giving assent to the condition of admission? That assent introduces the State into the Union, and pledges in the most solemn manner to the constitutional compact, which binds these States in one confederated body; imposes on her all its obligations, and confers on her all its benefits. Had this irregular, self-constituted assemblage the authority to perform these high and solemn acts of sovereignty in the name of the State of Michigan? She could only come in as a State; and none could act or speak for her without her express authority; and to assume the authority without her sanction, is nothing short of high treason against the State.

"Again; the assent to the conditions prescribed by Congress implies an authority in those who gave it to supersede in part the Constitution of the State of Michigan; for her Constitution fixes the boundaries of the State as part of that instrument which the condition of admission entirely alters, and to that extent the assent would supersede the Constitution; and thus the question is presented, whether this self-constituted assembly, styling itself a Convention, had the authority to do an act which necessarily implies the right to supersede in part the Constitution. But, further: the State of Michigan, through its legislature, authorized a Convention of the people, in order to determine whether the condition of admission should be assented to or not. The Convention met; and, after mature deliberation, it dissented to the condition of admission; and thus again the question is presented, whether this self-called, self-constituted assemblage, this caucus — for it is entitled to no higher name — had the authority to annul the dissent of the State, solemnly given by a Convention of the people, regularly convoked under the express authority of the constituted authorities of the State? [1]

"If all, or any of these questions," he continued, "be answered in the negative; if the self-created assemblage of December had no authority to speak in the name of Michigan; if none to supersede any portion of her Constitution; if none to annul her dissent to the condition of admission regularly given by a Convention of the people of the State, convoked by the authority of the people of the State, to introduce her on its authority would be not only revolutionary and dangerous, but utterly repugnant to the principles of our Constitution.

[1] Mr. Calhoun, in this speech, commits the error of supposing the second Convention, called by the so-called State legislature, to be regular. It has already been seen, that this was certainly not so, and it will be shown in a subsequent section, on high constitutional authority, that the position assumed on that subject, in previous sections, is the true one. See § 208, *post.*

The question then submitted to the Senate is, had that assemblage the authority to perform these high and solemn acts?

"The chairman of the Committee on the Judiciary holds that this self-constituted assemblage had the authority; and what is his reason? Why, truly, because a greater number of votes were given for those who constituted that assemblage than for those who constituted the Convention of the people of the State, convened under its constituted authorities. This argument resolves itself into two questions: the first, of fact, and the second, of principle. I shall not discuss the first. . . . . I come to the question of the principle involved; and what is it? The argument is, that a greater number voted for the last Convention than for the first, and, therefore, the acts of the last, of right, abrogated those of the first; in other words, that mere numbers, without regard to the forms of law or the principles of the Constitution, give authority. The authority of numbers, according to this argument, sets aside the authority of law and the Constitution. Need I show that such a principle goes to the entire overthrow of our Constitutional government, and would subvert all social order? It is the identical principle which prompted the late revolutionary and anarchical movement in Maryland,[1] and which has done more to shake confidence in our system of government than any event since the adoption of our Constitution; but which, happily, has been frowned down by the patriotism and intelligence of the people of that State."[2]

§ 205. On the same side followed the Hon. Mr. Ewing, of Ohio, in an argument so lucid and satisfactory that, at the risk of extending this discussion too far, I extract from it the following passage, relating to the evidence tending to show that the third Michigan Convention in fact represented the people of the Territory. He said: —

"An assemblage of the people, in meetings which are familiarly denominated caucuses, was held in some of the counties, and mutually agreed to call a new Convention. Committees

1 The movement referred to was one organized in Maryland to call a Convention "by the inherent and unalienable rights of the people, and, without a legislative Act, to alter and change the Constitution of the State." The ground on which it was justified, was, that the government of the State did not represent the voice of the numerical majority of the people, and that the authority of law and Constitution was nothing against that of numbers.

2 Benton's *Abr. Deb. in Cong.*, Vol. XIII. pp. 73, 74.

get together, and, after consultation, publish a time and place at which it is to assemble. The whole matter was utterly unauthorized, save by party organization, and was the effect of such organization. Will any man dispute it? Will any man pretend that this latter Convention was the effect of a simultaneous and spontaneous impulse of the whole people of Michigan?[1] Is there any the least proof of such being the fact? The Convention originated in county calls; and all the counties but two joined in the plan, and held elections for delegates. What evidence is there of any regularity in these elections? Let us look at the papers. We have, to be sure, the Act of the Convention itself, giving the assent of the State to the Act of admission, and which was transmitted to the President of the United States. And we have the certificate of General Williams, said to have been the presiding officer of the Convention, and the names of the delegates. But there is not any official act or signature of any officer known to the laws either of Michigan or of the United States; not the slightest proof of the election or qualification. That paper, containing the assent of Michigan in a matter so important, is not at all authenticated. Where do you find the law according to which it was conducted? There is none. It rests on nothing. There was a meeting of certain individuals held at a place called, I believe, Ann Arbor; and we have certain resolutions of theirs, which are to avail against the doings of a Convention held in pursuance of a law of the State, and all whose acts are fully and legally authenticated. I cannot recognize such a paper. I should do violence to my own judgment should I receive it. Even the chairman of the Judiciary Committee could not do it. He called upon the senators elect (and whose admission here is to follow the passage of the bill) to say that everything at this self-styled Convention was well and duly conducted; and they do say so, and give the private letters of certain individuals to that effect. And they give, further — and that I understand to be the evidence principally relied on — an article from a Detroit

[1] Had it been the effect of such an impulse, the case would have been no better. It will not do to admit, that the inhabitants of a Territory can, even by a perfectly unanimous vote, destroy a political organization set over them by Congress, and substitute for it one of their own creation.

newspaper, stating that such an election was had, such Convention held, 3000 more votes were given for the delegates to this last Convention than for those who constituted the first Convention.[1] This, sir, is the evidence to support an organic law of a new State about to enter the Union! Yes, of an organic law, the very highest act a community of men can perform. Letters, referring to other letters! and a scrap of a newspaper!"[2]

§ 206. On the other hand, among the numerous and able speeches maintaining the regularity of the Convention, that which expounded most fearlessly the principle upon which alone it could be justified, was that of Senator Niles, of Connecticut. He said: —

"The question before the Senate he regarded a very simple one; it was really a question of facts; merely, whether the condition of the Act of Congress of last session, providing for the admission of Michigan into the Union, had been complied with. In considering this question, gentlemen had gone into the first principles of government, and made what he regarded a bold attack upon popular power, on the fundamental principle of popular sovereignty, which lies at the foundation of all our institutions. These doctrines were rather antiquated; they belonged to the school of the Restoration in England, and the political writings of Sir Robert Filmer; they were the present doctrines of the conservatives in all the governments in Europe . . . . the doctrines to which the 'Alien and Sedition laws,' and other kindred measures, owed their origin. . . . . And what were those doctrines? They were, that the people could not be trusted; that they were their own worst enemies; that all the disorders, real or imaginary, that prevailed, were attributable to a wild spirit of democracy — to popular frenzy. An honest and fearless expression of opinion concerning men and measures, was denounced as a spirit of insubordination, disorganization, and rank jacobinism. A distinguished leader of that party, now no more . . . . I allude . . . . to Fisher Ames . . . . declared, that the disease which threatened general and universal ruin to our institutions and our future prospects, was rooted

1 By the first Convention, the speaker means what I have designated the second.

2 Benton's *Abr. Deb. in Cong*, Vol. XIII. p. 78.

deep; that it had found its way into the very hearts of the people. This disease was democracy; it was the will and sovereignty of the people. . . . . And it was the aim of those in authority to put down that wild spirit of democracy by the strong arm of power, and to maintain their authority, not through the public will, and as an emanation from it, but in opposition to it; in defiance of it. It was for this purpose that the Alien and Sedition laws were passed. . . . . But that great scheme failed; and are its exploded, reprobated doctrines now to be revived? Are we now to be told that there is no political power remaining in the people; that having established and put in operation governments, they have parted with all political power whatever; that they cannot revise or new-model this form of government they have themselves established, unless in pursuance of a provision in the Constitution, or in accordance with a law of the legislature? This is maintaining that sovereignty resides in the constituted authorities and not in the people at large; it is raising the creature above his creator; the agent above the principal. It is exalting the legislature above, and making it independent of, the constituent body. The Constitutions of most of the States contain some provisions for altering or amending them; some, through the agency of a Convention, and some, otherwise. But such constitutional provision is not inconsistent with, and cannot take away, the right and power of the people, acting in their primary, original capacity, to change their system of government. This is a right which they have not delegated, and which, of course, must abide with the people at large. Conventions of the people may be called, and often are, in pursuance of a law of the legislature; yet this is a mere matter of convenience. But does the law confer on them their power? That is the question. If it does, then a legislature can grant to another body greater power than it possesses itself; even the power to change or destroy those very forms under which it exists; a power to destroy the legislature itself. This is preposterous, and shows the absurdity of the principle contended for. If a Convention does not derive its power from the legislature, from whence can it derive it except from the people in their primary, elementary capacity, and wholly independent of the legislature and constituted authorities? If this is not a true idea of a Convention of the people, he should like to be informed what a Convention is. The senator from South Carolina (Mr. Preston) asks, who and what are the people? . . . . The people, in one sense, are the whole population of a State; but, in a political sense, the people were that portion of the population which possessed the political power in a State; it did not mean women or children, but the whole body of citizens with whom the political power resided."[1]

§ 207. The question of the validity of the first Michigan Convention as well as of the Constitution and State government erected by it, have been the subject of judicial determination. The so-called legislature of Michigan, elected under the Constitution in anticipation of admission into the Union, met and organized on the 3d of March, 1835. On the 26th of March, 1836, ten months before Michigan was admitted into the Union, this legislature incorporated the members of "The Detroit Young Men's Society," and to that society accrued, as was claimed, the title to certain real estate in Detroit. Ejectment was brought and defended by the defendants in possession, on the ground that the society was not a corporation or body politic, in the law, capable to take or hold the premises in question, nor to exercise any corporate rights under color of the Act of incorporation, for the reason, that there was no legal State government, and, consequently, no State legislature competent to pass laws, at the time the Act was passed, within the Territory of Michigan. The argument, in brief, was, that a Territorial and State government cannot coexist within the same Territory; that the former having been established by Congress, with whom rests the exercise of Territorial sovereignty, it must continue to exist, until regularly superseded by the power which created it, which, in the case of Michigan, did not occur until the State was admitted into the Union, January 26, 1837; or, at the earliest, until the Act of conditional admission of June 15, 1836.

The Supreme Court of Michigan, however, held that the Society was a valid corporation, the Territory having been, it was said, transformed into a State on the adoption of the Constitution by the people, October 5th, 1835; that the legislature, organized in November following, was a legitimate legislature;

[1] Benton's *Abr. Deb. in Cong.*, Vol. XIII. pp. 90-92.

that Article V. of the compact contained in the Ordinance of 1787, "secured absolutely and inviolably to the people of the Territory of Michigan, as established by the Act of Congress of January 11, 1805, the right to form a permanent Constitution and State government, whenever said Territory should contain sixty thousand free inhabitants; that that right could in no way be modified or abridged, or its exercise controlled or restrained, by the general government; that the assent of Congress to the admission of Michigan into the Union, was only necessary, because the older States, represented in Congress, possessed the physical power to refuse a compliance with the terms of compact contained in the Ordinance of 1787, and there was no third party to which the State could resort to enforce such compliance; and that the right to such admission, secured by Article V. of the Ordinance, became absolute and unqualified, on the adoption of the Constitution of the State, and the organization of the State government." [1]

Upon this decision a writ of error was taken to the Supreme Court of the United States, by whom the case was dismissed *for want of jurisdiction.* In deciding the case, the Court held, that an objection to the validity of a statute, founded upon the ground that the legislature which passed it were not competent or duly organized under Acts of Congress or the Constitution, so as to pass valid statutes, is not within the cases enumerated in the twenty-fifth section of the Judiciary Act, and, therefore, that the Court had no jurisdiction over the subject; that, in order to give the Federal Supreme Court jurisdiction, the statute, the validity of which is drawn in question, must be passed by a State, a member of the Union, and a public body owing obedience and conformity to its Constitution and laws; that if public bodies, not duly organized or admitted into the Union, undertake, as States, to pass laws which might encroach on the Union or its granted powers, such conduct would have to be reached either by the power of the Union to put down insurrections, or by the ordinary penal laws of the States or Territories within which these bodies are situated and acting, but that their measures are not examinable by the Supreme Court of the United States on a writ of error.[2]

1 Scott *v.* The Detroit Young Men's Society's Lessee, 1 Doug. Mich. R. 119.

2 Scott *v.* Jones, Lessee of the Detroit Y. M. Soc., 5 How. (U. S.) R. 343

§ 208. A very able dissenting opinion was, however, delivered by Justice M'Lean, in which he asserted the jurisdiction of the court. In the course of this opinion, he said: —

"No serious objection need be made, in my judgment, to the assemblage of the people in Convention" (the first Convention) "to form a Constitution, although it is the more regular and customary mode to proceed under the sanction of an Act of Congress. But, until the State shall be admitted into the Union by an Act of Congress, the Territorial government remains unimpaired. No act of the people of a Territory, without the sanction of Congress, can change the Territorial into a State government. The Constitution requires the assent of Congress for the admission of a State into the Union; and 'the United States guaranty to every State in the Union a republican form of government.' Hence the necessity, in admitting a State, for Congress to examine its Constitution. The Act 'to incorporate the Detroit Young Men's Society' was the exercise of sovereign power, a power totally repugnant to the sovereignty of the Union in its Territorial form. Until the 26th of January, 1837, Michigan was not admitted into the Union and recognized as a State. Whatever effect this admission may have, by way of relation, on the exercise of the political powers of the State prior to that time, is not now the question. The question of jurisdiction relates to the time the Act was passed and its validity. This Act of incorporation was repugnant to the Constitution of the United States, under which the Territorial government was organized. It was repugnant to the laws of Congress which formed that organization. It was an exercise of sovereignty incompatible with the sovereignty of the Union in all its legal forms. And this Act was declared by the Supreme Court of Michigan to be valid. I cannot conceive a clearer case for jurisdiction. . . . . The two sovereignties of the State and the Territorial government cannot exist at the same time within the same limits." [1]

For a decision, on the other hand, denying the validity of the State government of Michigan before the admission of the State into the Union, see Myers *v.* The Manhattan Bank, 20 Ohio R. 283, — a decision, for every reason, of authority at least equal to that of the Michigan Court.

[1] Scott *v.* Jones, Lessee, &c., 5 How. (U. S.) R. 380–382.

§ 209. As the majority of the court expressly announced in this case that they decided no point but that of jurisdiction, it cannot be assumed that they would have coincided with Justice M'Lean in the points discussed by him, had they sustained the jurisdiction. But certainly there is deducible from the opinion of the court an inference that the Territory of Michigan did not become a State for the purpose of giving rights, which might be the subject of litigation before the courts of the Union, in other words, did not become a State for all purposes, until admitted into the Union. The only observation I wish to make upon the case is, that our Constitution knows no purgatorial condition, intermediate between that of a Territory and that of a State.[1] So long as a political organization is a Territory, it is not in any sense or for any purpose a State, and, *vice versa*. Once a Territory always a Territory, until a change be effected by an Act of Congress. A Territory may seize upon the reins of power, and make of itself, *de facto*, a State, but when it does so it departs from legal and regular courses, and enters upon the field of revolution.[2]

§ 210. In the cases of the other States whose Constitutions were framed partly or wholly by Conventions called without enabling Acts, there are no circumstances that require extended notice, except in that of Kansas. Arkansas framed her Constitution in January, 1836; Florida, in January, 1839; Iowa, in November, 1844, but modified it, under the requisition of Congress, in relation to boundaries, in May, 1846; Wisconsin, in

[1] On this subject see a speech of Henry Winter Davis, in Appendix to Vol. XXXVII. *Cong. Globe*, pp. 261, 262.

[2] In connection with the subject discussed in the foregoing sections, see an opinion of Attorney-General B. F. Butler, officially given, respecting certain movements made in Arkansas in 1835, with a view to erect the Territory of that name into a State, without an enabling Act. The Governor of the Territory, apprehending that the Territorial legislature, or the people of the Territory, would call a Convention to form a State Constitution without the authority of Congress, wrote a letter to the President of the United States, asking instructions for his guidance in such a case. This letter being referred to the Attorney-General for his opinion on the constitutional and legal questions presented, that officer discussed at length two questions, stated by him thus: — 1. As to the power of the Territorial legislature to pass laws authorizing the formation of a Constitution and State government; and, 2. As to the right and authority of the citizens of the Territory to take measures for that purpose, and the extent to which such

February, 1848; California, in October, 1849; Oregon, in September, 1857; Nevada, in 1864; Nebraska, in 1866; and Colorado, in 1876. As we have already intimated, these States were all of them, excepting Oregon, formed under a claim of right arising from stipulations in treaties or deeds of cession directly binding the United States to admit them upon the happening of certain contingencies. Generally, the right thus secured was kept prominently in view in the discussions attending the transition from the condition of Territories to that of States, and many of the Conventions carefully recited in the preamble to the Constitutions framed by them the terms of the treaty or deed of cession by which their right was guaranteed. Thus the preamble to the Constitution of Arkansas contained the following recital: —

"We, the people of the Territory of Arkansas, by our representatives in Convention assembled, at," &c., ... "having the right of admission into the Union . . . . by virtue of the treaty of cession by France to the United States of the Province of Louisiana, in order to secure to ourselves," &c.

The Florida Constitution contained a similar clause, but basing the right to admission on the treaty with Spain, before referred to, as that of Tennessee had based the right in the case of that Territory, on the deed of cession from North Carolina.

Oregon, alone of all the States admitted into the Union, can

proceedings, if it be lawful to enter on them at all, may properly be carried, consistently with the Constitution and laws then in force.

The answers given to these questions are eminently sensible and instructive, but are too long for insertion here. To the first question, after considering the organic law of the Territory, and comparing it with the Federal Constitution, he answers, in substance, that to suppose such a power in the Territorial legislature, involving, as it would, that of altering or abrogating the Territorial government established by the Act of Congress, would be manifestly absurd. The second question he answers by saying, that the inhabitants can legally take no step toward the formation of a Constitution or State government that will be of any validity without the previous authorization of Congress. Still the people have a right, he says, to assemble and petition the government for a redress of grievances; and if they throw their petition into the form of a Constitution and accompanying memorial praying admission into the Union, he perceived no legal objection to their doing so, nor to any measures taken to collect the sense of the people in respect to the same. — *Opinions of the Attorneys-General*, Vol. II. p. 726. See also Webster's *Works*, Vol. VI. p. 485, where a similar sentiment is expressed.

point neither to an enabling Act of Congress authorizing her to form a Constitution and State government, nor to a stipulation giving her inhabitants the right to be admitted into the Union, on a contingency specified, and thus after a sort excusing them for a clamorous assertion of the right, when it seemed to be unreasonably withheld. The conduct of that Territory, therefore, in anticipating the action of Congress, was not only irregular and illegal, but inexcusable.

Respecting the mode in which the Conventions in these several cases were called, it is sufficient to say that it was, by the action of the Territorial legislatures, or of officers connected with the administration of the Territorial governments. Thus, those of Tennessee, Arkansas, Florida, Iowa, Oregon, and Nevada, were called by the legislative Assemblies of those Territories respectively, and that of California by General Riley, military governor of that Territory, acting at the instance of General Taylor, President of the United States.

§ 211. Of the four Conventions called to frame a Constitution for the State of Kansas, the first was assembled by a spontaneous movement among the inhabitants of the Territory, without the authority of law.

The first step was the calling of a meeting by "many voters," at Lawrence, on the 14th of August, 1855, "to take into consideration the propriety of calling a Territorial Convention preliminary to the formation of a State government, and other subjects of public interest." At this meeting were, passed resolutions requesting "all *bonâ fide* citizens of Kansas Territory" to elect in their respective election districts, in mass Convention or otherwise, three delegates for each representative in the legislative Assembly, according to the proclamation of Governor Reeder of the 10th of March previous, to assemble in Convention on the 19th of September, 1855, "*to consider and determine upon all subjects of public interest*, and particularly upon that having reference to a speedy formation of a State Constitution, with an intention of an immediate application to be admitted as a State into the Union of the United States of America."

Two weeks before the assembling of the Convention thus called, a second meeting was held at Big Springs, at which the project of holding a Convention for the purpose indicated was commended, and the determination expressed to resist unto blood the laws of the "spurious legislature" of the Territory, should peaceable remedies fail. The reference to the spurious legislature was aimed at the legislative Assembly of the Territory organized under the auspices of the United States government, ostensibly by the inhabitants of the Territory, but, as it was charged, in fact, by an invading horde of pro-slavery voters from Missouri. The meeting then proceeded openly to recommend "throughout the Territory the organization and discipline of volunteer companies," for the purpose of giving effect to the preceding resolutions.

In pursuance of the recommendation of these meetings, a Convention was held at Topeka on the 19th of September, at which it was determined to hold another Convention at the same place, on the fourth Tuesday of October, for the purpose of forming a Constitution and State government; and, to this end, such proceedings were had as were deemed necessary for giving the notices, conducting the election of delegates, making the returns, and assembling the Convention. The Convention met at Topeka on the fourth Tuesday of October, 1855, and formed a Constitution, which, being submitted to the people, was, by a large majority of those who voted, adopted.[1]

§ 212. In passing judgment upon the Topeka Convention, it is not within the scope of my design to inquire whether or not the facts of the situation justified the calling of that body, as one step in a revolution, but simply whether it was a legitimate Constitutional Convention. Viewed thus, in its legal aspects, it is impossible to regard it as other than illegitimate. It was called neither by Congress, the Territorial legislature, nor any officer connected with the public administration in the Territory, but in opposition to and in defiance of them all. Such a body will not for a moment bear examination on legal or constitutional grounds.

Neither the Convention itself, nor those who called it, so far as I am aware, ever pretended that they were proceeding in the line of law and precedent; but, despairing, as was openly intimated,

[1] See the Report of the Senate Committee on Territories of March 12, 1856; also the Minority Report, from the minority of the same Committee, respecting the proceedings of this Convention and the affairs of Kansas in general.

in the resolutions passed by the mass meetings which called that body, of securing their rights under a government foisted upon them by their pro-slavery enemies, they notified the world that they proposed to seek them at the point of the bayonet, and organized themselves into military companies, accordingly. Although, therefore, the friends of Kansas in Congress, in their eager endeavors to secure for its inhabitants their civil and political rights, by admitting them into the Union, under the Topeka Constitution, made use of arguments which seemed to vindicate the legality of the body which framed it, still candor compels me to admit, that the enemies of equal rights not only had the best of the argument, but alone used the language of truth and soberness. The case was, perhaps, the not uncommon one of the law and substantial justice appearing upon opposite sides in a controversy. However that may be, it is certain that President Pierce was right, when, in his message of January 24, 1856, relating to the proceedings of the Topeka Convention, he said of them: "No principle of public law, no practice or precedent under the Constitution of the United States, no rule of reason, right, or common sense, confers any such power as that now claimed by a mere party in the Territory. In fact, what has been done is of a revolutionary character. It is avowedly so in motive and in aim, as respects the local law of the Territory. It will become treasonable insurrection if it reach the length of organized resistance by force to the fundamental or any other federal law, and to the authority of the general government."

§ 213. In the mean time, the first Territorial legislature of Kansas had passed an Act to take the sense of the people on the question of calling a Convention to form a State Constitution, the vote to be taken at the election in October, 1856. At that election, accordingly, a vote was taken at which a majority of the votes cast — the free-State men not voting — was in favor of calling such a Convention. In pursuance of this vote, the Territorial legislature, on the 19th of February, 1857, passed another Act providing for the election, on the 15th of June following, of delegates to a Convention, to meet on the first Monday of September, for the purpose of framing a Constitution preparatory to admission into the Union. The election of delegates was held on the day appointed, the Free-State men still withholding their votes, the entire vote for delegates being about 2200. The delegates elected assembled at Lecompton on the 5th of September, adjourned over to October, and then reassembling, framed the instrument known as the Lecompton Constitution.

§ 214. Although there is no doubt that this Convention was called by the Territorial legislature, with the consent of the executive of the United States, still, Congress not having authorized it, it was unquestionably irregular and illegal. To use the language employed by President Buchanan at a later day, to characterize the action of the Topeka Convention, that of the Lecompton Convention was "a usurpation of the same character as it would be for a portion of the people of any State to undertake to establish a separate government within its limits, for the purpose of redressing any grievance, real or imaginary, of which they might complain, against the legitimate State government." To which he added, that "such a principle, if carried into execution, would destroy all lawful authority, and produce universal anarchy." The view thus entertained by President Buchanan, of the Topeka Convention, however, was not that taken by him of its successor, the Convention held at Lecompton, on the call of the Territorial legislature. In the same paragraph of his message, from which the above passage is extracted, the President vindicated the regularity of the latter Convention, on the ground that it had virtually been called in pursuance of an enabling Act. The foundation for this assertion he found in the provisions of the Kansas-Nebraska Act, as it has been called, which formed the organic law of the territory of Kansas. Section 14 of that Act declared it to be the true intent and meaning thereof, "not to legislate slavery into any Territory or State, nor to exclude it therefrom, but *to leave the people thereof perfectly free to form and regulate their domestic institutions in their own way*, subject only to the Constitution of the United States."

Respecting this clause of the Act, President Buchanan said: "That this law recognized the right of the people of the Territory, without an enabling Act, to form a State Constitution, is too clear for argument. For Congress 'to leave the people of the Territory perfectly free,' in framing their Constitution, 'to form and regulate their domestic institutions in their own way, subject only to the Constitution of the United States,' and then to say, that they shall not be permitted to proceed and frame the Constitution in their own way, without express authority from Congress, appears to be almost a contradiction in terms."

§ 215. For a refutation of this position of President Buchanan, — if that can need refutation which upon its face is absurd, — I shall avail myself of a speech of the Hon. Henry Winter Davis, of Maryland, made when the Lecompton Constitution was under discussion in Congress. Having considered the question whether Congress may not, in certain cases, with propriety, ignore irregularities and admit Territories into the Union whose Constitutions have been framed without the previous authorization of Congress, he proceeds as follows: —

"But the argument is irrelevant; for the question is not whether Congress *may*, in its discretion, recognize Constitutions formed by the people without authority of law; but whether a Territorial legislature has, *in point of law*, authority to legalize the election of a Convention, to give the Convention itself a legal existence, to vest *it* with *legal* power to bind not merely the people, but the *Congress?* No one denies the power of Congress to admit Tennessee and Florida, yet nobody ever asserted any legal validity in their proceedings before admission.

"The language of the organic Acts, and the proceedings of Congress thereupon, are decisive. The Territories divide themselves into two great classes. In Ohio, Illinois, Indiana, Missouri, Mississippi, Alabama, Arkansas, Tennessee, and Michigan, the legislature had 'power to make laws, *in all cases*, for the good government of the people of the said Territory, not repugnant to, or inconsistent with, the Constitution and laws of the United States.' In Wisconsin, Minnesota, Oregon, Florida, and Iowa, the power of the legislatures was declared to extend — in the identical words of the Kansas-Nebraska Act — 'to all rightful subjects of legislation, not inconsistent with the Constitution and laws of the United States.'

"Congress has construed both forms of expression by passing enabling Acts for both classes. Not only for Ohio, Louisiana, Missouri, Mississippi, Alabama, Illinois, and Indiana, but also for Wisconsin, Minnesota, and Oregon,[1] did Congress pass Acts

[1] This is a mistake. We have already seen, (§ 188, *ante*,) that Oregon called the Convention which framed her first Constitution, without an enabling Act.

specially *authorizing* them to call a Convention and form a State government; and, in every instance, excepting Wisconsin, those bills provided all the details of the Convention, the number of delegates, its time of assembling, the modes under which the delegates should be elected. It is plain, Congress thought the power of Congress 'to make laws in all cases,' necessarily extended '*to all rightful subjects of legislation.*' It is plain, Congress thought neither form of expression authorized the temporary Territorial government to create a Convention to form a Constitution, which would begin to operate only after the Territorial legislature itself had ceased. Its power to govern was confined to the Territory, a temporary contrivance for temporary purposes; involved in all the local interests and conflicts of Territorial politics, and not safely to be intrusted with the providing for a Constitution. In a word, they were authorized to make laws to govern the Territory; but a law for a Constitutional Convention was no law for governing a Territory at all.

"The case is stronger under the Kansas Act, for it reserves to Congress the power to make two or more States or Territories out of that Territory; and, if Congress have the right to make *two* States, it is absurd to suppose it gave the Territorial legislature power to make one State of it."[1]

§ 216. The application of the Territorial legislature, through its Convention for admission into the Union under the Lecompton Constitution, although seconded by President Buchanan, and in general by the administration party in Congress, was substantially unsuccessful. After a long contest, the friends of the measure were forced to consent to a conditional admission, the bill, known as the English bill, which was finally passed, providing for admission of the State into the Union, on condition that the people of Kansas should first vote to accept certain propositions, beneficial to their interests, *and* the Lecompton Constitution; but further providing, that should the propositions, *and*, with these, the Lecompton Constitution, be rejected, the people of the Territory should be at liberty to form for themselves a Constitution and State government by the name of Kansas, and might elect delegates for that purpose *whenever, and not before*, it should be ascertained by a census duly and legally taken, that the population of said Territory equalled or exceeded

[1] See Appendix to Vol. XXXVII. *Cong. Globe*, p. 262.

the ratio of representation for a member of the House of Representatives of the Congress of the United States. The Act then prescribed the mode in which the delegates, who might thus be elected, should proceed to form a Constitution, and provided for submission of the same to the people of Kansas, and for the admission of the State thus formed into the Union under it.

In pursuance of this Act, the people of Kansas went into an election on the 3d of August, 1858, the result of which was, that the propositions of Congress, and, consequently, the Constitution submitted, were rejected by over ten thousand majority.

By this vote, the condition in which the Territory of Kansas was left was this: An enabling Act, passed by Congress, authorized her people to form a Constitution and State government "whenever, and not before," it should be "ascertained by a census duly and legally taken," that her population equaled or exceeded the ratio of representation fixed by Congress for electing members of the national House of Representatives — that is, when its population should number 93,340.

In the mean time, a Convention, called by the Territorial Legislature, had met on the 23d of March, 1858, at Leavenworth, and had framed a Constitution prohibiting slavery. It was ratified by the people, but, on presentation to Congress, was refused consideration, on the ground that the Territory had not the requisite population.

Such, however, was the rapidity with which the Territory was peopled, that on the first Tuesday of June, 1859, a fourth Convention, called in like manner by the Territorial Legislature, met at Wyandotte, by which a Constitution was framed, — the population at the time of the call of the Convention exceeding the number limited by the Act above named. Under this Constitution the Territory was afterwards admitted into the Union, January 29, 1861.

§ 217. 3. The third variety of Conventions, called since March 4, 1789, consists of such as have been assembled for the revision of existing Constitutions of States, members of the Union.

These may be subdivided into several classes, as follows: —

(*a*). Such as have been convened, for legitimate constitutional purposes, regularly, that is —

I. By the legislatures of the respective States, acting either —

1. In pursuance of special provisions of such existing Constitutions, or —

2. If no such provisions exist, under their general legislative authority.

II. By the electors, choosing delegates to such Conventions, under the name of Councils of Censors, at fixed dates, in obedience to direct constitutional provision.

III. By such Councils of Censors, to adopt or to reject the Constitution or amendments framed by them.

(*b*). Such as have been called, for legitimate constitutional purposes, irregularly, — that is, either —

1. In disregard of constitutional provisions prescribing particular modes in which amendments to the Constitution should be effected, or —

2. In defiance of the existing governments of the States concerned, though in pretended conformity to constitutional principles.

(*c*). The so-called Secession and Reconstruction Conventions held before and since the late civil war.

These several classes will now be considered in the order indicated.

§ 218. (*a*). I. 1. Of the first subdivision of the first class, comprising such Conventions as have been regularly called by legislative authority, exercised in pursuance of express constitutional provisions, there have been held thirty-four Conventions.[1]

[1] The following Conventions belong to this list: Those of Alabama, 1875; California, 1878; Delaware, 1831 and 1852; Florida, 1885; Georgia, January, 1789, May, 1789, 1795, 1798, and 1877; Illinois, 1847, 1862, and 1869; Iowa, 1857; Kentucky, 1799 and 1849; Louisiana, 1844; Maryland, 1864 and 1867; Massachusetts, 1820; Michigan, 1850 and 1867; Mississippi, 1832; Missouri, 1875; Nebraska, 1875; New Hampshire, 1791, 1850, and 1876; New York, 1867; North Carolina, 1875; Ohio, 1850 and 1873; Tennessee, 1834; and West Virginia, 1872.

In reference to one of the Conventions placed in this list, that of Delaware, 1852, there has been much controversy in that State. The facts relating to the call of that body are as follows: — The Delaware Constitution of 1831 contained this clause, — "No Convention shall be called but by authority of the people; *and an unexceptionable way* of making their sense known will be for them to vote by ballot on the third Tuesday of May in any year, for or against a Convention; and if *a majority of all the citizens of the State having a*

As, in calling these Conventions, the requirements of the respective State Constitutions are believed to have been strictly complied with, it is necessary only to point out the circumstance that they were all called by the direct action of the State legislatures.

§ 219. 2. The second subdivision, consisting of Conventions called for legitimate constitutional purposes by the respective State legislatures, under their general legislative power, without the special authorization of their Constitutions, comprises twenty-seven Conventions.[1]

The question of the legitimacy of Conventions thus called, I shall have occasion to consider in other parts of this work, when treating of the relations of legislatures to Conventions,

right to vote for representatives vote for a Convention, the next General Assembly shall call one; the majority of all the citizens of the State having a right to vote for representatives to be ascertained by comparing the number of votes for a Convention with the highest number of votes cast at either of the three preceding general elections."

Feb. 26, 1851, an Act was passed by the General Assembly, taking the sense of the people as to the call of a Convention; and Feb. 4, 1852, was passed another Act, which, reciting that at the before appointed election there was a majority of votes for a Convention, called one accordingly, to meet at Dover on the first Tuesday of December following. Now, according to the rule laid down in the Constitution, there was not a majority of votes for this Convention, though there was a majority of all the votes cast. When the Convention met, therefore, the legitimacy of the call was denied by some, on the ground that *the unexceptionable way* pointed out in the Constitution was the only legal way that could be pursued. By those sustaining the legitimacy of the body, on the other hand, it was contended, that the clause of the Constitution was not peremptory, but recommendatory; and of that opinion was the Convention — with which I am inclined to concur.

I am indebted for the facts detailed in this note to the Hon. Willard Hall, of Wilmington, Delaware, who was a member of the Convention.

[1] The Conventions embraced in this list are the following: Those of Arkansas, 1874; Connecticut, 1818; Georgia, 1833 and 1839; Indiana, 1850; Louisiana, 1852 and 1879; Massachusetts, 1853; Missouri, 1845, 1861, and 1865; New Jersey, 1844; New York, 1801, 1821, and 1846; North Carolina, 1835; Pennsylvania, 1837 and 1872; Rhode Island, 1824, 1834, 1841, and 1842; South Carolina, 1790; Tennessee, 1870; Texas, 1876; Virginia, 1829 and 1850.

In regard to the Indiana Convention of 1850, it should be observed that, although there was contained in the Indiana Constitution of 1816 power to the legislature to call a Convention every twelfth year thereafter, that is, in 1828, 1840, 1852, &c., the power was not pursued, but a Convention was called independently of it by an Act approved January 18, 1850.

and of the powers of the former resulting from those relations.[1] I shall, therefore, here only observe, — 1. That, whenever a Constitution needs a general revision, a Convention is indispensably necessary; and if there is contained in the Constitution no provision for such a body, the calling of one is believed to be directly within the scope of the ordinary legislative power; and, 2. That, were it not a proper exercise of legislative power, the usurpation has been so often committed with the general acquiescence, that it is now too late to question it as such. It must be laid down as among the established prerogatives of our General Assemblies, that, the Constitution being silent, whenever they deem it expedient, they may call Conventions to revise the fundamental law.

In four or five of the Conventions of this class, the objection has been raised, that they were illegitimate bodies, because called by the legislatures without special authority in the respective Constitutions. This was the case in the Virginia Convention of 1829, the Pennsylvania Convention of 1837 and 1872, the New York Convention of 1846, and the Massachusetts Convention of 1853. But the objection has commonly been urged by a minority, whose party or other interests inclined them to look with disfavor upon any change of the existing Constitution. In a large proportion of these cases the objection seemed the more plausible, for the reason that there existed constitutional provisions for effecting specific amendments to the organic law in a more summary manner, by a vote of the people upon propositions made by the General Assembly. There having been provided, it has been said, a mode in which constitutional changes might be effected, it was a violation of legal analogy to infer a power to do substantially the same thing in another way, not authorized specifically by the Constitution, according to the well established rule, *expressio unius est exclusio alterius*. We shall, however, have occasion in subsequent chapters to consider the subject more at large, and shall there find that the maxim has no application to this case, since the legislative acts in question do not authorize the doing of the same, but of a different thing, in a different manner.[2] For our

[1] See *post*, ch. vi. §§ 376–418, and ch. viii. §§ 570–574 *f*.

[2] See *post*, ch. vi. § 395, and ch. viii. §§ 572–574 *c*.

For discussions of the supposed irregularity of the Conventions mentioned,

present purpose, it may be regarded as settled, that the legislature of a State has authority to provide for calling a Convention, whenever there is no Constitutional provision at all relating to amendments of the fundamental law, or the provisions are confined to the enactment of specific amendments, and a general revision is deemed necessary.

§ 220. II. Of Conventions chosen at fixed dates, by the electors, under the name of Councils of Censors, in obedience to direct Constitutional provision, and therefore called regularly for legitimate Constitutional purposes; and,

III. Of Conventions thus called by Councils of Censors to adopt or to reject the Constitutions or amendments framed by them, the only cases which have occurred, within the period mentioned, have occurred in Vermont.[1]

The first Vermont Constitution, that of 1777, provided, Sec. XLIV., that in 1785, and every seven years thereafter, there should be elected thirteen persons, to be called a Council of Censors, whose duty it should be to inquire generally into the public administration, and with power "to call a Convention, to meet within two years after their sitting, if there appears to them an absolute necessity of amending any article of this Constitution which may be defective, explaining such as may be thought not clearly expressed, and of adding such as are necessary for the preservation of the rights and happiness of the people."

Under this provision, Councils of Censors were chosen every seven years, from 1785 to 1869, by which numerous Conventions were called,[2] the regularity of which cannot be impeached. A

see *Deb. Va. Conv.* 1829, pp. 884, 885; *Deb. Mass. Conv.* 1853, Vol. I. pp. 35, 83; Vol. III. pp. 123, 124, Speech of the Hon. Joel Parker; *Deb. Pa. Conv.* 1837, Vol. I. pp. 183–187.

[1] Class II. comprises the Councils of Censors of 1785, 1792, 1799, 1806, 1813, 1820, 1827, 1834, 1841, 1848, 1855, 1862, and 1869.

Class III. comprises the Conventions of 1786, 1793, 1822, 1828, 1836, 1843, 1850, 1857, and 1870.

The Councils of 1799, 1806, 1813, and 1862 called no Conventions.

[2] See Appendix B. Although the Conventions of class III. are nominally the only Conventions, yet, considering that the function of the Councils is precisely that of a Convention, when confining itself to its normal duty of recommending Constitutional changes, I have reckoned those bodies in the list of Conventions. Viewing them thus, the so-called Convention in Vermont is but

similar provision was contained in the Pennsylvania Constitution of 1776, Sec. XLVII., but the Council held only two sessions, and failing to agree, no Convention was called. Afterwards, the legislature, in disregard of the Constitution, took upon itself to summon a Convention, which met in 1789 and abolished the cumbrous provision. It was also abolished in Vermont by the Convention of 1870.

§ 221. (*b*). 1. Of the next class of Conventions, comprising such as have been called for legitimate constitutional purposes, but irregularly, in disregard of constitutional provisions prescribing particular modes in which alone amendments to the Constitution should be made, there have been but three deserving of mention; that of Pennsylvania of 1789; that of Delaware of 1792; and that of Maryland of 1850. A brief history of these will be given in the order in which they occurred.

As stated in the last section, the Pennsylvania Constitution of 1776, Sec. XLVII., provided a special apparatus for revising or amending that instrument, through the instrumentality, first, of a Council of Censors, and, secondly, if deemed necessary by the latter, of a Convention to be called by that body. The terms of this constitutional provision were identical with those of Section XLIV. of the Vermont Constitution above quoted, and indeed were the model after which the latter was drawn. But beside this section, there was inserted in the preamble to the Pennsylvania Constitution the following important restrictive clause, namely:—

. . . . "We, the representatives of the freemen of Pennsylvania . . . . do, by virtue of the authority vested in us by our constituents, ordain, declare, and establish the following *declaration of rights and frame of government* to be the Constitution of this Commonwealth, and to remain in force therein forever unaltered, except in such articles as shall hereafter, on experience, be found to require improvement, and which shall, by the same authority of the people, fairly delegated, *as this frame of government directs*, be amended or improved," &c.

the people of the State, by a small body of representatives, at the second remove, instead of by the electors, at the first, ratifying the proposals of a Council performing the function of a Convention. As the Vermont Constitution styles this ratifying body a Convention it has been included in the list, on the same ground as were those which in the several States of the Confederation ratified the Federal Constitution.

§ 222. The Council of Censors having twice met — in 1783 and 1784 — and having failed by a constitutional majority to agree upon calling a Convention, to consider amendments deemed necessary by a majority of that body, adjourned September 25, 1784, to meet again on the day preceding the next general election; but in fact never again convened.

At the session of the General Assembly in March, 1789 — the year preceding the time fixed by the Constitution for the meeting of the next Council of Censors — resolutions were passed calling the attention of the people to the subject of amending their Constitution, and suggesting that, should they concur with the House in the opinion that a Convention should be called for that purpose, it would be "convenient and proper for them to elect members of a Convention of the same numbers and in the like proportions for the city of Philadelphia and the several counties with those of their representatives in Assembly, on the day of the next general election, at the places and in the manner prescribed in cases of elections of members of Assembly by the laws of the State." The resolutions further provided, that on the pleasure of the people in the premises being signified to them at their next sitting, they would provide by law for the expenses of the Convention, and, if requested, would appoint the time and place for the meeting thereof.

At the next session of the Assembly, in September following, it appearing to the satisfaction of that body, by petitions and the reports of members, communicating the results of their inquiries during the vacation of the Assembly, that a Convention was expedient and proper in the general opinion of the people of the State, resolutions were passed calling a Convention, to meet at Philadelphia on the fourth Tuesday in November, 1789. Delegates were accordingly elected, and, assembling on the day appointed, framed and established the Constitution of 1790.

§ 223. Article XXX. of the Delaware Constitution of 1776 provided as follows: —

"No article of the Declaration of Rights and Fundamental Rules of this State agreed to by this Convention, nor the first, second, fifth (except that part thereof that relates to the right of suffrage), twenty-sixth, and twenty-ninth articles of this Constitution, ought ever to be violated on any pretence whatever; *no other part of this Constitution shall be altered, changed, or dimin-*

ished, without the consent of five parts in seven of the Assembly, and seven members of the Legislative Council."

As the Assembly contained seven members only, and the Legislative Council nine members, it is evident that no change whatever could be made in the Constitution, legally and constitutionally, save by the direct action of both the Assembly and the Legislative Council, and then only by a majority of five-sevenths of the one and seven-ninths of the other. The phraseology being negative, no room was left for the employment of any alternative method. A *Convention* could not be called for the purpose of changing or abolishing the Constitution without a palpable infringement of its provisions.

Nevertheless, in 1791, amendments to the Constitution being very generally deemed necessary, the legislature passed an Act calling a Convention, with a view to effect them. In the preamble to this Act, the grounds upon which that body based its action are exhibited in the following terms: —

"By the thirtieth article of the Constitution of this State, the power of revising the same, and of altering and amending certain parts thereof, is vested in the General Assembly; and it appears to this House, that the exercise of the power of altering and amending the Constitution by the legislature would not be productive of all the valuable purposes intended by a revision, nor be so satisfactory and agreeable to our constituents; and that it would be more proper and expedient to recommend to the good people of the State to choose deputies for this special purpose to meet in Convention." Then follows the enacting clause authorizing the election of delegates to a Convention to change the Constitution. A Convention was accordingly elected, with the general approbation of the people of Delaware, by which a new Constitution was framed and put in operation in the following year.

§ 224. The action of the people of Maryland, in calling the Convention of 1850, was similar to that just described. Section LIX. of the Maryland Constitution of 1776, contained this provision: —

"That this form of government, and no part thereof, shall be altered, changed, or abolished, unless a bill so to alter, change, or abolish the same shall pass the General Assembly, and be published at least three months before a new election, and shall be confirmed by the General Assembly after a new election of delegates, in the first session after such new election."

The whole power of the State having, under the Constitution of 1776, come to be exercised by a minority of the citizens, efforts were repeatedly made, but without success, to induce the General Assembly to effect the needed changes in that instrument. In 1837, the impatience of the reform-party nearly led to hostile collisions with the existing government, — the former taking steps to call a Convention for the purpose of framing a new Constitution, without the authority and against the will of the General Assembly; and the latter, through the State executive, denouncing such an act as rebellious, and threatening with punishment all who should engage in it.[1] At length, at the session of the General Assembly held early in 1850, an Act was passed submitting to the people of Maryland the question, whether or not a Convention should be called to revise the Constitution. The vote was taken at an election held in May of that year, and resulted in a majority in favor of a Convention. The whole number of votes cast, however, was only about twenty thousand — the total number of voters in the State being over sixty thousand. A Convention was thereupon assembled, on the first Monday in November, 1850, which, in a session lasting until the 13th of May, 1851, adopted the Constitution known as that of 1851. This Constitution was, in pursuance of one of its own provisions, submitted to a vote of the people on the 4th of June following, and being ratified by a majority of those voting, went into operation on the 4th of July, 1851.

§ 225. Respecting the three Conventions of this class, I need only observe, that in respect of their origin, they were wholly illegitimate. The first — that of Pennsylvania — was not called in the mode provided by the Constitution, to which, whether wisely or unwisely, the people of the State had, by a solemn provision of that same instrument, specially restricted their agents and themselves. So also with that of Delaware. By its Constitution of 1776, no organic change could be made except upon the concurrence of two conditions: first, a favoring vote of five parts in seven of the Assembly; and, second, a like vote of seven of the nine members of the Legislative Council. Nor

1 M'Sherry's *Hist. Md.*, pp. 348–353.

could any such change be constitutionally made in Maryland except on the concurrence of three conditions: first, the passage, by the General Assembly, of an Act for that purpose; second, the publication of the proposed amendment for the information of the people, for at least three months prior to a new election of that Assembly; and, third, the confirmation of the Act by such new Assembly. Not one of the conditions mentioned was fulfilled in the case of either of those States. The legislatures, instead of proceeding to do what was desired, by their own direct action, as their respective Constitutions commanded, attempted to delegate the work to Conventions called by themselves — a thing clearly prohibited by those instruments. It is obvious, that to justify such proceedings, on legal grounds, would be to take away from the fundamental law that characteristic quality by which it is the law of laws — the supreme law of the land. If it be not the supreme law, for all the purposes of a Constitution, in the American sense, it might as well be a piece of blank paper.

In this discussion I do not meddle with the question, Whether, in the cases indicated, the course taken to effect constitutional changes was necessary or not? in other words, Whether the revolution consummated by the legislatures of those States was unavoidable, and so morally defensible? It may be admitted, that the constitutional provisions I have quoted were injudicious; that in communities like ours, rapidly increasing in wealth and population, they were certain, sooner or later, to lead to heart-burnings, if not to outbreaks of revolutionary violence. But this does not affect the legal question I am discussing, namely, Whether, tested by the principles of our constitutional system, the mode of securing the desired reforms did not involve a flagrant usurpation on the part of those legislatures? There is, in my judgment, no way in which the action of those bodies, in those cases, can be justified, except by affirming the legal right of the inhabitants of a given territory, organized as a body politic, to meet at will, as individuals, without the authority of law, and, on their own claim that they are the people of the State, to dictate to the government such changes in its laws, Constitution, or policy, as they may deem desirable. This question I do not stop here to discuss, as it will be necessary for me to consider it fully hereafter, when I come to treat of the remaining class of Conventions, called irregularly, though for legitimate constitutional purposes, to which I now pass.

§ 226. 2. The next variety of Constitutional Conventions, called irregularly, namely, those called in defiance of the existing governments of the States concerned, though in pretended conformity to constitutional principles, embraces but a single Convention, — the so-called "People's Convention" of Rhode Island, held in 1841.[1]

For nearly two centuries prior to the meeting of that Convention, Rhode Island had governed herself under a Charter of King Charles II., of a character so democratic that, at the Revolution, it was deemed unnecessary to alter or abolish it. As the State advanced in wealth and population, however, some of the provisions of the Charter became very unsatisfactory to a large portion of the citizens, particularly that regulating the right of suffrage; and naturally so; for at the time the agitation commenced, which resulted in the call of the People's Convention, the legislature of Rhode Island was elected by less than one half of the white male adult resident citizens of the State; and so far was the body from representing the people proportionately, that the majority of the Assembly was elected by about one-third of the freemen.[2] Rhode Island, moreover, originally agricultural, had undergone great changes, — many of its smaller towns becoming great manufacturing centres; while what were once its chief cities had become much diminished in population. Thus Newport, formerly the principal town, had sunk to a population of 8000, while Providence had risen to nearly 24.000; yet Newport continued to be represented by six, and Providence by four, representatives, which was also the number sent by Portsmouth, whose population was but 1700.[3]

To change this system, efforts had been made from time to time for many years. In 1824, a Convention was called by the legislature, and a Constitution framed and submitted to the people, but was rejected by them. Ten years later another Convention was called, but broke up without completing its task. In January, 1841, the legislature called a third Convention, which met in November following; but, adjourning for the express pur-

[1] Two Conventions were held in Rhode Island in 1841, one legitimate, before referred to (§ 219, *note* 1), and the other above described.

[2] *Democratic Rev. for* 1842, Vol. II. p. 70.

[3] Ibid.

pose, as was declared, of obtaining the opinion of their constituents on the expediency of extending the electoral franchise, assembled again in February, 1842, and framed a Constitution, which, being submitted to the people on the 21st, 22d, and 23d days of March, 1842, was rejected. Finally, in June, 1842, a fourth Convention was called by the legislature, which met in September, framed a Constitution, and submitted it to the people on the 21st, 22d, and 23d days of November, when it was ratified and put in operation.[1] In the mean time, however, before this successful result had been reached, the popular impatience had vented itself in revolutionary proceedings, having for their object the formation of a new Constitution without the consent or privity of the existing government. These proceedings will be described in the following section.

§ 227. The efforts of those citizens who desired an extension of the right of suffrage in Rhode Island, having failed, as it seems, through the unwise reluctance to diminish their own power, of those who were voters by existing laws, there were formed throughout the State, in 1840 and 1841, suffrage associations, the object of which was declared to be, "to diffuse information among the people, upon the question of forming a written republican Constitution."

On the 5th of July, 1841, a mass Convention of the friends of the suffrage movement met at Providence, at which were said to have been present six thousand free white male inhabitants of the State, of the age of twenty-one years and upwards. One of the results of the meeting was the appointment of a State committee with large powers in relation to the conduct of the reform agitation, and among them the power to call a Convention at a future day. On the 20th of the same month, accordingly, the State committee issued a call, "by virtue of authority in them vested by the said mass Convention," notifying the inhabitants of the several towns and of the city of Providence, to assemble together, and appoint delegates to a Convention, for the purpose of framing a Constitution for the State, and providing, that every American male citizen, twenty-one years of age and upwards, who had resided in the State as his home, one year preceding the election of delegates, should have a right to vote for delegates to said Convention, to draft a Constitution

[1] Bartlett & Woodward's *Hist. U. S.*, Vol. III. pp. 609, 610.

to be laid before the people of said State; and that every thousand inhabitants in the towns in said State should be entitled to one delegate, and each ward in the city of Providence, to three delegates.[1]

In pursuance of this notification, certain of the citizens of Rhode Island, having the prescribed qualifications, in August, 1841, elected delegates to a Convention, which met in Providence, in October of the same year, and drafted a Constitution, extending the right of suffrage to every white male adult citizen of the United States, who had resided one year in the State, and apportioning the representatives among the towns and cities of the State as nearly as possible in proportion to their actual population. Publishing the draft, the Convention adjourned to meet again in the month of November, 1841. On the 18th of November, the delegates again met and completed the draft. They then submitted their so-called Constitution to be voted upon by the people of Rhode Island; the voters to be American citizens, twenty-one years of age, and having their permanent residence or home in the State, but without any limitation of sex, color, place of nativity, or any fixed period of residence whatever. The voters were required to say whether they were qualified by the existing laws or not. The vote was to be taken on the 27th, 28th, and 29th days of December, 1841, in open meetings, and by an order of the Convention; every person who "from sickness or other cause," did not vote on those three days, was authorized to send his vote in to the moderator, within three days thereafter.[2]

§ 228. The Constitution thus framed, was submitted to the people, as thus determined, and received, as the returns showed, 13,944 votes in its favor — a clear majority of the whole number of adult male resident citizens, of whom there were in the State 23,000. Of the 13,944 votes cast for the Constitution, 4960 were given, it was claimed, by persons having a right to vote under the Charter and acts of the General Assembly, being a majority of all the voters qualified to vote by the existing laws of whom there were in all only about 9000.[3]

[1] Luther *v.* Borden, 7 How. (U. S.) R. 1.

[2] *Considerations on the Questions of the Adoption of a Constitution and Extension of Suffrage in Rhode Island*, by Elisha R. Potter, p. 19.

[3] *Democratic Rev. for* 1842, Vol. II. p. 71. On the other hand, it has been

The Constitution having been thus submitted, and, as was claimed, adopted, on the 12th of January, 1842, at an adjourned session of the Convention, there were passed the following preamble and resolution : —

" *Whereas*, by the return of the votes upon the Constitution, proposed to the citizens of this State by this Convention, the 18th day of November last, it satisfactorily appears, that the citizens of this State, in their original sovereign capacity, have ratified and adopted said Constitution, by a large majority ; and the will of the people, thus decisively made known, ought to be implicitly obeyed and faithfully executed ;

" We do therefore resolve and declare, that said Constitution rightfully ought to be, and is, the paramount law and Constitution of the State of Rhode Island and Providence Plantations; and we further resolve and declare, for ourselves and in behalf of the people whom we represent, that we will establish said Constitution, and sustain and defend the same by all necessary means.

" *Resolved*, That the officers of this Convention make proclamation of the return of the votes upon the Constitution, and that the same has been adopted and become the Constitution of this State; and that they cause said proclamation to be published in the newspapers of the same." [1]

The Constitution was proclaimed, as ordered by the Convention, an election of officers under it was held, at which Thomas W. Dorr was elected Governor, and a legislature was chosen, which met on the 3d of May, 1842, and having taken the proper initiatory steps to organize the new government, adjourned, leaving to the executive the responsibility of sustaining it against the attacks of the old government. This, the pretended Governor, Dorr, attempted to do. Two separate efforts were made to inaugurate by force the new government, — the first in May, 1842, and the last one on the 29th of June, 1842. The old government, however, prevailed ; Dorr was driven into exile, but finally returning, was tried for treason, convicted, and sentenced to imprisonment for life.

denied, apparently upon good grounds, that the people's Constitution received a majority of the votes either of all the American citizens in the State, over twenty-one years of age, or of the legally qualified freemen. See *Considerations*, *&c.*, by Elisha R. Potter, Appendix, No. 4, p. 57.

[1] Luther *v.* Borden, 7 How. (U. S.) R. 1.

§ 229. In several legal trials growing out of the movement just described, the question of the legitimacy of the "People's Constitution," was brought directly under discussion, both in the State and Federal courts.

The old government of Rhode Island caused prosecutions to be instituted in the courts of the State against some of the persons concerned in the forcible measures above indicated. In defending these actions, the parties prosecuted offered evidence of the proceedings, resulting in the formation of the new Constitution, and requested the courts to charge the jury, that "the proposed Constitution had been adopted by the people of Rhode Island, and had, therefore, become the established government; and, consequently, that the parties accused were doing nothing more than their duty in endeavoring to support it."

The State courts, however, uniformly held, that "the inquiry," as to the legitimacy of the new Constitution, "belonged to the political power of the State, and not to the judicial; that it rested with the political power to decide whether the Charter government had been displaced or not; and when that decision was made, the judicial department would be bound to take notice of it as the paramount law of the State, without the aid of oral evidence or the examination of witnesses; that, according to the laws and institutions of Rhode Island, no such change had been recognized by the political power; and that the Charter government was the lawful and established government of the State during the period in contest, and that those who were in arms against it were insurgents, and liable to punishment."

The same question was afterwards passed upon by the Supreme Court of the United States, in the case of Luther *v.* Borden, carried up by writ of error from the Circuit Court of Rhode Island. The facts of the case were briefly these: — The Charter government of that State had declared martial law, and raised a military force to protect itself against the attempts of the suffrage party to subvert it. On the 29th of June, 1842, at the time the second attempt was made by Dorr to inaugurate his pretended new government by military force, Luther M. Borden and others, composing a part of a regiment of militia, raised and acting under the authority of the Charter government, in obedience to orders from their commanding officers, broke and entered the dwelling-house of Martin Luther, an adherent of Dorr, for the purpose of arresting him as aiding and abetting the insurrection. Luther thereupon brought an action of trespass, *quare clausum fregit*, against Borden and his associates, in the Circuit Court of the United States for the District of Rhode Island, to try the question of the relative validity of the two governments. The defendants justified their entry by setting up the Charter of the colony, the establishment of the Union between Rhode Island, under the Charter, and the other States composing the United States, and the acts of the general government and of the several States, recognizing the State of Rhode Island as a member of the Union, under its said Charter. They showed further the assembling together of the suffrage party for the purpose of overthrowing the established government of the State, the declaration of martial law, and the organization of the military force under the Charter government, of which they constituted a part, and claimed that, in breaking and entering the dwelling-house of the plaintiff, they were acting under orders from the existing government, rightfully and lawfully issued.

§ 230. To this the plaintiff replied, exhibiting in detail the proceedings above described, resulting in the proclamation by the suffrage party of a new Constitution, and in the forcible attempts of Dorr to establish it. After offering evidence to prove the case on his part, as stated, the plaintiff requested the judge (the Hon. Joseph Story) to charge the jury, "that under the facts offered in evidence by the plaintiff, the Constitution and frame of government prepared, adopted and established in the manner and form set forth and shown, thereby was and became the supreme law of the State of Rhode Island, and was in full force and effect, as such, during the time set forth in the plaintiff's declaration, when the trespass alleged therein was committed by the defendants, as admitted by their pleas; that a majority of the free white male citizens of Rhode Island, of twenty-one years and upwards, in the exercise of the sovereignty of the people through the forms and in the manner set forth in the evidence offered by the plaintiff, and in the absence, under the then existing frame of government of the said State of Rhode Island, of any provision therein for amending, changing, or abolishing the said frame of government, had the right to reassume the powers of government, and establish a written

Constitution and frame of a republican form of government and that having so exercised such right, as aforesaid, the preëxisting Charter government, and the authority and assumed laws, under which the defendants in their plea claimed to have acted, became null and void and of no effect, so far as they were repugnant to and conflicted with said Constitution, and are no justification of the acts of the defendants in the premises." [1]

The court rejected the testimony offered, and refused to give the instructions asked by the plaintiff; but, on the contrary, instructed the jury, that the Charter government and laws, under which the defendants acted, were, at the time the trespass was alleged to have been committed, in full force and effect, as the form of government and permanent law of the State, and constituted a justification of the acts of the defendants, as set forth in their pleas.[2]

To this decision of the court exceptions were taken, and the case was carried by writ of error to the Supreme Court of the United States.

Before giving the decision of the latter upon the case, it should be noted, that, at the time the people's party assailed the Charter government with military force, the executive of the latter government made application to the President of the United States for aid in maintaining the same, under the fourth section of the fourth article of the Constitution, guaranteeing to each State of the Union, on the application of its legislature, or, when the legislature could not be convened, on that of its executive, protection "against domestic violence;" and the President promised the necessary support, and took measures to call out the militia to sustain the Charter government.

§ 231. Upon these facts, the Supreme Court, Chief Justice Taney, delivering the opinion, held —

First. That the question involved in the case related altogether to the Constitution and laws of one of the States of the Union, and that it was the well-settled rule in the courts of the United States, that the latter adopt and follow the decisions of the State courts in questions which concern merely the Constitution and laws of such States; that the courts of the United States have undoubtedly certain powers under the Constitution

[1] Luther *v.* Borden, 7 How. (U. S.) R. 1.

[2] Id. p. 38.

and laws of the United States, which do not belong to the State courts, but that the power of determining that a State government has been lawfully established, which the courts of the State disown and repudiate, is not one of them; that, upon such a question, the courts of the United States are bound to follow the decisions of the State tribunals, and that, inasmuch as the courts of Rhode Island had affirmed the validity of the Charter government, and the invalidity of the pretended new one seeking to supplant it, the courts of the United States must, therefore, regard the Charter government as the lawful and established government "during the time of this contest."[1]

Secondly. That the fourth section of the fourth article of the Constitution of the United States provides, that the United States shall guarantee to every State in the Union a republican form of government, and shall protect each of them against invasion; and, on the application of the legislature, or of the executive (when the legislature cannot be convened), against domestic violence; that, under this article of the Constitution, it rests with Congress to decide what government is the established one in a State; for, as the United States guarantee to each State a republican government, Congress must necessarily decide what government is established in the State before it can determine whether it is republican or not; and when the senators and representatives of a State are admitted into the councils of the Union, the authority of the government under which they are appointed, as well as its republican character, is recognized by the proper constitutional authority, and its decision is binding on every other department of the government, and could not be questioned in a judicial tribunal. So, too, as relates to the clause of the Constitution providing for cases of domestic violence, it rested with Congress to determine upon the means proper to be adopted to fulfil this guarantee. They might, if they had deemed it most advisable to do so, have placed it in the power of a court to decide when the contingency had happened which required the Federal government to interfere. But Congress thought otherwise; and by the Act of Feb. 28, 1795, provided, that "in case of an insurrection in any State against the government thereof, it shall be lawful for the President of the United States, on application of the legislature of

[1] Luther *v.* Borden, 7 How. (U. S.) R. 40.

such State, or of the executive (when the legislature cannot be convened), to call forth such number of the militia of any other State or States as may be applied for, as he may judge sufficient to suppress such insurrection;" that this power, conferred upon the President by the Constitution and laws of the United States, belonged to him exclusively; that the President had acted in the case of Rhode Island, not, it was true, by actually calling out the militia, on the application of the Governor of Rhode Island, under the Charter government, but by recognizing him as the executive of the State, and by taking measures to call out the militia to support his authority, if it should be found necessary for the general government to interfere; that this interference of the President by announcing his determination, was as efficient as if the militia had been assembled under his orders; that it ought to be equally authoritative; and that no court of the United States would, knowing this decision, be justified in recognizing the opposing party as the lawful government.[1]

For these reasons, the judgment of the circuit court, acquitting the defendants, was affirmed.

§ 232. It is perhaps unfortunate that the question involved in this case could not have been decided by the Supreme Court of the United States, directly upon principle. As in the case which went up from Michigan, involving the legitimacy of the State government organized in the territory of that name in 1835,[2] so, in that of Luther *v.* Borden, the question discussed was treated in the Supreme Court as one simply of jurisdiction, the court abstaining from expressing any opinion on the points most interesting to us in this discussion. Upon the merits of the controversy, therefore, judicial authority is wholly wanting, save as it is derived from the adjudications of the courts of the State, which obviously cannot be considered as conclusive. To determine, then, the question as to the right of the citizens of a State to alter or abolish their political Constitution, without the consent of the existing government, we are compelled to recur to fundamental principles. For such a discussion we are happily not without abundant materials. In the argument of Luther *v.* Borden in the Supreme Court, Mr. Webster and Mr. Hallett, counsel respectively for the Charter government of Rhode Island,

[1] Luther *v.* Borden, 7 How. (U. S.) R. 44.

[2] *Ante*, §§ 207, 208.

and for the plaintiffs in error, representing the Dorr government, met the case fairly and squarely, expounding with very great ability the principles involved, upon which alone they sought to rest the cause of their clients. Perhaps I could not better exhibit the true doctrine on the question than by transcribing, within reasonable limits, and contrasting the arguments of those gentlemen, who, to eminent ability and learning as lawyers, added a special fitness for this discussion, as being leading members of the two great political parties of the time, which had ranged themselves, in the main, upon opposite sides in the Rhode Island controversy.

§ 233. In behalf of the plaintiff in error, Martin Luther, Mr. Hallett urged: — That the fundamental principle of the American system of government is, that government is instituted by the people, and for the benefit, protection, and security of the people, nation, or community; and that when any government shall be found inadequate or contrary to these purposes, a majority of the community has an indubitable, inalienable, and indefeasible right to alter or abolish the same, in such manner as shall be judged most conducive to the public weal; that the terms "community," "society," "state," "nation," "body of the community," "great body of the people," are used by early political writers as synonymous with the word "people;" and that all the American writers use the term "people" to express the entire numerical aggregate of the community, whether state or national, in contradistinction to the *government* or *legislature;* that in the people, as thus defined, resides the ultimate power of sovereignty; that it is the people, or sovereign, that has the sole right to establish government, and, when deemed necessary, to alter or abolish it; and that according as well to the teachings of the best political writers as to the positive affirmations of many of our Constitutions, the people may meet when and where they please, and dispose of the sovereignty, or limit the exercise of it; that the doctrine that legislative action or sanction is necessary, as the mode of effecting a change of State government, is anti-republican and novel, having been broached for the first time under the United States government, in the debate in Congress upon the admission of Michigan, December, 1836; that, in the United States, no definite uniform mode has ever been established for either instituting or changing a form of

State government; that the State legislatures have no power or authority over the subject, and can interfere only by usurpation, any further than like other individuals, to recommend; that the great body of the people may change their form of government at any time, in any peaceful way, and by any mode of operations that they for themselves determine to be expedient; that, even where a subsisting Constitution points out a particular mode of change, the people are not bound to follow the mode pointed out, but may, at their pleasure, adopt another; that, where no Constitution exists, and no fundamental law prescribes any mode of amendment, then they must adopt a mode for themselves; and the mode they do adopt, when ratified or acquiesced in by a majority of the people, is binding upon all; that it is a well-settled rule in the United States, that a State Constitution, being the deliberate expression of the sovereign will of the people, takes effect from the time that will is unequivocally expressed in the manner provided in and by the Constitution itself; that is, from the time of its ratification by the vote of the people, which, in the language of Washington, is of itself "an explicit and authentic act of the whole people;" that this right of the people to change, alter, or abolish their government, in such manner as they please, is a right not of force but of sovereignty; that whatever may be the case with the Federal government, no right of revolution, in the common and European sense of the term, implying a change by force, is anywhere sanctioned, so far as the individual States are concerned, in the Constitution of the United States; that a revolution by force, inasmuch as it includes insurrection and rebellion, which constitute "domestic violence," against which, by the Federal Constitution, Congress is bound to guarantee the States, can never be resorted to within the limits of that Constitution, while a State remains in the Union; that, therefore, when our best writers and our Constitutions affirm the existence of the right above asserted in the people, they affirm a right to be exercised, not by force, but by peaceful and constitutional methods; that, as a consequence of these principles of government and sovereignty, acknowledged and acted upon in the United States and the several States thereof, at least ever since the Declaration of Independence, the Constitution and frame of government, prepared, adopted, and established by the "People's Convention" in Rhode Island, as above set forth, was and became thereby the supreme fundamental law of the State of Rhode Island, and was in full force and effect as such, when the trespass alleged in the plaintiff's writ was committed by the defendants.[1]

§ 234. The argument of Mr. Webster in reply to this most ingenious defence of anarchical principles, consisted mainly in a masterly statement of the principles of the American system of government. It was in substance as follows: —

That without going into historical details, the principles on which the American system rests, are, first and chief, that the people are the source of all political power, government being instituted for their good, and its members, their servants and agents; and, secondly, that, as the exercise of legislative power and the other powers of government immediately by the people themselves, is impracticable, they must be exercised by representatives of the people; that the basis of representation is suffrage; that the right to choose representatives is every man's part in the exercise of sovereign power; to have a voice in it, if he has the proper qualifications, is the portion of political power belonging to every elector; that that is the beginning, the mode in which power emanates from its source and gets into the hands of Conventions, legislatures, courts of law, and the chair of the executive; that it begins in suffrage — suffrage being the delegation of power of an individual to some agent; that, this being so, there follow two other great principles of the American system: first, that the right of suffrage shall be guarded, protected, and secured against force and fraud; and, secondly, that its exercise shall be prescribed by previous law; that is, that its qualifications, and the time, place and manner of its exercise, under whose supervision (always sworn officers of the law) are to be prescribed by previous law; and that its results are to be certified to the central power by some certain rule, by some known public officers, in some clear and definite form, to the end that two things may be done — first, that every man entitled to vote may vote, and, second, that his vote may be sent forward and counted, and so he may exercise his part of sovereignty, in common with his fellow-citizens; that not only do the people limit their governments, National and State — it is another principle, equally true and important that they often limit them-

[1] Luther v. Borden, 7 How. (U. S.) R. 19-27.

selves; that they set bounds to their own power; securing the institutions which they establish against the sudden impulses of mere majorities; thus, by the 5th Article of the Constitution, Congress, two-thirds of both Houses concurring, may propose amendments of the Constitution, or on the application of the legislatures of two-thirds of the States, may call a Convention— the amendments proposed, in either case, to be ratified by the legislatures or Conventions of three-fourths of the States; that they also limit themselves in regard to the qualifications of *electors*, and in regard to the qualifications of the *elected;* they also limit themselves to certain prescribed forms for the conduct of elections,—it being required, that they shall vote at a particular place, at a particular time, and under particular conditions, or not at all; that it is in these modes we are to ascertain the will of the American people, and that our Constitutions and laws know no other mode; that we are not to take the will of the people from public meetings, nor from tumultuous assemblies, by which the timid are terrified, the prudent alarmed, and society disturbed; and that, if any thing in the country, not ascertained by a regular vote, by regular returns, and by regular representation, has been established, it is an exception and not the rule.

§ 235. Referring to the same principles, he continued: That it is true, at the Revolution, when all government was dissolved, the people got together and began an inceptive organization, the object of which was to bring together representatives of the people who should form a government; that this was the mode of proceeding in those States where their legislatures were dissolved; that it was much like that had in England upon the abdication of King James II.; he ran away, he abdicated, and King William took the government, and how did he proceed? He at once requested all who had been members of the old Parliament, of any regular Parliament, in the time of Charles II., to assemble; the Peers, being a standing body, could, of course, assemble; and all they did was to recommend the calling of a Convention, to be chosen by the same electors, and composed of the same numbers as composed a Parliament; the Convention assembled, and, as all know, was turned into a Parliament; that this was a case of necessity, a revolution, so-called, not because a new sovereign then ascended the throne of the Stuarts, but because there was a change in the organization of the government; that the legal and established succession was broken; the Convention did not assemble under any preceding law; there was a *hiatus*, a syncope, in the action of the body politic; this was a revolution, and the Parliaments that assembled afterwards referred their legal origin to that revolution.

Is it not obvious enough, he asked, that men cannot get together and count themselves, and say there are so many hundreds, and so many thousands, and judge of their own qualifications, and call themselves the people, and set up a government? Why, said he, another set of men, forty miles off, on the same day, and in as large numbers, may meet and set up another government, and both may call themselves the people. What is this but anarchy?

Another American principle growing out of this, said Mr. Webster, and just as important and well settled as is the truth, that the people are the source of power is, that when, in the course of events, it becomes necessary to ascertain the will of the people on a new exigency, or a new state of things or of opinion, the legislative power provides for that ascertainment by an ordinary act of legislation. Has not that been our whole history? The old Congress, upon the suggestion of the delegates who assembled at Annapolis, in May, 1786, recommended to the States that they should send delegates to a Convention to be holden at Philadelphia, to form a Constitution. No article of the old Confederation gave them power to do this, but they did it, and the States did appoint delegates, who assembled at Philadelphia, and formed the Constitution. It was communicated to the old Congress, and that body recommended to the States to make provision for calling the people together to act upon its adoption. Was not that exactly the case of passing a law to ascertain the will of the people in a new exigency? And this method was adopted without opposition, nobody suggesting that there could be any other mode of ascertaining the will of the people. The counsel for the plaintiff in error went through the Constitutions of several of the States. It is enough to say, in reply, that of the old thirteen States, the Constitutions, with but one exception, contained no provision for their own amendment. In New Hampshire, there was a provision for taking the sense of the people once in seven years. Yet there is hardly one that has not altered its Constitution, and it has been done by Conventions called by the legislative power. Now, what State ever altered its Constitution in any other mode? What alteration has ever been brought in, put in, forced in, or got in any how, by resolutions of mass-meetings, and then by applying force? In what State has an assembly, calling itself the people, convened without law, without authority, without qualifications, without certain officers, with no oaths, securities, or sanctions of any kind, met and made a Constitution, and called it the Constitution of the State? There must be some authentic mode of ascertaining the will of the people, else all is anarchy. It resolves itself into the law of the strongest, or, what is the same thing, of the most numerous for the moment, and all Constitutions and all legislative rights are prostrated and disregarded.

To these arguments he added another, founded on the provision of the Federal Constitution (Article 4, section 4), similar in its terms to that contained in the opinion of the Supreme Court, already referred to, showing that the Charter government of Rhode Island was the only one that could be recognized by the court or by the government of the United States, which, by its own Constitution, was pledged to protect and maintain it.[1]

§ 236. It seems presumptuous to attempt to add any thing to an argument so solid and conclusive as that of Mr. Webster, but I cannot forbear from remarking upon two or three points made by Mr. Hallett.

1. Combating "the doctrine that legislative action or sanction is necessary, as the mode of effecting a change of State government," as "anti-republican and novel," Mr. Hallett asserted, that, "in the United States, *no definite uniform mode has ever been established for either instituting or changing a form of State government*." This is true, if, by the establishment of a definite uniform mode, be meant the prescribing of such a mode by a provision of either the Federal or State Constitutions, so as to be binding upon the States. But it is not essential to the establishment of such a mode, that it should be done by constitutional provision. The common practice of all the States, as well as of the United States, rarely departed from even amidst the distractions of the Revolution, according to which the calling

[1] See *Great Speeches and Orations of Daniel Webster*, by E. P. Whipple (Little, Brown & Co., 1879), p. 538.

of Conventions for the purpose of "either instituting or changing a form of government," is left to the proper legislative authority in each case, is itself a part of the common law of the land, from which, except in cases of necessity, to be judged of only by the same legislative authority, no departure ought to be tolerated. Such a mode is not only established, but it is as definite and uniform as any mode can be, consistently with safety.

§ 237. 2. The capital point in Mr. Hallett's argument, however, was, that *it is a right of the people to change, alter, or abolish their government, in such manner as they please*," and that *this right* "*is a right, not of force, but of sovereignty.*"

Now, if in this extract, by the word "people," be meant the nation, considered as a political unit, I observe that, conceding the right claimed for it to exist, the exercise of that right would be wholly impracticable. The people, in that sense, never did, and never could act directly; it could act only by a delegation of its authority, as, to the legislature, to the electors, and the like, — the terms and conditions of that delegation being prescribed in the Constitution. The right of the people then, in this sense of the term, if it exist, is a right that never has been, and never can be exercised; that is, is, practically, not a right at all.

But, were there no such inherent impracticability; if the entire population of a State could, as it is often expressed, "meet upon some vast plain," so long as that population was organized under a Constitution, like those with which we are familiar though it would be physically able to carry into execution such ordinances as should get themselves passed at its tumultuous parliament, it clearly would have no *constitutional* or *legal* right to pass an ordinance at all. Such an assemblage would not constitute, in a political sense, The People. The people of a State is the *political body* — *the corporate unit* — in which are vested, as we have seen, the ultimate powers of sovereignty; not its inhabitants or population, considered as individuals. It is never to be forgotten, that the *individuals*, constituting a State, have, *as such*, no political, but only civil, *rights*. Except as an *organized body*, that is, *except when acting by its recognized organs*, the entire population of a State already constituted, were it assembled on some vast plain, could not constitutionally pass a law or try an offender.

§ 238. If, on the other hand, by the term "people," be meant that part of the population of a State, in whom is vested, by the Constitution, the *exercise* of sovereign rights, the *electors*, the doctrine, that they have "the right to change, alter, or abolish their government, *in such manner as they please*," is absurd and ridiculous — I mean, as a legal or constitutional right, or, as Mr. Hallett says, as a "right, not of force, but of sovereignty." They have a right, unquestionably, "to change, alter, or abolish their government," in the mode provided in the charter determining their powers, the Constitution, or, when that is silent, in such a mode as shall be conformable to the customary law of the land, and to the general principles of a republican representative system. By both these, as well as by the express provisions of such Constitutions as are not silent on the subject, movements of the people, with a view "to change, alter, or abolish their government," are never initiated but by the legislative authority of the State. Why this should be so, is shown by Mr. Webster in that part of his argument in which are exhibited the practical requisites to the authenticity of a vote.[1] If there is anywhere, in our political system, then, a power to change, alter, or abolish the existing government, as a *legal* right, it must reside in some branch of that government, by virtue of authority given in the Constitution; or, where there is no express authority given, in some body called for that purpose by the rightful law-making power of the State.

§ 239. Again: The argument of Mr. Hallett in support of the proposition, that the right of the people to change, alter, or abolish their government, in such manner and at such time as they may please, is a right, not of force, but of sovereignty, consists of two branches — a negative branch, and an affirmative branch.

The negative branch of the argument is, that the right cannot be a mere right of force or of revolution, because the Constitution of the United States nowhere recognizes the right of revolution, in the common and European sense of the term, so far as the States are concerned; but that, inasmuch as revolution by force involves insurrection and rebellion, which constitute "domestic violence," against which Congress is bound by that Constitution to guarantee the States, it can never be resorted

[1] § 234, *ante*.

to within the limits of the Constitution, while a State remains in the Union.

The facts stated are perfectly true, but the inference drawn from them is unwarranted. Revolution can never be resorted to under the Federal Constitution, or under any other Constitution, *legally;* but, when the evils under which a commonwealth languishes, become so great as to make revolution, including insurrection and rebellion, less intolerable than an endurance of those evils, it will be justifiable, although the Federal relations of that commonwealth may be such as to array against her forces vastly greater than they would be were she and the other States independent and isolated communities. The right of revolution stands not upon the letter of any law, but upon the necessity of self-preservation, and is just as perfect in the single man, or in the petty State, as in the most numerous and powerful empire in the world. This right, the founders of our system were careful to preserve, not as a right *under*, but, when necessity demanded its exercise, *over* our Constitutions, State and Federal.

§ 240. The affirmative branch of the argument is, that the right asserted must be a right of sovereignty and not of force, because it is specifically guaranteed in the Declaration of Independence and in the Bills of Rights of nearly all our State Constitutions.

To determine whether this inference from facts which cannot be denied is just or not, it is necessary to examine critically the documents indicated, as well as the historical circumstances attending their inception.

Now these documents are of three kinds. The first kind consists of such as assert the right clearly and unmistakably as a right of revolution.

Thus, the Declaration of Independence affirms, "that whenever any form of government becomes destructive" of the ends of government, "it is the right of the people to alter or abolish it, and to institute a new government, laying its foundation on such principles, and organizing its powers in such form as to them shall seem most likely to effect their safety and happiness."

Not only so, but it classes this affirmation among *the self-evident truths:* "We hold these truths to be self-evident."

Now, no truth can be self-evident, which becomes evident only under particular conditions, as when it is deducible only from the construction of legal instruments, or from the provisions of some positive code. It must be a truth independently of such conditions, as would be indispensable to give it rank as a *legal* truth. If the truth in question is a self-evident truth, it is one which would obtain equally whether asserted in the Constitution and laws or not.

Now, that a people, organized under a Constitution, which itself provides a particular mode for its own amendment, have a *legal* right to alter or abolish it *whenever* and *however* they please, is not a self-evident truth, and could never have been claimed to be such by any body of sane men.

Moreover, the circumstances, under which the Declaration of Independence was promulgated, and the clear import of its terms, indicate, that it was the right of revolution to which its authors referred. That instrument was the manifesto by which they declared that to be a revolution, which hitherto had been but a mere insurrection. Its language was that of justification for acts tending to the permanent disruption of the empire. "Prudence, indeed, will dictate," its authors say, "that governments long established should not be changed for light and transient causes; and accordingly all experience hath shown, that mankind are more disposed to suffer, while evils are sufferable, than to right themselves, by abolishing the forms to which they are accustomed. But when a long train of abuses and usurpations, pursuing invariably the same object, evinces a design to reduce them under an absolute despotism, *it is their right, it is their duty, to throw off such government, and to provide new guards for their future security.*"

Here, certainly, our fathers were not claiming, as guaranteed or existing by the laws of England, a right to disrupt the British empire, but a right older than those laws, the right of revolution.

§ 241. The second class of documents consists of the Bills of Rights of a large number of our Constitutions, containing broad general assertions of the right of a people to alter or abolish their form of government, *at any time, and in such manner as they may deem expedient.* The peculiarity of these documents is, that they *seem* to assert the right in question as a *legal* right; at least, they furnish a plausible argument for those who are willing to have it believed that the right is a *legal one;* when, in fact, it is a revolutionary right. The framers of those Constitutions generally inserted in them provisions for their own amendment. Had nothing further been said, it might have been inferred, that no other mode of securing needed changes was under any circumstances to be pursued, but that prescribed in those instruments. Such, however, was not the intention of their framers. They meant to leave to the people, besides, the great right of revolution, formally and solemnly asserted in the Declaration of Independence. They, therefore, affirmed it to be a right of the people to alter or abolish their Constitutions, *in any manner whatever ;* that is, *first*, *legally*, in the mode pointed out in their Constitutions, or by the customary law of the land ; and *secondly*, *illegally*, that is, for sufficient causes, by revolutionary force.

Thus, the Bill of Rights of Mississippi contains a provision, which is a type of that found in a great number of our State Constitutions, couched in the following terms: "We declare, ... that all power is inherent in the people, and all governments are founded on their authority, and instituted for their safety, peace and happiness. *For the advancement of these ends, they have, at all times, an unalienable and indefeasible right to alter, reform, or abolish their government, in such manner as they may think proper.*"[1]

But, let it be noted, that these Constitutions do not say, that every mode of exercising this right will be a *legal* mode. What they do declare is, in effect, this: The people cannot bind themselves or be bound, irretrievably, to continue a form of government, when it has ceased to answer the ends of its establishment. They may change it or set it aside *in any way whatever that circumstances may make necessary.* They may do it by force even, and, of course, by the mild and regular procedure laid down in their Constitution — calling things always, however, by their right names; when doing it in the latter mode, designating it as *legal* or *constitutional*, but when in the former, as *revolutionary.*

[1] Substantially the same is the declaration found in each of the following Constitutions: — Those of Massachusetts, 1780; Vermont, 1786; Connecticut, 1818; Maine and Alabama, 1819; Delaware, 1831; Mississippi, 1832; Tennessee, 1834; Arkansas, 1836; Pennsylvania, 1838; Florida, 1839; New Jersey, 1844; Texas, 1845; Missouri, 1846; California. 1849; Kentucky, 1850; Ohio, 1851; and Iowa, Oregon, and Minnesota, 1857. Where revisions have been made of these Constitutions, the provision is commonly inserted therein without modification.

§ 242. That the view I have taken of the two classes of documents specified is the correct one, is rendered more probable when we look into the state of opinion in England and America, previous to our Revolution, in reference to the duties of a people towards their rulers, embodied, in conformity to the views of the latter, in the famous doctrine of "Passive Obedience" or "Non-Resistance."

The substance of this doctrine was, that governments are of divine appointment, and hence that any resistance whatever to kingly authority (for it was to bolster up the institution of monarchy that it was invented), even when that authority is exerting itself in palpable violation of the laws, is sinful in the sight of God. This doctrine, originating in the Middle Ages, was held by the Tory party in England during the entire existence of the Stuart dynasty, their opponents, the Whigs, on the contrary, maintaining the essential principles of liberty, the independence of Parliament and of the people, and the lawfulness of resistance to a king who violated the laws. After the fall of the Stuarts, the doctrine was generally discredited, but in the alternations of parties which ensued, it was frequently revived, mainly through the influence of the Church, which repaid the favors lavished upon her by the crown, by inculcating doctrines tending to make the latter absolute master of the public liberties. During the long period of Whig ascendency, however, extending with few intermissions from the reign of William III. to that of George III., the slavish dogma of Passive Obedience became nearly extinct, being subjected to persecution by the party in power. In the reign of Queen Anne, Dr. Sacheverell was impeached for maintaining it in a sermon preached before the Commons.[1] At the accession of George III., however, there came a great Tory reaction, and the doctrine of Non-Resistance was again preached by all of that numerous party which thought what was pleasing to the ruling monarch. At the time

[1] In his answer to the Articles of Impeachment, the Doctor said: — "The said Henry Sacheverell, upon the strictest search into his said sermon preached at St. Paul's, doth not find that he hath given any the least colourable pretence for the accusation exhibited against him in this first article, but barely by his asserting the utter illegality of Resistance to the Supreme power upon any pretence whatsoever; for which assertion, he humbly conceives he hath the authority of the Church of England." 15 *How. St. Trials*, p. 42.

our Revolution broke out the minds of men everywhere throughout the British empire were oppressed by scruples, resting on the teachings of revered names in the Church, as to the sinfulness of resistance to the usurpations of the King, even when he was evidently laying violent hands on the very temple of freedom itself.[1]

§ 243. Among the most difficult tasks of the men of our Revolution, therefore, was to disabuse the public mind of the heresy of Passive Obedience or Non-Resistance. The discussions preceding the revolt are filled with arguments tending to make it clear to tender consciences in the colonies, that in entering upon a course of opposition to King and Parliament, they were not guilty necessarily of a sin or a crime.[2] In this great work, naturally, the clergy of the period bore a conspicuous part. It was left to no particular class, however, to clear up a doubt, which strikes the mind in our day as absurd. It was preached down in the pulpits, argued against in the halls of legislation and upon the stump, and, to make sure that it should be deprived of all further power to mislead, it was nailed to the wall for public reprobation in the great manifesto of our Revolution, and in our Bills of Rights.

When the fathers, therefore, in the Declaration of Independence, solemnly affirmed the right of a people to alter or abolish their government, whenever it should have become destructive of its proper ends, "laying its foundation on such principles, and organizing its powers in such form, as to them should seem most likely to effect their safety and happiness," they were fighting the old dragon of Passive Obedience, now long since dead; to our age, the shadow of a peril long past and apparently so baseless, that we can scarcely realize that it ever existed. By this declaration, in other words, the statesmen of the Revolution meant merely to deny, that the people could not, without mortal sin, arrest their rulers in a career of usurpation, even if their opposition should terminate in blood; and to affirm, that government being instituted for the good of the people, and not the people created as slaves to the government, obedience was due

[1] On the whole subject of Non-Resistance, see Macaulay, *Hist. Eng.*, Vol. I. pp. 37, 38, 324–326; May, *Const. Hist. Eng.*, Vol. I. pp. 15–104; Hallam, *Const. Hist. Eng.*, pp. 237, 238, 491, 493; Hume, *Hist. Eng.*, VI. pp. 133, 134.

[2] See Bancroft, *Hist. U. S.*, Vol. V. pp. 195, 206, 288, 289, 324, 325.

from the one to the other only so long as it was not destructive of the ends of government.

The same motives which led to the insertion of the clause in the Declaration of Independence, induced the framers of our Constitutions to place it in the Bills of Rights prefacing those instruments.

§ 244. A confirmation of this construction of this clause in our Constitutions is found in the context to it in some of those instruments. Thus, the Maryland Constitution of 1776, the New Hampshire Constitution of 1792, and the Tennessee Constitution of 1834, contained immediately after the clause in question the following declaration:—

"*The doctrine of non-resistance against arbitrary power and oppression, is absurd, slavish, and destructive of the good and happiness of mankind.*"

§ 245. It remains now to notice the third and last kind of documents referred to, namely, Constitutions containing clauses in some respects resembling those commented upon above, but of which the effect is different, or the reverse. These are the Constitutions of Virginia, Rhode Island, and Maryland.

In the Bills of Rights of the various Virginia Constitutions is found the following declaration:—

"That government is, or ought to be, instituted for the common benefit, protection, and security of the people, nation, or community. Of all the various modes and forms of government, that is best which is capable of producing the greatest degree of happiness and safety, and is most effectually secured against the danger of maladministration; and that when any government shall be found inadequate or contrary to these purposes, *a majority of the community* hath an indubitable, inalienable, and indefeasible right to reform, alter, or abolish it, in such manner as shall be judged most conducive to the public weal."

Now, the authors of this declaration evidently intended by it to assert for "a majority of the community" either a *legal* or a *revolutionary* right. If it was the latter, why confine to a majority a right which belongs to one man or a hundred men as perfectly as to a million, or to a majority of all the citizens?

Again: unless by the term majority be meant that which is greater, not in numbers, but in force, the clause, as declaratory of a revolutionary right, is absurd. Nature knows no majority but that of force. The majorities, of which we hear so much, of the male adult citizens invested with the suffrage, are matters of positive regulation. Does Nature determine the age at which a citizen becomes an adult citizen? or does she confine the exercise of the suffrage to males only?

As, however, that use of the word majority is unprecedented, it is clear that the words referred to were intended to assert a legal right. But if the right belongs to a majority to alter or abolish the existing form of government as a legal right, it must be to a majority of the electors, acting in pursuance of some law passed according to the forms of the Constitution. No other *majority* and no other *people* are known to the laws, nor could the action of any other majority or any other people be denominated *legal*. I conclude, therefore, that the clause refers merely to the ordinary and accepted modes of amending or repealing Constitutions, leaving a choice of them to the existing government.

That the words referred to have been generally considered objectionable, as liable to misconstruction, may be inferred from the fact that, although a great number of the Constitutions formed in other States have copied the Virginia declaration, not one of them has ever retained those words. One instance will suffice. The Vermont Bill of Rights declares "that *the community*" — not "a majority of the community," as in that of Virginia — "hath an indubitable, inalienable, and indefeasible right," &c.[1]

§ 246. In the Rhode Island Constitution, framed in **1842**, is found the following declaration: —

"In the words of the Father of his Country, we declare, that 'the basis of our political systems is the right of the people to make and alter their Constitutions of government; but that the Constitution which at any time exists, *till changed by an explicit and authentic act of the whole people*, is sacredly obligatory upon all.'"

So, also, to a similar effect, is a clause in the Maryland Constitution of 1851, which declares, —

[1] See also the Constitutions of Connecticut, 1818; Alabama, 1819; Mississippi, 1832; Tennessee, 1834; Arkansas, 1836; Pennsylvania, 1838; Florida, 1839; Texas, 1845; Kentucky, 1850; and Oregon, 1857, — in which the same omission is observable.

"That all government of right originates from the people, is founded in compact only, and instituted solely for the good of the whole; and they have at all times, *according to the mode prescribed in this Constitution*, the unalienable right to alter, reform, or abolish their form of government, *in such manner as they may deem expedient.*"

In these two Constitutions there is no declaration of the right of revolution, those clauses which are usually so worded as to assert that right being, in these, confined by restrictive clauses, so as to make the right involved a mere *legal* right to alter or abolish forms of government *in modes appointed by law.*

It is obvious — recurring to the clause in the Rhode Island Constitution — that, if a form of government remains unaltered until "changed by an explicit and authentic act of the whole people," it will remain so forever, unless the modes and instrumentalities employed to effect the change are appointed and regulated by positive law. The whole people cannot meet in Convention. No declaration of their will can be explicit, no representation of them by a few can be authentic, unless made and authorized through some organ empowered to utter their voice.

In the Maryland declaration it is difficult to give any effect at all to the concluding words, "in such manner as they may deem expedient." Referring to the debates preceding the adoption of the section, it is apparent that the effect of inserting the clause restricting alterations of the Constitution "to the mode prescribed in this Constitution," was not well considered. Striking out from the clause, as it now reads, the restrictive words, it conforms closely to those inserted in so many of our Constitutions of which I have before spoken. As Maryland had suffered from revolutionary attempts to alter her Constitution, her Convention desired to narrow within safe limits that important right. It therefore inserted the restrictive words, but neglected to strike out those which are significant only as declaratory of the old revolutionary right, thus seeming to negative its own intention. The only construction that can be given to the section which will allow all of its parts to stand, is to refer the clause, "in such manner as they may deem expedient," to the words "alter" and "reform," and not to the nearer word "abolish." It would then mean that the people have an inalienable right, in the mode prescribed in the Constitution, to alter or reform the same in such manner as they may deem expedient — that is, make *such changes* therein as they please — or the right wholly to abolish it. Thus, by a sacrifice of grammatical accuracy, the work of the Convention is redeemed from self-contradiction.

§ 247. (*c.*) The last variety of Conventions which I shall mention consists of those exceptional bodies by which were effected, first, the so-called secession of certain slave States from our Union in 1860 and 1861; and secondly, the reconstruction of those States preparatory to a resumption of their normal relations to the Union in 1864, 1865, 1866, and 1868.

The States concerned, in the order in which their ordinances of secession were passed, were South Carolina, Mississippi, Florida, Alabama, Georgia, Louisiana, Texas, Arkansas, Virginia, Tennessee, North Carolina, and Kentucky — the ordinance of the first having been passed in December, 1860, and that of the last in November, 1861.

It is not my purpose to enter fully upon the history of the Secession Conventions, since the view I take of them renders only a few of the leading facts relating to the call of these bodies important.

The Secession Conventions were called avowedly to effect, by revolutionary means, the disruption of the American Union, established by the war of Independence, and confirmed by the Federal Constitution of 1789. The election of Mr. Lincoln upon a platform deemed menacing to the interests of those States, was the wrong, to redress which the rupture of their constitutional relations to their sister States was attempted. By concert among the leading men of the South, and perhaps in pursuance of a long cherished purpose, Conventions were called in every State but one above named, as soon after the announcement of Mr. Lincoln's election as the popular attachment to the existing government could be made to give way to a desire for Southern Independence. Tennessee called no Convention, but as her legislature assumed to act as a Convention, and in that capacity passed a pretended Ordinance of Secession, I have reckoned that body amongst the Secession Conventions.

§ 248. The mode of calling these Conventions was as follows: The legislatures of many of the States meeting, by law, not far from the time of the Presidential election, the friends of secession easily secured the passage of Acts calling Conventions in those States. Where those bodies were not soon to assemble, it became necessary to prevail upon the governors of the States to call extra sessions of their legislatures — a thing easily accomplished, as most of those officers were ardent champions of the secession cause, and perhaps, for that reason, had been chosen to fill their respective places. When assembled, these bodies found little difficulty in falling in with the current and calling Conventions, generally declaring the object of them to be to consider the "relations between the government of the United States, the people and governments of the different States, and the government and people" of the State concerned. "and to adopt such measures for vindicating the sovereignty of the State and the protection of its institutions" as should appear to be demanded.[1] In most of the States, the question of calling those Conventions was not submitted to the people, though in Tennessee and North Carolina it was so submitted, and was voted down, the electors in the latter State, nevertheless, at the same time, with a singular inconsistency, electing delegates as required, but choosing such as favored the Union. The Convention met, and at its first session refused to vote an Ordinance of Secession; but, after the bombardment of Fort Sumter, the cause of the Union appearing hopeless, the same body was reassembled, and voted the State out of the Union unanimously!

In Texas, the Governor, Houston, refused to call the legislature together, but some sixty of the conspirators against the Union, signed a document convening that body, and a Convention was thereupon called, and an Ordinance of Secession passed. In Alabama the Convention was called by Governor Moore, in pursuance of an Act of the legislature, passed in anticipation of the election of a Republican to the office of President of the United States, authorizing and requiring him on the happening of that contingency to call a Convention, to take such steps as should protect the power and interests of the State.

In none of these States were the Ordinances of Secession sub-

[1] Act calling the Missouri Convention of 1861, sec. 5. That Missouri did not secede was probably no fault of the pro-slavery legislature which passed this Act.

mitted to the people, save in Texas, Tennessee, and Virginia, and in those cases they were submitted under systems of fraud and violence ingeniously contrived to insure, as they did insure, the adoption of the ordinances, at all events.

§ 249. Admitting, however, that the Secession Conventions were all called in pursuance of the legislative authority of their respective States, they are nevertheless to be set down as Revolutionary Conventions for two reasons: —

1. The legislatures had constitutionally no authority to call them to inaugurate secession. The Constitution of the United States was a part of the Constitution of each of those States, and all the State officers, legislative, executive, and judicial, were bound by oath to support it. In taking steps to overturn that Constitution and to disrupt the Union, every member of the State legislatures calling Conventions with the ulterior purpose of passing secession ordinances in any event, was entering upon a course of revolution, and became guilty of perjury and of moral, if not technical, treason.

2. The Secession Conventions did not confine themselves to the recommending, or even to the enacting of changes in their several State Constitutions, which, as we have seen, is the utmost limit of the powers of Constitutional Conventions; but they severally assumed general powers of administration and government. All of them changed more or less the existing State Constitutions; but they did more, — they appropriated moneys out of the State treasuries, raised troops, and appointed officers, with a view to an armed conflict with the United States, should the latter dispute their right to secede. When the convention of delegates which met at Montgomery, Alabama, to frame a Constitution for the Confederacy of the seceding States, submitted its project to the States for ratification, the State Conventions took it upon themselves to ratify that instrument, not only without express instructions, but in evident violation of those which were implied in the Acts calling them together.

Like the Provincial Conventions, therefore, which effected our separation from Great Britain, the Secession Conventions were simply provisional organizations resting upon a revolutionary basis, and exercising such powers as were deemed requisite by the insurgent populations to insure the success of the revolution upon which they had entered. In one respect, however, they differed from the Conventions of 1776. The existing establishments, the State organizations, were, in 1861, all conducted in the interest of the rebellion; it was, therefore, unnecessary for the Conventions, running a parallel course with the various departments of the State governments, to assume so wide governmental powers as did the Provincial Conventions in 1776, to which the colonial governors and Assemblies were generally hostile.[1]

§ 250. The Secession Conventions being thus purely Revolutionary Conventions, as defined in the first chapter, they must depend for their justification solely upon the success of the revolution which they originated. That revolution, it is now a matter of history, did not succeed in any one of the eleven States. The armies engaged in the attempt to wrest those States from the Union were overthrown, having succeeded only in dismantling those States, and placing them in abnormal relations to the Union. Precisely what those relations were, at the moment the rebel armies surrendered, it is not easy to determine; nor, perhaps, is it necessary, further than to state, that the revolting States were found to be under the sway of certain so-called governments, how formed does not matter, which were alien to the Union, the State Constitutions, under which the initial steps in the rebellion had been taken, having been severally overthrown. Such governments obviously could not be recognized by the Federal authorities as existing at all, for any purpose.[2]

Here, then, were brought again into relations of practical subjection to the Union, certain integral populations, which had once been Constitutional States, but which having, by truancy from constitutional courses, lost something necessary to that character, were such no longer — were, indeed, little more than "geographical denominations;" communities, which, although as much in the Union, territorially, as ever, were properly neither constitutional States, nor constitutional Territories, but States which had, *sua sponte*, for purposes of ambition, divested themselves of their constitutional apparel, and donned that of treason and rebellion, and so had forfeited their prerogative as States to

[1] Penn *v.* Tollison, 26 Ark. R., 545.

[2] The State of Texas *v.* White, 7 Wall. R., 700, 717; S. C. 25 Texas R. (Supplement), 465, 591.

participate in governing the Union, and been relegated to a condition analogous to that of Territories — a condition in which they belonged to the Union, but had rightfully no governing function whatever, local or general.

§ 251. Standing thus, it is evident, there were necessary to lead off in any movement with a view to the rehabilitation of such States in their normal relations to the Union, Conventions to provide them with Constitutions. This was universally admitted, but how to call those Conventions, was a question upon which there were wide divergences of opinion.

But four modes of calling such Conventions were possible.

1. The inhabitants of the rebel States might, by a spontaneous movement, without the intervention of any recognized authority whatever, have called Conventions to reconstruct their governments. This course would have required, obviously, the tacit consent of Congress, but, as explained in the first part of this chapter,[1] it would have been liable to great practical objections, and would, besides, have been wholly irregular, not to say revolutionary.

2. The second course was for the so-called legislatures of the seceded States, elected under the rebel *régime*, to initiate, with the consent or connivance of Congress, the movements for reconstruction in their respective States. This course, however, was politically impossible. The government of the United States could not recognize the rebel legislatures, as possessed of any political functions whatever, without, by implication, admitting the validity of the act of secession. If those bodies were to meet, it must be as so many individuals liable to the penalties of treason, and having no rights which the government of the Union was bound to respect, except such as they held in common with other public enemies.

§ 252. 3. As a third course, the Congress of the United States might have inaugurated the movement toward reconstruction by calling Conventions in the lately insurgent States.

Undoubtedly, this course would have been irregular, since Congress has power to pass enabling Acts only for Territories, strictly so called, and not for States. It is true, as we have seen, that the rebel communities, on the surrender of the Confederate armies, were not constitutional States. But neither

[1] See *ante*, §§ 114, 115.

were they constitutional Territories. They were States whose practical relations to the Federal whole were in a state of disruption. In other words, they were *quasi* States, so far as their historical relations to the Union were concerned, but *quasi* Territories, in relation to the exercise of Federal rights.[1]

Being neither States nor Territories, but communities presenting, in their different relations, the aspects of both, Congress could not regularly act toward them as though they were either. It could not permit them to call, nor could it itself regularly call for them, Conventions to reconstruct their subverted governments.

4. Finally, the requisite nucleus for reconstruction might have been provided by the President of the United States, acting in his capacity of Commander-in-Chief of the national armies, engaged in crushing the rebel Confederacy.

With reference to this mode, however, it is evident, that it would have been legitimate only as a war measure, the power of the President to act in the manner supposed, being simply a war power, and therefore proper only whilst the war should last. On the coming of peace, all political structures built up by, and under the shelter of the military arm for the temporary government of the conquered districts, would melt away, save as the law-making power of the Union should recognize and confirm them. They would not have been legally or regularly formed. Judged from a constitutional point of view, they would have been based simply on the will of the commanding general, and, therefore, have been akin to institutions purely revolutionary, as founded without the authority of law. That this is so, becomes the more probable, when it is considered, that it has never, in any one of the States of the Union, or in the Union itself, been recognized as within the competence of the executive branch of the government to call a Convention: that is, of the executive, as such. Considered as the commander of armies in the field, on the other hand, and, in that capacity, called upon to provide for the government temporarily of the territory overrun, because the President could do any thing, he could doubtless call a Convention to frame a provisional Constitution; or, should he prefer to do so, could himself, in general orders, establish a Constitution.

[1] See The State of Texas *v.* George W. White *et als.*, 7 Wall. R., 700, 717 S. C. 25 Tex. R. (Supplement), 465, 591.

But, the point insisted upon is, that such a Convention would lack the essential requisites of legitimacy, as a Constitutional Convention. The act of the President would be justifiable only upon the ground of its necessity, and hence the body convened would stand on the same footing as the English Convention, called by William of Orange on the abdication of James II., which was unquestionably a revolutionary body.

§ 253. These four modes of proceeding being all liable to objections, the question arises, which, on the whole, was preferable?

The answer is — that mode which, beside being attended by the fewest practical evils, was most conformable to established precedents in the United States, in times of peace and constitutional order.

Tried by this test, it is, in my judgment, beyond question, that the third mode, that by the direct intervention of Congress, was to be preferred.

Congress was the grand Council of the nation. Its interference in the business of reconstruction, though irregular, would be effected by some formal Act or Resolution, in which could be provided, to the satisfaction of the nation at large, guarantees not only for the private rights of the citizens of the States concerned, but for the public liberties. Besides, in one aspect of the case, there would, in the intervention of Congress, be an intrinsic propriety, sufficient almost to stamp the act as constitutionally rightful and regular. The legislature of the Union is, as we have seen, as to Federal relations, the legislature of each State. As the rebel States, when admitted to full participation in the government, at once assume a governing relation to the other States, co-members with them of the same Federal whole, the question of their reconstruction, as a practical question, is a Federal one, and ought to be settled by Federal authority. Of all the departments of the general government, Congress is undoubtedly the one to which can be most safely intrusted the power of calling the Conventions necessary for that purpose. As, in such a case, these bodies would be called in each State by that legislature which had supreme jurisdiction over the Federal relations of such State, the departure from the strictest constitutional precedents would be but nominal.

§ 254. The mode at first adopted was the fourth, by the intervention of the President of the United States, save in Virginia, where reconstruction was inaugurated by the spontaneous action of the loyal citizens of the State. In all of them, therefore, the Conventions called for the purpose indicated were, it is conceived, irregular.

The history of the call of those bodies, considering separately such as were convened before and such as were convened after the close of the secession war, is as follows.

The particulars of the call of the Virginia Convention of 1861, by which a loyal government, recognized by the President and represented in Congress, was established in Virginia, have been given in previous sections of this chapter, when treating of the formation of the State of West Virginia,[1] and need not be here repeated. A little later, proceedings to reconstruct the government of Tennessee were sanctioned by President Lincoln. The victories of the Union forces at Forts Donelson and Henry, and the consequent capture of Nashville, compelled the removal of the rebel State government to Memphis. A large part of the State having been restored to Federal authority, Andrew Johnson was appointed military governor by President Lincoln, and assumed the duties of the office in Nashville, on the 12th of March, 1862. September 19, 1863, President Lincoln authorized Governor Johnson to exercise such powers as might be necessary and proper to enable the loyal people of Tennessee to present such a republican form of government as would entitle the State to the guarantee of the United States therefor, and to be protected under such State government by the United States against invasion and domestic violence, "all according to the 4th section of the 4th article of the Constitution of the United States." On the 9th of January, 1864, a State Convention, called by a committee of "Union" men in Middle Tennessee, assembled at Nashville, and proposed amendments to the Constitution, which were ratified by the people on the 22d of February following. Under the Constitution as thus amended the State was admitted to representation in Congress by a joint resolution approved July 24, 1866. This resolution, reciting the performance of certain conditions imposed by Congress and of other acts denoting loyalty, declared the State of Tennessee restored to her former proper, practical relations to the Union, and entitled to be represented by Senators and Representatives in Congress.

[1] *Ante*, §§ 179–182.

§ 255. In two other States, those of Louisiana and Arkansas, a so-called reconstruction took place, under the Proclamation of President Lincoln of December 8, 1863. That proclamation was addressed to the ten then remaining rebel States, but its terms were accepted and acted on only by Tennessee, as above, and by the two other States named, before the assassination of Mr. Lincoln. The proclamation made known to the citizens of the rebel States that, "whenever a number of persons therein, not less than one tenth in number of the votes cast in any such State at the Presidential election in the year 1860, having each taken a prescribed oath, and being a qualified elector of the State immediately before the so-called act of secession, should establish a State government republican in form, such shall be recognized as the true government of the State." With characteristic caution and prudence, the President added these words: "This proclamation is intended to present the people of the States wherein the national authority has been suspended . . . a mode in and by which the national authority and loyal State governments may be reëstablished within said States; . . . and while the mode presented is the best the executive can suggest with his present impressions, it must not be understood that no other possible mode would be acceptable."

§ 256. In pursuance of this proclamation, Louisiana and Arkansas were provided with loyal State governments; the people of the former having been called upon to take the necessary steps by a proclamation of Major-General N. P. Banks, of January 11, 1864. The first step was, under that proclamation, to elect State officers on the 22d of February, 1864; and the second to choose delegates to a Convention, on the first Monday of April following, to revise the Constitution of the State. The particulars of the proceedings in Arkansas were similar.

Were any argument needed to show that the supposed reconstruction of these rebel States, based as it was on the proclamation of the Commander-in-Chief of the armies of the United States, was irregular, it would be found in the statement of General Banks in his proclamation, by which the proceedings in Louisiana were justified, that *the fundamental law of the State was martial law*. The only law in the State was the arbitrary will of the commanding general, which was no law at all. The proceedings, therefore, though not illegal in the sense of contravening any positive law then in force, *were wholly without law*, and so revolutionary.[1]

§ 257. The first series of the Reconstruction Conventions called in North Carolina, Mississippi, Florida, Alabama, Georgia, Texas, Tennessee, and South Carolina were all convened after the close of the war, in pursuance of the authority of President Johnson. As the proceedings in all these cases were similar, I shall refer only to those that occurred in North Carolina, the first State, in the order of time, in which attempts at reconstruction were made.

On the 29th of May, 1865, the following proclamation, relating to the reorganization of North Carolina, was issued by President Johnson, namely: —

"*Whereas*, the 4th section of the 4th Article of the Constitution of the United States declares, that the United States shall guarantee to every State in the Union a republican form of government, and shall protect each of them against invasion and domestic violence; and *whereas*, the President of the United States is, by the Constitution, made Commander-in-Chief of the army and navy, as well as chief civil executive officer of the United States, and is bound by solemn oath faithfully to execute the office of President of the United States, and to take care that the laws be faithfully executed; and *whereas*, the rebellion which has been waged by a portion of the people of the United States against the properly constituted authorities of the government thereof, in the most violent and revolting form, but whose organized and armed forces have now been almost entirely overcome, has, in its revolutionary progress, deprived the people of the State of North Carolina of all civil government; and *whereas*, it becomes necessary and proper to carry out and enforce the obligations of the United States to the people of North Carolina, in securing them in the enjoyment of a republican form of government:

"Now, therefore, in obedience to the high and solemn duties imposed upon me by the Constitution of the United States, and for the purpose of enabling the loyal people of said State to organize a State government, whereby justice may be established, domestic tranquillity insured, and loyal citizens protected in all

[1] See *ante*, §§ 109–113, where the signification of the term "revolutionary," as used by me, is given.

their rights of life, liberty, and property, I, Andrew Johnson, President of the United States, and Commander-in-Chief of the army and navy of the United States, do hereby appoint William W. Holden Provisional Governor of the State of North Carolina, whose duty it shall be, at the earliest practicable period, to prescribe such rules and regulations as may be necessary and proper for convening a Convention, composed of delegates chosen by that portion of the people of said State who are loyal to the United States, and no others, for the purpose of altering or amending the Constitution thereof; and with authority to exercise within the limits of said State all the powers necessary and proper to enable such loyal people of the State of North Carolina to restore said State to its constitutional relations to the Federal government, and to present such a republican form of State government as will entitle the State to the guarantee of the United States therefor, and its people to protection by the United States against invasion, insurrection, and domestic violence: *Provided that*, in any election that may be hereafter held for choosing delegates to any State Convention as aforesaid, no person shall be qualified as an elector, or shall be eligible as a member of such Convention, unless he shall have previously subscribed the oath of amnesty, as set forth in the President's proclamation of May 29th, A. D. 1865, and is a voter qualified as prescribed by the Constitution and laws of the State of North Carolina in force immediately before the 20th day of May, A. D. 1861, the date of the so-called Ordinance of Secession; and the said Convention, when convened, or the legislature that may be thereafter assembled, will prescribe the qualification of electors and the eligibility of persons to hold office under the Constitution and laws of the State, a power the people of the several States composing the Federal Union have rightfully exercised from the origin of the government to the present time."

§ 258. In pursuance of this proclamation, Governor Holden summoned a Convention, which met at Raleigh on the 2d day of October, 1865, and remodelled the Constitution of North Carolina.

Under proclamations from time to time issued by the President in terms substantially identical with those above given, Conventions met in all the States which were in a disorganized condition at the close of the war, and in like manner reformed their Constitutions.

With the question which has so agitated the Union, as to the proper department of the government *to recognize the reconstructed State organizations*, framed by those Conventions, whether the executive, under the Act of 1795, passed to give effect to Article 4, section 4, of the Federal Constitution, above quoted, or the Congress of the United States, I do not propose to meddle. What I have to do with here is the previous question as to the legitimacy of the Conventions by which those governments were formed, — a question totally distinct and depending on different principles; for it is evident, that, whatever be the proper authority to recognize those governments, the act of recognition might give legitimacy to organizations formed by Revolutionary, no less than by regular and lawful, Conventions.

As I have before intimated, the Conventions called by the provisional governors appointed by President Johnson are believed to have been, all of them, irregular and illegitimate. They were called by the Commander-in-Chief of our armies in the exercise of the war power given to him by the Constitution. While that exercise of power was not, in the technical sense of the term, *illegal*, — for nothing is illegal to him who has by law an absolute discretion, — it was, nevertheless, from the very nature of the case, without the law and the Constitution, *extra legem*, — resting for its limitations, as for its justification, solely upon the necessity of the case. The only differences between the arbitrary acts of a military commander, under the Constitution, and acts strictly revolutionary, are, first, — that the former are done with a view to the conservation and defense, and the latter with a view to the disruption or overthrow, of the State; and, secondly, that the former, therefore, are not, and the latter are, punishable as crimes under the penal code. In their essential nature the acts are identical, as being *lawless* acts, acts done *ad arbitrium* and not *ad legem*. Let a military commander step but a hair's breadth beyond what is demanded by necessity, shedding a single drop of blood when the shedding of blood is no longer demanded, and his act is a crime, or, if it have a political intent and bearing, an act of revolution, in the bad sense of the term, as truly as that of one who attempts to subvert the Constitution of the State. This shows that the two kinds of acts are substantially the same.

But, however this may be, it is clear that it is not regularly or constitutionally one of the duties of an executive magistrate to call Conventions to alter or amend the Constitution, and, particularly, is this true of the President, with reference to Conventions in the States. For such a magistrate to do it is, to say the least of it, irregular, and to permit it, except under the pressure of an overruling necessity, — a necessity such as would excuse any act, however unauthorized or revolutionary, — is dangerous.

§ 258 *a*. It is well known that the reconstruction of the governments of the late rebel States, supposed to have been accomplished by the proceedings detailed in the foregoing sections, was not satisfactory to Congress. By three acts (one approved March 2, 1867; one amendatory thereof, approved March 23, 1867; and one approved July 19, 1867[1]) it was declared by Congress that all the existing governments in the rebel States, excepting that established in Tennessee, were not legal State governments, and that they were to be continued thereafter subject in all respects to the military commanders of the respective districts, and to the paramount authority of Congress. By the same acts, provision was made for the reconstruction of such States, upon certain conditions, by means of Constitutional Conventions, to be called and held under the protection of the military authorities quartered in those States. Conventions were accordingly held, by which the Constitutions were framed or amended, and put in force, as required in those acts; and under them the States were, with the exception referred to, admitted into full participation in the government of the Union, by the reception of their Senators and Representatives in the Congress of the United States.

§ 258 *b*. Among the conditions imposed by Congress, which were formally accepted by the Conventions of the several States, were, that the delegates to said Conventions should be elected by the male citizens of such States, twenty-one years old and upwards, of whatever race or previous condition, who had been resident in their respective States one year previous to the day of such election, except persons disfranchised for participation in the rebellion, or for felony at common law; that they should provide in their Constitutions that the elective franchise should be enjoyed by all such persons as had the qualifications above

[1] See 14 U. S. Sts. at Large, p. 428; 15 id. pp. 2, 14.

stated for electors; that such Constitutions should be ratified by a majority of the persons voting on the question of ratification who were qualified as electors of delegates; that such Constitutions should be submitted to Congress for examination and approval; that Congress should approve the same; and that said States, by a vote of their several legislatures elected under said Constitutions, should adopt the amendment to the Constitution of the United States proposed by the 39th Congress, and known as Article XIV. When said article should have become a part of the Constitution of the United States, the acts declared that their said States should be declared entitled to representation in Congress, and that Senators and Representatives should be admitted therefrom on their taking the oath prescribed by law.

§ 258 *c.* The mode of calling the Conventions actually pursued was, in Alabama, Florida, Georgia, Arkansas, South Carolina, Mississippi, and North Carolina, as follows: The military commanders of the districts in which those States were situated ordered elections to be held to determine whether the voters, already registered under military authority, were in favor of holding a Convention, and to elect delegates thereto; and, the majority of such voters favoring such a Convention, a further order was issued for the delegates so elected to meet, at a time and place named in the order, for the purpose of framing a Constitution and civil government, according to the provisions of the Acts of the 2d and 23d of March, 1867. Lists of the delegates elected were also made out at department headquarters, and in some cases elections declared to have been irregularly held, or to have been infected by fraud, were set aside by the commanding general, and new elections to fill vacancies ordered.[1]

§ 258 *d.* In respect to the regularity of these Conventions, it need only be remarked, that they were called by, or at the invitation of, Congress, in the acts above recited, in substantial conformity to the principle set forth in sections 252 and 253 of this work, and there described as the third of the four possible modes of bringing about a reconstruction of the rebel govern-

[1] *Jour. Ark. Conv.* 1868, pp. 27–31, containing orders of General Ord for the elections in Arkansas and Mississippi, comprised in his military district, the fourth; also *Jour. N. C. Conv.* 1868, pp. 3–9. On the whole question of reconstruction, and of the *status* and relations of the rebel States to the Union during and at the close of the secession war, see Texas *v.* White, 7 Wall. R., 700, 722.

ments, and as being the mode which, beside being attended by the fewest practical evils, was most conformable to established precedents in the United States, in times of peace, and constitutional order. If the course adopted was irregular, and the means employed not strictly in accordance with principle, they were as little so as was possible under the peculiar circumstances of the case.[1]

§ 259. In concluding this survey of the various Conventions thus far held in the United States, it will be proper to refer to the so-called Convention held at Montgomery, Alabama, in 1861, to frame a Constitution for the Confederacy of seceded States. This Convention was not called to frame a Constitution for either the United States, a State in the Union, or a Territory seeking admission into the Union, but for an imaginary commonwealth, — the dream for a third of a century of the States Rights School of politicians, and for four years the supposed realization of that dream on the banks of the James River, — and for that reason not proper to be classed with either of the varieties of Conventions I have been considering. In the same category are to be placed all such Conventions as were held in the separate States of the "Confederacy" between the years 1861 and 1865, to alter or abolish the so-called Constitutions of those States, as members of the imaginary commonwealth referred to — all equally fictitious Constitutions for commonwealths that had no substantial basis either in law or in fact.

My only purpose in mentioning these bodies is to note that, so far as they seemed to possess a *de facto* character as Constitutional Conventions, that is, so far as they were not mere schools of abstractionists, engaged, for their own recreation, in framing imaginary Constitutions, they were wholly illegitimate and revolutionary.

§ 260. Having thus considered, from the two points of view

[1] "After two years of trial of the fourth method of reconstruction," (described in section 252, *ante*), "the people of the North, learning from sad experience, have come to adopt Judge Jameson's opinion, and Congress has just enacted a law" (the Act of March, 1867, commonly called the Reconstruction Act) "to provide for the more efficient government of the rebel States," meaning a law in conformity with the method recommended in section 253, *ante*, and called the third method of reconstruction. *N. A. Rev.* for April, 1867, p. 654. The first edition of this work, thus referred to, was published in October, 1866, though on the title-page the date given was 1867.

indicated in the opening part of this chapter, the question, How should a Convention be called? I pass to the other question there propounded, namely —

II. By whom should Conventions, to be legitimate, be elected?

This question will be considered from the same two points of view as the former, namely, (*a*), from that of principle, and, (*b*), from that of historical precedents.

(*a*). Upon principle, the question, by whom Conventions should be elected, is one of little difficulty.

1. The sovereign body, we will suppose, is already organized under a government, which of course is one of its own appointment, comprising the usual departments for its actual administration. Having established it, the sovereign retires from view, leaving in the hands of that government full powers not only to operate, but to initiate the movements necessary to modify, repair, or renew, the system.[1] One of the departments in every adequate system of government is the people, in its narrow sense, meaning the body of persons named by the sovereign to be the immediate depositaries of governmental powers, the electors. By this body, or by some individuals selected from it, according to established laws, every function of government, every political act, must regularly be performed, and by no others. The electoral circle determined by the Constitution, so long as that instrument remains unchanged, is a closed one. It is a circle, moreover, which can be opened and enlarged only by the sovereign body itself, acting in the modes prescribed by the Constitution or by the customary law of the land.

Suppose, now, a Convention is to be chosen to change the fundamental law, its members must be elected by the body invested with political functions, the electors, or by some determinate portion of it, in conformity to the laws and customs of the commonwealth. The legislature, as we have seen, is the proper body to direct the election and assembling of the Convention. Common sense would indicate that delegates intended to represent, first, the electoral body, and, through that, the sovereign, if they are to represent truly the different phases of opinion current among the people at large, should be chosen by the entire electoral body. Thus, the requirements of principle and

[1] See *ante*, § 25.

of expediency would be fully satisfied. To authorize persons outside the circle of the electors to participate in the work, would be to extend the exercise of political functions to persons excluded by the Constitution; that is, by an act of a mere department of the government, to modify or repeal a solemn provision of that instrument, by which its own powers are determined. On the other hand, although, strictly speaking, delegates should be chosen by the entire electorate, yet, were the legislature, in calling a Convention, to limit the right of voting for them to the electorate less certain designated classes of persons deemed unfitted to exercise that right intelligently, or with safety to the state, such action, although a departure from strict principle, would be less objectionable than action which should extend the right beyond the electoral circle. A Convention so elected would still represent the electors and nobody else; and as it would merely recommend, but of itself conclude nothing, there would be no danger of the government being swamped by the unauthorized intervention of non-electors. This mode of choosing delegates is therefore considered as, on the whole, not illegitimate.

§ 261. 2. If, on the contrary, the sovereign political body be in a state of disorganization, its Constitution overthrown, and the departments of the public administration deposed from all authority, and a Convention is to be called to rebuild the fabric of government, by whom then should the delegates be chosen?

As, in the case supposed, all action would be the direct exercise of sovereign power,[1] and in its essential nature revolutionary, there would be no law to govern the election but that of expediency. Such persons might then be permitted to vote as should at the time seem fitted to exercise the franchise wisely. In general, however, a people thus situated would find it expedient to confine the right of voting to the class, by the laws of the land now obsolete, invested with the franchise — the basis and apportionment of representation according to those laws being just and equal. Where they were unjust or unequal, the right of the people to change or abolish them could not be questioned as a right of revolution.

§ 262. (*b.*) It is believed that the precedents developed thus far in our history, as well in times of constitutional order as in those of revolution, conform to the principle just announced.

[1] See *ante*, § 23.

1. The Conventions called to revise old or to frame new Constitutions, during the period intervening between 1783 and the present time, excluding the Secession and Reconstruction Conventions, have, with scarcely any exception, been elected by the persons by existing laws entitled to exercise the suffrage at the general State elections. Let us look, first, at the provisions of our Constitutions; and, secondly, at the various acts calling Conventions, to ascertain the qualifications required by them for the electors of delegates to Conventions. Of the Constitutions, few in number, which have contained provisions on the subject, some have authorized to vote for delegates "citizens," or "voters," or "qualified voters entitled to vote for representatives;"[1] some, "persons having the qualifications to vote for members of the General Assembly;"[2] some, "the qualified electors;"[3] some, "the towns and places, or incorporated places;"[4] one, "each senatorial district," without further specification;[5] and the residue, "the freemen of this State."[6] Coming now to the precedents developed in the actual call of Conventions: Convention Acts have in some cases designated the voters for delegates as "the electors of the State, qualified to vote at general elections;"[7] or have authorized to vote "all persons qualified to vote for members of, or representatives to, the General Assembly;"[8] or "the

[1] Constitutions of Delaware, 1792 and 1831; Illinois, 1848; Kansas, 1857; Kentucky, 1792, 1799, and 1850; and Louisiana, 1812.

[2] Constitutions of Florida, 1865; Illinois, 1818 and 1870; Ohio, 1802; and Tennessee, 1796.

[3] Constitutions of Mississippi, 1817 and 1832.

[4] Constitutions or amendments of New Hampshire, 1784, 1792, 1850, and 1876.

[5] Constitution of Missouri, 1875.

[6] Constitutions as amended by the Vermont Councils of Censors of 1785, 1792, 1799, 1806, 1813, 1820, 1827, 1834, 1841, 1848, 1855, 1862, and 1869. These amendments were required to be submitted to Conventions called by such Councils, for the purpose of adopting or rejecting them. Of these Conventions, nine had been called when the system was abolished, in 1870. See § 220, *ante*, and appendix B, *post.*

[7] Convention Acts of Nebraska, 1875; Pennsylvania, 1837; and Rhode Island, 1824, and November, 1841.

[8] Convention Acts of California, 1878; Delaware, 1831 and 1852; Georgia, 1833, 1839, and 1877; Illinois, 1847, 1862, and 1869; Indiana, 1850; Kentucky, 1849; Louisiana, 1844; Massachusetts, 1780, 1820, and 1853; Michigan, 1850; Mississippi, 1832; Missouri, 1861 and 1865; Nebraska, 1864 and 1866; Nevada, 1864; New York, 1846 and 1867; North Carolina, 1835, 1861, and 1875;

qualified electors, or legal voters, of the State;"[1] or "persons having the qualifications of members of the General Assembly;"[2] or "inhabitants qualified to vote for Senators;"[3] or "the free citizens of the State, aged twenty-one years and upwards;"[4] or "the people of the State or of the several counties;"[5] or "the inhabitants of the county qualified to vote for Governor and Senators;"[6] or "the freeholders."[7] In most of these cases, it turns

South Carolina, 1860; Virginia, 1829, 1850, and 1861; and West Virginia, 1872. To these may be added, in general, the enabling Acts passed by Congress authorizing Conventions to frame Constitutions for Territories seeking to become States. The first of these was passed for Ohio, in 1802, and authorized to vote for delegates all male citizens of the United States, of full age, resident one year in the Territory, who had paid a Territorial or county tax, and all persons having in other respects the qualifications to vote for Representatives in the General Assembly of the territory. 2 U. S. Sts. at Large, p. 173. The enabling Acts of Louisiana, id. 641; Indiana, 3 do. 289; Mississippi, id. 348; Illinois, id. 428; Alabama, id. 489; Missouri, id. 545; Nevada, 13 do. 30; Nebraska, id. 47; Colorado, Act of March 3, 1875, were substantially the same; those of Louisiana, Mississippi, and Missouri, however, containing the word "free" before the words "male citizens," and those of Illinois and Alabama not requiring the payment of a tax. In the enabling Act of Wisconsin, and in the Acts of Congress and of the Republic of Texas relating to the admission of the latter into the Union, the Conventions were to be called or elected by "the people." 9 U. S. Sts. at Large, p. 56. In that of Minnesota, "the legal voters in each Representative District" were authorized to elect delegates to the Convention. 11 U. S. Sts. at Large, p. 166.

[1] Convention Acts of Alabama, 1861 and 1875; Arkansas, 1874; Connecticut, 1818; Florida, 1885; Iowa, 1857; Kansas, 1859; Kentucky, 1799; Louisiana, 1852; Maryland, 1850, 1864, and 1867; Michigan, 1836 and 1867; Minnesota, 1857; Mississippi, 1832; Ohio, 1850 and 1873; Pennsylvania, 1789, 1837, and 1872; Texas, 1875; and West Virginia, 1861. The case of the West Virginia Convention of 1872 may be placed in the same category, although the phraseology of the Convention Act is different. The latter authorizes to vote for delegates every person qualified to vote for delegates to the legislature, resident one year in the State and thirty days in the county in which he offers to vote, with certain exceptions of minors, paupers, persons convicted of treason, felony, bribery at an election, and of unsound mind. The Constitution of 1861, Article III., sec. 1, authorizes all white male citizens, with the same exceptions, to vote at all elections within the districts where they reside.

[2] Pennsylvania, 1789.

[3] New Hampshire, 1850 and 1876.

[4] New York, 1801. Street's Council of Revision, p. 46.

[5] Arkansas, 1861; and Delaware, 1776.

[6] Maine, 1819.

[7] Virginia, 1829.

out, upon inspection of the Constitution or laws regulating the right of suffrage, that by the classes indicated were meant the general body of the electors of the States respectively. In the Act calling the Louisiana Convention of 1844, and in several of the State Constitutions which provide for the election of Conventions, the delegates are required to be chosen "in the same manner as members of the General Assembly;" or the elections to be held "in the same manner and under the same regulations" as antecedent elections held to determine the expediency of calling Conventions, at which latter the persons qualified to vote were the "voters," "qualified voters," "qualified electors," "electors qualified to vote for members of the General Assembly," &c.[1] Generally, however, in the cases last described, the provisions were, that if the result of the prior elections, at which the classes of persons named had voted, should be in favor of calling Conventions, the General Assemblies of the respective States should call the same, to be thereafter elected by the people; from which it may be inferred that the same voters are to figure in both elections.[2] In a few cases, all white male citizens of the United States, twenty-one years of age and resident in the county or election district a fixed period of time before the election, varying from three months to a year, were authorized to vote for delegates to the Convention.[3]

§ 263. 2. The rule which seems thus to be well-nigh universal in times of peace and order, has generally, in substance, obtained in those of revolution. During our first revolution, extending from 1775 to 1783, although it is not easy to determine the question with accuracy, enough is known to make it probable that the Conventions were elected by the persons authorized under the laws of the several colonies to vote at general elections. In some cases, however, special qualifications were required to

[1] Constitutions of Minnesota, 1857; Ohio, 1851; and Tennessee, 1834 and 1861.

[2] Constitutions of California, 1849; Iowa, 1844 and 1857; Kansas, 1859; Michigan, 1850; West Virginia, 1863; and Wisconsin, 1848.

[3] The residence in the county, voting district, or Territory required was, in Florida, 1838, six months; Kansas, 1857, three months; Michigan, 1835, six months, and the word "free" was inserted before the word "white"; New Jersey, 1844, one year in the State and three months in the county; Tennessee, 1870, six months; Wisconsin, 1846 and 1847, six months in the Territory. In the enabling Act of Nevada, 1863, no length of residence was specified.

insure the loyalty of such as were allowed to vote. Thus, in Pennsylvania, the conference of committees, by which the Convention of 1776 was called, required, in addition to the qualifications of electors generally, an oath abjuring allegiance to George III., and undertaking not to oppose the establishment of a free government by the proposed Convention. Such a requirement, at a time of public danger, may be accepted as a proper exercise of legislative power. Indeed, to omit such a provision would be inexcusable.

In a few cases, the right of suffrage was given generally to the "freemen of the counties,"[1] to "the people,"[2] or to "the several parishes and districts,"[3] — terms which indicate the existence of election laws determining both the voters and the modes of proceeding to collect and return their votes.

To these instances may be added those of the first series of Reconstruction Conventions called in 1864–66, under the proclamations of Presidents Lincoln and Johnson, referred to in previous sections.[4] The persons authorized by these proclamations to vote for delegates were the electors qualified as voters by the laws of their respective States before the secession ordinances were passed, each having taken and kept the amnesty oath prescribed by those proclamations.[5]

The second series of Reconstruction Conventions, held in 1867 and 1868, in pursuance of the so-called Reconstruction Acts of Congress of March 2d and 23d and July 19, 1867, belong to a different class, and will be considered in a subsequent section.[6]

§ 264. A few cases must now be mentioned in which there was a departure from the principles and the current of the precedents set down in the preceding sections. The first of these was that of the Georgia Convention of 1788, which, as we have seen, was elected directly by the legislature.[7] The second case was that of the New York Convention of 1821. By the New York Constitution of 1777, sec. vii., the following persons were

[1] Act calling the Delaware Convention of 1776.

[2] Acts calling the North Carolina Convention of 1776 and the Vermont Convention of 1777.

[3] Act calling the Georgia Convention of 1776.

[4] See *ante*, §§ 254–258 *d*.

[5] See 13 U. S. Sts. at Large, pp. 737, 760.

[6] See *post*, § 266.

[7] *Ante*, § 148, 149; *post*, § 266.

made electors, namely: all male inhabitants of full age, personally resident in one of the counties of the State for six months immediately preceding the day of election, if during that time possessed of a freehold of the value of twenty pounds within said county, or of a leasehold interest of the yearly value of forty shillings, and if they had been rated and actually paid taxes to the State; with a reservation of a right to vote, within their places of residence, to the freemen of the cities of Albany and New York made such before the 14th of October, 1775.

The Act of Assembly of March 13, 1821, calling the Convention of that year, made essential changes in the qualifications of electors, by authorizing to vote for delegates to that body all free male citizens of the State, of the age of twenty-one years or upwards, who should possess a freehold within the State; or who should have been rated and paid taxes to the State; or who should have been actually enrolled in the militia of the State, or in a legal volunteer or uniform corps, and should have served therein either as an officer or private; or who should have been or then were by law exempt from taxation; or who should have been assessed to work on the public roads and highways, and should have worked thereon, or should have paid a commutation therefor, according to law.

The effect of this act was considerably to increase the body of the electors authorized to vote for delegates, beyond those given the right of suffrage by the existing Constitution, although it deprived of it negro slaves, to whom, if possessed of the requisite property qualification, that Constitution had given the right.

§ 265. The next instance of exceptional legislation in the matter of electing delegates to Conventions occurred in Rhode Island.

By the charter of Charles II., in force in Rhode Island until 1842, the right to determine the qualifications of voters was committed to the General Assembly. We have already seen that, at the date mentioned, in consequence of changes of the population not attended by corresponding changes in the basis of representation, or in the qualifications for the suffrage, great inequalities had arisen in the political power enjoyed by different parts of the State and by different classes of the population. As a consequence, the suffrage movement was set on foot, culminating, as already explained, in the formation of the so-called

People's Constitution, the election of State officers under it, and in an attempt by the pretended Governor, Dorr, to establish the new government, in the place of that existing under the Charter, by military force.[1] This revolutionary attempt was easily suppressed, but the legitimate government did not confine itself to forcible measures to maintain its own supremacy, and to restore the public tranquillity. The Constitution framed by the legitimate Convention, called by the General Assembly in 1841, having, through the efforts mainly of the suffrage party, been rejected, another Convention was called by the same body in the following year, by which the present Constitution of the State was framed. To appease the discontent of the "People's Party," the General Assembly, in calling this Convention, extended the right of suffrage for the election of delegates, repealing the clauses of existing laws making property, payment of taxes, and military service qualifications for the exercise of that function, and retaining as the only requisite for it three years' residence in the State, and authorized to vote for delegates all persons qualified by existing laws to vote for general officers, and all native male citizens of the United States (except Narragansett Indians, convicts, paupers, persons under guardianship and *non compos mentis*), who were of the age of twenty-one years and upwards, and who should have had their permanent residence or home within the State for the period of three years next preceding their voting, and in the town or city wherein they should offer to vote for the period of one year next preceding such voting, and who should have had their names recorded with the town or city clerk of the town or city in which they should offer to vote, in a proper book to be kept for that purpose, at least ten days before the day of voting.[2]

§ 265 *a*. Several other instances of a departure from the principles generally recognized in calling Conventions have occurred since that in Rhode Island. In calling the New Jersey Conven-

[1] See *ante*, §§ 227, 228.

[2] *Considerations on the Questions of the Adoption of a Constitution and Extension of Suffrage in Rhode Island*, by E. R. Potter, p. 21. The persons authorized to vote for delegates to the People's Convention were as follows . "All male American citizens (natives and foreigners, and without distinction of color) aged twenty-one years, and who had resided in the State one year." These qualifications were fixed by the committee of citizens calling the Convention.

tion of 1844, the legislature authorized to vote for delegates every white male citizen of the United States above the age of twenty-one years resident in the State one year, and in the township three months, next preceding said election. The Constitution then in force, that of 1776, contained no provision of any kind for amending that instrument, or for calling a Convention, and it gave the right of suffrage for Representatives in Council and Assembly, and for all other public officers elected by the people of the county at large, to all inhabitants of the colony, of full age, who were worth fifty pounds, proclamation money, clear estate in the same, and who had resided within the county in which they claimed a vote for twelve months immediately preceding the election.[1] So the act under which the Maryland Convention of 1867 assembled, provided for the election of delegates to that body by the registered voters of the State. The last Constitution, that of 1864, had given the right of suffrage to the white male citizens of the United States, twenty-one years old and upwards, resident in the State one year, and in any county or legislative district of the city of Baltimore, six months next preceding the election. It also provided for a registration of voters, under an act of the Assembly, and excluded from voting persons convicted of larceny or other infamous crimes, and all rebels and rebel sympathizers. To this clause, however, was appended a proviso, that persons thus disqualified by disloyalty might be restored to the full rights of citizenship by an act of the General Assembly, passed by a two thirds vote of all the members elected to each house.[2] The Constitution further provided (Art. XII., sec. 2) that, should a Convention be called to revise or amend that instrument, it should "consist of as many members as both houses of the General Assembly," to be "chosen in the same manner." With a view, it was claimed, to place the State of Maryland in the hands of the sympathizers with, and participators in the late rebellion, the legislature in 1867 "enfranchised," and caused to be registered, "all white men, no matter what treason they had committed, and thus added to the voting population about 30,000 persons who had only lately ceased an armed resistance to the government."[3] This was charged to have been done "by a

[1] Sec. IV., New Jersey Constitution, 1776.

[2] See Article I., secs. 1–4, of the Maryland Constitution of 1864.

[3] Memorial of Republican members of the Maryland Legislature to Con-

doubtful construction of a clause of the Constitution," but the legislature proceeded further to acts more clearly violative of that instrument. The basis of representation being the white population, less those disfranchised for rebellion and not reinstated in their rights by the legislature, the latter, in its call for the Convention of 1867, gave to certain old counties, the seat of a large rebel population, an increased representation, by which the oppressor was "to represent the oppressed against his will, and by which a minority of the people of the State" were "to hold in their proposed Convention the same power as the majority."[1] This action was claimed to be in violation of the clause of the Constitution relating to the mode of choosing members of Conventions, quoted above, that they should be chosen "in the same manner as members of both houses of the General Assembly,— that is, upon the same basis of representation."

Another instance of departure from principle is that of the Act calling the Tennessee Convention of 1870. Article IV. of the Constitution of 1834, which contained no provision for calling a Convention, had given the right of suffrage to every free white man, etc., but provided that no person should be disqualified from voting in any election, on account of color, "who is now, by the laws of this State, a competent witness in a court of justice against a white man." In calling the Convention of 1870, the legislature authorized to vote for delegates "every male person not convicted and rendered infamous for crime," thus admitting colored votes, and extending the suffrage established by the Constitution.

§ 266. To the instances referred to in the last section must be added those of the second series of Reconstruction Conventions, called under the authority of Congress in 1867 and 1868. The enabling Acts of March 2d and 23d and July 19, 1867, by which the Constitutions and governments established under the first series of Reconstruction Conventions were declared to be illegal, and new Constitutions and governments were authorized to be established in the States of Virginia, North Carolina, South Carolina, Georgia, Mississippi, Alabama, Louisiana, Florida, Texas, and Arkansas, provided that the Conventions called

gress, presented to that body March 25, 1867. McPherson's *History of the Reconstruction*, p. 246.

[1] Memorial, etc., above referred to.

under those acts should be elected by the male citizens of those States, twenty-one years of age and upwards, of whatever race, color, or previous condition, resident one year in the State, except such as were disfranchised for participation in the rebellion, or for felony at common law; provided, that no person excluded from holding office by the XIV. admendment should vote. The persons thus excluded were those who, having previously taken an oath, as a member of Congress or of any State legislature, or as an executive or judicial officer of any State, to support the Constitution of the United States, should have engaged in insurrection or rebellion against the same, or given aid or comfort to the enemies thereof. By all the Constitutions in force in those States before the rebellion, or framed for them by the first series of Reconstruction Conventions, the right of suffrage was confined to the free white male citizens of the United States. The Federal statutes referred to, therefore, by enfranchising the blacks, extended the right to vote for delegates much beyond the circle of the electors under existing laws. They also narrowed that circle, very properly, by the clauses disfranchising persons for rebellion or felony at common law. A careful search among the Constitutions and Convention Acts, prescribing the qualifications of voters for delegates to Conventions, reveals only the few departures from what we regard as the principle that ought to govern in such cases, explained in the last three sections. And it is remarkable that, in every instance but three, — those of Georgia, 1788, Rhode Island, November, 1841, and perhaps Maryland, 1867, — the departure was upon this side or that of what we may call the "color line" in our politics, and resulted from efforts on the one side to disfranchise, and on the other to enfranchise, the negro race. The enlargement beyond, or the restriction within, the limits fixed for the suffrage by the several Constitutions, was in these cases, therefore, but the working of the old leaven of revolution, which finally burst forth in the war of secession, and is not properly a precedent for other times. This remark applies equally to the Conventions called by the States and those called under the Reconstruction Acts by Congress, or by its authority.

The case of the Georgia Convention of 1788, to which the delegates were chosen directly by the legislature, it need not be said, was a violation of all principle, and as a precedent would be fraught with extreme danger. So universally has this action of the Georgia legislature been discountenanced, that it has never been imitated in that or any other State. In the Rhode Island case, the departure from principle was little more than nominal, since, although the General Assembly enlarged the list of those authorized to vote for delegates to the second Convention of November, 1841, as well as to that of 1842, beyond the limits of the existing laws, that body had, by the charter of Charles II., as we have seen, the right to determine the qualifications of voters, and it was clearly a wise exercise of its legislative discretion to extend the franchise to those citizens whose just discontent had lately precipitated them into revolution.

In the case of New Jersey, it does not appear whether the electorate was, on the whole, increased or diminished. The Act calling the Convention of 1844, on the one hand, restricted the right of voting for delegates to the white citizens, instead of to all the inhabitants of full age, who had that right under the Constitution of 1776; but it increased the number of voters by removing the property qualification required by the same Constitution. It certainly, however, violated principle in thus giving the right of choosing delegates to persons not entitled to vote under the existing Constitution.

As to the Maryland Convention of 1867, it may be observed that, if it enfranchised the citizens who had been involved in the rebellion, and been disfranchised by the Constitution of 1864, in a manner or by a majority forbidden by that instrument, as is charged by the memorial above referred to, or if it caused those citizens to be registered contrary to law, and to be represented in the Convention by a disproportionate representation, as is also charged, the case is clearly one of a departure from principle, and ought not to be drawn into precedent. The case is put thus hypothetically because the statement of facts made in the memorial may be exaggerated or untrue.

CHAPTER V.

OF THE ORGANIZATION AND MODES OF PROCEEDING OF CONVENTIONS.

§ 267. THE Convention having been called, our next inquiries relate to the general structure or constitution of the body, to its internal organization and to its modes of proceeding.

The constitution of a Convention may be considered with reference, first, to its membership — the qualifications therefor — and, secondly, to the question of its subdivision into separate chambers, possessed of a mutual negative upon each other.

1. The first question — Who may be members of a Convention? — receives an explicit answer in but few of our Constitutions. The Kentucky Constitution of 1850, Article XII., requires that they shall be "possessed of the same qualifications of a qualified elector;" that of California of 1879, and that of Florida of 1865, that they shall have "the same qualifications as members of the General Assembly;" and that of Illinois of 1870, "the same qualifications as members of the Senate," which differ from those prescribed for the electors in the requirement that Senators shall be of the age of twenty-five years, citizens of the United States, resident in the State five years, and in the district in which they were elected two years, next preceding their election; whereas for electors, a residence of one year in the State, ninety days in the county, and thirty days in the election district, next preceding any election sufficed, thus increasing the qualifications for delegates above those prescribed for electors. These are the only Constitutions which have prescribed the qualifications of the delegates to Conventions.

In the Acts under which Conventions have assembled, however, the qualifications of the delegates have been more frequently specified. The most common requirement is, that they shall possess the qualifications of "electors," or "voters," or "which would entitle them to vote for Representatives to the General Assembly;"[1] or "the qualifications of members of the House of Representatives;"[2] or "those required of members of the General Assembly;"[3] or "those of Senators;"[4] or that they shall be "discreet and proper persons;"[5] or "free male citizens of the State twenty-four years of age and upwards;"[6] or "free white men, twenty-one years of age, resident one year in the State, provided that they possess the freehold required of a member of the House of Commons,"[7] or "persons entitled, under the Act calling the Convention, to vote for delegates;"[8] or "white male citizens of the United States having certain qualifications of age or residence in the State or Territory,"[9] or "having the qualifications of voters under existing laws;"[10] or "persons resident in the county, or delegate district," — of the former, the same number as of the members of the House of Delegates, and two of the latter;[11] or that "the elections of delegates should be conducted in the same places and manner, and under the same regulations, and the result be certified and declared in the same manner as prescribed for members of the House of Representatives.[12]

Some Convention Acts prescribe the qualifications of delegates

[1] Convention Acts of Colorado and New Hampshire, 1876; Florida, 1861; Indiana, 1850; Kansas, 1857; Michigan, 1867; Nebraska and Nevada, 1864; Ohio, 1850 and 1873; Rhode Island, 1824 and 1834; and South Carolina, 1860.

[2] Convention Acts of Arkansas, 1861 and 1874; Maryland, 1864; and North Carolina, 1875.

[3] Convention Acts of Georgia, 1877; and Louisiana, 1852.

[4] Convention Acts of Alabama, 1875; and Iowa, 1857.

[5] Convention Act of Virginia, 1850.

[6] Convention Acts of Delaware, 1831 and 1852.

[7] Convention Act of North Carolina, 1835.

[8] Convention Acts of Georgia, 1877; New York, 1821; Rhode Island, 1824, and November, 1841.

[9] Convention Acts of Florida, 1838, requiring twelve months' residence; Georgia, 1833 and 1839, requiring the age of twenty-five years, an inhabitancy of the State of seven and three years respectively, and a residence in the county of one year: Iowa, 1844 and 1846, requiring six months' residence in the Territory; Michigan, 1835, requiring twenty-one years of age; and Virginia, 1861, requiring twenty-five years of age.

[10] Enabling Act of Nevada, 1863.

[11] Convention Act of West Virginia, 1872.

[12] Convention Act of Michigan, 1836.

in negative terms, as, that no person excluded from the privilege of holding office by the XIV. amendment to the Constitution of the United States should be eligible as a member of the Convention:[1] or no person who is not twenty-one years of age, a citizen of the State twelve months, and of the district from which he is sent six months, preceding the election:[2] or no person not twenty-four years of age, a free white male citizen of the United States, a citizen of the State two years, and of the district one year, before his election.[3] In these cases, doubtless, all citizens qualified to vote at general elections, and not embraced within the prohibited classes, would be eligible to the Convention.

The Acts calling the Maryland Conventions of 1850 and 1867 required for delegates to those bodies the same qualifications as for members of the House of Delegates. But the former declared to be eligible, also, "Senators or Representatives in Congress, State Senators, and civil officers of the State or the United States, residing within the State twelve months preceding the election;" but the latter excluded "clergymen, ministers of the gospel, preachers of any denomination, Senators and Representatives in Congress, Judges of Circuit, Superior, Common Pleas, and Criminal Courts, State's Attorneys, Auditors of the city of Baltimore, Clerks of Courts, Registers of Wills, and Sheriffs," from seats in the Convetion.

Finally, the Act calling the New York Convention of 1867 made a wholly new departure in authorizing to sit as a delegate in said body any citizen of the State, whether a resident of the district for which he was elected or not. Whether this Act could be construed as authorizing the election of women, or persons under age, may perhaps be doubted. If not, it does little more than authorize the election of male citizens of New York of mature years, whether resident in the same election district or not. From the above citations it may be stated that in no case has any Constitution or Convention Act authorized to sit as a member of a Convention any person not a citizen of the State, and a qualified voter or elector according to the existing law; or any person

[1] Act of March 2, 1867, under which the second series of Reconstruction Conventions assembled. U. S. Sts. at Large, vol. 14, p. 428.

[2] Acts calling the Tennessee Conventions of 1861 and 1870.

[3] Convention Act of Missouri, 1861–63.

not a resident in the election district from which he seeks an election as delegate, save in the single case just noted of New York.

§ 268. In the Constitutions of several of the States, now in force, after making provision for calling Conventions under certain circumstances, the delegates thereto are required to be "chosen in the same manner, at the same places, and at the same time," as the representatives to the General Assembly, and the same or equivalent phraseology is found in many of the Acts of the State legislatures by which Conventions are called. So, also, in the enabling Acts passed by Congress, authorizing Conventions in Territories, there is commonly inserted a provision requiring the elections to be "conducted in the same manner as is prescribed by the laws of the Territory regulating elections therein for members of the House of Representatives." To these add, what is believed to be the fact, that in no case has any person ever been elected as a delegate to a Convention in the United States who was not a citizen-elector, resident in the State where the Convention was called, and the case, upon one side, is presented. If it does not establish the fact, that, as a general rule, no one, not possessing at least the general qualifications of an elector, is eligible to a Convention, it certainly raises a strong implication to that effect.

§ 269. Against these facts should be set off the declarations of certain authorities, in and out of Conventions, laying down an opposite rule, according to which the electors may choose whom they will to represent them in those bodies, whether qualified electors or not, even if non-residents of the State, and that, whether restricted by the Act calling the Convention or not. Thus, the opinion has been expressed, that "the delegates may be individuals from any class, including the ministers of religion, the Governor, and other public functionaries, and the judges"[1] — persons, by many of our Constitutions, excluded from occupying seats in our General Assemblies, or from holding any other places of honor or profit. So, in the Pennsylvania Convention of 1837, it was intimated that, had the county of Philadelphia elected Albert Gallatin, a citizen and resident of New York, as its delegate, it would have been competent for that body to admit him to a seat, in the face of the Act of the legislature, above referred

[1] Hinton's *Hist. U. S.*, Vol. II. pp. 324–327.

to, localizing the elections of its members.[1] Those who advocate this freedom of election might, perhaps, with some plausibility claim, that, inasmuch as the function of a Convention is to recommend, not to enact, constitutional changes, free scope should be allowed to the electors to employ the best talent they can find, wholly without restriction; and that what reason thus indicates to be expedient, the fact that most of our laws and Constitutions are wholly silent as to who may, and who may not be members of Conventions, demonstrates with sufficient clearness to be according to the intent of those who framed them.

§ 270. 2. In relation to the question of subdividing Conventions into two chambers, with a check upon each other, after the plan of our legislative Assemblies, it is not my purpose to enlarge. So long as those bodies confine themselves to their legitimate function, of advisers, and abstain from acts of legislation, which belong to another department, the legislature, their present constitution, in a single chamber, is without danger, and, having the merit of simplicity, is doubtless preferable to any other. Such has uniformly been the constitution exhibited by them thus far. The idea, however, has been advanced, that a Convention of two houses would better answer its constitutional purpose than of one. In the New York Convention of 1846, Mr. Ruggles introduced a resolution recommending, that all future Conventions called in that State should consist of two chambers. It was received with little favor, however, and was not pressed. In 1857, the Convention of Minnesota realized as a fact the constitution which had only been elsewhere imagined. The two political parties in the Convention, Republicans and Democrats, disagreeing as to the organization of the body, formed separate Conventions, which ran parallel courses, each claiming to be the only legitimate Convention. Two Constitutions were reported, and it seemed that the people were to be embarrassed by the necessity of choosing between them, when, toward the close of their respective sessions, a conference was had between the two bodies, and a single Constitution reported to, and adopted by them both. It seems clear, that this mode of organizing has decided advantages. A Constitution, accept able to all political parties in a State, must be free from partisan

[1] *Deb. Pa. Conv.*, 1837, Vol. I. p. 400.

legislation; must contain, as it ought, only measures whose policy or expediency had been thoroughly settled in the public mind.

§ 271. By a very remarkable exhibition of moderation, what, in Minnesota, resulted from disagreement, was in New Jersey, in 1844, substantially effected by amicable arrangement between political parties. Those parties did not separate after assembling in Convention, but, by an arrangement recommended by the members of the legislature, in concurrence with influential persons throughout the State, delegates were elected to the Convention from all the districts, save one, by each of the parties.[1] It is impossible to commend too highly an example which must have sprung solely from a view to the public good. Where all parties were, in point of numbers, on a par, it could be only by combinations, not reasonably to be expected, that measures having a party bearing could be carried in Convention. Although it is not so stated, the inference is, that the delegates elected sat together in a single chamber.

§ 272. I pass now to consider the internal organization of Conventions.

The call under which a Convention assembles, may contain specific directions in reference to its organization, in which case, it will be the duty of the body to follow those directions to the letter. As the case has never occurred in which it has been attempted to prescribe more than a few of the most important particulars, and as no attempt is likely to be made to hamper such a body by minute regulations, the subject will be dismissed without further comment. The alternative is, that the Act calling the Convention should be silent as to the points indicated. This case embraces most of the Conventions thus far held in the United States, the call generally confining itself to the time and mode of electing the delegates, the qualifications of the electors, the time of assembling of the Convention, and such other particulars as either fall more naturally within the scope of legislative authority, or as require to be definitely settled before the body meets. Such, on the other hand, as are incidental to the exercise of the functions of the Convention, as such, are commonly left to the discretion of the body itself.

[1] Mulford, *Hist. N. J.*, pp. 495, 496.

§ 273. The usual mode of initiating the organization of a Convention, is for some member elect to call the body to order and move the election of a presiding officer *pro tempore.* In nearly all the Conventions whose proceedings have been published, such has been the course pursued.[1] In a few instances, the body has been called to order by some person who was at once a member of the Convention and an officer of the existing government. Thus, in Massachusetts, in 1820, the Convention was called to order by the Lieutenant-Governor, William Phillips, who was also member for the town of Boston. The California Convention, held in 1849, and that formed by the Democratic members of the Minnesota Convention of 1857, were respectively called to order by the Secretaries of the Territorial governments, sitting as members of the Conventions. Except in the case last named, in which there was a split in the Convention, no stress, so far as I am aware, has ever been laid on the fact, that the Convention had or had not been called to order by an official person. In that case, there was a strife to establish for the several fragments into which the body was divided, a character as the legitimate Convention. The Democratic members, who had receded from the hall where the Convention was to assemble, on finding it occupied by the Republicans, by whom an organization had been, as was charged, prematurely effected, claimed for their Convention, subsequently organized in another place, a higher legitimacy, because opened by the Secretary of the Territory. The Act under which the Convention met, however, contained no directions requiring the Secretary, as such, to attend the Convention. Being a member, his action, therefore, must be presumed to have been in that capacity, and not in that of Territorial officer.[2]

[1] This was the course in Illinois, in 1847 and 1862; in Kentucky, in 1849; in Ohio, in 1850; in the Republican Convention of Minnesota, in 1857; in Virginia, in 1829 and 1850; in Wisconsin, in 1847; in Massachusetts, in 1853; in Pennsylvania, in 1837; in Iowa, in 1857; and in Louisiana, in 1844 and 1852. Some Convention Acts prescribe, that the Secretary of State shall attend the Convention to furnish a list of the members elect. Such was the case in New York, in 1821 and 1846; in Michigan, in 1850; and in Illinois, in 1847. In New York and Michigan, the Secretary read the list of members, and then some member moved the election of officers *pro tem.*, after which the body was called to order.

[2] The disruption of this Convention was occasioned by the fact that the enabling Act had named no hour at which the Convention was to assemble. Moved

§ 274. The officers of a Convention are either *temporary* or *permanent.* In most Conventions, the first proceeding, after the call to order, has been the appointment of a president, a secretary or secretaries, a sergeant-at-arms, and occasionally some other officers, *pro tempore.* The mode of appointment has been uniformly by *viva voce* vote, as, at this stage of the organization, is proper and necessary. On the basis of this temporary organization a permanent one is then effected. The permanent officers of a Convention are usually a president, one or more clerks or secretaries, sergeant-at-arms, door-keeper, and messengers.[1] In a majority of cases these officers have been elected by ballot, either with or without a requisition to that effect in the call of the Convention. In about one-third of the cases, however, they have been elected *viva voce*, and in a few, the President has been elected by ballot, and the inferior officers by *viva voce* vote, or by resolution.[2] Beside the permanent officers above named, in most Conventions there have also been appointed a chaplain or chaplains, a printer, and one or more reporters. As to the first of these officers, the chaplain, the practice is not uniform. In a few instances, a single person has been elected to that office for the session; but in far the greater number, a resolution has been adopted early in the Convention, inviting the clergy of the different denominations, resident in the places where the Conventions were sitting, to officiate as chaplains in rotation.[3] So, in

by alleged threats, that the Democratic members would seize the hall of the Convention at an early hour and forestall the organization, the Republican members in a body took possession of it during the night preceding, and held it until the usual hour for organizing such bodies arrived.

1 In all the Conventions in Massachusetts, the first officer elected was a secretary; and, in that of 1853, it was strongly contended that such a course was the most proper one. *Deb. Mass. Conv.*, 1853, Vol. I. p. 9.

2 They were elected by ballot, in New York, in 1821 and 1846; in Virginia, in 1829; in Massachusetts, in 1820 and 1853; in Pennsylvania, in 1789; in Illinois, in 1847; California, in 1849; in Michigan, in 1850; in Louisiana, in 1844; in Ohio, in 1850; and in Wisconsin, in 1847; and by *viva voce* vote in Illinois, in 1862; in Kentucky, in 1849; in Indiana, in 1850; in Minnesota (Republican Convention), in 1857; in Pennsylvania, in 1837; in Louisiana, in 1852; and in Iowa, in 1857. In the Minnesota Democratic Convention, in 1857, they were elected by resolution.

3 A chaplain was elected in the following Conventions; both those of Minnesota, in 1857; those of Massachusetts in 1820 and 1853, and in that of Maryland, in 1850; while in the following, the resident clergy officiated as stated; those of Kentucky, 1849; Illinois, 1847 and 1862; California, 1849; New York,

regard to printer, the practice has been various. In a few cases the Act calling the Convention has required or authorized it, when convened, to elect a printer, either unconditionally, or upon certain prescribed terms.[1] In much the greater proportion of the cases, however, the enabling Acts have been silent on the subject, and those bodies have elected such persons, and on such terms, as they thought best. In two or three instances, the printer so selected has been the official printer of the State or Territory. The Act calling the Michigan Convention of 1850, required the State printer to do the work of the Convention, and that body acquiesced in the provisions of the Act. In the Illinois Convention of 1862, the same spirit was not manifested. The Act under which it assembled, made it the duty of the Secretary of State "to cause such printing to be done as the Convention shall from time to time require." Although this Act was not couched, perhaps, in such terms as to leave the duty of the Convention free from doubt, since it seemed to be optional with that body to make or not, as it should see fit, requisitions upon the secretary for printing; still it is, on the whole, clear enough, that the legislature intended to put the printing of the Convention into the hands of a public officer of the State. The Convention evidently so interpreted the Act, for, in the discussions which followed the motion to elect a printer, it was assumed that such was the intention of the legislature. The Convention took its stand upon a question of power, contending that the legislature was incompetent to fetter the discretion of that body in the appointment of its own officers. It consequently refused to obey the Act as thus interpreted, and elected a printer of its own.

§ 275. In Conventions, some provisions have generally, and very properly, been made for preserving, for general circulation, reports of their debates and proceedings. In all, or nearly all,

1821 and 1846; Michigan, Ohio, and Indiana, in 1850; Virginia, 1829 and 1850; Wisconsin, 1847; Pennsylvania, 1837; Iowa, 1857; and Louisiana, 1844 and 1852. In Massachusetts, in 1779, the clergy who were members of the Convention officiated.

[1] Such was the case in Illinois, in 1847; Kentucky, in 1849; and Iowa, in 1857; in which no terms were prescribed; and in New York in 1846, and Michigan and Ohio in 1850, in the first two of which the Conventions were limited in the amount to be paid to the rate paid for the legislative printing, and in the latter, to a designated sum.

their journals have been published. In a much smaller number, have been published full reports of their debates. In the latter cases, the Conventions have commonly elected official reporters among their regular officers, without any special authorization of the legislature calling them.[1] In a considerable number, no official reporter has been appointed, but the reports published have been the work of private enterprise.[2] In the case of the Indiana Convention of 1850, the Act calling it had required the Governor to engage the services of a stenographer for the Convention. This was done, and the Convention received and employed him; though not without questioning the right of the legislature to dictate to that body who should act as its officers. Of the Ohio Convention of 1850, the reporter was appointed, before the Convention assembled, by the State legislature. On his presenting himself to the Convention, however, a similar discussion arose, as to the right of appointment, but the Convention acquiesced in the action of the legislature. The Act calling the Pennsylvania Convention of 1837, specially authorized that body to engage the services of a competent stenographer, a course probably wiser than any other, as avoiding discussion.

§ 276. It is obvious that in a numerous assembly, convened as a result of popular elections, some system is necessary for determining who have been elected, and are consequently entitled to take part in its deliberations. In the various Conventions, the practice on this point has been far from uniform, though there is apparent in them, after all, a sort of regularity. In a considerable proportion of them, generally the same in whose organization the initial step had been the appointment of officers *pro tempore*, a list of the members, furnished by the Secretary of State or other officer of the existing government, to whom the official returns of the elections had been made, or drawn up by the officers of the Convention themselves, has been called over immediately after the temporary organization, and

[1] This was the case in the following Conventions. Massachusetts, 1853; Wisconsin, 1847; Kentucky, 1849; Missouri, 1820; Michigan, 1850; Iowa and the two Minnesota Conventions, 1857; California, 1849; Louisiana, 1844 and 1852; and Illinois, 1862.

[2] In this class are the Conventions of Massachusetts, 1820; New York, 1821 and 1846; Virginia, 1829; and Illinois, 1847.

the credentials of the members have thereupon been presented and approved.[1] The list having thus been verified, the Convention has been prepared to enter upon business. In some cases, the list of delegates has been presented by some officer of the government, and read in the first instance, before the temporary organization has been effected.[2] In others, after the temporary organization, the first business transacted has been the raising of a committee on credentials, upon whose report the list of members for future use has been founded.[3]

In those Conventions, on the other hand, in which no temporary organization has been made, the practice has been equally varied. In Pennsylvania in 1776 and 1789, in New York in 1821, and in Indiana in 1850, a list of the delegates elected, furnished by the Secretary of State or other officer of the government, was read in the first instance, before any attempt at organization. In Maryland in 1776, and in Massachusetts in 1820 and 1853, a committee on credentials was raised, in the first case after, but in the two Massachusetts Conventions before, the permanent organization; and in one case, that of the Virginia Convention of 1829, the roll was not called or verified until after the completion of the permanent organization.

§ 277. The question whether the members of a Convention should be sworn before entering upon their duties, has been variously answered in different Conventions. Of the whole number whose proceedings have been accessible to me, about one half only have administered an oath. These were the following Conventions: those of Pennsylvania, 1776; North Carolina, 1835; New Jersey, 1844; Missouri, 1845; Illinois, 1847 and 1862; California and Kentucky, 1849; Ohio and Indiana, 1850; Iowa and the two Minnesota Conventions, in 1857; and Maryland, in 1864. On the other hand, an oath was not administered in the following Conventions: Maryland, 1776 and 1850; Tennessee, 1796 and 1834; Virginia, 1829 and 1850; Pennsylvania, 1789 and 1837; New York, 1821 and 1846; Massachu-

1 This was done in Illinois in 1847 and 1862, Kentucky in 1849, Ohio and Virginia in 1850, California in 1849, Pennsylvania in 1837, Iowa in 1857, and Louisiana in 1852.

2 These were the Conventions of New York in 1846, and Michigan in 1850.

3 In Minnesota in 1857 (both Conventions), in Wisconsin in 1847, in Iowa in 1857, and in Louisiana in 1844.

setts, 1779, 1821, and 1853; Michigan, 1850; Wisconsin, 1847; and Louisiana, 1812, 1844, and 1852. In those Conventions in which an oath has been administered, the most common form has been substantially that used by the Illinois Convention of 1847, which was as follows: "You do solemnly swear, that you will support the Constitution of the United States, and that you will faithfully discharge your duty as delegates to this Convention, for the purpose of revising and amending the Constitution of the State of Illinois." That administered in Maryland, in 1864, beside the foregoing, contained an oath of allegiance to the government of the United States. A more restricted form was employed in the California Convention of 1849, and in the Minnesota Republican Convention of 1857, namely: "You do solemnly swear that you will support the Constitution of the United States."

§ 278. In several of the Conventions in which an oath has been administered, opposition has been made either to taking any oath at all, or to taking one in the form proposed by the Convention, or prescribed by the Act under which it assembled.

1. It has been urged that no oath was necessary or proper; that if the Convention was a mere committee, with powers only of proposing amendments, it was a useless ceremony to bind it by oaths to do or not to do acts which it could do only on the hypothesis that it possessed a power of self-direction inconsistent with its supposed character; that it was even dangerous so to do, as involving an admission, that, without an oath or some positive prohibition, it would have power, and perhaps be at liberty, to act definitively. On the other hand, if the Convention was an embodiment of the sovereignty of the State or nation, empowered to pull down and reconstruct the edifice of government, as freely as the sovereign could itself do, were it possible for it to act in person and directly, then an oath would be doubly futile, since it could not fetter a power that was practically unlimited and uncontrollable.

In reply to this, however, it has been forcibly urged that, if not necessary, it is proper that a body like a Convention, intrusted with important public duties, should deliberate under the obligation of an oath; that it could do no harm, and might operate to restrain members from doing, for selfish or partisan ends, that by which the interest of the people at large might be jeopardized. This would become more apparent, when it was considered that an oath derives its efficacy more from its tendency to remind the taker of his obligation to a higher power, than from any liability the taking of it may impose upon him to punishment for perjury.

§ 279. 2. What form of oath should be used has, however, been more frequently the subject of dispute than whether any oath was proper. In Conventions to frame State Constitutions, assuming that an oath is to be administered at all, it is generally conceded to be proper that it should embrace an undertaking to be faithful and obedient to the Constitution of the United States. This could not well be contested, since the State Constitutions are, by the terms of the Federal charter, to be valid only when conformable to its provisions. It is also generally admitted to be proper, if an oath be taken at all, that the members should be sworn honestly and faithfully to perform their duties as members of the Convention. A question of more difficulty is, whether the oath should contain a clause to support the Constitution of the State. This question has been raised in several Conventions, and has been uniformly decided in the negative.[1] The reasonings of the opposite parties upon this question have been based on their respective conceptions of the nature and powers of a Convention. Those who have opposed taking the oath have done so on the ground, that to do so would be inconsistent with their duties as members of a Convention; that they were deputed by the sovereign society to pull to pieces, or, as some have expressed it, "to trample under their feet," the existing Constitution, and to build up instead of it a new one; that to take an oath to support the Constitution of the State, would be to swear that they would not perform the very duty for which they were appointed.

§ 280. On the other hand, it has been contended, that it is no part of the duty of a Convention to pull to pieces the existing Constitution of the State; that by the true theory of such a body, it is advisory merely; having power to overhaul the Constitution, search out its defects, and recommend such changes

[1] It arose in the Louisiana Convention of 1844, in the Ohio Convention of 1850, the Iowa Convention of 1857, and the Illinois Convention of 1862. In the last case the oath to support the Constitution of the State had been prescribed by the Act calling the Convention.

as should in its view promise to remedy them, but to conclude nothing; that in this view of a Convention, the Constitution is in full vigor and operation as much when that body, having completed its task, should suffer dissolution, as when it first assembled; that, in the mean time, if unrestrained, a Convention might, under a claim of power to exercise sovereign rights, "trample under its feet" every one of those liberties secured against ordinary usurpation by the Bill of Rights; it might suspend the writ of *Habeas Corpus*, raise a standing army and quarter it in peace upon the citizens without their consent, destroy the liberty of the press, declare those who should offend its dignity to be guilty of felony and punish them, by its own hands, with death. Surely, if such usurpations are possible, no matter what the theory of their powers may be, Conventions ought to be placed under all the restraints that can be devised to prevent them. Undoubtedly one of the most powerful of these is an oath to support the Constitution, in which are bound up these liberties, and which therefore must first be infringed before those liberties can be violated.

§ 281. To the Conventions of North Carolina, 1835 and 1875, and of Illinois, 1862 and 1869, the Acts under which those bodies assembled prescribed the form of the oath to be taken. In the former, great opposition having existed to the call of a Convention on the part of a powerful minority in the State legislature, in the Act finally passed restrictions were imposed upon the Convention as to the extent and nature of the amendments it should propose, requiring it to report amendments upon three points, and giving to it discretionary authority to propose others upon nine points particularly described in the Act. The Act then proceeded to require that no delegate should be permitted to take his seat in Convention until he should have taken and subscribed an oath or affirmation as follows: "I, A. B., do solemnly swear (or affirm, as the case may be) that I will not directly or indirectly evade or disregard the duties enjoined or the limits imposed to this Convention by the people of North Carolina, as set forth in the Act of the General Assembly, passed in 1834, entitled 'An Act to amend the Constitution of the State of North Carolina,' which Act was ratified by the people."

To the taking of this oath, objection was raised in the Convention, on the ground that the legislature had no right to impose it, some being of the opinion that, if taken, it would bind the members to concur in all the amendments proposed. Others thought it would merely restrict the Convention to the consideration of those amendments, without at all prescribing the view it should adopt respecting them. At length it was pointed out that there was absolutely no escape from taking the oath; that by the terms of the Act no delegate should be permitted to take his seat in the Convention until he had taken the prescribed oath. It was a condition precedent to their organization; and if it was objected that the legislature had transcended its authority in imposing the condition, it might be answered that the Act rested not alone on the authority of the legislature, but on that of the people to whom it had been submitted. This view prevailed, and the oath was taken by all the members.[1]

The requirements and restrictions contained in the Convention Act of 1875 were similar to the foregoing, as was also the form of the oath prescribed. Though some of the delegates were opposed to taking the oath, they did so, but entered a formal protest, denying the power of the legislature to impose it.[2]

§ 282. In the Illinois cases, the Convention Acts had both prescribed that the members, before entering upon their duties, should "each take an oath to support the Constitution of the United States, *and of this State*, and to faithfully discharge his duties as a member of said Convention." The taking of this oath was strenuously opposed, on the two grounds before mentioned, that the legislature had no power to impose it, and that the clause relating to the Constitution of the State was inconsistent with the general tenor of the Act calling the body together *as a Convention*. The result of the discussion was, that the Convention of 1862, by a formal vote, refused to obey the Act under which it assembled, in regard to the form of the oath to be taken by its members. The oath actually administered was substantially the same as that taken by the Illinois Convention of 1847, and differed from that prescribed mainly in omitting the words, "and of this State," upon which the debate arose. The Convention of 1869, though inclined to disobey, finally took the oath prescribed by the Act, with the words, "so far as its provisions are compatible with and applicable to my position,"

1 *Deb. N. C. Conv.* 1835, pp. 4–8.

2 *Journal N. C. Conv.* 1875, p. 1.

etc., added to the words, "and of this State;" thus, in substance, obeying the Act.

§ 283. Upon the question involved in the Illinois cases, I shall make but a single observation, and that in relation to the alleged incongruity between the undertaking contained in the oath, and the actual business of the Convention.

When a member of a Convention swears to support the Constitution of his State, what Constitution is it he swears to support? Is it the written instrument — the Constitution considered as evidence of an organic growth — or the organic growth itself — the actual Constitution? Substantially, the latter only. He calls God to witness that, while inspecting the written Constitution, to see if it adequately expresses the real Constitution, to which the Commonwealth has grown since the last revision, he will not violate, but will protect and defend, those essential rights, and respect and conform to those particular limitations and adjustments, which make up that real Constitution; though he doubtless adds that, pending the utterance of the *fiat*, by which obsolete or inadequate provisions of the written Constitution are stricken from its pages, he will respect them also as the fundamental law of the land. But, suppose every copy of the Constitution, considered as an instrument of evidence, were destroyed, and the memory of its contents utterly blotted out, the real Constitution would remain, the Constitution to which the oath mainly refers. So that, if we were to admit that it is the duty of a Convention to eradicate from the written Constitution, and to trample under its feet such part thereof as the Commonwealth has outgrown, the oath would still refer to that greater part which is living and operative.

The charge, then, that there is any inconsistency between the oath supposed, and the function of a member of a Convention, however broad the powers of the latter be conceived to be, is a gross absurdity, resulting from confusion of ideas as to the real meaning of the term Constitution. Much more is it an absurdity in view of the fact, that a Convention is a body of very narrow powers, charged only with pointing out defects and recommending remedies, but with a right, ordinarily, to conclude nothing.

§ 284. Immediately after the permanent organization, there is generally appointed a committee to report a body of rules for the government of the Convention, or to facilitate the transaction of its business. Pending the preparation of this report, in about half the cases, a resolution has been carried to adopt for their government, for the time being, the rules of the last House of Representatives of the State, so far as applicable. In a few instances, the rules of the last Convention have been temporarily put in force, and in one case, that of California, in 1849, those laid down in Jefferson's "Manual of Parliamentary Law." As to the character of the rules adopted, it may be said, in general, that they are, in substance, the same, so far as they are strictly rules of order, and not rules determining the modes of proceeding, as those by which our legislatures are commonly governed. The differences are such as result either from the special and limited character of Conventions, as compared with legislative Assemblies, or from the relative importance of their respective duties. In the former, for instance, there is not, probably, a necessity for the same safeguards against haste, surprise, or inadvertence, as in the latter, inasmuch as the volume of the laws to be passed upon is smaller, or against the combinations of interested parties, as the legislation performed by them is less near to the interests or the party prejudices of their members or others. Thus, it is sometimes provided, that clauses may be adopted as parts of the proposed Constitution, upon a less number of readings than would be safe, or than is usual, in case of ordinary laws. On the other hand, by reason of the vastly greater importance of the subjects of deliberation in Conventions, the rules often grant a much greater facility for reconsideration than in legislative Assemblies. Thus, in the Massachusetts Convention of 1853, on motion of the Hon. Henry Wilson, the ordinary rule requiring a motion for reconsideration to be made by one who voted with the majority, was so modified, as to permit any member to make it, whether he had voted with the majority or not. Greater latitude is, also, in many cases, allowed, as to the time within which that motion must be made.[1]

[1] The relaxation of the rule as to time seems to be much more reasonable than as to the mover. As was well said by Mr. Quincy, in the Massachusetts Convention of 1820, it is proper, before allowing a reconsideration, to require some evidence that a reconsideration would lead to a different result from that already attained, else it would be a mere loss of time; and a motion by one of the majority to reconsider, is proper evidence of that fact. The Convention of 1820, after some discussion, refused to modify the general rule as to reconsiderations.

§ 285. The Convention having organized, by the appointment of officers and the adoption of rules of order, and, therefore, being ready to proceed to business, a question of great perplexity and of great importance thereupon arises: "What shall be the mode of proceeding? — a question, in short, of method.

This question involves two subordinate ones, which I will take up in their order, namely, first, What arrangements, if any, shall be made whereby the labor of the Convention may be facilitated by subdivision? — a question properly of instrumentalities; and, secondly, In what manner shall those instrumentalities prosecute the task apportioned to them?

First. Of the first question, two practical solutions may be given.

1. The Convention may enter upon its task — the framing or the amending of a Constitution — directly, in Convention, as it is called — that is, without resolving itself into a committee or committees. In this mode of proceeding the course of business would be, to take up the existing Constitution of the State, or that of some other State, or some model or project presented by individuals, subject it to a round of discussions in Convention, and finally to adopt it as the proposed Constitution, or as an amendment thereto. The disadvantages attending this mode are so patent and so numerous, that it is doubtful if it would ever be adopted, as it is believed that it never has been adopted. The leading objection to it is, that the deliberations of any numerous assembly, which should adopt it, would be at once protracted and fruitless. It is obvious that every member might present his scheme, and rightfully claim for it regular and orderly consideration; and, in the absence of the concert of action secured by committees, a great number of schemes, turning out ultimately to be futile or inadequate, would undergo protracted discussion, which, with a proper mode of proceeding, would be nipped in the bud. Besides, the immense labor of maturing, in all its details, a large number of connected fundamental Acts, would have to be done, according to this mode, by the entire Convention — an arrangement, for business efficiency, to be equalled in absurdity only by a military plan, which should require to be detailed for every duty of camp or field, however trivial, the entire force of all arms in the command.

§ 286. 2. The alternative is, the employment of one or more

committees to prepare and report a Constitution, or parts thereof, or amendments thereto, for the consideration of the Convention. And, as intimated above, this course has been adopted with perfect unanimity by the Conventions to whose proceedings I have had access. Upon one point, however, there has been very great divergence of opinion, and that is, in relation to the number, and, if more than one, the mode of appointment of those committees.

§ 287. (*a*). As to the number of committees, a very common opinion, when the subject is first discussed, is that there should be, for convenience and despatch of business, but a single committee — the committee of the whole. Those who advocate this mode of proceeding claim for it simplicity and directness as well as efficiency, and they usually propose that the Constitution which is to be taken as a model for imitation or the basis for amendments, should be read; that each member should thereupon be allowed perfect freedom of discussion; and, when it has been determined what the views of the body are, that the committee should report, and the whole matter be at once, as it could readily be, concluded. At the same time it is commonly admitted, that this course would be impracticable in an ordinary legislature, by reason of the complexity and multifariousness of the subjects brought up for its action; but this is supposed not to hold true of a Convention, because, it is said, its business is relatively simple and homogeneous. Hence, in almost every Convention ever held, so far as I am aware, there have been advocates of a reference of its whole business, in the first instance, to a committee of the whole.

§ 288. (*b*.) Another plan, adopted in a few cases in Conventions engaged in framing first Constitutions, is to appoint a single select committee of limited numbers, to digest from such materials as may be at hand, the models of political amateurs or the Constitutions of neighboring States, a draft of a Constitution to be considered by the Convention. As this plan involves the necessity either for great haste on the part of the committee, or of much delay and inactivity on that of the Convention, pending the preparation of the report, it has been rarely employed. Of all the Conventions whose records have reached me, only ten have adopted this plan, namely, those of Maryland, Virginia, New Jersey, and Pennsylvannia, held in 1776, those of New York and Vermont, held in 1777; those of Massachusetts, held in 1778 and 1779; that of Tennessee, held in 1796; and that of California, held in 1849.

§ 289. (*c.*) A third mode of proceeding by the use of committees, is for the Convention to apportion the work to be done among several committees, giving to each an article or other definite portion of the existing Constitution, embracing a distinct topic, as the Executive, Legislative, or Judicial department, the Finances, Education, Bill of Rights, and the like; each committee to report in the form of articles and sections such provisions as it shall deem necessary.

These are evidently all the modes of which the subject is capable; and the one last described is that which has very generally been adopted. The mode of proceeding by a committee of the whole, has been examined to some extent already; but it may be proper here to inquire with some particularity into the merits of that mode, as compared with that last described, by numerous committees — a question which has given rise to much discussion in several Conventions, and is likely to be again discussed hereafter.

§ 290. In favor of proceeding in committee of the whole, it has been urged, that if it be an object to save time or to secure the exercise of all the talent in the Convention, the best course is to make use of that committee; that, if a Constitution is to be adequately discussed, the appointment of several committees, in the first instance, to report upon distinct portions of it, would increase rather than diminish the time occupied in the session, since, while the reports were being prepared, the Convention would be forced to remain idle; and the several reports being likely to be incongruous and more or less unacceptable to the Convention, every part of them would need to be amended and brought into harmony with other parts and with the sentiments of the majority in the body; that the wisdom and experience of the entire Convention are at least equal to those of any committee chosen therefrom; that it is the proper province of the Convention, as it is of a legislature, to settle principles, and of committees to arrange details; hence, it is evident that, when the members of a Convention have learned, from a full and free discussion in committee of the whole, unembarrassed by the rules that must be enforced in Convention, the principles deemed by the collective body necessary to be embodied in the Constitution, they would be enabled, even if afterwards subdivided into committees, to act with greater expedition and with greater intelligence; that it is also no slight recommendation of the committee of the whole, that on account of its freedom from the stringent rules that hamper the Convention, and of the practice which usually prevails of not reporting fully, if at all, the speeches made in that committee, men unused to public debate are enticed from their benches, and encouraged to contribute their wisdom to the common stock; that it is also well not to forget, as one inducement to proceed in committee of the whole, that in all great legislative contests for freedom, the "Grand Committee," the committee of the whole, has been the instrument by which victory has been achieved; that the crowning argument, however, in favor of this committee, is, that if recourse be had to the alternative, the appointment of one or more select committees, it is difficult, if not practically impossible, to withstand their influence, or to modify their reports. A select committee naturally comprises the best talent in the house. When a report is brought in by it, pride of opinion leads it to defend its offspring, and this its skill and experience generally enable it to do successfully. In a free and unreported debate, however, in committee of the whole, in which the Constitution is taken up and read section by section, commented upon, and amended, no such danger need be apprehended. It is the opinion formally announced and published to the world, not the casual observation, unreported, and confessedly not mature, that its author defends with vigor and pertinacity.

§ 291. The objections to proceeding in committee of the whole, on the other hand, resolve themselves mainly into a question of time. It is said, that if every member of a Convention is permitted to introduce his scheme of a Constitution, or his proposition of amendment, with liberty and encouragement to discuss each and all of them *ad libitum*, the task of framing a Constitution would be endless; and not only so, but such a freedom of making and discussing propositions, instead of tending to harmonize the views of members, would introduce an element of division; that what a single member proposes in committee of the whole, is the conclusion of a single mind, in which no other mind may agree; whilst, on the other hand, the report of a committee of leading members is, at least, the consentaneous opinion of many minds, and probably will be that of the whole Convention when it has been brought by discussion to understand the subject; that it is not always true that the wisdom or the experience of a Convention will be equal to that of a few of its leading minds, when we speak of it as embodying itself in action, whatever may be the case in relation to counsel; in a Convention there will be, of course, a greater total of wisdom and talent than in any committee of it less than the whole; but in those qualities a small committee, or a single person, may surpass the residue of the body, and yet it may go for nothing, unless the majority be very tractable. Hence, it is far better that the Convention should listen to the matured opinions of its few leading minds before committing itself by expressing its own; that the committee of the whole undoubtedly has its eminent uses in a Convention, but it is rather after than before the reports of standing or special committees have come in.[1]

§ 292. In favor of proceeding by committees charged severally with distinct parts of the Constitution, it has been urged, that it is the appropriate duty of a committee to prepare and lay out business for the deliberative body appointing it, and that neither a Convention nor a legislature can successfully proceed without them; that they contribute essentially to simplify the complex matters referred to them, and thus to expedite the labors of the Convention; that a committee chosen from a numerous assembly, and embracing a variety of talent and experience, will be able readily to prognosticate the determinations of the Convention, by divining its wishes, which are quite likely to accord with those of any fairly selected committee; that this consideration disposes of the objection, founded, perhaps, in part, upon the observed accordance between the votes of a numerous body and the recommendations of a committee of its leading members, namely, that committees are undesirable as possessing too

[1] For full discussions of the advantages and disadvantages of proceeding in committee of the whole, in the first instance, see the *Debates* in the following Conventions: Kentucky, 1849, pp. 39–54; New York, 1846, pp. 20–37; California, 1849, pp. 22–24; Michigan, 1850, pp. 20, 21; Ohio, 1850, pp. 47, 48; Pennsylvania, 1837, Vol. I. pp. 65, 66, 77, 95.

much influence, and as too much inclined to use that influence to secure the adoption of their own recommendations; that, thus viewed, committees do not so much dictate to those who appoint them, as discover to them in a few moments what is likely to be their own better judgment after floundering, perhaps, for weeks or months, in useless discussion; that, at all events, there need be no fear of excessive influence in committees, for the reason that, when their reports come in, they are open to debate and amendment if not satisfactory, precisely like propositions made by individual members, and so are likely to receive modification, if prejudiced or unreasonable.

§ 293. The objections to the use of committees have already, in part, been suggested. It is contended, that their reports are likely to want consistency and congruity, when considered as parts of a whole; that a Constitution built up by the action of a large number of committees is liable to lack provisions of essential importance, through inadvertent omissions; that however that may be, the labor of melting down into a consistent unit the heterogeneous reports of many committees, of discovering and supplying defects, and trimming down redundancies, is not less than that so much apprehended in committee of the whole; but it is chiefly objected, that when such committees do the work, the Convention loses its power of control over it; they will be organized in such a manner as that the talent and influence to be found in the Convention will be brought to bear upon particular propositions, and that individuals will be powerless to countervail them.

§ 294. The reasonings in favor of the mode of proceeding in committee of the whole, without standing committees, of which I have given an outline, however plausible they seem, have failed, in most cases, to convince the Conventions to which they were addressed, and those bodies have adopted, as have all the Conventions but one whose proceedings have reached me, the mode of proceeding by one or more standing committees, in preference to it. The Pennsylvania Convention of 1789, alone pursued the other plan, taking up the Constitution of 1776 in committee of the whole, and inquiring, during a large part of the session, "whether and wherein" it required alteration or amendment.[1]

[1] *Jour. Pa. Conv.* 1789, p. 143, *et seq.* In the North Carolina Convention of 1835, Mr. Speight said he believed the Convention which framed the old Consti-

§ 295. The precedents established in the various Conventions in relation to the number of committees, and of members apportioned to each, have been far from uniform. With the exception of the ten Conventions already specified, in which a single committee was raised to draft and report a Constitution, and of the Pennsylvania Convention of 1789, in which, as I have just stated, the subject was taken up in committee of the whole, all the Conventions ever held, so far as I am advised, have appointed several committees, the least number being four, and the highest thirty-one.[1] The number of committees has commonly been determined by the views entertained by members as to the number of distinct parts of the Constitution, or separate topics embraced in it, needing revision. To the committees charged with these, is commonly added a number of business committees, as on Printing for the Convention, and the like. In determining the number of members in each committee, regard is generally had to the importance of the subjects committed, and the number of delegates in the body, the work being commonly so apportioned as to give each member some share in the committee-labor.

§ 296. How the number of standing committees, and of the members of which each shall consist, shall be determined, has in many cases been the subject of vehement discussion. This has been the consequence mainly of jealousies between the friends and the opponents of the reforms contemplated in calling the

tution, first proceeded in committee of the whole, and then made a reference of the different subjects to their appropriate committees. *Deb. N. C. Conv.* 1835, p. 17.

[1] The Virginia Convention of 1829 had four Standing Committees, — one on each of the departments, Legislative, Executive, and Judicial, and one on the residue of the Constitution, including the Bill of Rights. The Illinois Convention of 1862 had thirty-one committees, upon the following subjects: Executive Department; Legislative Department; Judiciary; Judicial Circuits; Bill of Rights; Congressional Apportionment; Legislative Apportionment; Federal Relations; Banks and Currency; Revenue; Finance; Railroad Corporations; Counties; Municipal Corporations; Miscellaneous Corporations; Education; Militia and Military Affairs; Elections and Right of Suffrage; Schedule; Revision and Adjustment of the Articles of the Constitution; Internal Improvements; Roads and Internal Navigation; Public Accounts and Expenditures; Township Organization; State Institutions, Buildings, and Grounds; Canal and Canal Lands; Penitentiary; Retrenchment and Reform; Manufactures and Agriculture; Printing and Binding; and Miscellaneous Subjects.

Conventions. In the Pennsylvania Convention of 1837, the New York Convention of 1846, and the Kentucky Convention of 1849, the mode of determining the committees, which was finally adopted, was vigorously opposed as calculated to favor particular views of reform. That mode was to appoint a select committee to report generally upon the best mode of proceeding, including such a scheme of committees as should in its view cover the whole ground of needed changes in the Constitution. This course evidently remits the entire question of methods and instrumentalities, in the first instance, to a committee of the Convention, with the well understood purpose of conceding to its recommendations, unless clearly unjust or impracticable, a decisive influence. It has, nevertheless, been generally deemed the most satisfactory one that could be adopted, though in two of the three cases in which it was most largely discussed, another course was pursued. It was followed in the two Virginia Conventions, held in 1829 and 1850; the New York Conventions of 1821, and 1846; the North Carolina Convention of 1835; the New Jersey Convention of 1844; that of Missouri, of 1845; the Ohio, Michigan, and Indiana Conventions of 1850; that of Wisconsin, of 1848; the two Minnesota Conventions, and the Iowa Convention held in 1857; and the Massachusetts Convention of 1853. Where this mode is pursued, the preliminary committee is usually appointed immediately after the permanent organization of the Convention, and commonly consists of one or more members from each senatorial or other political division of the State. In its report, this committee generally contents itself with recommending a list of standing committees based on its view of the prospective work of the Convention, though sometimes there is added a resolution relating to the disposition of propositions of amendment introduced in Convention. Where this mode is not pursued, the committees are commonly appointed either on the motion of some member,[1] or upon the recommendation of the committee on rules, a list of them in such cases forming a part of its report.[2]

[1] They were thus appointed in the Louisiana Conventions of 1844, 1852, and 1864; in that of Kentucky of 1849, Maryland of 1864, Massachusetts of 1820, Texas of 1875, and Georgia of 1877.

[2] This was the case in the Pennsylvania Conventions of 1837 and 1872, and in those of Illinois of 1847, 1862, and 1869, in the New York Convention of 1867, the Ohio Convention of 1873, and the California Convention of 1878.

The persons to compose the Standing Committees are usually designated by the President of the Convention.

To the Standing Committees, thus appointed, the part of the Constitution they are severally to consider is apportioned by the Convention either in the original resolution appointing them, or by special motion ordering the reference to be made. In a few instances the existing Constitution has been taken up and read in Convention, section by section, and such parts as were deemed to require revision, have been referred to the appropriate committees.

§ 297. Secondly. The remaining question relates to the mode of proceeding of the Convention and its committees. After the work has been placed thus in the hands of committees, since the reports expected from them require time for their preparation, it is usual for the Convention to occupy itself in the interim, whilst the committees are in session, in miscellaneous business, as in considering cases of contested elections, or in discussing, in a general way, resolutions relating to the principles to be embodied in the new Constitution. Often resolutions of the latter character contain instructions to the standing committees, now in session, to institute inquiries in reference to the expediency of particular amendments. Usually, however, until the reports of its committees begin to come in, the Convention is in a more or less chaotic condition, proposing and voting upon a variety of resolutions relating to reforms conceived desirable, or to modes of proceeding imagined to be more advantageous than those adopted. But this period is generally short, for the reason, that reports upon parts of the Constitution not needing much change, are early presented, and thus the Convention is enabled to commence its work without delay.

§ 298. The mode of reporting in Conventions is different from that adopted commonly in legislatures. In the former, reports of committees usually consist merely of articles and sections, drawn up in the precise form the committees propose they shall bear as parts of the Constitution; whilst in legislative bodies they generally comprise discussions of facts and principles, intended to justify particular conclusions, appended in the form of resolutions, though sometimes to those abstract

The Maryland Convention of 1850 appointed Standing Committees, but upon whose recommendation does not appear, no report of the first two months of the session of that body having been published.

discussions, instead of resolutions, are added drafts of bills proposed for enactment. Of prefatory argumentation, the reports made to Conventions contain, as a general rule, nothing whatever. In about one-third of the cases, instances have occurred in which one or more committees have accompanied their reports by illustrative argument in writing, but that has been confined to reports upon topics of unusual importance or interest.[1] This mode of reporting, in the earlier Conventions, pursued without rule or order to that effect, has in some of the later ones been specially required, as in the New York Convention of 1846, the Illinois Convention of 1847, the Maryland Convention of 1864, and perhaps others. The earliest instance I have found in which the subject was mentioned was in the New York Convention of 1821, where Gen. Tallmadge, chairman of the committee on the Council of Revision, on presenting a report from his committee, stated that they had not gone into any explanation of the reasons which influenced them in making the report. This, he admitted, was a departure from the parliamentary usage, but the committee had done it not without consideration; "they had omitted to do this, because, in their opinion, the Convention might be induced to adopt the amendment for different views from those assigned by the committee. The reports of committees would remain of record, and might hereafter be used to give a false and imperfect construction to the proceedings of the Convention." He added, that the committee "hoped it would be considered by the other committees as a precedent."[2]

§ 299. In the case mentioned there was no discussion, and apparently no feeling upon the subject. Not so in the Convention of the same State in 1846. Early in the session a resolution was introduced, and, without much discussion, carried, declaring it to be "inexpedient for the several committees on the Constitution to accompany their reports with written explana-

[1] Reports without written or other illustration were made in the following Conventions: Massachusetts, 1779; New York, 1821 and 1846; Louisiana, 1844; Illinois, 1847 and 1862; California and Kentucky, 1849; Ohio and Indiana, 1850; the two Minnesota and the Iowa Conventions, 1857. In the following Conventions written arguments or illustrations in a few cases accompanied reports: Massachusetts, 1820 and 1853; Pennsylvania, 1837; Virginia, 1829; Wisconsin, 1847; Michigan and Maryland, 1850; and Louisiana, 1852.

[2] *Deb. N. Y. Conv.* 1821, p. 42.

tions of the reasons which may have influenced them in agreeing thereto." A week later, a motion was made to reconsider this resolution, which, after a debate, the spirit and pertinacity of which it is difficult to understand, was negatived. In this discussion, in addition to the reason for the restriction given by Gen. Tallmadge, it was urged, that if all the reports were acaccompanied by statements of the reasons which induced the committees to adopt them, the records of the Convention would become excessively voluminous; that if not so much so as to cause them to be wholly neglected, of which there was danger, they would be likely to be consulted mainly for the sake of the reports which would thus have imparted to them too powerful an influence; that the committees being composed of leading members, likely to be most eminent in debate, to allow them to express their reasons in writing would be to commit them to the opinions advanced, and for the reasons therein mentioned, and that it would be nearly impossible for the Convention to convince or to refute them; so that, in truth, it was not a question of gagging the committees so much as whether the committees should be allowed to gag the Convention; that the true course was, to let the members of the committees stand on the same footing as the other members of the Convention, each giving his opinion orally in debate; that thus, the remarks of all being reported with proportionate abbreviation, each would secure for his views the public estimation which they deserved, and no more.

§ 300. Against the restriction it was urged, that the work of a Convention was unlike that of a legislature; that it was to go before the people in the shape of recommendations, to be by them either adopted or rejected; that, therefore, the people ought to know the grounds on which they had been made; that those would be best determined from perusing the carefully drawn reports of committees, giving to the subjects committed to them calm and mature consideration; that such had ever been the parliamentary course, and, besides, it would be absurd to appoint committees to report conclusions, and to suppress the information — often consisting of statistics, or scientific or historical *data* — upon which they were based; that, in regard to the Convention itself, it was idle to talk of the excessive influence of committees, they, as a general thing, having no influence which they do not deserve to have; that there wano danger of their abusing the privilege proposed to be denied them of expressing in writing their reasons for their recommendations; that the natural indolence of every man would lead him to avoid the task, always irksome, of drawing up long written reports, and to rely for explanations of his views, except in rare and important cases, upon speaking rather than writing; that when cases of real importance arose, it was for the interest no less of the Convention than of the committees, to arrive at clear and definite ideas in the shortest time possible, upon the subjects in hand; that to this end it was highly desirable that committees should be allowed and encouraged to present their views in writing, in order that the members might take the reports with them to their rooms and examine them without the distraction of mind so inevitable in the Convention itself; and, finally, that by allowing written reports, many members who had no skill in debate, but who could wield their pen with real ability, would be able to make to the public counsels valuable contributions.[1]

§ 301. Without stopping to consider particularly the arguments above detailed, it is proper to say, that the true course seems to be that pursued by most Conventions, and recommended by Gen. Tallmadge in the New York Conventions of 1821 and 1846, to leave the matter of reporting their reasons in writing, or not, to the committees themselves, without any rule to fetter their discretion. Thus left, it is probable, in a majority of cases, committees would prefer to report merely articles and sections, trusting to debate to illustrate and enforce their recommendations. When a case, however, arises, in which, from the abundance or complexity of the *data* on which the conclusions of the reports are founded, and by which, if at all, they are to be justified, it is deemed important that those *data* should be marshalled in a succinct and orderly array, it will be an act of folly to interdict it, since only when thus presented can they be grasped and appreciated.[2]

[1] See *Deb. N. Y. Conv.* 1846, pp. 97–99, 131–138, 142–149.

[2] A writer in the *Democratic Review* for November, 1846, p. 340, referring to the New York Convention of that year, impeaches the motives of those who concurred in defending this restriction, declaring them, under the circumstances under which the proposition was initiated, to have been "discreditable in the highest degree." The course recommended by General Talmadge was adopted by the New York Convention of 1867.

§ 302. On the coming in of the reports of committees, the first proceeding commonly is to lay them on the table and order them printed, preparatory to their being submitted to the action of the Convention. In some cases this preliminary is dispensed with, and the reports are at once referred for consideration and discussion to a committee of the whole. This reference, either at this or at a later stage, after the reports have been printed, is nearly universal, there being in all the Conventions whose journals or proceedings are known to me only two or three exceptions to it. In those cases, the reports were taken up directly in Convention, and put on the way to final passage, without referring them to a committee of the whole. When so referred, after full and often very extended discussion in that committee, the reports, as amended by it, are passed through their several stages to final adoption, as in case of other laws, by the Convention itself.

§ 303. Before the scattered reports of the standing committees, amended by the committee of the whole, and afterwards by the Convention, are put upon their final passage, it is usual to refer them to a committee of revision, or on phraseology and arrangement, whose duty it is to file them down to uniformity of style, and establish the proper *locus* of each section in the Constitution. A committee charged with this duty is sometimes appointed among the standing committees, and sometimes is raised toward the close of the session, when the occasion for its services arises. It has been usual to regard this committee as of very slight consequence, as though its operation could only be to add to the polish of the instrument, or to the perfection of its logical arrangement, but I am persuaded the idea is a mistaken one. It is always in the power of such a committee — perhaps I might say it is liable, even without intending it, in the process of manipulating a Constitution for the purpose indicated — to change its language so as materially to alter its legal effect. In the hurry of its final passage, such a change would be apt, unless very conspicuous, to escape detection. It is said, I think by Mr. Jefferson, that Gouverneur Morris, to whom the duty of revising the style of the Federal Constitution was intrusted, in performing it, insensibly gave a cast to that instrument which it did not bear when it passed into his hands, and that the Convention did not discover the change. The same thing, as I am informed,[1] occurred in the case of the first Constitution of Michigan, in which very important changes were effected, perhaps unintentionally, in the manner I have indicated.

§ 304. The Constitution, coming from the hands of the committee of revision, and being adopted as a whole, it is usual for the entire body of the delegates, beginning with their president, to subscribe their names to it, in attestation of its genuineness. In a few instances it has been signed by the president and secretary only, and in a few others by such members only as voted for it upon its final passage. It is not apparent why members should ever refuse to subscribe to the Constitution which has been matured by the Convention, if the act be construed, as I think it should be, as an act of attestation, and not as a declaration of approval.

[1] By the late Gov. Robert McClellan, of Michigan.

CHAPTER VI.

OF THE POWERS OF CONVENTIONS.

§ 305. We approach now by far the most important question relating to Conventions, namely, What are their powers?

It is hardly necessary to apprise the reader that, by the term power, as applied to an institution charged with governmental functions, is meant not physical ability, but legal ability, or that moral competence which Burke describes as "subjecting, even in powers more indisputably sovereign, occasional will to permanent reason, and to the steady maxims of faith, justice, and fixed fundamental policy."[1] In language more familiar to ears trained in our constitutional schools, it means competence by law or by the principles of our political Constitution. What a Convention can do legally, that is, by the express provisions of some law, or what, in the absence of such a law, it can do consistently with the principles of our Constitutions, among which are to be reckoned its own, it has, in general, power to do, and nothing further.

§ 306. The general conception of a Convention is, that it is a body of delegates, chosen by the electors of a State, to perform certain legislative duties connected with the enactment of the fundamental law. The extent of those duties, whether it be to frame, establish, and put in operation that law, or only to take certain steps toward its establishment, leaving others to be taken by other agencies, is mainly the question we are to determine. In the general definition of a Convention, just given, the term "delegates" is used advisedly, and is intended to be taken in its legal sense, as distinguished from the word "representatives," which is defined by Lord Brougham to be a body of persons, chosen by the people, to whom the power of the people is parted with, and who perform that part in the government

[1] *Reflections on the Revolution in France.*

which, but for this transfer, would have been performed by the people themselves.[1]

§ 307. Two widely different theories of this important institution, from which have been derived divergent conceptions of its powers, have of late years been in vogue.

First. One theory is, that the Convention is *a strictly representative body*, acting for and in the name of the sovereign, and possessed, by actual transfer, of all the powers inherent in that sovereign, limited, however, in the case of Conventions in the several States, by the Constitution of the United States; that it is "a virtual assemblage of the people," of whom, by reason of their great numbers and remoteness from each other, an actual assemblage, imagined by political speculatists, is impossible,—the most that can be effected being a gathering together in convenient numbers of deputies, empowered to represent the people, and clothed with all the power the sovereign itself would have were it assembled *en masse.*

Secondly. The second theory is, that the Convention is *a collection of delegates* appointed by the sovereign, through the agency of one or more branches of the existing government, to perform certain determinate duties in relation to the formation or revision of the fundamental law; what those duties are, depending upon the tenor of the commission under which it convenes, or, when that is silent, upon sound constitutional principles and precedents. According to this theory, the members of a Convention are not, accurately speaking, *representatives*, but *delegates;* and it is their function, not to enact, but simply to recommend, constitutional changes,—unless, indeed, as is sometimes the case, the warrant for their assembling should contain authority to act definitively, in which case their power would, perhaps, be coextensive with the terms of the grant. In other words, in its last analysis, a Convention, according to this second theory, is a mere committee, sitting for a specified purpose, under the express mandate of the sovereign, and possessed of such powers only as are expressly granted, or as are necessary and proper for the execution of powers expressly granted. This theory evidently discards the notion, so much cherished by the advocates of the former, that the Convention is clothed with sovereign attributes, though doubtless intrusted to some extent,

[1] *Political Philos.*, Vol. III. ch. vi. p. 33.

under strict regulations, intended to secure responsibility, with their exercise.

§ 308. As I am unwilling to misstate the two theories, above propounded, I extract from the debates of our Conventions, or from the writings of our public men, passages in which the one or the other has, more or less completely, been maintained.

Thus, in the New York Convention of 1821, Mr. Livingston, advocating a proposition to deprive the few blacks in the State of the right of suffrage accorded to them by the existing Constitution, said: "We have been told by the honorable gentleman from Albany (Mr. Van Vechten) that we were not sent here to deprive any portion of the community of their vested rights. Sir, the people are here themselves. They are present by their delegates. No restriction limits our proceedings. What are these *vested* rights? Sir, we are standing upon the foundations of society. The elements of government are scattered around us. All rights are buried; and from the shoots that spring from their grave we are to weave a bower that shall overshadow and protect our liberties."[1]

The Hon. George M. Dallas, in a letter published in "The Pennsylvanian" of September 5, 1836, said: "A Convention is the provided machinery of peaceful revolution. It is the civilized substitute for intestine war. . . . When ours shall assemble, it will possess, within the territory of Pennsylvania, every attribute of absolute sovereignty, except such as may have been yielded and are embodied in the Constitution of the United States. What may it not do? It may reorganize our entire system of social existence, terminating and proscribing what is deemed injurious, and establishing what is preferred. It might restore the institution of slavery among us; it might make our penal code as bloody as that of Draco; it might withdraw the charters of the cities; it might supersede a standing judiciary by a scheme of occasional arbitration and umpirage; it might prohibit particular professions or trades; it might permanently suspend the privilege of the writ of *habeas corpus*, and take from us . . . . the trial by jury. These are fearful matters, of which intelligent and virtuous freemen can never be guilty, and

[1] *Deb. N. Y. Conv.* 1821, p. 105, ed. New York, November, 1821. It does not appear which of the two Livingstons who were members of the Convention, Peter R., or Alexander, uttered this opinion.

I mention them merely as illustrations of the inherent and almost boundless power of a Convention." [1]

So, in the Illinois Convention of 1847, Mr. Peters said: "He had and would continue to vote against any and every proposition which would recognize any restriction of the powers of this Convention." "We are," he continued, "the sovereignty of the State. We are what the people of the State would be, if they were congregated here in one mass meeting. We are what Louis XIV. said he was, 'We are the State.' We can trample the Constitution under our feet as waste paper, and no one can call us to account save the people." [2]

But two further extracts will be given upon this side of the question, taken from the proceedings of the Illinois Convention of 1862. A committee, composed of some of the leading jurists in that body, in a report upon the subject of electing a printer, said: — "When the people, therefore, have elected delegates, ... and they have assembled and organized, then a peaceable revolution of the State government, so far as the same may be effected by amendments of the Constitution, has been entered upon, limited only by the Federal Constitution. All power incident to the great object of the Convention belongs to it. It is a virtual assemblage of the people of the State, sovereign within its boundaries, as to all matters connected with the happiness, prosperity, and freedom of the citizens, and supreme in the exercise of all power necessary to the establishment of a free constitutional government, except as restrained by the Constitution of the United States." [3] 'In a speech in the same body, General Singleton said: — "Sir, that this Convention of the people is sovereign, possessed of sovereign power, is as true as any proposition can be. If the State is sovereign the Convention is sovereign. If this Convention here does not represent the power of the people, where can you find its representative? If sovereign power does not reside in this body, there is no such thing as sovereignty." [4]

§ 309. On the other hand, the theory which regards Conven-

[1] To a similar effect are remarks of Mr. Mitchell, in the Kentucky Convention of 1849, *Deb. Ky. Conv.* 1849, p. 863; also of B. F. Butler in the Massachusetts Convention of 1853, *Deb. Mass. Conv.* 1853, Vol. I. pp. 78, 97.

[2] Illinois *State Register* of June 10, 1847.

[3] Id. of January 10, 1862.

[4] Id. of January 17, 1862.

tions as advisory bodies simply, with limited powers, has been broached in equally explicit terms. The earliest case in which the powers of such bodies were brought into discussion, was that of the Federal Convention of 1787. The credentials of the delegates to that body, as is well known, contemplated only a revision of the Confederation, leaving it still a mere confederate system. On assembling, however, those delegates were generally satisfied, that any government, formed by patching up the old Confederation, would be wholly inadequate, and that what was wanted was a firm national government. But then arose the embarrassing question, was it competent for that body to disregard its instructions and frame such a system as it deemed absolutely necessary for the salvation of the country? The answer given to this question marks, indisputably, the sense of the statesmen of the Revolution as to the real nature of the Convention. Their answer was, in substance, that by strict law the Convention had no power nor right to disregard the instructions of the legislative Assemblies by which they were deputed, on whose call they had assembled; but that, under the controlling necessities of the times, they would venture to disregard those instructions, since, after all, the power of ultimate decision was to be in the people, the Convention having authority only to recommend, not to act definitively. Thus, Mr. Wilson, of Pennsylvania, one of the profoundest jurists our country has ever produced, said: — "With regard to the power of the Convention, he conceived himself authorized to conclude nothing, but to be at liberty to propose any thing."[1] So, Governor Randolph, of Virginia, referring to his own plan of a national government, which was afterwards made the basis of the Constitution, as adopted, said: "The resolutions from Virginia must have been adopted on the supposition that a federal government was impracticable. And it is said, that power is wanting to institute such a government; but when our all is at stake, I will consent to any mode that will preserve us. . . . . Besides, our business consists in recommending a system of government, not in making it."[2] Mr. Madison, also, contrasting the plan of Mr. Randolph with the federal plan introduced by Mr. Paterson, of New Jersey, said: "The principal objections against that of Mr. Randolph were the want of power, and the want of practica-

[1] Elliott's *Deb.*, Vol. V. p. 196. [2] Elliott's *Deb.*, Vol. I. p. 416.

bility. There can be no weight in the first, as the *fiat* is not to be here, but in the people."[1] In this most important Convention, then, of which many of the founders of our institutions were members, the power proper only for a sovereign, of definitive legislation, was not only not claimed for that body, but it was expressly disclaimed.

§ 310. Similar views have been expressed by members of later Conventions. In the Virginia Convention of 1829, John Randolph said: "Sir, we have been called as counsel to the people — as State physicians to propose remedies for the State's diseases, not to pass any Act which shall have in itself any binding force. We are here as humble advisers and proposers to the people."[2] In the Illinois Convention of 1847, a resolution was introduced by Mr. Singleton, containing his views of the powers and duties of that body, as follows: — "*Resolved*, that this Convention is limited in its purposes and powers; its object being to propose, for the acceptance of the people, such changes in their present Constitution as to the Convention may appear

[1] Elliott's *Deb.*, Vol. V. p. 216.

[2] *Deb. Va. Conv.* 1829, p. 868. Even if the legislature, in its Convention Act, had assumed to give the Convention unlimited power, Mr. Randolph maintained that it could not exercise it. Thus, in the Virginia Convention Act of 1829, the Convention was authorized to submit the amended Constitution to the voters of the Commonwealth qualified under its own provisions. Adverting to this authorization, Mr. Randolph denied that either the legislature had power to give, or the Convention to act upon it. Upon this point, he said: "Does not the gentleman from Frederick distinctly see that, if his doctrine be correct, we are giving a Convention power to bind conclusively the people of Virginia *quoad* the right of suffrage? . . . I shall be told that we have been clothed with this power. Are we? The legislature, I grant, have been very kind in clothing us with a power they did not possess. If the gentleman's doctrine be correct, then the legislature of Virginia — who cannot touch the subject without an act of treachery themselves — have given to the Convention power, as to the right of suffrage, to bind the people of Virginia; converting us . . . from an advisory into a controlling council. . . . If that be true, then, by a juggle between the legislature, who were without power themselves, and a Convention, who were called only to advise the people, an act is to be done by which the people are to be finally bound. . . . In the all-important question of the right of suffrage, this Convention is to exert an absolute power to decide, without consulting the people at all. How do we derive it? From a Virginia legislature who never possessed it. To refer to the legislature is only putting a tortoise under the elephant. Thus power rests upon the elephant, the elephant upon the tortoise, and the tortoise upon nothing. Sir, this won't do. It won't do."

necessary, limited, in these changes, by the true principles of a republican government, and, in the conduct of its body, by the Constitution of this State, as far as it is applicable. That this Convention has no power to repeal or modify any Act of the General Assembly of this State, otherwise than by constitutional provision, subject to the ratification of the people, or do any other act not necessary to the discharge of the trust confided to it."[1] Upon this resolution an animated debate arose, in the course of which the two theories of the Convention I have explained were distinctly propounded; the most outspoken and extravagant assertion of sovereign powers for the Convention being that made by Mr. Peters in the terms quoted in a preceding section. The result of the debate was, the adoption of a mild resolution which avoided the disputed points, as a substitute for the foregoing one, by a vote of 87 to 64. Other extracts might be added, from the debates of other Conventions, and particularly that held in Illinois in 1862, in which the two theories of the powers of those bodies were elaborately discussed. Enough, however, has been given, to answer my purpose, which is simply to illustrate, by actual examples, the scope and tenor of the divergent theories entertained on the subject.

§ 311. Of these two theories, it is important now to note, that the first, which attributes to the Convention powers amounting sometimes — the State alone considered, in which the body meets — to absolute sovereignty, is of modern origin. The records of our Conventions reveal no trace of it earlier than the New York Convention of 1821, from which an extract has been given.[2] In 1829, it again made its appearance in the Virginia Convention, but obscurely and hesitatingly. A question arose as to the power of that Convention to disregard positive instructions of the legislature relative to the submission of the fruit of its labors to the people, in the discussion of which, doctrines were propounded which afterwards ripened into the theory in question. The next appearance was in the letter of Mr. Dallas, from which an extract has been given above, and in the Convention held in Pennsylvania in the following year — the latter the fruit of the seed sown by that gentleman. The theory, however, was but partially propounded in the Convention, traces of it lurking in a

[1] *Journal Illinois Conv.* 1847, p. 13.

[2] See *ante*, § 308.

scarcely recognizable form in certain assertions of power, made for particular purposes. The boldness of the position taken by Mr. Dallas had excited opposition in the State, and caution was necessary. In the struggles preceding the meeting of that Convention, the advocates of reform had succeeded in inducing the legislature to call the body, but subject to stringent limitations, in regard to the submission of its amendments to the people. On assembling, a discussion arose between the advocates and opponents of reform as to the extent and nature of the powers of the Convention, thus limited; whether it was or was not restricted to submitting amendments, or whether it might not, on the one hand, frame a new Constitution, or, on the other, adjourn without proposing any change whatever. During this discussion, opinions were occasionally expressed, which indicated that the theory of conventional sovereignty had been making progress since its first appearance in New York a few years before.

Ten years afterwards, this theory was enunciated, in the terms we have seen above, by Mr. Peters, in the Illinois Convention of 1847.[1] In 1849, it made its appearance in the Kentucky Convention, and four years later, in that of Massachusetts, under the patronage of Messrs. Hallett and Butler. In 1860–1861, it produced its legitimate fruits in the so-called secession of the eleven slaveholding States from the Union, a movement matured and consummated by its aid; and finally, in 1862, its echo was heard in the free State of Illinois, some members of whose Convention unwisely seized upon a time of national peril to endorse a disorganizing dogma, in the general adoption of which at the South that peril had originated.[2]

[1] *Ante*, § 308.

[2] The notions entertained in the seceding States, as to the powers of Conventions, may be inferred from the following extract from a speech made by the Hon. William L. Yancey, in the Alabama Convention of 1861. The question being on the submission of the Ordinance of Secession to the people, that gentleman said: —

"This proposition is based upon the idea, that there is a difference between the people and the delegate. It seems to me that this is an error. There is a difference between the representatives of the people in the law-making body, and the people themselves, because there are powers reserved to the people by the Convention of Alabama, and which the General Assembly cannot exercise. But in this body is all power — no powers are reserved from it. The people are here in the persons of their deputies. Life, Liberty, and Property are in our hands. Look to the Ordinance adopting the Constitution of Alabama. It

§ 312. Such has been the career of this famous political dogma, as exhibited in Conventions recognized by their respective States as legitimate. In the mean time, in Maryland, in 1837, coupled with the heresy that a mere majority in numbers of the adult male citizens, without regard to legal provisions, can at any time call a Convention to alter or abolish the Constitution, it came near flaming into actual revolution — a call for a Convention being issued by private individuals, who only desisted from their illegal purpose, upon the appearance of a proclamation of the Governor denouncing it as treasonable. Five years later the same doctrines ripened and produced their legitimate fruits in Rhode Island, in the Dorr rebellion, of which a history was given in a preceding chapter. In that State, a Convention, called by unofficial persons, and claiming to represent the people of Rhode Island, because deputed by a majority of all the male citizens of twenty-one years of age, resident in the State, though not by a majority of the legal voters at a regular election, framed a Constitution, and attempted by force of arms to maintain it as the legitimate Constitution of the State.

In these proceedings, the alarming position was taken, that not only could a Convention be got together in defiance of the existing government, but, when assembled, it could remodel that government, — eject from office those charged with its administration, without their consent or that of the electoral body, on which the whole political structure was immediately bottomed. Such was the first conspicuous practical application of the theory of conventional sovereignty. The second has been already referred to, as exhibited on a more imposing scale, in 1860–1861, when eleven States sought, under its inspiration, to break in pieces the temple of the Union.[1]

states, 'We, the people of Alabama,' &c., &c. All our acts are supreme, without ratification, because they are the acts of the people acting in their sovereign capacity." — *Hist. & Deb. Ala. Conv.* 1861, p. 114.

[1] Comparing the dates of the various Conventions, in which the theory of conventional sovereignty has been propounded, with those of the successive tides of pro-slavery fanaticism in the United States, it is difficult to resist the conviction, that the assertion of that theory was connected with the great conspiracy which culminated in the late Secession war. Was it foreseen, that to carry out the design of disrupting the Union, with an appearance of constitutional right, new conceptions must become prevalent, as to the powers of the bodies by which alone the design could be accomplished? And conceding the existence of such

§ 313. Admitting, however, that the theory in question is a novelty, it is not always true, especially in politics, that "whatever is new is false," and it is therefore fairly incumbent on those who reprobate that theory, not alone to denounce it as novel, or to array against it the invectives of its opponents, but to refute it. This, it is my hope, in what follows, to be able to do. The refutation, however, will be much of it inferential, depending on the consideration not only of general principles, but of particular questions, relating to the power of Conventions in special cases, which either have actually arisen or are likely any day to arise.

§ 314. The powers of Conventions, including in that term both positive and negative powers, that is, both powers and disabilities, may be most conveniently discussed by considering them with reference,

I. To the external relations of those bodies; that is, their relations to the political society in which they are assembled; or, more particularly, —

(*a*). To the sovereign, or to the rights of sovereignty.

(*b*). To the government of the state, as a whole.

(*c*). To the electors, or most numerous branch of the government.

(*d*). To the three great departments of administration, — legislative, executive, and judicial; — and

II. To their internal relations — to the perfecting of their organization, to the maintenance of discipline over their own members or over strangers, and to the prolongation or perpetuation of their existence.

To this discussion will be devoted the remainder of this chapter.

§ 315. I. (*a*). The powers of Conventions, considered with reference to the sovereign, or to sovereignty, may be best exhibited by answering this question: Are Conventions possessed to any, and what, extent of sovereign powers? If a Convention is pos-

a conspiracy, to be carried through by such means, were the eminent names cited above the willing tools or the dupes of the far seeing traitors who hatched it?

Even in the case of Mr. Livingston, who broached the theory in the New York Convention of 1821 (see *Deb. N. Y. Conv.* 1821, p. 105) the imputation of pro-slavery fanaticism would seem not entirely unjust. The purpose of Mr. L. in propounding the theory was to satisfy the Convention of its power to abridge the right of suffrage accorded by existing laws to the free blacks of New York

sessed of sovereign powers, it must be either, first, because, while its members have no individual or personal sovereignty, the body has received sovereign powers, by actual transfer from their original source, the sovereign, and holds them absolutely, by right of representation; or, secondly, because its members, in common with all the citizens, or, at least, with all the electors, are possessed of individual or personal sovereignty, and, accordingly, when assembled in Convention, wield sovereign powers absolutely, both in their own right and in that of their co-sovereigns, outside of the body, whom they represent. Of these two alternatives, the first supposes sovereignty to be alienable, which, in a former chapter,[1] we have seen to be incompatible with its nature. Sovereignty was there shown to be inherent in the political society; and it was stated that, although two or more sovereigns might become merged into one, sovereignty is indivisible and incommunicable. It is impossible that a sovereign society should transfer its inherent sovereignty to any other society, or to a part of itself, so as to render the receiving body or person absolute sovereign over it. The mind refuses to conceive of a political society in a fit of apathy or of frenzy, parting with its birthright beyond redemption. And to suppose such an alienation made to citizens of the State, however eminent, would be scarcely less abhorrent than to aliens. It is not to be imagined that, were such an alienation possible, it could be made by the sovereign society itself directly; it must be made by some part of it, claiming a right to act for it by representation, as by some branch of the government now existing. But that the electors, or either of the three administrative departments of the government, should be able by any *hocus pocus* to transfer those transcendant powers which belong to the political society as such, is incredible; certainly without an express warrant from the sovereign to that effect. And supposing such a warrant were a thing possible to be given, what consideration could there exist sufficient to sustain, in any court, whether of law or of abstract morality, so unconscionable a contract? It is this view which justifies the revolts now so common in Europe, of subjects against their servants, calling themselves their sovereigns. Intrusted with the government, those servants or their ancestors, in some former age, upset the balance of the

[1] See *ante*, § 22.

Constitution, and proclaimed themselves to be the true sovereigns. But such a proclamation cannot alter the fact, which is, that the nation as a unit is the only sovereign. Force or fraud on the part of the servant, or pusillanimity on that of the nation, may have given the prestige of success to the usurpation of the former, but cannot have divested the inalienable rights of the latter. No truth is becoming more clear, in our day, than that in demanding everywhere the supreme direction of the commonwealth, and in asserting a right to determine the modes and instruments of its administration, the people — the nation — are but reclaiming their own.

§ 316. It seems clear, then, that if there is claimed for a Convention the possession of absolute sovereignty for the time being, it must be, not on the *de jure* ground of actual transfer, but on the *de facto* one of successful usurpation or revolution which, as divesting the rights of the people, we have just seen, is of no force or validity whatever.

And here it is proper to note a distinction which is made by those who maintain the derivation of sovereign powers to Conventions by transfer from the true sovereign, namely, that if not absolutely sovereign with reference to the political society, they are so with respect to the objects for which they are respectively convened, namely, the framing anew, altering, or amending of the fundamental law. Thus, in the Illinois Convention of 1862, the committee, whose report on the powers of that body has been already mentioned, conclude that remarkable document as follows: —

"Your committee, therefore, have come to the conclusion, that, after due organization of the Convention, the law calling it is no longer binding, and that the Convention then has supreme power in regard to all matters necessary and incident to the alteration and amendment of the Constitution." Here, if words mean any thing, the Convention is claimed to be sovereign in a sphere of operations which is limited, relating to the enactment of the fundamental law. But, it is certain that that Convention was not sovereign, nor even supreme, in that sphere, but subject to the Constitution of the United States. That was distinctly admitted, on numerous occasions, by members of that Convention who were loudest in their assertions of sovereign powers, and by the committee itself above referred to, in their report, from which that extract was made. In another paragraph the committee say:—"It" (the Convention) "is a virtual assemblage of the people of the State, sovereign within its boundaries as to all matters connected with the happiness, prosperity, and freedom of the citizens, and supreme in the exercise of all power necessary to the establishment of a free constitutional government, *except as restrained by the Constitution of the United States.*" What kind of a sovereignty is that, which is limited, in respect of its sphere of action, to alterations of the fundamental law, and limited within that sphere by the Constitution of a distinct society, by which it is forbidden to meddle with important subjects of legislation, such as war and peace, treaties, &c., proper for any body which is really sovereign? Moreover, this very Convention, which refused to obey the injunction of the statute, under which it assembled, relating to its printer, deemed itself compelled, as well by the injunction of that same statute as by the customs in such cases established, to submit to the people for ratification or rejection the Constitution it had matured. If a body thus hampered and subordinated is a sovereign power, so are their grooms and their bootblacks, since each of those menials has committed to him absolute power to perform the duties assigned him, subject to the limitations contained in his commission and to the laws of the land.

§ 317. The other alternative, which supposes every citizen, or, at least, every elector possessed of sovereign powers, according to the loose political jargon of our times, and that Conventions represent them in their sovereign character, each of their members being a sovereign in his own right as well as in the right of representation of sovereigns, involves two fundamental errors, which indeed are its only foundation. The first error is in supposing that there is any such thing as the personal sovereignty of individuals in any political society whatever. In relation to political rights and obligations, the unit is not the individual or the family, unless indeed the family constitute a patriarchal government, but the state. In the matter of civil rights and obligations, on the other hand, the unit is the individual citizen We have pointed out in the chapter on sovereignty the absurd consequences flowing from the hypothesis either of many sovereigns in the same political society, or of a divided or fractional sovereignty in the separate citizens of a state. In either case, each citizen would be equal to every other citizen, and there would be no common superior — a condition of things in which government would be impossible, and laws and Constitutions become what Mr. Burke styled the Bill of Rights of the French Constitution of 1793, but "a digest of anarchy."

§ 318. The second error in the hypothesis of conventional sovereignty based on the representation of individual sovereigns, is in supposing that such a sovereignty of the individual could be alienated, were it conceded to exist. It is evident that the hypothesis that every citizen is vested to some extent with the attributes of sovereignty, is founded on transcendental views of the dignity of the individual, resulting from an extension to every person considered as a part of a political society, of relations, rights, and duties, analogous to those which are conceived as attaching to him in the domain of morals. But this is erroneous, and is one of many instances showing the dangers of reasoning by analogy in matters of political concernment. But supposing such a sovereignty of the individual to be a fact, to alienate it would be to impart to another powers which belonged to the giver only by virtue of his individual manhood, which were essential attributes of his personality, and which consequently he could not give, nor another receive. If a Convention of several of those individual sovereigns were possessed of sovereignty, it would be a contradiction to suppose that transcendent power to be left still existing in the persons whom it represented. The result is, then, that in no intelligible sense of the word sovereign can it be properly applied to a Convention.

§ 319. Before leaving this branch of the discussion, it is proper to note, that although Conventions are not sovereign bodies, they are intrusted by the sovereign society with the *exercise* of an important sovereign power, that of legislation, of a certain kind, and to a certain extent. The substantive powers of government, such as those of enacting, expounding, and executing the laws, are all sovereign powers. But when it is said that the several agencies constituting a government are permitted to exercise sovereign powers, it is far from asserting that those agencies are possessed of original sovereignty. While they are wielding powers that belong to the sovereign society that society is conceived of not only as existing, but as clothed continually with all the rights of source of power, and of final arbiter in all questions relating to its extent or exercise.[1] The argument, therefore, which should seek to infer sovereignty in the Convention from the fact of its being vested to some extent with the exercise of sovereign powers, would prove too much; it would prove that, in any well-constructed government in our times, there were numerous sovereign bodies or persons, the legislature, the king, president or emperor, and the bench of judges.

§ 320. (*b*). We are next to inquire into the relations of Conventions to the government of the state, as a whole, and the powers growing out of those relations.

As to the former, the substance of what I desire to say, may be comprised in the discussion of a single question,— Is a Convention a component part of the governmental system of the state?

If it is not a part of that system, certainly the difficulties of locating it and of ascertaining its powers are infinitely enhanced, for the only alternative is to consider it as *imperium in imperio*; a body whose powers cannot be delineated, because practically unlimited; a body having only an incidental relation, by reason of the necessities attending its birth, to the ordinary governmental agencies — the government, indeed, sustaining to it the relation not of parent or guardian, but of midwife merely — a body, finally, standing in necessary connection only with the sovereign for which it acts, or, rather, whose successor it is. On the other hand, nothing could conduce more to simplicity of view, than to consider this institution as a branch of that system by which the state, considered as a political society, works out its will in relation both to itself and to the citizens of which it is composed. And this, although the subject is not free from difficulty, I am satisfied is the correct view to take of the question. We have seen in the first chapter, that, in England — and the same is true generally in all foreign states — the power of fundamental legislation belongs to the Parliament, precisely as does that of ordinary legislation; and that, for special reasons which were there detailed, a different plan has been adopted in the United States, namely, that of distinct bodies for the two species of legislation. The fact, however, that, except with us,

[1] See *ante*, § 308.

the two species are always united, demonstrates that there is no natural incompatibility between them. Though variant in character and importance, fundamental laws and municipal laws equally conform to the definition of laws. And certainly, the enactment of laws is the proper function of the government of a state. If it be objected, that the idea of a system depending for its own renovation upon itself, involves a contradiction, the reply is, that there is in it no contradiction, *whenever, as in every political society, the system is one operated by vital forces.* This is a matter of common experience in the strictly analogous case of the animal kingdom. In the animal, those organs by which are discharged the functions of reparation and reproduction are clearly as much parts of the organism as those by which it defends itself from hostile attack, or adjusts itself to changes of its physical condition. Why should that body of functionaries which legislates for the governors, as such, be denied a place in the state governmental system any more than that which legislates for the governed? The circumstance that the former assembles only occasionally, though it doubtless leads to much of the misconception prevalent regarding it, is really a matter of no consequence in determining its true character. The frequency or infrequency of its assembling is rather one of those matters of practical detail which are determined from time to time, as may be necessary to render the Convention system harmless as well as efficient. But the fact that Conventions always regularly assemble on the call of the legislatures of the states concerned, indicates decisively, that the Convention has a place in the governmental system. Had it been the design of those who framed that system originally, to make of the Convention a power outside of the circle of government, why make it dependent for its existence upon an act of a single department of that government, thus stamping upon its very front indubitable evidence of its filial relation to it?

§ 321. The probability that Conventions were intended to be parts of the systems of government amongst us, is increased by looking at the practical consequences of the contrary hypothesis. If they are not parts of those systems, they must be independent of them, practically, and those theorizers may be right, who proclaim the incompetence of legislatures to bind Conventions by their enactments. To the legislature, in that view, belongs the ministerial duty of issuing the *fiat* by which the Convention is spoken into being, but there its power ends. Once assembled and organized, that body slips its leash and bounds into a condition of absolute uncontrollability. It becomes potentially, at least, a realization of that remorseless monster in the human form which the fancy of Mrs. Shelley has depicted in her Frankenstein — a product of transcendent mechanical and philosophical skill, endowed with life and intelligence, but destitute of moral instincts or of practical accountability; a monster with powers so surpassing those of the philosopher who created it, that it was wholly beyond his control — he could not even kill it. In short, on this hypothesis, a Convention would exhibit the anomaly of an institution, manifesting all the traits of an absolute despot, occasionally springing up alongside of a system of laws, and, during its unregulated and indeterminate existence, compelling from that system complete obedience. If this be thought to be an extreme view of the possibilities of such an institution, the answer is, that in estimating the character of any political power, it is extremes that must be considered; for to them it is the tendency always to run. A political system can be safely characterized only by transcribing its least favorable feature, precisely as the strength of a machine is to be gauged, not by that of its strongest, but by that of its weakest, part.

§ 322. In the Illinois Convention of 1862, a question arose involving a practical application of these principles. By the Constitution of that State, Art. V. Sec. 10, it was provided, that the judges of the Supreme and Circuit Courts should not be eligible "to any other office, or public trust, of profit," in the State or the United States, during the term for which they were elected, nor for one year thereafter; and that all votes for either of them for any elective office (except that of judge of the Supreme or Circuit Court) given by the General Assembly or the people, should be void. One of the delegates, Mr. O'Melveny, having been a judge of one of the Circuit Courts, within one year prior to his election to the Convention, his competitor contested his seat, on the ground, that he was incapable of sitting as a member of that body under the above provision of the Constitution. The Convention having at first, without a division, decided that he should retain his seat, a motion was made on the following day, to reconsider that vote, upon which arose a spirited debate, the question being, whether to be a member of a Convention was to hold "an office, or public trust of profit" in the State. On the part of those who sustained the sitting member, it was contended, that the words "office, or public trust," referred particularly to the distribution of powers contained in the Constitution, according to the first section of the second article of which, the powers of the government of the State were confided to three separate bodies of magistracy, the legislative to one, the executive to another, and the judicial to a third. To which of these departments, it was asked, did the delegate to the Convention belong? Certainly, it was answered, it could not be contended that he belonged to either of them, for all the officers belonging to each were specially enumerated in the Constitution. The only plausible argument that could be urged against this view, it was said, was, that there was another provision of the Constitution, that relating to amendments, which provided for the election of delegates to the Convention, from which it might be attempted to infer, that those persons, being chosen in pursuance of the Constitution, were as much holders of office or public trust under it, as were the judges or the governor; but that the reply was, that the constitutional provision referred to did not, either in terms or spirit, define the qualifications of delegates, as it did those of the judges, members of the legislature, etc.; it simply left the people to choose whomsoever they might desire, without regard to age or other qualifications; whereas, had the framers of the Constitution regarded the members of the Convention as State officers, they would have inserted particular provisions, prescribing not only the persons to be elected, but the time and mode of their election, and perhaps their powers and duties.

§ 323. On the other hand, it was contended by those who favored the contestant, in substance, that if membership of a Convention was not an office, which was not conceded, it certainly was a public trust, and that, of the greatest magnitude. Every constable, and every justice of the peace, — functionaries whose duties were comparatively trivial, — was conceded to be an officer, and in a position of public trust, because it had been found not impracticable to specify in the Constitution the classes of persons who should fill those places and the full scope of their duties; but those public servants, whose business so far transcended in importance that of all others that it was deemed impracticable or inexpedient to limit it by prior description, and upon the fidelity of whom, to their constituents, depended the liberties, to say nothing of the existence, of the Commonwealth, were not only not officers, but they were denied to be holders of a public trust in the State which they thus served! Besides, what was the reason for inserting the prohibitory clause in the Constitution? Clearly, to furnish a guaranty of the purity and independence of the State judiciary; qualities which could not well exist, if, while invested with the judicial robes, the judges were allowed to participate in the scramble for Federal or State offices. But did the framers of the Constitution intend that those officers whom they forbade to accept another position of profit under the State, or the United States, for an entire year after sitting as judges, lest the honor of the bench might be sullied, should be at liberty to enter a Convention to new-model the fundamental laws, — amongst them, perhaps, those regulating the tenure and emoluments of their own offices?

§ 324. In my judgment, there can be but little doubt, that a member of a Convention is, in the enlarged and proper acceptation of the term, an "officer" of the State. This follows, not simply from the reasonings in the Illinois Convention, of which, somewhat developed into details, an abstract has been given, but especially from the principles explained in preceding sections. A Convention is a part of the apparatus by which a sovereign society does its work as a political organism. It is the sovereign, as organized for the purpose of renewing or repairing the governmental machinery. That same sovereign, as organized for the purpose of making laws, is the legislature; as organized for the purpose of applying or carrying into effect the laws, it is the judiciary or the executive. These successive forms into which the sovereign resolves itself, are but systems of organization having relation more or less directly to the government of the society. Together, they constitute the government. And yet they do not each constitute the government. One branch of the governmental system may perform no governing function at all, in the ordinary sense of the term — may not operate or administer the government. Thus, under those Constitutions which directed the election of a Council to the Governor, merely as an advisory body, such Council, though clearly a branch of the government, did not govern. The government of a commonwealth is the totality of those instruments through whose ministry its political organization is begun and continued. It is that totality which governs, and not necessarily either of its members, precisely as it is the body of an animal which lives and acts, and not the separate parts, though, doubtless, of these, one masticates the food, another digests it, a third performs locomotion, a fourth thinks, and so on. And, as in the living body, each organ, contributing by no matter how humble or obscure a function to the common life, or development, is a member of the organism; so in the commonwealth every citizen or body of citizens, charged with any duty looking to the defence, the operation or the renewal of the political system, is an organ of that commonwealth for purposes connected with its government, and must be ranked amongst its officers. In other words, if the nutritive and reproductive apparatus is properly reckoned as a part of the animal economy, the corresponding apparatus, in an organized state, must be accounted a part of the political structure.

§ 325. The relations of Conventions to the state as a whole being ascertained, three practical questions will now be considered, from which their powers, growing out of those relations, may be determined, namely —

1. Can a Convention appoint officers to fill vacancies in the various governmental departments? [1]

2. Can it eject from office persons holding positions in the government by regular election or appointment? [2]

3. Can it direct such officers in the discharge of their duties? [3]

[1] In the Louisiana Convention of 1844, a resolution was introduced providing that certain specified officers should fill the offices of Parish Judges and District Judges, "now vacant by the election of said officers to this Convention." The resolution was defended by its mover on the ground of necessity; but the Convention deemed the assumption of the power unwarranted, and rejected the resolution by a vote of sixty-eight to one. — *Deb. La. Conv.* 1844, pp. 26, 27.

[2] This question was raised in the Illinois Convention of 1862, but the power was not exercised.

[3] This question was raised in the Louisiana Convention of 1864, and the power of instruction asserted by a vote of sixty to fourteen. It notified the proper authorities to raise the salaries of loyal ladies engaged in "teaching the

If a Convention has power to do either of these acts, what is the extent of its power, and in what mode must it be exercised?

The power to fill vacancies in the government must be denied to a Constitutional Convention in any case. A sufficient reason for denying it is, that it is not necessary, since, running a parallel course to that body, and in full life and activity, is the ordinary appointing power, in its several departments, to whom the duty of filling such vacancies, by the Constitution, belongs. To assume the power would be justifiable only under a pressure of circumstances such as would necessitate usurpation, and convert the Constitutional into a Revolutionary Convention. Even supposing the body invested with definitive powers to establish a Constitution, without submission to the people, the selection of officers to fill vacancies, however occurring, could not be shown to be necessary to the fulfilment of such a commission. That duty could be better done by those to whom it is usually committed; and when to this it is added, that it would be unsafe to intrust power so extensive to a single assembly, an express warrant must be demanded before assenting to its exercise.

§ 326. To the two remaining questions, so far as they relate to direct action of the Convention, the same answer must be given. That body cannot remove from office, or instruct those holding office, by any direct proceeding, as by resolution or vote applying to particular cases. It is its business to frame a written Constitution; at most, to enact one. It has no power, under such a commission, to discharge the public servants, except so far as their discharge might result from the performance of its acknowledged duty. Indirectly, therefore, by constitutional provision of general application, unquestionably the power of removal must exist. A Convention may abolish existing offices, and thus effect the removal of those who fill them. So, in reference to instructing officers in relation to their duties, so far as the discharge of its admitted function, the framing of fundamental laws, is concerned, there is no doubt a Convention may modify at pleasure the regulations under which the government is administered in all its departments. But to attempt to issue instructions, in relation to

youth of our country." The Convention, however, as we have seen, was a revolutionary body.

matters of current policy, to particular officers, would be to blend with its ordinary and normal function those belonging properly to the legislature. Especially would this be improper, when the Convention meets under a call of the usual character, containing no power but to frame and submit to the people, for their adoption or rejection, a draft of a Constitution.

§ 327. Such, I think, upon principle, must be the answer to the questions indicated.

In relation to the power of a Convention to remove from, or appoint to, office, an interesting discussion has lately arisen in Missouri, to which attention must for a moment be directed.

By the Act of the General Assembly, calling the Missouri Convention of 1865, Sec. V., the delegates elected to that body were required to meet and organize, and thereupon to proceed "to consider, first, such amendments to the Constitution of the State as may be by them deemed necessary for the emancipation of slaves; second, such amendments to the Constitution of the State as may be by them deemed necessary to preserve in purity the elective franchise to loyal citizens, *and such other amendments as may be by them deemed essential to the promotion of the public good.*"

No further directions were given in the Act as to the nature of the amendments to be considered by the Convention, nor was that body required specifically to submit the fruit of its deliberations to the people.

The Convention met on the 6th of January, 1865, and adjourned on the 10th of April, having in the meantime prepared divers amendments to the Constitution, which, being submitted to the people on the 6th of June following, were adopted. Beside these, it also, on the 11th of January, adopted and put in operation, without submission to the people, an Ordinance "abolishing slavery in Missouri." In like manner, on the 17th of March, it adopted and put in operation, without submission, an Ordinance "providing for the vacating of certain civil offices in the State, filling the same anew," &c., of which the material portion was as follows: — "Be it ordained, &c.

"Section I. That the offices of the Judges of the Supreme Court, of all Circuit Courts, and of all Courts of Record, established by any Act of the General Assembly, and those of the Justices of all County Courts, of all Clerks of any of the aforesaid courts, of all Circuit-Attorneys and their assistants, and of all Sheriffs and County Recorders, shall be vacated on the first day of May, one thousand eight hundred and sixty-five, and the same shall be filled for the remainder of the term of each of said offices, respectively, by appointment by the Governor."

In pursuance of this Ordinance, each of the offices specified was filled by the Governor — the prior incumbents having been first, with force or otherwise, ejected therefrom. A vehement outcry was thereupon raised, charging the Convention and the Governor with having exceeded their authority. Whether they did so or not must depend on the question, whether the vacating Ordinance of March 17, 1865, was *an amendment to the Constitution or not.* If it was, it was within the express letter of the commission under which the Convention proceeded, the Act calling it together. If it was not, that body, clearly, was guilty of usurpation, since it is only laws of a fundamental character, that a Convention has power to enact or recommend.

§ 328. Of the question stated, whether the Ordinance of March 17, 1865, was an amendment to the Constitution or not, the following considerations seem to me to be decisive: —

1. An amendment to a Constitution is an Act, passed by competent authority, modifying *permanently* the structure, the operation, or the guarantees of the government. An Act which relates only to its *temporary administration*, to the *particular individuals* who shall or shall not fill its offices, or which, leaving the Constitution in its letter intact, merely suspends its action for a time, on some great emergency, cannot be called an amendment to its Constitution. It is rather an *administrative* Act, in the large sense of the term; or, where its effect is merely to suspend the action of the Constitution, it is, in substance, an executive Act, proper especially for an officer charged to see to it, that the Republic receives no detriment. In short, to borrow a figure which perfectly expresses the distinction I am contending for, it is an Act proper, not for the *millwright*, but for the *miller*.

2. That the Ordinance of March 17th was of this temporary, administrative character, lacking the essential characteristics of a *fundamental Act*, is apparent from its terms. In the first place, as I have stated, it ousted from office not *a class of persons*, but *particular individuals;* declaring, not that citizens

lacking specified qualifications should be thenceforward incapacitated to hold the office of judge, &c., but that Judges Bay and Dryden,[1] &c., then holding office, should vacate the same. Secondly, the Ordinance required the Governor to fill the offices thus vacated "*for the remainder of the term of each of said offices.*" It thus recognized the term fixed by the Constitution as still existing, and limited its own operation to the part thereof yet unexpired. In so doing, it obviously contemplated that, at the expiration of that term, the same offices should be filled as the Constitution provided, the Ordinance notwithstanding. In other words, it did not modify the Constitution, but suspended its operation for a limited time, after which it was again to be in full force.

§ 329. 3. That the Convention itself did not regard the Ordinance in question as an Act of fundamental legislation, is apparent from the fact, that it did not submit it to the people with the amendments to the Constitution, on the 6th of June, but put it in operation by its own authority. If it be objected, that the Convention also withheld from submission to the people the Ordinance of January 11, 1865, abolishing slavery in Missouri, clearly an Act of fundamental legislation, and that, if non-submission indicates decisively the character of the one Ordinance, it ought to do so of the other, the answer is, that although the better course would have been to submit the slavery Ordinance, yet, as the Convention Act was silent on the subject of submission, and as it expressly required the Convention to pass such amendments to the Constitution as they should deem necessary to emancipate the slaves, the cases are wholly different, and the objection is, therefore, groundless. In the one case, that body passed, but did not submit to the people, an Ordinance, which the people, through the legislature, had required it to pass; and in the other it passed, without submitting to the people, an Ordinance which it had not been required to pass, and of their authority to pass which, *as an amendment to the Constitution*, there is the gravest doubt.

§ 330. If the action of the Convention was not in the line of fundamental legislation, the alternative is, that it was one of revolution; for, in that case, it was one belonging to some

[1] The names of two of the judges ousted under the Ordinance, by whom prosecutions were brought to test its validity in the courts of Missouri.

branch of the existing government — an Act of administration or of ordinary legislation, coming within the province of some other department. And that it was of this character is, in my judgment, susceptible of no doubt.

In denying to the Convention, however, the power in question, it is not meant to imply, that the particular acts authorized by the Ordinance of March 17th were not necessary, but merely that they were not legal or constitutional. The Journals of the Convention of 1861, in the same State, are filled with evidences that Missouri was at that time in a revolutionary condition. Acts were done by that body, which were proper only for a strictly Revolutionary Convention, one which had assumed in a time of crisis, when the wheels of the regular administration were blocked, the functions of a provisional government. One of the earliest Ordinances of that Convention was one to vacate the offices of Governor, Lieutenant-Governor, Secretary of State, and members of the General Assembly, and, of its own authority, to appoint persons to exercise the duties of the first-named officers, until others, with a new General Assembly, should be elected in the November following.[1] It also, on the same day, passed an Ordinance repealing certain Acts of the General Assembly, approved in the early part of the year 1861.[2] So, also, it usurped the function of a General Assembly by passing an Ordinance for the organization and government of the Missouri State Militia,[3] and several Ordinances for the appropriation of moneys out of the State treasury.[4] All these acts were clearly usurpations of authority properly belonging to other departments of the State government. That that government was in treasonable hands might justify the Convention, on moral grounds, in seizing, by revolutionary force, powers not its own, but could not alter the legal character of its acts. In 1865, the same necessity perhaps existed, and, if so, might justify acts clearly of the same general character, legally considered, as those of its predecessor of 1861. But, as I have said, upon this question I pass no opinion. If the acts characterized as revolutionary were strictly necessary, it was not the first time in history that a party, having morally and politically the better case, had legally the worst of the argument.

[1] Ordinance of July 30, 1861. See Journal of the session of the Convention held in June of the year 1862, Appendix, pp. 3, 4.

[2] Id. p. 4. [3] Id. p. 7. [4] Id. pp. 18, 19.

§ 331. (*c*). I pass now to consider the relations of Conventions to the separate agencies or departments of the government, and the powers resulting to them from those relations. Of those departments, that which is the most numerous and which stands nearest in order to the sovereign, is the *electors*.

By the term electors, according to the American Constitutions, generally, with which alone we are now concerned, is meant that body of citizens who, by the Constitution or laws of the State, have been invested with the rights, first, of choosing the most important administrative[1] officers of the government, and, secondly, of determining, by its direct vote, the expediency of constitutional changes, and of enacting them. The electoral body, as already observed, is by far the most numerous corps of functionaries in the State. It never assembles in a single body, as does the legislature, but exercises its prescribed functions in determinate subdivisions of the public area, each of which constitutes an electoral circle, where alone the electors resident within it can exercise their franchise. Beyond the limited sphere of duty laid down for them in the fundamental law, this most important body has no power or official character whatever. It cannot pass an ordinary statute, or render a judgment, or execute a criminal. Its individual members, except in the simple act of casting their vote in the cases prescribed by law, represent nobody, and hence, theoretically, are entitled to no more weight than the still more numerous body of non-electors, comprising the residue of the people. But, although, while acting within their proper province, the electors, by their vote, are deemed to utter the voice of the sovereign, it is only the aggregate vote of the State, or what I might describe as the resultant of all the separate votes of its individual electors, which can be thus characterized, not the vote of the individual, or of the subordinate circle, which, as such, has generally no official validity whatever.

§ 332. Within the sphere allotted to the electors in the scheme of government, they constitute a strictly representative body. But it is only one of a number of such bodies. The three ordinary departments of a government — the legislative, executive, and judicial — are also representatives of the same constituent,

[1] I use the word "administrative" here in its broad sense, to designate all officers concerned in operating the government, — legislative, executive, and judicial.

the sovereign. That is, the functions severally committed to these four systems of agencies are, in general, committed to them absolutely, with respect both to each other and to the sovereign; the latter parting with the right to exercise the power, though not with the right to withdraw the grant, or to chastise those who abuse it. Because, judging from the visible operations of government, the electors seem to be the basis of the entire system, they are usually denominated *the people*. From this circumstance has arisen a common misapprehension, to the effect, that the electors are the source and possessors of all sovereign rights — the real sovereign. When it is considered, however, that this body is a variable one, the number and qualifications of those who compose it depending on the determinations from time to time of that power lying still further back, by whom the Constitution itself is enacted, the position of electoral sovereignty is seen to be untenable. The electors merely represent the sovereign, and are under all the conditions of responsibility and of limitation of power which attach to the departments at the next remove from the source of sovereignty, generally denominated the government.

§ 333. To determine the relations of Conventions, in general, to this primordial body of functionaries, let us first recall the genesis of the former. Conventions, as we have seen, are bodies chosen by the electors, at the instance of the legislature. They are thus, in one sense, the offspring of those two governmental agencies. But, on a broader view, they are to be regarded as the appointees of the sovereign itself. It is only through agents that the latter can act, and hence there is no system of functionaries amongst all those organized in a State, that, if considered with reference to its immediate source and origin, is not the child of the government of that State. They all depend upon each other, and run more or less into each other, trenching upon each other's power and jurisdiction. Still, in case of some of those agencies, it would not be denied that they are selected and commissioned by the sovereign, and if some, so, virtually, are they all. So far, then, as the genesis of Conventions is concerned, they must be set down as bearing to the electors substantially the same relations as does a legislature. It is a creature of the same political society, acting, as it can only act, through some one or more of its accustomed organs.

§ 334. Secondly, to determine the relations of Conventions to the electoral body, we must take into view their relative functions. The normal conception of the Convention is that of a body appointed by the sovereign to mature a scheme of fundamental law, to be submitted to that sovereign for ratification or rejection. But the sovereign neither on the one hand appoints, nor on the other ratifies or rejects, by its direct action. These exercises of sovereignty it can perform only through agents, and for that purpose it employs the electors, as being the most numerous, the most disinterested, and the nearest to itself, of any in the Commonwealth. Hence it follows, I think, that although in respect of their common origin from the sovereign, the Convention and the electoral body may be considered as in a certain sense coördinate, they are nevertheless, in another respect, to be ranked as unequal. A sort of primacy must be conceded to the electors, since, so far as the work of the Convention is concerned, they wield the actual sovereignty; for it is they who pass upon it, enacting it or otherwise, as to them seems best. Thus the electors stand between the Convention and the sovereign, whose rays of power they intercept and gather into a focus of their own. In a word, then, the Convention stands related to the electoral body thus: in point of origin, so far as other parties are concerned, they are coördinate, as both deriving their existence from the same source of power, the sovereign; but, with respect to each other, the electors are the more dignified and the more nearly sovereign body, since they receive their appointment directly, through the Constitution, from the sovereign, whilst the Convention receives it from the sovereign indirectly, through the same electors, to whom also it is bound to submit the fruit of its deliberations for approval or disapproval.[1]

§ 335. In the light of these principles, it will not be difficult now to furnish answers to such questions, depending on the relations just explained, as it may be useful to discuss.

1. Of these, the first which I shall consider is this: Can a Convention disfranchise any part of the electoral body?

This question may receive two different constructions. It may mean, Can a Convention, by virtue of its ordinary commission — to recommend, not to enact, constitutional changes

[1] For an exposition of this duty see *post*, Chapter VII.

— divest of the electoral franchise, by its direct action, any person qualified as an elector by the existing Constitution? In this sense, it is evident, the power does not exist, for reasons similar to those already given, in considering the power of a Convention to make removals from office. The question, on the other hand, may mean, Can a Convention effect the disfranchisement of subsisting electors by an indirect proceeding, as by constitutional provision, altering the qualifications for the exercise of the suffrage? This is a question of more difficulty. If the so-called "right of suffrage" is a natural right, and not a mere delegated power or duty, it is clear, that a Convention cannot rightfully divest of it persons coming within the limits by which it is defined. But if, on the contrary, it is no right at all, by nature, but rather a function or office, with which certain designated classes are charged by the sovereign, for its own purposes, it is equally clear, that, for what are deemed sufficient reasons, the charge may be withdrawn. In that case, inasmuch as the Convention is the agency through which the sovereign either effects constitutional changes or initiates them, reserving to itself, through the electors, the enactment of its recommendations, it follows that that body may, according to the terms of its commission, either withdraw or recommend the withdrawal of such charge.

§ 336. Which, then, is the true theory of the suffrage? Is its exercise that of a natural right, or is it merely the performance of a duty, resting simply upon positive law? The answer to this question can be based only upon presumptions, and, judging by them, suffrage is not a natural right. In the first place, there is the presumption arising from the fact, that no political community has ever existed in which the right to vote has been conceded to be the natural right of all the citizens. I mean, conceded, not as a matter of speculation, but as one of practical administration. This is believed to be true in the ancient democracies, as it has been in those modern governments, in which circumstances have enabled their founders to carry into effect most perfectly the theory of equal rights. In the cabin of the Mayflower it was the Pilgrim fathers, not the Pilgrim mothers, who framed the first Puritan commonwealth. In the second place, there has never been an instance, it is believed, in which a State, whatever its theories of the suffrage may have been, has not somewhere drawn a line of exclusion from its actual exercise, and drawn it, too, above the point which marks the extreme limit of practicability. In other words, no commonwealth, based upon popular suffrage, or admitting its exercise at all, has ever allowed it to the utmost extent that was practicable under the circumstances. Finally, suffrage, considered as a natural right, would be universal suffrage; and universal suffrage is an utter impracticability. For, admitting the force of the argument which attributes, by the law of nature, an equal right to vote to every citizen, nevertheless, when the statesman comes practically to establish the right, insuperable difficulties arise. Some are too weak or too young to exercise it at all, or with the requisite intelligence. A line must be somewhere drawn. Where it shall be drawn is a question of expediency, to be determined by the existing government, like any other measure involving mixed questions of justice and of policy. The principle of exclusion being once established, whether it shall be confined to considerations of age, or be extended to those of sex or social condition, is a matter of practical detail to be settled by the political power.

§ 337. The "right of suffrage" comes thus to be practically only a right of one man to represent many other men. Overlooking the absurdity of such a right, if asserted as a natural right, it comes at once into conflict with another right existing equally by the law of nature — the right of the State to determine who shall and who shall not discharge a function, which not all citizens can discharge. But a right of one man to do that which another has an equal right to prevent him from doing, is either a solecism or it is a right which subsists only upon conditions to be determined by that other; in other words, a right which is such only when it rests on some positive law ordained by that other.

Thus viewed, it is evident, that in the present condition of mankind, in which, for the public good, the principle of exclusion must be exercised, there is no such thing as a *right* of suffrage. Suffrage is not a right at all; it is a duty, a trust, enjoined upon, or committed to, some citizens and not to others. The only rights connected with the exercise of the suffrage, are, first, the right of the commonwealth, the collective body to be administered, for good or for evil, by the electors, to determine who those electors shall be; secondly, the right of every citizen, without distinction, derived to him through the commonwealth, to be fairly and adequately represented by the electors.

The conclusion at which I arrive then is, that a Convention may, by constitutional provision, effect the disfranchisement of existing electors. Of course, with the question of the policy of doing so, in any case, I do not concern myself.

§ 338. 2. Another question is, Can a Convention take upon itself the function of the electors to fill vacancies in its own ranks? This is substantially the same question before discussed in relation to the power of that body to fill vacancies in the ordinary departments of the government,[1] and should receive the same answer unless a different one ought to be given, because, in the case of appointing to an executive or judicial office, it would wrongfully assume the relation of electors to a third body, and in the other case, that of electors to itself. In the case last supposed, the Convention would be *pro tanto* self-appointing, and would maintain the attitude of at once constituent and delegate, which is that of a body *de facto* sovereign. So that the two cases would differ, but only in the degree of their common impropriety; the exercise by a Convention of the power to fill its own vacancies being far more unwarranted and dangerous than that of filling vacancies in other departments, as it would more flagrantly violate that system of mutual checks which is so indispensable to the safe action of popular institutions. It is evident, that of all possible checks, the most effectual, amounting practically to the power of complete control, is that of selecting the persons to constitute the body. This power it will never do for the electors on any consideration to resign.

§ 339. 3. The principles just settled enable us to answer another question, namely, Can a Convention authorize the colleagues of resigning or deceased members to name their successors? It is clear that, on general principles, what a Convention cannot do as a whole, it cannot authorize any of its members to do. But suppose, as was the case in the Virginia Convention of 1829, the Act of the General Assembly, under which the body convened, contained a special authorization to fill vacancies in that manner, could it then be allowed by the Convention? The answer must depend on the power of the legisla

[1] *Ante*, § 325.

ture to make such a provision, of which, to say the least, there is much doubt. The matter lies in a nutshell, thus: Where Constitutions have given to legislative bodies power to call Conventions, and have specified the electors of delegates thereto, they have with great uniformity named the persons qualified to vote at the general State elections.[1] Where no constitutional provision has existed governing the case, the same class has usually been designated by law.[2] Such has been the practice. Theoretical principles indicate with the utmost clearness that no other class could properly be permitted to act as electors in such a case. Could a legislature itself name the delegates to constitute the Convention? That would be to make of itself *the people*, to violate all the analogies of our republican system, and to trample under its feet the safeguards of our liberties. For, if it could appoint the delegates, it might name a committee of its own members, or of others, small in number, and likely to be equally, in either case, subservient to the power which created it. A Convention thus composed would virtually be but the legislature itself, which would in that case possess the uncontrollable powers of the English Parliament, those, namely, of constructing the government, and then of regulating its administration. It cannot be, then, that a legislature has power to remit the election of conventional delegates in the first instance to any body of persons but the electors. And if not in the first instance, it is equally doubtful whether it could do it afterwards to fill vacancies. These ought to be filled by the constituencies left unrepresented, which are not the colleagues of the retired members, but the electors in the proper districts. These considerations are confirmed by the observation that exceptional modes, even if convenient, cannot in any high sense of the term be said to be necessary. The absence of a delegation is not likely to be a very serious evil, in case no provision by law for calling a new election has been made in a form that is free from objection, and if the power to order one without such a law be doubted.

§ 340. 4. If a Convention cannot, when vacancies occur in its ranks, fill them itself, or authorize or permit a part of its members to fill them, can it issue precepts to the constituencies of the retired delegates directing new elections to fill them?

[1] See *ante*, §§ 262, 263. [2] Ibid.

This question touches to the bottom the powers of Conventions in relation to the electoral bodies which depute them, and will therefore be considered at length. It arose as a practical question in the Massachusetts Convention of 1853, and I cannot, perhaps, better illustrate the principles by which it ought to be decided, than by presenting an outline of the facts of that case, and of the discussions which it elicited.

§ 341. The Hon. Henry Wilson having been elected a delegate for both the town of Natick and the town of Berlin, chose to sit for the former, whereupon an order was passed that a notice be given by the Secretary of the Convention to the town of Berlin, that the Hon. Henry Wilson, who was returned as a delegate from that town, declined to act in that capacity. Thereupon the Hon. B. F. Butler submitted a form of a notice to be sent by the Secretary, as follows: —

"HALL OF THE CONSTITUTIONAL CONVENTION,
"BOSTON, May —, 1853.

"*To the Selectmen of the Town of Berlin:*

"GENTLEMEN, — The Hon. Henry Wilson, late delegate for Berlin in the Convention for revising the Constitution, having tendered his resignation as such delegate, which has been accepted by the Convention, and his seat being thereby vacated, I am directed, by a vote of the Convention, to request you to convene the qualified electors of your town, as soon as may be with a due regard to notice, in order to their electing and deputing a delegate to represent them in this Convention, in the manner prescribed by the second section of the Act calling the Convention, adopted by the people on the second Monday in November, A. D. 1852.

I am, &c."

[Signed by the Secretary.]

This form involved an evident departure from the principle of the order just adopted, inasmuch as it contained an assertion of a threefold power in the Convention, of which no trace was to be found in the order: first, a power to direct, or at least to request, the town authorities, and through them the electors, to exercise their electoral function at a particular time, and upon a particular subject; secondly, the power to accept the resignation of delegates duly elected to its own body; and, thirdly, the power to direct the electors as to the manner in which they were to proceed to elect their delegates to the Convention, as, that it should be done in conformity to a particular Act of the legislature.

§ 342. The question being upon the adoption of this form, a substitute was moved, that in notifying the town of Berlin of the vacancy, the Secretary be directed to forward to that town a certified copy of the order adopted by the Convention upon that subject. This substitute was rejected, and the form proposed by Mr. Butler adopted, opposition being made at every step, on the ground that it was beyond the power of the Convention even to notify the town of the vacancy, much more to direct the election of a delegate to fill it. On the following day a reconsideration of the last vote was moved, upon which arose a very long and interesting discussion of all the questions involved, but ending finally in a vote of nearly two to one refusing to reconsider the vote adopting the form of notice proposed by Mr. Butler.

Of the three questions indicated as involved in the form of notice adopted, the first, as to the power of a Convention to issue a precept, request, or notice to a town, with a view to induce it to fill a vacancy in its delegation, is the only one I purpose here to consider.

§ 343. That the Convention possessed the power to issue such a precept was claimed by Mr. Butler and others, as evident from the nature and functions of that body.

Thus, in favor of the form of notice presented by him, Mr. Butler said: —

"We are told that we assume the power, and that we are merely the agents and attorneys, of the people. Sir, we are the delegates of the people, chosen to act in their stead. We have the same power and the same right, within the scope of the business assigned to us, that they would have, were they all convened in this hall. In my judgment, we have every incidental power necessary to do the business of the people. If the people were all assembled here in their primary capacity, they would surely have the capacity to notify unrepresented towns, that they might participate in the business of the Convention and, by implication, we have just the same powers, duties, and necessities, no more and no less, conferred upon us, that the people would have were they here in their primary capacity. We are not acting as a court of referees. The power with which we are vested comes not from the legislative government; but the people, through the agency of the ballot-box, have given it to us. We are not men who have no interest in the matter, but have all the powers of the people whom we represent. If they chose, being assembled in their primary capacity, to add to their number by admitting a portion of the people at first not assembled with them, could they not do it? And, if they now see fit to send men to act with us, have they not the power to do it? I look upon this whole proceeding of calling a Convention as a mode of revolution by which we may peaceably accomplish that which in other countries is attained by the sword and by force. Here, through the medium of the ballot-box, the people take to themselves the supreme control of the whole machinery of the government, and they determine who shall come here and act for them."[1]

§ 344. On the same side, professedly, but shifting the ground assumed by Mr. Butler, if not, in substance, surrendering the power claimed by him, Mr. B. F. Hallett said: —

"Speaking strictly with reference to the authority under which this Convention is assembled, I confess that I have great doubts whether the Convention has power to send to any town an order or a direction in the form of law, calling upon them to send a member to this Convention. . . . . Taking this question as the issue, as to the power of the Convention, it resolves itself entirely, in my mind, into the simple power of a body to reproduce itself — that is, to fill vacancies occurring within itself by death or resignation; and whether that power be or be not incident to such a body, is a matter which may admit of different opinions, but with regard to which, it seems to me, the preponderance of opinions must be, that, in the absence of a prohibition to fill such vacancy, and where no mode is provided by law, the body must necessarily have the power to supply such deficiency — that is, to reproduce itself. In this point of view, therefore, the resignation of a delegate, causing a vacancy, would stand differently from a call upon towns to send delegates here in cases where no vacancies had existed except such

[1] *Deb. Mass. Conv.*, 1853, Vol. I. p. 78.

as arose from a mere failure of a town to elect a delegate. I should be content, therefore, to take this proposition as a proper one, and invite the town of Berlin to send a delegate here, upon the ground that we as a body have a right to fill our own vacancies, occurring since our organization as a body; and that is all the power we have got, if we have got any, in the premises. I am perfectly clear that we have no direct power under the Convention Act of 1852, in relation to supplying any vacancies in this Convention. That is our charter; it is the Constitution of this body of delegates, and we must act under it." [1]

§ 345. To these arguments, so discrepant in their principles, the Hon. Marcus Morton replied as follows: —

"We are a delegated body; if we have any authority it has been delegated to us. We are the agents or the attorneys of the people of this Commonwealth, and, if we have any power at all, it comes from them, and is contained in the power of attorney which authorizes us to come here. If we have the power or authority to act in this matter, let any gentleman put his finger upon the passage in the Act and point it out. And, if the authority cannot be found, then where do we get it? In acting upon this subject we should be assuming power which has not been delegated to us. It would be a downright usurpation, and it would be more than a usurpation of power by a legislative body, because there is nobody behind us to make it right. There is no way of correcting the evil. If gentlemen assume the power to act in this matter, — if the Convention is to send out precepts for new elections, and to admit individuals who may be chosen in this manner, they may assume power to send for the Common Council of the City of Boston, and bring them in here to act with us and to participate in our deliberations, and nobody can countervail, — nobody can set it aside. . . . . If we have power to act in this case, it is contained in the Act by which we are convened; and now I ask gentlemen to point out the power in that Act. I can find a strong indication that no such power was intended to be given. All that has been brought to show the existence of such a power has been drawn from precedent and the practice of other bodies." [1]

§ 346. To the same effect was the speech of Hon. Joel Parker. He said: —

[1] *Deb. Mass. Conv.*, 1853, Vol. I. p. 131.

"And now two questions seem to arise. One is, whether any action can rightfully be taken for the purpose of filling the vacancy, and having another delegate elected to represent the town of Berlin; and, if such action may be taken, the question occurs upon the form, whether it should be by a writ, or by a notice, that we will admit the delegate whom the town shall elect, and who shall present himself here, claiming the right to a seat by virtue of that election. In relation to this last question I have no difficulty. So far as the mere form is concerned, it seems to me to be altogether immaterial. I have not been persuaded by the remarks of the gentlemen who have preceded me, that it would not be competent, if a vacancy exists which can rightfully be filled, for the Convention to issue a writ or precept to the town of Berlin to elect a member; but a mere notice to that town that a vacancy exists, would be equally effective of that object, in my opinion. If the town of Berlin have a right, upon the resignation of their delegate, to proceed to a further election, they would have the same right upon receiving a notice that a delegate coming here and claiming a seat in the Convention would be admitted as a matter of right. And, if a writ should be issued, I do not understand that it would confer any power upon the town; it would be nothing more than issuing a precept in that particular form, to signify to the town that they might elect, and that their delegate would be admitted when he presented himself. We are to consider this question, Mr. President, solely as a question of right. . . . . But as it comes to us as a question of right, we are called upon to determine what the right is.

"If we are in a state of revolution, — peaceful and bloodless, but still a revolution, — I must say that I know not what limit there is to the power of a revolution, when it is brought into exercise; and, if the question is to be put upon that basis, . . . I shall not deny the power of a revolution. The town of Berlin may be represented, and anybody else may be admitted as a delegate whom the people may choose to send here. If we are a revolutionary body, acting without a Constitution, or any thing of that nature to guide us, — if citizens are to come here and act their pleasure, without regard to the manner in which they are proceeding, they may admit one person or another to

[1] *Deb. Mass. Conv.*, 1853, Vol. I. p. 74.

take part in that revolution. The whole community may take part in it, and the question would come up, Where are you to find room for them to assemble and carry on their operations? Sir, it is well known that the argument has been advanced that this Convention was revolutionary in its character, because the Constitution provided no such mode in which a Convention could legally assemble; that there was one mode provided by the Constitution for the revision of that instrument, and any other mode was in its nature revolutionary. For myself personally, I do not entertain that opinion. I believe this Convention to have been lawfully assembled, and that it is bound to proceed according to law; and that, when it departs from law knowingly and understandingly, then will its proceedings be revolutionary in their nature."[1]

§ 347. To this discussion I shall add but a single observation. Supposing the power in question not to have been given expressly in the Act calling the Convention, and looking at the question of right alone, has a Convention, by virtue simply of its essential nature and functions, power to issue precepts to the electors in the case of a vacancy, directing an election to fill it? It certainly has no such power, unless we invert all our conceptions of the office and relations of the two bodies. To accord that power to a Convention, in such a sense as that its mandate would be binding on the electors, is to suppose the former to be, if not sovereign, an agency of the sovereign with general discretionary powers of a legislative character, beyond the scope of its special business — to be, in short, strictly a legislature. On the contrary, as we have seen, both reason and authority concur in assigning to the Convention a particular function, limited by the Act under which it convenes, which is its charter or Constitution — a peculiarity of that body which will be more fully illustrated in a subsequent part of this chapter. If this be a correct estimate of the nature of Conventions, the remark of Judge Parker is just, that it is essentially immaterial what form the precept or notice to the town might assume. It might be a writ directing, or a notice requesting, that an election should be held to fill the vacancy in its ranks. But in neither form would it be of the least binding force. It would be, in substance, merely an extra-official intimation that the Convention would

[1] *Deb. Mass. Conv.*, 1853, Vol I. p. 83.

acquiesce in whatever action the electors should deem themselves authorized to take. The real power, if it existed at all, would be in the electors, and would find its source in the existing Constitution and laws, and not in the mandate of the Convention.

§ 348. 5. It being determined that if a vacancy can be filled at all, it must be done by the electors, by virtue of power derived not from the Convention, but from some other agent of the sovereign, as the legislature, the next question — seemingly unrelated to the subject of this treatise, but necessary to a complete discussion of the question next following — is, Can the electors fill such a vacancy at any time and in any manner they may think fit, or must they look to the law for their power to act, and consequently conform strictly to its provisions ?

If we have not mistaken the relations of the electors to the sovereign, and to the several agencies employed by the sovereign to conduct the government, it is clear that little discretion is left to them in the discharge of their functions, except as to the individuals whom they shall, within legal limits, select to fill the offices of the State. Their duties are always prescribed by the Constitution, or by some statute passed in pursuance of it, as that, on such a day or days, the electors shall assemble and choose citizens, having determinate qualifications, for particular offices or duties. In obeying this mandate they discharge a trust. To allow them to enlarge or vary the terms of the trust would be to subvert the relations of dependence imposed by the Constitution, and to invest them with the power of self-direction — that is, measurably, of sovereignty. To some of the agencies of government, the sovereign, indeed, gives large discretionary powers; but then those powers are of the essence of the grant, and not to use them would be to frustrate the purpose of the political society which made it. The grant of legislative power is a grant of that kind. With the electors the case is different. Their functions, as we have seen, are twofold : first, to elect persons, generally of their own number, to office ; and, secondly, to pass, affirmatively or negatively, upon proposed changes in the fundamental law. In the latter, which is an occasional function, they are invested with a limited discretion, a discretion either to approve or reject; in the former they have no discretion as to measures, but only to name, out of the whole body of eligible citizens, those who are to fill the public offices. And it is apparent that they could not safely be intrusted with any greater power. Never assembling *en masse*, but exercising their functions in isolated fragments, without concert or interconnection, their determinations could have coherence and efficacy only when made in subordination to a less numerous body, possessed of adequate powers of looking before and after, of deliberation, as well as of announcing authoritatively the sovereign will. Such a body only is the legislature, to which, in the absence of constitutional provisions, is committed the duty of performing that very office.

§ 349. Now, to apply these principles practically, take the case of the Massachusetts Convention of 1853, last referred to. The Act of the legislature calling that Convention, provided, as such Acts commonly do, that the inhabitants of the cities and towns within the State entitled to vote for representatives to the General Court, should assemble *on the first Monday of March*, A. D. 1853, *and elect one or more delegates*, &c., Sec. 1.; and that "*the persons so elected delegates*" should meet in Convention in Boston on the first Wednesday in May, &c., Sec. 3. Under this Act, would any delegates, not "so elected," be entitled to seats in the Convention? Evidently not. But what is comprised in the terms "so elected?" The answer, it seems, should be, "elected at the time and place, in the manner, out of and by the class of persons respectively prescribed in the Act." If, in regard to any one of these particulars, as, for instance, the time of holding the election, any departure from the Act be allowable, who is to determine when the electors in their several districts shall meet? Must the meetings in the several towns and cities, if held on another day than that appointed in the Act, be called or "notified" by the public authorities in the same manner as the regular meetings? If so, how can this necessary preliminary be secured? The public authorities might, in some places, in the absence of positive instructions by law, refuse to act. Would such a refusal be a breach of official duty? That could hardly be maintained, since, if the time were not fixed by a law binding upon all, or were fixed by a law whose terms could be disregarded, it must be because the time of holding the meetings was intended to rest in the discretion of those authorities, and they ought not to be blamed for exercising it.

An objection of scarcely less magnitude would be, that if elections were to be called at the discretion of the town or city authorities in respect to the time of their assembling, as each might act independently, the electors would be likely to assemble on different days, and thus render abortive some of the most important safeguards of the elective franchise.

Again: when an election has once been held according to the terms of the Act, the power of the electors has been exhausted. It is impossible to hold that they may, on any accident giving rise to a vacancy in the office filled by them, of their own motion reassemble to fill it again. If, on the other hand, at the time and place appointed for the election, they failed to exercise the power given by the Act, how can it be contended that they may, at their will, attempt to repair the deficiency in their representation? Such a proceeding would most clearly be an abuse of their position and power as electors. In a word, the difficulties attending the allowance of spontaneous and unconnected elections, at the instance of the local authorities, without the authorization of law, are so great, that the right of the electors to hold them must be wholly denied.

§ 350. 6. Another question, related to the foregoing, is, Can a Convention receive, as lawful delegates, persons elected at a time or in a manner not provided by law? If we have succeeded in reaching sound conclusions in relation to the questions thus far discussed, the answer to this is at hand. If the Convention cannot itself fill its own vacancies, and if the electors cannot, without special authority of law, or cannot in contravention of law, fill them, the former would have no power to accept as lawfully elected delegates persons unlawfully elected by the latter. Two bodies of functionaries cannot, by clubbing their separate usurpations, give a legal character to what is otherwise illegal. The Convention is usually, by the Act calling it, or by the customary law of such bodies, made the judge of the elections of its own members; that is, it is authorized to pronounce on the conformity to law of the proceedings by which its ranks are filled; a power which, of course, leaves to it practically a large discretion; but that discretion is, like that of a judge, a legal one, not its arbitrary will. When a delegate, therefore, presents himself and claims a seat, if he cannot exhibit evidence of his having been elected according to law, he ought to be rejected. The Convention owes to the electors no such courtesy as to wink at their usurpations of power.

§ 351. 7. The next question, involving the relations of Conventions to the electors, is, Can a Convention limit the discretion of the electors in the discharge of their appropriate duties; as, by determining what classes of persons they may, and what classes they shall not, elect to office?

This question might have been discussed appropriately in a preceding part of this chapter, in which were considered the relations of Conventions to the sovereign. Indeed, it has very often been put in this form: Can a Convention limit or restrict the sovereign in the choice of its servants, as by requiring that they shall be citizens of a prescribed age or nationality, to be eligible to office?

We will consider the question in both the forms indicated, beginning with the latter.

First. Can a Convention restrict the sovereign in the choice of its servants? Strictly speaking, the question is absurd. The Convention is but a subordinate, whilst the sovereign is the superior, from whom is derived all its power to act, and without whose ratifying voice what it does is wholly destitute of validity. The one is a mere agent, with power only to do what it is bidden; the other, the supreme source of power in the state, able, within the limits certainly of a moral competence, to do any thing it may please. Of course, then, a Convention cannot really, to any extent, bind the sovereign. It may recommend constitutional provisions, which, if adopted and put in force by the sovereign, will bind the latter, so far forth as it can be bound at all, but in that case it would be the sovereign which would limit or restrict itself, not the Convention which would bind it. And that the sovereign can limit or restrict itself is a well-settled principle. The bonds, however, by which it can bind itself, are doubtless only moral ones, since under whatever limitations the nation may have placed itself by voluntary regulation, it has evidently at all times the physical ability to disregard them. In one view, however, those bonds are of immense practical efficacy; it is only the sovereign body which can disrupt them with impunity. Its servants, the various departments of the government, are obliged to respect them or render themselves obnoxious to punishment for disobedience. As an admirable exposition of the truth that the sovereign body can restrict itself, I extract a passage from an argument made by Daniel Webster, in the celebrated case of Luther *v.* Borden, in the Supreme Court of the United States.[1]

He said: "I have said that it is one principle of the American system that the people limit their governments, National and State. They do so; but it is another principle, equally true and certain, and, according to my judgment of things, equally important, that the people often *limit themselves.* They set bounds to their own power. They have chosen to secure the institutions which they establish against the sudden impulses of mere majorities. All our institutions teem with instances of this." After specifying the 5th Article of the Federal Constitution, restricting the right of the people to amend that instrument, he continued: "But the people limit themselves also in other ways. They limit themselves in the first exercise of their political rights. They limit themselves by all their Constitutions, in two important respects: that is to say, in regard to the qualifications of *electors*, and in regard to the qualifications of the *elected.* In every State, and in all the States, the people have precluded themselves from voting for everybody they might wish to vote for; they have limited their own right of choosing . . . . They have also limited themselves to certain prescribed forms for the conduct of elections. They must vote at a particular place, at a particular time, and under particular conditions, or not at all."

§ 352. *Secondly.* Taken in the other form, namely, Can a Convention restrict the electors as to the persons they shall choose to fill the public offices? the question, on the principles before announced, is too clear for argument. Since, whatever a Convention should regularly do by recommending to the sovereign, if adopted by the latter, would be the act of that sovereign, it certainly might restrict the choice of public servants to be made by the electors to any class it might deem best fitted for that duty. As the sovereign is distinct from the electors, who, like all officers of the government, are its agents, it may of course dictate law or rules of action to them as to the others, and it can without doubt do it through a Convention. But the reservation must be again made, that in affirming that a Con-

[1] 7 How. R. 1, contained in Vol. VI. of Webster's *Works*, pp. 217, 224.

vention has power to limit or restrict the electors, it is meant that it may do so by constitutional provision, enacted according to the principles of our Constitutions; that is to say, by the Convention recommending it, the *fiat* being left to the people, or by the Convention alone enacting it directly, as its commission should determine.

§ 353. In one or other of its two forms, this question has several times been made the subject of discussion in our Conventions. It was very ably considered, upon abstract principle, in the New York Convention of 1846, and I deem it of sufficient interest to warrant me in giving a few extracts from speeches made in that body upon the different sides of the question. A section had been proposed to be embodied in the new Constitution, by which eligibility to the office of Governor was to be confined to citizens of the United States, thirty years of age, who should have been five years resident in the State prior to their election. Opposition was made to it on the grounds, first, that it was improper or inexpedient; and, second, that it would prove futile, inasmuch as the sovereign could not be bound by such restrictions.

Upon the general question, Mr. Charles O'Connor said: "Let us, however, for a moment, recur to principle, and see whether there is a propriety in retaining any of these qualifications. In every democratic state, the constituent body is the supreme power, and in it repose all the powers of government that men can legitimately exercise over themselves or others. In such a state, it is the province of the fundamental law to ascertain what persons shall form the constituent body or governing power in the state, and then to limit and define, with as much exactitude as practicable, the powers and duties of the agents of the people, or, in other words, the several departments of the government, to the end that the rights of individuals may suffer no detriment from their exercise. It was the proper province of such an instrument," he repeated, "to ascertain the constituent body, in which resided the supreme power. In the nature of things, that body never could embrace all within the protection of the state, and who were to be governed by its laws. Some must be too young to participate in the governing power. Others, again, too advanced in life to take part in it. It was a question whether females should constitute part of the governing body. It was a proper subject of consideration whether persons convicted of crime shall be permitted to form part of the governing body. It was a proper subject of consideration whether particular classes of persons — he would mention negroes, Indians, aliens, and, if you pleased, naturalized citizens — should form part of the constituent body. And, in laying down rules for determining who were the constituent body, we did not lay restraints on the people — we only ascertained who the people were. And, having ascertained that, it was a principle not to be departed from, that in a democratic form of government no restraint should be laid on them in their sovereign capacity, where the whole people acted for the purposes of the government. This doctrine was quite consistent with the existence of provisions declaring what persons should be eligible from a particular precinct to the Senate or Assembly; for a portion was not the whole people, and where power was thus delegated to a portion of the people to elect a member of Assembly, who might enact laws affecting the interests of the whole, the latter having no other check on the election in the precinct or district, might rightfully retain the selection to individuals having prescribed qualifications. What restraints ought to be imposed in such cases was another question. But, when we come, as in case of the Governor, to an election in which all participate, an exercise of the power of choice by the whole people, acting in their sovereign capacity, every one of the constituents or governing body having a vote, he insisted that no restraint should be imposed. The field of selection should be free and unrestricted."[1]

§ 354. On the other hand, the very evident fallacies contained in this reasoning were ably exposed by Mr. Ruggles, Mr. Marvin, and Mr. Porter. The last-named gentleman, after showing that the right of suffrage and of eligibility to office are derivative and not natural rights, adverting to the argument of Mr. O'Connor, said: —

"I submit to that gentleman, that in his argument there was a fatal fallacy. The gentleman says it is our right to determine who the people are, by fixing the qualifications of electors. That, having determined who the people are, we cannot restrict their power to elect. Sir, the electors are not the people. They are only a part of the great whole. The people comprise

1 *Deb. N. Y. Conv.*, 1846, p. 201.

all. You have a Bill of Rights to protect them in the enjoyment of life, property, and liberty. Does this extend only to qualified electors? No, but to every man, woman, and child within the dominion of your laws. These constitute the people, and we are their representatives. The gentlemen deny our right to restrict any thing but delegated power. Why, sir, the power of the electoral body itself is a delegated power; not in form, but in effect[1] — by the necessity of the social compact. We were elected only by qualified voters. But we are the representatives of all. Those electors themselves were but the representatives of the people. Four hundred and fifty thousand electors act for two millions and a half of citizens. Nay, more; two hundred thousand electors may constitute a plurality. Shall those two hundred thousand — a minority even of the electoral body — without restriction or barrier, select whomsoever they please to rule over two and a half millions of freemen? We have a female population of one million two hundred and ninety-three thousand, — three times the number of your whole electoral body. They have as deep an interest in this government as you, — nay, a deeper interest. If your laws prove dangerous to liberty, you can unmake the work of your own hands. You are clothed with the power of the ballot-box. You have the strong arm to resist unto blood. They are voiceless, powerless, defenceless. Are not we their representatives here? There are more citizens under than over twenty-one years. They have more interest than we in the Constitution we are to frame. They are to survive us and the electors who sent us here. . . . . We represent not the mere party which nominated, not the mere voters who elected us, but the whole people of New York, of every sex, and of every age and condition — aye, and the succeeding millions, whose constitutional rights we are now asserting. . . . . When, therefore, we convene as the representatives of a free people, to discuss elementary principles of constitutional law, let us discard the spirit of the demagogue. . . . . It devolves upon us to perpetuate the privileges of our citizens, and to guard our institutions from danger in the distance, whether menaced by legislative corruption, by popular excitement, by partisan frenzy, or by the encroachments of power."[2]

[1] It is clearly so, both in form and effect.

[2] *Deb. N. Y. Conv.*, 1846, pp. 249, 250.

The result of the debate was, that a clause containing the restriction indicated was embodied in the Constitution.

§ 355. In the Louisiana Convention of 1844, the same question was considered in its relations to the Constitution of the United States. The standing committee upon the executive department reported to that Convention a provision, the material part of which was as follows: "No person shall be eligible to the office of Governor or Lieutenant-Governor, except a *native citizen of the United States*, or an inhabitant at the time of the cession to the United States of that portion of territory included in the present limits of the present State of Louisiana, ... and who shall not have arrived at the age of thirty-five years." A motion was made to strike out all after the word "except," down to the words "State of Louisiana," upon the ground, that the proposed restriction was repugnant to the Constitution of the United States. A debate thereupon sprung up, which was participated in by the ablest men in the Convention, Mr. Brent, Mr. Soulé, Mr. Benjamin, and others, and which resulted in modifying the clause so as to require a person, to be eligible to the office of Governor or Lieutenant-Governor, to have attained the age of thirty-five years, and to have been fifteen years a citizen and resident of the State — the friends of the restriction thus sustaining a defeat.

The course of argument upon the question was as follows: —

§ 356. By those who were opposed to the restriction indicated, it was urged, that the clause objected to was repugnant to the Constitution of the United States; that if the Convention could confine eligibility to native citizens of the United States, it might also confine it to native citizens of Louisiana; that by the fourth paragraph of the eighth section of the first article of the Federal Constitution, it was declared, "that Congress shall have power to establish an uniform rule of naturalization throughout the United States;" that by the first paragraph of the second section of the fourth article, it was provided, on the other hand, that "the citizens of each State shall be entitled to all the privileges and immunities of citizens in the several States;" that, by the paragraph first cited, the several States ceded to the general government all control over the subject of naturalization, and that the legislation of Congress on the subject, therefore, if any had been had, must be regarded as paramount and supreme; that two questions thereupon arose — Had this power been exercised by the general government? and if so, Could its action be nullified by the authority of one of the States? That to the first question the answer was, that Congress had exercised the power, by declaring that immigrants to this country who should reside here five years, and pursue certain formalities, should be entitled to all the rights and privileges of American citizens; that to the other question, the only response was, that the legislation of Congress on the subject could not be counteracted or set at nought by any exercise of power on the part of the States; that it could not be doubted that the Convention had power to prescribe any qualification it pleased for him who aspired to the office of Governor, provided, however, that it did not contravene the provision cited from the fourth article, by making any distinction between American citizens; that the effect of the proposed restriction would be to discriminate against the naturalized citizen; that a foreigner, naturalized, let it be supposed, in the State of Illinois, under the Act of Congress, and so admitted to all the rights of citizenship, and eligible, under the laws and Constitution of that State, to all offices created by them, would instantly, on removing to the State of Louisiana, be struck with disability, and be disqualified to hold the office of Governor, whereas no such prohibition would extend to the native citizen of that or any other State; which would clearly violate that clause of the Federal Constitution which declares that "the citizens of each State shall be entitled to all the privileges and immunities of citizens in the several States."[1]

§ 357. On the other hand, the advocates of the proposed restriction contended, that the provision of the Federal Constitution, that "the citizens of each State shall be entitled to all the privileges and immunities of citizens in the several States," did not mean that they should be invested with all the rights which could be enjoyed by any citizen, but such only as flowed from the mere fact of citizenship, irrespective of other qualifications; that, accordingly, under this clause of the Constitution, no citizen of one State, migrating to another, could there claim to be a oter or to be eligible to office, unless mere citizenship, without ɔther conditions, under the Constitution or laws of such

[1] See speeches of Messrs. Beatty, Brent, and Soulé, in *Deb. La. Conv.*, 1844, pp. 206, 207, 211.

other State, entitled its citizens to those privileges; that the conduct of the founders of the Federal government indicated that it was not their intention, by the provision in question, to throw open all political rights to all citizens without qualifications, for they restricted eligibility to the offices of President and Senator in Congress to persons having prescribed qualifications as to age and citizenship; that, although it was true, that the Constitutions of most of the States contained no clause similar to the one proposed, such a clause was contained in six of those Constitutions, amongst them that of Virginia, framed in 1829–30, by a Convention which reckoned among its members some of the ablest men ever known in the Union, one of them a delegate to the Federal Convention of 1787, such as Monroe, Madison, Marshall, Patrick Henry, John Randolph, and Giles; that in that Constitution it was provided, that no man should be Governor of Virginia unless he was, — 1st, thirty years of age; 2d, a native-born citizen of the United States; 3d, five years a resident of the State; that, moreover, the action of Congress in admitting into the Union States whose Constitutions contained the restriction complained of was evidence tending to the same result; that the three States of Arkansas, Missouri, and Alabama, were the States referred to, and it being absolutely necessary, before they could be admitted, that their Constitutions should have been submitted to the Congress of the United States, to determine that no provision had been inserted therein which would clash with the Federal Constitution, when Congress had passed upon those instruments and admitted those States under them, no other or stronger evidence could be desired, that they did not conflict with the Federal Constitution; that to hold the contrary would be to maintain, that on three several occasions the Representatives and Senators in Congress and the Presidents of the United States had asserted an unconstitutional restriction to be a constitutional one.[1]

§ 358. Notwithstanding the adverse decision, if it must be so regarded, of this question in Louisiana, I am satisfied they were right who maintained the existence of power in the Convention to make the restriction.

1. It is important to note, that in the provision of the Federal Constitution, that "the citizens of each State shall be entitled

[1] *Deb. La. Conv.*, 1844, p. 220.

to all the privileges and immunities of citizens in the several States," the words, "in the several States," qualify the word "entitled," and not the nearer word, "citizens;" so that, arranging the words according to their grammatical relations, the passage would read thus: "the citizens of each State shall be entitled in the several States to the privileges and immunities of citizens." Were those words to be taken as qualifying the word "citizens," the Federal Constitution would be made to give to every citizen, wherever he might be in the Union, all the privileges and immunities enjoyed by citizens in any State; that is, supposing the office of Governor were, in the State of Alabama, thrown open to all the citizens of Alabama, the Federal Constitution would then step in and secure the same privilege to the citizens of each State, in their several States. The phraseology used, however, properly understood, has no such wide operation. By it, a citizen, migrating from any State to another State, would be entitled, in the latter, to such privileges as were there accorded to the possession of mere citizenship, under its laws. Thus, a citizen of New York, migrating to New Jersey, would not be an alien, but a citizen of New Jersey, and, as such, entitled to enjoy such privileges and exercise such rights, as the State of New Jersey allowed indifferently to all its citizens.

§ 359. It is, therefore, a matter of importance to ascertain what are "the rights of citizens in the several States;" that is, the rights attaching in the several States to naked citizenship; for such rights only are guaranteed by the constitutional provision cited.

It is believed, that the rights attaching in the several States to the possession of mere citizenship exist not by positive law, but by the principles of the common law, or by those of public law. It is then in the decisions of courts of law, and in the writings of publicists and jurists, that we must look to determine what those rights are.

A clear exposition of those rights was made at an early day by Mr. Justice Washington, in a case which has been a leading authority upon the subject ever since.[1] The State of New Jersey having passed an Act confining the right of fishing for oysters in its waters to its own citizens, the question was raised in that case, whether the Act was not in violation of Art. IV. § 2, of

[1] Corfield *v.* Coryell, 4 Wash. C. C. R. 371.

the Federal Constitution. After stating the question, Justice Washington said:—

"The inquiry is, what are the privileges and immunities of citizens in the several States? We feel no hesitation in confining these expressions to those privileges and immunities which are in their nature *fundamental;* which belong, of right, to the citizens of all free governments; and which have at all times been enjoyed by the citizens of the several States which compose this Union, from the time of their becoming free, independent, and sovereign. What these fundamental principles are, it would perhaps be more tedious than difficult to enumerate. They may, however, be all comprehended under the following general heads: protection by the government, the enjoyment of life and liberty, with the right to acquire and possess property of every kind, and to pursue and obtain happiness and safety; subject, nevertheless, to such restraints as the government may justly prescribe for the general good of the whole. The right of a citizen of one State to pass through or to reside in any other State, for the purposes of trade, agriculture, professional pursuits, or otherwise; to claim the benefit of the writ of *Habeas Corpus;* to institute and maintain actions of any kind in the courts of the State; to take, hold, and dispose of property, either real or personal; and an exemption from higher taxes or impositions than are paid by the other citizens of the State, may be mentioned as some of the particular privileges and immunities of citizens, which are clearly embraced by the general description of privileges deemed to be fundamental; to which may be added the elective franchise, *as regulated and established by the laws and Constitution of the State in which it is to be exercised.*"

§ 360. That the right to vote or to be elected to office, irrespectively of the qualifications prescribed by the laws of the State to which a citizen may remove, is not one of the privileges and immunities intended by the Federal Constitution, is clearly inferable from the last clause of this extract. The same opinion has been expressed by our best constitutional lawyer, Daniel Webster. Thus, in an argument before the Supreme Court of the United States in the case of The Bank of the United States *v.* Primrose,[1] Mr. Webster, referring to the article of the Constitution in question, said:—

[1] Webster's *Works*, Vol VI. p. 112.

"That this Article in the Constitution does not confer on the citizens of each State political rights in every other State, is admitted. A citizen of Pennsylvania cannot go into Virginia and vote at an election in that State; though when he has acquired a residence in Virginia, and is otherwise qualified, as required by her Constitution, he becomes, without formal adoption as a citizen of Virginia, a citizen of that State politically. But for the purposes of trade, commerce, buying and selling, it is evidently not in the power of any State to impose any hindrance or embarrassment, or levy any excise, toll, duty, or exclusion, upon citizens of other States, or to place them, coming there, upon a different footing from her own citizens." [1]

§ 361. From the reasonings above given, it is plain, that mere citizenship of a State does not carry with it a right to enjoy all the privileges and immunities conferred upon any citizen, but only certain civil rights, resting on natural law, but needing for their practical enjoyment the guaranty of government. It would, perhaps, express the whole truth to say, that the rights to which one is entitled from the naked fact of citizenship, are those usually guaranteed by our Bills of Rights. It is equally apparent that there are privileges and immunities enjoyed by some citizens, by reason of special qualifications, that are not conferred upon all citizens, though none but citizens can enjoy them — privileges and immunities that spring from positive law, such as to vote and to hold office. The former are denominated civil, the latter, political rights.

In assuming, then, as did the Louisiana Convention of 1844, to restrict eligibility to the office of governor, to native-born citizens of the United States, that body did not, in my view, transcend its power or contravene the Federal Constitution. The question as to the expediency of such a restriction, is a different one, which it is unnecessary here to discuss.

§ 362. 8. The last question, involving the relations of Conventions to the electors, which I propose to consider, is — Have

[1] To the same effect, see Amy *v.* Smith, 1 Littell R. 333; Campbell *v.* Morris, 3 Har. & McHen. R. 554; Murray *v.* McCarty, 2 Munf. R. 398; Austin *v.* The State, 10 Mo. R. 592; and the opinion of Justice Curtis in the case of Dred Scott *v.* Sandford, 19 How. (U. S.) R. 580–584. See also the remarks of Chief Justice Spencer, Col. Young, Mr. Radcliff and others, to the same effect, and of Mr. Jay, Mr. Van Vechten, Mr. Livingston, Mr. Kent (Chancellor Kent) and others, to the contrary, in the New York Convention of 1821, in *Deb. N. Y. Conv.* 1821, pp. 183–202.

the electors power to instruct their delegates, and if so, to what extent, or under what conditions?

This question arose as a practical one in the Ohio Convention of 1850, but was not discussed, the member, for whom the instructions were intended, refusing to obey them, but resigning his office, with the acquiescence of the Convention. As I deem the right of instruction, as asserted in this case, more than doubtful, a brief statement of the facts, and of the principles which, in my view, ought to govern it, will not be out of place.

The Ohio Convention of 1850 having been called, in anticipation of the election of delegates thereto, a public meeting was held "of the democracy of Butler County," at which resolutions were passed instructing the delegates who should be chosen from that county, to support, in the Convention, the doctrine of the repealability of charters of incorporation, as well those then existing as those that might be granted in the future. Mr. Vance, a candidate for the Convention, from Butler County, in a communication to his constituents, published before the election, refused to subscribe to the platform thus laid down for him, but was nevertheless elected by a large majority. The Convention having assembled, a clause was proposed to be inserted in the Constitution, giving to the legislature unlimited power of repealing such charters. The course of Mr. Vance upon this subject, not being satisfactory to the "democracy of Butler County," a meeting of the latter was again called, at which the instructions to their delegates were repeated and emphasized, and those delegates were requested to adhere to them strictly or to resign. Mr. Vance chose to do the latter, not distinctly admitting the instructions to be binding on him, but being unwilling to be placed in a position which would carry with it even the appearance of disobedience to the will of his constituents.

§ 363. As bearing on the general question of the right of instruction, the following observations seem to me to be pertinent to this case.

1. The function of a Convention being, when considered in the light of theory, advisory merely, and that of the particular Convention in question having been made so by the Act of Assembly, under which it convened, since the latter expressly required the submission of the Constitution to be framed by it to the people, it would seem to be an act of absurd inconsist-

ency for the people, or any part of the people, forming an electoral district, to instruct its delegates. It would be simply to ask advice, but first to dictate to the advising body what its advice should be!

2. But the Ohio case was more absurd than that. It was not the people of Ohio, or, even, what might by analogy be called the people of Butler County, that assumed to issue instructions in that case. It was "the democracy of Butler County," the members of one of its political parties, — comprising, perhaps, a majority of its legal voters, and perhaps not, — who presumed to discharge that delicate duty. It is doubtful if the dogma of squatter-sovereignty ever produced an act of greater insolence or absurdity than this. Whatever the delegates to the Convention represented, they certainly did not represent the "democracy of Butler County," who, therefore, had no more right to instruct them than had the milkmaids or the barbers of Butler County. If those delegates represented anybody within the county, it was the electors there residing, without distinction of party, of whom the election expressed the collective will. If the right of instruction were conceded to any designated section of the electors, acting, not as electors, but in a party or other private capacity, it could not be denied to every individual voter. For, in such a case, the right would be accorded to them, not as being the majority of the electors, since the term majority is relative to the entire electoral body only, but as constituting the party or section, whether less or more than the majority — a right which could rest only on the sovereignty of the individual elector.

§ 364. 3. Finally, I observe, that the right of instruction, if it exists at all, must inhere either in the sovereign, or in some body representing the sovereign, and that in either case, the electoral body of any particular district would be incapable of exercising the right. The electors are not the sovereign, though as a body they unquestionably are the representatives of the sovereign, and whatever they do, as such, within constitutional limits, must be considered as done by the sovereign itself. If that body were to publish instructions to a Convention in reference to the measures it should consider or report, whatever might be thought of the expediency of its interfering thus, neither their right to do so, nor the consequent duty of obedience on the part of the delegates could well be denied.[1] But with the electors of any particular electoral circle, the case is widely different. They do not, in a strict sense of the term, represent the sovereign. They, together with their co-electors throughout the State, are its representatives. Their voice, therefore, though an element in that which is to be taken as the voice of the sovereign, is not itself that voice. The voice of the sovereign is a chorus, made up of the separate voices of all the electors; it is the resultant of those separate voices. It follows, therefore, first, that instructions, if given by the electors at all, must emanate from the entire electoral body, as no otherwise could they be authentic; and, secondly, that they must be addressed to the assembly of the delegates and not to the single delegate, or to a less number than the entire body.

With the question, Whether instructions can be given to a Convention by any body of persons in the State beside the electors, as by the legislature, I do not now concern myself, since it will be the subject of special inquiry in the following chapter of this work.

§ 365. Thus far, I have considered the relations of Conventions to the sovereign body, and to the electors, its immediate representatives. I proceed now to discuss the relations of those bodies to the other governmental agencies, commonly styled the Legislative, Executive, and Judicial Departments, and to inquire into the powers and disabilities resulting to them severally on account of those relations.

§ 366. (*d*). 1. With the Executive and Judiciary of a State, a Convention has, in the ordinary and normal operation of its government, no direct relations. Neither of these departments has any thing to do with calling it together, except in perhaps rare cases, in which some specific and extraordinary duty has been prescribed to it by the legislature; and neither of them, while a Convention is in session, has any occasion to come in contact with it. The only cases in which either of those departments could be brought into direct relations with that body, would be where the latter should attempt to direct it in the discharge of its constitutional duties, — a case which has already been considered, — or in which one of the former should attempt to revolve outside its proper orbit, and thus bring about

[1] See *post*, §§ 376–383, where this question is more fully considered.

collisions with the latter. Inasmuch, however, as neither of the three could with any show of right do any act which should result in such a collision, except when acting in assumed conformity to some law, giving to usurpation an apparent legality, no questions could arise between them as to their respective powers, which would not resolve themselves into questions as to the relative powers of Conventions and legislatures, the only law-making bodies, save the electors, which have been already considered, known to our Constitutions. I shall therefore spend no time in considering the relations of those two departments to Conventions, but pass to those which the latter bear to legislatures, and the powers resulting therefrom, which belong to each of those bodies.

§ 367. 2. From a variety of causes, the relations of a Convention in any State to its legislature give rise to questions of the greatest moment and of the greatest difficulty. It is possible to comprehend and to estimate, relatively to each other, these two bodies, only by ascertaining, first, their respective relations to the sovereign; and, secondly, their mutual resemblances and differences of structure and function. Of these, the first has so frequently been the subject of consideration in previous chapters, that it is now only necessary to recapitulate some of the leading features of those bodies as they stand related to the political society in which they are convened. We have seen that both Conventions and legislatures are agencies appointed by the sovereign for purposes of its own, connected with the formation, the renewal, or the operation of government, the function of each being a legislative one; that to the former are intrusted certain duties relating to the framing of the fundamental laws, extending in some cases, according to their commissions, to the definitive enactment of them; and to the latter the enactment of the ordinary or statute law; that, laying out of view those rare cases in which powers of definitive action are given, Conventions are not strictly representative bodies, but rather collections of delegates, so confined and restricted by the nature of their duties and by the customary law pertaining to them, that they are essentially nothing but mere committees: that, on the other hand, legislatures are invested with so wide a discretion, and such power of definitive action, that they are entitled to be ranked as *par excellence* representative bodies;

that both are, nevertheless, responsible for the exercise of power to its source, the sovereign, but to a different extent and in a different manner; the responsibility of the former being ordinarily more direct, inasmuch as its office is "to recommend, but to conclude nothing," submitting the fruit of its deliberations to the electors; that of the legislature, on the other hand, being remote and indirect, since its function is to determine absolutely the right and the expedient in the current life of the State, subject only to reversal, or, in extreme cases, to punishment for error or malfeasance in that office. Both Conventions and legislatures, then, equally sustain the relation of instruments through which the sovereign executes its will; they are both creatures of the Constitution, the principles and provisions of which are, during their existence, in full operation, and constitute their charter; and hence they are to be viewed as parts of a system of coördinate but mutually inter-dependent agencies, the powers and jurisdiction of which are to be ascertained from a study of that system and not of each agency dissociated from the others.

§ 368. In point of structure, the two species of bodies differ widely from each other. The Convention is composed of a single chamber, and the legislature, in all the American governments, and in most liberal ones abroad, of two chambers, coördinate in authority, but representing different constituencies, and often different interests. By this diversity a Convention is readily seen to be theoretically less adapted for final action than a legislature. It is liable to the objection so fatal to single legislative assemblies, that it is prone to hasty and passionate determinations, and is, therefore, a ready instrument of faction and revolution. In matters which should appeal directly to the prejudices of its members, it could not be relied upon as just or wise. Such, so far as its structure is concerned, is likely to be the character of a Convention. A compensating influence, however, is afforded by the subject-matter of its deliberations. The fundamental law, while it is infinitely more important than the ordinary municipal law, to frame which is the province of a legislature, bears less nearly upon the dominant interests or passions of men, and hence it might so far be left safely to be moulded by a single chamber, even were its action to be final. When it is considered, however, that the action of Conventions is ordinarily not final, but recommendatory merely, the objections to their structure which have been noted are seen to be of much less weight.

§ 369. An important analogy between Conventions and legislatures relates to the qualifications for membership of those bodies. As we have already seen, the members of our legislatures are uniformly required to be elected from citizens of prescribed age, sex, and social conditions, that is, from the body of the electors. This is a matter which is carefully ascertained in our Constitutions. In relation, on the other hand, to the persons who shall be eligible as delegates to our Conventions, those instruments are commonly silent.[1] From this fact the inference has been drawn, that, in the absence of specific qualifications, it was intended that the electors should exercise perfect freedom of choice, and that it would be competent for them to depute as their delegates minors, or females, or citizens of other States. But this is a matter of doubt; for, as shown in a previous chapter, analogy, as well as the principles of popular government, seem to restrict the holding of public functions to the class in whom rests, as the nearest representatives of the sovereign, the practical exercise of sovereign rights, namely, that of the electors. Accordingly, as there stated, equally when the qualifications of delegates have, and when they have not, been prescribed, the choice of them has been almost uniformly confined within the limits determining the *minimum* qualifications of the electoral body.

§ 370. In respect of their functions, there is also an analogy, which is at the same time a contrast, between Conventions and legislatures. Both, as we have seen, belong to the *genus* legislature. That is, they are both charged with the elaboration or the enactment of laws. Where they differ is in the kind of law with which they are concerned, and in the extent of their agency in its formation.

1. A Convention participates directly in the enactment of the fundamental law only. Indirectly, it may determine the limits or the general character of the municipal law, but it never rightfully assumes to enact, or even to recommend it, except when that law has passed over from the experimental to that which is truly fundamental. Whatever it does, however, in the

[1] See *ante*, §§ 267–269, in which the exceptions are stated, where the qualifications of delegates are prescribed.

sphere accorded to it, it does merely by way of recommendation to the body behind it, by whom its recommendations are to be adopted or rejected. A Convention, therefore, is a legislative body only *sub modo*, having some, but not all, legislative functions.

2. A legislature, on the other hand, is a body possessed of much broader powers. Though responsible to the sovereign that created it, it is its function to express authentically the will of the sovereign in relation to all emergencies of the social state, so far at least as it has not been manifested by the Constitution. It is the body which pronounces the statute law of the State. All measures relating to the conduct or to the rights of individuals, to the administration, or defence of the government, which are not prohibited by the fundamental law or by the moral code,[1] and which yet are deemed, on a large view of the public interests, to be expedient, are within the competence of a legislature with the general powers of legislation conferred by our Constitutions.

§ 371. To this general statement of the extent of the power of our legislatures, the *proviso* must be appended, that the measures passed by those bodies must not be of the character denominated fundamental. The necessity of this *proviso* is apparent from the character of the American governments, before referred to, as distinguished from that of Great Britain, after which they were modelled. The Parliament of Great Britain is possessed of all legislative powers whatsoever. It can enact ordinary statutes, and it can pass laws strictly fundamental. Not so with our legislatures. Saving the single case, to be noted in a subsequent chapter, in which, by express constitutional provision, they act in a conventional capacity, in the way of recommending specific amendments to their Constitutions, they have no power whatever to amend, alter, or abolish those instruments. Subject, however, to this limitation, a legislature, under our system, may expatiate through the whole domain of the expedient, as fully as the sovereign itself could do, were it to act in person.[2] The propriety of such an adjustment

[1] But, that a Convention has power to trample on the moral code, or, as it is termed, "to annul perfect rights," see M'Mullen *v.* Hodge, 5 Texas R. 34. See also Warren *v.* Sherman, id. 441.

[2] This description of the limits of legislative power is applicable only to the

of powers is apparent from the consideration, that whatever is expedient to be done, within the limits imposed by the fundamental law, and whatever, therefore, it may presume the sovereign, in the case supposed, would order to be done, some agency, in all governments pretending to be adequate to perpetuate their own existence, must have authority to do. The formation and establishment of the fundamental law is, in all the American Constitutions, regularly the work of Conventions acting in conjunction with the electors. On the other hand, no fact is better settled than that, beyond the province thus specially set apart for them, neither Conventions nor the bodies of electors have any legislative power. They can neither of them pass any law comprised within the sphere of ordinary legislation.[1]

§ 372. In relation to legislatures proper, however, we repeat, it is well settled, that under the general grant of legislative powers contained in our State Constitutions, they are competent to pass all laws whatsoever, not fundamental in character, and not prohibited either by the laws of morality or by the Constitutions to which they are subject, State and Federal. Within these limits, the only question our legislators are bound to ask is, Is the law proposed an expression of what is truly expedient to be done? Nor is there any subject so sacred but that legislation may be made to affect it, provided the boundaries above prescribed be not passed. And although a legislature is but one of many coördinate departments in the government of a State, to each of which a separate and generally well-defined sphere of activity is set apart, it is yet possessed of powers the most wide-reaching of all — powers most nearly sovereign, and in a certain sense supplementary to those of all the others. Some of these powers are vested in the legislature in express terms by the Constitution, and others devolve upon it by necessary implication, as being involved in the general grant of legislative

State legislatures. That of the Congress of the United States is more limited, being confined to legislation upon subjects expressly defined in the Federal Constitution.

[1] The debates of our Conventions are full of disavowals of a right on the part of those bodies to pass ordinary laws. In a few cases, nevertheless, it must be admitted, that right has been claimed as a part of a general claim of all sovereign powers. It has never been practically asserted, however, except in a few doubtful cases, which will be considered hereafter.

power. Thus, to the legislature it is commonly left to determine the details of the organization, and often the operation of the other departments; as, for instance, the times of assembling of the electors and of the judiciary; the modes of their procedure, and in the case of the latter, the establishment of its circuits and of its inferior tribunals; the election, in certain cases, of executive or judicial officers; in other cases there is cast upon it or upon its presiding officers the exercise of the functions of those two departments. Instances of these powers occur on every page of our Constitutions.

§ 373. Of powers implicitly granted, instances are equally numerous. The most striking are those which occur daily upon the happening of unexpected events requiring instant legislative interposition to prevent evil consequences or to make them subservient to the public good. In all such cases it is the legislature that is called upon, as alone possessing the power to do or to authorize what is deemed necessary to be done. Such conjunctures commonly find the executive of the State or the judges inert, because powerless, unless indeed they should seize the power to do without law what law alone could render legitimate. The theory of our governments leaves no necessity for such usurpation, except in the single case of inadequate constitutional power; as, where the acts clearly necessary for the public safety have been directly prohibited by the Constitution. Bating this extreme and perhaps improbable case, there remain those, infinite in number, in which our legislatures, under a grant of general legislative powers, are enabled to supplement the other departments of the government, and to make lawful provision for the unforeseen exigencies of the State.

§ 374. Now let it be noted, that for the purposes and in the crises indicated, the legislature is the only agency competent to act. The electors certainly could not do it, for it is their sole and exclusive function — and they are adequate to no other — to elect to office and to pass in a general way upon propositions for constitutional change; the executive could not do it, for its business is simply to carry into effect laws passed by the proper law-making authority; it cannot deliberate; nor could the judiciary do it; for their province is limited to the interpretation of laws, and to their application to the complicated maze of facts arising in life and business. If neither of these is competent to authorize what is expedient to be done in political or social emergencies, unless the legislature could do so, the State would be left utterly powerless, except where there could be shown an express constitutional provision covering the case — a condition likely to be but rarely fulfilled.

§ 375. Finally, in any crisis calling for legal authority to act, and where no constitutional provision, either permissive or restrictive, exists, if the legislature take upon itself, within the limits of a wise expediency, the power to act, to give the requisite authority and direction, there is no department of the government that can question its right to do so; and not only that, but a failure to act would stamp it as false to its duty. Having all legislative power within the limits indicated, the making of such provisions of law as are needed to save the State from inconvenience, loss, or danger, defines precisely the legitimate exercise of that power. To do it is its imperative duty. For that it is constitutionally competent, and all departments of the government, all agents and representatives of the sovereign, charged with collateral functions, are bound, within the scope of that power, to obey its behests, as the authentic expression of the will of that sovereign.[1]

§ 376. Having thus two legislative bodies, whose spheres of operation are distinct, though conterminous, it is obvious that numerous questions may arise between them as to their relative jurisdictions and powers. Of these, such as it is desirable for us now to consider are reducible to the following heads, which will be considered in their order, namely: —

(*a*). Questions relating to the power of legislatures to bind Conventions, or, what is the same thing, of Conventions to nullify Acts of their respective legislatures; and

(*b*). Questions as to the power of Conventions to legislate or to exercise functions imposed by the Federal Constitution especially upon legislatures.

(*a*). 1. Among the questions of the first class the most general and important is this: admitting the right of a legislature to call a Convention into being by some legislative Act, has it the further right to impose conditions, restrictions, or limitations upon its action, to dictate to it its organization or modes of proceeding; in short, to subject it in any way or to any ex-

[1] Vattel, *Law of Nations*, Book I. ch. iii. §§ 34, 35.

tent to the restraints of law? If so, wherein, and to what extent?

§ 377. The theory of those who deny to a legislature power thus to bind a Convention, is simply the theory of conventional sovereignty, to which allusion has been so frequently made in preceding pages. According to this theory, a Convention is a virtual assemblage of the people, a representative body charged by the sovereign with the duty of framing the fundamental law, for which purpose there is devolved upon it all the power the sovereign itself possesses; in short, that, for the particular business with which it is charged, a Convention is possessed of sovereign powers, by virtue of which it overtops all the other governmental agencies. Hence, while it is admitted, that by reason of the occasional and extraordinary character of the Convention, the word by which its assembling is to be made a legal act must be spoken by the legislature, yet it is contended, that, beyond that, it has no power whatever; or if, as the ultimate concession, it be admitted that the supervisory power of the legislature continues until the organization of the Convention is completed, that that body, when organized, being in a condition to act independently, all right of external control over it *eo instanti* ceases, and the career of its omnipotence begins.[1]

§ 378. By those, on the other hand, who assert the right of a legislature to bind a Convention, it is contended, that the latter is in no proper sense of the term and to no extent sovereign; that it is but an agency employed by the sovereign to institute government; that as such, even if it were invested with power to act definitively to an equal extent with some other departments of the government, there would be no special sacredness attaching to it by reason of its framing the fundamental law — no such dignity as ought to invest it with a primacy before all other State agencies; but that, when it is considered, on the contrary, that a Convention has no such power to act definitively, but that it is a body having the general characteristics of a legislature, but with the functions and organization only of a committee, it would be not only preposterous to give to it the rank of a sovereign power, but absurd to consider it entitled to any preponderating influence whatsoever; that, inasmuch, therefore, as a Convention is a body whose assembling is occasional and dependent on considerations of expediency, it follows that

[1] See Appendix C, *post*.

the legislature, whose function it is especially to declare and enforce the expedient, is the proper body to determine the time and conditions of such assembling; that in doing so it would not set itself above the Convention; it would simply announce the will of their common sovereign in relation to the scope of the business committed to a coördinate agency; and that in the absence of constitutional provisions, the extent to which a legislature may prescribe the conduct of a Convention must rest in its own discretion, subject to the limitation, that its requirements must be in harmony with the principles of the Convention system, or, rather, not inconsistent with the exercise by the Convention, to some extent, of its essential and characteristic function.

§ 379. Conceding, then, that a legislature may by its enactments bind a Convention, it remains to determine to what extent it may do so, and in what particulars. In relation to the extent of its power, it may be said that that is exactly commensurate with what is necessary for the public safety, for which that body is constitutionally responsible; hence, that it may prescribe whatever a prudent foresight may indicate as necessary for the welfare of the State. At the same time, doubtless, the legislature ought, generally, to leave the Convention at liberty to discharge, in some measure, its essential function of deliberation. By universal custom, as well as by the express provision of most of the American Constitutions, no person or body in a State has power to call a Convention but the legislature; and none but the legislature can either prescribe or indicate the purposes for which it is to assemble. Accordingly, as we shall see, our legislatures nearly always expressly declare, with more or less precision, those purposes, whether to make a general revision of the Constitution, or to consider specific subjects, accompanying that declaration sometimes with a prohibition to consider other subjects. While a legislature, however, has a clear constitutional right, in its discretion, to prescribe the scope of the duties of the Convention it calls, it would seem to be unwise to hamper, by too stringent limitations, a body which, if it meet at all, ought to meet for some rational purpose, and that, in general, it could not do if its work were laid out for it too minutely in advance, by imperative provisions of law.

§ 380. On the other hand, the legislature is the sentinel on duty. It cannot rightfully abdicate that position. In convening an extraordinary assembly, constituting unquestionably the weak side of our institutions, and therefore the one upon which usurpation may be expected to make its assaults, it must see to it that the Republic not only do not receive, but be placed in no danger of receiving, any detriment. It cannot excuse itself from insisting that a Convention shall be composed of members elected from amongst the most intelligent citizens of mature age, according to regulations fitted to secure a fair representation; that its numbers shall be limited; that the body shall assemble at a prescribed time and place; that it shall be organized in a particular manner; that its obedience to the laws shall be secured by an oath, or other effectual sanctions; that its expenses shall be certified in such a manner, and by and to such officers, as shall make it reasonably certain that the public funds will not be squandered or diverted to partisan or treasonable uses; and finally, what is incomparably more important than all else, that it shall propose, instead of enacting, constitutional changes, — in other words, that the fruit of its labors shall be so submitted to the people as to ascertain authentically their will in relation to it. In short, it is in general the right and the duty of a legislature to prescribe *when*, and *where*, and *how* a Convention shall meet and proceed with its business, and put its work in operation; but whether, under any and what circumstances, it may dictate what it shall do, or shall not do, is a question of some difficulty, respecting which the precedents and authorities will be examined hereafter. Doubtless, without restrictions as to the former particulars, the Convention would be wholly independent of the existing government; with restrictions as to the latter, it would ordinarily be, *pro tanto*, a mere echo of the legislature which called it together.

§ 381. Instead of attempting, therefore, to detail specifically the particulars in respect to which a legislature may bind a Convention, we pass to consider the precedents which have arisen in our constitutional history bearing on the question, and showing what limitations legislatures have placed upon the Conventions called by them, and how the latter have met and acted upon such limitations. This we shall do at the greater length, because those precedents will throw light upon a most perplexing and vital question, upon which there have been doubt and controversy. We shall pass over, in the main, the limitations imposed in regard to the organization and internal structure of Conventions, and the other subordinate details referred to in the last section, which are never omitted from such Acts, and in respect to the propriety of which no doubt has ever been entertained. Mention should be made, however, of one subject coming within the category of things relating to the organization of Conventions, which has led to occasional opposition, and even revolt, in these bodies, and that is, the attempts of legislatures to bind the members of Conventions to take a prescribed oath. Reference was made to this subject [1] when we were considering the organization of Conventions; but attention must now be directed to the precedents bearing on the question of power in legislatures thus to bind Conventions. Convention Acts containing such oaths were those calling the following Conventions: Georgia, 1833; North Carolina, 1835 and 1875; and Illinois, 1862 and 1869.[2] The first called the Convention of 1833 for the purpose of reducing the number of the General Assembly of the State, and required its members, before taking their seats, to subscribe an oath not to attempt to add to or take from the Constitution, or to change or alter any other section, clause, or article than those touching the representation in the General Assembly. It further provided, that no person elected to a seat, who should refuse to take the oath, should be allowed to take his seat in the Convention. The Act calling the North Carolina Convention of 1835 required that body to propose four, and authorized it, at its discretion, to propose a number more of specified amendments, but positively forbade it to make alterations and amendments in any other particulars than those enumerated. It then required the members to take an oath not directly or indirectly to evade or disregard the duties enjoined, or the limits fixed to the Convention by said Act. The Act calling the Convention of 1875 prescribed the same oath, and then provided that no delegate should be permitted to sit, or be entitled to a seat, in said Convention, until he should have subscribed the same.

In the Illinois cases, the Acts calling the Conventions had prescribed that the members, before entering upon their duties,

[1] See §§ 279–286, *ante*.

[2] See § 283, *ante*.

should "each take an oath to support the Constitution of the United States, and of this State," etc.

In all these cases, the oaths prescribed were taken by the members of the Conventions, save in those of Illinois, in the first of which they refused to retain the clause binding them to support the Constitution of the State, but took the oath prescribed after striking out that clause; and in the last, the Convention of 1869, they took a modified form of the oath, in substance, however, the same as that prescribed, — a few members afterwards taking also the oath in the form required.[1]

§ 381 *a*. We come now to the question of imposing limitations as to the work of a Convention, or as to the recommendations or ordinances it shall or shall not make.

1. First, we will cite the enabling Acts passed by Congress with a view to the formation of Constitutions in the Federal Territories; or Acts for the admission of the same into the Union as States, or Acts for the admission into the Union of such Territories which had framed Constitutions without enabling Acts. Of the first there have been, up to this time, fourteen,[2] and of the two last, seven.[3] In all the enabling Acts of Congress authorizing Territories to form Constitutions, were embodied restrictions, or conditions of the nature of restrictions, upon the action of those bodies. These related to the boundaries of the proposed States; to the nature and principles of the Constitutions they were to frame; to their domestic institutions; to the future action of such States in relation to taxation, the public lands, salt-springs, etc.; to jurisdiction over adjacent waters; to the language in which the laws were to be promulgated, and judicial proceedings to be conducted; to the number and election of delegates to the Conventions, the time and place of assembling; or to conditions to their right to act as Conventions, as that they should, on behalf of their respective States, adopt the

[1] See *ante*, § 282.

[2] The fourteen are Ohio, Louisiana, Indiana, Mississippi, Illinois, Alabama, Texas, Wisconsin, Minnesota, Missouri, Kansas, Nevada, Colorado, and Nebraska.

[3] The seven are Tennessee, Michigan, Arkansas, Iowa, Florida, California, and Oregon. Kentucky, Vermont, Maine, and West Virginia do not belong to this class, as they were severally States formed from territory belonging to States in the Union, in pursuance of sec. 3, art. iv. of the Federal Constitution. See *ante*, §§ 170-185.

Constitution of the United States.[1] Besides these there were, in the enabling Acts of several of the Territories, provisions that their Constitutions should not be repugnant to the Ordinance of 1787;[2] and in that of Minnesota, one requiring the submission of the Constitution framed by the Convention to the people of the Territory, — a provision for the first time inserted in such Acts, probably on account of the then recent troubles in Kansas.

To these restrictions and conditions the several Conventions were required by Congress to give their express assent, and only upon strict compliance with them were the Territories admitted into the Union.[3]

In many of the Acts admitting into the Union Territories which had framed Constitutions without enabling Acts, in like manner, were contained conditions in regard to the disposition of the public lands therein, to their boundaries and jurisdiction, similar to those contained in the enabling Acts above described, and to

[1] See the enabling acts of Ohio, 2 Sts. at Large, 173; Louisiana, Id. 641; Indiana, 3 do. 289; Mississippi, Id. 348; Illinois, Id. 428; Alabama, Id. 489; Missouri, Id. 545; Texas, 5 do. 797; Wisconsin, 9 do. 56; Minnesota, 11 do. 166; Kansas, Id. 269; Nevada, 13 do. 30; Colorado, Id. 32; Nebraska, Id. 47.

[2] See the enabling Acts of Ohio, Indiana, Illinois, Mississippi, Alabama.

[3] In relation to the binding force of conditions imposed by Congress upon Territories under the circumstances stated in the text, see the case of *Brittle* v. *The People*, reported in 2 Nebraska R. 198. The Supreme Court of the State, after its admission, held that "when a Constitution has been adopted by the people of a Territory, preparatory to admission as a State, and Congress prescribes certain changes and additions to be adopted by the legislature as part of the Constitution, and such changes and additions are declared to be fundamental conditions to the admission of the State, and the legislature accepts such changes, additions, and conditions, and the State is thus admitted, they become thereby a part of the Constitution, and binding as such, although not submitted to the people for their approval."

It follows from this position, doubtless, that such fundamental conditions, thus imposed and accepted, are irrepealable without the consent of Congress. The condition infringed was one declaring that within the State of Nebraska there should be no denial of the elective franchise, or of any other right, to any person by reason of race or color, excepting Indians not taxed. By a law of the Territory still in force after its admission into the Union, none but white males were allowed to sit upon juries. On the trial of a criminal, a colored man was allowed to sit on the jury which convicted the offender, and the case came before the Supreme Court upon exception to the ruling which permitted him to sit as such. It was held that the fundamental condition referred to gave colored men the right to vote and to sit on juries.

these the Territories were compelled to assent by their Conventions or legislatures, as a condition of their admission into the Union.[1] Though, as we have said, the conditions thus imposed have always been complied with, it has not always been done without a struggle to avoid them, especially in relation to boundaries, as in the case of Michigan.[2]

§ 382. 2. Passing to Conventions called by the States, we observe, that while, in comparison with the whole number of Conventions thus far held in the United States, those which legislatures have attempted to bind in respect to what they should do or should not do, by directions, restrictions, or prohibitions, are few in number, yet cases of the kind have arisen which can but have some bearing upon the question of power we are considering, and which, therefore, we feel compelled to examine somewhat minutely.

We will first consider cases in which Conventions have been called to do a specific thing, defined in the Convention Acts, with an express or implied inhibition to do anything beyond that.

Among the cases of the kind are those of the Georgia Convention of January 4, 1789, and of the last eight Conventions of Vermont. These bodies were all called for the purpose only of passing upon amendments framed by previous Conventions, or by Councils of Censors having the functions of Conventions.[3] In those held in Vermont the limitations contained in the ordinances calling them were strictly observed; those bodies, though in some instances rejecting the amendments proposed by the Councils, never venturing to propose amendments, or to do any other official act themselves. In the Georgia case, on the other hand, although the Convention was "for the sole purpose of adopting and ratifying or rejecting" a Constitution submitted to it by a Convention held in November preceding, it proposed cer-

[1] See the acts admitting Michigan, 5 Sts. at Large, 49, 59, 144; Arkansas, Id. 50, 58; Kansas, 12 do. 126; Iowa, 5 do. 742, 788, 789; Florida, Id. 742, 782, 789; California, 9 do. 452; Oregon, 11 do. 383.

[2] We have omitted the case of the Federal Convention, which in point of date precedes those of the States hereafter cited, because it is not certain that it was a case of restrictions imposed by legislative authority upon a Convention. As we shall see, it was denied by Mr. Hamilton that it was such a case. We shall, in a subsequent section, cite the arguments on both sides of the question. See § 383, *post*.

[3] See § 220, *ante*.

tain alterations of the form laid before it, which were finally adopted by a third Convention that met May 4, 1789. No objection seems to have been made to this departure from the line of duty prescribed by the legislature; but less weight should be given to this circumstance, because at that early day the duties of Conventions, and even the proper mode of selecting them, were ill understood, the delegates to that of the preceding November, which framed the amendments submitted to the Convention of January 4, having been appointed by the State legislature.[1]

So the New York Convention of 1801 was called "for the purpose of considering the parts of the Constitution . . . respecting the number of Senators and members of Assembly, . . . and with power to reduce and limit the number of them," "and also for considering and determining the true construction of the 23d section of the Constitution, . . . as to the right of nomination to office, but with no other power or authority whatsoever."

In like manner, the Georgia Convention of 1833 was called by an Act which required it "to submit to the people such amendments, alterations, or new articles as they may make for the objects of reduction and equalization of the General Assembly only." The limitations thus imposed upon these Conventions were strictly observed, and the recommendations made by them were, on submission to the people in New York, adopted, but in Georgia rejected. The same may be said of restrictions contained in the Acts calling the New York Convention of 1867 and the California Convention of 1878, which in nearly identical terms authorized those bodies severally to punish as a contempt, and by imprisonment or otherwise, a breach of its privileges, or of the privileges of its members; but provided that such power should not be exercised except against persons guilty of one or more of certain offences specified. Both bodies confined themselves to the limits thus imposed.[2]

[1] See *ante*, § 148.

[2] For a powerful argument to the effect that a legislature may, in the Act calling a Convention, limit it to certain specific subjects, see the opinion of Harper, J., in The State *ex rel.* McDaniel, etc., 2 Hill S. C. (Law) R. 270–273 (* paging). The Convention in question, however, was not a Constitutional Convention, and the decision of a majority of the judges was adverse to the positions taken by Justice Harper upon the question under consideration, which was that of State sovereignty and State allegiance. The Convention was the Nullification Convention of 1832.

§ 382 *a*. Similarly, in several cases legislatures, in calling Conventions, have given to them positive directions to frame certain specific amendments to their respective Constitutions. Thus the Act calling the North Carolina Convention of 1835 required that body to "frame and devise amendments to the Constitution. . . . 1, so as to reduce the number of members of the Senate;" 2, "so as to reduce the number of members of the House of Commons;" 3, "prescribing the qualifications of voters for members of the Senate and House of Commons." By a subsequent section it further required the Convention to provide in what manner amendments should in future be made to the Constitution. So, it was provided by the Act calling the Maryland Convention of 1867, that it should insert in "the new Constitution and Form of Government a clause prohibiting the legislature from making any law providing for making payment by this State for persons heretofore held as slaves." So the legislature of Pennsylvania, in calling the Convention of 1872, required that body to submit to the people for ratification or rejection the amendments to the Constitution framed by it, but prescribed that the election to decide for or against them should "be conducted as the general elections of this commonwealth are now by law conducted." As the Convention was to submit the amendments by an ordinance to be passed by it, the above provision amounted to a direction to adopt an ordinance submitting them in the manner prescribed.

Finally, in the Act calling the Alabama Convention of 1875, the legislature made it the duty of the Convention, in the Constitution which it should frame, "to provide for a system of common schools, as liberally as the means of the State will permit, and to be enlarged as those means shall increase." In connection with these cases may be mentioned those in which Convention Acts have contained directions to make a certain disposition of the work of the respective Conventions, as to submit it to a vote of the people for adoption or rejection, — a provision nearly always inserted in the later Acts.[1] In many of these cases there

[1] See Convention Acts of the following Conventions: Massachusetts, 1780, 1820, and 1853; Pennsylvania, 1790, 1837, and 1872; New York, 1821, 1846, and 1867; Virginia, 1829 and 1850; Georgia, 1833 and 1877; North Carolina, 1835 and 1875; New Jersey, 1844; Michigan, 1850 and 1867; New Hampshire, 1852 and 1876; Ohio, 1852 and 1873; Illinois, 1847, 1862, and

was a direction not only to submit to the people, but to submit separately propositions not so related that they must stand or fall with others as a whole.[1]

To these cases of positive directions given absolutely may be added that of a direction, to take effect conditionally, contained in the Convention Act of the Pennsylvania Convention of 1872, that the Convention should submit any change or amendment agreed to by it to a vote of the people "separately and distinctly," if required so to do by a vote of one third of all the members of the Convention.[2]

1869; Indiana, 1850; Maryland, 1850, 1864, and 1867; Iowa, 1857; Missouri, 1861; Tennessee, 1870; West Virginia, 1872; Alabama, 1875; Nebraska. 1875; California, 1878; and Florida, 1885.

[1] See the Convention Acts of the following Conventions: Pennsylvania, 1790 and 1872; Virginia, 1829 and 1850; New Hampshire, 1850 and 1876; Illinois, 1862 and 1869; Tennessee, 1870; North Carolina, 1875; Alabama, 1875.

[2] Two Convention Acts, those calling the North Carolina Conventions of 1835 and 1875, contained, besides those considered above, peculiar provisions which, on their face, seem to be unnecessary, as they certainly are unusual. The former authorized the Convention to propose, in their discretion, nine specified amendments, "or any of them," to which, by a supplemental act, were afterwards added seven other amendments; and the latter, after forbidding the Convention of 1875 to vacate offices filled under the existing Constitution before the same should expire under existing law, authorized that body, nevertheless, to recommend "the abolishment of any office when the present term therein should expire, or vacancies occur," and that it might "provide for filling such vacancies otherwise than as now, and for limiting the terms thereof." The preamble to the Act of 1835, however, explains the anomaly of that Act, since it shows decisively that the legislature intended to restrict the Convention absolutely to twenty amendments, four of which it was required, as we shall see, to recommend, and the remaining sixteen it might recommend or not as it should deem best, but it was required and bound by a very stringent oath to recommend no others. It is not so easy to explain the propriety of the provision of the Act of 1875, because that Act called the Convention "for the purpose of considering and adopting such amendments as they should deem necessary and expedient, subject only to the restrictions hereinbefore provided," which, as we shall see in the following section, forbade the Convention absolutely "to consider, debate, or propose" twelve specified particulars. It would seem that the general power previously given authorized the adoption of any amendment not covered by the restrictions. But as one amendment, in respect to which a discretion was given the Convention, related to one phase of a subject, another phase of which had been withdrawn from the consideration of that body, the specification was, perhaps, inserted in the Act out of abundant caution, so as to avoid objection to a provision not intended to be forbidden.

All the directions and requirements contained in the acts referred to in this section were complied with and obeyed by the respective Conventions, save those embodied in the Pennsylvania Act. Of these, one was disobeyed, — that prescribing the mode of holding the election for the adoption or rejection of the amendments, which, in the city of Philadelphia, the Convention changed so as to require the election to be held, not as the general elections were by law conducted, but by a board of special commissioners named by the Convention and not known to the law; the other, relating to separate submission, was not obeyed, as, on the one side, it was denied, though on the other asserted, that the condition on which the separate submission was to be made had been fulfilled. These proceedings of the Pennsylvania Convention led to important litigation in the courts of that State, and to decisions as to the relative powers of legislatures and Conventions of great interest, which will be fully considered in subsequent sections, when we come to examine the bearing of judicial decisions upon the question now under discussion.[1]

§ 382 *b*. There remains to be considered another class of restrictions or limitations imposed by legislatures upon Conventions, — those by which the latter are directly or indirectly prohibited to recommend certain amendments or to do certain acts; and it is in regard to the binding force of such inhibitions that the principal doubt and controversy has arisen.

Thus, the Act calling the Pennsylvania Convention of 1872 provided, that nothing in the Act contained should authorize the Convention "to change the language, or to alter in any manner the several provisions of the ninth article of the present Constitution, commonly known as the Bill of Rights," but that the same should "be excepted from the powers given to said Convention," and should "remain inviolate forever;" and that it should have no power "to create courts with exclusive equity jurisdiction."

To the same effect, though less explicit, is the provision of the Act calling the North Carolina Convention of 1835, which, after requiring the Convention to propose four, and authorizing it to propose nine, specified amendments (to which were afterwards, by a supplemental act, added seven others, making twenty in all), provided as follows: "but they shall not alter any other

[1] See §§ 409 *a*–409 *e*, *post*.

article of the Constitution or Bill of Rights, nor propose any amendments to the same, except those hereinbefore enumerated." Beyond the twenty amendments specified, this Act, doubtless, operated as a direct prohibition to propose any change or alteration of the Constitution whatever.

So, the Act calling the North Carolina Convention of 1875 provided, that said Convention should "have no power to consider, debate, or propose any amendment to the existing Constitution, or ordinance, upon the following subjects." Here followed twelve particulars, the homestead and personal exemptions, the mechanics' and laborers' lien, the rights of married women, as now secured by law, etc.

Of an indirect prohibition the following instance appears in the Act calling the Maryland Convention of 1850. The first section provided, "that for the purpose of ascertaining the expediency of calling a Convention to frame a new Constitution and form of government, except so far as regards the rights and relations existing between master and slave as now established by the Constitution and form of government of this State, it is hereby recommended to the legal voters of the State" to vote as to the expediency of making such a call, and providing for the election at the same time of delegates to meet in Convention for the purpose indicated, if a majority of such voters should vote in favor thereof. The result of the vote was in favor of a Convention, which accordingly met and framed the Constitution of 1851. The exception embodied in the Act undoubtedly operated indirectly as a prohibition upon the Convention to adopt any amendment or ordinance affecting the rights and relations therein referred to.

To these may be added a few instances in which legislatures have indirectly prohibited any attempt, on the part of the Conventions called by them, to put the Constitution or amendments which they might frame in force without submitting the same to the people. Thus, the Act calling the Pennsylvania Convention of 1837 provided, "that for the purpose of ascertaining the sense of the citizens of this commonwealth on the expediency of calling a Convention of delegates to be elected by the people, with authority to submit amendments of the State Constitution to a vote of the people for their ratification or rejection, and with no other or greater power whatsoever, it shall be the duty," etc.

To the same effect was a provision of the Act calling the Missouri Convention of 1861, that "no act, ordinance, or resolution of said Convention shall be deemed to be valid to change or dissolve the political relations of this State to the government of the United States, or any other State, until a majority of the qualified voters of this State voting upon the question shall ratify the same."

Finally, the Act calling the Alabama Convention of 1875 provided, that the Convention should not "be authorized to make any ordinance, rule, or law, which shall be binding on the people of this State, or any part of them; nor to deprive any person in office of his right to said office, as now held by him under the Constitution and laws of this State; nor to place any property or educational qualification upon the right to vote in this State; nor to do any act but to frame and recommend for adoption a Constitution amendatory and revisory of the Constitution now in operation in this State."

The Conventions to which the prohibitions described in this section were directed, in every instance save one, observed and conformed to them. The Pennsylvania Convention of 1872, in the face of the prohibition against altering, adding to, or taking from, the Bill of Rights, recommended a change of one section of it, and the recommendation was ratified subsequently by the people.[1]

§ 382 *c*. A careful search among the Acts passed for the call of Conventions has brought to light only the foregoing restrictions, limitations, or directions imposed upon them by legislatures. What inference are we authorized to draw from these precedents in regard to the power of legislatures to bind Conventions by their enactments? The fact that but three Conventions — that of Georgia of January 4, 1789, that of Illinois of 1862, and that of Pennsylvania of 1872 — have ventured to disobey the legislative directions, or disregard or evade the limitations imposed, even in respect of matters of comparative unimportance relating to the organization and methods of procedure of Conventions, indicates, on their part, either a spirit of docility not generally characteristic of such bodies, or a conviction that the Acts calling them constituted the charters from which alone their powers were derived, and by which they were to be bounded. In regard to

1 See *post*, §§ 409 *a*–409 *e*.

the first case, that of the Georgia Convention of January 4, 1789, enough has been said in preceding sections[1] to demonstrate that it is of very slight importance as a precedent. While there was, doubtless, an assumption of power not warranted by the Act calling it, there appeared in it no spirit of disobedience, no insurrection against the law-making power, such as showed itself in the two other cases. The revolt of the Illinois Convention of 1862 was against the taking of the oath, prescribed by the Act calling it, to support the Constitution of the State, — a refusal which was absurd, and could have taken its rise only in minds swayed by pride and ignorance, or by unworthy motives. Naturally, the people of Illinois rejected at the polls a Constitution whose inception was tainted by such influences. The disobedience of the Pennsylvania Convention of 1872 related to two, and perhaps three, directions or injunctions of the legislature touching, 1, the mode of conducting the elections for the adoption or rejection of the Constitution it should recommend; 2, the alteration of the Bill of Rights; and 3, the separate submission of parts of it upon a certain contingency. The conduct of the Convention resulted from an admixture of some of the same subjective conditions described as swaying the minds of the Illinois Convention, with an insolent and disobedient spirit, together with a desire for partisan advantage, disguising itself as an aspiration for reform. It will be shown in a subsequent section how that, of the two acts of disobedience of the Pennsylvania Convention, one was rebuked, and the measure to which it led discredited and annulled by the highest court of the State, and the other only not declared unauthorized and set aside by the same tribunal, because the people had seen fit, in the mean time, by an act of political power, to condone the offence of the Convention. As for the third act of the body, it was left doubtful, on the evidence presented to the Supreme Court, whether it was an act of disobedience or not, and that tribunal, therefore, declined to pronounce it to be such an act. The conduct of the Convention in this matter, so discreditable to its intelligence, was followed by an act which strongly impeached its patriotism. Learning that the commissioners appointed by it to conduct the election in Philadelphia had been served with notice of an application for an injunction to stop their proceedings, it thought fit to utter threats of abolishing the court

[1] See §§ 148–149, *ante*.

in case its decision should be adverse to the measures it had taken. Better counsels, however, prevailed, and it contented itself with issuing a declaration of the powers belonging to it as a Convention, which went to the length of claiming for itself nearly unlimited sovereignty.[1]

One remark further in regard to the inference we are authorized to draw from these precedents as to the power of legislatures to bind Conventions: The old maxim that "one may lead a horse to water, but cannot make him drink," is, in general, applicable to the case of Conventions placed under unpalatable restrictions. Legislatures may impose such restrictions, but it is impossible, without special and most stringent provisions addressed to that end, to compel obedience to them. It has been done, however, and can be done again. In the cases of the Georgia Convention of 1833 and the North Carolina Conventions of 1835 and 1875, restrictions were imposed under such conditions that, until the members had solemnly sworn to observe and obey them, they could not take their seats, nor the Conventions be organized. Such a provision might form a part of all Convention Acts. If, beside this, the provisions of some of the latest of those Acts declaring any member who should be guilty of violating any oath required to be taken by him as such, liable to indictment for perjury, were inserted in all Convention Acts, nothing further would be needed effectually to bind Conventions to exact obedience. While the policy of imposing minute and stringent limitations upon such bodies is doubtful, there is no doubt whatever of the impolicy of imposing them, and then of permitting those sought to be bound by them to disobey with impunity. The general introduction, however, of such limitations is to be strongly reprehended, save where there exists a clear and cogent necessity, for the peace or safety of the State.

§ 383. Having thus reviewed the precedents bearing on the question, whether legislatures have the power to bind Conventions by their Acts, we pass to the consideration of cases in which that question has been made the subject of discussion in legislative bodies or in Conventions, or of judicial opinions touching it rendered by the judges of our courts.

The earliest discussion of the question arose in the Federal

[1] See the resolutions adopted by the Convention upon its reassembling after the judgment of the court had been rendered, § 409 *d*, *post*.

Convention of 1787. It is well known, that the credentials of the delegates to that body restricted them to the simple duty of revising and reporting amendments to the Articles of Confederation. With some difference of phraseology, they all, with the exception of those of the delegates from New Jersey, which State seems to have taken a wider view of the perils and necessities of the situation than any other, substantially accorded in this limitation.[1] The credentials of the delegates from New Jersey thus prescribed the purpose of the meeting: — "For the purpose of taking into consideration the state of the Union, as to trade *and other important objects*, and of devising such *other provisions* as shall appear to be necessary to render the Constitution of the Federal government adequate to the exigencies thereof."

The credentials of the delegates from Massachusetts and New York authorized them to meet "for the sole and express purpose of revising the Articles of Confederation, and reporting to Congress and the several legislatures such alterations and provisions therein as shall, when agreed to in Congress, and confirmed by the States, render the Federal Constitution adequate to the exigencies of government and the preservation of the Union." It would be difficult by any fair construction to find in this language power to do more than to patch up the old Confederation; and there is no room for doubt, that the views of the people at the time the Acts were passed which resulted in the assembling of the Convention, went no further than that. But the leading statesmen in that body became early convinced, that the only hope for the Union was in superseding the worthless system then in operation by a national government with large powers. Accordingly, on the introduction of what is known as Mr. Randolph's plan, soon after the organization of the Convention, and from that time on to the close of its sessions, it was never doubtful that the predominant sentiment of the body favored that plan, as containing avowedly the features of a national government. And it thus favored it against the vigorous protest of many members, who, coming from the smaller States, opposed such a plan as likely to lessen their proportionate weight in the Union. By the latter, the argument was strongly pressed, and, but for the circumstances of the times, it would have prevailed, that the Convention was bound by the

[1] Elliott's *Deb.*, Vol. I. p. 163.

terms of the Acts under which it assembled to confine itself to the limits they prescribed. The majority of the Convention, however, resolved, in spite of those restrictions, to recommend a national government; but they did it on the ground of necessity, as the only hope left for preserving peace and the Union, and many of them despaired even then of preserving either the one or the other.

§ 384. Thus, in the debate on Mr. Randolph's plan, as contrasted with that reported by Mr. Paterson, known as the New Jersey plan, which proposed simply a modification of the existing Confederation, to the objection, that the powers of the Convention did not extend to the adoption of a national government, Mr. Randolph said: —

"The resolutions from Virginia must have been adopted on the supposition that a Federal government was impracticable. And it is said that power is wanting to institute such a government; but when our all is at stake, I will consent to any mode that will preserve us."[1] . . . . "There are reasons certainly of a peculiar nature when the ordinary cautions must be dispensed with; and this is certainly one of them. When the salvation of the Republic was at stake, it would be treason to our trust not to propose what we found necessary."[2]

Mr. Mason "thought with his colleague, Mr. Randolph, that there were . . . . certain crises in which all ordinary cautions yielded to public necessity. He gave, as an example, the eventual treaty with Great Britain, in forming which the commissioners of the United States had wholly disregarded the improvident shackles of Congress; had given to their country an honorable and happy peace; and instead of being censured for the transgression of their powers, had raised to themselves a monument more durable than brass."[3]

§ 385. On the other hand, Mr. Hamilton deemed the establishment of a national system to be within the scope of their powers under their credentials. In support of that view he said: — "Let us now review the powers with which we are invested. We are appointed for the sole and express purpose of revising

[1] Yates' *Minutes*, in Elliott's *Deb.*, Vol. I. pp. 415, 416.

[2] Elliott's *Deb.*, Vol. V. p. 197. (Madison's Report.)

[3] Id. p. 216.

the confederation, and to alter or amend it, so as to render it effectual for the purposes of a good government. Those who suppose it to be fèderal, lay great stress on the terms *sole* and *express*, as if those words intended a confinement to a Federal government, when the manifest import is no more than that the institution of a good government must be the *sole* and *express* object of your deliberations. . . . . I have, therefore, no difficulty as to the extent of our powers."[1]

In this construction of their credentials, however, Mr. Hamilton was alone, and, as we have said, it was concedeđ with almost perfect unanimity, both in the Federal Convention and in those held in the States to pass upon the Constitution framed by it, that in recommending that instrument, instead of merely proposing amendments to the Articles of Confederation, the delegates to the former had exceeded their powers.

§ 386. For the purposes of this inquiry, it is sufficient to note respecting the action of the Federal Convention in this case, —

1. That it is, at the worst, a case of refusal by a Convention to obey the instructions of the legislative authority by which it was convened, in relation to the scope and general character of the system it should mature; but,

2. That the Convention did not claim a right to disobey, to annul, or even to suspend the Acts under which it assembled; that, on the contrary, it admitted implicitly the binding force of those Acts, which yet it felt itself constrained by necessity to disregard. Admitting obedience to be due, it pronounced it under the circumstances to be impossible.

3. Finally, that whichever construction put upon the credentials of the Convention be the true one, that of Mr. Hamilton or that of Mr. Randolph and others, the action of that body is entitled to little weight as a precedent to establish the right of such a body to disobey the Act that convened it; for, on the construction of Mr. Hamilton, there was no disobedience, and on that of Mr. Randolph, the disobedience was confessed and regretted, but excused on the ground of necessity.

§ 387. The next case in which the question of the right of a legislature to bind a Convention by the Act calling it was considered was that of the North Carolina Convention of 1835, to which attention has already been called.

[1] Yates' *Minutes*, in Elliott's *Deb.*, Vol. I. pp. 417, 418.

By the Act of January 6, 1835, Secs. 12 and 16, it was provided that the Convention thereby called should frame and devise four amendments to the Constitution, namely, two to reduce the representation in the Senate and the House of Commons; one to change the qualifications of voters; and one to provide for making amendments to the Constitution. It then authorized the Convention, in its discretion, to propose sixteen other amendments specified, or any one or more of them. After providing for submitting such amendments as the body should propose to the people, the Act concluded by declaring that the Convention should not alter any other article of the Constitution or Bill of Rights, nor propose any amendments to the same, except those which were therein before enumerated. The 10th Section of the Act had provided that no delegate should take his seat in Convention until he should have taken an oath not to evade or disregard the duties enjoined, or the limits fixed to the Convention by that Act. A discussion arising, on the first assembling of the Convention, whether that body was bound by the Act to take the oath prescribed, it was contended by some that the legislature had no right to impose an oath, and that consequently they were not bound to regard the Act. It was also suggested that the Convention might go further and disregard the injunctions and limitations of the legislature in relation to the amendments it should propose, citing as authority for that view the alleged precedent, just commented upon, in the Federal Convention. Different counsels, however, at length prevailed. The Convention was reminded by the Hon. Mr. Gaston that it was only by obedience to the requirements of the Act in relation to the oath, that it could become organized. Without first having taken the oath, no member could take his seat; and having taken the oath, the limitations of the Act could not be disregarded without perjury. Unlike the Federal Convention, therefore, which was constrained by necessity to disobey the Acts under which it assembled, the North Carolina Convention was constrained by necessity to obey them, and hence the cases may be thought to be equally indecisive as precedents upon the question we are discussing.

§ 388. In 1833, a judicial opinion was delivered by the judges of the Supreme Court of Massachusetts, which has some bearing, perhaps, upon the question of the binding force of Acts of

Assembly upon Conventions. The facts of the case, as derived from the opinion, are, that the legislature of Massachusetts, having under consideration a proposition for calling a Convention to revise the Constitution, and desiring to limit the latter to particular amendments, entertained a doubt whether or not that body would be bound to respect the limits it should impose, and accordingly the House of Representatives requested the opinion of the Supreme Court upon the following question, namely, "Whether, if the legislature should submit to the people to vote upon the expediency of having a Convention . . . . for the purpose of revising or altering the Constitution of the Commonwealth in any specified parts of the same, and a majority of the people voting thereon should decide in favor thereof, could such Convention, holden in pursuance thereof, act upon and propose to the people, amendments in other parts of the Constitution not so specified?" Upon this question the Court said:— "Considering that the Constitution has vested no authority in the legislature in its ordinary action to provide by law for submitting to the people the expediency of calling a Convention of delegates for the purpose of revising or altering the Constitution of the Commonwealth, it is difficult to give an opinion upon the question what would be the power of such a Convention, if called. If, however, the people should, by the terms of their vote, decide to call a Convention of delegates, to consider the expediency of altering the Constitution in some particular part thereof, we are of opinion, that such delegates would derive their whole authority and commission from such vote; and upon the general principles governing the delegation of power and authority, they would have no right, under such vote, to act upon and propose amendments in other parts of the Constitution not so specified."[1]

§ 389. Whether the general idea contained in this opinion respecting the source of the validity of the supposed limitations upon the action of the Convention, namely, that it was to be sought alone in the vote of the people, be a correct one or not, will be the subject of consideration further on. Assuming for the present, however, that the idea was a mistaken one, and that those limitations derived their binding force from the Act of As-

[1] *Opinion of the Justices of the Supreme Judicial Court*, etc., 6 Cush. R. 572; also of the *Supreme Court of Rhode Island*, 14 R. I. R. 649.

sembly either alone or in conjunction with the subsequent expression of popular approval, the Act being considered, in either event, as an act of ordinary legislation, the views expressed by the Court would seem to indicate that a Convention might be bound by an Act of a legislature. The Court affirm, that, in the case supposed, the Convention would not be competent to overpass the limits imposed by the vote of the people by which it was called; from that vote "they would derive," say they, "their whole commission and authority;" "and upon the general principles governing the delegation of power and authority, they would have no right, under such vote, to act upon and propose amendments in other parts of the Constitution not so specified." But suppose it were demonstrated that the efficacy of the call, with its limitations, depended not on the vote of the people, but on the Act of the legislature, preceding and requiring such vote, can it be doubted that the Convention would be equally bound by it? The Act then would constitute its commission, the source from which all its authority would be derived; and the principles governing the delegation of power and authority would seem as much as ever to establish that, under such a law, it would have no right to act upon or propose amendments in other parts of the Constitution not specified in it. Nevertheless, it were well to determine, if possible, the true source of the validity of the call of a Convention made under such circumstances. Does it flow from the power of the legislature, or from the power of the people giving its sanction to what a legislature has recommended?

§ 390. This interesting and perplexing question has been the subject of extended discussion in several Conventions. It arose in New York, in 1846, upon the following facts. In 1845, the legislature of the State had passed an Act recommending to the people a Convention, and prescribing the manner in which it was to be elected and held. By this Act it was provided, that the people, at the fall election of that year, should pass upon the question of Convention or no Convention, and if they should decide for a Convention, that the delegates were to be chosen in April, 1846, and to assemble in June of the same year. It was also, by the seventh section, provided, that "the number of delegates to be chosen to such Convention shall be the same as the number of members of Assembly from the respective cities and counties in this State."

By the existing Constitution of New York, the apportionment of members of the General Assembly made in the spring of 1836, took effect for the purpose of electing the members in the fall of that year, but not for any other purpose, until the first day of January, 1837; and it was to remain unaltered for ten years. In other words, the representation from "the respective cities and counties" of the State, in the Assembly, from the commencement of the political and calendar year 1837, to the commencement of the political and calendar year 1847, was to remain the same. When the legislature met in the early part of the year 1846, after the Act calling the Convention had been ratified by the people, but before the delegates had been elected under it, an Act was passed making a new apportionment of representatives to the Assembly, increasing the number, and a bill was introduced for an Act providing that the number of delegates to be chosen in and by the respective cities and counties to the Convention, to be held by virtue of the Act of 1845, should be the same as the number of members of the Assembly, to be chosen in pursuance of the new apportionment. In other words, the Act calling the Convention was proposed to be modified by the body which had originally passed it, after it had been voted upon by the people.

§ 391. Upon this bill, a question was raised as to the power of the legislature — whether it could change the rule of apportionment, as applicable to the Convention, prescribed in the Act voted on by the people. The subject was referred to the judges of the Supreme Court of the State for their opinion, who decided —

First, that the new apportionment for members of the Assembly not taking effect until the first day of January, 1847, the provision of the Convention Act of 1845, to the effect, that "the number of delegates to be chosen to such Convention shall be the same as the number of members of Assembly from the respective cities and counties in this State," meant the number of members to which they were entitled under the apportionment in force when the Act of 1845 was passed, and which would be in force until after the delegates had been chosen and their labors terminated; and, secondly, that inasmuch as the existing Constitution had omitted to confer upon the legislature any power to call a Convention, the Act passed for that purpose and referred to the people was beyond its jurisdiction, and could operate only by way of advice or recommendation, and not as a law; that, under such circumstances, the calling of a Convention was an act proper only for the people themselves; and that, consequently, the Act of 1845 derived its obligation from the popular vote of ratification and not from the power of the legislature to pass it. From this, the inference was drawn that the legislature had no power to suspend or alter any of the provisions of that Act.[1]

§ 392. In the course of this opinion the Court say: —

"The legislature is not supreme. It is only one of the instruments of that absolute sovereignty which resides in the whole body of the people. Like other departments of the government, it acts under a delegation of powers, and cannot rightfully go beyond the limits which have been assigned to it. This delegation of powers has been made by a fundamental law, which no one department of the government, nor all the departments united, have authority to change. That can only be done by the people themselves. A power has been given to the legislature to propose amendments to the Constitution, which, when approved and ratified by the people, become a part of the fundamental law. But no power has been delegated to the legislature to call a Convention to revise the Constitution. That is a measure which must come from the people themselves. Neither the calling of a Convention, nor a Convention itself, is a proceeding under the Constitution. It is above and beyond the Constitution. Instead of acting under the forms and within the limits prescribed by that instrument, the very business of a Convention is to change those forms and boundaries, as the public interests may seem to require. A Convention is not a government measure, but a movement of the people, having for its object a change, in whole or in part, of the existing form of government.

"As the people have not only omitted to confer any power on the legislature to call a Convention, but have also prescribed another mode of amending the organic law, we are unable to see that the Act of 1845 had any obligatory force at the time of its enactment. It could only operate by way of advice or

[1] For this opinion see Appendix D, *post*.

recommendation, and not as a law. It amounted to nothing more than a proposition or suggestion to the people, to decide whether they would or would not have a Convention. That question the people have settled in the affirmative, and the law derives its obligation from that Act, and not from the power of the legislature to pass it. The people have not only decided in favor of a Convention, but they have determined that it shall be held in accordance with the provisions of the Act of 1845. No other proposition was before them, and of course their votes could have had reference to nothing else. They have decided on the time and manner of electing delegates, and how they shall be apportioned among the several counties.

"If the Act of the last session is not a law of the legislature, but a law made by the people themselves, the conclusion is obvious, that the legislature cannot annul it nor make any substantial change in its provisions. If the legislature can alter the rule of representation, it can repeal the law altogether, and thus defeat a measure which has been willed by a higher power."

§ 393. Now in reference to this opinion, which, as being that of highly respectable judges of the highest court in the most important State in the Union, seems to be possessed of very great authority, the following observations occur to me as justified as well by its tenor as by the circumstances under which it was rendered.

1. The opinion was extrajudicial. The Constitution of the State did not authorize the legislature, much less one of its separate houses, to refer questions arising in the course of its deliberations to the judiciary for adjudication. In point of legal authority, therefore, it is entitled to no greater weight than it deserves on account of its intrinsic wisdom.[1]

2. How much authority the opinion ought to carry with it on this account, may be inferred from the estimate put upon it by the judges themselves. In the concluding paragraph they say: —

"We cannot close this communication without expressing our regret that questions of so much delicacy and importance should be presented under circumstances which have given but a few hours for conferring together, and reducing our opinion to writing. Neither of us had either examined or thought of the

[1] See Appendix E, *post*.

questions until after the reference was made; and it was not until this day that we were able to meet and consult together on the subject."

3. What its authors thus seemed to regard as deserving of little consideration, was certainly so esteemed by the legislature. That body entirely disregarded the legal determinations of the Court on the question of power. It also disregarded, not without an appearance of contempt, a positive recommendation which the opinion contained. After declaring that the legislature had no power to pass the law then under consideration, the judges added, that "if, however, the legislature should think otherwise, it is then proper that we should take some notice of the bill which has been referred for our consideration." Accordingly, observing that the bill in its terms merely declared that the true intent and meaning of so much of the Convention Act of 1845, as related to the number of delegates to be chosen to the Convention, was, that that number should be the same as the number of members of the Assembly, according to the apportionment of 1845, the judges said that, in their opinion, such was not the true intent and meaning of said Act, and they therefore recommended that, if it was deemed expedient to legislate on the subject, there should be a positive enactment, instead of a mere declaration of opinion. In spite of this recommendation, however, the legislature passed the bill, in the precise form it bore when referred to the judges. To this it may be added, that the people in like manner disregarded the opinion; for they elected their delegates according to the new apportionment.

§ 394. 4. Coming to the substance of the opinion, there is contained in it, it is conceived, with much that is excellent, much also that is fallacious and of the worst possible tendency. With the latter are to be classed all those parts of it which relate to the power of a legislature to call a Convention; to the essential character and relations of the latter to the existing government, and to the source whence is derived the efficacy of a law calling a Convention under the circumstances detailed in the opinion. What I have to say upon the last point will be deferred till the case arising in the Massachusetts Convention of 1853, in which the same question was broached, is brought under discussion.[1] The two other points will be briefly considered here.

[1] See *post*, §§ 400–409.

I. The assertion, that where express authority to call a Convention has not been given by the Constitution, a legislature has no power to do it, I deem to be unfounded, for two reasons: first, as contravening sound political principles; and secondly, as falsified by well-established usage under the American system.

First. It has been seen in previous sections of this chapter, that under the general grant of legislative power found in our State Constitutions, a legislature is competent to provide by law for all exigencies requiring provisions of a legislative nature, so far as it is not restrained by the rules of morality, or by express constitutional inhibitions. This is believed to cover the whole case. The making of provision for the assembling of Conventions, and the hedging of them about with the restrictions needed as well for their efficiency as for the safety of the Commonwealth, is emphatically a matter of legislation. It is, moreover, a matter of legislation not fundamental in character, but of that species which our Constitutions apportion exclusively to the legislative departments created by them. The legislation necessary to initiate and to temper the operations of a Convention, no department of the government is competent to effect but the legislature; the sovereign itself could not do it, nor the electors, — bodies whose organization is such as to make deliberation upon the details of laws impossible.

§ 395. Nor is it true, as intimated by the judges in the opinion, that the giving to the legislature in a Constitution express power to recommend specific amendments to that instrument, involves, by implication, the denial to that body of power to call Conventions for a general revision of it. We shall see in a subsequent part of this work,[1] that such a grant is applicable only to disconnected and unimportant amendments. It is obvious that a grant of power to propose such amendments in a summary manner, and without the formalities ordinarily attending the enactment of fundamental laws, cannot be considered as an implied prohibition to effect a general revision of a Constitution in the only appropriate and practicable way, by a Convention. If it be not in the power of a legislature to call a Convention, that fact is not to be inferred from a positive authority to effect a different object in a different way. The idea advanced

[1] See *post*, §§ 538–540.

by the Court is based on the legal maxim, *expressio unius est exclusio alterius*, — a maxim doubtless of wide application in the construction of ordinary statutes, and of contracts between man and man, but whose applicability to the construction of fundamental laws has been denied or doubted by high authority.[1]

§ 396. *Secondly.* It is too late to deny the right of a legislature, in the absence of express constitutional authority, to call a Convention, and in general to impose upon it conditions in relation to its organization, and, to some extent, its proceedings. Though doubtless considered irregular in its earlier stages, the usage has become established for legislatures to take the initiative in such cases, as of course; and since the year 1820, when the New York Council of Revision vetoed a Convention Bill because the legislature had passed it without providing for a submission of it to the people, not as being beyond its power, but as inexpedient, the power has very frequently been exercised. The eminent judges composing that council did not question the right of the legislature to call a Convention, but insisted that it was "most safe and wise," and "most accordant with the performance of the great trust committed to the representative powers under the Constitution," that Conventions to alter that instrument "should not be called at the instance of the legislature without the previous sanction of the people;" and they cite numerous instances in which legislatures, desiring to call Conventions, were required by constitutional provision to submit the question of the expediency of so doing to a popular vote.[2] It is noticeable, moreover, that the General Assembly of New York had, at the time the opinion we are considering was delivered, twice exercised the power in that opinion declared to be so doubtful, — once in 1801, without submitting the question of a Convention to the people; and again in 1821, after an affirmative vote of the people, pursuant to the advice of the Council of Revision.

The first point, then, made by the Court, relating to the power of the legislature, was not well taken.

§ 397. II. The other point, touching the character and relations of the Convention to the existing government, was equally without force. The judges assert that "neither the calling of a

[1] See *post*, §§ 570–574 *e*.

[2] See Appendix F, for the entire opinion of the Council.

Convention, nor a Convention itself, is a proceeding under the Constitution." "It is," they say, "above and beyond the Constitution;" . . . . and they add, "a Convention is not a government measure, but a movement of the people, having for its object a change in whole or in part of the existing government."

Upon these extraordinary statements I remark —

1. That they all beg a question, which I deem to be the most important one in American constitutional law, whether, as Justice Wilson said in the Pennsylvania Convention to ratify the Federal Constitution, the sovereignty in our governments "is and *remains* in the people;" or whether, upon the call of a Convention, it shifts its *locus* into the hands of a majority of its members. Of the proposition that "a Convention is not a proceeding under the Constitution, but above it," what evidence is adduced except the mere *dictum* of the judges themselves, passing extra-officially upon a question of infinite magnitude, on which, as they admit, they had heard no argument, and about which they had never thought until the reference was made four days before, or consulted together until the very day the opinion was written?

So far from a Convention not being a proceeding under the Constitution, but above it, it is one of the chief excellencies of our system that, under it, those constitutional reforms which elsewhere have generally required for their consummation outbreaks of revolutionary violence, are anticipated and carried through by the voluntary and peaceable operation of the government itself. In this respect, one of our governments, as I have many times intimated, exhibits the qualities of a vital organism, in which are bound up distinct but interdependent systems, whose objects are respectively the defence, the growth, and the reparation or renewal of the economy.

On the other hand, the theory of the judges supposes in the Commonwealth two independent and mutually antagonistic orders of agencies: one constituting the government, charged with the regular administration of the laws, and responsible for the safety of the public liberties; and the other, forming the Convention, an eccentric and irresponsible body, somehow launched into the system, to play havoc with the Constitution and laws lying under its feet. It is enough to exhibit, side by side, the two theories of the state, to see which is the true one. The one regards it as a single, complete, living organism, possessing in itself all the powers necessary to insure its beneficent operation and its continuity. The other makes of it a dual system of unrelated and hostile organizations, whose tendency must be to conspire, not for the good of the whole, but for the destruction of each other.

§ 398. So, of the assertion that a Convention is not a government measure. If by that is meant that a Convention is an institution which can legitimately come into being, and run its career, in opposition to the government, or without its consent, supervision, or control, the statement is manifestly untrue, unless the Convention is itself the government. There is no escaping from this dilemma. If the government retains its powers at all, it must retain them wholly, and it must govern the Convention as well as individual citizens. If, when a Convention assembles, on the other hand, the government is shorn of its powers, or retains them only so far as they are not appropriated by the Convention, it ceases to be the government, — it is but a subaltern agency, existing only by the sufferance of another, which is supreme.

§ 399. Again. The judges say that the calling of a Convention "is a measure that must come from the people themselves." By the term "people" in this clause, must be meant either the whole body of the nation, that is, the sovereign, or the electoral body. Whichever was intended, nothing could be more absurd, if it was meant thereby to assert, that it is competent for the people to call Conventions and carry through constitutional changes, independently of the existing government. If the legislature, as the judges say, "is only one of the instruments of that absolute sovereignty, which resides in the whole body of the people," the coördinate departments which, together with the legislature, constitute the government, must be authentic representatives of that absolute sovereignty; *and a Convention can be nothing more.* Whatever, then, comes from the government, acting within the scope of its powers, comes from the people. This is as true of legislatures as of Conventions. The one are no less "instruments of absolute sovereignty," referred to, than are the other. But admitting the competency of the people to call Conventions, it would be impracticable, except through legislative interposition. All they can do is, to pass upon propositions submitted to them, under the direction of some agency having power to deliberate, and not too numerous to assemble and act for the whole. Any other course would lead to local and conflicting determinations. It is perfectly true, that the calling of a Convention is a measure that must come from the people themselves, but from the people acting through their accustomed and recognized agents, not through persons or bodies, unknown to the law, self-elected and irresponsible.

§ 400. In the Massachusetts Convention of 1853, a similar question arose, and led to a very elaborate discussion, upon a state of facts not unlike those above detailed.

In a former part of this chapter,[1] we have seen, that a question was started in that Convention as to its power to issue a precept for the election of a member to fill a vacancy, from the town of Berlin; that the Convention decided to issue, not a precept, but a simple notice, informing the town of the vacancy, and that, on motion of Mr. Butler, of Lowell, it adopted a form of notice, of which the concluding and material part was as follows — addressed to the selectmen of the town: — . . . . "I am directed, by a vote of the Convention, to request you to convene the qualified electors of your town, as soon as may be with a due regard to notice, in order to their electing and deputing a delegate to represent them in this Convention, *in the manner prescribed by the second section of the Act calling the Convention, adopted by the people on the second Monday in November,* A. D. 1852."

Of the last clause of this notice, upon which the discussion arose, the meaning is this: By the Act of May 7, 1852, the question of calling a Convention to revise the Constitution of Massachusetts, was to be submitted to the people of the State on the second Monday of the following November, the Convention, if voted for, to be elected on the first Monday of March, 1853, and to meet on the first Wednesday in May, 1853. It was further provided, that all the regulations for voting at the general elections of State officers, should apply to the election of delegates to the Convention, one of which regulations was, that all ballots were to be cast in sealed envelopes, and, if tendered without them, were to be neither received nor counted.

[1] See *ante*, §§ 340–347.

§ 401. Under this Act, a vote of the people was taken on the second Monday of November, 1852, Yes or No, on the following question prescribed therein: — "Is it expedient that delegates should be chosen to meet in Convention for the purpose of revising or altering the Constitution of government of this Commonwealth?" The result of the election was a majority of about seven thousand in favor of a Convention. On the first day of March, 1853, a few days before the delegates to the Convention were to be elected, in pursuance of the foregoing Act, the legislature of Massachusetts, then in session, passed an Act, leaving it optional with the voters at all elections held in the State, to use the sealed or open ballots, as they might choose. It was not disputed, that the intention of the legislature was, that this rule should govern the election of delegates to the Convention. When, therefore, Mr. Butler moved, as above stated, that the town of Berlin be requested to elect a delegate "in the manner prescribed by the second section of the Act calling the Convention, adopted by the people on the second Monday in November, A. D. 1852," it was his intention to insinuate that the Act of March 1, 1853, modifying that of May 7, 1852, was for that purpose inoperative and void, and to recommend that it be disregarded by the electors in the Berlin election, though its validity as to all other elections was not denied. This raised the question as to the power of the legislature to modify or repeal the Convention Act, after it had been adopted by the people; in other words, the question, whence does an Act passed with the formalities indicated, derive its efficacy? Is it from the legislature, or is it from the people acting in their primary capacity? — a question, evidently, of great importance; for, if the validity of such an Act comes alone from the legislature, that body might repeal it at its pleasure; whilst, if it be derived from the people, the people alone would have power to alter or annul it.

§ 402. By Mr. Butler, Mr. Hallett, and others, who favored the restriction of the voters of Berlin to the mode of voting prescribed by the Act of 1852, the opinion of the New York judges above commented on, was cited as a decisive authority for that restriction, — the ground being taken by them, for the reasons stated in the opinion, that the legislature was incompetent, by its Act of March 1, 1853, to change the provisions of the previous Act passed upon by the people. They contended, that when the people adopted the Convention Act in November, 1852, they adopted the whole law, and not simply answered the question, whether it was expedient that delegates should be elected to a Convention to revise the Constitution; that consequently every provision of that Act was adopted by them and in force, and that those provisions severally derived their efficacy from the same source, the people, through the vote taken upon them; that the same conclusion would follow from a view of the powers of the legislature; for that, by the Constitution of the State — Article Nine of the Amendments of 1820 — a mode had been provided, in which, by the recommendation of the legislature, followed by a vote of the people, "any specific and particular amendment to the Constitution" might be made, and that, beside that, the Constitution contained no grant of power to the legislature to meddle with the Constitution, much less to convene any other body with authority to do it; that, accordingly, when the legislature submitted to the people the Act of May 7, 1852, it submitted it not as a law, since it had been drawn up outside the proper province of that body, but as a recommendation merely, to be rendered effectual and valid as a law only by the *fiat* of the people; that, consequently, the legislature, having had no authority to pass, were equally incompetent to repeal or modify the law, when put in force by the popular vote.

§ 403. On the other hand, it was contended by Mr. Choate, and Judges Parker and Morton, that the order respecting the mode of voting to fill the vacancy from Berlin, could be defended only on one of these two grounds: either, first, that the Act of March 1, 1853, was wholly void, so far as related to the mode of voting for delegates to the Convention, because the legislature had no constitutional power to enact it; or, secondly, that although it was admitted to be a valid Act, and one which could be enforced in a court of justice, the Convention, by some transcendent power, might, for its own action, at least, annul it; that, as to the first hypothesis, it was perfectly clear, that a legislature possessed, at any moment, exactly the powers which the then existing Constitution gave it, or allowed to it, neither less nor more, — its power over subjects of public concernment remaining the same, so long as the Constitution remained the same; that, assuming that the legislature, which, by the Act of May 7,

1852, ordained, that the sealed envelope should be used in voting for delegates to the Convention, had power to make such a provision — which nobody had yet called in question — then the legislature which sat in March, 1853, had power to modify that provision, if the Constitution which existed in May, 1852, existed without change in March, 1853; in other words, if one legislature could constitutionally prescribe the use of one kind of ballot for a future election, a subsequent legislature, at any time before such election, might prescribe the use of a different kind of ballot, if the whole and every part of the Constitution continued all the while unchanged; that the power of a legislature to pass such a law was derived from that provision of the Constitution which empowered the general court to pass all manner of laws deemed by it to be "good and wholesome;" that the moment a Convention is authoritatively called, whether, under the Massachusetts Constitution, the legislature could call one or not, then — in the absence, at least, of a mode of voting prescribed by the sovereign power — the power of the legislature to make good and wholesome regulations touching times and places and modes of voting, the place of the sitting of the Convention, and the like, attached and was quickened into activity, and continued perfect, at least till the elections were consummated; that the alleged power of the people to enact a law about sealed envelopes or any thing else, does not exist, in the light either of the Constitution or of historical facts;[1] that, laying aside the former, the fact was, that the legislature caused to be presented to the people, according to the forms of law, the question, whether they deemed it expedient that a Convention should be called to consider of revising the Constitution; that the people answered *Yes*, and there they rested; that they never passed upon the sealed envelope, or any other detail of the law whatever; that the second hypothesis referred to, of some transcendent power in the Convention, by virtue of which it was enabled,

[1] Reference is here made evidently to ordinary laws. Of the power of the people to enact fundamental laws there is not only no doubt, but it is clear that no other body has power to enact them, except by express warrant for the particular occasion. For an exposition of the general principle stated above, that the people have not the power of ordinary legislation, under our Constitutions, and cannot be invested with it by the legislature, see the cases cited below, § 418, *note*.

although the law of March 1, 1853, was valid, to annul it, was equally unfounded; that if the power existed, so far as the Convention's own action was concerned, disobedience to it by the selectmen of Berlin, under the recommendation of the Convention, would not for that reason be lawful or go unpunished; that the power, however, was not admitted, but tested, as it must be, by its consequences and results, it was extravagant and absurd; that its exercise was without precedent in the history of American constitutional liberty; that no Convention, called together under a statute of the existing government to revise a Constitution — and all American Conventions, or all, with scarcely an exception, had been so called — had ever yet assumed to nullify the law of election prescribed by the authority which called it together; that, finally, the people, by the vote ratifying the Act of May 7, 1852, willed two things: first, that there should be a Convention; second, that it should be called by the legislature, sitting as a legislature, as part of the established government; and that the elections of its members should be conducted exactly as that legislature should prescribe in the exercise of its ordinary unfettered discretion — conclusions that flow directly from the fact that the people had responded favorably to the proposal of a Convention; they rested there, thus leaving it, by irresistible implication, to the legislature to carry out their will in its own way, and that then two successive legislatures assumed to make the needful regulations for electing the Convention accordingly, and the people assembled, pursuant to custom, and under those regulations cast their votes and retired.[1]

§ 404. To these arguments I shall add one or two observations, calculated, as I think, to place the subject under consideration in a still clearer light. The principal point made by the judges of the New York Supreme Court, before referred to, and by the advocates of the sealed envelope in Massachusetts, citing the decision of those judges as their main authority, was, that the Acts passed by the legislatures of those States respec-

[1] See speeches of Messrs. Choate, Parker, Morton, and others, in *Deb. Mass. Conv.* 1853, Vol. I. pp. 73, 83, 116, 117. 144. In this debate Judge Parker contended, that not only could a legislature modify the Act calling a Convention, under the circumstances detailed in the text, but that it could wholly repeal the Act, even after the Convention had commenced its session, thus putting an end to its existence. Id. p. 155.

tively, and adopted by the people, derived their sole efficacy from the popular vote, and were therefore incapable of a subsequent repeal or modification by the same or another legislature. Whether this was so or not depends mainly upon the terms of those Acts, ascertaining the extent to which the people were required to pass upon them. Those Acts consisted of two parts: first, of one or more sections submitting to the people a single question, Whether or not they deemed it expedient to call a Convention and, secondly, of sections prescribing the time, mode, and conditions of the election at which the question was to be answered; and, in case of an affirmative answer, providing for the election of the delegates, and the assembling, organization, and conduct of the Convention. The same is true of all the Acts calling Conventions which have come to my knowledge, except the few which contained no provision for a preliminary vote of the people on the question of Convention or no Convention. Thus the terms of the Massachusetts Act of May 7, 1852, are as follows: —

The first section is, in substance, that "the legal voters of the State, at the November election, 1852, *shall give in their votes* by ballot on this question, 'Is it expedient that delegates should be chosen to meet in Convention for the purpose of revising or altering the Constitution of government of this Commonwealth?'" The last clause contains absolutely every thing that was submitted to the people. The Act then proceeds as follows: The Governor and Council *shall count the votes*, and on the first Wednesday in January, 1853, *shall make known the result;* and if a majority of the votes are in favor of a Convention, *it shall be taken to be the will of the people* that a Convention should meet accordingly; and the Governor *shall call upon the people to elect delegates* to meet in Convention, &c. The second, third, fourth, and fifth sections are in the same imperative terms: "*the inhabitants shall elect one or more delegates*"; "*every person entitled to vote for representatives*, &c., *shall have a right to vote;*" "*the same officers shall preside at such elections*," &c.; *the votes for said delegates* "*shall be received, sorted, and counted*, &c., in the same manner as is now provided," &c; "*all laws now in force shall apply and be in full force;*" "*the persons so elected shall meet in Convention*," at a time and place specified; "*they shall be judges of the returns* and elections of their own members; they *shall proceed*, as soon as may be, to organize themselves in Convention;" "and such alterations or amendments, when made and adopted by the Convention, *shall be submitted to the people*," &c.; "and, if ratified by the people, in the manner directed by said Convention, the Constitution *shall be deemed and taken to be altered and amended accordingly*;" "and if not so ratified, *the present Constitution shall be and remain* the Constitution of government of this Commonwealth."

The New York Act was substantially identical with the one just described, differing from it only in the unimportant particular, that, at the preliminary election, the inspectors of election were required to prepare ballots, on which should be written, "Convention," and "No Convention," and all citizens were "allowed" to cast one or the other of them, as they should deem best. Should the result of the election be a vote in favor of a Convention, the remaining twelve sections of the Act, consisting of imperative provisions, similar to those above quoted, were to take effect.

§ 405. Now, although it is true that, in these Acts, the imperative provisions were most of them pivoted upon the contingency of an affirmative answer to the question of "Convention or no Convention," and that, in case a negative answer should be given, they would lose their entire force as laws, yet it is also true that, so far as those Acts were ever to have force as laws, they were to derive it from the legislature. They were couched in the language of laws, of commands, addressed by a superior, able to enforce them, to inferiors; they differed from other laws merely in being made conditional, *as to their taking effect*, upon the happening of a future event, the affirmative vote of the people upon a single question. If the event did not happen, the laws would remain inoperative; if it did happen, they would at once go into effect.

Now, what degree of efficacy is to be attributed to such conditional Acts, and what the source from which that efficacy is derived, are legal questions, upon which, fortunately, there is no lack of authority. Our State legislatures have, within the last twenty years, in many cases, passed Acts relating to the sale of intoxicating liquors, to schools, railroads, &c., and required, before they should take effect, that they should be submitted to the people. If approved by the people, they should be enforced, and if not, they should not. By our Constitutions, the power of passing laws having been exclusively committed to our General Assemblies, the objection has been raised, in these cases, that the Acts were unconstitutional, as attempting to transfer to the people the right to make laws. The courts, however, have, in many of the cases, sustained the action of the legislature, on the ground that the laws were perfect and complete as such, when passed by that body, but were made contingent, as to their taking effect, upon the happening of a future event — the approving vote of the people.[1] When, on the other hand, by the terms of the Acts, the *fiat* which is to make them laws is to be spoken by the people, they have been holden to be unconstitutional.

The analogy between these cases and those of the Convention Acts of New York and Massachusetts, is, in my judgment, complete. These Acts were in terms imperative, *per verba de presenti*, and but for the contingency provided for of a popular vote, they would have gone into immediate effect. With that provision, however, they stood thus: If the people should, at the election provided for, vote that a Convention was inexpedient, none would be held; and of course those provisions requiring an election of delegates to form one, would not go into effect; otherwise they would.

§ 406. Again: When a Convention Act is submitted to the people, it is clear that it is the mere question of the expediency of a Convention that is passed upon. The people have no power of deliberation, or of suggesting amendments, but merely of pronouncing upon single propositions, yea or nay. An affirmative vote declares it to be expedient, a negative to be inexpedient, to call a Convention — a declaration which has neither the form nor the effect of a law. The language of a law is "*fiat*" — *let it be done;* that of such an Act of the people is "*videtur*" — it seems good, — "*desiderandum est*" — it is desirable — a mere expression of opinion, not the uttering of a command. The contrary, however, is true of those parts of such Acts which relate to the details necessary to give practical effect to a Convention Act. There is no expression of opinion,

[1] Barto *v.* Himrod. 4 Seld. R. 483; with which compare The People *v.* Collins, 3 Mich. R. 343. See *post*, § 419, and cases cited in note.

but the uttering of positive commands to the officers of the government, voters, &c., contingent, as to their taking effect, upon the opinion expressed by the electoral body.

§ 407. That the construction contended for is the proper one to give to such Acts, is inferable from the adjudication of the Supreme Court of Illinois upon cases that have arisen in that State. By the existing Constitution of the State, that of 1847, no Act of the General Assembly authorizing corporations or associations with banking powers could go into effect or in any manner be in force, unless the same should be submitted to the people at the general election succeeding the passage of the same, and be approved by a majority of all the votes cast at such election for and against such law.[1]

In 1851, a General Banking Law was passed by the General Assembly and submitted to the people, agreeably to the constitutional provision, and ratified by them. To that part of this law prescribing the mode in which taxes should be assessed against the corporations thereby created, and the amount of their taxable property be ascertained, an amendment was made by the General Assembly in 1857, but the amendment was not submitted to the people. Against the validity of this amendment the objection was raised by one of the banks affected by it, that it was void, because it had not been ratified by the people as required by the Constitution; that the General Assembly had no power to repeal or modify any clause of the General Banking Law which had been submitted to and adopted by the people, without the same solemnities that attended its original passage. In substance, it will be observed, this objection was precisely the same as that taken to the New York and Massachusetts Acts referred to, namely, that, in ratifying the General Banking Law, the people had ratified every clause of it alike, and so placed all parts of it equally beyond the reach of a legislative repeal. The case coming before the Supreme Court, it was held by that body, that the vote of the people did not render the clause in question irrepealable by the General Assembly. The Court, speaking of the effect of the vote of the people, say: —

"That vote gave to this clause no additional sanction. The subject of taxation and the revenue are, by the Constitution,

[1] *Ill. Const. of* 1847, Art. X. § 60.

placed in the hands of the legislature alone. Upon this subject they have complete jurisdiction to legislate independently of the popular vote, *and such vote in approval of laws which might take effect without it, could not place the law beyond or above the jurisdiction of the General Assembly.*" [1]

§ 408. In this case the clause in question was held not to have been made irrepealable by the popular vote upon the law of which it formed a part, because it related to a subject-matter properly cognizable by the General Assembly under its general powers granted by the Constitution. And it was so held, although the Court expressly admitted that the clause sought to be amended had been submitted to and voted on by the people of the State. The Court say: —

"We are clearly of opinion that some of the provisions of this law which was submitted to the people are subject to legislative interference and control, and among them is the one in question. We may safely say that the Constitution did not require that the mode of assessing the property of the bank for the purposes of taxation should be submitted to the people, *and its submission to them was a work of supererogation.*"

Although, then, an Act in all its parts be submitted to the people, and they pass upon it throughout, it is not placed beyond legislative repeal, as to such parts of it as are within the general cognizance of the General Assembly, when there is nothing in the Constitution requiring the subject-matters comprised within those parts to be submitted to a vote of the people.

It is clear, then, from this decision, that had the New York and Massachusetts Convention Acts been submitted to and voted on by the people, *in toto*, section by section, they would still have been, in the main, subject to legislative repeal or modification. But, as we have seen, it is doubtful whether those Acts ever were submitted as a whole. It is pretty certain that in neither case was any part of them submitted except that relating to the expediency of the call of a Convention.

And with reference to the Illinois case, it is conceived, that the decision might have been placed upon broader and more solid

[1] Bank of the Republic *v.* County of Hamilton, 21 Ill. R. 53; afterwards confirmed by the same Court in Reaper's Bank *v.* Willard, 24 Ill. R. 433, and in Smith *v.* Bryan, 34 Ill. R. 364.

constitutional ground by holding simply that the Constitution of the State required only the question of the expediency of incorporating banking institutions to be passed upon by the people, leaving all questions of details to the General Assembly, to which, as involving the exercise merely of a legislative discretion, they belonged.

§ 409. The result of the discussion in the Massachusetts Convention, it should perhaps be stated, was that that body adopted by a large majority the notice to the town of Berlin offered by Mr. Butler, and the town accordingly elected a delegate to fill the vacancy, in the manner pointed out in "the Act calling the Convention, adopted by the people on the second Monday of November, 1852." The force of this action of the Convention, however, as a precedent, is much impaired by the fact that all the amendments proposed by it were repudiated by the people.

§ 409 *a*. The question as to the power of legislatures to bind Conventions by the Acts calling them received a very extended discussion, also, in the highest court of Pennsylvania, in 1873, since the previous editions of this work were published.[1] The facts essential to a comprehension of the questions raised are, that the legislature, at its session in April, 1872, passed an Act calling a Convention "to amend the Constitution," without a special warrant in the existing Constitution, which contained no provision for amending that instrument save by the action of the legislature followed by a ratification by the people; that, antecedently to the passing of such Act, however, the question of calling a Convention had, by the legislature, been submitted to the people, and had been answered in the affirmative; that the Act passed in pursuance of that vote had provided that the Convention should have power to propose to the people of the State, for their approval or rejection, a new or amended Constitution, subject to the following provisions: first, that one third of all the members of the Convention should "have the right to require the separate and distinct submission to a popular vote of any change and amendment proposed by the Convention," and that that body should submit the amendments agreed to by it to a vote of the people "at such time or times and in such manner as the Convention should prescribe, subject, however, to the limitation as to the separate submission of amendments contained

[1] Wells *v.* Bain, and Donnelly *v.* Fitler, 75 Pa. St. R. 39, 55, 56.

in this Act;" secondly, that the election to decide for or against the adoption of the new Constitution or amendments should "be conducted as the general elections of this commonwealth are now by law conducted;" thirdly, that nothing in the Act contained should authorize the Convention "to change the language, or to alter in any manner the several provisions, of the ninth article of the present Constitution, commonly known as the Bill of Rights," but that the same should "be excepted from the powers given to said Convention," and should "remain inviolate forever."

Notwithstanding these restrictions, the Convention made the following proposals and dispositions directly at variance with them: It proposed to the people an amended Constitution, to be voted on as a whole, although one third of all the members of the Convention, as it was claimed, demanded that Article V., relating to the judiciary, should be separately submitted. It also disregarded the requirements of the Act in respect to the mode of conducting the election to be held for the adoption or rejection of the Constitution. It created, by ordinance, a special board of commissioners for the city of Philadelphia, who should conduct the election, instead of the proper election officers of the commonwealth, by whom its elections were by law to be conducted. Finally, it proposed alterations in several provisions of the Bill of Rights. Bills in chancery were filed in Philadelphia, by two different parties, praying for injunctions to prevent the holding of the elections in that city under the ordinance, upon two grounds, both relating to the mode in which the Constitution was submitted to the people, — the first, that the ordinance for submission under the direction of special commissioners was void, as in violation of the express limitations contained in the Act of the legislature, which was claimed to be mandatory; and the other, that the submission of the Constitution as a whole, and not in separate parts, as required, it was claimed, by one third of all the members of the Convention, demanding the separate submission of Article V., was in like manner void. The injunctions prayed for were allowed unanimously by the full bench of the Supreme Court, sitting at *nisi prius*, upon the first ground, the court holding that the legislative restrictions were mandatory and absolutely binding. As to the question of separate submission of Article V., the decision of the judges was adverse to the plaintiffs, not on the ground that the limitation was not mandatory, but that it was not clearly shown that one third of the members of the Convention had required Article V. to be submitted separately; that, as "the Convention was clothed with express power to act upon the question of submitting the amendments in whole or in part, the question of a separate submission, being one committed to the whole body, of which the requiring third was a part, it must be presumed that the decision of the body as a whole was rightly made, and either that the request was not made by a full one third of all the members, or, if made by one third, that it was not made in a regular or orderly way.[1]

§ 409 *b*. In relation to the principal point involved in the cases, as to the power of the Convention to disregard and in effect to repeal the clause of the Convention Act touching the mode of conducting the election, the court, per Agnew, Ch. J., said: —

"Since the Declaration of Independence, in 1776, it has been an axiom of the American people, that all just government is founded in the consent of the people. This is recognized in the second section of the declaration of rights . . . of Pennsylvania, which affirms that the people have at all times an inalienable and indefeasible right to alter, reform, or abolish their government in such manner as they may think proper. A self-evident corollary is, that an existing lawful government of the people cannot be altered or abolished unless by the consent of the same

[1] Wells *v.* Bain, and Donnelly *v.* Fitler, 75 Pa. St. R. 39, 55, 56. It is difficult to reconcile this statement of the court with the fact, clearly apparent from the proceedings of the Convention, where it was charged on numerous occasions, and never denied, that more than one third of all the members of that body had demanded the separate submission of the judiciary article. It does not appear, however, from the proceedings, that any formal presentation of that fact in writing, which was at one time suggested though disapproved, was ever made; and when propositions for such submission were presented by way of amendment to the report of the committee on submission, they were uniformly voted down. The pretence was, that they ought to have been presented in some other way. Nothing in the matter, however, is entirely clear but that the majority of the Convention were resolved that the Constitution should be submitted as a whole. The presumption, therefore, indulged by the court, that the Convention, which, in the same opinion, it was pronouncing guilty of disobedience to law, was, in respect to the matter of separate submission, obedient, because it was not affirmatively shown to have been the contrary, though technically correct, perhaps, goes but little way to exculpate the majority of that body. For the whole debate, see *Deb. Pa. Conv.* 1872, Vol. VIII. pp. 620–712.

people, and this consent must be legally gathered or obtained. The people here meant are the whole, — those who constitute the entire State, male and female citizens, infants and adults. A mere majority of those persons who are qualified electors are not the people, though, when authorized to do so, they may represent the whole people. The words 'in such manner as they may think proper,' in the declaration of rights, embrace but three known recognized modes by which the whole people, the State, can give their consent to an alteration of an existing lawful form of government, viz.: —

"1. The mode provided in the existing Constitution.

"2. A law, as the instrumental process of raising the body for revision and conveying to it the powers of the people.

"3. A revolution.

"The first two are peaceful means through which the consent of the people to alteration is obtained, and by which the existing government consents to be displaced without revolution. The government gives its consent, either by pursuing the mode provided in the Constitution, or by passing a law to call a Convention. If consent be not so given by the existing government, the remedy of the people is in the third mode, — revolution."

From these premises the court draw the following conclusions:

"The people, that entire body called the State, can be bound as a whole only by an act of authority proceding from *themselves*." The authority to speak for them, in a state of peace, the people "confer upon a part only, at an election authorized by law, and the electors at such election must be those who possess the qualifications sanctioned by the people in order to represent them; otherwise they speak for themselves only." "As it is not pretended that the Convention was sitting as a revolutionary body, and as it did not proceed in the mode provided for amendment in the Constitution, it was therefore the offspring of *law*. It had no other source of existence.

"The legislature having adopted a proceeding by law as the means of executing their will, and that law being thus the instrument chosen to express their will, it necessarily became the channel of their authority, and the only chart" of the Convention's powers. "In a state of peace a law is the only means by which the will of the whole people can be collected in an authorized form, and by which the powers of the people can be delegated to the agents who compose the Convention." "The form of the law is immaterial. It may be a law to confer general authority, or to confer special authority. It may be an invitation, in the first place, to meet in primary assemblies to select delegates, and confer on them constituted powers; or a law to take the sense of the people on the question of calling a Convention, and then a law to make the call, and confer the powers the people intend to confer upon their agents." To the question, What powers were conferred upon the late Convention? the answer must be that "by the first Act," that of 1871, "entitled 'An Act to authorize a popular vote upon the question of calling a Convention,' the one subject of both title and text is the *question of calling* a Convention. That question was authorized to be submitted to a popular vote. That question was answered in the affirmative: the people, answering the legislature, said, 'You may call a Convention.' This was all the vote expressed." "It is evident that, had the matter dropped there, and the legislature had made no call, no Convention and no terms would ever have existed. Not a line, nor a word, nor a syllable in this Act expresses an intent to make the call themselves, or on what terms it shall be made, or what powers shall be conferred. Did the people by this Act, without an expressed intent and by mere inference, intend to abdicate all their own power, their rights, their interests, and their duty to each other, in favor of a body of mere agents, and to confer upon them, by a blank warrant, the absolute power to dictate their institutions, and to determine finally upon all their most cherished interests?" "When, therefore, the people elected delegates under the second Act, they adopted the terms it contained by acting under it. The delegates so elected are clearly estopped by the record itself from denying the terms under which they hold their seats, for they hold them under that Act and no other." Among the terms contained in the Act is one that "the election to decide for or against the adoption of the new Constitution, or specific amendments, shall be conducted as the general elections of this commonwealth are now by law conducted." . . . "This section of the law is mandatory, and is so for the best of reasons, — it is the only legally authorized means of taking the sense of the people upon adoption of the amendments which can bind the whole people." "It is therefore clear to our minds that the ordinance relating to the election in the city of Philadelphia is flatly opposed to the Act of 1872, and is therefore illegal and void."[1]

§ 409 *c.* Afterwards a bill was filed in Pittsburgh, in another county, praying for an injunction against holding any election in that county, upon the same grounds set out in the bills above described, and upon the further ground, that the action of the Convention in altering several of the provisions of the Bill of Rights, contrary to the limitations imposed by the Act calling it, was illegal. The lower court refused the injunction, on the ground, that these limitations were not binding upon the Convention, since that body, it said, was possessed of sovereign power; and that, conceding the ordinance for holding the election in Philadelphia to be illegal, it had no bearing upon Allegheny County, and the court would not entertain a bill for an injunction filed by parties as to whom the legality or illegality of the ordinance in reference to Philadelphia, in another county, was a mere abstract question. On appeal to the Supreme Court, this judgment of the court below was affirmed. This decision of the Supreme Court, at first sight, appears to be a reversal of its previous decision in Wells *v.* Bain and Donnelly *v.* Fitler, described in the preceding section, but it was in fact a confirmation of the principles announced in that decision. After the former, and before the present decision was rendered, the Constitution framed by the Convention had been submitted to and adopted by the people, including the change recommended to be made in the Bill of Rights; and thus, however irregular, or even revolutionary, its inception had been, it had become the fundamental law of the State, and the Supreme Court must accept it as such. But while the court held that the Constitution as a whole was binding upon that tribunal because ratified by the people, it proceeded, in a most impressive and luminous judgment, to repudiate the doctrine propounded by the court below as to the possession by the Convention of sovereign power. After rehearsing the facts above stated, the court say: —

"The change made by the people in their political institutions by the adoption of the proposed Constitution since this decree" (was entered by the court below) "forbids an inquiry into the merits of this case. The question is no longer judicial, but in affirming the decree we must not seem to sanction any doctrine

[1] Wells *v.* Bain, and Donnelly *v.* Fitler, 75 Pa. St. R. 39, 55, 56.

in the opinion dangerous to the liberties of the people. The claim for absolute sovereignty in the Convention, apparently sustained in the opinion, is of such magnitude and overwhelming importance to the people themselves that it cannot be passed unnoticed." After stating that in the preceding case of Wells *v.* Bain it had been claimed for the Convention that it had the power to ordain ordinances having the present force of law, and the instant power to proclaim a Constitution, binding without ratification, irrespective of the manner adopted by the people of exercising their right to alter or amend their frame of government, and that this imputed sovereignty in a Convention called and organized under a law, as the very means adopted by the people to exercise their reserved right of amendment, was not discussed in that case with the fulness the importance of the question to the people demanded, the court say: —

"A Convention has no inherent rights; it exercises powers only. Delegated power defines itself. To be delegated it must come in some adopted manner to convey it by some defined means. The right of the people is absolute to alter, reform, or abolish their government in such manner as they may think proper. This right being theirs, they may impart so much or so little of it as they shall deem expedient. It is only when they exercise this right, and not before, they determine, by the mode they choose to adopt, the extent of the powers they intend to delegate. Hence the argument which imputes sovereignty to a Convention, because of the reservation in the Bill of Rights, is utterly illogical and unsound. The Bill of Rights is a reservation (by the people) 'of rights out of the general powers of government to *themselves*, but is no delegation of power to a Convention. If, by a mere determination of the people to call a Convention, whether it be by a vote or otherwise, the entire sovereignty of the people passes *ipso facto* into a body of deputies or attorneys, so that these deputies can, without ratification, alter a government and abolish its Bill of Rights at pleasure, and impose at will a new government upon the people, without restraints upon the governing power, no true liberty remains. . . . The people have the same right to limit the powers of their delegates that they have to bound the power of their representatives. Each are representatives, but only in a different sphere. It is simply evasive to affirm that the legislature cannot limit the right of the people to alter or reform their government. Certainly it cannot. The question is not upon the power of the legislature to restrain the people, but upon the right of the people, by the instrumentality of the law, to limit their delegates. Law is the highest form of a people's will in a state of peaceful government. When a people act through a law, the act is theirs, and the fact that they used the legislature as their instrument to confer their powers makes them the superiors, and not the legislature. The idea which lies at the root of the fallacy that a Convention cannot be controlled by law is, that the Convention and the people are identical. . . . The calling of a Convention and regulating its action by law is not forbidden in the Constitution. It is a conceded manner through which the people may exercise the right reserved in the Bill of Rights. . . . The right of the people to restrain their delegates by *law* cannot be denied unless the power to call a Convention by law, and the right of self-protection, be also denied. . . . If the authority of the people passes to the Convention outside of the law, the people are left without the means of self-protection except by revolution. . . . In conclusion, we find nothing in the Bill of Rights, in the vote under the Act of 1871, or the authority conferred in the Act of 1872, nothing in the nature of delegated power, or in the constitution of the Convention itself, which can justify an assumption that a Convention so called, constituted, organized, and limited, can take from the people their sovereign right to ratify or reject a Constitution or ordinance framed by it, or can infuse present life and vigor into its work before its adoption by the people." [1]

§ 409 *d*. The judgment of the Supreme Court allowing the injunction in *Wells* v. *Bain*, though not rendered until the 5th of December, 1873, two days after the Convention had completed its labors, had been, it seems, so far anticipated by that body that it adjourned to the 27th of the same month, at which time the election for the adoption or rejection of the Constitution, fixed by the Convention for the 16th, would have been held. The purpose of this action, as declared by the resolution of adjournment, was to examine the returns of votes polled for and against the new Constitution before proclamation should be made by the Governor, and to take cognizance and dispose of frauds, if any should be practised at said election, and to transact "such

[1] Wood's Appeal, 75 Pa. St. R. 71.

other business as may be deemed necessary and proper." The last clause doubtless concealed, in its general terms, the real design of the Convention to take further action in the line of its function as a Convention, and of its claim of powers to nullify the Act of the legislature, and not simply to examine the returns and to dispose of frauds, — an exercise of power not only needless, but, until it was thus specified, unheard of. Whatever its purpose, as the Constitution was adopted by the people, it became unnecessary to do either of the things stated in its resolution. After having audited and allowed, therefore, a bill presented for expenses incurred by the commissioners appointed by the Convention to conduct the election in Philadelphia, whose proceedings had been stopped by injunction, it merely passed resolutions respecting the powers belonging to it, which it deemed infringed by the action of the legislature and of the Supreme Court, and then adjourned *sine die.*

The resolutions were as follows: —

"1. *Resolved*, That this Convention was called by the authority of the people, as determined by their vote under the Act of 1871 declaring that a Convention should be called to amend the Constitution of this commonwealth; and that this vote was a mandate to the legislature, which that body was not at liberty to disobey or modify.

"2. *Resolved*, That the Constitution of this State is the only recognized form of its government; and the people having expressly reserved to themselves the right to alter, reform, or abolish their government in such manner as they think proper, and having in distinct terms excepted this right out of the general powers of government, and declared that such right shall forever remain inviolate, this Convention deems it to be its duty to declare, that it is not in the power of any department of an existing government to limit or control the powers of a Convention called by the people to reform their Constitution; and that the Convention, subject to the Constitution of the United States, is answerable only to the people from whom it derived its power."

One member of the committee which reported the resolutions, however, dissented from the action of the majority, on the ground that, "since the submission to and adoption by the people, the labors and duties of the Convention had practically ceased, and that it was unwise and inexpedient at that time to make any enunciation of Constitutional Convention powers, which, not being submitted to or acted on by the people, would only be an expression of the opinion of a majority of the Convention."[1] To this the minority might have added that, when the Convention had completed the Constitution it proposed for adoption, and had submitted it to the people, its function as a Convention had ceased and determined, and that its adjournment to a future day, to take further action, was not authorized by the act either of the people or of the legislature. The former, to adopt the phraseology of the Convention, had recommended the call of a Convention "to amend the Constitution of this commonwealth," but it had given no further power; and the latter, in making the call, had declared its purpose to be "to revise and amend the Constitution of this State," with further provisions for submitting the same to the people, but with no other or greater powers, and it made no mention of adjourning to a day certain, subsequent to the election by the people. Its assumption of the power thus to adjourn was, therefore, a usurpation on the part of the Convention.[2]

§ 409 *e.* The importance of the subject may justify a further remark in regard to the matter in controversy between the Pennsylvania Convention of 1872, on the one hand, and the legislature supported by the Supreme Court, on the other. Looking at it from the side of the legislature, the impolicy of the restriction it imposed in respect to altering the Bill of Rights is very apparent. Both Acts resulting in the election of the Convention — that submitting the question of calling it to the people, and that making the call — expressed the purpose to be "to amend," or "to revise and amend," the Constitution. In the term "Constitution" is generally embraced, as the term is now used, both the Constitution in its narrower sense — that is, the "Frame of Government" — and the Bill of Rights. The legislature might well have anticipated, therefore, that a Convention disposed to stand upon its extreme rights would claim authority to alter or amend one as well as the other. The changes in the Bill of Rights recommended by the Convention and adopted by the people, though not very extensive or radical, constituted valuable additions to the existing securities of private rights: that to Section 7, for in-

[1] See *Deb. Pa. Const. Conv.* 1872, Vol. VIII. pp. 732, 742, 743.

[2] See §§ 473–478, *post.*

stance, forbidding convictions for newspaper libels relating to the conduct of officers or men in a public capacity, or to any other matter proper for public investigation or information, when the fact that such publication was not maliciously or negligently made should be established to the satisfaction of the jury, instead of the provision of the existing Constitution permitting the truth to be given in evidence in such suits; and the amendment to Section 17, which, to the provision of the existing Constitution forbidding *ex post facto* laws, or laws impairing the obligation of contracts, added the words, "or making irrevocable any grant of special privileges or immunities." The other amendments were either slight or incapable of enforcement, as aimed at the interference of the United States in State elections when not invited by the State authorities.

The legislature therefore, in forbidding any change, must be presumed to have been ill-advised as to the wishes of the people in regard to altering that part of the Constitution. It clearly would have been better for it to trust the Convention than to attempt to restrict it in regard to what it should or should not propose when that body could point to a general authority that appeared to authorize amendments to the whole Constitution. The legislature, in other words, attempted that in which the chances were equal that it would fail, and in which it did fail. Such a contest, save where public opinion backing the legislature was largely preponderant, and the matter prohibited to the Convention was of vital importance, should have been avoided. But, if it were deemed advisable to risk a contest, the possibility of a defeat should have been forestalled by requiring the members of the Convention to subscribe an oath of obedience to the behests of the legislature, as a condition of their taking their seats, and by declaring disobedience, after subscribing the same, to be a felony.

So far of the case from the side of the legislature. From that of the Convention: what course, then presenting itself to that body, was the most patriotic one for it to pursue? It was not pretended that there was urgent need or pressure for the amendment of the Bill of Rights. It was stated in the Convention as a fact that the committee on the Bill of Rights was appointed rather as a declaration on the part of the Convention that it could not be limited by the legislature, than because the members desired to make any change in that article.[1] The people adopted it when proposed, but as the Constitution was submitted as a whole, to vote against the proposed amendment was, perhaps, to defeat the Constitution, which as a whole was highly acceptable to the people. They ratified it by a vote of two to one, but it is improbable that many votes were gained for it, and probable that many were lost, because of the change proposed in the Bill of Rights. When disobedience to an impolitic, or even an unjust, act of legislation is likely to yield no material benefit, but to become a precedent of indiscriminate disobedience hereafter, it is the part of wisdom and of patriotism to obey. That principle might well have led the Convention to leave the Bill of Rights unchanged, thus obeying the mandate of the legislature in regard to the Bill of Rights, as it did that relating to the creation of courts "with exclusive equity jurisdiction," which had also been interdicted.

As to the other restrictions imposed by the legislature touching the mode of submitting the new Constitution to the people, one and, perhaps, two of which the Convention disregarded, there can be no question that the legislature had but exercised its rightful jurisdiction in imposing those restrictions, and that the Convention was clearly wrong in disregarding them or either of them. As we have seen, it is not unusual to insert in Convention Acts positive directions as to the time and mode of submitting the Constitution to be framed by a Convention to the people, and it is not unfrequently required that the proposed amendments shall be submitted separately, unless the Convention shall be of opinion that they are so connected with, or dependent upon, other provisions, that, if voted on separately, the system might be rendered inharmonious; and in no case, it is believed, save that of the Pennsylvania Convention, has the direction of the legislature in that regard been disobeyed. The precedents, therefore, on the point, are against the Convention. Considered on principle, the question is still clearer against that body. To submit a Constitution to the people requires the services of the various State functionaries now in office, who know not the Convention as a source of authority to command them, but who know only the legislature and the people, through whom they received their commissions. The act of submission is an act of

[1] See *Deb. Pa. Conv.* 1872, Vol. VIII. pp. 54, 57, 647.

ordinary legislation to which the legislature is competent, and to which the Convention, unless expressly authorized, is incompetent. Where, of the possible and usual modes of submission, some are expressly interdicted, as in the Pennsylvania Act, no such authority as to those interdicted could be pretended. As intimated by the Supreme Court of that State, the source of the Convention's powers is the Convention Act alone; and when that specially denies to it certain powers, it cannot exercise them without a violation of law. It is simply a question of power.[1]

§ 410. 2. The principles settled by the preceding discussion make it easy to answer another question relating to the power of a legislature over a Convention, namely, Can the former bind the latter to submit the fruit of its labors to a vote of the people? If it be granted that a legislature can bind a Convention in any particular, it is plain that the power ought to exist more especially in such matters as relate to its modes of organization

[1] On the power of a legislature to bind a Convention in relation to submission to the people, see, further, §§ 410-414, *post*. One of the ablest lawyers in the Pennsylvania Convention, who participated in the discussion of a report recommending the appointment of a Committee on the Bill of Rights, was the late Judge Jeremiah S. Black, the delegate from York. Upon the question of the power of that body to alter the Bill of Rights, and so in relation to the propriety of appointing such a committee, Judge Black said: "I only want to say now that we are not a revolutionary body, but a body that is acting under and in pursuance of law. Suppose the legislature had seen proper to say we should not assemble at all, or that we should make no amendments to the Constitution, — that the Constitution should stand just as it is; then the question is, whether we could, in defiance of that mandate, assemble ourselves together in Convention representing as we do the whole people of the Commonwealth, and, against the will of the people and against the authority of the organized government now existing, proceed to alter the body of it. I say we could not do that. That would be revolutionary. Where do we get the power? Where does it come from? Nobody will deny that we are sitting here in pursuance of certain Acts of the legislature, — the two Acts of the legislature, — one which first authorized a vote by the people upon the question, and the other one which authorized the election of delegates to the Convention. If we derive our power from that source, is it possible that we can take it without the limitations that were imposed upon it by those who created it? I don't think that question can be answered in any but one way." *Deb. Pa. Conv.* 1872. Vol. I. pp. 57, 58. It may be observed that there are but two alternatives: either the law is as stated by Judge Black, or a Convention, once convened, is absolutely supreme over the existing government of the State; and if it submit its work to the people for adoption or rejection, it is of its mere grace and favor, which, if it please, it may entirely withhold.

and proceeding, — that is, to questions of method; and that the region of greatest doubt would commence when questions began to arise touching *what* the Convention should or should not consider or recommend. Among questions of the former kind, relating to its method of procedure, that which is by far of most vital consequence is, What disposition shall be made by the Convention of the work of its hands?

Two courses only are possible:

First. The Convention might finish its deliberations, and, without further ado, publish its work as the supreme law of the land; or,

Secondly. It might regard its action as only inchoate or provisional, and accordingly submit the fruit of it to the people, its master, for approval or disapproval.

§ 411. Of the two courses indicated, the first is wholly inadmissible in any case whatever, that alone excepted in which it should be adopted under the express authority of law. The reason is, that it would make of the Convention a simple despot; and if despotic authority is desired, it would be far better to have the concentrated vigor of an absolute monarch, whose rule is commonly "tempered," if no otherwise, "by assassination," into a sort of practical responsibility to the people, or the temperate administration of a legislature of two houses, in which passion and ambition would, by a system of checks, be rendered least dangerous to the Commonwealth. The history of liberty has shown, that the most direct road to the ruin of a free state is to make a single popular assembly the dispenser of its ordinary statute law. But to intrust such a body, without check, with the enactment of its fundamental law, would be but to discount the national life, — to antedate that final overthrow which history shows to be in store for all nations.[1]

§ 412. The second course is for the Convention to recognize the limitation upon its powers, imposed, if not in express terms by the Act calling it, then by the principles of constitutional government, as well as by the customary law regulating the action of such bodies in America, and to submit the propositions it may mature to a vote of the people. By this course only can there be assured to the sovereign or nation at large that firm hold upon its liberties, that practical dominion over all function-

[1] See Parker *v.* The Commonwealth, 6 Barr, 509.

aries empowered to act in its stead, which constitutes a government of law as distinguished from a revolutionary tribunal, in which no law is obeyed but the passions or interests of those who direct it.

§ 413. These two courses being the only possible ones, it needs no argument to show, not only that the Convention ought to follow that which is compatible with the continued healthy life of the state, but that there ought to be provided some mode in which it may be compelled to follow it — some power by which, the possibility of its refusal to do so being anticipated, provision may be made against a career of usurpation — by which treasonable conduct may be averted by denouncing against it summary punishment. Undoubtedly, for this purpose, the legislature is the department having power to make the requisite provisions. To deny to that body the right to hedge about the institutions in which our liberties are embodied, would be to make it adequate to the transitory and more trivial subjects of legislation, but inadequate to those which, while they are no less strictly matters of legislative cognizance, far transcend in importance all others that can arise.

§ 414. As a practical question, the right of a legislature to require a Convention to submit its recommendations to a vote of the people has been several times discussed, and intimations have been thrown out that the latter body might disregard the requirement, but no attempt has ever been made, so far as I am aware, to carry that supposed right into effect. In the Illinois Conventions of 1847 and 1862, it was contended by a few members that the Convention was, for the purposes for which it was assembled, sovereign, and that, although an act of legislation was doubtless needful to bring the body into existence, yet, when once born, its sovereignty attached, and it could disregard all the provisions of the Act at its pleasure. Hence it was concluded, that those bodies might or might not submit the result of their labors to the people, notwithstanding the positive injunctions of the legislature, as their own views of expediency should dictate.

In reply to these arguments, I do not deem it necessary to adduce any considerations other than those so often urged in preceding pages, to refute their fundamental principle — that of conventional sovereignty. Those arguments seem to have had little effect upon either of the bodies to which they were addressed, and possibly were propounded merely to pave the way for certain aberrations in the mode of submission to the people, which will be hereafter discussed; for the Constitutions framed by those Conventions were each submitted to the people in substantial compliance with the Acts under which they assembled, except a few sections which, for special reasons, and contrary to the spirit, if not to the letter, of those Acts, were withheld from submission, or submitted in an unusual and exceptionable manner.

§ 415. 3. Connected with the subject of legislatures by their Acts binding Conventions, as well as that of submitting Constitutions to the people just referred to, is a question that arose in 1857–8, in Kansas, during the struggle that finally resulted in the admission of that State into the Union, namely, whether, if a Convention has taken upon itself to submit a Constitution framed by it to the people, on a particular day and in a particular manner, the legislature of the State may alter the time and mode of such submission? This question evidently involves directly that of legislative supremacy as between legislatures and Conventions, and, therefore, although it might appropriately be discussed in other relations than the present, I deem it proper to consider it in this connection. The facts under which the question arose are as follows: —

In 1855, the first territorial legislature of Kansas passed an Act to take the sense of the people at the election in October, 1856, on the call of a Convention to form a State Constitution. Accordingly, an election was held, at which about 2500 votes, cast mainly by pro-slavery voters, were polled, the Free-State men not voting. At this election a new legislature was elected, all pro-slavery, which met in January, 1857, and in conformity with the vote of the 2500 at the preceding October election, passed an Act providing for an election of delegates on the 15th of June, to meet in Convention in September following. The delegates elected assembled in Convention at Lecompton, September 5th, but soon adjourned over to October, to await the result of the general election to be held on the first Monday of that month. At this election both parties nominated candidates, and after rejecting fraudulent votes, the Free-State party carried the Territorial legislature and the delegate to Congress. The

Convention reassembled in October, after this election, formed the Constitution afterwards so famous as the Lecompton Constitution, and submitted only a portion of it to the people — that portion relating to slavery — and that in a form and under a test oath which would prevent the Free-State people from voting. December 17th following, the legislature, containing a Free-State majority, assembled and passed an Act to submit the Lecompton Constitution fairly to a vote of the people, on the 4th of January, 1858. On the 21st of December, 1857, the vote was taken in the manner prescribed by the Convention, and resulted as follows: —

For the Constitution with slavery	6266
For the Constitution without slavery	567

January 4, 1858, in accordance with the Act of the Territorial legislature, the people voted as follows: —

For the Lecompton Constitution with slavery	138
For the Lecompton Constitution without slavery . .	24
Against the Lecompton Constitution	10,226

§ 416. Here the discrepancy being so enormous, and the apparent results, though contradictory, so decisive, the question becomes of great importance, Which of the two elections was authorized by law and which was not? This question evidently depends, as a legal one, on the power of a legislature, or the successor of a legislature, by which a Convention has been called, to alter a regulation made by the latter in relation to the time and manner of submitting a Constitution to the people. And this again depends upon the question whether the making of regulations touching the submission of Constitutions to the people is an exercise of ordinary or of fundamental legislation. If it be the former, it belongs exclusively to the legislature, whether that body claims it or yields it to the Convention. And, if the right to submit belongs exclusively to the legislature, any Act of a Convention having for its purpose such submission would be wholly invalid, unless ratified by such legislature, or by the acquiescence of the people. From this it follows, that if the legislature were to dissent from the dispositions made by a Convention and to make new ones, the latter would in effect be rather original Acts than alterations of Acts previously passed; that is, in them alone would there at any time be any validity whatever. Doubtless, Conventions have been sometimes empowered to make such provisions as they may deem advisable respecting the submission of the fruit of their labors to the people, in terms which seem to give them a discretion to submit or not, as they please, and perhaps no great evil has as yet practically resulted from so doing. But such legislation is believed to be ill-judged, and it may be dangerous. To demonstrate this, it is necessary only to advert to a single circumstance, which is, that whenever the providing for submission to the people is remitted to a Convention, the power is given to that body absolutely. There is no such thing as taking the sense of the people on the propriety of any provisions the Convention may make, for they are to take effect prior to, or at latest, contemporaneously with, the popular vote, with the single exception of such as relate to the returning and counting of the votes. The result is, that a body whose function is, and can safely be, at most, only that of a committee, is vested with an absolute discretion in a point of infinite importance to the public welfare. This would be eminently unsafe, were the trust confined to ordinary legislation; but it is not. It has a decisive influence upon the passing or not passing of the fundamental law, and may even determine its character.

§ 417. The principal reasons why such legislation as is necessary to submit to the people the fruits of the deliberations of a Convention, should be performed by the legislature, are, first, that that legislation is not fundamental in its character; and, secondly, that a legislature, and no other body, is, under our Constitutions, competent to perform that work, and that the legislature has no constitutional authority to delegate the right to perform it to any other body.

The principles upon which the first of these propositions rests have been the subject of extended examination in a former chapter, in which was considered the distinction between the two kinds of legislation specified.[1] It needs therefore only to be remarked here, that in an Act having for its purpose the submission of fundamental laws to the people, there is nothing whatever of a fundamental character. It is a simple exercise of ordinary legislation — an adapting of means to an end —

[1] See *ante*, §§ 85-87.

depending for its particular character upon current views of expediency. Hence it is worthy of note, that such Acts, even when passed in the shape of ordinances by Conventions, are generally not accounted parts of the Constitution. They are commonly made to figure in the Schedule, which, as we have seen, is the repository of provisions intended to facilitate the transition from an order of things going out with an old, to that coming in with a new, Constitution. Hence such Acts, being temporary in purpose and effect, are not really proper to rank as constitutional provisions, though they have been held to be as binding upon the various departments of the government as if they had been embodied in the Constitution.[1]

§ 418. In relation to the second proposition, it is so purely a legal one, and is so well settled, that there is even less need of dwelling upon it at length. No position is better established in American law than that ordinary legislation belongs exclusively to the legislature proper, and cannot be delegated even to the people or electors, who are in one sense superior to both legislatures and Conventions. Thus, the Supreme Court of Delaware, in a case where the question arose as to the constitutionality of an Act of the legislature entitled, "An Act authorizing the people to decide by ballot whether the license to retail intoxicating liquors shall be permitted among them," upon that question, said: —

"It is . . . . clear that neither the legislative, executive, nor judicial departments, separately nor all combined, can devolve on the people the exercise of any part of the sovereign power with which each is invested. The assumption of a power to do so would be usurpation. . . . . The powers of government are trusts of the highest importance; on the faithful and proper exercise of which depend the welfare and happiness of society. These trusts must be exercised in strict conformity with the spirit and intention of the Constitution, by those with whom they are deposited; and in no case whatever can they be transferred or delegated to any other body or persons; not even to the whole people of the State; still less to the people of a county. . . . . If the legislative functions can be transferred or delegated to the people, so can the executive or judicial power. The absurd spectacle of a governor referring it to a

[1] Stewart *v.* Crosby, 15 Texas R 546; see also § 103 *a*, *ante*.

popular vote, whether a criminal, convicted of a capital offence, should be pardoned or executed, would be the subject of universal ridicule; and were a court of justice, instead of deciding a case themselves, to direct the prothonotary to enter judgment for the plaintiff or defendant, according to the popular vote of a county, the community would be disgusted with the folly, injustice, and iniquity of the proceeding. All will admit that, in such cases, the people are totally incompetent to decide correctly. Equally incompetent are they to exercise with discernment and discretion collectively, or by means of the ballot-box, the power of legislation; because, under such circumstances, passion and prejudice incapacitate them for deliberation."[1]

If weight is to be given to this and numerous other decisions of our courts, according with it in principle, it is clear then that the function, often assumed by Conventions, of submitting to the people the results of their deliberations more properly belongs to the legislature, the latter being the only body which can constitutionally make the requisite legislative provisions. It follows, therefore, that if the provisions made by a Convention for submitting its work to the people are deemed to be inexpedient, whether made with or without authority of law, the proper law-making authority of the State may repeal or alter them at pleasure.[2]

§ 419. (*b.*) In the preceding sections have been considered

[1] Rice *v.* Foster, 4 Harr. (Del.) R. 479. See also the following cases, in which the same rule is maintained: Bradley *v.* Baxter, 15 Barb. R. 122; People *v.* Collins, 3 Mich. R. 343; Case of the Borough of West Philadelphia, 5 W. & S. R. 281; Barto *v.* Himrod, 4 Seld. R. 483; Maize *v.* The State, 4 Porter's (Ind.) R. 342; Parker *v.* Commonwealth, 6 Barr's R. 509. But see Smith *v.* Bryan, 5 Gilm. (Ill.) R. 1.

[2] For a consideration of the question whether, when a legislature has passed an Act calling a Convention, it may modify or repeal it, see *ante*, §§ 389–409. If it has that power, up to what point of time it continues to exist, and whether it may be exercised to abolish a Convention already in session, by repealing the Act calling it, and ordering the members of the Convention to disperse, is one that has never arisen practically, and upon which, therefore, it may be useless to speculate. If the safety of the State, endangered by treason in the Convention, seemed to demand it, it is not easy to see how a legislature or a valid State government, charged with the defence of the public liberties, could excuse itself for permitting the treason to ripen unopposed. That a legislature has that power was maintained by Judge Joel Parker in the Massachusetts Convention of 1853. *Deb. Mass. Conv.* 1853, Vol. I. p. 155. But see Appendix D, *post.*

the general relations of legislatures to Conventions, and the power of the former, by their enactments, to bind the latter, concluding with a discussion of some questions involving an application of the principles which determine those relations and limit that power. Another and not less important aspect of the same relations remains to be considered, namely, that in which the Convention is regarded as the active body, exercising powers, or assuming functions; while the legislature, to which that action is conceived to be relative, is passive, or out of sight.

Under this phase of the subject various questions arise, but they all resolve themselves substantially into the following, which I purpose, therefore, to discuss at some length, namely —

1. Is a Convention possessed of legislative powers?

2. Can a Convention act as a legislature in matters by the Federal Constitution required to be transacted by the legislatures of the several States?

3. Can a Convention fetter a discretion confided to the State legislatures by the Federal Constitution?

§ 420. 1. We have seen that, in the United States, the constitutional Convention belongs to the *genus* legislature, — by which is meant that its proper function is to elaborate, to a certain extent, to be determined by the tenor of its commission, the fundamental law, much as the legislature enacts the ordinary municipal law. Of these two species of law, the distinction between which has been already explained, it is the important thing to note, that the one denominated fundamental is, generally speaking, the work only of a Convention, a special and extraordinary assembly, convening at no regularly recurring periods, but whenever the harvest of constitutional reforms has become ripe; while, on the other hand, the ordinary statute law, whose provisions are tentatory and transient, is, regularly at least, the work of a legislature, — a body meeting periodically at short intervals of time. It is thoroughly settled that, under our Constitutions, State and Federal, a legislature cannot exercise the functions of a Convention, — cannot, in other words, take upon itself the duty of framing, amending, or suspending the operation of the fundamental law.[1] Being the supreme law of

[1] The same also is true of the legislatures of all constitutional governments, excepting, perhaps, that of England. Vattel, *Law of Nations*, Bk. I. ch. 3, §§ 34, 35

the land, all departments of the government are subject to its control, for from and under it they derive both their commissions and their existence; and to permit either of them to modify it would be to invert the relations of dependence on which the safety of the whole system depends. This has never been doubted since the early days of the Republic.[1] Does an analogous rule prevail in relation to the Convention, the framer of the fundamental law? Or may it, by virtue of some transcendent power inherent in it, or of well-established custom or precedent, overleap all bounds interposed to limit its competence, and take upon itself the function of legislation in general?

§ 421. This question will be examined upon both of the grounds indicated, in their order, namely, first, upon that of inherent power; and, secondly, upon that of custom or precedent.

First. The reasoning of those who assert for the Convention a general power of legislation is, in its last analysis, that by which is vindicated the doctrine of conventional sovereignty, of which, in its general form, a refutation has already been attempted.[2] The particular argument in this connection is, that the business of a Convention is extraordinary, beyond the competence of either of the recognized ordinary agencies of the sovereign; that that body receives its commission from the same source as do those agencies, and, therefore, on the whole, is entitled to outrank them all; that, although as a prudent precaution against dissatisfaction or cavil, it is doubtless better for a Convention to forego the exercise of extreme rights and to submit its work to the judgment of the people, yet, that it is not true that it lacks power directly and definitively to enact the supreme law of the land; that if this be conceded, it needs only to analyze the general power thus described into its constituents to find the power in question; that the fundamental conception of the business of a Convention is, that it takes to pieces, or, as it is sometimes expressed, "tramples under its feet," the existing Constitution of a State, and out of the old materials, or out of

[1] It is true, some confusion existed on this subject in some of the States, under their first Constitutions; but the question of the power of their legislatures was soon settled by the courts, as above indicated. See Kamper *v.* Hawkins, 1 Va. Crim. Cas. 20.

[2] See *ante*, §§ 315–319.

old and new together, erects a structure to fill its place; that with the Constitution falls, of course, the government of the State; that, starting thus, potentially, at least, according to its own will, with a clean slate, to deny to the body possessing such omnipotence the power of legislation, would be to deny that the greater includes the less; that, if it can enact the fundamental law, why not also the ordinary statute law, of which the nature, it is true, is somewhat dissimilar, but whose importance is vastly inferior? that a Convention is competent, by constitutional provision, to abolish all existing agencies of government, and to fill their places with others, constructed on different principles; is it then conceivable, it is asked, that it cannot do directly what it can do indirectly, or that the right to exercise so exalted a prerogative is conditioned upon its exercise in a particular mode? that as a matter of fact, the Convention, through its relations to the several departments of the government, as in turn their destroyer and their creator, can exercise at will the functions of each of them; that being "a virtual assemblage of the people," it wields all the powers which the people themselves would possess were it, in the nature of things, possible for them to act directly; hence, that, within the bounds fixed by its own discretion, a Convention may make laws, or may interpret or execute them.

§ 422. To this argument, the following considerations constitute, in my judgment, a complete answer: —

If "the safety of the people is the supreme law," — of which there is no doubt, and which I affirm, — the maxim involves both a grant of power and a limitation of power. It is a grant of power, inasmuch as it authorizes and requires all public functionaries to protect and defend the people at whatever cost; to do it, however, by adhering, first, to the letter, and secondly, to the spirit of their instructions, that is, of the Constitution and laws; and, thirdly, to the principles on which the social edifice is bottomed. When the letter of the law is silent, or its spirit doubtful, the principles indicated are the only chart by which official conduct can be regulated, and are the first in validity and sacredness, since they are the sum of the letter and spirit of positive law, as well as of that unwritten law which presided at the genesis of the social state anterior to all positive law. Hence, it is plainly the duty of such functionaries always to conform to those principles, since a disregard of them involves, in substance, a violation of the letter and spirit of the positive law, and, at length, the ruin of the Commonwealth. Do what necessity requires, and ask for indemnity for technical breaches of law, is the rule of practical conduct dictated by the maxim under consideration.[1]

As a limitation of power, the same maxim is of extensive application. In cases of doubtful construction of constitutional provisions, or in which there are no express provisions determining grants of power, it is the most important touchstone in our whole system. Starting with the postulate of representative republican institutions, the two following propositions must be accepted, — first, that whatever manifestly endangers the safety of those institutions must be forborne, though authorized by an express grant of power; and, secondly, that no act whatever must be done or tolerated, in the absence of such a grant, of which the tendency, or, still more, the direct effect would be to endanger them. In the case last supposed, no power to do the act could be implied, under any circumstances whatever, no matter how clearly it might seem, for the time, to be expedient.[2]

§ 423. Now, in the light of these principles, is the exercise by a Convention of legislative, or other governmental powers, in addition to those clearly belonging to it, to be considered as within its competence, as a constitutional body? Is such an assumption of power one which threatens no danger to the Commonwealth? By the theory of those who accord to it such powers, as soon as the Convention is assembled, the control of the existing government over it is at an end; the Constitution lies torn into fragments under its feet; and while the work of its instauration is in progress, that body alone constitutes the state, gathering into its single hands the reins ordinarily held by the four great systems of agencies constituting the government, to whose functions it succeeds. If this be so, what, but its own sense of justice, is to restrain such a body from running riot as did the Thirty Tyrants at Athens? The jurists of the Illinois Convention of 1862, as we have seen, affirmed, that the Act under which such a body assembles, is no longer binding,

[1] See Rice *v.* Foster, 4 Harrington's R. 479 (485).

[2] Rice *v.* Foster, *ubi supra.*

when once it has become organized. If, at that moment, it has also cast upon it, by virtue of its great commission, all governmental powers, how easy to extend the scope and the period of the exercise of those powers, under the plea that expediency demands it. The expedient is the appropriate domain of a legislature. If, at the moment of organizing, a Convention is endowed with legislative powers, it may be deemed expedient to subvert the system of guarantees by which our liberties are assured to us, and at the same time to withhold from the popular vote the constitutional provisions by which the change is to be effected. Such a consummation would be not merely possible; it would be probable. And, clearly, the possibility of its occurring with an appearance of rightfulness, is enough to stamp as dangerous that theory of conventional powers from which it must flow. In the science of politics, it is an important point gained to have settled the limit where normal action under the Constitution ends, and revolution begins. To have done that is practically, in most cases, to have rendered revolution impossible.

The result is, that a Convention cannot assume legislative powers. The safety of the people, which is the supreme law, forbids it. Even, if we suppose the body expressly empowered by the legislature to exercise such powers, the right so to do must be denied, because the same supreme law places an absolute interdict on such a grant; it is beyond the power of a legislature to delegate any such authority.

§ 424. To these general considerations, tending to discredit the claim of Conventions to legislative powers, must be added the decisive circumstance, that our Constitutions, as well State as Federal, have vested all the power of ordinary legislation the people have chosen to grant at all, in our legislatures. The construction put upon these provisions of our Constitutions by the courts, is, that the grant is exclusive, and that the power can neither be delegated by the legislatures, nor exercised by the people, not even by the whole people.[1] It is doubtless true, that neither in the cases establishing the construction referred to, nor in our Constitutions, is there any reference to the exercise of legislative power by Conventions; but neither is there any mention of its exercise by the people. The conclusion that the

[1] For the cases establishing this construction, see *ante*, § 418, *note* 1.

general grant of legislative power to our legislatures, is implicitly an interdict upon the exercise of that power by the people, is derived mainly from the same general considerations relating to the safety of the Commonwealth, above specified, and of course tends to justify an extension of the interdict to all other bodies with respect to which the same reasons apply.

§ 425. Were additional arguments needed to demonstrate that a Convention has no power of ordinary legislation, reference might be made to the fact, that the possession of such a power would be extremely inconvenient, on account of the necessarily temporary and experimental character of such legislation, on the one hand, and the difficulty of effecting changes in the enactments of Conventions, on the other. Every Ordinance, or constitutional provision, passed by a Convention, assumes a form nearly as rigid as that of the Medan laws; they can be repealed only in the formal way in which they were enacted. It would be impossible to administer with success any government so crippled in its legislative arm. The result would inevitably be, that laws would be constantly disregarded, or that Conventions would become so necessary and frequent that they would ultimately supplant our legislatures.

§ 426. *Secondly.* In relation to custom and precedent — it is not denied by those who attribute to Conventions a general power of legislation, that that view receives little countenance from the practice of those bodies, in former times. But the lack of precedents is explained away by the consideration, that the actual exercise of such a power would naturally be infrequent and exceptional, as it would ordinarily occur only when great crises demanded instant legislative remedies, the legislature itself being either not in session, or controlled by treasonable influences. Moreover, it is plausibly argued, that the fact that a power is usually, because, perhaps, more conveniently, exercised by one of two bodies, is no reason for denying the existence of it in the other. To hold thus, it is said, would be to maintain, that the inherent rights of an assembly, which preëminently represents the sovereign, are forfeited by *non-user;* rights, of which the exercise, on account as well of the extraordinary character of the body possessing them, as of the conditions under which only they are likely to be asserted, must be occasional. Still, however infrequent, it is claimed that precedents exist, and there are pointed out to us three classes of cases, in which Conventions have, it is said, exercised the general power of legislation. These are — first, the cases of the Conventions which framed the first Constitutions of some of the States, during the Revolution, upon the exceptional and irregular character of which comment has already been made; secondly, cases in which Conventions have undertaken, in non-revolutionary times, by ordinance, to regulate matters of ordinary administration, or to do other acts manifestly legislative in character; and, thirdly, cases in which Conventions have inserted in Constitutions provisions partaking rather of a legislative than fundamental character, as relating largely to matters of detail.

§ 427. In relation to these classes of cases, I observe that they are none of them deemed of much weight as precedents.

1. It is true, that many of the earliest Conventions, even where called expressly to frame and establish Constitutions, were also charged with, or assumed, other functions, to wit, those of provisional governments. Accordingly, the journals of those bodies are filled about equally with their proceedings in discharge of governmental functions, and of their special office as Constitutional Conventions — propositions to be embodied in their Bills of Rights, or Constitutions, for instance, being mixed up with measures relating to the internal police, to the raising of troops or of revenue, or to the punishment of their Tory opponents. Obviously, cases like these, arising in revolutionary times, cannot properly be cited as precedents for the conduct of similar bodies in times of peace and constitutional order. But when it is considered, that the moment the Conventions referred to overstepped the limits which bounded their jurisdiction and entered upon the domain of actual administration, that is, of government, they became bodies of a wholly different character, to wit, Revolutionary Conventions,[1] it is clear, that the alleged precedents are of no value whatever.

§ 428. As to the second class of cases, in which a few Conventions have, by ordinance, legislated outside of their special province, their value as precedents is of less account, because they have been of infrequent occurrence, and the subjects of that legislation have been commonly trivial. A Convention being in session, and the progress of business developing a

[1] See *ante*, §§ 7–10.

necessity for further legislation, to avoid the delay and expense attending the regular course of proceeding in the legislature, that body has sometimes ordained the regulations required, and the government and people have acquiesced. Here, it may be, that it was not thought expedient to insist too rigidly upon precise conformity to principles in matters of small concern; and, perhaps, in the infancy of our institutions (for they are yet in the gristle) it has not always been seen that a Convention is so radically distinct from a legislature as it unquestionably is. Considering the ignorance still prevalent, even among educated men, respecting the theory of Conventions, it is not strange that it should be thought competent for them to do what history shows the Conventions of the revolutionary period certainly did. And, in truth, the only way of breaking the force of those cases as precedents, is to deny the normal and constitutional character of the latter Conventions, which, as we have seen, may very justly be done. The Conventions of our Revolution were, in many of the States, the governments of those States. If they legislated, they did so in this their exceptional character. If the Conventions of our day can also legislate, and if the evidence that they can do so is derived from the practice of those early Conventions, they must, also, potentially, at least, be the governments of their respective States — which is the doctrine of conventional sovereignty.

§ 429. So, in the third class of cases, where the jurisdictions of legislatures and Conventions clash, because, having a common frontier, cases arise in which it is doubtful to which body they belong, it is unfair to make an assertion of jurisdiction by either a binding precedent as to the right. A Convention is authorized to embody in the Constitution general provisions establishing principles, but leaving details dependent on considerations of temporary expediency to be determined by the legislature. Thus, take the provision relating to Homestead Exemption, as it is called; a Convention is competent to recommend the adoption of the principle, in such a form and under such conditions, as are consonant with the general conception of fundamental legislation, and no further. It may indicate what has become the settled policy of the State, but, if it go beyond that, developing principles into minute provisions, likely, as circumstances shift, to need modification, it trespasses upon the domain of the legislature. Doubtless, a Constitution, stuffed with legislative details, may acquire legitimacy, by its being ratified by the people; for, where a Constitution contains a positive provision, the courts cannot ignore it, or annul it; but the impropriety of such legislation would not thereby be disproved or lessened. If legislative provisions are thrust into a Constitution and passed upon by the people, ought they to have the force of laws any more than when submitted to the people disconnected from provisions truly fundamental? In the latter case, we have seen, that our courts pronounce them wholly without validity as laws. If the same judgment be not given respecting a constitutional provision consisting of legislative details, it is simply because it would be in effect to permit our judiciary to annul the charters under which they act, under the pretext of striking from them provisions not properly fundamental.

§ 430. With these remarks upon the general question of the power of Conventions to legislate, I pass to a consideration of certain practical questions which have arisen, involving an application of the principles I have developed.

(*a*). The first of these which I shall mention, arose in the Illinois Convention of 1862, under the following state of facts. About a year before the Convention assembled, the legislature of Illinois had passed three Acts relating to the city of Chicago, or to the townships over which it extended, which were obnoxious to a portion of its citizens, and particularly an Act, approved February 21, 1861, entitled "An Act to establish a Board of Police in and for the City of Chicago, and to prescribe their Powers and Duties," the force and effect of which were to turn out of office the old city police, and to vest the police powers of the city in a board of commissioners elected by the voters of the county in which the city was situated. The two other Acts related to matters entirely foreign from the mode of electing or appointing city officers. The Convention met in January, 1862, and toward the end of its session, March 21, adopted an Ordinance providing for an election to be held in the city of Chicago on the third Tuesday of April following, at which the legal voters of said city were to cast ballots on which should be printed or written the words, "For the city of Chicago electing its own officers," or the words, "Against the city of Chicago electing its own officers." The Ordinance then went on to provide, that, in case a majority of the electors voting at said election should be in favor of said city electing its own officers, then it should not be lawful for any officers of that city to be chosen in any other manner than by a vote of the people of said city, or appointed in any other manner than by the mayor and aldermen, as provided by present laws, *and that the three Acts referred to should be, and the same were, each and all of them, thereby repealed.*

§ 431. After the adjournment of the Convention, on the third Tuesday of April, 1862, the electors of the city of Chicago, as required by this Ordinance, voted on the question of electing their own officers, and, as was, of course, foreseen by its framers, voted affirmatively. So far, admitting the propriety of the action of the Convention, the obnoxious Acts of the legislature would seem to have been repealed. But other facts still further complicate the case. The Act of Assembly calling the Convention had required that body to submit to a vote of the people the alterations or amendments proposed by it, and had declared, that said alterations or amendments should not take effect "unless adopted by a majority of the legal voters voting at such elections." Accordingly, the Constitution framed by the Convention, including, as a part of its Schedule, the Ordinance above described, *in totidem verbis*, was, by the Convention, submitted to a vote of the people of the whole State, at an election held on the 17th day of June, 1862, at which election the entire instrument, save a few provisions not involved in this discussion, which were separately submitted, was rejected by a decisive vote. An important circumstance, to be noted, to aid in determining the effect of these various proceedings is, that immediately succeeding the Ordinance, as embodied in the Schedule, was the following clause, viz.: — "The provisions of this Constitution, required to be executed prior to the adoption or rejection thereof, shall take effect and be in force immediately."

§ 432. Upon these facts embarrassing questions arose: When the people of Chicago had voted in favor of electing their own officers, were or were not the three legislative Acts referred to in the Ordinance, thereby repealed? Was there any police system in force in that city, and if so, which was it, the city police or the county police? If by the action of the Convention, or of the Chicago electors, or of both combined, the repeal of the obnoxious laws was effected, what influence upon them had the subsequent vote of the whole people of the State, rejecting the Constitution, Ordinance and all, with the exceptions indicated? Did not the additional clause, giving immediate effect to such provisions of the Constitution as were required to be executed prior to the adoption or rejection thereof, save the Ordinance from the fate reserved for the rest of the instrument, especially as that Ordinance had been passed upon and adopted by that part of the people of the State who were to be affected by it?

To settle these questions, an application was made to the Supreme Court of the State for a mandamus to compel the board of police commissioners, appointed under the Act of 1861, to vacate their offices and to give place to commissioners to be elected by the legal voters of the city in pursuance of the Ordinance. The case was very ably and elaborately argued, and a decision was finally rendered denying the writ, upon the ground, as is understood,— for no opinion was ever filed by the court,— that by the vote of the people rejecting that instrument, the entire Constitution and Schedule were swept away and became of no force or effect for any purpose. At all events, the Acts, sought to be repealed by the Convention, were continued in force until repealed by the legislature, and hence the decision of the court involved practically the following conclusion, that the Convention was not competent, even with the coöperation of that part of the people to be affected by it, to repeal an Act of the legislature, local in its scope and operation.[1]

§ 433. A brief abstract of the arguments of counsel in this case, relative to the power of the Convention to repeal laws, may be of interest.

On the part of the relator it was contended, that about the intention of the Convention in passing the Ordinance of March 21st, and hence relative to the extent of power which that body meant to assert, there could be no doubt; it certainly claimed the right to legislate; the only question was, Had it that right? That in relation to that question, it was clear, that it was competent for that body to prohibit the appointment *thereafter* of

[1] People of the State of Illinois, *ex rel.* The City of Chicago *v.* A. C. Coventry *et al.*, April Term, 1862, of the Supreme Court of Illinois. Case not reported.

any person to any office for the city of Chicago by the Governor or General Assembly; that, at least, the power of the Convention to deliberate and act upon such a question, had not been disputed, and it would be difficult to show, that it could not so far change or abrogate existing statutes as to make the legislation of the State conform to the supposed new order of things; that the repealed Acts were in palpable conflict with the principle of the new provision about to be adopted by the Convention as a part of the fundamental law, and therefore the Ordinance declared, that "the powers and duties of all officers appointed under and by virtue of said Acts, shall immediately cease;" that so far as respected the legislating of those officers out of office, the power to do that had been frequently exercised, as in the Illinois Constitution of 1848, and had never been questioned; that the effect of every new Constitution was to annul all existing statutes in conflict with its provisions, and if any statutes were continued in force, they were, strictly speaking, reënactments by that Convention, to which alone we must look as the source of their validity;[1] that if that body could thus reënact statutes, or continue them in force for a prescribed period only, it was idle to deny to it the right in express terms to repeal them; that, if it was admitted that the Convention possessed legislative functions for any purpose, no limit could be assigned to its exercise of them; that the extent of its power to legislate must be subject only to its own discretion, which no other tribunal, legislative or judicial, had power to review; that the business of a Convention was to make a Constitution — to ordain organic laws. But what were organic laws? Who was to decide? The answer was plain and free from difficulty; the Convention had the sole power of determining what should be the organic law, and whatever it prescribed (subject, in some cases, to the ratification of the people) became a part of the Constitution; that the courts could not control or annul its decision, except in the single case where enactments were repugnant to the Federal Constitution; that, with that exception, no provision inserted in the organic law could be annulled by any power on earth save by the people acting in their highest sovereign capacity.

§ 434. For the respondents, it was contended, that the Conven-

[1] Woods v. Blanchard, 19 Ill. R. 40.

tion, in passing the Ordinance in question, had set at defiance the provisions of the Act of the legislature under which the delegates to it had been elected, and had assumed to be vested with the supreme authority of the people of Illinois; that the supreme authority of a community includes executive and judicial as well as legislative powers, all of which it might with equal justice claim a right to exercise without control, if it were really the sovereign body it pretended to be; that the claim of powers so extensive was discredited by the best writers on government, and by the examples of the fathers throughout our entire history, all of whom had united in the sentiment forcibly expressed by the authors of the "Federalist," "that the accumulation of all powers, legislative, executive, and judiciary, in the same hands, whether of one, a few, or many, and whether hereditary, self-appointed, or elective, may be justly pronounced the very definition of tyranny;" that, clothed with such powers, the Convention was subject to no Constitution or law, and might have perpetuated its own existence and powers, and the people could have escaped from its tyranny only by a revolution resulting in a dethronement of the usurpers of their power; that the principles of our government led to no such disastrous results; but that those results were, on the contrary, the fruits of a perversion of those principles; that the fundamental idea of our system of governments was, that the sovereignty resided in the people, who, for its practical exercise, confided it, or so much of it as they deemed desirable, to separate agencies; that all acts of either of those agencies, within the sphere of its powers, were acts of the people; that in general the powers granted to each of those agencies or departments were exclusively its own, liable to be resumed by the people, but, so long as vested in the several departments, not to be rightfully exercised even by the people themselves; that from these principles it followed, not only that the people might and did limit the powers delegated to their representatives, but that they equally might and did limit their own powers; and, consequently, even if the Convention wielded all the powers of the people, it could not perform an act of ordinary legislation, because the people had by the Constitution granted the power of legislation to the General Assembly, and had thereby limited their own power in that behalf.[1]

[1] The argument, so far as it proceeded upon the ground that the people

§ 435. (*b*). The next practical question to which I shall advert, is one of intrinsically so much moment, and of such frequent occurrence, that I shall devote to it considerable space. namely: Have Conventions power to appropriate money? The power to appropriate money, when asserted at all, has been uniformly claimed upon the ground that a Convention is possessed, subject only to the Federal Constitution, of sovereign powers, and consequently, as involved in that grant, of all special administrative or governmental powers, legislative, executive, and judicial. On the other hand, legislative power has been generally denied to it on the ground that the Convention is not in any sense sovereign; that it is even, in the extent of its powers, inferior to the legislature, by which Acts may be definitively passed, while our Conventions are invested, save in exceptional cases, with a recommendatory power only, — being, in truth, but mere committees charged with a certain legislative function, but not with that of legislation in general, much less with those of the executive or judicial departments. To this are commonly added considerations of the danger of intrusting the public purse to an assembly consisting of a single chamber, and of the improbability, therefore, that the founders of a system so guarded and balanced as ours, would have left it in the control of such a body, without a single check against usurpation. I shall, therefore, only give a short statement of some cases in which the question has arisen, or the power been exercised, and of the decisions and results thereof, so far as known.

§ 436. Resolutions or ordinances have been passed by Conventions, appropriating the public moneys, for the following purposes: —

1. To pay the salaries of the officers or members, and to defray the incidental expenses of those bodies.

2. For benevolent, charitable, or other purposes, outside the scope of their special duties or business, as Conventions.

1. The precedents in the earliest Conventions, excepting those which clearly acted as provisional governments, are not in favor of the power in question. Thus, in that of Massachusetts, of

could limit themselves by the Constitution, was mainly that of Mr. Webster before the United States Supreme Court, in the case of Luther *v.* Borden, 7 How. R. 1. For the full argument, see Webster's *Works*, Vol. VI. p. 221, *et seq.*

1779–80, a committee was appointed "to apply to the General Court for the payment of the members of this Convention, to be made out of the treasury of the State," and also "for payment of such charges as have arisen, or may arise, in prosecuting the business of this Convention." The action of the Federal Convention of 1787 was similar. Instead of assuming the power to determine their own salaries and to vote money to pay them, the whole subject was referred to Congress. On the 5th of September, it was "*Resolved*, That the United States in Congress be requested to allow and cause to be paid to the secretary and other officers of this Convention such sums in proportion to their respective times of service as are allowed to the secretary and similar officers in Congress." This resolution was followed by an order directing the secretary of the Convention to make out and transmit to the treasury office of the United States an account for the said services and for the incidental expenses of the Convention. The Act calling the Illinois Convention of 1847, authorized that body to elect a printer, and fixed his compensation at the rate received by the public printer from the General Assembly. A proposition was made in the Convention for a committee to receive proposals for doing the printing of that body, and directing that it be let to the lowest responsible bidder. This motion was resisted, on the ground of a want of power to vary the enabling Act; that the proposition to do so involved the right to appropriate the sums agreed to be paid, since they could not be claimed under the Act, if the latter were repudiated. The motion was for that reason laid upon the table. On a similar ground, a motion made in the New York Convention of 1846, to appoint stenographers, was negatived.

§ 437. On the other hand, propositions of the kind specified have often been adopted and acted on by Conventions. Thus, the Pennsylvania Convention of 1837, in the course of each of its two sessions, passed a resolution appropriating money as a compensation to the clergymen who officiated therein, though not without vigorous protest on the ground of want of power. So, in the Louisiana Convention of 1844, a resolution was carried authorizing the State Treasurer to advance to its printer the sum of one thousand dollars, "for the subscription to the Reporter," a daily paper containing a report of its debates. The

Convention of 1864 of the same State made similar appropriations, to a large amount, to be paid out of "the funds in the public treasury not otherwise appropriated," for extra services rendered by its officers. In the Indiana Convention of 1850, the question of its power to appropriate money arose on a motion to elect a printer to the Convention. This motion was opposed on the two grounds, — 1, that, under the laws of Indiana, there was a State printer, under bonds to do the public printing, who claimed, and was in law entitled, to do that of the Convention; and, 2, that the Convention was not competent to appropriate money to pay a printer, should it elect one. After a long discussion, which turned mainly on the question whether the State printer, elected by the General Assembly, and under bonds "for the prompt, accurate, and workmanlike execution of the public printing, and the faithful performance of all the duties required of him by law," was *ex officio* printer to the Convention, it was determined that he was not, and that body proceeded to elect one to fill that office, without, however, making any provision for his payment. To this action a formal protest was made by a minority, and entered on its journal, affirming the right of the State printer to do the printing of the Convention, and denying the power of the latter to appropriate money to pay the printer elected by it. The Illinois Convention of 1862, toward the end of its session, adopted a resolution, almost unanimously, making appropriations to certain State officers for extra services in relation to the Convention. A doubt being expressed in regard to the power of the Convention to make the appropriation, it was answered, that the legislature had appropriated money to defray the expenses of the Convention, and provided, that for the compensation of its officers — the amount to be determined by the Convention — the president should issue his certificate to the auditor of public accounts, who should issue warrants for the sums mentioned therein, upon the State Treasurer. It is obvious, however, that this provision did not cover the case of extra or other compensation to State officers, who were specially directed by law to perform certain services for the Convention in their official capacity, but who were not mentioned in the Act as entitled to compensation. And of this opinion, evidently, was the State Auditor, for on presentation of the resolution of the Convention making the appropriation, that officer refused to issue his warrant for payment of the money. By special Act, however, the General Assembly afterwards ordered compensation to be made to the officers named for the same services — the Act reciting as a reason for the appropriation the refusal of the State Auditor.[1]

§ 438. In regard to the above appropriations, it is to be noted that they were made under an assumption of power to do so inherent in those bodies, and without special authorization to that effect in the Acts calling them. But, were it true, that appropriations thus loosely made were honored by the State authorities, they would amount to but little, in my judgment, as settling the question of power. They have not, however, commonly thus been honored. It has been a usual consequence of the meeting of Conventions that our legislatures have followed it up with appropriations out of the treasury to meet what have been styled appropriations by those bodies. It is probable that, practically, those formal Ordinances disposing of the public funds have been regarded rather as recommendations than as mandates of an authority having the right to enforce its will. To bring the question to a test, it is only necessary to conceive a custodian of the public moneys receiving a warrant from a Convention — a body by whom he was not appointed and to whom he is not by law made responsible — directing him to turn over to the bearer the public funds in his hands. Is it possible that any officer, so situated, would feel authorized to obey such a warrant? And, suppose he were to obey, would that warrant be pleadable in bar of an action on a Treasurer's bond to the State, if he should have failed on demand to turn over such funds to his successor, appointed in the manner laid down in the Constitution? Yet, the power in a Convention to appropriate one dollar of the public money is a power to seize and to use as it may please the entire treasure of the State.

§ 439. 2. In relation to the second class of cases, in which Conventions have assumed to make appropriations from the treasuries of their respective States, for general objects, foreign from the special purpose of those bodies, less need be said, as the arguments against the right are the same, and apply with increased force, whilst the instances in which it has been as-

[1] Act of January 28, 1863, Illinois Laws of 1863, pp. 11, 12.

serted are fewer in number. In the absence of legislative provision, it is doubtless often convenient, that Conventions should assume the power to appropriate, or, at least, go through the forms of appropriating, money, in the execution of their commissions; and where the power is exercised only to facilitate the transaction of their proper business, it is, if unauthorized, obnoxious to less serious objection. But the case is different in relation to matters outside the business assigned to them. There, it seems clear, that, no matter what the circumstances might be under which the power should be exercised, it would be a power usurped. Accordingly, it will surprise no one, that in the better days of the republic, following the Revolutionary period ending with the adoption of the Federal Constitution, few instances of such legislation have occurred, and those mainly within the last five years. Of these I shall mention but two.

§ 440. The Illinois Convention of 1862, in a paroxysm of patriotic zeal, just after the capture of Fort Donelson, passed the following remarkable Ordinance: —

"Be it ordained by the people of the State of Illinois, represented and assembled in Constitutional Convention, —

"That the sum of five hundred thousand dollars, or so much thereof as may be necessary, be, and the same is hereby, appropriated out of the Treasury of the State of Illinois, for the exclusive purpose of relieving the wants and sufferings of the brave sons of Illinois, who have been or may be wounded in the battles fought by them and their brothers in the defence of the Union and the Constitution."

Sections two and three authorized the issue by the governor, auditor, and treasurer of Illinois, of State bonds for that amount, and provided for the disbursement of the money by those officers jointly with a committee to be appointed by the Convention. Praiseworthy as the object of this Ordinance was, the assumption in it of general powers of legislation was so glaring that some of the firmest friends of the soldier in the body were constrained to oppose its passage. They united in a protest, setting forth, that, in their opinion, the Convention had no power to authorize appropriations from the State Treasury, and that the assumption of such a power in so important a matter as the issue of State bonds, was an evidence of a loose administration of public affairs, and directly calculated to injure the credit of the State. The intention of those who passed the Ordinance was declared to be to issue the bonds immediately, but for some reason this was never done. What might have been attempted, had the Constitution framed by the Convention been adopted, cannot be known, but as that instrument was rejected, the bonds were never issued — and that was, perhaps, all that the friends of the Ordinance intended.

§ 441. Another instance of this kind of legislation occurred in the Convention of 1864 for the reconstruction of Louisiana. An appropriation of thirty-five thousand dollars was made by it from the State treasury for purposes of charity, to be distributed by a board of almoners appointed by the Governor, of which he was to be *ex officio* president, the money to be drawn upon his warrant. Afterwards a resolution was adopted, directing the payment out of the State treasury of the sum of ten thousand dollars for expenses incurred "in the formation of the free State of Louisiana." On the same day, upon the recommendation of the finance committee, it was resolved to draw from the general fund in the State treasury the amount necessary for the payment of members, employés, and contingent expenses until the end of the session; also to pay to the State librarian, for services rendered by him in furnishing books and documents to the Convention, the sum of five hundred dollars.

In reference to the precedents drawn from this last Convention, it should be noted that they are of no weight at all by reason of the exceptional character of that body. That Convention, like those which followed it in the other States that attempted to secede from the Union, was, as we have already seen,[1] the creature of the military law, and so, in its inception, not to be ranked as legitimate. It was, besides, in essential character, a provisional government, and not a Constitutional Convention. In this exceptional character, it wielded whatever powers it chose to assert, subject only to the dictation of the military commander, being in fact the only civil government existing in the State. The legislature had perished along with the other departments of the government, in the act of seceding, so that, if there were funds in the State treasury, there was no civil authority, save the Convention, that could claim the right to disburse them. The analogy, therefore, was close between the

[1] See *ante*, §§ 247–249.

Louisiana Convention and those of the American colonies, to which reference has been made, which, while they exercised some of the functions of Constitutional Conventions, were simply Revolutionary Conventions, and, therefore, the former can properly furnish no precedents to bind such Conventions as are strictly constitutional bodies.[1]

§ 441 *a*. In several cases which have arisen since the first edition of this work was published, the power of Conventions to appropriate money has been directly passed upon and denied by high legal authority. The earliest of these arose in New York,

[1] A different question from those discussed above, as to the legality of a legislative appropriation for the salaries and other expenses of a Convention, was raised in the Pennsylvania Convention of 1872. In the original Act calling the Convention, the legislature had fixed the salary of the members at one thousand dollars, and appropriated a specific sum for other expenses, but directing the Convention to fix the compensation of the clerks and other officers. Warrants for these allowances were to be drawn by the president, and countersigned by the chief clerk, upon the treasurer, for payment. While the Convention was in session, the legislature again convened, and, in an Act to provide for the expenses of the government, embodied a section repealing so much of the Act calling the Convention as fixed the amounts of the compensation of its members, officers, and employees, and of its incidental expenses, and in lieu thereof appropriated the sum of five hundred thousand dollars, "or so much thereof as may be necessary," for the payment of the expenses of the Convention, including the pay of the members, clerks, and officers, to be settled by the Auditor General, — the amount of the salaries, and pay of the members and officers thereof, to be fixed by the Convention, and the money to be paid by the treasurer on warrants drawn by the president, as in the previous Act. Upon the report of a committee appointed to designate the amounts to be allowed for salaries and compensation, to be drawn from the fund thus provided, a discussion arose, in the course of which the Hon. Jeremiah S. Black denounced the appropriation thus made of a lump sum, out of which the Convention were to take as much as they pleased for their own salaries, as illegal. The objection was not sustained by the Convention, which, by a vote of sixty against forty-four adopted the report. See *Deb. and Proc. of Pa. Conv.* 1872, Vol. IV. pp. 696–710. Giving his reasons, Judge Black said: "I maintain that this is no appropriation within the meaning of the Constitution, which forbids that public money shall ever be paid out of the treasury except in accordance with appropriations made by law. If the legislature should say that a certain sum, a million of dollars, — I do not care what words they use, — shall be placed at the disposal of a person who has a claim against the commonwealth, whether for work or anything else, and that he may take as much of it as he pleases to satisfy himself, that would be no appropriation." Id. p. 704. His conviction that the appropriation was illegal was so strong that he refused to receive a dollar for his *per diem*, and at length resigned his seat in the Convention. *Deb. and Proc. Pa. Conv.* 1872, Vol. VII. p. 436.

during the session of its Convention of 1867, under the following circumstances. The Act of March 29, 1867, calling that Convention, provided, Sec. 5, that the delegates to the Convention should "be entitled to six dollars per day for every day, from the first day to the last day, of the session thereof, and the same mileage as is now paid to the members of the legislature." It then further provided, that the amendments or Constitution which might be proposed should "be submitted by the Convention to the people for adoption or rejection at the next general election, to be held on the Tuesday after the first Monday of November next." On the 7th of October, 1867, the labors of the Convention being unfinished and promising to continue beyond the day fixed by the Act for submitting the Constitution to the people, the Comptroller of the State submitted to the Attorney General for his opinion the following questions: "1. Can the Convention continue its sessions after the time fixed in the legislative Act . . . for a submission of its work to the people has expired, or has that body a discretionary power as to the time of submission, beyond the control of the legislature? 2. On either of the suppositions of the preceding inquiry, is not the legislative Act binding on the Comptroller in all its provisions, so far as they impose duties on that officer, and, if so, can he properly pay the members and officers of the Convention for attendance after the time indicated in the Act for a submission to the people?"

To these inquiries, the Attorney General, the Hon. J. H. Martindale, replied, in substance, that the voluntary sessions of the Convention after the date fixed for the submission were not prohibited by any law; that the legislature, at its next session, might recognize its work and submit it to the people; that, whatever might be the primary source of the authority of the Convention, whether it derived its vitality primarily from the present Constitution, or from the legislative Act providing for the election and assemblage of its members, if the legislature should submit the result of its deliberations to a general election of the people, and they should approve, the amendments or Constitution so proposed or adopted would be established in the State; and that it was unnecessary to consider the effect of such a submission without a legislative Act. As to the second question, the Attorney General answered that the authority of the Comptroller "to pay members and officers for attendance after the time indicated in the Act for a submission to the people" was confined by narrower and more precise limitations; that he was not authorized to draw his warrant on the Treasurer for any moneys except in conformity to law; that, by the provisions of the Act in question, the members were each entitled, etc. (reciting the terms of the Act); and that the amendments or Constitution which might be proposed should be submitted (reciting also its terms as to submission); that the law in effect told the Comptroller to pay the members six dollars per day for every day of the session of the Convention, but that the session must be ended before the next general election; that such, in his opinion, was the intention of the legislature in passing the Act, and such was the popular, and he thought the true, construction of it; that all the right of the members to their compensation was derived from, and must be limited by the terms of, the legislative Act under which they were convened; that all the Comptroller's authority to pay them was conferred and imposed by the same Act; that they had discretion to prolong their voluntary session, and to trust to some future legislative enabling Act; that in doing so they violated no law; that the Comptroller had no official discretion to transcend the limitations of the present Act, nor to draw his warrant in anticipation that it would be extended by the next legislature; that in doing so he would violate the Constitution, which prescribes that "no money shall ever be paid out of the treasury of this State, or any of its funds, or any funds under its management, except in pursuance of an appropriation by law;" that the next legislature might, in its discretion, pay the members, for their attendance after the 5th of November, six dollars, or one dollar, per day, or refuse to pay any sum whatever; that the construction which derived the authority and rights of the Convention, including the pay of its clerks and members, from the Constitution, regardless of the limited period prescribed to its session in the legislative Act, would permit continued sessions without limit, and impose the duty on successive legislatures, by the high obligations of "good faith," to make appropriations for its expenses until the Convention determined to conclude its labors; that he thought such a construction was erroneous, and advised him to decline to pay the members and officers of the Convention for attendance after the time indicated in the Act for a submission to the people.

Accordingly, on the 20th of November, the Convention being still in session, the Comptroller advised it of his correspondence with the Attorney General, and of his unwillingness to take the responsibility of continuing to draw warrants on the treasury for the payment of the expenses of the Convention without further legislative action.

So, the Georgia Convention of 1867, having by ordinance authorized its disbursing officer to receive and receipt for a certain sum of money from the State Treasurer, that officer, although ordered by General Pope, in command of the military district comprising the State of Georgia, to make such payment, declined to comply with the provisions of the ordinance, stating as his reasons that, "holding his office under the Constitution of Georgia adopted in 1865, being sworn to perform its duties according to that Constitution and the laws of the State, by which he was forbidden to pay money out of the treasury except upon warrant of the Governor and sanction of the Comptroller General, and having entered into heavy bonds for the faithful performance of the duties so prescribed, he was compelled to decline making the payment ordered by the Convention." [1] Afterwards it appears that both the Treasurer and the Governor of the State were removed by General Meade, then in command of the district, because they "declined to respect the instructions of, and failed to coöperate with, the major-general commanding the Third Military District." [2] Although the Constitution and government of Georgia, under which those State officers had been appointed, were provisional, as was finally declared by Congress, the Treasurer was unquestionably right legally in refusing payment, though had he complied with the order he doubtless would have been indemnified by the Federal or State authorities when the reconstruction of the State should have been completed. But, although in a suit on his bond he might have pleaded the compulsion of military force, and have been justified morally in yielding to it, it is more than doubtful whether he, or the sureties on his bond, could have succeeded in resisting judgment upon such a plea, because technically the Convention, backed by the army of the United States, would not have been the legislature of Georgia, nor its ordinance or a military order the law of the State; nor would any payment

[1] See *Jour. of Geo. Conv.* 1867, pp. 78, 79.

[2] Id. p. 131.

the Treasurer should have made been made upon the warrant of the Governor, nor with the sanction of the Comptroller General.

§ 441 *b*. In like manner, the legislature of Georgia having, in 1877, in the act calling the Convention of that year, appropriated the sum of twenty-five thousand dollars to pay the expenses of the same, and authorized the Governor to draw his warrant therefor, and this sum proving insufficient, the State Treasurer, under the official advice of the Attorney General, the Hon. R. N. Ely, declined to pay the members of the Convention their *per diem* and mileage to an amount exceeding the sum appropriated by the legislature.

In both the New York case and the last Georgia case the Conventions acquiesced in the opinions of the Attorneys General, and procured, in the former case, from the Commercial Bank of Albany, and in the latter from the Hon. Robert Toombs, a member of the Georgia Convention, loans of the sums needed to pay all the expenses of those bodies, upon the faith that legislative provision to meet them would afterwards be made.

Finally, the same question arose in the Pennsylvania Convention of 1873, under the following circumstances. We have seen that that body, in submitting the Constitution it had framed to the people, instead of directing the election to be conducted "as the general elections were by law conducted," as the Convention Act had required, appointed a special board of commissioners to conduct the election in the city of Philadelphia, but that the proceedings of that board were stopped by the injunction of the Supreme Court.[1] The commissioners obeyed the mandate of the court; but upon the reassembling of the Convention, after the decision had been rendered and after the election had been held, they sent in to that body a bill for expenses incurred before the injunction was served, which, after deducting an unexpended balance of the sum of five thousand dollars already advanced by the Convention, amounted to nearly seven thousand dollars. A resolution that a warrant be drawn for that balance on the State Treasurer, in favor of the election commissioners, was adopted by the Convention.[2] Upon presentation of the warrant to the State Treasurer, the Hon. R. W. Mackey, he referred the question of the power of the Convention to issue the same, and of his duty

[1] See *ante*, § 409 *a*.

[2] *Deb. Pa. Conv.* 1872, pp. 749–754.

to pay it, to the Attorney General of the State, who answered both questions in the negative. Payment, therefore, was refused. By an Act of the Pennsylvania legislature, approved April 29, 1874, however, the bill presented by the commissioners was ordered paid, it appearing that the items embraced in it were for expenses incurred by commissioners before the Supreme Court of the State had pronounced the ordinance for their appointment to be illegal and void.

§ 442. 2. I pass now to the second class of questions proposed for discussion in this chapter, namely, Can a Convention act *as a legislature* in matters by the Federal Constitution required to be transacted by the *legislatures* of the several States?

There are two cases:

(*a*). Can a Convention assume, *as a legislature*, to prescribe the "times, places, and manner of holding elections for Senators and Representatives" in Congress?

(*b*). Can a Convention assume, *as a legislature*, to ratify proposed amendments to the Federal Constitution, when the ratification is required by Congress to be made by the State legislatures?

(*a*). The fourth section of the first article of the Federal Constitution provides, that "the times, places, and manner of holding elections for senators and representatives shall be prescribed in each State by the legislature thereof."

In the Illinois Convention of 1862, a question arose in relation to the power of that body to personate the State legislature, under this section. Soon after the result of the census of 1860 was announced, the legislature of Illinois had districted the State for thirteen members of Congress, on the basis of that announcement, and had adjourned. In March, 1862, while the Convention was in session, an Act was passed by Congress allowing the State an additional representative. An election for members of Congress being about to take place in November of that year, it was deemed desirable, if possible, to correct the erroneous apportionment, without summoning together the legislature. Accordingly a resolution was introduced into the Convention instructing the judiciary committee to inquire whether that body had power to establish districts for the election of members of Congress. Upon that committee was placed the best legal talent in the Convention, and a report was promptly made, maintaining that the power of the Convention to establish districts was undoubted.

§ 443. The ground taken by the majority of the committee was simply that the true construction of the clause of the Constitution which requires that "the times, places, and manner of holding elections for members of Congress" should be prescribed by the legislature, was, that the people of the different States should have the right to prescribe through their proper representatives, the particulars indicated; that the ordinary construction of the clause was founded upon the assumed technical signification of the word "legislature," according to which, the clause in question could only refer to the General Assembly; that, on the contrary, the word "legislature," from its derivation, construction, and general use, was not confined in its meaning to limits so narrow, but denominated a body of persons having the power to lay down laws, — in common acceptation, to make laws; that it was, therefore, properly applied to any body having and exercising the power of making laws; that the Congress of the Revolution was a legislature; that the Convention which framed the Federal Constitution was the first legislature which ever convened and acted in America, having made and established, by the subsequent approval and ratification of the States, the supreme law of the land; that in organizing new States out of Territories, the Conventions called for that purpose had exercised this power without question; that the Convention of Illinois was a legislature, authorized to create laws which might abolish other legislatures; change, annul, or reëstablish existing laws; in short, was superior in power, in the act of making laws, to any ordinary legislature, and hence might, at least, do, in the way of changing or abrogating the Acts of a former legislature, whatever a subsequent legislature might do.

Upon the report of this committee, and almost without debate, the Convention instructed its committee on Congressional apportionment to redistrict the State at once for members of Congress. This was done, and there was consequently embodied in the Constitution a scheme of districts satisfactory to the majority of the Convention.

§ 444. In relation to the arguments advanced by the committee, it is worthy of note —

1. That, although, as stated by the committee, the spirit of

the clause of the Federal Constitution in question doubtless is, that the people of the several States should have the right to determine the time, place, and manner of electing their representatives in Congress, still it is explicitly required by that clause that the *legislatures* shall be the bodies by which that determination shall be made. The real question is, what is meant by the term "legislature?" The words "legislature" and "Convention" are used in the Federal Constitution, the former ten times, and the latter four times. The signification intended by the word "Convention," it is impossible to mistake, since it is used only in reference to framing or ratifying a body of fundamental laws for the United States. The word "legislature" is always preceded by the article "the," as importing an institution well understood, and is uniformly coupled with the term "State." Moreover, from the context, it is impossible not to infer that the term is used technically, to designate the ordinary law-making power, and not a Convention, or other body. It may also be noted, that whenever reference is certainly made to the ordinary law-making power, the term "legislature" is employed; and that whenever reference is certainly made to that body of persons whose duty it is to frame the fundamental law, the term "Convention" is employed.

§ 445. 2. The statement of the committee, that the Congress of the Revolution was a legislature, though true, is exceedingly unfortunate for their purpose. The Congress of the Revolution constituted a provisional government, and as such was possessed of not only legislative, but executive and judicial powers; it was precisely such a body as the Convention Parliament of 1689 in England, composed of citizens collected irregularly, charged with the duty temporarily of protecting and governing the nation left without an organized government, and to that end authorized to exercise such powers as should seem to them to be necessary. A body of a similar character, so far as its legal *status* is concerned, was the National Convention of France; though, it must be admitted, that assembly, composed of men unpractised in public affairs, was, in point of political wisdom, infinitely inferior to both the Convention Parliament and the Continental Congress. But the point is, that they were all of them Revolutionary Conventions, wielding provisionally all powers whatsoever. It is worse than idle to compare our

Constitutional Conventions with such bodies. Constitutional Conventions are not governments at all; they wield no administrative powers, and of such as are denominated legislative powers, they wield only such as relate to the organic law, and in respect to that, their powers are limited to recommendations merely. In other words, the Continental Congress, referred to by the committee, was not a Convention, in the sense intended by them, at all; and, therefore, no inference as to the powers of such a body can be drawn from the fact that that Congress did or did not possess particular powers.

§ 446. The committee say, that, in organizing new States out of Territories, the Conventions, called for that purpose, exercise, without question, the power of apportioning such States for members of Congress, and thence infer that all Conventions may exercise the same powers. It is true, that, in many cases, such has been the practice. There being as yet no State, and, of course, no State legislature, unless the Convention could make a temporary arrangement for the election of members of Congress, the new State must, after its admission into the Union, be unrepresented in that body, until a State legislature could be elected and could pass the necessary laws, — a condition involving often a considerable delay. In such cases, accordingly, the custom has been for the Convention to anticipate the action of the legislature, — a course which, on account of its obvious convenience, has been commonly acquiesced in. These cases, however, form exceptions to a rule which is general, — that it is the State legislatures which apportion their several States for Congressional elections. I have failed to find a single exception to that rule save in the cases of Territories seeking to become States, or of States standing substantially on the same footing as Territories.[1]

Besides, in one view of the subject, such action of the Territories, taken in connection with that of Congress following it, involves no impropriety, if it is not strictly regular. Immediately following that clause of the Federal Constitution giving

1 The Louisiana Reconstruction Convention of 1864, which stood on a footing in some respects similar to that of a Territory preparing itself for admission into the Union, apportioned the State for the election of members of Congress. We have seen, however, that that body was a revolutionary one, — a provisional government, — erected under the sanction of the military arm. See *ante*, §§ 247-249.

the power of determining the "times, places, and manner of electing senators and representatives" to the State legislatures, is the important reservation, "but the Congress may at any time, by law,.make or alter such regulations, except as to the place of choosing senators." Hence, having the power to make or alter, Congress doubtless might ratify such regulations, however made; or, if a State, actual or inchoate, were in such a condition, that it had no lawful legislature, Congress might itself, for the sake of convenience, establish them by its direct action. This it does, in substance, by anticipation, in those cases in which it accepts and admits into the Union Territories, presenting themselves with Constitutions containing the apportionments referred to.

§ 447 (*b*). Similar considerations enable us to dispose of the second case relating to the power of a Convention, as a legislature, to act upon proposed amendments to the Federal Constitution. Article V. of that Constitution provides, that Congress, whenever two-thirds of both houses shall deem it necessary, shall propose amendments to that instrument, or, on the application of the legislatures of two-thirds of the several States, shall call a Convention for proposing amendments, which in either case shall be valid as parts of the Constitution, "when ratified by the *legislatures* of three-fourths of the several States, or by Conventions in three-fourths thereof, as the one or the other mode of ratification may be proposed by Congress."

By a joint resolution of Congress, approved March 2, 1861, an amendment was proposed to the Constitution of the United States, inhibiting any amendment to such Constitution which should authorize Congress "to abolish or interfere within any State, with the domestic institutions thereof, including that of persons held to labor or service under the laws thereof." The mode of ratification proposed by Congress was by the action of "the legislatures of three-fourths of the several States." The legislature of the State of Illinois, having at its session held in 1861 failed to ratify this amendment, the Convention of that State, of 1862, attempted to supply a remedy. After a discussion, in which the difficulties attending the assertion of the power in question were considered on constitutional grounds, the Convention, by a decisive vote, passed a resolution ratifying the proposed amendment.

Respecting this action of the Convention, I deem it unnecessary to say more, than that there is not, in my judgment, on legal grounds, a shadow of reason for the construction given to the Constitutional provision, and that party zeal alone could have led the eminent men who composed that body, to the position assumed in the discussion.

§ 448. 3. The last practical question proposed for discussion, is whether a Convention has power, by constitutional regulation or otherwise, to limit a discretion confided to a State legislature by the Constitution of the United States?

This question arose in the Massachusetts Convention of 1820, under the following circumstances. Mr. Austin, of Boston, introduced into that body a resolution affirming the expediency of electing representatives in Congress and presidential electors, in districts to be determined by the legislature, instead of by general ticket, as it is called, and requiring that body, immediately after every apportionment of representatives by Congress, to provide by law for so electing them. By the second section of the Federal Constitution, it is directed, that the members of the National House of Representatives shall be chosen "by the people of the several States," and by the fourth section, that "the times, *places*, and *manner* of holding elections for senators, &c., shall be prescribed in each State by the legislature thereof."

By the mover of this resolution, it was not denied that it was by the legislature, and not by a Convention, that the times, places, and manner of electing senators, &c., were to be determined; but he contended that the latter had a right to limit the former in the exercise of its discretion; that the legislature was bound to exercise all its powers under the direction of the Constitution, and that the people had at the same time the right to impose upon the legislature such terms and conditions as they should deem advisable; that admitting the right of imposing the particular restriction in question, the expediency of it was beyond dispute; for, it was said, that "when electors and representatives are chosen in large districts, the rights of the minority are destroyed. It is only by dividing the State into small portions, that there can be a fair expression of public opinion."[1]

§ 449. On the other hand, Judge Story contended that the proposed restriction was in conflict with the Federal Constitu-

[1] *Deb. Mass. Conv.* 1820, pp. 106–108.

tion; that by the latter instrument a discretion as to the choice of electors was given to the legislature; that that discretion was unlimited, and yet the proposition before the Convention went directly to destroy that freedom of choice, and compelled the legislature to resign all manner of choice but one; that it was bound to exercise its authority according to its own views of public policy and principle; but that the proposition in question compelled it to surrender all discretion; that a strong objection to that proposition, moreover, was that if it should be adopted by the Convention, and ratified by the people, the legislature would probably follow the rule presented by the proposed amendment; that the members of the legislature were under oath to support the Constitution of the State; that they were also under oath to support the Constitution of the United States; but would it not, it was asked, be a violation of their oaths to bind themselves not to choose representatives in any manner that the Constitution of the United States allowed, except that stated in the amendment? As to the question of policy, he admitted that a uniform mode of choosing representatives and electors by districts throughout the United States, would be a great improvement in the National Constitution; but he urged that the question before the Convention was not of that nature; that it went to limit Massachusetts to a particular mode of choice, leaving the rest of the United States free to adopt any other, the result of which would be, on the most important occasions, to deprive that State of all the influence to which her talents, character, and numbers entitled her.

In these views, Mr. Webster, also a member of the Convention, coincided, and the proposed amendment was not adopted.[1]

[1] See *Deb. Mass. Conv.* 1820, pp. 109–112. An interesting question discussed at great length in the Pennsylvania Convention of 1837, mainly as one of expediency, relates to the adoption of a provision in a State Constitution requiring State officers to take an oath to support the Constitution of the United States. A committee had reported an oath of office not containing such a clause to be taken by all State officers, and the debate arose upon an amendment proposing to insert it. The result was that not only the amendment, but the report of the committee recommending an oath of office, was defeated, and the Constitution framed by the Convention contained no provision for an oath of office. *Deb. Penn. Conv.* 1837, Vol. I. pp. 195–215. As bearing on the propriety of inserting in State Constitutions provisions supplementing or enforcing that of the United States, see remarks of Webster in the Massachusetts Convention of 1820, quoted *ante*, § 95.

§ 449 *a.* 4. A question not unrelated to that discussed in the last two sections is, whether a State Convention can prescribe what legislature shall act upon an amendment to the Constitution of the United States proposed by Congress; as, that it shall be a legislature elected after such amendment has been submitted to the States? This question arises upon a constitutional provision adopted by the Tennessee Convention of 1870, and subsequently ratified by the people of that State. As embodied in the Constitution, it is known as Article II., Sec. 32, of that instrument, and is as follows: —

"No Convention or General Assembly of this State shall act upon any amendment of the Constitution of the United States, proposed by Congress to the several States, unless such Convention or General Assembly shall have been elected after such amendment is submitted."

So far as relates to Conventions the prohibition is futile and inoperative, if the conclusion we have reached in the preceding section is correct; for no State Constitutional Convention, whether authorized or not by the Act calling it, could discharge the function of a legislature in the case supposed. Does the constitutional inhibition operate to deprive a legislature, existing at the time an amendment to the Constitution of the United States is submitted to the States, of power to act upon it? It is conceived that it does not, but that such inhibition is void as attempting to modify the Federal Constitution or to control the operation of a Federal Act or resolution, and that the consequences attending upon a void provision must follow. If the existing legislature were to assemble according to law and to pass upon the proposed amendment, its action would be valid and effectual to bind the State, notwithstanding the inhibition, if its action were affirmative of the amendment; and if its action were negative of it, that action would have the same effect as that of any State legislature which should have negatived the amendment.[1] On the other hand, doubtless, were the existing legislature to decline or fail to act upon the proposed amendment and go out of existence, the State legislature next elected according to law would have power to consider and act upon it.

In the Illinois Convention of 1869 a resolution to the same

[1] As to the effect of the negative action of a State legislature in such a case, see §§ 576–581.

effect, after which perhaps that of Tennessee was modelled, was introduced, but, after an adverse report by the Committee on Federal Relations, to which it had been referred, it was changed by its mover into the following form: —

"Article ——. The General Assembly shall not ratify any amendments to the Constitution of the United States until a general election for members of the General Assembly shall have been held, after such amendments shall have been proposed by Congress to the legislatures of the respective States." The proposed article was thereupon rejected by the Convention.[1]

§ 450. II. The preceding sections of this chapter have been devoted to a delineation of the powers of Conventions, resulting from what may be called their external relations; that is, their powers with reference to the sovereign society at large, and to the government of the State, both in general, and as divided into several distinct departments. It remains now to inquire what powers belong to them by reason of their internal relations, having reference, for example, to the perfecting of their organization, to the maintenance of discipline over their members or over strangers, and to the prolongation or perpetuation of their existence.

The powers of Conventions, considered from this point of view, are, first, such as are expressly given by the Act under which they assemble; or, secondly, such as are implied as being necessary to the exercise of these express powers, or as incidental to the complete execution of their commission.

§ 451. *First.* With respect to powers expressly given, it is unnecessary to speak at much length. In general, a power expressly granted to a Convention by a legislative Act or by a Constitution, is a power, the right to exercise which cannot be denied to it. Whether this rule is one whose application is universal, is a question of some delicacy which may be worthy of a short examination. To ascertain whether the rule has limits, an extreme case may be put. Let us suppose, that in calling a Convention, the legislature has authorized or required it to enact or to recommend measures subversive — 1, of the laws of morality; or, 2, of the guaranties of the public liberties, not extending, however, to the abrogation of republican forms. Would the Convention have power — not would it be obliged,

[1] *Deb. Ill. Conv.* 1869, pp. 161, 1152–1155, 1763–1771.

but would it be competent — to obey? 1. As to measures *mala in se*, the answer is, that the Convention would derive from such an Act no power whatever, for no body of men can give to another power to do what neither can rightfully do independently, — power in extent greater than is possessed by the giver.

§ 452. 2. More difficulty exists in relation to measures of the second class, which, in general, would be merely *mala prohibita*, though, doubtless, some of them, by destroying safeguards long recognized as essential to liberty, might be considered as tainted with positive immorality. But assuming that all such measures would, on *à priori* moral grounds, be indifferent, would a Convention then be competent to enact or recommend them? The answer clearly must be in the affirmative. Thus, were a legislature to require or authorize a Convention in the Constitution it should frame to repeal the entire Bill of Rights, or to insert clauses empowering the legislature to establish a censorship of the press, or the judiciary to issue general warrants, although the measures indicated would endanger some of our most valued rights, yet not being necessarily incompatible with the existence of republican government, or within the range of direct Federal prohibition, they would not be beyond the competence of the Convention.

§ 453. *Secondly.* It is the implied or incidental powers, claimed by or attributed to Conventions, that are of principal interest in this discussion; powers, that is, involved in the general grant of authority to assemble in Convention to revise the fundamental law. Conceiving of Conventions, then, as we must, as mere committees, what powers have they resulting by implication from their general character or from the nature of their business in relation to the points indicated? The general rule is undoubtedly this: — as Conventions are commonly numerous assemblies, containing, in most cases, the same number of members as the State legislatures, they are possessed of such powers as are requisite to secure their own comfort, to protect and preserve their dignity and efficiency, and to insure orderly procedure in their business. For the attainment of these ends, they are not without the authority possessed by agents in general, and, in my judgment, they are possessed of no other or greater. Thus, they must have a suitable hall, adequately warmed and lighted; and, though the Acts calling them were silent on the point, they would unquestionably have power to engage one, and to pledge the faith of the State for the rental thereof. So, there can be no doubt, a Convention would be authorized to appoint such officers and servants as the custom of public assemblies in free communities has sanctioned, or as may seem under the circumstances to be necessary.

§ 454. In respect to a president and secretary or secretaries, there can be no question. The convenience of members and the despatch of business would point also to messengers or pages as requisite. The same may be said perhaps of one or more door-keepers, since, if the hall where the session is held, were accessible to everybody, at all hours, the functions of the Convention might be seriously interrupted, and its dignity insulted. With respect to a sergeant-at-arms, some doubt exists. It is a universal practice in Conventions to appoint such an officer, and the right of doing so for certain purposes cannot be denied. The doubt arises in relation to his powers, which of course involves the competence of those bodies to vest him with them. A sergeant-at-arms is defined to be "an officer who executes the commands of the house in apprehending delinquents or offenders, and in preserving order," &c.[1]

As to one of these functions, that relating to the preservation of order, some officer charged therewith would doubtless be necessary in any assembly; but if it be true, as we shall attempt to show hereafter, that Conventions have no magisterial powers whatever beyond those possessed by every public meeting, it is doubtful whether a sergeant-at-arms is not a useless piece of ostentation in those bodies. In the case of a legislature, that officer discharges all the functions indicated by the definition. Moreover, the name sergeant-at-arms was undoubtedly derived from the sterner duties of his office, involving the arrest of delinquents, whether members of the body or strangers. For the present, however, I shall assume that the sergeant-at-arms of a Convention lacks the function which gives to the name of the corresponding officer of a legislature its appropriateness, and is a functionary, like a secretary or door-keeper, destitute of proper police powers. In his limited capacity, however, his duties are important. "He attends upon the Convention, maintaining order among those present, serving its processes and executing

[1] Worcester's *Dict. in verb.* "Sergeant."

its orders, giving notice to the presiding officer of persons attending with messages, or other communications; he has the appointment and supervision of the various officers of his department — and, as housekeeper of the house, has charge of all its committee rooms and other buildings during its sitting."[1] In short, he is the principal executive officer of the Convention.

How this officer came to be called a sergeant-at-arms, with powers so inferior to those indicated by his title as well as to those wielded by his namesake in the legislature, is shown by the origin of Conventions. We have seen that the first Convention, the type, in some respects, of all that have followed, was a Parliament irregularly called and constituted — a revolutionary assembly, modelled after the legitimate legislative branch of the government, with the same officers, and, in general, the same modes of proceeding. Of this original perversion of a Parliament, called the "Convention Parliament," our earliest Conventions, during the Revolution, were close imitations, both in structure and organization; and when, upon the foundation of our constitutional system, those exceptional and revolutionary bodies were transformed and introduced into it as part of the regular constitutional apparatus, their scheme of officers and rules and modes of proceeding were also adopted, without substantial modification.

§ 455. The power of a Convention to supply its members with stationery is perfectly clear; but in reference to the public journals there has been some doubt, though upon precedent as well as upon principle, the power must probably be admitted. It has been the practice of nearly all the Conventions held in the present century, to order, as well for the use of the members, as for distribution among their constituents, one or more newspapers for each member during the session. The reason usually assigned for this expenditure is, that it is important there should be a direct and constant communication between the people and their delegates in the Convention, in order that the latter may as perfectly as possible reflect the public will. If all that is proposed and discussed, be submitted immediately to the

[1] Cushing's *Law and Prac. of Legisl. Assemb.*, 2d ed., p. 131. The description quoted above is adapted from that given by Cushing of the sergeant-at-arms of a legislature.

people, with the reasons for and against, a thing possible only through the medium of the press, the delegates would be guided and moulded by a reflex wave of sentiment which would be fresh and unmistakable. Every thing which, within reasonable limits, conduces to that end, and at the same time conforms to the usages and is not foreign from the purpose and nature of the Convention is, by a liberal construction of its powers, authorized.

§ 456. The same principle applies to the case of phonographic reports and printing for the Convention. It would be a most niggardly policy which should refuse the expenditure necessary to the preservation of most full and accurate reports of its debates and proceedings. Upon this subject, however, there has been very great difference of views in different Conventions. In many of the States, volumes have been published, containing both the journals and the debates of all their Conventions. In others, the subject seems not to have been regarded as of any consequence whatsoever; and what little has been preserved has been owing to the private enterprise of the newspaper press. The result is, that the memorials of the most important public bodies ever assembled in those States, are often very meagre, and more often confused and inaccurate. Such a policy is "penny wise and pound foolish." In after years, when it has become impossible to replace what has been lost, more enlightened public opinion commonly finds cause to regret a paltry economy which deprives history of its most important data. It should be remembered, that our Conventions lay the foundations of States, many of which are to rival the greatness and glory of Rome, of England, and of France. In a hundred years from now, what treasures would they not expend, could they purchase therewith complete copies of their early constitutional records — documents standing to their several organizations in the same relation as would the discussions of those ancient sages who framed the Twelve Tables of the Roman law, to the Republic of Rome.

§ 457. And here I may be indulged in a remark or two in relation to the character and value of the debates of our Conventions.

Doubtless, to the listener, few public assemblies would exhibit so little that is attractive as those bodies. There are, of course, in them, much garrulity and much ignorance, and the topics of discussion are abstract and unfamiliar. Accordingly, the published conventional debates are dreary wastes of platitudes, dotted here and there with gems of wisdom and eloquence. So well is their prevailing character known, that in some of the later Conventions particular pains have been taken to discourage speech-making by the establishment of rules limiting debate — prominent delegates in one case, where there were no rules, directing the reporters to omit the speeches they themselves should make. But I am persuaded that a diffuse style, tainted in every period with rhetorical vices, is not incompatible with a high degree of political wisdom, and that all such attempts, however well-meant and, on grounds of taste, deserving of general sympathy, are ill-judged and harmful. When measures are under deliberation, which rest on principles alone, the opinions of commonplace men are frequently of as much value, and are likely to be quite as original, as those of the more gifted debaters. At all events, it is eminently useful to a public assembly to listen to the observations upon any subject, of many men of various callings, and of unequal attainments. If their thoughts are not generally profound, they are often suggestive; and, in a deliberative body, it is not so much the remarks of those who speak, as the reflections upon them of those who listen, which ripen its measures. The truth of this is seen in perusing the printed reports of the debates in our Conventions. One cannot go through the discussion of any important measure, in which men of ordinary minds participated, without being surprised to find fresh light constantly flowing over the subject from speeches, which not all the polishing of the reporter could make otherwise than offensive to a cultivated taste. In my judgment, therefore, it is unwise, where questions relating to the fundamental law, always more or less abstract, are under discussion, to limit or discourage debate to the same extent that might be advisable in a legislature, in which the measures proposed are commonly such as carry their policy or impolicy upon their faces; or, at least, in reference to which, if a mistake be made, the consequences are not so disastrous or so lasting. Hon. Henry A. Wise is said to have declared in the Virginia Convention of 1850, that "he would not give a fig for any Constitution that was framed in less than twelve months," — a remark involving some exaggeration, but indicating a much more proper appreciation of the importance of mature deliberation in organic legislation than the contrary extreme. There are no greater enemies to their respective States than those foolish delegates who are no sooner seated in Convention than they begin to clamor for less speech-making and more voting, with a view to an early adjournment and a light bill for Convention expenses.[1]

§ 458. In relation to the printing for the Convention, the case is very clear. If the Act calling the body provides for it, or requires it to be done in a particular manner or by a designated person, or limits it in amount or in cost, doubtless the Act should be obeyed. But, unless thus restricted, the power of the body to order its printing to be done, is as undoubted as to engage a hall or the requisite executive officers. The only alternative is, the employment of secretaries enough to furnish written copies of all papers and documents used in the course of its business. This would be possible, and such provision would, after a sort, answer the purpose. But it is certain, that the measures proposed would be neither so well understood nor so rapidly matured, if thus presented, as if they were printed. To this may be added, that the expense of printed would be much less than of written copies, and that the length of the session would probably be reduced by the use of them. The employment, then, of printed matter, being clearly within the power of the Convention, as incident to the speedy and convenient execution of its commission, the extent of it rests in the discretion of that body, and it can bind the government, within reasonable limits, by its contracts therefor.

§ 459. A Convention having provided itself with the officers needed to do or to expedite its work, its attention would be next directed to the subject of maintaining order in the transaction of its business, and in the conduct of its members. For this purpose, rules of order are necessary. There is sometimes inserted in the Act calling the Convention, a power to establish such rules as should be deemed requisite; but, without such a clause, a Convention would clearly be authorized so to do. It is usual, before rules have been reported by the special committee

[1] On this subject, see the excellent remarks of Hon. Mr. Sergeant, President of the Pennsylvania Convention of 1837, in *Deb. Penn. Conv.* 1837, Vol. I. pp. 304, 305.

for that purpose, to adopt temporarily those of the last Convention, or of the last State House of Representatives. In the absence of such a vote, it has been said, that the *lex parliamentaria*, as laid down in the best writers, is in force. If by this is meant, that the maxims of common sense, having reference to the protection of the rights of minorities, to the preservation of order, and to the speedy transaction of the business in hand, as the same are determined by the experience of public bodies, are to be taken as a guide, the proposition may be accepted, since the *lex parliamentaria* is but a body of practical rules founded on those very maxims. However that may be, it is undeniable that that law remains in force only at the discretion of the Convention. It may at any time be abrogated, partly or wholly, though it is certain that, if abrogated, there could not be substituted for it a system which, in its leading principles, should be contrary to the spirit of that law. So far as it should be so, it would operate as a device either to fetter the Convention in the exercise of its unquestioned powers, or to rob of their rights a minority of its members. It is not my purpose to inquire farther into the nature or extent of the rules of order which it is in the power of Conventions to adopt, but I pass to a question, not unrelated to that inquiry, though of vastly greater importance, namely, whether Conventions have power to arrest or to punish for offences committed against themselves or against their members, and to what extent?

§ 460. This question may be considered in reference

1. To offences committed by their own members, in their own presence; and

2. To offences committed by strangers, outside their walls, including the power to compel obedience to their mandates.

Before proceeding to consider these questions, however, I shall premise a few words in relation to the general principles which limit or determine the power of Conventions in this regard.

As a Convention is not a legislature, though a body, by delegation, exercising some legislative functions, but of so limited and subordinate a character as to entitle it to rank only as a legislative committee, it cannot do, even for its own defence, acts within the competence only of a legislature, or of a body with powers of definitive legislation. It can do, or authorize to be done, such things only as every assemblage of citizens is competent to do, as being necessary to the enjoyment of the right of freemen peaceably to assemble, guaranteed by our Constitutions. These would differ in different circumstances. If a mob were to enter the hall of a Convention and seek to overawe it, the body would doubtless be authorized to eject it, if practicable without a breach of the peace. On the other hand, were a riotous assemblage to gather in the vicinity of a Convention, threatening its members with bodily harm, or assailing them with abusive epithets, it is conceived that the body would have no power to disperse it, or to arrest or otherwise punish the persons composing it — at most, no greater power than would be possessed by any citizen or body of citizens. Its duty would be to call upon the constituted authorities forming the government of the State. It is true, cases may be imagined in which such a rule would place Conventions at the mercy of the populace, the government being unable or unwilling to interfere to vindicate the rights of those bodies. But those would be extreme cases, only existing where revolutions were impending. The liability to be so interrupted is shared by Conventions with all civic gatherings for social or political purposes. It would not be pretended, that, because the latter are liable to be disturbed by evil-disposed persons, they are authorized to exercise general police powers. Why then attribute those powers to the former? The laws are equally open to both, and there are, ever vigilant and ever ready, administrative officers charged to apply those laws to preserve the peace, and to give to every citizen, whatever his function, that protection which shall enable him to exercise it.

§ 461. It may be said, that legislatures wield powers much more extensive than those to which we seek thus to limit Conventions, and it may be asked, Why, if those powers are deemed necessary to the former, they should be less so to the latter? The answer is, *because the former possess them.* If they exist anywhere in the government, it is enough; and not only so, but the fact that they exist in one department or agency, is evidence that they do not, and a reason why they should not, exist elsewhere.

So, the inference that Conventions ought to have within themselves all the powers necessary for any emergency of violence or sedition, because our courts of justice and our corps of administrative officers have authority to vindicate their own dignity and independence, is wholly unauthorized. Not to mention that those bodies are largely dependent on our legislatures for the measures most effectual to protect them from insult and violence, they are radically different from Conventions — *they are political agencies in the actual exercise of functions of government.* It is proper that they should be vested with original powers of self-protection, since otherwise there could not exist that independence of each other in which alone safety would be possible. The three ordinary departments of a government need to be armed for self-defence against each other, at all points, because their spheres of action are conterminous, and they stand ever in each other's presence. Not so with Conventions, in relation to other State agencies; they are occasional, exceptional, and subaltern assemblies, charged with a special and limited function, and, therefore, have far less need of the powers indicated than either of those departments; or if those powers should be thought to be indispensable to their safety or efficiency, they must be wielded and exercised by the governmental agencies in which our Constitutions have vested them.

§ 462. 1. The power of a Convention to discipline its own members for offences committed in its presence is undoubted, and of considerable extent. The order and dignity of public deliberative bodies may, in many ways, be so assailed as seriously to interfere with the progress of business, if not wholly to interrupt it, yet without the commission of any misdemeanor for which the offenders would be amenable to the laws. A Convention, having no power to make laws giving the magistrates jurisdiction of such offences, unless it could, by sanctions of its own, enforce its rules for the preservation of order, it would be at the mercy of such members as chose to do the work of violence, but to do it in such a manner as to elude the penalties for a breach of the peace. To prevent this is the principal object of rules; and every public assembly, by its very nature, must have power to make and to enforce them in some modes appropriate to its own Constitution. To Conventions, however, it must be admitted, the range of sanctions is not very wide. For minor offences, it would be confined, probably, to reprimand, and for the more heinous, to expulsion from the body; or, in cases of actual violence to arrest and tradition to the public authorities.

Power to this extent I conceive to be indispensable to the existence of any deliberative assembly; and, without assuming the character of a legislature, with power to create and to invest officers and tribunals with jurisdiction to punish offences, I can imagine it possessed of no greater. The power to arrest an offender, in the case supposed of actual violence, would involve that of safely keeping, and, if necessary, of confining him until he could be delivered to the officers of the law. So, the power to expel a member would carry with it that of suspending, which is less, or of suspending with forfeiture of pay, temporarily or altogether, according to the degree of the offence. But the power could not be claimed, in the former case, to imprison as a punishment, or for a longer time than should be necessary to secure the arrested member until he could be transferred to the magistrates, on complaint regularly made;[1] or, in the latter, to pass from a forfeiture of pay (if that be regarded as allowable) to the imposition of pecuniary mulcts.

§ 463. In reference to the question of punishing offences by forfeiture of pay, if within the competence of a Convention at all, its action would be, like its proceedings in general, recommendatory, and not final. By directing its president or other proper officer to withhold from a delinquent his certificate, a Convention would make it impossible for him to draw his pay, unless it were specially awarded to him by a subsequent legislature.

§ 464. The offences by which members may subject themselves to whatever power of discipline a Convention possesses, are of various kinds, not differing materially from those that may occur in a legislature, which have been described by Cushing as follows: —

"Members may be guilty of misconduct, either towards the assembly itself, towards one another, or towards strangers. Misconduct of members towards the assembly, besides being the same in general as may be committed by other persons, consists of any breaches of decorum or order, or of any disorderly con-

[1] To our legislatures, our Constitutions sometimes expressly give power to imprison as a punishment for offences, but without such express provision they are understood to possess the power, and it is the punishment commonly resorted to by those bodies in cases requiring some degree of severity. See Cushing's *Law and Pract. of Legisl. Assemb.*, p. 267.

duct, disobedience to the rules of proceeding, neglect of attendance, etc.; or of any crime, misdemeanor, or misconduct, either civil, moral, or official, which, though not strictly an attack upon the house itself, is of such a nature as to render the individual a disgrace to the body of which he is a member. Misconduct of members towards each other consists of insulting remarks in debate, personal assaults, threats, challenges, etc., in reference to which, beside the ordinary remedies at law or otherwise, the assembly interferes to protect the member who is injured, insulted, or threatened. Offences by members towards other persons, of which the assembly has cognizance, consist only of injurious and slanderous assertions; either in speech or by writing, which, as there is no other remedy,[1] the assembly itself, if it thinks proper, takes cognizance of, and punishes."[2]

§ 464 *a*. The Acts calling the New York Convention of 1867 and the California Convention of 1878 provided, in substantially identical terms, that those bodies should have the power severally to expel any of its members, and to punish its members and officers, for disorderly behavior, by imprisonment or otherwise, but that no member should be expelled until the report of a committee, appointed to inquire into the facts alleged as the ground of his expulsion, should have been made; and that, in all cases in which they should punish any of their members or officers by imprisonment, such imprisonment should not extend beyond the session of those bodies respectively.

§ 464 *b*. In the Georgia Convention of 1867 a special committee was appointed to report upon a charge made by a newspaper against one of its members, that he had been convicted in New York of seduction. The chairman of the special committee submitted a minority report, giving the evidence collected, and closing with a resolution of expulsion. The majority, acquiescing in the report of their chairman as to the identity of the person and the facts as charged, were not prepared to recommend what the Convention should do. In their report they say: "There is

[1] The statement that "there is no other remedy," is applicable only to legislatures, and is justified by the principles established in relation to the privileges of such bodies. Custom has ordained that it is a breach of privilege to question a member of a legislature for words spoken in the house in debate, and many of our Constitutions expressly recognize the protection. Cushing's *Law and Pract. of Legisl. Assemb.* p. 250.

[2] Id. p. 259.

no law fixing any qualifications for membership of this body except the Act of Congress of March 2, 1867. That Act makes but one qualification, — conformity to the third section of the proposed constitutional amendment," known as the XIV. amendment. "It is true," they continue, "that Act prescribes conviction of felony at common law as a disqualification of a voter. Seduction is not felony at common law, nor is simple seduction felony by the laws of Georgia at all. It appears to us that this Convention would be adopting a dangerous rule to prescribe guilt of any offence as a disqualification for a seat. A Convention is in its nature a body which meets above all rules except those prescribed in its call. Perhaps half of the members of this Convention, as well as that of 1865, are held by the United States to have been guilty of treason. It is true that they have been pardoned, but we greatly doubt if the pardon is at all necessary to make them eligible. This Convention has, without doubt, power to expel a member guilty of a serious crime whilst a member; but we are not clear that it can, within the scope of its powers, examine into the past history of one of its members, and, finding it grossly immoral or criminal, go behind the vote of the people and expel him." And they conclude: "We are not prepared to say what should be the action of the Convention in this matter."[1] Afterwards, the resolution being called up, the accused member, in some remarks made by him to the Convention, insinuated that he had a letter in his possession charging a like offense upon the president of that body. He was thereupon by an unanimous vote expelled therefrom.[2]

§ 465. 2. In relation to the power of a Convention to vindicate its safety or its dignity by disciplining strangers, there is greater difficulty. The right to exercise such a power must be inferred either from the fact that it is held and exercised by legislatures, or that it is absolutely necessary to the exercise of powers admitted to belong to Conventions.

In probably all the State legislatures, the power is asserted to imprison persons not members for contemptuous or disorderly behavior in their presence; for threatening, assaulting, or abusing any of their members for any thing said, done, or doing in either house; or for a breach of their privileges, in making ar-

[1] *Journal Geo. Conv.* 1867, pp. 274, 275.

[2] Id. pp. 295, 296.

rests for debt, or in assaulting or disturbing their officers in the execution of any process or order of the houses; or in assaulting a witness or other person ordered to attend upon them, or rescuing persons arrested by their order, knowing them to be such. But it is a noticeable circumstance, that in a great proportion of the cases in which the power is exercised by legislative bodies, it is done in pursuance of express authority given in their respective Constitutions. This fact might cast a doubt on the right, where no such provision exists, were it not that it has become thoroughly established by prescriptive usage, as Mr. Cushing has said, "that in all the States, as well those whose Constitutions do not, as those which do contain" a clause authorizing its exercise, "each of the legislative branches has jurisdiction, according to the common parliamentary law, of all offences committed against it by persons not members."[1] But the fact that no law or Constitution has ever recognized the existence of such a power in Conventions, authorizes a doubt in regard to it. Those bodies are governed by the parliamentary law, but as all other public assemblies are, that is, so far only as is consistent with their special character and functions. Not all provisions of what is called the parliamentary law are in force in relation to all deliberative assemblies. The English Parliament differs, in this respect, from our Congress, and the latter from the State legislatures, which again differ from Conventions of all kinds, amongst which last, finally, there are characteristic differences. It is for this reason, that no work relating to the law and practice of any one of those bodies can be followed as an absolute guide in any other. In some measure the functions, and to a very great extent, the powers, of all those bodies differ, and thus necessitate different laws and usages. The fact, then, that the power in question is commonly exercised by our legislatures, has no tendency to prove that it belongs also to Conventions.

§ 466. Is the power to arrest or imprison persons, not members of Conventions, for offences committed outside of their halls, indispensable to the exercise of the powers confessedly vested in those bodies? In my judgment, this cannot be pretended. For a moment forgetting the danger of vesting such a power in a single chamber, a power involving, of course, that of holding,

[1] Cushing's *Law and Pract. of Legisl. Assemb.*, pp. 270–272.

in spite of courts and legislatures, persons declared by it guilty of violating its privileges or of contempt of its authority, is there substantial ground for pronouncing the power to be necessary? If it were admitted, that both the government of the State in its various departments, and the government's master, the sovereign, were hostile to the Convention, interested and determined to compass its overthrow, there would be plausibility in claiming for it the power as a means of self-defence. But the hypothesis is at variance with all the facts. If the Convention be legitimate, it is the offspring of the government, deriving its origin from an Act concurred in by both the legislature and the executive, and exists constantly under the guardianship of those two friendly powers, which, in point of time, preceded it, and which accompany and will survive it, so that at no moment can it be at the mercy of hostile influences, and, therefore, stand in need of the extraordinary powers claimed for it.

§ 467. Very little light is thrown upon the general question above discussed by precedents. One or two cases, however, have arisen bearing upon it, to which reference will be made.

The Illinois Convention of 1862, on a suggestion that a reporter for one of the daily journals had imputed to a large proportion of its members complicity with a disloyal society, known as the "Knights of the Golden Circle," appointed a committee to investigate the charge, *with power to send for persons and papers, and to swear witnesses*, which, of course, involved the power to compel obedience to its summons, by arrest or imprisonment, if necessary.

As may be inferred from the high tone of that Convention, in respect of its prerogatives, the power was exercised without reserve; witnesses were summoned from all quarters, and their statements taken under oath. It does not appear that the powers of the committee were questioned, and, therefore, whatever weight a precedent, established by a Convention disposed to magnify its office, but whose entire labor was repudiated by the people, may be thought to deserve, it must be allowed to have. As the instances are very rare, if any have occurred since the Revolutionary period, in which Conventions have claimed such powers, their propriety may be doubted, unless shown to be indispensable to the practical working of the Convention system. Whether it was so or not in Illinois, may be inferred from the considerations before presented, and also from the particular facts of the case. The substance of the offence charged against the reporter, was the publication of libellous imputations upon the members of the Convention. But it is not easy to see how a libel, contained in a newspaper outside of the organization whose members were assailed, and relating to those members not in their character as delegates, but as citizens and patriots, could in any way interfere with the orderly and complete execution of the commission of the collective body. The presumption of the necessity of such a power is much weakened when it is considered how a committee acting under such circumstances would be likely to protect and vindicate the public interests. The discussion in the Convention on the subject of appointing a committee, indicated that the libel was thought to reflect on members belonging to only one of the political parties in the body. That party was in a majority in the Convention. Hence the charges in substance imported that a large number, perhaps a majority, of the party dominant in that body was connected with a disloyal society, whose aim was to revolutionize the State. Suppose those charges to have been well founded; would an inquest, ordered and conducted by a majority of which a large proportion were traitors, furnish to the public interests adequate protection against their own treason? If, on the other hand, there were no truth in the charges, would it comport with the public interest or dignity, that an important deliberative assembly should lend itself to purposes of private revenge, or squander its time in tracing the pedigree of slanders propagated by nameless scribblers in the public journals, and affecting not the body itself, but its members as individuals? Have we no judicial tribunals for the very purpose of conducting such inquiries whenever a responsible accuser can be found, or are those bodies, standing aloof from partisan strifes, less fitted to conduct them than a Convention, whose functions, whatever else they may be, are certainly not judicial?

§ 468. In regard to the power given to the committee to administer oaths, but a word is necessary. There can be no question, that the appointment of a committee with such a power involved an exercise of ordinary legislation, to which the Convention was not competent. Unless its action should have the effect of a law, by which a witness could be compelled to take the oath, and be made liable to the penalties of perjury in case it were broken, it was wholly nugatory. Would our courts pronounce guilty of perjury any man who should falsely take an oath thus authorized? Would not the act of administering such an oath be within the statutes against extra-judicial oaths?

§ 469. The only instance I shall mention in which a Convention has assumed to exercise the power of arresting persons, not members of its own body, occurred in Louisiana, in 1864; and I refer to it rather because it furnishes a convenient text in connection with which to consider the conventional power of arrest, as a practical question, than because the precedent is of much value in itself.

On the 22d of July, near the close of the session of that Convention, there appeared in the New Orleans "Times" newspaper, an article containing severe strictures upon the president and other members of that body, — in plain language imputing to the former, on the preceding day, drunkenness in his chair, and to the latter, riotous and unseemly behavior. On the morning of its appearance, the president arose to a question of privilege and called the attention of the Convention to the article in the "Times," which he declared to be a libel against himself as well as the Convention. The following resolution was thereupon offered by Mr. Cutler, and adopted: —

"*Resolved*, That Thomas P. May, editor of the New Orleans "Times," be brought before this Convention forthwith, by the sergeant-at-arms, and that he be required to purge himself of the contempt and libel on this body, as published in the issue of July 22, 1864, or that he be otherwise dealt with as the Convention may deem proper and just."

Mr. May, surrounded by his friends, refused to be arrested, and an order was thereupon procured from General Banks, then in command of the Department of the Gulf, with his headquarters at New Orleans, directing the Provost Marshal to arrest him and take him before the Convention. Brought, on the following day, to the bar of that body, the president read the foregoing resolution, and asked Mr. May what reply he had to make; whereupon that gentleman read the following paper: —

"I am here with the Provost Marshal to obey a military order issued by General Banks, and not in obedience to a resolution of this Convention. At the proper time, in the proper place, and in pursuance of the forms of law, I will answer to any charge made against me and my paper, the 'Times.'"

Mr. Henderson moved that this answer be considered as an additional contempt, which, after some discussion, was adopted. The Convention then, after a preamble charging upon Mr. May disloyalty to the government, and a gross libel against the president and members of the Convention, as well as contempt of its authority, by a vote of 49 to 31, adopted the following resolution: —

"*Resolved*, that Thomas P. May, Esq., for his said contempt committed upon the president and members of this Convention, in publishing in said paper said libel, shall be imprisoned in the parish prison of the Parish of New Orleans for the space of ten days, unless the Convention sooner adjourns; and that the sergeant-at-arms be directed and authorized to carry this resolution into effect."

To this resolution there followed others *requesting the military authorities to suppress the publication of the "Times," and the President of the United States to remove Mr. May from a federal office held by him.*

§ 470. In connection with the above resolutions, it is proper to note, that by Article 23, of the existing Constitution of Louisiana, that of 1852, each house of the legislature was empowered to "punish by imprisonment any person, not a member, for disrespectful and disorderly behavior *in its presence*, or *for obstructing any of its proceedings*," such imprisonment not to "exceed ten days for each offence."

It is probable, that, in the outset, the Convention deemed itself to be substantially within this constitutional provision, though a newspaper libel could hardly be considered disrespectful or disorderly behavior in its presence or as obstructing any of its proceedings. It accordingly commenced operations with a vigor calculated to impress the unthinking with high ideas of its power. But at this stage of the case, and before any attempt was made to imprison the culprit editor under the order specified, a second order from General Banks released him from custody, and he was not further molested. Thus, this dignified body, with the full purpose of humbling the offending editor, after putting in operation all the machinery in its possession by which it could hope to accomplish that end, retired from the unequal conflict, ending, in truth, where it ought to have begun, by calling upon the government to do for it what it could not accomplish by its own officers. But in these proceedings it was not only chargeable with imbecility; it was guilty of usurpation of unusual and dangerous powers. How far the exceptional condition of the State at the time might have palliated that usurpation, had not circumstances shown it to be unnecessary and foolish, need not be definitely settled. As the grasp of the Convention upon its pretended powers was not secure enough to bring success, but it was found necessary to call upon the existing government to aid in maintaining its dignity, it is demonstrated beyond question that it could do its appointed work without those powers, namely, by calling upon the public authorities for aid whenever the powers inherent in all public assemblies were found insufficient to protect it from insult or to expedite its business.[1]

§ 470 *a*. The New York Convention of 1867 met under an Act which prescribed the offenses for which it might punish strangers. It provided that that body should have power to punish as a contempt, and by imprisonment or otherwise, a breach of its privileges, or of the privileges of its members, but that such power should not be exercised except against persons guilty of one or more of the following offenses: —

1. The offense of arresting or imprisoning a member or officer

[1] For an excellent discussion of the proceedings of this Convention in this case, see Speech of Mr. Casabat, a member of the body, in *Deb. La. Conv.* 1864, p. 509.

As to the general question discussed in the text, it is proper to remark that in all the Conventions thus far held in the United States, some one hundred and ninety-two in number, I find no instance of the exercise of the power of arresting or imprisoning persons not members of those bodies, except in those whose character and proceedings were such as to rank them as Revolutionary Conventions. To this remark the instance in the Louisiana Convention of 1864, as I regard that body, is no exception. During the Revolution, the Conventions which framed the first Constitutions of their respective States were nearly all of them of the revolutionary stamp; and in many of those which clearly were such, the power in question was exercised, and, so far as I am aware, in no others. For an instance of this, see the proceedings of the New Jersey Convention of 1776, concerning the arrest and imprisonment of the royal governor, William Franklin, in *Jour. N. J. Conv.* 1776, pp. 10–13, 22, 23.

of the Convention, by civil process, in violation of his privilege from arrest as therein before declared.[1]

2. That of disorderly conduct in the immediate view or presence of the Convention, and directly tending to interrupt its proceedings.

3. That of publishing any false and malicious report of the proceedings of the Convention, or of the conduct of a member in his delegated capacity.

4. That of refusing to attend or be examined as a witness, either before the Convention or a committee, or before any person authorized by the Convention, or by a committee, to take testimony in the proceedings of the Convention.

5. That of giving or offering a bribe to a member, or of attempting by menace or by any other corrupt means or device, directly or indirectly, to control or influence a member in giving his vote, or to prevent him from giving the same.

To these provisions were appended the following limitations in regard to the punishment the Convention might inflict, that in all cases in which that body should punish any of its members or officers, or any other person, by imprisonment, such imprisonment should not extend beyond the session of the Convention.

The Act calling the California Convention of 1878 contained similar provisions, differing only in the specification of the first and fourth offences, but making no material modification thereof.

§ 471. It may be useful now to append a few remarks in relation to the question of privileges, as applicable to Conventions. Are the members of a Convention, or is the body itself, entitled to claim the immunities usually accorded to the legislature, and to its individual members, such as exemption from legal process, from service as jurors or witnesses, or from legal question tending to impair the freedom of their debates and proceedings? It is doubtless essential, in order to enable a legislature, or any other public assembly, to accomplish the work assigned to it, that its members should not be prevented or withdrawn from their attendance, by any causes of a less important character; but that, for a certain time at least, they should be excused from obeying any other call, not so immediately necessary for the welfare or safety of the State; they must also be always protected in the exercise of the rights of speech,

[1] For the declaration referred to, see § 472 *a*, *post*.

debate and determination in reference to all subjects upon which they may be rightfully called to deliberate and act; it is absolutely necessary, finally, that the aggregate body should be exempted from such interferences or annoyances as would tend to impair its collective authority or usefulness.[1] The immunities thus indispensable are, in the case of legislatures, commonly secured by rules and maxims or constitutional provisions, and are styled privileges, as being rights or exemptions appertaining to their office, to which citizens generally are not entitled.

§ 472. Out of the catalogue of privileges above given, it is not easy to select one with which a Convention or its members could safely dispense. It ought never to be, as without them it would frequently be, in the power of the enemies of reform to prevent or postpone it by arresting, harassing or intimidating the delegates to the body by whom it is to be accomplished. But the real difficulty is, not to determine whether or not a Convention ought to enjoy those privileges, but to ascertain how and by whom they should be protected and enforced.

Upon this point, there is, in my judgment, but one position that can be maintained with safety, and that is, that Conventions must stand upon the same footing with jurors and witnesses; they must look to the law of the land and to its appointed administrators, and not to their own powers, for protection in their office. If a juror or a witness, going or returning, is harassed by arrest, he does not himself or with his professional associates cite the offending officer before him for punishment, but sues out a writ of *Habeas Corpus*, and on pleading his privilege procures his discharge. Beside this, for personal indignity or injury, he may appeal to the laws for pecuniary compensation. The same course is doubtless open to any member of a Convention, and it furnishes for all ordinary cases a practical and sufficient remedy. Behind those bodies stands continually, armed in full panoply, the state, with all its administrative and remedial agencies, ready to protect and defend them. If experience, however, should at any time show that Conventions could not rely for defence upon laws and magistrates alone, the proper remedy would be an application to the legislature for an increase of powers. But such a necessity is not likely to arise. Except, perhaps, in revolutionary times, interference with the privileges of Conventions need not be

[1] Cushing's *Law and Pract. of Legisl. Assemb.*, §§ 529, 530, 531.

apprehended. The business that engages them is not one that appeals very strongly to the passions of men. If a member is occasionally arrested or libelled, it is absurd to pretend that our legal tribunals are not competent to give adequate and seasonable redress. And if the times be revolutionary, it is better that such an assembly as a Convention should be armed only with the weapons of its ordinary warfare — which are the weapons of peace — since experience has abundantly shown that, having others, it is quite as likely to wield them in the interests of revolution, as any other body in the State.

§ 472 *a.* The members of the New York Convention of 1867 were, by the Act under which they assembled, declared entitled to the following privileges: that every delegate should be privileged from arrest on civil process during his attendance at the sessions of the Convention, except on process issued in any suit brought against him for any forfeiture, misdemeanor, or breach of trust in any office or place of public trust held by him; that each delegate should enjoy the like privilege for the space of fourteen days previous to any such session, and also while going to or returning from such session, provided that the time of such going or returning did not exceed fourteen days; that each delegate should enjoy the like privilege after any adjournment of the Convention, until its next meeting, when such adjournment should not exceed fourteen days; that each delegate should enjoy the like privilege while absent with leave of the Convention; that no officer of the Convention, whilst in actual attendance upon the same, should be liable to arrest on civil process; and that for any speech or debate in the Convention, the members should not be questioned in any other place.

The California Convention of 1878 assembled under an Act copied from that of New York, described above, so far as relates to the offences and the punishments thereof specified in the Act, but differing from it in its enumeration of the privileges of the members of the Convention. It provided that every delegate to the Convention should have the like privileges from arrest and from civil process as members of the legislature then had by law; and that for any speech or debate in the Convention the delegates should not be questioned in any other place.

§ 473. The only remaining point proposed for discussion in this chapter relates to the extent of the power of Conventions, of their own motion, to prolong or to perpetuate their existence.

Upon the general question, I shall only observe, that when the Act of Assembly under which a Convention meets, expressly or by reasonable implication prescribes the work expected of it, as, "to revise and propose amendments to the Constitution," or simply "to meet in Convention," where the purpose of the meeting has been clearly made known by preliminary discussion, when that work has been accomplished, the body *eo instanti* becomes *functus officio;* and has no power to prolong its existence a moment, for any purpose whatever. The only difficulty is to determine when its work has been accomplished. Where these bodies have confined themselves to the limited sphere of duty in foregoing sections asserted to be alone proper for them, that of recommending to their constituents changes in the fundamental law, the question I am considering could not arise. It is only when, through the ignorance or negligence of the legislatures calling them, no provision has been made for taking the sense of the people upon the fruit of their labors, or for putting it in operation, and it is therefore deemed necessary for the Conventions themselves to perform that duty, that any reason could be discovered for prolonging an existence which properly ends when its constitutional function has been discharged.[1] In a few cases, accordingly, where such has been the state of facts, Conventions, after completing their scheme of fundamental modifications, have adjourned to meet at a future day, with a view either to amend it, should the popular sense have pronounced against it in any part, or to put it in operation, if it should have met with general approval. But this has rarely been done without a more or less direct authorization from the legislature which called them. Thus, the New Hampshire Convention of 1781 and the Pennsylvania Convention of 1789, having framed Constitutions, adjourned with a view to collect the

[1] By an ordinance of the Virginia Convention of 1775, for regulating the election of delegates to the Convention which framed the Constitution of 1776, special authority was given to the president, or, in case of his death or absence, to Robert Carter Nicholas, Esq., or to the Committee of Safety, to call the members of the Convention together again when it should appear to them "that a meeting of the Convention is necessary sooner than the time to which they stand adjourned." Hening's Va. St. at Large, Vol. IX. p. 53. It thus seems to have been doubtful in 1775 whether a power, which it might be necessary to exercise in times of public danger, could be assumed by the Convention without special authority in the Act calling it.

public sense in regard to their work; and at a subsequent session either prepared and submitted a new Constitution to the people, or declared the one already submitted to be the Constitution of the State, according to the vote of the people thereon. In New Hampshire, a previous Convention, that of 1778, had submitted a new Constitution to the people, and, as it had no authority to adjourn to a day subsequent to the vote upon the Constitution, it had adjourned *sine die* before such vote was taken. That Constitution was rejected by the people. In 1781 an Act was passed calling another Convention, and in it was inserted a provision that, "if the first proposed system or form of government should be rejected by the people, the same Convention shall be empowered to proceed and make such amendments and alterations from time to time as may be necessary; *provided* always that after such alterations the same be sent out for the approbation of the people." In pursuance of this authority the Convention framed and submitted to the people a Constitution which was rejected; it thereupon twice reconvened, and submitted to the people, successively two new Constitutions, one of which was rejected, and the other, the third framed by it, was adopted, and accordingly the last was by the Convention declared to be the civil Constitution of New Hampshire, to take effect on the first Wednesday of June, 1784.

The Act calling the Pennsylvania Convention of 1789 was to the effect that that body should review, and, if it should see occasion, alter and amend, the Constitution of the State; and that "it would be expedient, just, and reasonable that the Convention should publish their amendments and alterations for the consideration of the people, and adjourn at least four months previous to confirmation."

That calling the Kentucky Convention of 1849 required it to meet "for the purpose of readopting, amending, or changing the Constitution," and expressly gave it "power to adjourn and reassemble at such times as it may deem proper." Accordingly the Convention adjourned to a future day, in order that in the interim the people might vote upon the question of its adoption or rejection, and, on its being adopted, reassembled and put it in operation.

From these provisions, it was evidently the intention of the legislatures of Pennsylvania and Kentucky that the Conventions should adopt definitively and put in operation the Constitutions or parts of Constitutions framed by them. Until that work was accomplished, then, they had a right to sit, or, having adjourned for a reasonable time and purpose, again to assemble. Their work concluded, however, without special authority, it would, doubtless, have been wholly beyond their power to prolong their existence a moment, still more to reconvene, after having once dispersed.

§ 473 *a*. Several other cases have also occurred in which the same question, or some phase of it, has arisen, to which attention should be briefly directed. These are of two kinds: cases in which Conventions of States in a peaceful and orderly condition have prolonged their existence without authority from the legislatures which called them; and cases in which Conventions called in States in a revolutionary condition have exercised the same power. Of the former, there have been three: the Conventions of Maryland, of 1864; New York, of 1867; and Pennsylvania, of 1873. The facts in the two last of these cases have already been stated in the preceding sections treating of the power of legislatures to bind Conventions, and that of Conventions, by ordinance, to appropriate money.[1] Of the New York case it need only be said, that the Convention continued its sessions beyond the day on which the Act calling it had required its work to be submitted to the people, for the reason that its work was not yet completed. This the Convention was advised by the Attorney General that it derived from the Act no authority to do, but that there was no law forbidding it to continue its sessions; and that, although it would have no power itself to submit its work, when finished, to the people, a subsequent legislature might do so. With this view of the law and of its powers, the Convention deemed it expedient to go on and complete its work. In Pennylvania, the Convention, although it had completed a new Constitution and submitted it to the people, and had thus exhausted its powers under the Convention Act, nevertheless assumed the power to prolong its existence beyond the day fixed for the vote of the people, with a view, doubtless, to ulterior measures in case that vote should be adverse. The question of the legality of some of its proceedings had been submitted to the Supreme Court of the State, and the Convention, apparently

[1] See *ante*, §§ 435–441 *b*.

anticipating that its judgment might be adverse, made threats to abolish the court, should such be the result; and, in that condition of things, it adjourned to the 27th of December, a date some ten days after the vote of the people would have been taken. There being in the Act calling it no power thus to adjourn, or to prolong its sessions beyond the time of completing its work, its assuming to do so was clearly an usurpation of powers belonging only to the legislature. Happily, perhaps, for the peace of the State, the Constitution was ratified by the people, and some of the principal points of difference withdrawn rather than settled by the political power; the Convention, therefore, upon reassembling, contented itself with shooting a few "Parthian arrows," in the shape of resolutions setting forth its view of Conventional powers, and with ordering the commission it had appointed to hold the election in Philadelphia, which the Supreme Court had declared illegal, to be paid the expenses incurred by it; and thereupon it adjourned *sine die*.

The circumstances under which the Maryland Convention of 1864 voted to prolong its existence, by adjourning subject to the call of its president, are thus stated in the resolution of adjournment, passed August 21, 1864: —

"*Resolved*, That, in view of the uncertain condition of affairs in this State, owing to the possibility of an invasion by the public enemy, which may interfere with the expression of the popular will on the day to be fixed for voting on this Constitution, that this Convention, when it adjourns, for the purpose of taking the sense of the people on this Constitution, stand adjourned subject to the call of the president, and in case of the death or disqualification of the president (H. H. Goldsborough), Frederick Schley, of Frederick County, Joseph B. Pugh, of Cecil County, Henry Stockbridge, of Baltimore city, William T. Purnell, of Worcester County, be and they are hereby authorized, in the order in which they are named, to act as president and call the Convention together; but should the day appointed for the adoption or rejection of this Constitution pass without interruption, then the president shall declare, through the public press, the final adjournment without day of this Convention, and no *per diem* shall be allowed for the recess."[1] The vote on the new Constitution was fixed by the Convention for the 12th

[1] *Deb. Md. Conv.* 1864, vol. iii. p. 1876.

and 13th days of October, 1864. On the 1st of November of the same year, the president, H. H. Goldsborough, through the public press, announced that the balloting upon the question of adopting the Constitution had been peaceful and uninterrupted, and that, in pursuance of the foregoing resolution, he proclaimed the Convention adjourned *sine die.*[1] The only provision of the Convention Act bearing on the question of continuing the Convention was, that that body should "continue in session from day to day until the business on which said Convention shall have been assembled shall have been fully completed and finished." The business on which the Convention had been assembled was "to frame a new Constitution and form of government, to be voted on by the people on a day or days to be named by the Convention itself." That work had been fully completed and finished on the day of its conditional adjournment, the 6th of September preceding. The Convention, therefore, by the terms of the Act, was on that day *functus officio*, and its assumption of power to continue its existence beyond that time was wholly unwarranted. The reasons stated for the course pursued, that the condition of affairs in the State was uncertain, owing to the possibility of an invasion by the public enemy, and that such invasion, if it occurred, might interfere with the expression of the popular will on the day to be fixed for voting on the Constitution, were precisely such as would justify the assembling of the legislature by the Governor of the State, both of whom, together with the State officers generally, were at that time loyal to the Union, and created no necessity for the Convention's transcending its proper functions, or usurping a jurisdiction not granted, — in other words, for seizing revolutionary powers.

§ 473 *b*. The second class of cases referred to in which Conventions have assumed to prolong their existence after the special work they were called to do had been completed, have been those in which the Conventions met in States at the time in a revolutionary condition. Of these, all but one were Conventions called in the late rebel States, to effect either a secession of the same from the Union, or their reconstruction after the close of the secession war. The exception was the Convention of Missouri of 1861–63; an exception more nominal, however, than real, since,

[1] *Deb. Md. Conv.* 1864, vol. iii. p. 1902.

as we have seen,[1] that State, during the entire period covered by that Convention, was in a condition that bordered closely on revolution. In fact, the Convention is believed to have been called as a secession Convention. At its first session it was presided over by one afterwards a distinguished rebel general, and there was always in it a powerful minority not loyal in spirit or purpose to the Union. Constantly anticipating and called upon to counteract, therefore, the schemes of traitors within and without its own body, the Convention seized the reins of power, and entered upon a course of action proper only for a strictly revolutionary Convention, assembled during a temporary eclipse of the established powers of government. It vacated the offices of Governor, Lieutenant Governor, and Secretary of State, the incumbents of which, between the first and second sessions of the Convention, had gone over to the rebels, and were actually leading a hostile force into Missouri; it appointed a provisional governor and other civil officers, raised military forces, and provided the means for equipping and paying them. During the three years occupied by its sessions it was four times reconvened, as the public exigencies seemed to demand; once, for its second session, by the majority of a committee appointed to summon the members, if thought necessary, before the day to which it had adjourned should arrive, and three times by the provisional governor of the State, the Hon. H. R. Gamble, making five sessions in all. It need not be said that the acts and proceedings of a Convention thus called and conducted, however loyal or even necessary its action may have been, can be no precedent for Conventions not thus provisionally charged with all the powers of government, at a time of public danger. The Conventions of rebel States forming the residue of this class were those of Georgia, 1861, 1865, and 1867; South Carolina, 1860; Louisiana, 1864 and 1867: North Carolina, 1865; Virginia, 1867; Mississippi, 1865; and Arkansas, 1861[2] and 1868. Of those held in 1860 and 1861, it

[1] See §§ 327–330, *ante*.

[2] This Convention adjourned March 10 to the 19th of August, subject to the call of its president, "in an exigency in his opinion requiring it." It was, accordingly reconvened on the 6th of May, by its president, David Walker, by a proclamation issued April 20, for the reason that "preparations are being made for a war between the citizens of the free and the slave States." McPherson, *His. Rebellion*, 399.

After its reconstruction, the Supreme Court of that State held, in Penn *v.*

need only be said that they were all avowedly revolutionary bodies, called to effect a dismemberment of the American Union. In prolonging their existence after their first session by adjourning subject to the call, in the Georgia case, of the president of the Convention, and, in the South Carolina case, of the Governor of the State, they exercised revolutionary powers, and their action can be a precedent only for a revolutionary Convention. Omitting for the present such of the Union Conventions as assembled under the proclamations of Presidents Lincoln and Johnson, those of Louisiana, 1864, Georgia, Mississippi, and North Carolina, 1865, we pass to consider those called in pursuance of the Reconstruction Acts of March, 1867, which stand in some respects upon a different footing. The following Conventions, after the completion of the work of framing a Constitution, adjourned, that of Georgia, 1867, and Arkansas, 1868, subject to the call of their respective presidents;[1] that of Louisiana, 1867, subject to that of a quorum of its members; and those of Virginia, 1867, and Missippi, 1868, subject to the call of a committee of five of their delegates. There is nothing in those Acts authorizing such adjournments, and they must in each case be regarded as a usurpation, unless, from that provision of the Act which requires the president of each Convention, when the result of the vote of the people on a Constitution has been to adopt the same, "to transmit a copy of the same, duly certified, to the President of the United States," authority to continue in session may be inferred. Doubtless, speaking strictly, were the Conventions to have adjourned *sine die* immediately after submitting their Constitutions to the people, not only those bodies, but their presidents and other officers, would have ceased in the eye of the law to exist. Now, if the naming of the president of the Convention to transmit the Constitution was intended merely to designate a private person who should be charged with that duty, and not an officer chosen in pursuance of a Federal law, it is difficult to justify the exercise of such a power by Congress. It would follow that, to enable

Tollison, 26 Ark. R., 645, that that body "might have had power to adjourn from day to day, but the president had no power to convene it at will; and that, as a Convention, it was *functus officio* when it adjourned on the 10th of March, and all its acts subsequent to that time were absolutely null and void, and without authority or sanction on the part of the people."

[1] To the Arkansas resolution was afterwards added a *proviso* that, if not convoked within one year, the Convention should stand adjourned *sine die*.

the person who had been chosen president of a Convention to comply with the Act as such, the Convention would need to continue in session until after the vote upon the Constitution had been taken and announced. If it be objected that many of the Reconstruction Conventions adjourned *sine die* at once after completing their work of framing new Constitutions, and hence could not have complied with the law as above construed, the answer is, that if the person who had been president of a Convention, but was now a private citizen, had transmitted the Constitution to the President of the United States, after its adoption, and it had been accepted without objection by the latter, and approved by Congress, the irregularity would have been waived. On the other hand, if the clause of the Act quoted, properly construed, gave those Conventions no power to continue their existence for the purpose indicated, their acts were without warrant of law.

§ 474. Recurring now to the cases of the Convention of Louisiana, 1864, called under the proclamation of President Lincoln, and of North Carolina, Georgia, and Mississippi, called in 1865 under that of President Johnson, the three last will be first considered. The North Carolina Convention, having as it supposed restored the State to its normal relations to the Union by certain amendments to the Constitution framed by it, and submitted to and adopted by the people, adjourned on the 9th of October, 1865, to the 6th of May, 1866. On that day it reassembled and proceeded to make further changes in the Constitution, deemed to be necessary to secure admission into Congress for her Senators and Representatives, and adjourned *sine die* on the 25th of June, 1866. The amendments framed by it, however, were rejected by the people. The Georgia Convention of 1865, having in like manner finished its labors by drafting and submitting to the people a Constitution, adjourned subject to the call of its president, "should a contingency arise in regard to the Federal relations of the State, or other cause, which in his judgment would make it necessary for the Convention to be again convened, *provided* that the call should be made within six months; if not made within that time, then the Convention to stand adjourned *sine die*."[1] So, the Mississippi Convention of 1865, having finished a revision of the Constitution of that State, adjourned subject to the call of its president, "if in his judgment necessity

[1] See *Journal Geo. Conv.* 1865, p 194.

should arise for reconvening it." In these three cases the action of the Conventions in providing for a continuance of their sessions was, perhaps, authorized by the terms of President Johnson's proclamation, which described the purpose and powers of the Conventions, that might be called in the several rebel States in pursuance of it, to be to alter and amend the Constitutions thereof, and with authority to exercise, within the limits of said States, all the powers necessary and proper to enable the loyal people thereof to restore said States to their constitutional relations to the Federal Government. As, however, the reconstruction attempted in these and other States under this proclamation was, by the Acts of Congress of March, 1867, declared to be unauthorized, and the governments established in pursuance of it to be provisional only and not legal governments, the action of those Conventions, whether authorized or not, must fall with them, and thus cannot be properly considered as valid precedents.

The case of the Louisiana Convention of 1864, which was called under the proclamation of President Lincoln, while in the respect just stated it was equally invalid with those of the three States named, is in some other respects subject to a more stringent rule, and will require a more extended consideration. Nothing contained in the proclamation of President Lincoln gave the Convention any authority to do more than to take steps for the reëstablishment of a loyal government in Louisiana and the other States named. Under date of December 8, 1863, proclamation was made that whenever certain specified classes of persons within the rebel States, including Louisiana, having taken a prescribed oath and kept it, "shall reëstablish a State government which shall be republican," etc. . . . "such State shall be recognized as the true government of the State." It makes no mention of a Convention as one of the means that might be used to compass the end desired. The Convention was called by General Banks, in command of the Department of the Gulf, by a general order, of which the only clause determining the powers and functions of the Convention was the following: —

"I. An election will be held on Monday, the 28th of March, at 9 o'clock, A. M., in each of the election precincts established by law in this State, for the choice of delegates to a Convention to be held for the revision and amendment of the Constitution of Louisiana."

In pursuance of this order, delegates were elected, assembled on the day named, revised and amended the Constitution of Louisiana, submitted the same for adoption or rejection to a vote of the people, and on the 25th of July following adjourned. It did not, however, adjourn *sine die.* On the last day of its session, by a vote of 62 to 14, it adopted the following resolution: —

"*Resolved*, That when this Convention adjourns, it shall be at the call of the president, whose duty it shall be *to reconvoke the Convention for any cause*, or, in case the Constitution should not be ratified, for the purpose of taking such measures as may be necessary for the formation of a civil government for the State of Louisiana. He shall also, in that case, call upon the proper officers of the State to cause elections to be held to fill any vacancies that may exist in the Convention, in parishes where the same may be practicable."[1]

When the Convention adjourned, accordingly, it "adjourned subject to the call of the president, in pursuance of the resolutions this day adopted."[2]

After its adjournment, the Constitution framed by it was submitted, as required by Article 152, to a vote of "the good people" of the State, and adopted.

§ 475. By the Constitution thus framed, the State was governed, so far as she had a civil government at all, from the time of its adoption until it was declared to be provisional merely by the reconstruction Acts of March, 1867, and superseded by the Constitution of 1868, framed in pursuance of those Acts.

Early in the month of July, 1866, however, an attempt was made to reassemble the Convention of 1864. The objects to be effected by it, as declared by the proclamation of the person assuming to call it, referred to below, were to revise the Constitution, and to take measures for the ratification of an amendment to the Constitution of the United States, proposed to the *State legislatures* by the 39th Congress.[3]

To this end, the president of the Convention was requested by a caucus of its members, to call that body together in pursu-

[1] *Journal La. Conv.* 1864, p. 170.

[2] Id. p. 171.

[3] Had the latter been the only object of the reconvocation of the Convention, it would have been alone sufficient to stamp it as illegal. See *ante*, § 447.

ance of the resolution above recited, but refused so to do. The caucus thereupon declared the office of president vacant, and elected Judge R. K. Howell president *pro tem.*, by whom a call was issued requiring the delegates to reconvene in Convention on the 30th of July following. There being, from various causes, also a large number of vacancies in the Convention, the Governor of the State, J. Madison Wells, in alleged pursuance of the same resolution, issued his proclamation, requiring the proper officers of the State to issue writs of election for delegates in unrepresented parishes. The Convention accordingly assembled at New Orleans on the day appointed, but was dispersed by a mob, led by the police of the city.

§ 476. Upon these facts the question arises, Was the body which met at New Orleans on the 30th of July, 1866, legally a continuation of the Convention of 1864?

The answer must be that it was not.

Looking at the resolution of the Convention, it is clear that no authority to call the body again together was derived from that part of it which empowered the president "to reconvoke the Convention . . . . in case the Constitution should not be ratified," for it was ratified. If the body was legally reconvoked, it was under that clause of the resolution which declared it to be the duty of the president to reconvoke "the Convention *for any cause.*"

Now, in reference to this clause, —

1. Supposing that it authorized the president of the Convention, at his discretion, to call that body together at any future time, the trust was personal and official, and could not be discharged by another, even if the president was unable or unwilling himself to discharge it. In fact, however, the president exercised the trust — the discretion committed to him — for, on application, he refused to reconvoke the body.

2. But, admitting that the trust might, under some circumstances, be shifted to, or assumed by, another, a rightful successor to it must have been the legal appointee of the Convention; and to fulfil that condition, the Convention must first have been legally reconvoked. But, clearly, in its dispersed and dormant condition, neither the body itself nor any caucus of its members could do an act which was necessary as a precedent condition to its reconvocation. In other words, the appointment of

a president *pro tem.* by a caucus of the delegates, was but the act of individuals, and of no validity whatever under the resolution. Who composed the caucus? Conceding that all the delegates were present, — which was not the fact, — by what authority did they sit in caucus? When a Convention acts, it does so, not by a caucus, but by its whole body. That it could not so act is a proof that, except as individuals, its members could not act at all.

§ 477. 3. But a stronger argument against the validity of the act of reconvocation is found in the terms of the clause of the resolution in question. Its words are, — "Whose duty it shall be to reconvoke the Convention *for any cause.*"

Within what limits was this power to be exercised — limits, that is, as to time and occasion? Was the president of the Convention to hold this most important prerogative during life? Might he call the body together, as he might his hounds, for ordinary purposes of party or of administration, or must the extraordinary assembly be reserved for extraordinary occasions? When and for what the call should be made, was left entirely to the discretion of the president, a single person, no longer even an officer, unless indeed the Convention be regarded as sitting *en permanence.* Such a discretion defines precisely that which, under our Constitutions, is lodged with our General Assemblies — a legislative discretion. That a Convention in the last stages of dissolution, having completed its work, should attempt to give such a discretion, was not only unconstitutional, it was impudent. Imagine a conflict between the General Assembly and the president of the Convention, on the question of calling that body again together. The General Assembly passes an Act requiring the Convention to reassemble. The president issues his proclamation forbidding it to convene. The delegates obey the latter, for, by the terms of the resolution, the discretion to call them was lodged with the president. Or, the General Assembly, twenty-five or fifty years after the adjournment, resolves to call a new Convention. The president deems the old one an abler or a more available body, and issues his order reconvoking it. Which is the legal Convention? Is the air peopled with defunct Conventions, waiting the magic word from their defunct presidents, to clothe themselves again in flesh to rule us? Yet such may certainly be the case, unless when its function is discharged the Convention dies — if, at its decease, it can lodge with its presiding officer, for life, a discretion to revive the body at his own pleasure and for his own purposes.

§ 478. On a review of the cases cited in the last seven sections, it appears that of the eighteen Conventions which have prolonged their existence by adjourning after the completion of their work, either to a day certain, or generally, subject to the call of their president or of a committee, twelve were sitting at a time when their States were in a revolutionary condition, so that their action, though perhaps excusable on moral grounds, is without weight as a precedent for Constitutional Conventions in general. It also appears that, of these twelve Conventions, two called under the proclamation of President Johnson, and five which met in pursuance of the reconstruction Acts of 1867, were perhaps, by a fair construction of those documents, authorized to do what they did. Of the six Conventions, whose sessions, with the possible exception of that of Maryland, 1864, were held in peaceful times, the three earliest — New Hampshire, 1781, Pennsylvania, 1789, and Kentucky, 1849 — had from the Convention Acts under which they assembled authority, either express or plainly implied, to adjourn on the completion of the Constitutions they should frame, and to reconvene after the vote of the people thereon, for the purpose of further amending or of putting them in force. There are left three Conventions not subject to any of the conditions stated. Of these, that of New York, 1867, prolonged its session, in no spirit of revolt against the Act under which it assembled, as expounded to it by the Attorney General, but, perhaps admitting its want of legal authority, with a hope of receiving the sanction of the legislature at a subsequent day, and of thereby saving the great expense of another Convention — a hope in which it was not disappointed. The Maryland Convention of 1864 and the Pennsylvania Convention of 1873 occupy the bad eminence of being the only bodies of the kind which, called to do a defined work under a law constitutionally passed, have completed that work, and then, laying claim to unlimited powers, instead of quietly dissolving, have assumed the right to continue an existence which, from the moment it adjourned, became a menace and a danger. To one who cannot read between the lines it may seem, that the motive in both these cases was a desire to promote the public good; but in fact it was the public good in a party sense, to be compassed by partisan methods; and while, in Maryland, it would be natural to sympathize with the extreme Union men who attempted, by the action we are discussing, to bring and to keep that State in the hands of the thoroughly loyal part of its people, it was sought to be effected by a proceeding fraught with a danger to the country at large, by establishing a wrong theory of conventional power, greater than would be a temporary subjection of a loyal community to rebel control. In Pennsylvania, there was not even that poor excuse for the action of the Convention, though doubtless there had been great abuses in the elections in the city of Philadelphia, to remedy which was the motive for its illegal mode of submission in that city. But for its disobedience to the mandate of the legislature in regard to the altering of the Bill of Rights, if it were even admitted that the limitation was injudicious, there was neither in law nor in morals any justification whatever; for the judiciousness or injudiciousness of the law was not a question for the Convention, any more than it was for the Masonic order in Pennsylvania. The law was the source of all the power the body had, and if its terms were unreasonable, appeal should have been taken, not to the sciolists in constitutional law who proclaimed the power of Conventions to be illimitable, but to the people, to rebuke the legislature by returning to it men who would give to a new Convention larger powers. When it is considered, moreover, that more than one member of the Convention who advocated the appointment of a committee to revise the Bill of Rights, notwithstanding the interdict of the legislature, declared in substance that they did so for the purpose of showing that body that the Convention would not be trammelled by it,[1] it is impossible to respect either the statesmanship or the patriotism of the majority controlling the Convention which failed to place upon such a declaration the stamp of its disapproval.

[1] See *Deb. Penn. Conv.* 1873, Vol. I. pp. 53–62.

CHAPTER VII.

OF THE SUBMISSION OF CONSTITUTIONS TO THE PEOPLE.

§ **479.** An important part of the duty of a Convention is to submit to the sovereign, for its approval or disapproval, the propositions of constitutional law which it has matured.

The duty of submission grows out of the nature of our institutions.

In the American political system, the edifice of government rests on the people. Two ideas pervade that system: first, that of the absolute right of the people, under God, and, in the States, subject to the Federal Constitution, themselves to determine and to carry into operation the policy, laws, and government, in all its departments; and, secondly, that of the solemn obligation resting on those through whom the people act, not only to obey their will, but to keep themselves constantly in a condition of perfect responsibility to them, save in the single case where a discretion has been in terms given them. In other words, if the safety of the State, as constituted in America, requires, as it certainly does, that the people should possess a curb upon their agents, it requires no less that those agents should recognize that curb as existing, and facilitate its application. We have seen that our Conventions are in substance but mere committees, destitute of the power of self-direction, and by their organization as little fitted as in theory designed for independent or definitive action. If, therefore, in the face of these principles, the people were so far to forget what is essential to the safety of their institutions as to be willing to throw the State, without check, into irresponsible hands, the Convention is the last body to which should be committed so grave a trust. This follows from the fact, if from no other, that it consists of but a single chamber. But the Convention, as we have seen, is of revolutionary parentage; it was originally the child of illegality, and has come into the constitutional household by adoption, and hence has been ever the subject, in all questions of power and competence, of fatal misconceptions. It is, of all our institutions, the one through which sedition and revolution would most naturally seek to make their approaches. Instead of deserving confidence, such an institution merits distrust and repression. In a word, to apply the principles above announced, it is the interest of the Commonwealth that no discretion liable to be abused should be left to a Convention, without careful provision for repressing and correcting its abuses; or, viewed on the side of the Convention, it is for such a body a sacred duty, in no case unbidden to assume to exercise a discretion, upon an abuse of which there is not reserved to the people an instant and effectual check. Such a check (and it is practically the only one possible) is involved in the submission of the fruit of its labors to the judgment of those for whom they act — the people.

§ 480. The general propriety and necessity of submission being conceded, there are three cases in which doubts may arise as to the duty of Conventions in that regard. It may be useful to dwell a few moments upon each of them.

The first case is, where both the Constitution and the Act of Assembly, under which the Convention met, are silent in respect of submission:

The second, where, by one or both of those instruments, submission is expressly required; specific directions, perhaps, being also, at the same time, given as to the mode:

The third, where, in the Act calling the Convention, submission is expressly dispensed with.

§ 481. I. Where neither the Convention Act nor the Constitution requires the Convention to submit its work to the people, the duty of that body to do so is, nevertheless, upon sound principles, believed to be perfectly clear. Obviously, a Convention is bound to regard itself as limited to the exercise of such powers as are expressly given to it, or as are necessary to the exercise of such as are expressly given. But, in the case supposed, no express power relating to submission is contained in its commission. Both the duty and power of the body are then to be determined by the general scope of that commission, so interpreted as to harmonize with the spirit of the institutions of the country, and to assure to them, in the greatest possible degree, exemption from the evils and dangers to which they are liable. Under such a rule, the question whether submission is or is not a duty, is one mainly of presumptions. Is it probably the safer constitutional precedent to establish, that a body, consisting of a single chamber, and charged with legislative duties of supreme importance, may shape their work as their own interests or prejudices may dictate, and then put it into practical operation, wholly without responsibility to the people; or, that the measures they may mature shall be regarded as advisory merely, as having no force or validity beyond that of simple recommendations, until ratified by those for whom they act? This is the whole subject in a nutshell, and it is impossible for a moment to doubt which is the safer, and, therefore, the only proper course. Conventions are bound to give to the people an opportunity to negative inexpedient or dangerous constitutional provisions. They may know their members to be honest, and may believe them to be wise, and their enactments salutary or even necessary; but they will not fail to recognize the two cardinal truths, — first, that however virtuous or wise men may be, they are liable to fall into errors, which may entail upon the State no less disaster than would treason itself; and, secondly, that the action they may take in any particular, whether right or wrong, is likely to become a precedent for succeeding Conventions.

§ 482. II. The second case, which has already formed the subject of consideration in a previous chapter, in another relation, presents less difficulty; that is, where submission of the Constitution to the people is expressly required by law. If the Constitution contained provisions to that effect, probably no one would be hardy enough to maintain that there could be any alternative to obedience but revolution. And if it prescribed special modes or forms, it is presumed no power would be thought competent to dispense with a punctilious conformity to its terms.[1] It is only in relation to Acts of the legislature that question could arise. Would a Convention be bound by the Act under which it assembled, without regard to its own views of propriety or necessity, to submit the product of its deliberations to the people, if the Act required it? As this

[1] In the Ohio Constitution of 1851, and in the West Virginia Constitution of 1863, provisions are inserted declaring amendments to those instruments to be of no force unless submitted to the people.

question has already been the subject of consideration, to some extent, in a preceding chapter,[1] it is necessary here only to indicate briefly the arguments which were there adduced.

§ 483. The Act of Assembly under which a Convention meets, is its charter. Whatever, not inconsistent with the Constitution or the principles of the Convention system, the former prescribes, the latter must do. It is the law, passed by the competent law-making power, within the limits that bound its jurisdiction. What is a Convention, that it should assume to be exempt from obedience to that department of the government which is charged with higher sovereign attributes — is more nearly sovereign — than any other in it? Does it claim to be itself above the legislature? Let it show its warrant for a claim so exorbitant, for upon it must rest the burden of proving what contradicts all political analogies, and the first principles of constitutional government. It cannot find that warrant in the mandate of the power by whose *fiat* it came into being, for, by hypothesis, that is expressly to the contrary. It cannot find it in claims set up by Conventions, and allowed by the people, in the best days of the Republic, for, with scarcely an exception, during that happy period, when party conflict had not succeeded in perverting our statesmen into mere politicians, it was universally conceded, that the Convention was the child of the law, and, as such, bound to obey literally its requirements. Nor can a warrant for the claim be found in the principles which preside over the genesis and healthy growth of free communities, for those principles, as we have seen above, require Conventions to rank themselves as the servants, not the masters of the people; and when the will of the people is known, to conform themselves scrupulously to it; but when it is unknown, to presume that to be required of them which most conduces to the safety of the Commonwealth.

§ 484. III. The third case, — that in which submission is expressly dispensed with, and the Convention authorized or required to put the Constitution into operation without referring it to the people, — would seem to present less occasion for doubt. The case has not very frequently arisen, but, so far as I am aware, Conventions have never questioned, either the competence of the legislature so to provide, or their own right and duty to obey

[1] See *ante*, §§ 410-417.

It is only when our General Assemblies have imposed restrictions upon them, that Conventions have been disinclined to recognize their right to command. Precedents of the exercise of such a power have, as we shall soon see, arisen, sometimes with and sometimes without special legislative authorization. Perhaps, therefore, the question whether such a body can rightfully obey a command of the legislature requiring it to act definitively, ought not to be regarded as an open one. And it may be, that no very serious exception could be taken on principle to an Act containing such a provision, provided the precaution had been employed to take upon it in advance the sense of the people. This might be accomplished in two ways: first, by proposing the Convention Act in one legislature, and laying it over to be finally acted on by a succeeding one, in the mean time publishing it and calling to it the public attention; or, secondly, by actually submitting to a vote of the people the question of calling a Convention. Of these two modes, either of which would fulfil the conditions requisite for the public safety, the second is unquestionably the preferable one, and it has the high sanction of the New York Council of Revision, in 1820, of which Governor Clinton, Chancellor Kent, and the judges of the Supreme Court, were members. The majority of this Council, deeming it "most accordant with the performance of the great trust committed to the representative powers, under the Constitution, that the question of a general revision of it should be submitted to the people, in the first instance, to determine whether a Convention ought to be convened," vetoed a bill providing for a call of a Convention, which had been passed by the legislature, on the single ground that it did not propose to submit the question to the people.[1] The same principles that govern the call of a Convention, ought, evidently, to apply to a grant to such a body of unusual powers in the Act by which it is called. It does not admit of a doubt that the safest and wisest course, in one case no less than in the other, would be to submit the questions referred to to the determination of the people.

§ 485. But, suppose there has been no submission to the people, no means used to collect their opinion upon the question, aside from precedents, would the legislature then be competent to authorize definitive action by a Convention, or the latter be empowered to take it? The answer must be in the negative.

[1] For this veto, see *post*, Appendix F.

1. When a legislature calls a Convention, without the special authorization of the Constitution, it steps to the very verge of its power. It does an act which, as it can show no express warrant for it, it can justify only on the ground that it was a necessity, and that it was itself the only department of the government clearly not incompetent to do it. But an Act which can be justified only by necessity, must conform to that necessity in its character and limitations; so far as it goes beyond it, the Act is unnecessary, and, therefore, unjustifiable. If the calling of a Convention is necessary, it certainly is not necessary to call it in such a way as to make of it a despot — to let it loose upon the community without check against the assumption of dangerous powers. A legislature may always prescribe that a Convention shall content itself with proposing, and that to its propositions there shall be communicated the force of law only by the *fiat* of the people. *What is practicable under such conditions, is to be taken as the measure of its duty*, and it is as binding on that body as though it had been expressly embodied in the Constitution.

§ 486. 2. If, on the other hand, the Constitution, like most of our later ones, were to authorize the legislature, in general terms, "to call a Convention," and, if in doing so, that body were to insert in its Act a provision permitting the latter to frame and put in force a Constitution, without submission, would the legislature exceed its power, or would the Convention be warranted in availing itself of the permission? Laying the precedents referred to out of sight, the answer must still be in the negative, and for substantially the reasons above given. Although, from the generality of the constitutional provision, power might properly be inferred in calling a Convention, to exhaust the categories of time, place, and mode of assembling, organizing, and proceeding, as well as to fill out the outlines of an expedient limitation of its powers, with a view to the safety of the state and the facilitation of its business — such details being authorized as fairly implied in the general grant of power to call the Convention — nothing is authorized which is not thus implied, or which is opposed to the spirit of republican institutions.

If I have not misconceived, then, the considerations bearing upon the question, it is the duty of Conventions, in all cases, not even excepting that, perhaps, in which they are authorized to act definitively, to submit the Constitutions they frame to the people; certainly to do so, whenever submission is not expressly dispensed with by the Constitution, or by the Convention Act.

§ 487. Let us now see to what extent the precedents have conformed to what I have announced as the theoretical principles relating to the submission of Constitutions; that is, of the Conventions which, since the foundation of our government, have been concerned in framing Constitutions, or parts of Constitutions, how many have, and how many have not, submitted them to the people?

I have in this work, generally, for the sake of completeness of view, reckoned as Conventions all bodies which have framed or ratified Constitutions or parts of Constitutions, either for the Union or for States, now members of the Union, as well as a few which have met to frame Constitutions, but have failed to do so. As thus defined, the list of those bodies thus far held in the United States comprises one hundred and ninety-two Conventions.[1]

From this list, for our present purpose, must of course be struck out, first, those Conventions which have been called simply to ratify propositions made by other Conventions, or by bodies having functions analogous to those of Conventions, twenty-eight in number;[2] and secondly, such as have proved abortive, having met and adjourned without maturing any amendments to the fundamental code, seven in number.[3] There would then remain one hundred and fifty-seven Conventions. Of these, one hundred

[1] See *post*, Appendix B, for a full exhibit of these Conventions, in which are distinguished those which did, from those which did not, submit their work to the people.

[2] They were the following Conventions, held, —

(*a.*) To ratify the Federal Constitution of 1787: Connecticut, Maryland, Massachusetts, New Hampshire, New York, North Carolina, South Carolina, and Virginia, 1788; Delaware, Georgia, New Jersey, and Pennsylvania, 1787; North Carolina (second Convention), 1789; Rhode Island, 1790; and Vermont, 1791.

(*b.*) To ratify State Constitutions, or parts thereof, either framed by previous Conventions or dictated by Congress: Georgia (two Conventions), 1789; Michigan (two Conventions), 1836; and Vermont, 1786, 1793, 1822, 1828, 1836, 1843, 1850, 1857, and 1870.

[3] These were the Conventions of Nebraska, 1864; Pennsylvania, 1783 (Council of Censors); Rhode Island, 1834; and Vermont, 1799, 1806, 1813, and 1862 (Councils of Censors).

and thirteen have submitted the fruit of their labors to the people,[1] and forty-four have not.[2]

§ 488. From this exhibit, it is evident that the prevailing sentiment of the country, from the earliest times, has favored the submission of Constitutions to the people. That such has been the general feeling is confirmed by an examination into the political situation and opinions of our fathers, at different times during our history, and into the particular circumstances attending those cases in which submission has not been made, to

[1] The submitting Conventions were as follows: —

(*a.*) Such as were concerned in framing the first Constitutions of their respective States, or of the Union, including those whose work was rejected by the people: The Continental Congress, 1775–1781; California, 1849; Colorado, 1864, 1865, and 1875; Iowa, 1844 and 1846; Kansas, 1855, 1857, 1858, and 1859; Maine, 1819; Massachusetts, 1778 and 1789; Michigan, 1835; Minnesota, 1857; Mississippi, 1817; Nebraska, 1866; Nevada, 1863 and 1864; Oregon, 1857; Texas, 1845; West Virginia, 1861; and Wisconsin, 1846 and 1847.

(*b.*) Such as were revising Conventions: Alabama, 1868 and 1875; Arkansas, 1864, 1868, and 1874; California, 1878; Colorado, 1876; Delaware, 1852; Florida, 1868 and 1885; Georgia, 1788, 1833, 1839, 1861, 1865, 1867, and 1877; Illinois, 1847, 1862, and 1869; Indiana, 1850: Iowa, 1857; Kentucky, 1849; Louisiana, 1844, 1852, 1864, 1867, and 1879; Maryland, 1850, 1864, and 1867; Massachusetts, 1779, 1820, and 1853; Michigan, 1850 and 1867; Mississippi, 1832 and 1868; Missouri, 1845, 1865, and 1875; Nebraska, 1875; New Hampshire, 1778, 1781, 1791, 1850, and 1876; New Jersey, 1844; New York, 1821, 1846, and 1867; North Carolina, 1835, 1865, 1868, and 1875; Ohio, 1850 and 1873; Pennsylvania, 1837 and 1872, Rhode Island, 1824, October, 1841, November, 1841, and 1842; South Carolina, 1868; Tennessee, 1834, 1861, 1865, and 1870; Texas, 1861 (ordinance of secession submitted, but not the amendments to the Constitution), 1866, 1868, and 1875; the Federal Convention, 1787; Vermont, 1785, 1792, 1820, 1827, 1834, 1841, 1848, 1855, and 1869; Virginia, 1829, 1850, 1861 (Secession Convention), 1861 (Reconstruction Convention), and 1867; and West Virginia, 1872.

[2] The non-submitting Conventions were as follows: —

(*a.*) Such as framed first Constitutions: Alabama, 1819; Arkansas, 1836; Delaware, Georgia, Maryland, New Jersey, New York, North Carolina, Pennsylvania, and Virginia, 1776; Florida, 1838; Illinois, 1818; Indiana, 1816; Kentucky, 1792; Louisiana, 1811; Missouri, 1820; New Hampshire, 1775; Ohio, 1802; South Carolina, 1775; Tennessee, 1796; and Vermont, 1777.

(*b.*) Such as were revising Conventions: Alabama, Arkansas, Florida, Kentucky, Louisiana, Mississippi, Missouri, and North Carolina, 1861; Alabama, Florida, Mississippi, and South Carolina, 1865; Delaware, 1792 and 1831; Georgia, 1795 and 1798; Kentucky, 1799; New York, 1801; Pennsylvania, 1789; South Carolina, 1778, 1790, and 1860; and Virginia, 1864.

those of which most directly bearing on the point under discussion, a short space will be devoted.

The science of politics, as specially adapted to our system of republics, scarcely existed at the time that system originated. American statesmen were doubtless well acquainted with the principles of freedom as developed in English institutions, and were thus, in a general way, prepared for the new development of them about to manifest itself in America. But the task of the statesman then was to apply old principles to a wholly new situation — always a work of difficulty, in which much must be trusted to time and experience. Of all the prominent statesmen of the Revolution, John Adams seemed best and earliest to forecast the form our institutions must assume, as well as their foundation and peculiar spirit. He saw that a republic alone would satisfy the wishes or harmonize with the genius of our people, and he was wise enough and fortunate enough to point out seasonably and with great precision the method in which the edifice of government, in the several States, must be erected. He was convinced it must be founded upon the people, by the people, and for the people. "I had looked," he says, "into the ancient and modern confederacies for examples, but they all appeared to me to have been huddled up in a hurry by a few chiefs. But we had a people of more intelligence, curiosity, and enterprise, who must be all consulted; and we must realize the theories of the wisest writers, and invite the people to erect the whole building upon the broadest foundations. . . . This could only be done by Conventions of representatives chosen by the people in the several colonies, in the most exact proportions. It was my opinion that Congress ought now" (1775) "to recommend to the people of every colony to call such Conventions immediately, and set up governments of their own, under their own authority; for the people were the source of all authority, and original of all power."[1]

§ 489. These views, so mature for that early day, were, in most respects, adopted and carried into effect by the several colonies. As we saw in a former chapter, a scheme of a Constitution, suitable, in the author's opinion, for the incipient States, was prepared and extensively circulated by Mr. Adams, during the winter and spring preceding the general framing of

[1] Adams's *Works*, Vol. III. p. 16.

Constitutions that took place in 1776.[1] To this fact is doubtless due much of the family likeness apparent in the Constitutions that afterwards appeared. But circumstances prevented, in nearly all the colonies, a strict conformity to the spirit of Mr. Adams' recommendation; though they called Conventions, they did not always consult the people in relation to the Constitutions they matured. In many of these colonies no submission was made to the people, because it was not, by the friends of the Revolution, deemed safe to submit, though the propriety of such a step, in general, seems not to have been denied. While the Convention of New York was in session, the enemy were actually, in large force, invading that and the adjoining State of Vermont, whose Convention was also in session about the same time. In those States, therefore, for that reason, it was thought to be perilous to attempt to take upon their respective Constitutions a vote of the people. Not only was there danger from the public enemy, but the enemy within was, in both States, numerous, and, in organizing the new governments, might occasion serious embarrassment, if their establishment were made dependent upon an affirmative vote of the whole people. Their first Constitutions were, therefore, put in operation by Ordinances of their Conventions alone.

§ 490. This action of their Conventions, however, seems not to have met with entire approval, at least in Vermont, whose people were not satisfied that a Constitution thus adopted possessed the force of law. As we have seen, accordingly, in a previous chapter, the General Assembly of that State endeavored, by two separate Acts, passed in different years, to impart to their fundamental law the validity which it was supposed to lack.[2] This incident shows two things: first, that a very general distrust, founded on a considerable knowledge of safe political principles, prevailed in relation to the validity of the Constitution; and second, that, at the same time, the views of the people in reference to the relations of the legislature to the Constitution, under which it assembled, were very immature. The first Constitution of New Hampshire had, in like manner, been put in operation by the Convention which framed it, though all the subsequent revisions of it, of which there have been several,

[1] See *ante*, §§ 128, 129.

[2] See *ante*, § 154.

have been submitted. The same causes probably operated to cause the first Constitution to be withheld from submission, as in the States above named; and they, doubtless, had their influence, generally, during the Revolution. The Tory party was strong enough in all the States to occasion serious embarrassment, in case a vote should be taken to determine upon the establishment of a new government independent of the crown; and in some of the States it was a matter of doubt whether it might not outnumber the friends of independence. Consequently, of the first Constitutions framed prior to the ratification of peace with England, none were submitted except that of Massachusetts, framed in 1778. This Constitution, however, was rejected by the people, and it was not until two years later that the leading Northern State was enabled to frame for herself a satisfactory fundamental code. Her first failure, however, furnished striking evidence of the existence amongst her people of sound practical views of Constitution-making, since that failure resulted from dissatisfaction with the mode in which the proposed Constitution had been concocted. The Constitution of 1778, as stated in a former chapter, was framed by a committee of the legislature, appointed in 1777, and on being submitted to the people, was, for that reason alone, rejected by an overwhelming vote — the people of that Commonwealth deeming the General Court, as the legislature was called, unauthorized to take the step indicated.[1] Afterwards, a Convention was, in a regular and formal manner, called by the General Court, by which the Constitution, known as that of 1780, was framed.

§ 491. Two Conventions, classed with non-submitting Conventions, — those of South Carolina of 1778, and of Pennsylvania of 1789, — might, perhaps, without impropriety, have been classed with those which submitted their work to the people. The legislature of South Carolina, which met in January, 1777, having been elected with the understanding that it should revise the Constitution of 1776, proceeded at its first session to perform that duty. Though, by the tenor of its commission, that body might have deemed itself authorized to enact its proposed Constitution at once, without in any manner taking the sense of the people in relation to it, it did not do so. It ma-

[1] See *ante*, § 156.

tured the instrument, and delayed the formal act of adopting it for a whole year, in the mean time publishing it for the consideration of the people at large.[1] "From the general approbation of the inhabitants, the new Constitution received," as was believed, "all the authority which could have been conferred on the proceedings of a Convention expressly delegated for the purpose of framing a form of government."[2] And, had the body by which it was finally adopted been elected during the year following its publication, with a view to its ratification or rejection, there would have been a substantial submission of it to the people. As it was, there was the possibility that a body, wedded naturally to its own views of the public necessities, embodied in its project of a Constitution, would fail accurately, by its intercourse with the people, to gather, or would refuse to obey, the public will.

The course of the Pennsylvania Convention was, in respect of submission, similar, though, on the whole, more exceptionable than that of South Carolina. In the resolutions by which it was convened, there was a clause declaring it to be, in the opinion of the legislature, expedient "that the Convention should publish their amendments and alterations for the consideration of the people, and adjourn at least four months previous to confirmation."[3] In obedience to this suggestion, the Convention matured a Constitution toward the close of February, 1790, and adjourned over to the 9th of August following, publication of the same being in the mean time made in the newspapers. On the day last named, the body again assembled, and, after a session of twenty-four days, finally adopted the Constitution of 1790. Thus there was the semblance of taking the sense of the people upon the Constitution, and, perhaps, a virtual submission to them of that instrument. But, how far it fell short of what a submission ought to be, is evident from the fact, that after the Convention assembled the second time, it spent twenty-four days in reviewing and amending the instrument upon which the people had been informally consulted. What changes the people as a whole desired in the scheme as published was not, and could not be, accurately known, nor,

[1] Ramsay, *History of the Revolution of South Carolina*, pp. 128, 129.

[2] Ibid.

[3] *Conventions of Pennsylvania*, p. 134.

consequently, whether the delegates obeyed or disobeyed the public voice. Both cases, therefore, have been set down as those in which Conventions did not submit their work to the people.

§ 492. Of the reasons inducing the Conventions of South Carolina, held in 1790; those of Delaware in 1792 and 1831; those of Georgia in 1795 and 1798; and that of Kentucky in 1799, which were revising Conventions, to withhold the Constitutions framed by them from submission to the people, I am not advised. In relation to the New York Convention of 1801, it may be said, that the objects of calling that body were, — first, to reduce the number of senators and representatives in the General Assembly; and secondly, to determine the true construction of the twenty-third Article of the Constitution relative to the right of nomination to office. From the language of the Act calling the Convention, it is obvious that submission of its determinations was not only not expected, but was virtually dispensed with. Without raising again the question as to the power of the legislature thus to authorize the Convention to act definitively,[1] it is clear that the case must be ranked as an exceptional one, so far as relates to the question of submission, and can form no precedent for cases in which the circumstances should be different.

§ 493. Of the forty-four non-submitting Conventions, those which remain are the Missouri Convention, whose sessions ran through the years 1861, 1862, 1863, and the so-called Secession and Reconstruction Conventions held in 1860, 1861, 1864, and 1865.[2]

The force of these cases as precedents is broken by the very peculiar circumstances which attended the call of those Conventions. It is unnecessary to rehearse here a history familiar to every reader. The States in which those Conventions assembled were in a thoroughly revolutionary condition. To this remark the State of Missouri, in the period covering the existence of the Convention of 1861, is no exception. Indeed, there is probably no doubt that that body was called in the interest of the Secession faction, and that, but for the determined stand taken by its Union members, it would have carried the State, so far as a State

[1] On this question see §§ 484–487, *ante*.

[2] See list, note 2 to § 487, *ante*, page 497.

can be carried, out of the Union. Nevertheless, there were limits beyond which the legislature, in calling the Convention, durst not go without providing for a reference to the people; accordingly, it prescribed in the Convention Act, that no Act or resolution of the Convention should be deemed to be valid to change or dissolve the political relations of the State to the government of the United States, or any other State, until a majority of the qualified voters of the State voting upon the question should ratify the same.[1] As the contingency referred to did not arise, no ordinance or amendment to the Constitution adopted by the Convention was submitted to the people, and judging from the action of the Secession Conventions in other States, had a secession ordinance been adopted by the Convention, we may be permitted to doubt whether it would have been submitted as required by the above Act. Respecting the condition of the other States at the time of their secession, there can be no doubt; it was avowedly revolutionary. When towards the close of the war, and after it, the first attempt was made to reconstruct their governments under the proclamations of Presidents Lincoln and Johnson, many causes operated to deter the Union citizens from submitting the amended Constitutions to a general vote of the people: in some the electoral machinery was more or less disorganized, and in all there was fear that it would be impossible to secure the approval, by a popular vote, of those measures relating to debts contracted in aid of the rebellion, and to the abolition of slavery without compensation to the late owners of slaves, which it was believed would be insisted on by Congress; the bulk of the people being as yet unripe for accepting the conditions absolutely necessary for the restoration of the Union, as at the time of the Secession Conventions they had been thought to be unripe for its demolition. Admitting, however, for the sake of the argument, that the Conventions held in the seceding States in the years mentioned were regular, they were held in exceptional circumstances; and the fact that they found it inexpedient or impossible to submit their work to the people, is clearly no precedent for non-submission in times of peace and constitutional order. "The extreme medicine of the Constitution," as wisely hinted by Burke, ought not to be made "its daily bread."

[1] Section 10 of Act approved January 21, 1861.

§ 494. Certain peculiarities in the mode of submission will now be noticed. The first is that required by the Federal Constitution for amendments to that instrument proposed by Congress. Article V. provides that amendments proposed by Congress, or by a Convention called by that body, shall be valid "when ratified by the legislatures of three fourths of the several States, or by Conventions in three fourths thereof, as the one or the other mode of ratification may be proposed by the Congress."

The other peculiarities in the mode of submission have been exhibited in the States, or in Territories seeking admission into the Union as States. Of these, two are deserving of mention, of which the first is that for over ninety years practised in Vermont.

By the forty-third section of the Vermont Constitution of 1777, provision was made for the election, every seven years, of a Council of Censors, of thirteen members, one of whose powers should be to call a Convention, to meet within two years after their sitting, if there appeared to them an absolute necessity of amending any Article of the Constitution. It was further provided, that the Articles to be amended, and the amendments proposed, and such Articles as were proposed to be added or abolished, should be promulgated at least six months before the day appointed for the election of such Convention, for the previous consideration of the people, that they might have an opportunity of instructing their delegates on the subject.

Here a Council of thirteen matured the proposed amendments, and the Convention was charged with the duty merely of passing upon them such a judgment as the people should have instructed them to do, or as the delegates should deem most accordant with the general voice. Such a mode of submission is the same in its general character as that commonly adopted, where, as we shall see, the whole body of the electors are called upon to adopt or reject amendments to the Constitution. The only difference is that, in Vermont, the electors choose a body of delegates to do for them, and in their names, what elsewhere is done by the electors directly. Considering the dangers of faction and corruption, always greater in small than in large bodies of men, there can be no doubt that, although the Vermont mode is theoretically unexceptionable, practically it is less to be commended than the one with which it is contrasted.

§ 495. The remaining case, presenting peculiarities in the mode of submission, is that of Territories framing their first Constitutions, preparatory to entering the Union as States. These are commonly, but, as I am confident, erroneously, cited as cases of non-submission. Assuming, for the present, that it is to the people — the sovereign — that Constitutions ought to be submitted, the question, To whom, in particular, should those framed for Territories be submitted? admits of a ready answer. The sovereign authority in the Territories is the people of the United States. When a Constitution, then, is framed for a Territory, if submitted at all, it should be to the people of the United States, in some one of the ways recognized as proper for ascertaining its will. The best way, as we have shown, would doubtless be to take a vote upon the question of the electors throughout the Union; but the practice of the government, under the Constitution of the United States, has been uniformly to leave the adoption or rejection of a Territorial Constitution to the Congress of the United States, the principal representative of the general sovereignty of the Union. This seems, implicitly at least, to be required by those clauses of the Constitution which provide that "new States may be admitted by Congress into this Union," and that "the United States shall guarantee to every State in this Union a republican form of government."[1] Beside this, which, in my judgment, is the normal and sufficient mode of submission, another has of late years come into use in these cases. In all, or nearly all, the enabling Acts of Congress authorizing Conventions in Territories of the United States, passed since the troubles in 1855–9 in Kansas, a clause has been introduced requiring those bodies to submit the Constitutions framed by them to the inhabitants of the respective Territories. This course, though theoretically not requisite, is highly proper, since otherwise Constitutions might be forced upon Territories by packed Conventions, in league with the majority of Congress, to which the people to be governed by them were hostile. It is to be understood, however, that the adoption of this mode is not obligatory upon Congress, and that the action of the territorial inhabitants is

[1] *Const. U. S.*, Art. IV. §§ 3, 4.

petitory only, the power of absolute disposition remaining in Congress. It is not probable that the latter would, after the events which occurred in Kansas, ever sanction a Constitution condemned by a vote of a majority of the inhabitants of the Territory fairly taken.

§ 496. Having thus considered the importance of submission in general, and the extent to which it has been practised in our constitutional history, it is proper now to inquire what is involved in the term "submission."

The term "submission," considered as designating a political act, involves, according to the point of view from which it is regarded, two distinct though related conceptions: first, that of something to be done by the submitting body; and, secondly, that of something to be done by those to whom it is submitted. To an adequate exposition of the subject, it is necessary that each of these conceptions should be analyzed, and its several features separately considered; and this, I think, may be conveniently done by discussing in their order the following subjects: —

I. By whom the particular regulations necessary for submitting Constitutions ought to be made.

II. To whom they ought to be submitted.

III. The nature of the act performed by the person or body to whom submission is made.

IV. In what manner Constitutions should be submitted.

V. The final proclamation or announcement by which the act of submission is crowned or consummated.

§ 497. I. In reference to the body by whom the regulations for submitting Constitutions ought to be made, it seems, laying out of view all questions of convenience or economy, that the most proper body is that by which the Convention is called, that is, the General Assembly. That body is in constant direct relations with the people, and with their more immediate representatives, the electors. Its voice is not only known to them, but it is in an emphatic sense their own voice. Moreover, as has been already shown,[1] the legislature has undoubted authority, under its general grant of legislative power, to pass the Acts necessary to submit a Constitution with such restrictions as shall secure respecting it an authentic expression of the public will; to which

[1] See *ante*, §§ 482, 483.

end it may provide by law for punishing such as attempt to cast illegal ballots, or to disturb the quiet of the election. With a Convention, the case is widely different. Conceding to it equal wisdom and experience, its power to legislate is denied by most, and doubted by all, respectable authorities; certainly, its power, by legislation, both to provide for submission with the necessary safeguards, and to enforce by penalties the observance of its requirements. If a Convention has any power at all in the premises, it is confined to that which is indispensable to the complete execution of its commission. It cannot extend to such special considerations as the exigencies of time and place may require, and to meet which, a wide legislative discretion alone is adequate. For, even if no clause of the Convention Act indicates the disposition to be made by the Convention of its work, common sense would seem to require that it should report its proposed Constitution to the body that called it, to deal with as it might deem advisable.

§ 498. The precedents, however, have not conformed precisely to the principles enunciated in the last section. Of the whole number of submitted Constitutions, one hundred and thirteen in all, more than one-half have been submitted in pursuance of their own express provisions, or of ordinances appended to them, containing sometimes specific instructions as to the mode of taking the votes of the people, but generally requiring the same to be taken as in ordinary elections, or leaving the time and mode of conducting the election to the discretion of the respective legislatures.[1] In some cases, submission has been required both by the Constitutions themselves, and by the Convention Acts in pursuance of which they were framed.[2]

[1] These Constitutions are the Articles of Confederation, 1781; the Federal Constitution, 1787; those of Arkansas, 1864, 1868, and 1874; California, 1849 and 1879; Florida, 1839 and 1885; Georgia, 1877; Illinois, 1848, 1862, and 1870; Iowa, 1857; Kansas, 1855, 1857, 1858, and 1859; Louisiana, 1845, 1852, 1864, and 1868; Maryland, 1864 and 1867; Massachusetts, 1821 and 1853; Michigan, 1835, 1850, and 1867; Minnesota, 1857; Missouri, 1865 and 1875; Nebraska, 1865 and 1876; Nevada, 1864; North Carolina, 1868; Ohio, 1851 and 1874; Oregon, 1857; Pennsylvania, 1873; Tennessee, 1834, 1865, and 1870; Texas, 1845 and 1868; the last nine Constitutions of Vermont; Virginia, 1830, 1851, and 1870; West Virginia, 1872; and Wisconsin, 1848.

[2] These were the following Constitutions: Arkansas, 1874; California, 1879; Florida, 1885; Georgia, 1877; Illinois, 1848, 1862, and 1870; Iowa, 1857; Kansas, 1857; Louisiana, 1845 and 1852; Maryland, 1864 and 1867; Massa-

A careful search has not enabled us to determine, in the remaining cases, by whom the submission of Constitutions has been made. The ordinances of Conventions have not always been preserved. It is safe, however, to say that it has generally been the work of Conventions acting either under express authority of law, or in obedience to the tacit understanding that submission should be made, which has prevailed in this country. The motives which have, doubtless, led to the acquiescence of the people in these acts of legislation by Conventions have been considerations of convenience and economy, both of which are promoted by them.

§ 499. When not done by the Conventions, submission has been commonly effected through the medium of the General Assemblies. It was so done in Virginia, in 1830, though under the direction, or at the request, of the Convention; so, also, in Indiana, in 1851, and in many other cases. The Federal Constitution was submitted by the Congress of the Confederation, in pursuance of the request of the Convention of 1787. In Virginia, the Act under which the Convention of 1850 assembled required it to transmit a certified copy of the Constitution to the General Assembly, in order that provision might be made by law for submitting the same to the people, and for organizing the government under it. This provision, however, was changed by the following legislature, which passed an Act requiring the certification of the Constitution to the Governor, who was authorized to call an election to pass upon its adoption or rejection.

§ 500. II. As to the body to whom submission should be made, it is evident, in general, that no one can be entitled to pass upon the fundamental law but the sovereign itself; or, in the States, some person or body of persons, to whom, by the nation at large, has been committed the exercise of sovereign rights, in local affairs. This would point to the peoples of the several States. But, because it is impracticable to submit it to such bodies, a choice must be made among the various orders of functionaries who represent the sovereign within the several States, or a special body must be deputed to act for them in the matter;

chusetts, 1821 and 1853; Michigan, 1850 and 1867; Missouri, 1865; Nebraska, 1865 and 1876; Nevada, 1864; North Carolina, 1868; Ohio, 1851 and 1874; Pennsylvania, 1873; Tennessee, 1865 and 1870; Virginia, 1830, 1850, and 1870; West Virginia, 1872; and Wisconsin, 1848.

and, as the submission must thus, at best, be virtual, it is the duty of the authorities charged with the business of perfecting a fundamental code to see to it that, in selecting the representative to whom submission is to be made, one be chosen who will act therein at once the most honestly, the most intelligently, and the most safely. Applying this test, it is evident that neither of the three ordinary departments of the government, legislative, executive, and judicial, ought to be selected for that office. Not to repeat arguments already sufficiently presented, tending to show the impropriety of confiding fundamental legislation to that department which enacts our ordinary laws, to that which interprets and applies them, or to that which executes them,[1] it is apparent that the electors, the most numerous order of functionaries in the State, withdrawn most completely from the passions and temptations of actual administration, and standing nearer to the people than any other, are the best fitted for that delicate duty. Their number is so great, and they are, withal, so evenly diffused, that the views they may at any time hold may reasonably be presumed to be those of the sovereign, — a presumption, indeed, lying at the foundation of our whole suffrage system, — yet they are not so numerous or so diffused as to render a collective ballot by them impracticable. By naming the electors to this office another advantage is gained, — one of the utmost importance to all governments founded upon a popular basis, — and that is, that substantive powers are not accumulated in a few hands, or in a single department, but are distributed, and thus made to counterpoise each other. The legislature, forbidden itself to meddle with it, calls a Convention to revise the fundamental law. The Convention matures a scheme of amendments which it deems necessary, and recommends them, but ventures to conclude nothing. The electors, the ultimate body of functionaries, take up the *projét* which the Convention has forged into shape, and temper and vitalize it by a power derived from the sovereign itself, and which they wield as its immediate representatives. Such is the distribution of functions exhibited in the work of fundamental legislation.

§ 501. It is to the people, then, that is, to the electors — for

[1] See §§ 367–372, *ante;* also speech of Daniel Webster in the case of Luther *v.* Borden, 7 How. 1, in *Great Speeches of Daniel Webster,* by E. P. Whipple (Little, Brown & Co., 1879), p. 543.

when we speak of the actual administration of government, it is they whom we mean by the term people — that Constitutions are properly to be submitted. How far this principle has been carried out in practice may be inferred from the requirements, first, of Convention Acts, and secondly, of Constitutions, as to the persons to whom Constitutions were to be submitted.[1] These will be considered in their order, beginning with Convention Acts.

1. Of the Constitutions submitted in pursuance of special provisions of the Convention Acts, some were submitted to the qualified electors or voters of the State;[2] some, to the people;[3] one, to the freeholders and inhabitants qualified to vote for representatives;[4] two, to the freemen of the several towns;[5] two, to persons entitled to vote for members of the General Assembly;[6] and ten, being those framed by the second series of Reconstruction Conventions, to the male citizens of the several States, twenty-one years of age and upwards, of whatever race or previous condition, resident in such States one year previous to the election, except persons disfranchised for rebellion or for felony at common law.[7]

[1] Obviously the best evidence on this point would be the Acts or resolutions of the legislatures or Conventions describing the persons who were to vote on the question of adopting or rejecting the proposed Constitutions. As most of the submissions made have been made by Conventions, some by provisions inserted in the schedules attached to such Constitutions, and some by ordinances subsequently passed, which are often published neither in the journals or proceedings of the Conventions, nor in the collections of State statutes, we must content ourselves with the best *data* that are accessible, which are believed to be the Convention Acts and the Constitutions.

[2] Convention Acts of Alabama, 1875; Connecticut, 1818; Delaware, 1852; Florida, 1885; Georgia, 1833 and 1839; Illinois, 1847, 1862, and 1869; Indiana, 1850; Iowa, 1844 and 1857; Maryland, 1850, 1864, and 1867; Missouri, 1861; Nebraska, 1875; Nevada, 1863; New York, 1846; North Carolina, 1875; Ohio, 1850 and 1873; and Pennsylvania, 1837 and 1872.

[3] Convention Acts of Massachusetts, 1820 and 1853; Michigan, 1850 and 1867; New Hampshire, 1781, 1850, and 1876; North Carolina, 1835; Tennessee, 1865 and 1870; Virginia, 1850 and 1861; West Virginia, 1872; and Wisconsin, 1846.

[4] Convention Act of Massachusetts, 1780.

[5] Convention Acts of Rhode Island, 1824 and 1834.

[6] Convention Acts of California, 1879; Georgia, 1877; and Iowa, 1846 and 1857.

[7] Convention Acts of Alabama, 1867; Arkansas, Florida, Georgia, Louisi-

The Convention Acts of a few States contained special provisions of an unusual character. Thus, that of the New York Convention of 1821 required the Constitution it should frame to be submitted to the citizens entitled to vote for delegates under that Act, which, as we have seen,[1] had extended the right to vote to citizens not before entitled, and at the same time had disfranchised certain classes of colored voters. So, the Convention Act of New Jersey, 1844, required submission to be made to the persons qualified by the same Act to vote for delegates — a class much larger than the electorate established by the existing Constitution, that of 1776, because of the omission of the property qualification required by the latter. In like manner, the Act calling the Virginia Convention of 1829 had directed the submission of the new Constitution to the persons authorized by it to vote for members of the most numerous branch of the legislature. The same was, in substance, true of the Acts calling the two legitimate Conventions of Rhode Island, of 1841 (November) and 1842, both of these Acts extending the franchise as fixed by the charter, and requiring the Constitutions which should be framed to be submitted to the persons by those Acts qualified to vote for delegates, and to those declared entitled to the suffrage by the new Constitution. The call of the People's Convention of the same State, held in 1841, extended the suffrage to all male American citizens aged twenty-one years, who had resided in the State one year, and required the Constitution framed by the Convention to be submitted to the voters as thus described, upon certain days named, and added the remarkable provision, that every person who, "from sickness or other causes," did not vote on one of those days, might send his vote in to the moderator within three days thereafter." The New York Convention Act of 1867 required the submission to the persons entitled by law to vote for members of the General Assembly, but provided that no person should vote who would not, if duly challenged, take and subscribe a prescribed oath of fidelity to the United

ana, Mississippi, North Carolina, South Carolina, Texas, and Virginia, 1868. Very similar were the provisions of the Act calling the Kansas Convention of 1857, save as to the residence required, which was thirty days in the Territory and ten days in the county, and save that it did not include a provision for disfranchisement.

[1] *Ante* § 264.

States. Mention has already been made of the call of the Pennsylvania Convention of 1789, which recommended by the Act calling it to publish the amendments and alterations it should propose, and adjourn at least four months previous to confirmation of the same; a proceeding which might be considered as nearly equivalent to a submission to the people.[1]

§ 501 *a*. 2. Constitutional provisions respecting submission have been of two kinds: first, such as required the submission of the instruments of which they formed a part, and, secondly, such as required the submission of the Constitutions which should be framed by future Conventions.

Of the former variety, nineteen have directed submission to be made to the qualified electors or voters of the State;[2] four, to the citizens of the State entitled to vote for members of the General Assembly;[3] and one, to the people without further description.[4] In three cases of Territorial Constitutions, submission was required to be made to the white male inhabitants of the respective Territories over twenty-one years of age resident in the district in which they offered to vote.[5] One Territorial Constitution framed in 1864, that of Nevada, required submission to be made to the persons qualified by the laws of the Territory, on certain dates mentioned, to vote for representatives to the General Assembly, including soldiers in the army of the United States in or out of the Territory. Three Constitutions, framed by Conventions called under the Reconstruction Acts of March and July, 1867, were required to be submitted to the voters of the State

[1] See *ante*, § 491.

[2] These are: Arkansas, 1874; California, 1849; Florida, 1838; Indiana, 1851; Iowa, 1846 and 1857; Kansas, 1855; Louisiana, 1864; Maryland, 1851 and 1867; Missouri, 1875; Nebraska, 1866 and 1875; Ohio, 1851; Oregon, 1857; Pennsylvania, 1873; Tennessee, 1834 and 1870; and West Virginia, 1872.

In the cases of Indiana, 1851, and Maryland, 1851 and 1867, the provisions touching submission were indirect and inferential, since they merely regulated the submission which was assumed rather than directly required. The class of persons authorized to vote were, however, indicated with sufficient clearness to be those stated in the text. In Tennessee, 1865, the taking of a stringent oath of loyalty was made a condition of the right to vote.

[3] Constitutions of California, 1879; Illinois, 1848 and 1862; and Michigan, 1850.

[4] Constitution of Kansas, 1858.

[5] Constitutions of Kansas, 1857; Minnesota, 1857; and Wisconsin, 1848.

registered and qualified as required by those Acts.[1] The Arkansas Constitution of 1864 directed submission thereof to be made to the white male citizens, over the age of twenty-one years, of the county, or in case of a military company, of the State, presenting themselves to vote, and not excepted in the proclamation of President Lincoln, who should take the oath prescribed in that proclamation. Several Constitutions required submission to the persons qualified as voters under the same, or under both the old and new Constitutions.[2] The Missouri Constitution of 1865 required submission to the qualified voters of the State who should take a prescribed oath of loyalty, including soldiers serving in the armies of the United States, their votes to be taken by messengers sent to them for that purpose. By the Vermont Constitutions of 1785, 1792, 1820, 1827, 1834, 1841, 1848, and 1855, they were severally to be submitted to Conventions called for that purpose only. It is only of this class of provisions that a question could be raised. In the absence of constitutional authority, no Convention or legislature could properly submit a Constitution, or an amendment thereof, framed by it, or under its authority, to any persons but the electorate established by the existing Constitution.

Of Constitutions containing specifications of the persons to whom amendments or revised Constitutions thereafter proposed by legislatures or Conventions should be submitted, seventy in in number, thirty-seven have required submission to be made to the electors or voters or qualified electors or voters of the State;[3]

[1] Constitutions of Louisiana and Texas, 1868, and Virginia, 1870.

[2] Constitutions of Arkansas, 1868; Illinois, 1870; Kansas, 1859; Louisiana, 1845 and 1852; Maryland, 1864; Michigan, 1835; Tennessee, 1834; Texas, 1845; and Virginia, 1851. The Tennessee Constitution also limited the right to vote, formerly given to freemen having a certain length of residence and a certain freehold interest, to free white men, provided that no person should be disqualified on account of color who was a competent witness in a court of justice against a white man.

[3] Constitutions of Alabama, 1865 and 1875; Arkansas, 1874; California, 1879; Colorado, 1876; Connecticut, 1818; Georgia, 1777 and 1868; Indiana, 1851; Kansas, 1855, 1858, and 1859; Louisiana, 1845, 1852, 1864, and 1868; Maryland, 1864 and 1867; Massachusetts, 1780; Minnesota, 1857; Mississippi, 1832 and 1868; Missouri, 1865; Nebraska, 1875; New Hampshire, 1784 and 1792; New York, 1867; North Carolina, 1876; Ohio, 1851; Oregon, 1857; Pennsylvania, 1838 and 1873; Rhode Island, 1842; South Carolina, 1868; West Virginia, 1863 and 1872; and Wisconsin, 1848.

twenty two, to the persons voting, or qualified to vote, for representatives or members of the General Assembly;[1] nine, to Conventions called by Councils of Censors;[2] one, to the freemen of the State;[3] and one, to the inhabitants voting in town meeting.[4]

Some of the provisions touching the submission of Constitutions described in this and the preceding section relate to the first Constitutions of States formed out of territory of the United States, and the phraseology referred to indicates the persons to whom, not the regular submission required by the Federal Constitution, was made — for that, as we have seen,[5] is always to the Congress of the United States — but that supererogatory submission authorized by Congress of late years, for the purpose of securing the settlers in our Territories against a recurrence of the outrages which so foully disgraced the American name in Kansas. In all cases of Territories framing their first Constitutions, it is believed, that submission can with strict legal propriety be made only to the people of the United States represented in Congress, and they have all of necessity conformed to this rule; that is, no Territories have ever been admitted into the Union under Constitutions without the submission of the same to that body for approval, and without its previous consent to their admission as States.

§ 502. Among the instances of submission given, are a few which deserve special attention on account of their exceptional character. Of these, the first that I shall mention are the two cases of Constitutions framed for the United States. The Constitution, improperly so-called, of the Confederation, comprised in thirteen articles, was the Constitution of a league of States, each of which expressly reserved to itself "its sovereignty, freedom, and independence." It was, therefore, a mere treaty, and, of course, its framers, the Continental Congress, were bound to

[1] Constitutions of Alabama, 1819 and 1867; Arkansas, 1868; California, 1849; Florida, 1868; Iowa, 1846 and 1857: Michigan, 1835, 1850, and 1867; Nevada, 1864; New Jersey, 1844; New York, 1821 and 1846; North Carolina, 1835 and 1868; Tennessee, 1834 and 1870; Texas, 1866, 1868, and 1876; and Virginia, 1870.

[2] Constitutions of Pennsylvania, 1790, and Vermont, 1785, 1792, 1820, 1827, 1834, 1841, 1848, and 1855.

[3] Constitution of Vermont, 1870.

[4] Constitution of Maine, 1820.

[5] See *ante*, § 495.

submit it to the States, of which they were the representatives. This course was followed, and that instrument was ratified by the States as political societies, each acting by its legislative Assembly. The Federal Constitution, on the other hand, was a Constitution based not only on States, but on individuals, and so far involved the substitution, for the principle of a league, of that of a national government. It had been found that the system of the Confederation was so powerless as to make it nearly useless for many purposes of government. Necessity required the enlargement of the plan, and not a mere revision or amendment of the government framed on the existing plan. Accordingly, although nothing was swept away which had shown itself useful, unless clearly incompatible with the plan demanded by the public necessities, the system proposed was, in its most characteristic particulars, a radically new one. It was a national government with federal features, instead of a mere league, with scarcely any features at all of an effective government. While it preserved the States, as political communities, they entered into the new system shorn of many of their most important powers. The new government was, in its essence and organization, a popular government, and not a mere sleazy union between popular governments; and in it first emerged into prominent political self-assertion The People of the United States, in whose name it purported to be framed.

§ 503. The sources, then, from which the Federal Constitution must seek ratification, were three: first, the existing government of the Union, embodied in the Congress of the Confederation; secondly, the States, as political organizations, represented by their legislatures; and thirdly, the people of the United States, by that Constitution made the inheritors of many of the powers and responsibilities of the two former. The necessity of securing a ratification of the new system by the Congress of the Confederation and by the States is apparent, as well from the fact that they were required by it to yield, the first all, and the second much, of its power to that system, as because the 13th Article of the existing Constitution expressly forbade the making of any alteration in its terms, " unless such alteration should be agreed to in a Congress of the United States, and be afterwards confirmed by the legislature of every State." Submission to the people of the United States, on the other hand, was demanded by the consideration that they were really the principals, in whose name the great act was to be consummated, whilst all others, the Congress and the States, were subordinates and accessories.

Accordingly, the Convention of 1787 provided for a submission which should satisfy all these conditions, in the following resolution: —

" *Resolved*, That the preceding Constitution be laid before *the United States in Congress assembled*, and that it is the opinion of this Convention that it should afterwards be submitted *to a Convention of delegates, chosen in each State by the people thereof, under the recommendation of its legislature*, for their assent and ratification."

By acting according to this resolution, it is evident that both the government of the Confederation and those of the States would express their assent to the new Constitution. The provision that the people of the several States should elect delegate Conventions to pass upon it, fulfilled the remaining condition, since thus, and thus only, could the people of the United States vote upon the proposed Constitution as a whole, that is, by voting in groups by States.

§ 504. The next cases deemed exceptional which will be considered are those of Constitutions submitted by legislatures or Conventions, without constitutional authority, to a class of persons differing from that of the electors qualified to vote at general elections. Of these, the largest proportion were cases in which submission was made to the electors *plus* certain designated classes of persons previously not entitled to vote at such elections, and the residue, of cases in which submission was made to the electors *minus* certain classes of persons thus entitled, according to existing laws.[1] To these should be added two cases in which submission of Constitutions was made to an electorate both increased and diminished, as compared with that qualified by the

[1] Of the first description were the Constitutions of Illinois, 1870; Kansas, 1859; Louisiana, 1845 and 1852; Michigan, 1835; New York, 1821; Rhode Island, November, 1841 and 1842; Texas, 1845; Virginia, 1830 and 1850; and West Virginia, 1863.

Of the second, was the Maryland Constitution of 1864. To this may be added the case of the Chicago Ordinance, so-called, submitted to the voters of Chicago by the Illinois Convention of 1862. See § 508, *post.*

existing Constitutions. Thus, the Tennessee Convention of 1834, in submitting the Constitution of that year, restricted the suffrage given by the Constitution of 1796, by inserting the word "white," and enlarged it by no longer requiring a freehold as a qualification for an elector, as did the Constitution of 1796. The Arkansas Convention of 1868, on the other hand, in submitting its Constitution, enlarged the previous suffrage by striking out the word "white," and restricted it by disfranchising persons who were electors according to existing laws, for offences connected with the war of the rebellion. In a few cases, the Conventions, by schedules or ordinances, required submission to be made to the electors qualified to vote according to both the existing and the amended Constitutions.[1] In most of these cases the effect was, on the whole, doubtless to increase the existing electorate. In five of them the Convention Acts expressly authorized the Conventions to submit in the manner described,[2] but in the residue no such authority was given or pretended.

It is evident that, in these cases, a new principle was introduced, namely, that of submitting proposed changes in the fundamental law to persons other than the body entrusted with the electoral function under existing laws; in some cases, to citizens forming no part of the existing governmental system; in others, to a part only of the citizens comprised in that system. Such a submission, especially, when made to persons not forming a part of the existing electorate, it is conceived, was not only a novelty but a capital innovation, upon which might hang, for the States concerned, the most weighty consequences: and, unless the principles which ought to govern in the enactment of fundamental laws are misconceived, it was unconstitutional and in the highest degree dangerous. In those cases in which the Convention Acts had authorized such a submission, the respective Conventions, acting upon the authority given, are chargeable with a less offense against constitutional principle than those which assumed the power without legislative warrant. But though the authorization of the legislatures was, in terms, ample, it was one which those bodies, with the single exception of Rhode Island,

[1] These were the Constitutions of Louisiana, 1845 and 1852; Texas, 1845; and Virginia, 1850.

[2] These were the cases of New York, 1821; Rhode Island, 1841 and 1842; and Virginia, 1830 and 1850.

had very clearly no constitutional power to give. By its charter of 1663, the General Assembly of that State was authorized "to make, ordeyne, constitute or repeal . . . such laws, statutes, orders, and ordinance . . . as to them shall seeme meete, for the good and wellfare of the sayd company," — terms, doubtless, covering the definition of the right of suffrage. In the absence of such constitutional authority, however, for a legislature, by its mere action as such, either to enlarge or to diminish the classes entitled to the right of suffrage as determined by the Constitution, is to repeal or to modify the fundamental law, and so beyond their competence.

§ 505. In neither of the cases in which the body of the citizens to whom submission was made was increased, without constitutional authority, was the propriety of such action discussed, save in that of the Virginia Convention of 1829. In that Convention a powerful opposition was made to it by some of the leading members, Leigh, Giles, Nicholas, Mason, John Randolph, Tazewell, and Upshur. A brief synopsis of the arguments advanced by both sides may be useful, — premising merely that there had been passed by the General Assembly of Virginia two Acts relating to that Convention: first, an Act submitting to the people the question of calling a Convention; and, second, after the people had, by a large majority, sanctioned such a call, an Act to call and organize the Convention, in which was inserted the provision relating to submission before referred to.

§ 506. By the friends of the mode of submission proposed by the committee of the Convention on that subject, in conformity with the authorization of the General Assembly, it was argued, that when an affirmative answer was given by the people to the simple question propounded by the General Assembly, whether they desired a Convention or not, it was their intention that the Assembly should give expression to the public will, as well with respect to the manner in which the Convention was to proceed as to the purposes for which it was to be holden; that here, then, was the authority of the constituent body; here was the voice of the principals, to whom the legislature were but agents; that, acting under that authority, they declared the manner and purpose of the Convention; that that declaration, however, was not obligatory, had no sanction, did not bind the freeholders to send delegates; that, if it contained anything which the freeholders did not approve, they might have arrested the proceeding; that they had the same authority to give counter instructions as they had to give original instructions; that they could have gone to the polls again, and commanded the legislature to repeal the Act; but that, as the case was, if the legislature acted at all in the matter, it had plainly to prescribe the objects of the Convention, and how they were to be attained; that the whole subject had been referred to them — there being no other way to do it — and that the only remedy was to arrest the matter *in pais;* that such being the case, what had been done? that the second Act, when presented to the freeholders, had been acquiesced in by the election of members everywhere, without complaint or remonstrance; that, if there was any other mode in which the people could express their approbation, it might be said the Act was still unratified; when, therefore, it was complained, that the Convention was proceeding to act definitively upon the right of suffrage, by admitting persons to vote on the new Constitution, without consulting their constituents, the answer was, that it was true, but that their constituents had authorized them so to do; that it would not be pretended that their constituents had no such power, because it had never been supposed that the principal was necessarily bound to retain the right of ratifying the acts of his agent; that it might have been unwise in the people to grant such a power, but that was a question for the constituent body alone; that, finally, it was too late to assert such a limitation of the power of that body, since the existing Constitution of the State had never been submitted to the constituent body for their ratification; that, if that instrument was valid, as the supreme law, it was because the people had tacitly expressed their assent to it by electing officers under it, and by acquiescing in its provisions.

§ 507. On the other hand, by Mr. John Randolph, Nicholas, and others, it was contended, that, conceding the right of the General Assembly, by its second Act, to provide for the call and organization of the Convention, it transcended its power in authorizing that body to submit the result of its labors to any body but to the freeholders themselves. Thus, Mr. Randolph said: —

"By whose authority did the legislature pass the . . . . Act

. . . . under which we are assembled here? By the authority of their constituents. And who are their constituents? The freeholders of the Commonwealth. By whose authority do we sit here? Whence is our power? From our constituents. And who are *our* constituents? The same answer must be given, — the freeholders of the Commonwealth. Now, the freeholders of the Commonwealth having given their sanction to the . . . . Act of the legislature — I refer to the first as well as the second Act on the subject of a Convention — and deputed us here to propose amendments to the old Constitution, or the draft of a new one, to whom, I ask, in the nature of things, did the freeholders suppose the new Constitution was to be submitted for adoption or rejection? Must it not have been to that original authority, to that source and fountain, from whence is derived all our authority as a Convention? — I mean to themselves? Let me suppose a case. A majority of the freeholders of Virginia . . . . being the body politic of Virginia, have consented that a Convention shall assemble for the purpose of devising amendments to the existing Constitution or proposing a new Constitution in its stead. Now, sir, the freeholders of Virginia have not yet decided — though they have decided that amendments shall be submitted to them — that, with worse than the stupidity of Esau, they shall be deprived of their birthright. The Convention are proposing that the former limits of the right of suffrage shall be extended, I will say, *ad indefinitum.* Who is to decide on this question? Those to whom we propose to extend that right? Unquestionably, no; no more than the people of Ohio or Pennsylvania have a right to decide it. They have no right whatever; they have not a shadow of right. . . . . Sir, it is as plain as any proposition in Euclid, — sir, it is plainer — it is self-evident — that no other power on earth, save that power from which this Convention derives all its authority to propose any Constitution at all, can rightfully pronounce on the validity of our acts, or decide upon the acceptance or rejection of such Constitution as we shall make."[1]

§ 508. The same principles that govern the foregoing cases, in which submission was made to the electors *plus* citizens not within the electoral circle, will settle that of submission to a part of the electors, not representing the whole body.

[1] *Deb. Va. Conv.* 1829, pp. 866, 884, 885. See also Speech of Mr. Nicholas, id. p. 891.

This latter mode was attempted, in a case already referred to, by the Illinois Convention of 1862.[1] In that case, an Ordinance was passed, entitled "An Ordinance to secure to the citizens of Chicago and the corporate authorities thereof the right to elect and appoint their own officers." By its terms this Ordinance was to be submitted, on the third day of the ensuing April, to the legal voters of the city of Chicago, and, if adopted, was to have the effect of repealing certain statutes obnoxious to a portion of the inhabitants of said city and vicinity. The Ordinance was, moreover, incorporated into the Schedule appended to the Constitution, and with it was directed to be submitted to a vote of the people of the State at an election to be held on the 3d Monday of June, about two months after the separate vote on the Ordinance alone. The object designed to be effected by the foregoing provisions is apparent at a glance. It was intended to parcel out the Constitution, submitting one part of it to the citizens of Chicago, and the residue to the people of the State at large, and to cause the former, temporarily at least, to take effect independently of the latter. The question is, Was it within the competence of that body to submit its work, or any portion of it, to the citizens of Chicago, or to any number of the electors less than the whole?

§ 509. That such a submission is improper becomes evident when it is considered that it is the sovereign, the political society or people, as a unit, whose function it is to pass upon the fundamental law. The electors of a single district have no power to speak for that great constituency, for they neither constitute nor represent it. The voice uttered by them, when they speak by their ballots, is but an element in the voice of the people, having no force of itself whatever, but only as it contributes to swell the chorus which alone is the people's voice. The voice of the people is one freighted with a single sentiment or command, not a multitude of voices, each uttering a sentiment or command of its own. It is the resultant of all the separate voices of the individuals constituting the people. When, therefore, the electors of Chicago voted upon the Ordinance in question, they did not utter the voice of the people of the State, in whom alone rests the power of making and unmaking Constitutions, but of a minute fraction of it, having no authority to represent the whole. However respectable they were in point of numbers and intelli-

[1] See *ante*, 430–434, 505.

gence, they were as destitute of power to speak officially for the people of Illinois as the two London tailors, whose petition to Parliament commenced in these words, "We, the people of England," were to speak for the latter.

§ 509 *a*. Allied to the exceptional cases mentioned in the preceding sections are those in which submission of Constitutions has been made to persons qualified to vote, provided they should take an oath of a more or less stringent character as to their loyalty to the United States. Such an oath was required by the supplementary reconstruction Act of Congress of March 23, 1867, regulating the submission of the Constitutions framed in pursuance of the Act of March 2, 1867.[1] After a declaration by the person proposing to vote, that he had not been disfranchised for participation in any rebellion or civil war against the United States, nor for felony at common law, the Act required him to swear that he had "never taken an oath as a member of the Congress of the United States, or as an officer of the United States, or as a member of a State legislature, or as an executive or judicial officer of any State, to support the Constitution of the United States, and afterwards engaged in any insurrection or rebellion against the United States, or given aid or comfort to the enemies thereof;" and finally, to pledge on his part future obedience to the same.[2] Beside these cases there are those of the Conventions of Maryland, 1864, Missouri, 1865, and New York, 1867, which, in submitting the Constitutions framed by them, in like manner required the voters to take an oath of loyalty, past and future, to the United States. This oath, which was in substance the same in all the cases named, in that contained in the Missouri Constitution, after referring to the second section thereof, in which was specified a great number of acts of disloyalty and unfriendliness to the United States, continued as follows: "That I have never, directly or indirectly, done any of the acts in said section specified; that I have always been truly and loyally on the side of the United States against all enemies

[1] For this oath see sect. 1 of the Act of March 23, 1867, 15 U. S. St. at Large, p. 2.

[2] To the list of rebel State Conventions called under that Act, and subject to its conditions, may be added those of Arkansas, 1864, and Tennessee, 1866, called by executive proclamations which prescribed a similar oath to the persons authorized to vote on their Constitutions.

thereof, foreign and domestic; that I will bear true faith and allegiance to the United States," etc.[1]

So far as the Conventions called under State laws are concerned, it is believed that nothing could justify the imposing of such a condition which would not justify an act of revolution; accordingly, it is observable that most of the States in which such action was taken were at the time either actually in the throes of revolution, or were striving to recover from the effects thereof, or to counteract the treasonable designs of those in their midst who sympathized with revolution in other States. The means by which alone it was deemed practicable to accomplish these purposes was the depriving of citizens, by the letter of the law entitled to vote, of the power to do so, without a judicial trial or sentence, but by an edict bearing the semblance of a law. This, clearly, the Conventions in question had no power to do. Even had the Convention Acts provided that they might make such a submission, the case would not have been different, because the legislatures would have had no power to pass such acts. In these cases, therefore, the action referred to, justifiable perhaps morally, was in its character revolutionary. Happily we are not left without decisive authority upon this question. By the terms of the Missouri Constitution a citizen must have taken the oath prescribed before he could vote at any election, serve as an attorney, or as a priest, clergyman, or minister of any religious denomination, etc. A Catholic priest refused to take the oath, was indicted, convicted, and sentenced to pay a fine of $500 for acting in that character without taking the oath. On appeal to the Supreme Court of Missouri this judgment was affirmed. The case was taken on a writ of error to the Supreme Court at Washington, by which, at the January term, 1867, the judgment of the Supreme Court of Missouri was reversed, and the cause remanded with directions to the Missouri Supreme Court to enter a judgment reversing that of the Circuit Court which had originally tried the case.[2] The court held that the oath required by the Missouri Constitution was a test oath unexampled in our history, and was a violation of that provision of the Federal Constitution which provides that "no State shall

[1] Article XIII. Missouri Constitution, 1865, sect. 6.

[2] See Cummings *v.* Missouri, 4 Wall. 277. See, also, Ex parte Garland, id. p. 333.

pass any bill of attainder or *ex post facto* law;" that the clause of the Missouri Constitution prescribing the oath and forbidding the doing of the acts referred to, save on condition of taking the oath, was a bill of attainder, which the court defined to be a legislative Act which inflicts punishment without a judicial trial; and that, being an Act imposing a punishment, by way of disqualifying from office or from the pursuit of a lawful occupation, for an act which was not punishable at the time the act was committed, or imposing additional punishment to that then prescribed, it was an *ex post facto* law. The court, per Field J., say: "The clauses in the Missouri Constitution which are the subject of consideration do not in terms define any crimes, or declare that any punishment shall be inflicted; but they produce the same result upon the parties against whom they are directed as though the crimes were defined and the punishment was declared. They assume that there are persons in Missouri who are guilty of some of the acts designated. They would have no meaning in the Constitution were not such the fact. They are aimed at past acts, and not future acts. They were intended especially to operate upon parties who, in some form or manner, by actions or words, directly or indirectly, had aided or countenanced the rebellion, or had endeavored to escape the proper responsibilities or duties of a citizen in time of war; and they were intended to operate by depriving such persons of the right to hold certain offices and trusts, and to pursue their ordinary and regular avocations. This deprivation is punishment. Nor is it any less so because a way is opened for escape from it by the expurgatory oath. The framers of the Constitution of Missouri knew at the time that whole classes of individuals would be unable to take the oath prescribed. To them there is no escape provided; to them the deprivation was intended to be and is absolute and perpetual. To make the enjoyment of a right dependent upon an impossible condition is equivalent to an absolute denial of the right under any condition, and such denial, enforced for a past act, is nothing less than punishment imposed for that act. It is a misapplication of terms to call it anything else.

"Now some of the acts to which the expurgatory oath is directed were not offences at the time they were committed. It was no offence against any law to enter or leave the State of Missouri for the purpose of avoiding enrollment or draft in the military service of the United States, however much the evasion of such service might be the subject of moral censure. Clauses which prescribe a penalty for an act of this nature are within the terms of the definition of an *ex post facto* law, — 'they impose a punishment for an act not punishable at the time it was committed.'

"Some of the acts at which the oath is directed constituted high offences at the time they were committed, to which, upon conviction, fine and imprisonment or other heavy penalties were attached. The clauses which provide a further penalty for these acts are also within the definition of an *ex post facto* law, — 'they impose additional punishment to that prescribed when the act was committed.'

"And this is not all. The clauses in question subvert the presumptions of innocence, and alter the rules of evidence which heretofore, under the universally recognized principles of the common law, have been supposed to be fundamental and unchangeable. They assume that the parties are guilty; they call upon the parties to establish their innocence; and they declare that such innocence can be shown only in one way, — by an inquisition, in the form of an expurgatory oath, into the consciences of the parties." [1]

The reasoning of the court in this case is equally applicable to the oath prescribed in the other State Constitutions referred to, excepting, perhaps, those framed by the reconstruction Conventions. The action of Congress in calling those bodies, irregular at best,[2] was hardly rendered more so by a provision for submitting their work to the people, in a manner demanded by political necessity, as calculated to secure the supremacy of those loyal to the Union.

§ 509 *b*. In the provisions of some of the States for submitting Constitutions framed during or just after the late civil war, they were to be submitted to the qualified voters of the State, but with the *proviso* that should persons otherwise entitled to vote at elections be absent from the State, as soldiers in the armies of the United States, their votes might be received at the points where the armies were encamped, and apparatus was provided for taking such votes, and reporting them to the State authori-

[1] Cummings *v.* Missouri, *ubi sup.*

[2] See *ante*, § 253.

ties at home. Such provisions were adopted in the Constitutions of Nevada and Maryland, 1864, Missouri, 1865, and Tennessee, 1866.[1] Were a legislature or a Convention to adopt such a law or ordinance at the present time, when *arma silent inter leges*, not a voice would be raised in favor of the constitutional competence of either body to take such action. But, under the circumstances in which the States named were then laboring, — a civil war still raging, or, though nominally ended, not having as yet given place to a stable peace, or been followed by a reconstruction of the shattered institutions of the rebel States, — much may be pardoned to the errors of men struggling to maintain the substantial rights of the people, imperilled by the return to their homes of multitudes of citizens fresh from armed conflict to subvert those rights. But while this may morally furnish an excuse for the Acts or Ordinances in question, it forms legally no justification for them whatever. So clear is this that it may be confidently predicted that the spectacle will never again be witnessed of commissioners from New England gathering in the far Southwest the votes of New England men domiciled or commorant there. The Constitutions of the States, expressly or by clear implication, all require, as a condition of the right to vote at an election therein, an actual residence within their respective boundaries. A law permitting the reception of votes of supposed electors beyond those boundaries, without inquiry whether the *animus revertendi* existed or not, assumes that *animus* as a fact, contrary, in a great number of cases, to the real intention of the voters. It is well known that, at the close of the war, many Union soldiers remained at the South when their regiments were disbanded there. To reckon such persons as still resident citizens of the Northern States in which they enlisted was to violate the only rational presumption in the case, — that they intended

[1] A similar provision was contained in the Act calling the New York Convention of 1867. See Act of March 29, 1867, secs. 2 and 5. In like manner, the enabling Act of Congress, under which the Nevada Convention of 1864 assembled, gave the Convention express authority to receive the votes of soldiers in the Federal armies, within or without the said Territory, upon the question of the adoption of the Constitution. As no submission of the Constitution framed by the Convention to the people of the Territory was strictly necessary, but only to the Congress, the irregularity of taking the soldiers' votes was of less importance. It was enough that the Convention should adopt and Congress approve. See § 495, *ante*.

from the first what they finally did, namely, to take up their permanent residence at the South. It should be added, however, that the power of a Convention to provide for receiving the votes of soldiers on foreign service, in future elections, to occur after the adoption of the Constitution providing therefor, is not now denied, but only the power of such a body, without constitutional authority, to submit the Constitution, for adoption or rejection, to voters residing abroad, though in the public service of the country.

§ 510. III. We are now to determine the nature of the act performed by the persons or body to whom submission is made.

A convenient mode of conducting this inquiry will be to pass in review the various departments of a government, and to select from amongst them that one whose acts and functions correspond with those of the people in the act of passing upon a fundamental law.

The act in question must, I think, be comprised within one of the three classes of acts known as legislative, executive, and judicial. Let us see to which it belongs, commencing with the last.

(*a*). When the people pass upon a Constitution, the act done by them is so palpably not of a judicial character, that I spend no time in comparing or contrasting it with the exercise of judicial power.

(*b*). Understanding by the term executive acts, such as are usually performed by our executive magistrates, there are of such acts three separate classes: 1, administrative acts, relating to the carrying of laws into practical effect; 2, acts involving the exercise of the official negative, or *veto;* and, 3, acts of authentication, such as the signing of bills, &c. Does the act in question belong to either of these classes?

1. It cannot be pretended that the act of the people, in the case supposed, is an act of administration, which is possible only when the law to which it relates has been passed and approved. The purpose of an administrative act is to give to a law, already complete as such, the practical operation, without which it would remain a dead letter in the statute book. This is equally true of municipal laws, strictly so called, and of organic or fundamental laws.

§ 511. 2. Though the act of the people we are considering bears some resemblance to the exercise of the negative or veto power, still I am satisfied it is radically different from it; and the result is the same, whether it be compared with the true veto, as exercised by the Roman Tribunes, by the individual members of the Polish Diets, or by the English monarchs, or with the qualified veto, more properly called the negative, familiar to us in America. The veto proper was an absolute interdict upon the measure proposed, and it was nothing more. It never ratified or sanctioned, but always forbade. It consequently made of every functionary intrusted with the power a coördinate department with the legislature in the matter of rejecting, though not in that of confirming, laws. The negative of an American President or Governor is somewhat similar in its nature, but is much less extensive in its effects. It is, like that, a mere interdict; but it is an interdict that is only provisional, having the effect simply of compelling a reconsideration of the measure to which it has been applied, and, in the vote to be taken upon it, of enhancing, as if by a temporary amendment to the Constitution, the majority necessary to carry it. In most of the State Constitutions, as in that of the United States, it is provided, that a bill "returned with the objections" of the Executive may, notwithstanding, become a law, if, on a reconsideration, it be passed by a two-thirds vote in both houses.

That a vote of the people upon a Constitution is not in character like either of these executive acts, is perceivable at a glance. The vote of the people may be in the negative, or it may be in the affirmative; and in either event it is absolute.

Again: both the veto proper and the negative of an American executive officer, operate only upon a bill passed through all the forms of a law, by the two houses of the legislature, and submitted to him for his official sanction. It is impossible that a measure not thus originating should be the subject of the veto or of the negative. With a Constitution submitted to a vote of the people, it is different. A Convention might reject a particular form of a Constitution, and adopt and submit to the people another; but if the legislature were, in the mean time, before the vote upon it, to submit for the consideration of the people the rejected Constitution, it might be competent for them, at the same election, to adopt the latter and reject the former.

§ 512. 3. For similar reasons, the act of the people is not to be compared with the executive act of giving assent to bills by the formality of signing them. The latter is an act applicable only to bills passed by the legislative branch, and is only used to affirm, and not to negative, such bills.

§ 513. (*c*). The act of the people in adopting or rejecting a Constitution, on the other hand, is clearly legislative in its character. It either gives force to what comes to them as a mere proposition, or it rejects that proposition absolutely and definitively. A power thus to impart vitality to law, where before there was none, is a power of legislation. Conceding that the people have power to enact fundamental laws, all becomes simple and intelligible. Under its general power to enact a Constitution, the people may perhaps authorize a Convention to exercise the same power, without submitting it for ratification — that is, for what it may deem sufficient reasons, it may delegate that power to a Convention;[1] or, grasping more firmly the reins of power, and consulting more the safety of the Commonwealth, it may itself exercise its legislative function, rejecting or adopting a part or all of what is submitted, as it may think advisable.

Nor is the character, thus attributed to the people, of an extraordinary legislature, so far as concerns the fundamental law, inconsistent with their evident inability to mature laws by discussion, as in legislative assemblies. The same inability inheres to some extent in our legislatures. Without committees to inquire and report, to draft and mould into form fit for public action, bills for Acts, legislation as known amongst us would be well-nigh impracticable. As a body, a legislature is too numerous and unwieldy for the function of digesting such bills. The difficulty inherent in legislation by the people, though somewhat greater by reason of their greater number and dispersion, is of precisely the same character. The people, acting as legislators,

1 This, perhaps, needs explanation. As was observed a few pages back, it is perhaps too late to deny to the *people* this power of delegation. It has been too often exercised. But the right of a *legislature* to authorize a Convention to exercise the power in question is, on principle, more than doubtful. It certainly, in my judgment, does not exist. The most that can be conceded — and that rather on the authority of precedents than otherwise — is, that a legislature might pass a law providing for definitive action by a Convention, and if that law were submitted to the people so as fairly to draw out an expression of the public will on the point, it would be liable to no serious objection.

need the antecedent ministry of intelligent and skilful committees to gather and to embody in fitting forms their collective sense. Our Conventions are simply committees of such a kind. And if we look closely into the principles of legislation, the fact that the people never legislate in a single body, but in groups, assembled in separate districts, not to debate, but to vote upon, the measures proposed to them, does not constitute a radical difference between them and a legislature. The latter might enact the statute law in the same way; and to those familiar with the practices of such bodies, it may be doubtful whether legislation so conducted would not be more honest, if not more intelligent, than it is now.

It seems clear, then, that the act of the people in passing upon a Constitution is a legislative one, though, on account of the exceptional circumstances under which it is performed, an act unique in character.[1]

§ 514. IV. I pass now to consider briefly the manner in which Constitutions should be submitted.

In determining the manner of submitting Constitutions to the people, two things should be kept prominently and constantly in view: first, the obtaining, completely and as far as

[1] That the people act, in the case supposed, in a legislative capacity, has been repeatedly intimated by high authority. See the case of The People *v.* Collins, 3 Mich. R. 343, per Douglass, J.; 2 Am. Law Reg. p. 591, same case.

Mr. John Austin, in his profound work, *The Province of Jurisprudence Determined*, says, respecting a single State, what is true of all the States in the Union: — "In the State of New York, the ordinary legislature of the State is controlled by an extraordinary legislature. . . . . The body of citizens appointing the ordinary legislature forms an extraordinary and ulterior legislature, by which the Constitution of the State was directly established. . . . . That such an extraordinary and ulterior legislature is a good or useful institution, I pretend not to affirm. I merely affirm that the institution is possible, and that, in one political society, the institution actually obtains." — *The Prov. of Jurisp. Determined*, Vol. I. pp. 205, 206.

An anonymous writer in the *American Law Register*, published at Philadelphia, has attempted to cast ridicule upon this observation of Mr. Austin, as an instance of the ignorance prevailing among public men and writers abroad in regard to our institutions. But I am satisfied the writer referred to had not the slightest conception of Mr. Austin's meaning. We must not be the slaves of words. In substance, the electors, in the act of ratifying or rejecting a Constitution, are a legislature, — "an ulterior legislature," — as compared with the General Assembly. See Am. Law Reg, Vol. IV., New Series, p. 12.

possible in detail, of the public will; and, secondly, convenience, — the latter, however, being a consideration of inferior importance, when compared with the former. The general rule, undoubtedly should be, that every clause of both Constitution and Bill of Rights must be submitted to the people, those only excepted which are to take effect in the act of making the submission itself. No other rule can be adopted with safety; for if it were admitted that any other exceptions whatever could be made, and that provisions of minor importance might be reserved from the people, to be put in force by the Convention directly, the door would be thrown open to all manner of abuses. When is a constitutional provision of minor importance? The same provision, from a difference of circumstances, may be of vast moment in one, and of no moment at all in another, Constitution. *Obsta principiis* is, in such cases, the only safe maxim. If it be recognized as the duty of a Convention to submit its work to the people, either on the ground that the legislature has so directed, or that such a course is intrinsically proper, because its resolutions are recommendatory only, where can it find the right to discriminate between what should and what need not be submitted? — to draw the line beyond which it is within its own discretion to obey or to disobey the imperative provisions of law?

§ 515. A Constitution may be wholly new, or it may be an old one revised by altering or adding to its material provisions. It may, also, in a hundred separate subdivisions, contain but a fourth of that number of distinct topics, or each subdivision may be substantive and independent. It is obvious that the submitting body, weighing accurately the public sense, may determine whether the whole Constitution must stand or fall as a unit, or whether some parts, being adopted and going into effect without the rest, the new system would be adequate to the exigencies of the state, and may submit it as a whole or in parts accordingly. But it is perfectly clear that every distinct proposition, not vital to the scheme as a whole, or to some other material part, ought to be separately submitted.[1] If it were not

[1] In November, 1820, a bill for an Act calling a Convention was passed by both houses of the New York Legislature, but was returned by the Council of Revision with objections, one of which was, that the bill provided for submitting the Constitution to the people in mass, and not in separate sections according to

nearly impracticable, the best mode would be to submit every distinct proposition separately, so that each voter could vote *yea* or *nay* upon it, regardless of anything but its absolute propriety. In many cases, however, such a mode could not be safely adopted, since different measures might have been so adjusted to each other, that by the absence of either the balance of the system would be disturbed.[1] Such associated provisions ought, therefore, to be submitted in conjunction. On the other hand, where no material changes have been made in the existing Constitution, or such only as had been unequivocally demanded by the public voice, the more convenient and compendious mode of a submission in mass may, without material objection, be adopted. Every case, then, must, to a considerable extent, stand upon its own foundation. The problem is — Given one or more proposed changes of the fundamental law — to reconcile the indispensable requisite — a *bonâ fide* submission of them to the people, so as to ascertain their will in respect to each of them — with a reasonable degree of convenience. Submission must be so made, moreover, that the general scheme, if adopted, shall not limp from lack of a necessary member, — it being obviously better to be relegated to an old Constitution, which, though inadequate and partly obsolete, perhaps, is yet fully and consistently developed, than to be governed by a new one so mutilated, in the act of birth, as to lack necessary powers.

the various subjects embraced. The Council, stating this ground of objection, say: it is objected to, "Because the bill contemplates an amended Constitution to be submitted to the people, to be adopted or rejected *in toto*, without prescribing any mode by which a discrimination may be made between such provisions as shall be deemed salutary, and such as shall be disapproved by the judgment of the people. If the people are competent to pass upon the entire amendments, of which there can be no doubt, they are equally competent to adopt such of them as they approve, and to reject such as they disapprove; and this undoubted right of the people is the more important, if the Convention is to be called in the first instance without a previous consultation of the pure and original source of all legitimate authority." See *post*, Appendix E.

[1] On this subject, Daniel Webster, in the Massachusetts Convention of 1820, said: "When the Constitution of New Hampshire" (meaning that of 1783) "was revised," (in 1792,) "the Convention submitted the amendments to the people for their adoption separately, and it was found at the adjourned session of the Convention that some were adopted and some rejected, so as to make incongruous those which were adopted. The Convention then pursued the course . . . . of uniting in one article all that were necessarily connected, and no further difficulties occurred." — *Deb. Mass. Conv.* of 1820, p. 224.

§ 516. It must be admitted, that but little attention has been paid to the distinctions here indicated. In far the larger proportion of the cases in which submission has been made, it has been of the instruments entire. This was naturally true, in general, of all such as were first Constitutions of their respective States.

The earliest departure from this mode was in Massachusetts, in 1780, in which the Frame of Government and Bill of Rights were both submitted in such a way as to enable the people to reject the whole or any part of either, — a course followed by all the subsequent Conventions in that State, though the Act calling the Convention of 1820 left it to the discretion of that body to determine the mode in which the submission should be made. The example set by Massachusetts in 1780 was followed by New Hampshire in 1791, and in the subsequent revision in 1850. The Acts calling the New York Conventions of 1821 and 1846 required those bodies to submit their proposed amendments to the people, together or in distinct propositions, as to them should seem expedient. Accordingly, the Convention of 1821 provided that they should be submitted "together, and not in distinct parts;" and that of 1846, expressing the opinion that the amendments it proposed could not be prepared so as to be voted on separately, submitted them *en masse* excepting one, that relating to "equal suffrage to colored persons," which was submitted as a separate article. Under a similar discretion, the Pennsylvania Convention of 1837 submitted its amendments *en masse*. The Illinois Conventions of 1847 and 1862, and the Oregon Convention of 1857, pursued a course similar to that of the New York Convention of 1846, submitting the great body of their respective Constitutions entire, but a few articles relating to slavery, to the immigration of colored persons, the public debt, and other subjects considered of doubtful policy, separately. The Illinois Convention of 1847, though it submitted the bulk of its articles in the manner stated above, withheld one, relating to "commons," altogether from the consideration of the people, therein proceeding in direct violation of the Act under which it assembled, which expressly required it to submit its amendments to the people.[1]

[1] Some Constitutions contain an excellent provision requiring that, when two or more amendments shall be submitted at the same time, they shall be so sub-

§ 517. The subject of the proper mode of submitting Constitutions to the people, received an elaborate discussion in the case, now celebrated in our political annals, of the so-called Lecompton Constitution, framed for the State of Kansas. Concocted in a time of crisis by the partisans of slavery, by whom an attempt was made to force it upon that State against the wishes of the majority of its inhabitants, mainly emigrants from the free States, and desirous of establishing free-state institutions therein, that instrument had the singular fate to be twice, and a part of it three times, submitted to the people, by different bodies, and though once declared adopted, to have never in fact been established as the Constitution of that State. A brief sketch of the history of this case will not be without interest, and it will, it is believed, throw light upon the general doctrine of submission of Constitutions we are considering.[1]

On the 5th of September, 1857, there assembled at Lecompton, Kansas, at the call of the Territorial Legislature, but without an enabling Act of Congress, a Convention, by which the Constitution referred to was framed. The body was composed in the main of delegates elected in the interest of, if not by, the pro-slavery party in that and the neighboring State of Missouri, the free-state men of Kansas abstaining from the elections, in the expectation that whatever Constitution the Convention should agree upon would be submitted to the electors of the Territory. The Territorial Governor had, in fact, promised solemnly, in the name of the government which he represented, that the Constitution it should frame should be submitted to a fair vote of the people. This promise, however, was not redeemed; so far from it, the Convention enacted the farce of submitting it to the people, but did it in such a way as to compel them to vote for the Constitution or abstain from voting altogether — the vote, to be taken on the 21st of the ensuing December, being required to be, "For the Constitution with slavery," or "For the Constitution without slavery."

mitted as to enable the electors to vote upon each amendment separately. Constitutions of Alabama, 1875; Arkansas, 1868 and 1875; California, 1879; Indiana, 1851; Iowa, 1846 and 1857; Kansas, 1855, 1858, and 1859; Louisiana, 1845, 1852, 1864, and 1868; Maryland, 1867; Nebraska, 1875; New Jersey, 1844; Ohio, 1851; Oregon, 1857; Pennsylvania, 1838 and 1873; South Carolina, 1868; West Virginia, 1863 and 1872; and Wisconsin, 1848.

[1] See also §§ 415–418, *ante*.

In the mean time, a new Territorial election being held, and resulting in giving to the Free-State party a majority in the Territorial legislature, that body, on the 17th of December — about a week before the vote ordered by the Convention — passed an Act fairly submitting the Constitution as a whole, except the slavery clause, which was submitted as a separate article, to the qualified electors, at an election to be held on the 4th of January, 1858. Both these elections were held at the times fixed; that ordered by the Convention resulting in the adoption of the Constitution with slavery by a vote of 6266 to 567; and that held under the Territorial Act, in the rejection of the entire Constitution by a vote of 138 "for the Constitution with slavery," 24 "for the Constitution without slavery," and 10,226 "against the Constitution." Here, then, was a Constitution, adopted in the main by six thousand majority at one election, and at another, held two weeks later, rejected *in toto* by over ten thousand majority. Evidently, such results could only have been produced by fraud and management upon one side or the other. Each party claimed that the election, whose result was favorable to its own views, was the only valid one, but, inasmuch as the pro slavery party constituted the majority of the Convention, the Constitution was, under its direction and by its officers, forwarded to Congress as the expression of the will of the inhabitants of the Territory, with a petition for admission into the Union as a State under it.

§ 518. Accordingly, the Senate Committee on Territories reported a bill for that purpose, upon which arose a very excited and protracted debate. This bill simply provided for the admission of the Territory into the Union upon the usual conditions relating to the public lands, though in its preamble was inserted a recital recognizing the validity of the Lecompton Constitution. The opponents of the bill resisted it mainly on the ground that the Constitution had not been submitted to the inhabitants of the Territory *bonâ fide*, but in such a manner that no elector could vote against the provision establishing slavery, without voting at the same time for the residue of the Constitution as a whole. That instrument, it was said, contained, or might contain, provisions as distasteful to the people as that relating to slavery, and yet, in order to vote against the latter, they must vote in favor of the former, — a dilemma into which no Convention was justified in bringing those for whom they were pretending to act. Notwithstanding all these objections, the bill was carried through the Senate by a vote of 33 to 25. This bill being sent to the House, there was moved as a substitute for it another, providing for the admission of Kansas into the Union, but containing a clause requiring the Constitution to be again submitted to the people, and authorizing the inhabitants, in case of its rejection, to form for themselves a Constitution and State government. The first section, after the usual words importing the admission of the State into the Union, contained the following significant recital: "But, inasmuch as it is greatly disputed whether the Constitution, framed at Lecompton on the 7th day of November last, and now pending before Congress, was fairly made, or expressed the will of the people of Kansas, this admission of her into the Union as a State is here declared to be upon this fundamental condition precedent, namely: that the said constitutional instrument shall be first submitted to a vote of the people of Kansas, and assented to by them, or a majority of the voters, at an election to be held for the purpose," &c., &c. Then followed a specification of the mode of taking the vote, by ballots "for the Constitution," or "against the Constitution," and careful provisions for determining the qualifications of voters and for insuring an honest and complete vote.

The vote in the House on this substitute for the Senate bill was 120 to 112.

§ 519. The two houses being thus at variance, and refusing to agree, a committee of conference was appointed in the House by the casting vote of the Speaker, by which a bill was reported commonly known as the "English Bill," which was accepted by both houses April 30th, 1858, and became a law.

Although, as we have seen, strict principle did not require the submission of the Constitution, by Congress, to the inhabitants of the Territory at all, yet, as that body undertook, by the English Bill, to make such submission, it would be expected some mode would be adopted that should be fair and adequate. Such, however, was not the fact. After reciting the framing of the Constitution, and that the Ordinance accompanying it, containing propositions in behalf of the Territory for the acceptance of Congress, was unacceptable to the latter, the Act provided that the State of Kansas should be admitted into the Union under said Constitution, when its people should have voted to accept the proposition thereby made, which was twofold, first, donating to the new State, with great liberality, public lands, salt-springs, and the proceeds of the sales of the public domain within its limits, for various public purposes; and, secondly, limiting, in the terms usual in such Acts, the power of the State to interfere with the primary disposal of the lands of the United States, or to tax said lands or the property of the United States. The Act then provided, that at said election the voting should be by ballot, and by indorsing on his ballot, as each voter might be pleased, "Proposition accepted," or "Proposition rejected;" and that, if a majority of the votes should be for "Proposition accepted," the President of the United States should by proclamation announce the same, and the State thereupon, without further action of Congress, should become one of the States of the Union. But, should a majority of the votes cast be for "Proposition rejected," the Act further provided, that *it should be deemed and held, that the people of Kansas did not desire admission into the Union with said Constitution, under the conditions set forth in said proposition*, in which event they were authorized to form for themselves a Constitution and State government, *whenever, and not before*, it should be ascertained by a census duly and legally taken, that the population of said Territory *equalled or exceeded the ratio of representation required for a member of the House of Representatives of the Congress of the United States*, which, at that time, was one representative to 93,340 inhabitants.

The mode of submission thus skilfully devised was objectionable on three grounds: first, it was a submission *in solido* of an entire Constitution, generally acceptable, perhaps, but containing one or more clauses which were obnoxious to a large, if not to the major, part of the State. But, lest hostility to the clause establishing slavery should lead to the rejection of the whole instrument, and thus the opportunity be lost of bringing into the Union another slave State, there were provided, secondly, a *bribe*, to induce a favorable vote — the proposition above described containing unusually liberal donations of public lands to the State, in case it should accept the whole scheme — a proffer morally as nefarious as that made by Satan to the

Saviour of mankind, of all the kingdoms of this world, if He would bow down and worship him; and, thirdly, a *threat*, to deter from its rejection, involved in that provision of the Act, which authorized the Territory to frame another Constitution only when its population should be at least 93,340, — a condition which, if enforced, might exclude it from the Union for years.

§ 520. It is needless to say, that the inhabitants of Kansas contemned both the bribe and the threat, and rejected the Constitution finally, by an overwhelming vote.

In reviewing these proceedings, the wonder is, that Congress, having the power to admit the Territory, without submitting to its inhabitants at all, the Constitution, certified to it by a Convention of its people, as having been regularly adopted, should have thought it worth while to commit a piece of injustice so elaborate and so useless, as was involved in this act. But that it did so, indicates unmistakably, that the true principles of Constitution-making, one of which is, that submission should be made of every proposition to change or to establish a fundamental law, to those to be affected thereby, were well understood, and that those principles, upon an equitable view, were thought to cover as well the case of Territories, notwithstanding their condition of pupilage or subjection, as of States exercising the rights of sovereignty. The reason for the course taken by Congress was that, under the inspiration of pro-slavery fanaticism, it desired, while it seemed justly and fairly to apply those principles, in reality to trample them in the dust, in order that slavery might be planted on the soil of Kansas. Happily, however, "the engineer was hoist with his own petard" — a measure intended to fasten slavery upon the Union forever, was the step too far, which, inaugurating a bloody revolution, resulted in giving the death-blow to that institution itself. The lesson thus learned, at such infinite cost, exemplifying the maxim that "honesty is the best policy," is not likely to be soon forgotten. It has already been productive of good; for, since the discussions upon the admission of Kansas into the Union, all enabling Acts contain minute provisions for taking fairly the sense of the inhabitants of the territories upon the Constitutions thereby authorized to be framed.[1]

[1] A novel and very objectionable mode of ascertaining the result of a submission of a Constitution to the people was resorted to by the Arkansas Con-

§ 520 *a*. It has been made a question whether, if a Convention, disobeying the Act calling it, either in relation to the mode of its organization or to the nature or scope of the proposals it should make, should submit the same to the people, and the people should ratify them, they would or would not be valid as a Constitution or as a part thereof? If the question were to be considered as a naked one of constitutional law, irrespective of all circumstances of place or time, it would seem that the answer should be in the negative. But, to receive that answer, it must be raised at once, and be decided without reference to any act of validation of the supposed work of the Convention by acquiescence on the part of the sovereign. As the question, accordingly, has received conflicting determinations, it is conceived that that fact is due to the overlooking, in some cases, of the curative effect of acquiescence of the sovereign upon constitutional provisions otherwise void. Thus, in Pennsylvania, as we have seen,[1] the highest court of the State pronounced valid amendments proposed in direct disobedience to the Convention Act, on the ground that, although the Convention had no power to propose them, they had been adopted and acquiesced in by the people of the State.[2] The same question was discussed incidentally in the North Carolina Convention of 1835. The Act calling the Convention had required its members, before they could become organized as a Convention, to take a certain oath strictly limiting the number and scope of the amendments they might recommend to the people. Some of the members were reluctant to take the oath, and it was asked by Mr. Speight whether, if the Convention should agree to make amendments to the Constitu-

vention of 1868, and that was to entrust the ascertainment of the result to a commission of three persons, not holding any official relation to the government of the State, with very extensive powers, executive and judicial. Schedule, secs. 4–9, Ark. Const. 1868. It gave the commissioners power to inquire into the fairness or validity of the voting upon the Constitution, to count the votes, to reject all that were fraudulent or illegal; and when it appeared "that fraud, fear, violence, improper influence, or restraint were used, or persons were prevented or intimidated from voting, to take such steps, either by setting aside the election and ordering a new one, or rejecting votes, or correcting the result in any county or precinct, as might in such cases be just and equitable." Sec. 8, Schedule. With such machinery, any party or faction, however small, could adopt any Constitution, however objectionable.

[1] See § 409 *c*, *ante*.

[2] Wood's Appeal, 75 Penn. St. 71.

tion different from those suggested in the Act of Assembly, and should submit them to the people, and they should agree to them, they would not be valid? and he referred to what had been done by the Convention to revise the old Confederation, that, though the delegates were appointed only to revise the old Confederation, they transcended their limits, and actually formed an entire new Constitution, and that Constitution was sanctioned by the people.[1] On the other hand, Mr. Gaston said: —

"He would not pursue the inquiry which had been entered upon by the gentleman from Greene" (Mr. Speight) "as to the effect of our proceedings should we throw off the limitations imposed on us, form a Constitution, submit it to the people, and it should be approved by a majority of their suffrages. This would present a state of things never yet witnessed in this country. No doubt the people, as a collective body, assembled in Convention for that purpose, can adopt a Constitution and make it theirs, by whomsoever and whensoever it were drafted. But they do this acting collectively, and not as individuals voting at the polls. It was true, as stated by that gentleman, that the Convention which framed the Federal Constitution exceeded their powers, and therefore the Constitution as framed by them was regarded only as a proposition. It is said to have been submitted to the people in the several States, and, when ratified by them, to have become a Constitution. But how was it submitted to the people? They were not called to vote upon it as individuals. The proposed Constitution was presented to the then Congress of the United States, and by the Congress to the State legislatures. Conventions of the people were then called in each State to deliberate on the adoption or rejection of it. Adopted by the people in convention, it became a Constitution."[2]

§ 520 *b*. The Pennsylvania case well illustrates both principles stated in the preceding section. An Ordinance of the Convention had been passed in direct disobedience to the Convention Act as to the mode of conducting the election for the adoption or rejection of the Constitution in the city of Philadelphia. This Ordinance, before it had been approved by the people, or validated

[1] *Deb. N. C. Conv.* 1835, pp. 5, 6.

[2] *Deb. N. C. Conv.* 1835, pp. 7, 8. Compare remarks of Hon. Joel Parker in the Massachusetts Convention of 1853. *Deb. Mass. Conv.* 1853, Vol. I. p. 156.

by any action of the political power of the State, was brought before the Supreme Court, and pronounced void, and the commissioners named to conduct the election were restrained by injunction from doing so. The same Convention had also proposed an amendment to the Bill of Rights, in violation of the Convention Act, which forbade any such amendment. This amendment the people ratified, with the general acquiescence of the community; and thereafter the question of its validity was brought before the Supreme Court, and its validity affirmed, on the ground that the political power had spoken, and that the judiciary could but follow and sustain its acts, even though they should amount to revolution.[1] Doubtless, the same judgment that was pronounced in regard to the election Ordinance, by the Pennsylvania court, would have been rendered by the Supreme Court of North Carolina, in the case imagined by Mr. Speight, could the question of the validity of the supposed action of the Convention have been brought before that tribunal as it stood when the discussion arose, and before such action had received the sanction of the people or of the political power of the State.

It will be inferred from the foregoing that the acquiesence which may give validity to an excessive exercise of power by a Convention must involve more than a mere affirmative vote of the qualified electors. These have no power to authorize or to condone a breach of constitutional duty; they can neither make nor repeal nor suspend the operation of a law. They are not "the people" in any case where they act without law or beyond the law. The acquiescence which ratifies or validates an act otherwise void is that of no single department or functionary, save as that department or functionary is supported by the consenting judgment of the sovereign whose voice it speaks. It is the acquiescence of the sovereign community, clearly manifest and continuous, that is alone effectual. As to the particular acts which are to manifest that judgment, or the length of time over which they should extend, no precise rule can be given. The most that can be said is, that when the sovereign body has clearly moved, and that movement gives evidence of irresistible force and of continuance, the various systems of officials, constituting the existing government, must heed and bow to it, or go

[1] Wells *v.* Bain, 75 Pa. St. R. 39; Wood's Appeal, Id. p. 59; Luther *v.* Borden, 7 How. U. S. R. 1.

down before it. Acquiescence, though silent and scarcely visible, is such a movement.

§ 521. V. It now remains only to consider briefly the crowning act by which changes in the fundamental law are consummated, or the results of submission certified and announced. The necessity of some such act, which should be authentic and final, is apparent, when it is considered that, without it, painful embarrassments might arise, in the minds of both governors and governed, as to their powers or duties in particular cases. It is obvious, also, that the announcement that a new organic law or code of laws had been adopted and put in force, ought to emanate from some department of the existing government.

In the case of the ordinary statute law, the necessity for an authentic promulgation is always recognized, and it is carefully provided for. Before such a law can take effect, it must, by our Constitutions, have been separately passed by the two houses of the legislature, have been signed by their respective Speakers, and by the Executive; and, finally, must await the arrival of the day fixed for it to become in force. In the mean time provision is made for publishing it throughout the sphere of its operation. With all this extreme care, doubts not unfrequently arise whether or not a particular law was so passed as to be legally binding. To give still greater certainty, therefore, it is commonly required, that the various steps, as well legislative as executive, taken in the progress of a bill to a law, shall be made matters of record, so that courts and individuals interested may always determine with precision whether any proposition did or did not become a law. If such particularity and caution are necessary in ordinary statutes, of which the effects are temporary and partial, they would seem to be proportionately more so, when the laws are fundamental, and their effects permanent and general. In looking, however, at the precedents, we fail to find in many cases a conformity to the requisites of sound principles, while there is apparent, in regard to them, an amount of ignorance or indifference, for which it is difficult to account.

§ 522. Of some of the earliest Constitutions, proclamation was made by a solemn act of the public authorities, accompanied by appropriate ceremonies. Thus, in the case of the New York Constitution of 1777, adopted in Convention April 20th, publication was made on the 22d of the same month, at the

Court-House in Kingston, "from a platform erected on the end of a hogshead," the vice-president of the existing government presiding. The revised Constitution of New Hampshire of 1783, "was introduced at Concord by a religious solemnity;" and that of Pennsylvania of 1790, by an imposing procession of all the officers of the State, the members of the Convention, and of the civic societies of Philadelphia, in the course of which the Constitution was formally proclaimed at the Court-House in Market Street.

The above were all instances of Constitutions put in operation without submission, except that of New Hampshire of 1783. Where submission to the people has been made, the course very generally adopted has been to require the returns of the election to be made from the several districts to the Secretary of State, to be canvassed by him and the other great officers of the State, often in the presence of such citizens as may choose to witness the proceeding; and, finally, the results of the canvass have been announced to the people by a proclamation of the Governor — the Constitution thereupon taking effect as such.[1] In many cases the Constitution has required that the people should vote for or against the Constitution, and, if there should be a majority for it, the Governor should make proclamation of that fact, but provided no mode of certifying the returns of the election to that officer.[2] In the Virginia Conventions of 1829 and 1850, and in that of Maryland of 1864, provision was made merely for a proclamation of the result of the election by the governor.[3]

1 This course was pursued in the following Conventions:— New York, 1821; Louisiana, 1844, 1852, and 1864; Illinois, 1847 and 1862; Michigan, 1850; California, 1849; Tennessee, 1834; Ohio, 1850; and Oregon, 1857.

2 It was so done in North Carolina, 1835; Texas, 1845; Wisconsin, 1848; and Iowa, 1857.

3 In the last-named State, a question arose in 1864 respecting the nature of the power given to the Governor by the Convention Act to pass upon the returns of the election at which the Constitution of that year was voted on by the people, which has been the subject of adjudication by the Court of Appeals of that State. The Constitution having been submitted to the people under regulations restricting the right to vote, within the State, to qualified electors who should have taken a prescribed oath, but permitting soldiers in the service of the United States to vote outside the limits of the State, the returns of the election coming into the hands of the Governor to be counted, an applica-

§ 523. Some of the above modes of announcement are sufficiently indefinite. Others have been practised, however, that are still more so. Thus, in the Maryland Convention of 1850, and that of Minnesota of 1857, the Schedules merely provided that, if a majority of all the votes cast should be for the Constitutions submitted, the same should be deemed to be adopted as the Constitutions of those States respectively. The Massachusetts Convention of 1779, and that of Kentucky of 1849, adopted still a different mode of announcing the result of the submission to the people. Having matured their respective Constitutions, and provided for a vote of the people upon them on a certain day, they adjourned to a day subsequent to that fixed for the election, at which time they reassembled, received the returns of the elections, and announced their results to the people by proclamation. A different mode was adopted by the last two Conventions of Massachusetts — those held in 1820 and 1853. The returns of the elections were made to the Secretary of the Commonwealth, were canvassed, and the votes counted by committees of the Conventions, appointed for that purpose previously to their dissolution, and proclamation of the results made by the Governor. In the Pennsylvania Convention of 1837, the returns of the elections were opened by the Speaker of the Senate, in joint session of the two houses, the result publicly announced by him, and a formal certificate of that fact made and filed among the public archives.

§ 524. In case of the Territories, the proper authority to make the announcement is evidently the government of the Union, representing the people thereof. Accordingly, the mode of offi-

tion was made to the Superior Court of Baltimore City for a rule upon the Governor to show cause why a *mandamus* should not be issued commanding him, in ascertaining the number of votes cast at the said election, to count certain votes tendered and rejected because the required oath had not been taken, and to exclude certain others cast by soldiers beyond the limits of the State.

The application being refused, the case was carried to the Court of Appeals, by which the judgment of the court below was affirmed, a majority of the court holding that the power to pass upon the returns in such a case was a political and not a judicial power, and therefore was not subject to revision by the judicial tribunals. See Miles *v.* Bradford, Governor of Maryland, 22 Md. R. 170 (decided at the June Term, 1864). For a complete statement of the facts of this case, including the proceedings in the court below, see *Deb. Md. Conv.* 1864, Vol. III. Appendix.

cially making known the establishment of a new Constitution, and the contemporaneous birth of a new State, is for Congress either to pass an Act reciting the framing of the Constitution, that it is republican in form, and concluding with a declaration that the Territory is thereby admitted into the Union, or to anticipate the action of the Territorial Convention by providing that such a body might meet to frame a Constitution and State government, or to accept conditions of admission into the Union imposed by Congress, — their Constitution having been already formed, — and that, thereupon, if the action of the Convention should be favorable, its results should be announced by a proclamation of the President, and the admission of the Territory into the Union be complete.

Of all the modes of announcement above described, that by a formal proclamation is clearly the most conformable to theoretical principles, and the most satisfactory in a practical point of view. From this there is, however, a descent through various gradations until modes of promulgation are reached, which are so indefinite and so inadequate, that it seems a matter of the greatest good fortune that serious embarrassments have not followed their adoption. Thus, take the cases in which it was provided that the Constitutions should go into effect, if adopted by a majority of the votes cast at an election on a day fixed, but in which no provision whatever was made for a canvass of the returns of the election, or for a promulgation, by some recognized official authority, of its results. That disputes have not arisen involving the validity of the fundamental Acts thus loosely ushered into the world, is due, not to the sufficiency of the processes by which they were promulgated, but to the peace and order of the times, and the utter absence of motive to raise, respecting their validity, even a doubt.[1]

[1] A Constitution, or an amendment, takes effect on the day of its adoption by the people, unless otherwise provided in the existing Constitution, or by the Convention acting under legislative authority. Parker *v.* Smith, 3 Minn. R. 240; Campbell *v.* Fields, 35 Texas R. 751; Schall *v.* Bowman, 62 Ill. R. 321; State *v.* Williams, 49 Miss. 640. But see Williams *v.* Douglass, 21 La. An. R. 468; Foster *v.* Daniels, 39 Geo. R. 398; People *v.* Norton, 59 Barb. (N. Y.) 169; People *v.* Gardner, Id. 198.

CHAPTER VIII.

OF THE AMENDMENT OF CONSTITUTIONS.

§ 525. As the plan of this treatise extends only to a discussion of the Convention, the mode of initiating or calling, and of organizing it, its functions, powers, and modes of proceeding, the foregoing chapters would seem to complete the circle, and to render improper the consideration of other topics not strictly within that plan. But while this is, in the main, true, it may, nevertheless, be useful to touch upon the subject of constitutional provisions for amending Constitutions. And, in one view of it, a discussion of that topic may be regarded as logically involved in an exhaustive treatise upon the Convention system. We have seen, that the creation or renovation, by an organized political society, of its Constitution of government, is analogous to the exercise of the procreative function in animals — obviously, an important topic in their natural history — and, as the Convention is the principal organ through which the political body effects changes in its Constitution, whether extending to its transformation or to its mere reparation, no discussion of that organ would be complete which should overlook the Constitutional provisions regulating its use and operation, or which should omit to state its excellences and defects as compared with those of other modes of attaining the same ends.

§ 526. By the principles of general law, the right of a people, at any time, to recast their political institutions, cannot be denied. The questions upon which difficulties arise, are, as to the extent to which it may be done, under given circumstances, without endangering the entire system, as to the modes of doing it, and the instruments through which it shall be effected. These questions, recurring under all forms of government, receive various answers, according to their respective circumstances and conditions. The cluster of States forming the American system are so dissimilar to those of Europe, in any age, that little light can be drawn, in this respect, from the practice of the latter, or from the writings of their statesmen and publicists. Between England and the United States, there is, it is true, the sympathy of race, and the institutions of the former were the model after which those of the latter were built; but the imitation was not close, and in many of their most important features the institutions of the two countries are as variant as are those of England and Austria. The provisions of the English Constitution for effecting changes in itself are unique, being the fruits of the signal victory by which the Parliament in 1688 became the dominant power in the realm. Ever since that revolution, to that body has been conceded the power to enact fundamental, as it does the statute laws, by bill passed through the regular stages of legislation, and approved by the sovereign.

In America it was early felt in many of the States that although the governments succeeding to the colonial establishments were based upon the will of the people, limitations must be imposed upon the latter in regard to amending their Constitutions. The wisest statesmen of the time saw that, in a country where the people were admitted to a direct participation in the government, party passions and interests would be likely to lead to too much tampering with Constitutions, if effectual checks were not interposed. They, therefore, framed governments which, in this particular, departed from the English model. Their Constitutions, purporting to define the powers of the several branches of the government, in no case permitted definitive amendments by the legislature, and most of them omitted all mention of the power of amendment. A few, as the Articles of Confederation, the Federal Constitution, and those of Maryland and of Delaware, framed in 1776, gave that power to the legislature, but under restrictions which reduced it far below the power so familiar to our fathers in the Parliament; and two made provision for Conventions to be called for that purpose, also under restrictions, — those of Pennsylvania and Vermont.[1]

§ 527. But it would be wrong to imagine the existence among the people of the United States, during the Revolutionary

[1] That the American mode of effecting amendments is superior to that of England, see *Popular Government*, by Sir H. S. Maine, Essay IV. pp. 196–254.

period, of a ripened public opinion on the subject of amending their Constitutions. There was, even in the States most noted for their steadfast zeal in the cause of liberty, a great lack of sound views of the power of the people over the institutions they had founded, and of the safe methods of perfecting them. Thus, in Massachusetts, whose first Constitution contained no provision for amendments, the doctrine of the Revolution, that governments were founded by the people, and could be amended by them as they should think fit, was erroneously understood to warrant tumultuous assemblages of citizens, without legal authority, to dictate to the government not only its current policy, but amendments of the fundamental law. Shay's Rebellion was the natural outgrowth of such views, quickened, doubtless, by the distress almost universal in a community not yet recovered from the effects of a long war.[1] The first batch of American Constitutions, moreover, were many of them framed in extreme haste, for temporary purposes, when little was thought or known of the best modes of constructing or amending such instruments. In several instances the State governments were intended to be mere provisional organizations, to be laid aside, not when new and better ones should be provided, but upon the expected contingency of a peace with England, following as a consequence of a redress of grievances. The result was, that the Constitutions first framed generally contained no provision for their future amendment, since the necessity of amendment was not at that time apprehended.

§ 528. But silence upon a subject of such importance was liable to misconstruction, and was therefore dangerous. Hence the policy of regulating by express constitutional provisions the exercise of so important a power soon began to be generally apparent. In several of the States the clauses of the Constitutions relating to amendments have been couched in negative terms, interdicting amendments except in the cases and modes prescribed. In a majority of the cases, however, they have been permissive, pointing out modes in which Conventions may be called, or specific amendments effected, without terms of restriction, or allusion to other possible modes.

But however liberal these provisions may seem to be, restriction is really the policy and the law of the country. By the

[1] Curtis' *Hist. Const. U. S.*, Vol. I. pp. 261–264.

common law of America, originating with the system we are considering, and out of the same necessities which gave the latter birth, it is settled, that amendments to our Constitutions are to be made only in modes pointed out or sanctioned by the legislative authority, the legal exponent of the will of the majority, which alone is entitled to the force of law.[1] The mode usually employed is that of summoning a Convention; and it is clear that no means are legitimate for the purpose indicated but Conventions, unless employed under an express warrant of the Constitution. The idea of the people thus restricting themselves in making changes in their Constitutions is original, and is one of the most signal evidences that amongst us liberty means, not the giving of rein to passion or to thoughtless impulse, but the exercise of power by the people for the general good, and, therefore, always under the restraints of law.

§ 529. But, while the framers of our Constitutions have sought to avoid the dangers attending a too frequent change of their fundamental codes, they have adverted to an opposite danger, to be equally shunned — that of making amendments too difficult. With a view to obviate this danger, in all our late Constitutions there have been inserted special provisions, the tenor of which will be explained hereafter. The general principle governing their selection, and, in truth, lying at the foundation of the whole subject, as a branch of practical politics, is this: Provisions regulating the time and mode of effecting organic changes are in the nature of safety-valves, — they must not be so adjusted as to discharge their peculiar function with too great facility, lest they become the ordinary escape-pipes of party passion; nor, on the other hand, must they discharge it with such difficulty that the force needed to induce action is sufficient also to explode the machine. Hence the problem of the Constitution-maker is, in this particular, one of the most difficult in our whole system, to reconcile the requisites for progress with the requisites for safety.[2] This problem can-

[1] See Curtis' *Hist. Const. U. S.*, Vol. I. pp. 261–264. Compare Grote, *Hist. Greece*, Vol. XI. pp. 493, 509, 510.

[2] Mr. John Stuart Mill thus states the problem: "No government can now expect to be permanent unless it guarantees progress as well as order; nor can it continue really to secure order unless it promotes progress. It can go on, as yet, with only a little of the spirit of improvement. While reformers have

not be yet regarded as solved, though we are doubtless approximating to a solution. Every new Constitution gathers up the fruits of past experience, and in turn contributes something to the common stock. We have reached such a stage that the provisions of our latest Constitutions may be considered as adequate to all ordinary exigencies of our condition. No community of American citizens would be badly provided for, were it compelled to accept any one of a score of Constitutions now in force amongst us, without modification, save in subordinate particulars touching local matters.

§ 530. Having thus formed a general conception of the doctrine of amendments in the American system, I pass to inquire, — I. What modes have been provided by our various Constitutions for effecting them? II. What are their comparative excellences and defects?

I. There are two modes of effecting amendments thus far devised: first, that by the agency of Conventions; and secondly, that by the agency of our General Assemblies, without Conventions, — both regularly followed by a ratification by the people.

Of the one hundred and ninety-two Conventions thus far held, only one hundred and nineteen have matured Constitutions, or amendments thereof, which have gone into effect. The residue is made up of Conventions which adjourned without recommending any alteration of the Constitution; or whose propositions of amendment were rejected by the people; or which were called merely to ratify Constitutions proposed by previous Conventions; or, finally, which were revolutionary bodies, like the late Secession Conventions. Of the one hundred and nineteen Constitutions framed by that number of Conventions, nine have contained no provision for their own amendment or revision;[1] twenty-nine have contained provisions for their amendment or

even a remote hope of effecting their objects through the existing system, they are generally willing to bear with it. But, when there is no hope at all, — when the institutions themselves seem to place an unyielding barrier to the progress of improvement, — the advancing tide heaps itself up behind them till it bears them down." — *The French Revolution and its Assailants*, in "Miscellanies."

[1] These were those of New Hampshire, North Carolina, South Carolina, and Virginia, 1776; New York, 1777; Pennsylvania, 1790; and Virginia, 1830, 1851, and 1864.

revision through the agency of Conventions only;[1] thirty-five through the agency of the General Assemblies only;[2] and forty-six for their amendment through the agency of either Conventions or the General Assemblies.[3] In this list have been reckoned as well amendments as complete revisions of Constitutions. In treating of the two modes, that through the agency of the General Assemblies will be styled the legislative mode.

§ 531. From the foregoing statement, it is evident that the two modes of amending Constitutions are of about equal antiquity and about equal authority. The legislative mode originated with the Continental Congress, and its particulars were, in that case, determined by the relations of the Confederation to the States. The mode of amending or revising, by Conventions called for that purpose, was first adopted by Pennsylvania in 1776, from which State it was, in the following year, borrowed by Vermont. These two modes, devised thus in the first years of our independence, have kept pretty equal pace throughout the whole range of our constitutional history, some Constitutions adopting one mode and some the other; but, for the first sixty years, only four authorizing both modes, that of the United States of 1787, that of South Carolina, 1790, and those of Dela-

[1] These were Florida, 1865; Georgia, 1777, 1789, and 1865; Illinois, 1818; Indiana, 1816; Kansas, 1857; Kentucky, 1792, 1799, and 1850; Louisiana, 1812; Maryland, 1851; Massachusetts, 1780; Mississippi, 1817 and 1832; Nebraska, 1867; New Hampshire, 1783, 1792, 1850, and 1877; Ohio, 1802; Pennsylvania, 1776; Tennessee, 1796; Vermont, 1777, 1787, 1793, 1828, 1836, and 1850.

[2] These were Alabama, 1819; Arkansas, 1836, 1864, 1868, and 1874; Connecticut, 1818; Delaware, 1776; Georgia, 1798; Indiana, 1851; Louisiana, 1845, 1851, 1864, 1868, and 1879; Maine, 1820; Maryland, 1776; Massachusetts, 1822; Mississippi, 1865 and 1868; Missouri, 1820 and 1863; New Jersey, 1776 and 1844; New York, 1821; Oregon, 1857; Pennsylvania, 1838 and 1873; Rhode Island, 1842; South Carolina, 1778; Tennessee, 1834 and 1865; Texas, 1845, 1868, and 1876; and Vermont, 1870.

[3] These were the Federal Constitution, 1788; Alabama, 1865, 1867, and 1875; California, 1849 and 1879; Colorado, 1876; Delaware, 1792 and 1831; Florida, 1839, 1868, and 1885; Georgia, 1868 and 1877; Illinois, 1848 and 1870; Iowa, 1846 and 1857; Kansas, 1855, 1858, and 1859; Maine, 1820; Maryland, 1864 and 1867; Michigan, 1835 and 1850; Minnesota, 1857; Missouri, 1865 and 1875; Nebraska, 1875; Nevada, 1864; New York, 1846; North Carolina, 1835, 1865, 1868, and 1876; Ohio, 1851; South Carolina, 1790, 1865, and 1868; Tennessee, 1870; Texas, 1866; Virginia, 1869; West Virginia, 1863 and 1872; and Wisconsin, 1848.

ware of 1792 and 1831. During the period beginning with 1835 and ending with 1885, however, ten Constitutions have provided for amendments by Conventions only, twenty-two in the legislative mode only, and forty-one in both modes, showing a growing conviction that the legislative mode has advantages which make its more general adoption seem desirable, and yet that it alone is not adequate to the exigencies of the times, but needs to have coupled with it a provision for a Convention when the people should deem it necessary or expedient to make a general revision of the Constitution. Doubtless, as our Constitutions become riper and more perfect with time and experience, the necessity of employing the more expensive mode by Conventions will be found to be less and less. Such seems to have been the opinion of Mr. Webster, who, in the Massachusetts Convention of 1820, opposed the adoption of a provision for the call of a future Convention. . . . "With the experience which we had had of the Constitution," he said, "there was little probability that, after the amendments which should now be adopted, there would be any occasion for great changes. No revision of its general principles would be necessary, and the alterations which should be called for by a change of circumstances would be limited and specific."[1]

§ 532. II. To determine the excellences and defects of these two modes of amending Constitutions, they must be considered with reference to their tendency, respectively, to prevent or to alleviate the three great evils of popular government, — hasty legislation, excessive legislation, and partisan legislation. Let us consider, from this point of view,—

(*a*). The mode by Conventions.

It is obvious that, were the existing government of a State, or any branch of it, invested with the power, without condition or limit, to call Conventions to change the organic law, there would be cause to apprehend two dangers: one, that the permanent, and, therefore, paramount and sacred character of that law would be impaired; for, what the government could at any time procure to be changed or repealed, would, in effect, be but an ordinary statute; the other, that our Conventions would become the arenas, and our Constitutions the objects as well as the instruments, of party conflict. The right of the people, at

[1] *Deb. Mass. Conv.* 1821, p. 413.

any time to amend their Constitutions must be admitted; but as they can never do this directly, the necessity becomes apparent of checks, to render it probable that a movement to that end has been sanctioned by them, and that it has been done upon due consideration. What those checks should be, is a problem of which the conditions will vary with the circumstances of the case. In this country, the difference between States which differ most is but slight, and hence the results of their individual experience are in the main equally useful to all. Conventions being universally called amongst us by legislative authority, the checks must be such as will obviate the evils above enumerated, resulting from haste, excess, and partisan zeal, in legislation.

§ 533. The readiest mode of preventing these evils is either to increase the majority required to call a Convention, or to compel the submission to the people either of the legislative Act calling a Convention, or the question whether or not a Convention shall be called.

The first of these checks would doubtless be efficacious, unless the minority, invested with a veto upon the Act, were too small. On most questions, of whatever magnitude or character, if the vote of a party were sufficient to determine results, it would be likely to be cast as the interest of the party should require. In the see-saw of politics, it is rare that a party very much or very long outnumbers its antagonist. Hence, if party majorities were allowed free scope to tamper with our organic laws, there would be nothing stable in them. On the other hand, if a reform of the fundamental code be really needed, men of all parties will admit the fact, or enough men in all parties to effect it. Should the proposed amendments, however, assume a partisan character, or for any other reason be improper to be made now, or at all, there should be no room for danger of their adoption. It seems evident, then, that where the check is sought in numbers, a majority is too small, and a unanimous vote too large, for either practicability or safety. A mean must be sought not liable to these objections, and that not from *à priori* considerations, but from experience. What that mean has generally been in the practice of the several States, will be seen further on.

§ 534. The second check, which is found in a submission of

the question of calling a Convention to the people, seems more efficacious. By the term "people" is meant, theoretically, the political society, but practically, as we have seen, the body of the electors, which is its representative, at the nearest hand. The views of the latter, expressed in any mode adapted to its organization, may more fairly be presumed to be those of the political society than those of any body less numerous and further removed from it; and, therefore, whenever the electors have assented to the call of a Convention, its necessity or eminent propriety may be considered to be beyond doubt. Such a body may be swayed by passion, but it will not be by a passion that is local. A State, in which the passion of a majority of its electors, on high questions of fundamental law, is selfish and local, must be near its downfall. At all events, when a legislature is required to submit the question of the expediency of constitutional changes to the determination of a body that never assembles, that is not easily approached for unworthy purposes, and that is, this side the sovereign itself, the ultimate depositary of sovereign rights, there is one chance the more that such changes will not be ill-advised. That such a question ought in all cases to be submitted to the people, has been affirmed by what will be conceded to be high authority. The point arose in New York the year preceding the Convention of 1821. At an extra session of the legislature in November, 1820, an Act had been passed by both houses, by the provisions of which a Convention was to be called, without referring the question, in the first instance, to the people, — the delegates to be chosen in February, 1821, and the body to convene in June following. This Act having been submitted to the Council of Revision, composed of the Governor, the Judges of the Supreme Court, and the Chancellor, — a body invested by the Constitution with a negative on all Acts of the legislature, to be overcome only by a two-thirds vote of both houses, — it was returned with their objections, and thereupon failed to become a law. The objections were drawn up by Chancellor Kent, and received the concurrence of Governor Clinton and Chief-Justice Spencer, a majority of the Council. The first objection was stated to be, because the Act recommended to choose "delegates to meet in Convention for the purpose of making such alterations in the Constitution" as they might think proper, "without first having taken the sense of the people, whether such a Convention, for such a general and unlimited revisal and alteration of the Constitution," was, "in their judgment, necessary and expedient." Admitting as undoubted and as indefeasible the right of the people at all times to alter their Constitution, as to them should seem meet, the Council expressed great doubt whether it belonged "to the ordinary legislature, chosen only to make laws, in pursuance of the provisions of the existing Constitution, to call a Convention, in the first instance, to revise, alter, and perhaps remodel the whole fabric of the government, and before they have received a legitimate and full expression of the will of the people that such changes should be made." They remark, with great justice, that "the Constitution is the will of the people, expressed in their original character, and intended for the permanent protection and happiness of them and their posterity; and," they add, "it is perfectly consonant to the republican theory, and to the declared sense and practice of this country, that it cannot be altered or changed in any degree, without the expression of the same original will." The Council conclude by showing that in many of the Constitutions thus far framed in the leading States of the Union, it has been explicitly provided that no Convention should be called but by the concurrence of the people, expressed at an election at which the question of calling one should have been distinctly presented.[1]

§ 535. The wisdom of this decision it is impossible to doubt. How far it conforms to the constitutional practice of the country may be inferred from an examination of precedents, to which I now pass.

[1] For the whole of this very valuable document, see Appendix F.

Another check upon the calling of Conventions, mentioned by Mr. Madison, involves the concurrent action of any two of the three departments of the government; but, as it has never been employed, I have not enumerated it in the text. It is thus described by him: — "Another plan has been thought of, which might perhaps succeed better, and would at the same time be a safeguard to the equilibrium of the constitutional departments of the government; that is, that a majority of any two of the three departments should have authority to call a plenipotentiary Convention, whenever they may think their constitutional powers have been violated by the other department, or that any material part of the Constitution needs amendment." — Letter to John Brown (of Kentucky), dated Aug 23, 1785, Madison's *Works*, Vol. I. p. 177.

The provisions of our Constitutions relating to this subject are of four varieties: first, such as require the call of a Convention periodically or at a specified time; secondly, such as look to an expression of the sense of the people on the question of calling a Convention periodically or at a specified time; thirdly, such as look to a vote of the people on the question whenever the legislature should deem it advisable that a Convention should be called; fourthly, such as authorize the call of Conventions whenever the legislature should deem the amendment or revision of the Constitution to be necessary.

1. Of the first variety, the earliest instance is presented by the Pennsylvania Constitution of 1776, which provided for the call of a Convention every seventh year after its adoption. This provision was adopted by Vermont in its first Constitution, of 1777, and in all that followed down to and including the Constitution as amended in 1850. New Hampshire, in her Constitution of 1784, adopted the same term. The Georgia Constitution of 1789 required the call of a Convention in 1794.

2. Of the second variety, looking to an expression of the sense of the people on the question of calling a Convention periodically or at a specified time, are the Constitutions of Massachusetts, of 1780, requiring a vote of the people in 1795; of Kentucky, of 1792, requiring such a vote in 1797 and 1798; of New Hampshire, of 1792, requiring such a vote every seventh year; of Kansas, of 1858, requiring a vote in 1863 and every seventh year thereafter; of Iowa, of 1846 and 1857, requiring a vote in 1870 and every tenth year thereafter; of Maryland, of 1851, requiring a vote in every year succeeding the returns of each United States census; of Indiana, of 1816, a vote every twelfth year; of Michigan, of 1850, a vote in 1866 and every sixteenth year thereafter; of New York, of 1846, a vote in 1866 and every twentieth year thereafter; of Ohio, of 1851, in 1871 and every twentieth year thereafter; of Massachusetts, of 1853, in 1873 and every twentieth year thereafter; of Maryland, of 1864 and 1867, in 1882 and 1887 respectively, and every twentieth year thereafter; and of Virginia, of 1870, in 1888 and every twentieth year thereafter.[1] The Iowa Constitutions of 1846 and 1857, and

[1] The adoption of the term of twenty years was probably based on the calculation of Mr. Jefferson, that the people of a State, as a body, was wholly

the Michigan Constitution of 1850 contained also a provision that a vote of the people upon the question of calling a Convention might be taken at such other times as the legislature might by law prescribe. A novel provision for calling a Convention was made in the Massachusetts Constitution of 1853, beside the one described above. Its terms were, that, whenever towns or cities containing not less than one-third of the qualified voters of the Commonwealth should, at any meeting for the election of State officers, request that a Convention be called to revise the Constitution, it should be the duty of the legislature, at its next session, to pass an Act for the calling of the same, and submit the question to the qualified voters of the Commonwealth, whether a Convention should be called accordingly, saving, however, the power of the legislature to take action for calling a Convention without such request, as before practised in the Commonwealth.

§ 536. 3. Of the third variety, looking to a vote of the people upon the question of calling a Convention whenever the General Assembly, or a prescribed majority thereof, should recommend it, are a large proportion of the Constitutions which contain provisions for calling Conventions at all. Of these, some authorize such a vote at any time when the General Assembly may recommend it;[1] some, whenever a majority of all the members elected to each house may recommend it;[2] some, whenever two-thirds of the General Assembly, or of each house thereof, may recommend it;[3] some, whenever two-thirds of all the members elected

renewed once in about twenty years. See his Letter of July 12, 1816, to Samuel Kercheval, Jefferson's *Works*, Vol. VII. pp. 9–17.

[1] Constitutions of Tennessee, 1796 and 1870; Delaware, 1831; Iowa, 1846 and 1857; Wisconsin, 1848; Michigan, 1850; Missouri, 1865 and 1875; and Nebraska, 1867. The Delaware Constitution of 1792 contained a provision which authorized a vote of the people upon the question of holding a Convention, at a general election of representatives, without the previous action of the legislature, and requiring the latter, in case a majority of all the citizens of the State having a right to vote for representatives should have voted for a Convention, at its next session to call one.

[2] Constitutions of Kentucky, 1799 and 1850, and Louisiana, 1812, — each of two successive legislatures, — and West Virginia, 1863 and 1872.

[3] Constitutions of California, 1849; Florida, 1885; Georgia, 1877; Illinois, 1818 and 1870; Kansas, 1857 and 1859; Michigan, 1835; Mississippi, 1817; North Carolina, 1876; Ohio, 1802 (after 1806).

It has been held that two-thirds of each house means two-thirds of a quoto each house of the General Assembly may recommend it;[1] some, whenever it is recommended by three-fifths of the members elected to each house.[2]

4. Of the fourth variety are a few Constitutions which authorize the call of Conventions whenever the legislature, or a specified majority thereof, should deem the amendment or revision of the Constitution to be necessary.[3]

§ 537. In some cases, Constitutions impose restrictions upon the calling of Conventions, and among them are some of those comprised in the foregoing lists. Thus, in one Constitution it was provided that it should be altered or amended only by a Convention of the people, called for that purpose by Act of the General Assembly.[4] In several Constitutions it was declared that no Convention should be called unless by the concurrence of two-thirds of the members of each house of the General Assembly.[5] So, many Constitutions forbade the calling of a Convention, unless the question of Convention or no Convention should have been submitted to the people, and the vote have been in favor of a Convention;[6] or, that a Convention should be called in the election of delegates to which any person qualified by the Constitution to vote should be disqualified, and providing, that representation therein should be based on population, and that the right of suffrage should never be taken from any person

rum of each house. State *v.* McBride, 4 Mo. R., 303. But see Green *v.* Waller, 32 Miss. R. (3 George), 650, and remarks of Fisher, J., relative to the same case, 33 Miss. R., Appendix, 735.

[1] Constitutions of California, 1879; Colorado, 1876; Illinois, 1848 and 1862; Maryland and Nevada, 1864; Minnesota, 1857; Ohio, 1851; and South Carolina, 1868.

[2] Constitutions of Kansas, 1858, and Nebraska, 1875.

[3] The Georgia Constitution of 1865 gave general authority to call a Convention at any time. The following authorized such a call, without limitation, by a vote of two-thirds of each house of the General Assembly: Florida, 1839 and 1865; North Carolina, 1868; and South Carolina, 1790 and 1865; and the following by a vote of three-fourths of all the members of each house of the General Assembly, with the approval of the governor: Texas, 1866.

[4] Constitution of Georgia, 1865, Art. V. Sec. 11.

[5] Constitutions of Florida, 1839 and 1865; Georgia, 1877; North Carolina, 1835, 1868, and 1876; and South Carolina, 1790 and 1865.

[6] Constitutions of Alabama, 1865, 1867, and 1875; Delaware, 1792 and 1831: substantially, Georgia, 1777; Kentucky, 1792, 1799, and 1850; Louisiana, 1812; Missouri, 1865 and 1875; and West Virginia, 1863 and 1872.

qualified by the Constitution to vote;[1] or forbidding that a Convention should be called before a specified year;[2] or the recommendation of certain designated amendments or provisions, as affecting the immigration or importation of slaves, before 1808;[3] or introducing slavery or involuntary servitude otherwise than in punishment of crime;[4] or affecting the rights of property in the ownership of slaves;[5] or denying or in any way impairing the right of suffrage, or any civil or political right as conferred by the Constitution, except for causes which apply to all persons and classes without distinction;[6] or providing that no amendment or revision recommended by a Convention should take effect until submitted to the qualified electors, and approved by them.[7]

Some of the Constitutions referred to above contained also other special provisions which should be noted. Thus, the Kentucky Constitutions of 1792 and 1799 authorized a vote of the people upon the question of calling a Convention in two successive years, and, if both votes were in favor of the call, the General Assembly was required at their next session to make such call; but, if in either year the vote should be adverse to the call, no Convention should be called until two-thirds of both branches of the General Assembly should deem it expedient. The Constitutions of West Virginia framed in 1863 and 1872 surpass all others in the number and rigor of their restrictive clauses. No Convention is to be called, "having authority to alter the Constitution of the State," unless in pursuance of a law providing for an election to take the sense of the people, etc., as stated above; and no members of a Convention are to be elected until one month after the result of the poll shall have been ascertained and published. All acts and ordinances of any such Convention are to be submitted to the voters of the State, for ratification or rejection, and to have no validity whatever

[1] Constitution of Georgia, 1868.

[2] Constitution of Kansas, 1855, specifying 1865.

[3] Federal Constitution, 1788.

[4] Constitutions of Indiana, 1816; and Ohio, 1802.

[5] Constitution of Kansas, 1857.

[6] Constitution of Virginia, 1870.

[7] Constitutions of New Hampshire, 1783 and 1792; Ohio, 1851; Kansas, 1858; Maryland, 1864 and 1867; West Virginia, 1863 and 1872; Illinois, 1870; and Colorado, 1876.

until they are ratified; and in no event are they, by any shift or device, to be made to have any retrospective operation or effect.

A special interest attaches to these negative provisions, on account of an important constitutional question, considered elsewhere, to which they give rise, namely, whether, under those instruments, amendments can be effected through the agency of Conventions called in disregard of those restrictions?[1]

§ 537 *a*. Beside the four varieties of Constitutions containing provisions for the call of Conventions, described in the preceding sections, it may be useful here to mention another class which contain no provisions for that purpose, though some of them contain provisions for making amendments in the legislative mode[2] In relation to this class of constitutional provisions, also, the question, to be considered hereafter, arises, whether, under either of them, a Convention can be called.[3]

§ 538. (*b*.) The mode of effecting amendments to a Constitution through the agency of the legislature, without a Convention, would seem to be the most natural, because the most simple one. Our fathers, as we have shown, were familiar with its use in England. The peculiar nature of our system, however, made the adoption of the English mode, without material modifications, inadvisable, for by the latter constitutional changes are, as in case of ordinary legislation, the work of King, Lords, and Commons, acting in conjunction. In America, however, fundamental legislation, even when carried on by our General Assemblies, is conducted in a manner very different from

[1] See *post*, §§ 537, 563–569.

[2] To this list belong the following Constitutions: —

1. Constitutions containing no provisions for amendment at all: New Hampshire, North Carolina, South Carolina, and Virginia, 1776; New York, 1777; Pennsylvania, 1790; and Virginia, 1830, 1851, and 1864.

2. Constitutions containing provisions for amendments in the legislative mode, but none for the call of Conventions: Delaware, Maryland, and New Jersey, 1776; the Articles of Confederation, 1777; South Carolina, 1778; Georgia, 1798; Connecticut, 1818; Alabama, 1819; Missouri, 1820 and 1863; Maine, 1820; Massachusetts and New York, 1821; Tennessee, 1834 and 1865; Arkansas, 1836, 1864, 1868, and 1874; Pennsylvania, 1838 and 1873; Rhode Island, 1842; New Jersey, 1844; Texas, 1845, 1868, 1876; Louisiana, 1845, 1852, 1864, 1868, and 1879; Indiana, 1851; Oregon, 1857; Mississippi, 1865 and 1868; and Vermont, 1870.

[3] See *post*, §§ 563–574 *h*.

ordinary legislation. As, in calling Conventions, the legislature acts under checks unknown to it when exercising its usual function; so here, the restrictions upon its action are so numerous and important, and the departures from the processes of ordinary legislation so wide, that it has been made a question whether, in proposing amendments to the organic law, the legislature is engaged in an act of legislation at all, — a question which it will become our duty in due time to consider.

§ 539. Though this mode, under proper restrictions and in cases to which it is adapted, may be followed without danger, yet it is subject to obvious objections. The legislature is a body chosen for temporary purposes. It is a mirror of political passions and interests, and, with the best intentions, cannot be expected to be free from bias, even in questions of the highest moment. It is composed, moreover, in general, of politicians rather than of statesmen. Indeed, if a man shows himself, by culture and the breadth of his views, to be fitted for the highest trusts, it is nearly certain that he will not be found in the legislature, but be left in obscurity at home. But, when a Convention is called, it is sometimes possible to secure the return of such men. It is not necessarily because such a body is recognized to be, as it is, the most important ever assembled in a State, but because the measures it is expected to mature bear less directly on the interests of parties or of individuals. Party management, therefore, is not usually so much directed to the seeking of control of a Convention as of a legislature. Besides, the proper function of the latter body, that of municipal legislation, being one of the highest vested by the sovereign in any governmental agency, it cannot but be inexpedient, on a general view, that there should be added to it that of organic legislation, requiring different and higher gifts, and wider experience and study, thus threatening to unsettle the balance of the Constitution.[1]

§ 540. With proper safeguards, and under adequate checks, however, a legislature, as we have said, may be allowed to take part in fundamental legislation without endangering the safety of the State. In point of convenience, such an arrangement possesses many claims to acceptance. The calling of a Convention

[1] See Hildreth's *Hist. U. S.*, Vol. I. 2d Series, p. 231; remarks of the author upon the South Carolina Constitution of 1790.

is a measure attended commonly by much delay and expense, and is often compassed by very great difficulties. Reforms would often be foregone rather than resort to means so inconvenient. The needed amendments to our Constitutions are often of no great extent; a doubt has arisen, perhaps, as to the construction to be put upon a particular clause; a change may be desired in the qualifications for the suffrage, or in the basis of representation; a branch of the administration is found to be too cumbrous for use; or a new distribution among the agencies of government of their constitutional powers is thought to be advisable to facilitate the transaction of business, or to render public operations more safe or more economical. For amendments of such a stamp, separately considered, the mode by legislative action is well adapted; and it is adapted to no other. It ought to be confined, it is believed, to changes which are few, simple, independent, and of comparatively small importance. For a general revision of a Constitution, or even for single propositions involving radical changes as to the policy of which the popular mind has not been informed by prior discussion, the employment of this mode is impracticable, or of doubtful expediency.

The checks proper to be applied to a legislature, acting in a conventional capacity, are not different from those applied where it assumes to call a Convention. They consist of increased majorities, of repeated votes, and of publication and submission to the people. In many cases, as we shall see, all of these devices for preventing hasty action are employed simultaneously. When measures are thus initiated deliberately, in a right spirit and for proper ends, the conditions of safe legislation seem to be fulfilled.

§ 541. Of the Constitutions which permit amendments in the legislative mode, that is, by combined legislative and popular action without a Convention, a large proportion contain substantially the following provision, copied from the Michigan Constitution of 1835: —

"Any amendment or amendments to this Constitution may be proposed in the Senate or House of Representatives; and if the same shall be agreed to by a majority of the members elected to each of the two houses, such proposed amendment or amendments shall be entered on their journals, with the yeas and nays taken thereon, and referred to the legislature then next to be chosen, and shall be published for three months previous to the time of making such choice. And if, in the legislature next chosen as aforesaid, such amendment or amendments shall be agreed to by two-thirds of all the members elected to each house, then it shall be the duty of the legislature to submit such proposed amendment or amendments to the people, in such manner and at such time as the legislature shall prescribe; and, if the people shall approve and ratify such amendment or amendments by a majority of the electors qualified to vote for members of the legislature voting thereon, such amendment or amendments shall become part of the Constitution."

This provision has been selected because it contains nearly all the requirements and conditions to the exercise of the legislative mode of amending Constitutions found in any of those instruments.

§ 542. The points of difference presented by the various Constitutions, in respect to their provisions for amendments in the legislative mode, relate to the majority of the legislature required to recommend a change; the length of the notice to be given before the succeeding election, if any; the majority required in the legislature chosen at such election, and the body by which submission to the people, when required, shall be made. Thus, to recommend amendments, in certain Constitutions, a majority of three-fifths of all the members elected to each house of the General Assembly is required;[1] in some, a majority of all the members elected to each house only;[2] and, in all the remaining Constitutions, a majority of two-thirds of the members elected

[1] Constitutions of Florida, 1885; Kansas, 1858; Louisiana, 1845; Maryland, 1864 and 1867; Nebraska, 1875; North Carolina, 1835, 1868, and 1876; and Ohio, 1851.

[2] Constitutions of Arkansas, 1868 and 1874; California, 1849; Connecticut, 1818; Iowa, 1846 and 1857; Louisiana, 1864; Michigan, 1835; Minnesota, 1857; Missouri, 1865 and 1875; New Jersey, 1844; New York, 1821 and 1846; Oregon, 1857; Pennsylvania, 1838 and 1873; Rhode Island, 1842; South Carolina, 1778; Tennessee, 1834 and 1870; Vermont, 1870; West Virginia, 1863; and Wisconsin, 1848.

In most cases in which a simple majority is required, the Constitutions prescribe a reference of the proposed amendments to the General Assembly to be chosen at the next general election. The exceptions are the Constitutions of Louisiana, 1864; Minnesota, 1857; Missouri, 1865 and 1875; Pennsylvania, 1838 and 1873; Rhode Island, 1842; and South Carolina, 1778.

to each house.[1] Of the Constitutions requiring a second vote of the succeeding legislature, fourteen require a simple majority of all the members elected to each house;[2] two require three-fourths of all the members elected to each house;[3] and of the remaining Constitutions, some require two-thirds of each house;[4] and the rest, two-thirds of all the members elected to each house.[5]

Notice is required to be published in a large proportion of the Constitutions in question; in a few cases generally, without specifying the length of time;[6] in two, a notice of four weeks;[7] in one, of ninety days;[8] in two, of twelve months;[9] in nine, of six months;[10] in one, of four months;[11] and in the residue, of three months.[12] In the Massachusetts Constitution of 1821, two votes

[1] Alabama, 1819, 1865, 1867, and 1875; Arkansas, 1836 and 1864; California, 1879; Colorado, 1876; Delaware, 1792 and 1831; Florida, 1839 and 1868; Georgia, 1798, 1868, and 1877; Illinois, 1848 and 1870; Kansas, 1859; Louisiana, 1852 and 1868; Maine, 1820; Massachusetts, 1821 (of the House,— a majority of the Senate); Michigan, 1850; Mississippi, 1832 and 1868; South Carolina, 1790, 1865, and 1868; Texas, 1845, 1866, and 1868; Vermont, 1870 (of the Senate, — a majority of the House); and West Virginia, 1872.

[2] Constitutions of Arkansas, 1868; California, 1849; Iowa, 1846 and 1857; Louisiana, 1845; New Jersey, 1844; New York, 1846; Oregon, 1857; Pennsylvania, 1838 and 1873; Rhode Island, 1842; Vermont, 1870; West Virginia, 1863; and Wisconsin, 1848.

[3] Constitutions of Delaware, 1792 and 1831.

[4] Constitutions of Alabama, 1819, 1865, and 1867; Arkansas, 1836 and 1864; Connecticut, 1818; Florida, 1839; Georgia, 1798 and 1868; Massachusetts, 1822 (of the House, — a majority of the Senate); Missouri, 1820; North Carolina, 1835 and 1868; South Carolina, 1790, 1865, and 1868; Tennessee, 1834 and 1870; and Texas, 1845, 1866, and 1868.

[5] Constitutions of Florida, 1868; Illinois, 1848; Michigan, 1835; and New York, 1821.

[6] These are Connecticut, 1818; Massachusetts, 1821; Minnesota, 1857; Rhode Island, 1842; and Vermont, 1870.

[7] These are Missouri, 1875, and Oregon, 1857.

[8] South Carolina, 1778.

[9] Arkansas, 1836 and 1864.

[10] Arkansas, 1874; Florida, 1839; Georgia, 1798; Mississippi, 1832; North Carolina, 1835 and 1868; Ohio, 1851; and Tennessee, 1834 and 1870.

[11] Missouri, 1865.

[12] Constitutions of Alabama, 1819, 1865, 1867, and 1875; Arkansas, 1868; California, 1849; Colorado, 1876; Delaware, 1792 and 1831 (three to six months); Florida, 1868 and 1885; Illinois, 1848 and 1870; Iowa, 1846 and 1857; Kansas, 1858 and 1859; Louisiana, 1845, 1852, and 1868; Maryland,

in each of the two houses were required, of two-thirds of the house and a majority of the senate. In most of the Constitutions now under consideration is found a further provision, both for notice and to preserve a record of what is done, requiring the amendments recommended by the General Assembly to be entered on the journal, with the yeas and nays taken thereon.[1]

Another remarkable requirement appears in certain Constitutions, — that, in voting upon proposed amendments, the amendments shall be read three times on three several days, this requirement in most cases applying to both legislatures.[2]

In relation to the body by which the Act of submitting the Constitution to the people, when required, should be passed, in a majority of cases there was no specification, but a provision merely that it be submitted: in the remaining cases it was required that the Act should be passed by the legislature.[3]

On the popular vote to ratify the action of the legislature, a majority was required in all the cases but that of Rhode Island, 1842, which made a vote of three-fifths of the people necessary.

§ 543. There are a few cases which are not reducible to any

1864 and 1867; Michigan, 1835; Mississippi, 1868; Nebraska, 1875; New Jersey, 1844; New York, 1821 and 1846; Pennsylvania, 1838; South Carolina, 1790 and 1865; Texas, 1845, 1866, and 1868; Virginia, 1870; West Virginia, 1863 and 1872; and Wisconsin, 1848.

[1] Constitutions of Arkansas, 1868 and 1874; California, 1849 and 1879; Colorado, 1876; Florida, 1868 and 1885; Illinois, 1870; Indiana, 1851; Iowa, 1846 and 1857; Kansas, 1858 and 1859; Louisiana, 1845, 1852, 1864, and 1868; Maryland, 1864 and 1867; Massachusetts, 1821; Michigan, 1835 and 1850; Missouri, 1865 and 1875; Nebraska, 1875; New Jersey, 1844; New York, 1821 and 1846; Ohio, 1851; Oregon, 1857; Pennsylvania, 1838 and 1873; South Carolina, 1868; Tennessee, 1834 and 1870; Vermont, 1870; Virginia, 1870; West Virginia, 1863 and 1872; and Wisconsin, 1848.

[2] Constitutions of Alabama, 1819, 1865, 1867, and 1875; Florida, 1839; Georgia, 1798; Mississippi, 1832 and 1868; Missouri, 1820; North Carolina, 1835 and 1868 (to be read three times); South Carolina, 1790, 1865, and 1868; Tennessee, 1834 and 1870; Texas, 1845, 1866, and 1868; and West Virginia, 1863 and 1872.

[3] Constitutions of Arkansas, 1868; California, 1849 and 1879; Florida, 1868; Illinois, 1848 and 1870; Indiana, 1851; Iowa, 1846 and 1857; Louisiana, 1864; Maine, 1820; Maryland, 1867; Massachusetts, 1821; Michigan, 1835; Minnesota, 1857; Missouri, 1865 and 1875; New Jersey, 1844; New York, 1821 and 1846; North Carolina, 1835, 1868, and 1876; Oregon, 1857; Pennsylvania, 1838 and 1873; Rhode Island, 1842; Tennessee, 1834 and 1870; Vermont, 1870; Virginia, 1870; West Virginia, 1863 and 1872; and Wisconsin, 1848.

rule, that it may be useful to note separately. The first of these is that of the Delaware Constitution of 1776, by Section XXX. of which it was provided as follows: —

"No article of the Declaration of Rights and fundamental rules of this State, agreed to by this Convention, nor the first, second, fifth (except that part thereof that relates to the right of suffrage), twenty-sixth, and twenty-ninth articles of this Constitution ought ever to be violated, on any pretence whatever. No other part of this Constitution shall be altered, changed, or diminished, without the consent of five parts in seven of the Assembly, and seven members of the Legislative Council." [1]

Section LIX. of the Maryland Constitution of 1776 contains the following provision, in some of its points not dissimilar to those referred to in the preceding section: —

"That this form of government, and the Declaration of Rights, and no part thereof, shall be altered, changed, or abolished, unless a bill so to alter, change, or abolish the same shall pass the General Assembly after a new election, and shall be confirmed by the General Assembly, after a new election of delegates, in the first session after such new election; *provided*, that nothing in this form of government which relates to the eastern shore particularly shall at any time hereafter be altered, unless for the alteration and confirmation thereof at least two-thirds of all the members of each branch of the General Assembly shall concur."

The Articles of Confederation provided, Article XIII., that no alteration should at any time be made in any of said articles, "unless such alteration be agreed to in a Congress of the United States, and be afterwards confirmed by the legislature of every State."

The Federal Constitution provided still a different mode, though it bore in general a strong resemblance to the class first above mentioned, save in the mode of ratification by the people. It was as follows: —

"Congress, whenever two-thirds of both houses shall deem it necessary, shall propose amendments to this Constitution . . . . which . . . . shall be valid to all intents and purposes as parts

[1] The Legislative Council consisted of nine members, so that five-sevenths of the Assembly and seven-ninths of the Council were necessary to amend the Constitution.

of this Constitution, when ratified by the legislatures of three-fourths of the several States, or by Conventions in three-fourths thereof, as the one or the other mode of ratification may be proposed by Congress." [1]

[1] In connection with this clause of the Federal Constitution, it may not be out of place to consider the animadversions of a late writer respecting the mode thus provided for effecting amendments to that instrument as contrasted with that pursued under the English Constitution. I refer to Fisher, in his interesting work, entitled *Trial of the Constitution.* Justly admiring the English Constitution, and naturally entertaining great solicitude for the public safety during the perilous times through which we had lately passed, that writer has pronounced the Constitution of the United States to be in comparison with it, inadequate to a crisis like that of 1861–5, in that it does not contain a practicable provision for amendments. In his opinion, had the United States been in a condition to settle the vexed question of slavery through an amendment to its Constitution, effected by the direct action of Congress in its ordinary capacity, the late desolating war would not have fallen upon us. The result of his discussion is, an earnest recommendation of the English mode of fundamental legislation by mere parliamentary majorities, followed up by the formality of the executive sanction.

This view of the subject I regard as a mistaken one. Although it has been stated in general terms to be one of the functions of the English Parliament to enact amendments to the Constitution of the realm, yet that remark is but formally and superficially true, the function of that body being rather to register than to enact them. The fact is, that every considerable change in the English Constitution from Magna Charta down to our day, has been achieved by conflict outside the walls of Parliament — often by the blood of the English people. When victory has declared itself, the principle established by it has by Parliament been written down as a part of the fundamental code — the three estates of the realm as it were following in the train of the national armies, and gathering up and depositing among the treasures of the kingdom the fruits of their conflicts. Never, either in England or elsewhere, do the peaceful labors of the legislator produce changes that touch radically the passions or the interests of men. Force alone works out such changes. Accordingly, had the American Constitution contained the provision so lauded by Mr. Fisher, the terrible war through which we have just passed would not have been prevented. So soon as party tactics should have failed to guard our Constitution against amendments in the interest of freedom, by filling Congress and the high judicial tribunals with the devotees of slavery, the latter would, precisely as they have now done, have appealed to arms. To men bent upon accomplishing a purpose, a pretext alone is necessary. Had our Constitution distinctly permitted Congress to ordain amendments to the fundamental code, the range within which to seek a pretext for revolution would hardly have been lessened. It is only formal and unimportant amendments that can be thus carried through, by the peaceful action of the majority — amendments of such a stamp that they commend themselves as needful or as proper to all candid minds when first presented, and so appearing are readily acquiesced

§ 544. It has already been observed that, generally, whichever mode of amending Constitutions is adopted, the intervention of the legislature is required. It either proposes to the people the calling of a Convention, and, if they vote in favor of it, provides for its call; or it recommends specific amendments to be passed upon by the people in some one of the modes referred to.

To this rule there were exceptions, however, in the cases of the Pennsylvania Constitution of 1776, and of the earlier Constitutions of Vermont. In these cases the legislatures were allowed no participation in the business of concocting amendments, but they were effected by Conventions, called by a body styled the Council of Censors, which alone had power to propose them — a device which experience has shown to be more ingenious than useful. Among the powers of the Council, which was to meet every seventh year, was that of calling a Convention, to meet within two years after their sitting, if there should appear to them an absolute necessity of amending any Article of the Constitution which might be defective, explaining such as might be thought not clearly expressed, and adding such as were necessary for the preservation of the rights of the people; but it was wisely further provided, that the Articles to be amended, together with the amendments proposed, and such Articles as were proposed to be added or abolished, should be promulgated, at least six months before the day appointed for the election of such Convention, for the previous consideration of the people, that they might have an opportunity of instructing their delegates on the subject.

This plan, which seems excellent, was not found to work well in Pennsylvania; two stormy sessions of the Council resulting in a hopeless disagreement, after which it never met again, and was abolished in 1790.

§ 545. From Pennsylvania, in the mean time, in 1777, this peculiar provision had been borrowed by Vermont, by which it was retained in force until 1870. Although, at an early day, this Council did an essential service to the cause of constitutional government in Vermont, by the faithfulness with which

in, because of slight importance — not such as are vital to powerful interests, against which they are aimed, or which, at least, they will most injuriously affect.

it discharged certain censorial duties committed to it by the Constitution, and had been instrumental in initiating some very important constitutional changes, still, on the whole, it could not be regarded as a success. Of late years, it had been found to be too inflexible, serving rather as a shield to protect, than as a sword to cut down, abuses, and hence it gave place, as we have stated, in 1870, to a different scheme, which, although, perhaps, unwisely restrictive, is likely more readily to reflect the public will. The amendment of that year provides, that the Senate, in 1880, and every tenth year thereafter, may, by a two-thirds vote, propose amendments to the Constitution, which, if concurred in by a majority of the House, of the Senate and House, respectively, of the next General Assembly, and of the freemen of the State voting directly thereon, shall become a part of the Constitution. No provision being made for calling a Convention, the General Assembly can, doubtless, call one, whenever a general revision of the Constitution becomes necessary.

§ 546. With these exceptions, no Constitution has ever contemplated amendments except through the prior ministry of the legislature. In the Massachusetts Convention of 1853, Mr. Hallett, indeed, proposed a plan not subject to the objections existing to that of a Council of Censors, and which, nevertheless, avoided the necessity of legislative intervention in the matter of calling Conventions. His plan was to authorize the qualified electors, in the year 1873, and every twentieth year thereafter, at the general election then to be held, to vote on this question: "Shall there be a Convention to revise the Constitution, in conformity to the provisions of the Act of 1852, Chapter 188, relating to the calling a Convention of delegates of the people for the purpose of revising the Constitution?" If it should appear, by the returns made, that a majority of the qualified voters throughout the State, who should assemble and vote thereon, were in favor of such revision, the same should be taken to be the will of the people of the Commonwealth, that a Convention should meet accordingly; and thereupon delegates should be chosen, on the first Monday of March next succeeding, and such delegates should meet in Convention in the State House, on the first Wednesday of May succeeding, in the same manner, and with the same authority, as was provided in the second, third, and fourth sections of that Act.[1]

[1] *Deb. Mass. Conv.* 1853, Vol. III. p. 118.

Though doubtless possessed of some objectionable features, especially in regard to Conventions at fixed periods, and to the character of the Act referred to, the principle of this provision seems in some respects to be salutary. It certainly would obviate the difficulties experienced in many of the States in securing the consent of the legislature to the call of a Convention, to lessen, perhaps, their power and emoluments. One material question relating to it, however, it is now too early to answer definitively; and that is, whether or not such a provision unduly facilitates the alteration of the Constitution. For want of some such clause, the State of Rhode Island was, in 1842, thrown into a revolution, in which, as is not unusual, the law was on one side, and substantial justice on the other. On the other hand, it is possible, that had the States lately in rebellion against the Union, contained the provision offered by Mr. Hallett, and left no power in the legislatures to meddle with Constitutional changes at all, the inauguration of their revolution would have been prevented. To the leaders of the revolt, the alternatives would have been distinctly presented, either to wait on the movements of the electors in the several States, or openly to violate the Constitution — neither of which would have favored the secession scheme. But, as we have seen, it is, perhaps, now too early to pronounce upon a question which can be determined only by long constitutional experience.

§ 546 *a*. A novel device for effecting the amendment or revision of Constitutions by the employment of the legislative mode, without the calling of a Convention, has lately been adopted in several States, that by a "constitutional commission." It was first resorted to by the legislature of New York, in 1872; afterwards by that of Michigan, in 1873; by that of Maine, in 1875, and by that of New Jersey, in 1881. The New York Act authorizing the commission required the Governor of the State to appoint, by and with the advice and consent of the Senate, thirty-two "persons," four from each judicial district, who should constitute a commission, "for the purpose of proposing to the legislature, at its next session, amendments to the Constitution." The Michigan Act authorized the Governor to nominate and appoint eighteen "able and discreet citizens," no two of whom were to reside in any one congressional district as then organized, who should be authorized to examine into and report to the next session, either special or general, of the legislature, "such amendments and revision of the Constitution" as in their judgment might be necessary for the best interests of the State and the people. The Maine legislature, by resolution, authorized the Governor to appoint a commission, consisting of ten "persons," to consider and frame "such amendments of the Constitution" as might seem necessary, to be reported by them to the legislature for such action as might seem advisable, and for final submission to the people at the next annual election in September. A subsequent clause of the resolution required the commission to submit the result of their labors to the present legislature on or before the 15th of February next, — a period of thirty-four days. The Act of the New Jersey legislature required the Governor, during the current session of the legislature, to appoint three "persons," who, together with the president of the Senate and two "persons" to be designated by him, and the speaker of the House of Assembly and two "persons" to be designated by him, should constitute a commission, whose duty it should be "to prepare amendments to the Constitution of this State." The commission were to prepare and submit their report to the next legislature, in proper form for consideration. In all the States named the commissions were appointed and reported to their respective legislatures, as required, and those bodies, in all save New Jersey, adopted a part or all of the recommendations made to them. In New Jersey, no action has ever been taken upon the report submitted by the commission. The commissioners of New York were appointed by Governor Hoffman, — one half of the number from each political party, — and among its members were Lucius Robinson, afterwards Governor of the State, Francis Kernan, afterwards United States Senator, and other distinguished citizens. The Michigan commission was also strongly constituted, and contained several members of eminent ability, as it may be presumed did also those of Maine and New Jersey. The sessions of the commissions were brief, that of New York, which was the longest, being of about fourteen weeks, that of Michigan of about seven weeks, and that of Maine of about three weeks. The results of their labors were various: the New York commission reported a large number of amendments, based apparently upon a complete revision of the Constitution of 1846, which, somewhat changed by the legislature, were submitted to the people and in part adopted in November, 1874. It is noteworthy that one of the amendments proposed by the commission fixed the salary of members of the legislature at $1,000, but that the legislature increased it, before submission, to $1,500. Of the whole number of amendments recommended by the Maine commission, seventeen were endorsed by the legislature, but of these only nine were adopted by the people. The Michigan commission recommended a large number of amendments, which, upon submission to the people, were all rejected.

§ 546 *b*. Whether this device, if a constitutional one, is adapted to bring before the people a better-considered scheme of constitutional amendments than the old legislative mode, of which it is a modification, must depend largely upon the influences which employ and direct it. In theory, nothing could be nearer ideal excellence than the mode of constituting the commissions. Under all the Acts or resolutions authorizing them, save that of Michigan, the Governor was at liberty to appoint any persons, without limitation, though, perhaps, those selected must have been residents of the State, of full age, and of the male sex. In Michigan they were required to be "able and discreet citizens," not more than two resident in any one of the existing congressional districts. In New Jersey, to the three persons named by the Governor were added the presiding officers of the two houses of the legislature and two other persons named by each of them. If there were ability and experience anywhere in those States, it was possible, it should seem, to secure it. In two States, New York and Michigan, the reports were to be made to the next session of the legislature; in New Jersey, to the next legislature; and in Maine to the existing legislature, in season to be submitted to the people at the annual election in September of the same year. Sufficient time, therefore, seems to have been given to the people to acquaint themselves with the proposed amendments, before they were required to act upon them, save in Maine, where the commission, the legislature, and the people were together allowed but nine months in which to formulate, to recommend, and to adopt them. In this respect the plan of the New Jersey commission was the most to be approved. By requiring the report to be made to the next legislature, it gave the people ample time to consider the proposed amendments in advance, not only of the election at which they were to ratify or reject, but of that at which they were to choose the legislature which was to recommend. A serious question, however, remains, whether the employment of such a commission is consistent with the Constitution. The Constitutions of the four States which have employed commissions had provided that "any amendment or amendments," or, as that of New Jersey phrased it, "any specific amendment or amendments," to the Constitution. might be recommended by a majority,[1] or by two-thirds,[2] of both houses of the legislature, and that they should become parts of the Constitution, if approved by a majority of the electors voting at an election held for the purpose, or by a majority, first, of the members elected to each house of the legislature next to be chosen; secondly, of the electors voting thereon. Two of these Constitutions, those of Michigan and New York, contained also provisions that in 1866, and at stated periods thereafter, the question of calling a Convention for a "general revision of the Constitution,"[3] or to "revise the Constitution and amend the same,"[4] should be submitted to the qualified electors.

§ 546 *c*. In view of these various provisions, it is clear that, if the purpose of the legislature was to secure the adoption by the people of independent specific or particular amendments, no constitutional objection would lie against such action. But, on the other hand, if that purpose was, or if the result of the commission should be, to submit to the people a complete revision of the Constitution, very serious objection would exist. Under the Constitutions which provided for a revision by Conventions, those of Michigan and New York, the unconstitutionality of a revision by a commission is very apparent. We have seen elsewhere that, throughout the American Constitutions the legislative mode is confined exclusively to the proposing of amendments, and as such is sharply contrasted with that by Conventions, which is employed for revisions. For effecting the latter, the only appropriate, and hence the only constitutional, instrument is that body. The difficulty is to draw the line between "an amendment or amendments" and a "revised Constitution."[5] Per-

[1] Constitutions of New Jersey, 1844, and New York, 1846.

[2] Constitutions of Maine, 1820, and Michigan, 1850.

[3] Michigan Constitution of 1850.

[4] New York Constitution of 1846.

[5] See § 574 *c*, *ante*.

haps the best practical test of what was intended by those terms, as gathered from a fair construction of the constitutional provisions, would be to consider the relation to each other and to the existing Constitution of the proposed amendments, and the probable consequences of adopting all or either of them. If the amendments proposed by the commission were independent, whether few or many in number, as I have said, no objection is perceived to their adoption in this mode; for, if one or more of them were rejected by the legislature or by the people, the harmony and balance of the Constitution would not be disturbed, that instrument simply remaining so far unchanged. But the probability that so fortunate a result would follow would diminish as the number of the amendments increased. When that number should be so great as to leave the Constitution considerably changed or a new one, the maintenance of the harmony and balance referred to would be well-nigh impossible. Here lies the danger from the employment of commissions. Even if they are composed of wise and able men, and report amendments that are desirable, and, whether many or few, are congruous with the system as a whole, there can never be a certainty that they will be recommended by the legislature as received from the commission. In no case, so far, has the report of a commission been adopted by the legislature without material modification. This dilemma, therefore, always arises: The report of the commission must be exactly pursued by the legislature, or the benefit of their supposed superior wisdom and ability is lost; but if the legislature is bound to adopt the commission's report and to submit it to the electors without change, the function of the former would be merely a ministerial one; it would not be itself, but the commission, that would recommend, — a transfer of function which the Constitution certainly would not warrant. If it be supposed that the legislature has a constitutional right to discuss and to modify the amendment or system of amendments reported by the commission, the whole question of amending or of revising the Constitution would be relegated to the body supposed, by the very act of appointing a commission, to be unfitted for that work.

§ 546 *d.* Among the reasons adduced in favor of the employment of commissions are the expedition and the cheapness with which constitutional changes can, by means of them, be instituted and perfected. If the employment of commissions be held to be constitutional for revisions as well as for specific amendments of Constitutions, these reasons are likely very generally to prevail, with results to our republican system of the most dangerous character; our fundamental laws will be tinkered, at every session of our legislatures, in the interest of party, of corporate aggrandizement, and of fraud, as our statute law now too generally is. For the enactment of systems of constitutional law, of entire Constitutions, the incipient steps ought to be taken by Conventions called expressly for that purpose, under the sanctions and the limitations of the law of the land; and if, from considerations of cheapness and expedition, our States abandon the Convention system, it will not be long until our legislatures, like those of France, will claim conventional powers, to the complete subversion of our liberties.

It was, doubtless, considerations such as these that induced the people of Michigan to reject the revision of the Constitution of 1850 reported by the commission of 1873. The legislature, it will be remembered, had authorized the commission to report "such amendments and revision of the Constitution as in their judgment might be necessary," etc. In March, 1874, the legislature submitted to the people, not specific amendments, but an entire Constitution, in terms which compelled the electors to adopt the whole or none, and which did not specify the changes made or the parts of the Constitution affected by them. It was very generally believed that the authority given the commission to revise was unconstitutional, and for that reason, with others, the electors refused to ratify it.[1]

[1] . . . "There was," throughout the State, it is said, "a latent feeling that, although the processes by which it" (the Constitution) "was evolved might be within the letter of the Constitution, the commission, or the legislature, or both, had assumed too much in making a general revision; that a revision should spring from the wish of the people properly expressed through the ballot-box, and be made by a Convention chosen for the purpose, as contemplated by the Constitution itself, and not from the legislature, or from a body of its creation." — Letter to the author from the Hon. S. B. McCracken.

Of the doubtful constitutionality of this attempt to revise the Constitution by a commission, that body, as well as the legislature, seem to have been convinced, since, in Article XVIII. of the revised Constitution, after providing for a Convention to revise or amend that instrument, they added a provision "for a commission to be appointed by the Governor, by and with the advice and consent of the Senate," for the same purpose. This provision, however, was, with the rest of the Constitution, rejected by the people.

§ 547. It is a matter of interest now to ascertain, first, the nature of the participation of a legislature in the work of amending a Constitution — whether the act it performs is an act of legislation or a special ministerial act, finding its analogies in those of a Convention, which, as we have seen, are mere recommendations addressed to a body above and beyond it, which alone enacts them into laws; and, secondly, when that body recommends amendments to a Constitution, the extent of its power in that particular.

I. In relation to the first subject of inquiry, there will be found, I am confident, upon a careful survey of the whole field, two distinct cases: first, that in which legislatures intervene to call Conventions, or to require the people to vote upon the question of calling Conventions, or upon amendments which legislatures submit to them; and, secondly, that in which legislatures merely, by resolution, declare the adoption of specific amendments to be expedient, as a preliminary step towards submitting them to a vote of the people. In the first case, their action is believed to be strictly legislative; in the second, to be merely ministerial. These will be considered in their order.

In every case in which a legislature intervenes in the business of fundamental legislation, it does so by some vote or resolution; and to determine whether or not, in so doing, it performs an act of legislation, the readiest mode is to examine the result of its deliberations in detail. If it have the characteristics of a law, if it appear to have been passed by the law-making power within the scope of its authority as such, and to furnish a rule of action binding upon individuals, it must be classed with acts of legislation, whatever fine-spun theories may teach to the contrary.

It has been seen that our Constitutions usually provide for the call of Conventions by the legislature, either at their own discretion, or upon the expressed desire of the people voting on the question at some fixed time, or when requested so to do by the legislature. The essence of the provisions, however, is, that the legislature, when moved thereto by an evident expediency, or by the public voice constitutionally expressed, shall call a Convention. This course has been universally followed, and the call has commonly been made in very nearly the same terms. It generally provides for an election on a given day, to choose delegates for a Convention; it prescribes the duty of the delegates, namely, to revise the Constitution, sometimes descending to particulars, as, to amend that part of it relating to the basis of representation, or to the appointment and tenure of judicial offices; to determine the construction of a particular clause, and the like; it fixes the time and place of assembling; imposes limitations and restrictions upon its powers; ascertains the pay of its officers and members; and prescribes the disposition to be made by the Convention of the fruit of its deliberations, as, that it shall be submitted to the people, for ratification or rejection; that a copy of it shall be lodged with the Secretary of the Commonwealth, or be recorded in his office. Connected with the duties presented, or the limitations imposed, penalties are not unfrequently denounced, as, for illegal voting at the poll for ratifying or rejecting the Constitution, or for making false returns of the votes.[1]

Now, is it reasonable to deny to acts of the legislature, bearing thus the style and semblance of laws, containing mandatory clauses directed to public officers or to individual citizens, accompanied by penalties for such as should transgress or disobey them, the force of laws?

§ 548. Similar considerations apply, to some extent, to the action of a legislature in the initiation of specific amendments, or in the matter of submitting Constitutions to the people. The general course, in these cases, is for the legislature, after the appropriate preliminaries, to require the electors, on a day specified, to cast their votes for or against the propositions indicated by it, laying down for the direction of the public officers, as well as of the voters, the specific injunctions needed to secure an adequate and honest expression of the public will. Can a reason be conceived why the intervention of a legislature in this business, prescribing rules of conduct, and denouncing, as it commonly does, penalties for acts of disobedience, should not be considered an act of legislation as much as when it takes steps identical in character, but respecting interests that are temporary and trivial?

The soundness of this view may be tested by adverting to

[1] The Act of the New York Legislature, passed March 21, 1821, calling the Convention of that year, contained provisions on all these subjects, of the kinds indicated.

the consequences of denying to the Acts in question validity as laws, and conceiving of them as simple recommendations. What certainty could there be as to the result of an election, in which some of the voters should obey, and some should disobey the commands of the legislature, with reference, for example, to voting without prescribed qualifications, or to taking an oath to discharge the duty of inspectors of the election faithfully, and to make due returns thereof to the specified officers? Without the restraints of law, what are usually regarded as necessary safeguards of elections would rest merely in the discretion of the persons offering to vote; that is, they would practically have no existence; and, of course, the elections, considered as expressions of the public voice, would be a mere farce. As to those parts of the action of a legislature indicated, then, we are forced to concede that it is properly legislative.

§ 549. 2. On the other hand, when the legislative action consists simply in affirming, by a resolution intended only as a step preparatory to further and other action either of that or of some other body, the expediency of amending the Constitution, or in merely proposing such amendments as it deems desirable, such action cannot properly be called legislative. A mere declaration of opinion or a recommendation, to which the people may or may not, at their discretion, assent, it would be an abuse of language to style a command, or a rule of civil conduct. A good example of such recommendatory action, is that exhibited by Congress in proposing amendments to the Federal Constitution. When that body has proposed the amendments deemed by it to be desirable, its action is at an end. If the propositions it makes receive the ratification of the legislatures of three-fourths of the States, or of Conventions in three-fourths thereof, they become parts of the Constitution; otherwise, they fall to the ground.

Upon this point we are not without authority to which great respect is due. In the Massachusetts Convention of 1820, in a discussion of a report of a committee on the subject of future amendments by the legislative mode, on the recommendation of two-thirds of each house, Mr. Webster moved to amend by requiring two-thirds of the House, and a majority of the Senate, and in support of his amendment said:—

"The object of the mode proposed for making amendments . . . . was to prevent the people from being called upon to make trivial amendments, or any amendments, except when a real evil existed. A reason for requiring two-thirds of the House, and only a majority of the Senate, was, that the general sense of the people was better expressed by representatives from small districts, than from large ones. *This was not an exercise of legislative power — it was only referring to some branch the power of making propositions to the people.*"[1]

So, also, on the same subject, Mr. Lincoln said: —

"The whole power in relation to amendments, might as well be left to the Senate as to require the consent of two-thirds. . . . One-third of the Senate might be chosen by a little more than one-fifth of the people, and might prevent the wishes of the other four-fifths. . . . There was no danger of a political excitement continuing two years, so as to have a bad influence on the frame of government. *The proposing amendments was not a subject of legislation, and there was no need of a check.*"[2] The aim of these gentlemen was to show that in requiring more than a majority of the legislature or of some branch of it, to propose amendments to the Constitution, no principle was violated, as would have been the case had it been an exercise of ordinary legislation, for which, by the common practice of all free governments, a majority is sufficient. Being not an exercise of legislation at all, there was no impropriety in requiring a vote of two-thirds or of any other majority.

§ 550. In the Virginia Convention of 1829, one speaker, Mr Thompson, went beyond the position taken by Messrs. Webster and Lincoln, above explained, and denied that Acts of the legislature to take the sense of the people, *or to organize a Convention*, were Acts of ordinary legislation. He said: —

"No one ever supposed that the Acts to take the sense of the people, and to organize a Convention, were Acts of ordinary legislation; or, properly speaking, Acts of legislation at all, as little so as an election by that body of any officer. . . . . The truth is, the action of the ordinary legislature on this subject . . . is not of the character of ordinary legislation. It is in the nature of a resolve or ordinance adopted by the agents of the people, not in their legislative character, for the purpose of collecting and ascertaining the public will, both as to the call and organization of a Convention, and upon the ratification or rejection

[1] *Deb. Mass. Conv.* 1820, p. 407.

[2] Id. 405.

of the work of a Convention."[1] It being a matter of interest to know what such Acts were, if not Acts of legislation, the speaker thus explained his views on that subject: —

"The Acts spoken of were called for by their constituents, resulted from the necessity of the case, and were justified by that supreme and paramount law, the *salus populi.* In short, they supplied the only mode by which the original right of the people to meet in full and free Convention to reform, alter, or abolish their form of government, could be exercised without jeopardizing the peace, tranquillity, and harmony of the State."[2]

Thus, to escape the conclusion that the Convention Act was a law, binding upon the members of the Convention, the speaker based the Act of the legislature upon usurpation, and that of the people in pursuance of it, upon the right of revolution. To this hard necessity was he reduced to sustain the main position taken in his argument, that the submitting of the Virginia Constitution to the people, in a manner different from that prescribed by the General Assembly, was not an illegal act, or one which the Convention had no power to do.

§ 551. II. In relation to the extent of the power of a legislature to recommend specific amendments to a Constitution, in what I have styled the legislative mode, no reason is perceived why, in the absence of constitutional restriction, the legislature should not be at liberty to propose amendments to either part of the Constitution, the frame of government, or the Bill of Rights. And yet, doubtless, much might be said against the expediency of making very thorough or extensive changes in the Constitution, in a mode which is well adapted only to the enactment of few and simple amendments. The ground of this objection is that, in the legislative mode, there can ordinarily be no discussion worthy of the name in the presence of the electorate, the body with which lies the important and decisive function of giving to the proposals of the legislature the force of law. Instances have occurred, however, of restrictions which doubtless would bind the legislature not to make certain proposals. Thus, the Delaware Constitution of 1776 declared that no article of the declaration of rights, nor the first, second, fifth (except the part relating to the right of suffrage), twenty-sixth, and twenty-ninth articles of the Constitution ought ever to be violated on any

[1] *Deb. Va. Conv.* 1829, p. 887. [2] Ibid.

pretence whatever. It then specifies a mode in which changes may be made, in other parts of the Constitution, through the action of the assembly. Although this was not in terms a positive prohibition, it was such in intention and effect. Several Constitutions prohibit the proposing of amendments to the Constitution by the legislature oftener than once in so many years;[1] or before a specified time;[2] or the proposing of more than a certain number at the same time;[3] or providing that while an amendment or amendments, agreed upon by one General Assembly, shall be awaiting the action of the succeeding General Assembly, no additional amendment or amendments shall be proposed.[4] There can be no doubt that any amendment proposed in violation of these provisions would be declared by the courts to be void, for neither would the legislature have the power to propose nor the people to adopt them. To decide otherwise would be to hold that the legislature can constitutionally do an act expressly forbidden by the Constitution; and that the people by an unauthorized vote, a vote recommended in violation of the Constitution, which in effect would be a vote taken at their own instance alone, can enact a valid constitutional amendment. Among all the wild assertions of power in the people ever made, it has never been contended that they can enact an ordinary statute at all, and it has never but once been contended that they can enact a Constitution without the previous recommendation of the legislature, acting under the express authorization of the existing Constitution. The exception was in the case of the attempted revolution of the Dorr party in Rhode Island, in 1841, the character and result of which have been depicted in a former part of this work.[5]

§ 551 *a*. Two decisions of the Supreme Court of Arkansas which bear directly on the question of the extent to which a legislature may propose amendments to the Constitution will be here considered. As the discussion of them will tend to throw

[1] New Jersey, 1844, and Pennsylvania, 1838, not oftener than once in five years; Tennessee, 1834 and 1870, not oftener than once in six years.

[2] Mississippi, 1868, no amendment affecting the eighteenth section of the Bill of Rights, which forbade a property or educational qualification to be an elector, before 1885.

[3] Colorado, 1876; Illinois, 1848 and 1870; and Oregon, 1857, not more than one amendment at a time; and Arkansas, 1868, not more than three at a time.

[4] Indiana, 1851.

[5] See §§ 226–241, *ante*.

light upon a point in respect to which misapprehension has not infrequently existed, they will be examined at some length.

The 14th Section of the Bill of Rights of the Arkansas Constitution of 1836, contained the following provision: "That no man shall be put to answer any criminal charge but by presentment, indictment, or impeachment." By the 24th Section, it was declared as follows: "Every thing in this Article" (Article II., comprising the Bill of Rights) "is excepted out of the general powers of government, and shall forever remain inviolate." At its session in 1844, the General Assembly of Arkansas, in pursuance of authority given in the Constitution, proposed an amendment to the Constitution, which was finally adopted by the next succeeding General Assembly, in 1846, to the following effect: the amendment declares that "the General Assembly shall have power to confer such jurisdiction as it may from time to time deem proper, on justices of the peace, in all matters of contract, covenants, and actions for the recovery of fines and forfeitures, when the amount claimed does not exceed one hundred dollars; and in actions and proceedings for assault and battery, and other penal offences, less than felony, which may be punished by fine only."

For the purpose of carrying into effect the power thus conferred, the General Assembly, in December, 1846, passed an Act entitled "An Act to define the Jurisdiction and regulate the Proceedings of Justices' Courts in cases of Breaches of the Peace," of which the 1st Section declared, that "hereafter no assault and battery or affray shall be indictable, but such offences shall be prosecuted and punished in a summary manner, by presentment of a constable, or any other person, before justices of the peace, as hereinafter provided;" thus, contrary to the 14th Section of the Bill of Rights as it originally stood, putting persons arrested for assault and battery, or for an affray — both criminal charges — to answer without "presentment, indictment, or impeachment." At the October Term, 1847, of the Circuit Court of Carroll County, the grand jurors returned an indictment against Jackson A. Cox, for an assault and battery. Defendant pleaded to the jurisdiction of the court, alleging that by the Act of December 16th, 1846, the court was divested of jurisdiction of the offence, and jurisdiction thereof given to justices of the peace. To this plea the Attorney for the State demurred, the court overruled the demurrer, and the State appealed.

On the hearing in the Supreme Court, the point raised was, that the Bill of Rights had not been amended by the proceedings of the legislature, but was still in force, notwithstanding those proceedings, that body having no power to amend that part of the fundamental law, under the specific power given it to amend the Constitution, by Article IV. § 35, thereof; since by the terms of Section 24 of the Bill of Rights (Article II.) every thing contained in that Article was excepted out of the general powers of government.

§ 552. This objection the Supreme Court overruled, and sustained the judgment of the court below declaring the amendment valid and the Act constitutional. By Oldham J., they say: —

"To the general and ordinary powers of the government conferred by the Constitution, the prohibition extends, and no further, but does not limit the General Assembly, in the extraordinary and specific authority and power conferred upon it, to propose and adopt amendments to the Constitution. The Constitution, in prescribing the mode of amending that instrument, does not limit the power conferred to any particular portion of it, and except other provisions by declaring them to be amendable. The General Assembly, in amending the Constitution, does not act in the exercise of its ordinary legislative authority, of its general powers; but it possesses and acts in the character and capacity of a Convention, and is, *quoad hoc*, a Convention, expressing the supreme will of the sovereign people, and is unlimited in its power save by the Constitution of the United States. Therefore every change in the fundamental law, demanded by the public will for the public good, may be made subject to the limitation above named." [1]

§ 553. Three years later, the composition of the Supreme Court having undergone a change, another case, similar in its essential circumstances, except that the Circuit Court had pronounced against the validity of the amendment, notwithstanding the above decision, came before that tribunal on appeal taken by the respondent.[2]

After full argument, the main point decided by the court in The State *v.* Cox, was overruled, the judges holding, that the

[1] The State *v.* Cox, 3 English's R. 436.

[2] Eason *v.* The State, 6 English's R. 481.

provisions of the Bill of Rights constitute the essential principles of free government — the great landmarks of freedom — that the power to repeal or change them is not given to the General Assembly when acting either in the exercise of ordinary legislative authority or in the exercise of the higher power of amending the Constitution, but is reserved to the people themselves, acting through a Convention, lawfully called.

The principal argument by which this position was supported, rested upon a construction of Section 24, — the concluding section of the Bill of Rights, — a part of which has been given above, but which, entire, is as follows: —

"This enumeration of rights shall not be construed to deny or disparage others retained by the people; and to guard against *any encroachment on the rights herein retained*, or *any transgression of any of the higher powers herein delegated*, we declare, that every thing in this Article is excepted out of the general powers of government, and shall forever remain inviolate; and that all laws contrary thereto, or to the *other provisions herein contained*, shall be void."

By the court it was maintained, that one of "the higher powers herein delegated," was the power of amendment; since, they said, in those terms must be included all the powers delegated, whether they be denominated "general powers" or "specific powers;" "inevitably, therefore," it was said, "if these powers of amendment be a portion of the 'higher powers delegated,' which no one will attempt to gainsay, they must necessarily be as much within the controlling influence of the provisions of the Bill of Rights, as any others of these delegated powers." [1]

§ 554. Upon this decision of the court, I shall make but one or two observations.

That the reasoning of the court in relation to Section 24 of the Bill of Rights and the power of amendment, is utterly fallacious, becomes evident when that section is fairly interpreted, according to its terms, and considered in connection with the other sections of the Bill of Rights.

Read and interpreted as it should be, Section 24 is as follows: —

"This enumeration of rights shall not be construed to deny or disparage others retained by the people," — that is, the rule

[1] Eason *v.* The State, 6 English's R. 481 (490).

of law, "*expressio unius est exclusio alterius*," shall not obtain, as a rule of construction, in relation to this Bill of Rights, but the people shall hold and enjoy all such rights as belong to them, whether specified in this Bill of Rights or not; — "and to guard against any encroachment on the rights *herein retained*," that is, *in this Bill of Rights* specially reserved to the people; "or any transgression of any of the higher powers *herein delegated*," that is, *in this Bill of Rights* delegated; "we declare that every thing in this Article," that is, *in this Bill of Rights*, "is excepted out of the *general powers of government*, and shall forever remain inviolate," that is, the three departments of the government, created by the following Articles of this Constitution, legislative, executive, and judicial, and invested, severally, in general terms, with *governmental powers*, shall not, by reason of the generality of the grants of power to them, presume to encroach on the rights, or transgress any of the powers, *in this Bill of Rights* retained or delegated, but the same shall forever remain inviolate; "and" we further declare, "that all laws contrary *thereto*, or to the *other provisions herein contained*, shall be void," that is, that all laws, passed by the General Assembly, by virtue of its general power of legislation, contrary either to the rights retained, the powers delegated, or the other provisions contained *in this Bill of Rights*, shall be void.

§ 555. That this is the true interpretation of the section in question is evident from a careful inspection of the Bill of Rights as a whole. The interpretation given requires us to find in the Bill of Rights three classes of provisions: 1, such as *reserve* to the people *rights;* 2, such as *delegate powers;* and 3, *other provisions*, differing from both the other two.

Of the first class there are numerous examples, such as the *right* to bear arms, freely to assemble and to apply for redress of grievances, &c. Of *powers delegated*, instances are found in Section 23, which provides, that "the military shall be kept in strict subordination to the civil power;" and in Section 8, which permits the giving of the truth in evidence in prosecutions for the publication of papers investigating the official conduct of officers or men in a public capacity; and empowers juries "to determine both the law and the facts" in all indictments for libels. These provisions clearly involve a grant of power to the General Assembly to make laws in harmony with them, and to carry them into effect, making it at the same time its duty to do so. Of *other provisions*, examples are found in those clauses of the Bill of Rights which are couched in negative terms, and operate as restraints upon the various departments of the government, in the exercise of their acknowledged powers, rather than as substantive grants, or positive recognitions of rights or powers. Such are the provisions against *ex post facto* laws, the putting of persons twice in jeopardy of life or limb, for the same offence, and the like.

Having thus its full operation by applying it to the Bill of Rights alone, it is, in my judgment, erroneous to extend the provision of the 24th Section, as do the Court in the case under consideration, to that part of the Constitution relating to the making of amendments by the General Assembly.

Besides, it is noticeable, that it is "out of the general powers of *government*" that every thing enumerated in the Bill of Rights is excepted, not out of powers which are not powers of *government* at all, like that of amending the Constitution given to the General Assembly. A power of *government* is a power which expends itself in administering or operating the political machine established by the Constitution, not one which goes to the rebuilding of that machine itself; or, to use a metaphor already once employed by me, it is a power proper not for the millwright, but for the miller.

I need hardly say, therefore, that I deem the first decision of the Supreme Court, in the case of The State *v.* Cox, the better law. It expresses with admirable brevity, force, and clearness, the true doctrine in regard to the power of our General Assemblies under similar clauses of our Constitutions.

§ 556. III. The question has been raised, whether or not propositions of specific amendments to a Constitution, made by a legislature, under the constitutional provisions referred to, ought to be submitted to the executive for approval.

Judging of this question from *a priori* considerations, it seems that the answer should be, that whenever the propositions are coupled with provisions which impart to the legislative Act, in whole or in part, the force of law, according to the principles above explained,[1] they ought to receive the approval and the signature of the executive; but that when they bear only the

[1] See *ante*, §§ 547-550.

character of recommendations, they ought not to be submitted to the executive. The reason for this distinction is simple. By our Constitutions, all Acts of the legislature, before they can become operative as laws, must receive the sanction and signature of the executive branch of the government. An Act which is not legislative in its nature, and when perfect and operative to the full extent intended by its framers, is yet destitute of all vigor as a law, not coming within the terms of the constitutional provisions, would clearly not be subject to the same conditions.

1. This question, so far as relates to amendments to the Federal Constitution, has been several times the subject of discussion in Congress, and once of adjudication in the Supreme Court of the United States.

The clauses of the Constitution of the United States, bearing on the question, are as follows: —

"Art. V. The Congress, whenever two-thirds of both houses shall deem it necessary, shall propose amendments to this Constitution, ... which shall be valid to all intents and purposes as part of this Constitution, when ratified by the legislatures of three-fourths of the several States, or by Conventions in three-fourths thereof, as the one or other mode of ratification may be proposed by Congress."

Art. I. Sec. 7. "Every order, resolution, or vote, to which the concurrence of the Senate and House of Representatives may be necessary (except on a question of adjournment), shall be presented to the President of the United States; and, before the same shall take effect, shall be approved by him, or, being disapproved by him, shall be repassed by two-thirds of the Senate and House of Representatives, according to the rules and limitations presented in the case of a bill."

§ 557. It would naturally be supposed that a recommendation of amendments by Congress, by two-thirds of both houses, if not a bill, might properly be designated as a resolution or vote; and hence, that by the very terms of Art. I. Sec. 7, above quoted, such a recommendation ought to receive the approval of the Executive.

On the other hand, a close examination of Article V. shows that it contemplates nothing but a mere expression of opinion that amendments to the Constitution are necessary. That body being a numerous one, and representing the people, it is deemed probable that, whenever two-thirds of both its branches pronounce particular organic changes to be expedient, such is the sense of the people at large. There is to be no submitting of propositions to a vote of the people, consequently no directions for conducting an election, or making returns of votes, — in short, no prescribing of a rule of action to officers or citizens, for the reason that all action upon the subject is to be taken by separate agencies fully organized under State laws. In this view of the Constitution, then, the necessity of executive approval seems to be very doubtful; and of this opinion are the authorities generally.

Amendments to the Federal Constitution were proposed by Congress in 1789, in 1794, in 1803, and in 1866, and in neither case were they presented to the President for his approval.[1] The same is substantially true of the amendments relative to slavery proposed by the same body in 1865.[2]

The question we are considering was passed upon by the Supreme Court of the United States, in the case of Hollingsworth *v.* The State of Virginia,[3] in relation to the eleventh amendment, proposed in 1794. The validity of that amendment was denied by one of the parties in that cause, on the ground that it had "not been proposed in the form prescribed by the Constitution," in that it appeared, upon an inspection of the original roll, that "the amendment was never submitted to the President for his approbation." In support of this position, the language of the first article of the Constitution, above given, was mainly relied upon; and to the argument of the opposing counsel, that as two-thirds of both houses were required to originate the proposition, it would be nugatory to return it with the President's negative, to be repassed by the same number, it was answered that that was no reason for not presenting it to the President, since the reasons assigned by the latter for his disapprobation might be so satisfactory as to reduce the majority below the constitutional proportion. On the other side, beside the argument above specified, it was urged by

[1] See Speech of Senator Trumbull of Illinois, in the Senate of the United States, in *Daily Globe* for February 8, 1865. See also Hollingsworth *v.* Virginia, 3 Dall. R., 378.

[2] Ibid. [3] Ibid.

Lee, Attorney-General, that the case of amendments was evidently "a substantive act, unconnected with the ordinary business of legislation, and not within the policy or terms of investing the President with a qualified negative on the Acts and Resolutions of Congress."

On the day following the argument, a unanimous *per curiam* opinion was delivered, that the amendment had been constitutionally adopted. The only language used by the Court which appears in the report is that of Chase, Justice, who observed as follows:—"The negative of the President applies only to the ordinary cases of legislation: he has nothing to do with the proposition or adoption of amendments to the Constitution."

§ 558. The opinion thus expressed by the Supreme Court coincides with that entertained by the Senate, when the amendment of 1803, respecting the mode of electing President and Vice-President of the United States, was under consideration. From the journals of that body, it appears that the question was distinctly raised on a motion that the amendment should be submitted to the President for his approval. The following is the entry on that subject:—

"On motion that the Committee on Enrolled Bills be directed to present to the President of the United States, for his approbation, the resolution which has been passed by both Houses of Congress, proposing to the consideration of the State legislatures an amendment to the Constitution of the United States, respecting the mode of electing President and Vice-President thereof, it was passed in the negative—yeas 7, nays 23."

§ 559. In 1865, the amendment proposed by Congress, relative to slavery, having by inadvertence been presented to the President of the United States for his approval by a subordinate officer of the Senate, Senator Trumbull, of Illinois, chairman of the Judiciary Committee of that body, introduced the following resolution:—

"*Resolved*, That the article of amendment proposed by Congress to be added to the Constitution of the United States, respecting the extinction of slavery therein, having been inadvertently presented to the President for his approval, it is hereby declared that such an approval was unnecessary to give effect to the action of Congress in proposing said amendments, inconsistent with the former practice in reference to all amendments to the Constitution heretofore adopted, and being inadvertently done, should not constitute a precedent for the future; and the Secretary is hereby instructed not to communicate the notice of the approval of said amendment by the President to the House of Representatives."

Upon this resolution a discussion arose, in which were exhibited the reasons for and against presenting amendments in such cases to the President, with great fullness.

In favor of such presentation, it was argued, that the express language of the Constitution required it, for it said, "every order, resolution, or vote to which the concurrence of the Senate and House of Representatives may be necessary," which covered this case precisely. Propriety, moreover, sanctioned such a course; for, if the President should dissent, and present his objections to the two houses, it did not follow that the vote of two-thirds could be again had to repass the resolution. And there seemed a necessity, it was said, that the resolution should be presented to the President, since only through him, by the Secretary of State, could it readily be transmitted to the legislatures of the several States. Without special provision of law, unless it passed through the hands of the President, it would lie a dead letter. As to the decision of the Supreme Court, while it could not be denied that Justice Chase had said that the provisions of the Constitution applied only to ordinary acts of legislation, and that the Court concurred with him, yet not a single reason was given for that proposition, nor was the argument made by counsel against the validity of the amendment answered either by the opposing counsel or by the Court. Besides, it was noticeable, that in the vote which was taken on the question in 1803, among the names of those who voted for presenting the resolution to the President were those of Mr. John Quincy Adams and Mr. Pickering, and when such gentlemen affirmed a step to be necessary, some argument might fairly be required to show that it was not necessary. Finally, it was denied that the precedents were all opposed to the presentation to the President. The resolution passed in 1861 for an amendment to the Constitution interdicting attempts by Congress to interfere with slavery in the States, was submitted to the President, and approved by him, without objection, as in case of an ordinary law.[1]

[1] *Daily Globe* for Feb. 8, 1865, Speech of Senator Howe of Wisconsin.

§ 560. On the other hand, by Senators Trumbull and Reverdy Johnson, both profound lawyers and jurists, it was strenuously contended that it was unnecessary and improper to present the resolution to the President. Beside referring to the precedents explained above, it was urged that the object of the constitutional provision on the subject of amendments was simply to initiate a mode by which the people should decide whether there should be an amendment of the Constitution or not. The action of Congress to that end did not, it was said, operate as a law. The whole effect of it was to submit the question to the people for their determination. Precisely the same effect was given to amendments proposed by the legislatures of the States. It would not be contended that the President had any control over a Convention called by two-thirds of the State legislatures. The proposition was, that no proposal by Congress of an amendment to the Constitution, although having received the support of two-thirds of both houses, was to be submitted to the States, unless the President should approve it. Suppose the other mode of proposing amendments, by two-thirds of the State legislatures, should be adopted, would the President have anything to do with that? All would admit that he would not. Would Congress have anything to do with that? All would admit that their duty would be an imperative one — simply to call a Convention. So that the whole object of the clause seemed to be to provide a mode by which the people might be furnished an opportunity of deciding whether the Constitution should be amended or not.

Moreover, what made it still more obvious, it was said, that the Convention which framed the Federal Constitution did not intend that the President should decide upon a resolution of that description, was, that the resolution was not to be passed unless it was concurred in by two-thirds of each house. The constitutional provision which gives to the President the authority to veto any bill submitted to him says, that if he disapproves such bill or resolution, he is to send it back to the house in which it originated, and if passed by that house and the other by two-thirds, it is to become a law notwithstanding the veto. It was true, it did not follow that it would get the same vote after Congress had heard the President's objections; but, looking at the two provisions — that which gives to the President the right to approve or disapprove, and that which looks to the duty of Congress consequent upon his disapproval — it was evident, it was said, that what was intended to be submitted to the President was a question which was to be passed upon by more votes than were necessary before it was submitted.[1]

After these arguments, Mr. Trumbull's resolution was agreed to without a division.

§ 561. 2. The question has thus far been considered with reference only to amendments to the Constitution of the United States. Of cases where amendments have been made to State Constitutions, I have, after considerable research, been enabled to collect only the following precedents: —

In the Constitutions severally in force in Connecticut, Massachusetts, and New York, specific amendments may be proposed by the legislature by resolutions, which are then referred to the legislature next to be chosen. If adopted by the requisite majority, by such succeeding legislature, it is made the duty of the latter to submit the amendments to a vote of the people. The practice in those States has been not to present the resolutions containing the proposed amendments to the Governor for approval, but to present to that officer the subsequent Act by which they are submitted to the people. In New York, the propositions of amendment are sometimes incorporated in a bill, providing conditionally in one or more clauses for submission to the people, and in those cases the bill is submitted to the Governor for his approval. The existing Constitutions of Michigan and Minnesota provide that amendments may be proposed by a prescribed majority of the legislature, after which they are required to be submitted by that body to the people. In the former State, the practice has been to effect this by a joint resolution, and in the latter, by a bill; in both cases, however, combining the propositions and the clauses submitting them to the people in a single Act. In both cases, this Act is presented to the Governor for his sanction. In the Constitutions of Georgia and Rhode Island, amendments are permitted to be made by the action of two successive legislatures, without submission to the people; and in neither case are the resolutions proposing the amendments presented to the Governor.[2] In the Constitu-

[1] *Daily Globe* for Feb. 8, 1865, Speeches of Senators Trumbull and Johnson.

[2] The practice is the same in Alabama, though there the Constitution is

tion of Missouri authorizing amendments to be made in the same manner, the resolutions of the first legislature are presented to the Governor, and those of the second, not. In the Constitution of Maine, finally, amendments may be proposed by the legislature, which are then to be submitted to the people, the Constitution itself containing particular directions as to the time and mode of holding the election, and no action on the part of the legislature being requisite, except by resolution to notify the towns to vote on the proposed amendments as prescribed in the Constitution. It is the practice to present the resolutions embodying the amendments to the Governor.

In all these cases, the Constitutions give to the Governor a qualified negative, substantially like that of the President of the United States, except that of Rhode Island, which provides no negative whatever. One Constitution, that of Connecticut, gives to a majority of the legislature the power of passing over the Governor's head any measure returned with his objections.[1]

It thus appears that the practice of the legislatures of the several States is generally conformable to the theoretical principles proper to govern in such cases, as developed in previous sections of this chapter.

§ 562. While the foregoing are the only precedents bearing on the question under consideration which I have been able to find, indications of opinion respecting it may be drawn from the provisions of the Constitutions of Delaware of 1792 and 1831,

submitted to the people between the two successive legislatures. See Collier *v.* Frierson *et al.*, 24 Ala. R. 100.

The facts in the case of Collier *v.* Frierson are as follows: The General Assembly of Alabama having, at its session in 1844–5, proposed several amendments to the State Constitution, and submitted them to a vote of the people, and the people having voted in favor of them, joint resolutions were adopted at the next succeeding session of the General Assembly reciting these facts, and declaring that the people had accepted "the said amendments, which are in the words and figures following,"— setting them all out except one, which was entirely omitted, — and the usual clause was then added, enacting that "the aforesaid amendments to the Constitution, proposed as aforesaid, and accepted by the people as aforesaid, be ratified;" *held*, "that the amendment which was entirely omitted from the ratifying resolutions was not constitutionally ratified, and therefore failed."

[1] For the facts stated in this section I am indebted to the Secretaries of State of the several States mentioned therein. For the practice in Kentucky, see note to § 581, *post*. See, also, Koehler *v.* Hill, 60 Iowa R., 543, 558.

and that of Louisiana of 1845. Those of Delaware provided that amendments might be proposed by two-thirds of each house of the legislature, with the approbation of *the Governor.* They were then to be published, and if adopted by three-fourths of each branch of the succeeding legislature, they should be valid as parts of the Constitution. The provision of the Louisiana Constitution was the same, except that the successive legislatures were to adopt the amendments, the first by a vote of three-fifths, and the second by a majority only of the persons elected to each house, and they were then to be submitted to the people. In these cases, it is perhaps fair to infer that the action of the second legislature did not require the approbation of the Governor, else the clause requiring it for that of the first would have been so worded as to apply to both. Especially may this be inferred in relation to the Louisiana case, since the Constitution of that State referred to, while in one clause permitting the second legislature to adopt resolutions of amendment by a majority vote merely, in another required to overcome the negative of the Governor a vote of two-thirds, which, supposing a negative in such cases possible, would be inconsistent with the former provision.

§ 563. IV. Before concluding the discussion of the doctrine of amendments to the State Constitutions, I propose further to consider two questions several times alluded to in preceding pages, but particularly germane to the subject now in hand, namely, (*a.*) Whether, when a Constitution contains a provision for effecting its own amendment, in one of the modes above mentioned only, the other mode can be adopted, or whether the constitutional provision must alone be pursued for that purpose? (*b.*) Whether, when a Constitution contains no provision for amendments at all, either of the two modes may be pursued?

(*a.*) In respect to the first question, there may be two cases, according to the terms in which the constitutional provisions are couched.

1. The Constitution may contain clauses, in negative terms, forbidding amendments, except when effected in a prescribed mode. Instances of this kind have been given in this chapter,[1] of which that contained in the Constitution of West Virginia is the most striking. That Constitution, Art. XII., provides that

[1] *Ante*, § 537.

no Convention is to be called to amend the same, "unless in pursuance of a law to take the sense of the people on the question of calling a Convention, nor unless a majority of the votes of the people should be in favor of a Convention." It also provides that no members of a Convention are to be elected "until one month after the result of the poll should be ascertained and published;" and that all Acts and Ordinances of any such Convention are to be submitted to the voters of the State for ratification or rejection, and "are to have no validity whatever until they are ratified."

The question as to the force of such provisions may be determined by considering the case of a Convention called by the legislature of West Virginia, without submitting the question of calling it to the voters, as required by the Constitution. It is believed, it would be impossible to attribute to such a body any validity or legitimacy whatever. The Act by which it should be assembled would have been passed in direct and palpable violation of the paramount law of the State, and would, therefore, bind neither the magistrate nor the citizen; it would be an act of revolution. This is too plain for argument; and, doubtless, all cases depending on provisions of a similar character are to be governed by the same considerations.

§ 564. That the estimate formed in the last section of the force of the negative provisions in question is a correct one, may be inferred from the acts and expressed opinions of the members of the Federal Convention, in relation to the Articles of Confederation, in which a similar provision relating to amendments was contained. By the 13th of those Articles, it was provided that no alteration should at any time be made in any of those Articles, "unless such alteration (should) be agreed to in a Congress of the United States, and be afterwards confirmed by the legislature of every State." It is well known that the Federal Constitution of 1787 was, in direct violation of that Article, confirmed, not by the legislature of each State, but by Conventions called in the several States. It was provided, moreover, in that Constitution, in palpable contradiction to the same Article, that that instrument should go into operation as to the ratifying States, when they should comprise, not the whole thirteen States constituting the Confederation, but nine States, at least. In fact, the new Constitution went into operation on the 4th of March, 1789, when only eleven States had ratified it, North Carolina withholding her assent until the 21st of November following, and Rhode Island, until the 29th of May, 1790. But, the point to be noted is, that while the Federal Convention acted, in the particular mentioned, in evident violation of the existing Constitution, it frankly admitted that fact, and excused its illegal and revolutionary proceedings upon the ground of absolute necessity. Our fathers were convinced of two things: first, that the salvation of the United States depended on the substitution of a firm national government for the loose Confederation then existing; and, secondly, that to attempt to effect that change by the unanimous action of the State legislatures, as required by the 13th Article above quoted, would be to court failure, which would be nearly certain ruin. Hence the Convention, and hence its irregular provision for securing the adoption of the system it recommended.[1] In this case, then, it is clear, that the act of disregarding the provisions of the 13th of the Articles of Confederation, was done confessedly as an act of revolution, and not as an act within the legal competence of either the people or the Convention, under the Constitution then in force. It was truly a revolutionary act, happily, indeed, consummated without actual force, but involving, as possible elements of the problem, both violence and bloodshed, should they be needed to make the revolution effectual.

§ 565. There are certain cases, however, in which amendments have been effected in spite of such negative provisions, where attempts have been made to justify them on legal grounds. One of the most notable of these occurred in Delaware, in 1791–2. The first Constitution of Delaware, Article XXX., was as follows: —

" No article of the Declaration of Rights and Fundamental Rules of this State, agreed to by this Convention," (that of 1776,) " nor the first, second, fifth (except that part thereof that relates to the right of suffrage), twenty-sixth, and twenty-ninth articles of this Constitution, ought ever to be violated on any pretence whatever; *no other part of this Constitution shall be altered, changed, or diminished, without the consent of five parts*

[1] For the arguments relating to this subject in the Convention, by which the above statements are confirmed, see Elliott's *Deb.*, Vol. V. pp. 352–356, 499–502, 532–534.

in seven of the Assembly, and seven members of the Legislative Council."

As the Assembly consisted of only seven Representatives, and the Legislative Council of only nine members, this provision required, to amend the Constitution in those parts which were made liable to amendment, five-sevenths of the one, and seven-ninths of the other, and the amendments were to be effected through the agency only of the legislative branch. Nevertheless, in 1791, the legislature passed an Act calling a Convention to revise and amend the Constitution. Accordingly, a Convention was elected, assembled in 1792, and framed the second Constitution of the State.

Similar action was taken in 1850 in the State of Maryland. The Constitution of 1776, then in force, Sec. 59, provided that neither the Form of Government nor the Bill of Rights, nor any part thereof, should be altered, changed, or abolished, "unless a bill so to alter, change, or abolish the same should pass the General Assembly, and be published at least three months before a new election," &c.

After violent contests between the friends and enemies of a reform of the State Constitution, an Act was finally passed in 1850, in direct violation of this provision of that instrument, to call a Convention, the result of which was the election of such a body, and the adoption by it of the Constitution of 1851.

§ 566. Attempts, as I have said, have been made to defend this action of the States of Delaware and Maryland, on legal grounds. In the case of Delaware, the legality of the course pursued was distinctly asserted by Mr. Bayard, the Senator from that State, in a speech delivered in the Senate of the United States, in 1858, upon the Lecompton Constitution. As one reason why it would not be unjust to force that Constitution upon the people of Kansas against their will, he affirmed, that it would be in their power at any time to amend it, should it prove distasteful to them, notwithstanding positive provisions were contained in it forbidding amendments for a fixed period; and, to establish that position, he referred to the action of his own State in 1792; the broad principle being asserted by him, that a majority of a people could not be restrained by constitutional inhibitions from changing their fundamental law when and as they pleased. The reasoning, in brief, by which this remarkable proposition was sustained, was comprised in these political axioms, resulting, as he claimed, "from the nature of man:" first, that all powers of government rest ultimately in the people at large; secondly, that a majority of those who choose to act may organize a government; and, thirdly, that the right to change is included in the right to organize, and may in like manner be exercised at any time by a majority. According to these principles, as the Senator affirmed, "the right of a majority to organize a government, under the law of the social compact, precludes any power in that majority to render the government they form unalterable, either for twenty or ten years, or for one year; because such a restriction is inconsistent with their own authority to form a government, and at war with the very axiom from which their own power to act is derived."[1]

§ 567. So, in reference to the Maryland case, the Hon. Reverdy Johnson, United States Senator from that State, in a late letter respecting certain proceedings of the Maryland Convention of 1864, said:—

"No man denies that the American principle is well settled, that all governments originate with the people, and may by like authority be abolished or modified; and that it is not within the power of the people, even for themselves, to surrender this right, much less to surrender it for those who are to succeed them. A provision, therefore, in the Constitution of any one of the United States, limiting the right of the people to abolish or modify it, would be simply void. And it was upon this ground alone that our Constitution of '76 was superseded by that of '51. . . . . The Constitution of 1851, therefore, rests on the inherent and inalienable American principle, that every people have a right to change their government." Subsequently, referring to this principle, he says: "In its nature it is revolutionary, but, notwithstanding that, it is a legal principle."[2]

§ 568. Two points involved in these extracts deserve consideration.

1. The right is claimed for the people to establish and to

[1] Appendix to Vol. XXXVII. of the *Congressional Globe*, p. 188.

[2] Letter to William D. Bowie and others, dated October 7, 1864, published in the *N. Y. Daily Tribune* of June 5, 1865.

change their governments at pleasure — a right which cannot in general be denied. But who are the people? In the true sense of the term, it means the political society considered as a unit, comprising in one organization the entire population of the State, of all ages, sexes, and conditions. Unquestionably, it is the right of the people in this sense to found its institutions, and to determine how they shall and how they shall not be abolished or amended. Having ordained the mode, however, in which changes therein may, and in which they shall not, be made, clearly no mode can be *legal* which contravenes the express letter of that fundamental provision. The society has, it is true, the physical power to override its own restrictions. But such an act would most certainly be illegal, because in violation of the letter of the law. Even were the whole people, by unanimous action, to effect organic changes in modes forbidden by the existing organic law, it would be an act of revolution.

2. That whatever the people are authorized to do, a majority of them may do, is generally true — by the term majority meaning the greater number. But it is important to determine the stage at which that proposition holds good. Nature knows nothing of any majority but that of force. Anterior, then, to any positive institutions, and this side an appeal to force, nothing less than the whole can rightfully bind the whole. It is only when a political society, with positive laws and compacts, has been established, that the whole can be bound by the action of a number less than the whole; and the number to which shall be accorded the power to act for the whole, and the conditions under which it may so act, are matters of positive regulation, in which alone they find their warrant. From this it is apparent, that a mere majority in number of all the citizens of a State, or of the electors of a State, have no right whatever to act for the whole State, unless they can point to authority to that effect, express or implied, in the Constitution of the State; and that if the action taken or proposed by such majority is palpably in the teeth of a constitutional provision, it is usurping and revolutionary. This, it will have been observed, was admitted by Senator Johnson in the extract given above, although, it is true, that eminent lawyer gave utterance to the astounding paradox, that the action of the Maryland Convention was at once *revolutionary* and *legal* — a contradiction, which we have

a right not to expect from a man occupying the high position of a Senator of the United States, not to say, of the foremost lawyer of the Union.

§ 569. Whether or not the acts thus pronounced to be revolutionary were necessary or excusable, that is, on the whole expedient, even at the price of revolution, is a different question, which I do not decide. But that they were revolutionary is inferable from the preamble of the Act of the Delaware legislature calling the Convention of 1792, setting forth the grounds upon which it took that step. It did not pretend to have a legal right to call a Convention, but affirmed that it was expedient so to do. Its language was as follows: "By the thirtieth article of the Constitution of this State, the power of revising the same, and of altering and amending certain parts thereof, is vested in the General Assembly; and it appears to this house that the exercise of the power of altering and amending the Constitution by the legislature would not be productive of all the valuable purposes intended by a revision, nor be so satisfactory and agreeable to our constituents; and that it would be more proper and expedient to recommend to the good people of the State to choose deputies for this special purpose to meet in Convention."

There can be little doubt that this was true, and that the framers of the Constitution of 1776 acted indiscreetly in limiting amendments, in negative terms, to the General Assembly, and thereby, by irresistible inference, inhibiting the call of a Convention. But the real question was not, is it expedient that the Constitution be revised by a Convention, but can a Convention be called for that purpose, in the face of the provision, that no part of the Constitution (with certain exceptions not to the purpose here) should be "altered, changed, or diminished, without the consent of five parts in seven of the Assembly, and seven members of the Legislative Council?" This latter question the legislature itself answered implicitly in the negative, when it premised that the power of revising the Constitution and of altering and amending certain parts thereof was "vested in the General Assembly." The Constitution having no express provision for amendment in any save the legislative mode, the General Assembly might undoubtedly have called a Convention, had there been no clause in negative terms prohibiting it; for it is thoroughly settled that a grant of general legislative authority, alone considered, carries with it the power to call a Convention. But the power would have been an implied power, arising by inference from the general power of legislation expressly granted; and it need not be said that no power can be implied in the face of a direct and express prohibition. In such a case, the prohibitive clause could not be construed as directory, but must be taken to be absolutely mandatory.

§ 570. 2. The second case involved in the first of the two questions stated is that in which the constitutional provisions relating to amendments are permissive merely, without words restricting the legislature or the people to the mode or modes prescribed.

In this case, the answer to the question would vary according to the nature of the constitutional provisions: —

If the Constitution authorized its own amendment through the agency of a Convention, without further provisions, it is beyond dispute, that it could not be amended in what we have called the legislative mode. This proposition no one, so far as we are aware, has ever denied. Controversy has been confined to the case in which a Constitution has contained no provision for its own amendment, save in the legislative mode; and it has related to the question whether it could, nevertheless, be amended through the agency of a Convention, — a question of greater difficulty, and one of such importance that it deserves a careful consideration, to which we now proceed.

When the Constitution makes no provision, then, for amendments, save in the legislative mode, can a Convention be lawfully called? Looking first at the precedents, we have seen in a former chapter,[1] that numerous instances have occurred in which Conventions have been called by the legislatures of States under the circumstances indicated. In some of these, the provisions permitting amendments to be made, through the agency of the legislatures, in a particular manner, or at a designated time, had proved unsatisfactory, because they either required, to effect their object, too large a majority of those bodies or of the people, or authorized them to be made at a time too remote, so that the practical consequence seemed to be a closing of all avenues to a seasonable change. In other cases, men of ability and

[1] See *ante*, § 219.

experience had doubted the feasibility of effecting, in the legislative mode, so extensive and complicated changes as had been made necessary by the lapse of time. Seeing in neither case any peaceful alternative but the calling of a Convention, under the sanction of law, that course has been pursued, not always without doubt or protest, though generally with the consent of the wise, to which time has commonly added the acquiescence of all. Among the States which have called Conventions under these circumstances, have been some of the most important in the Union, and that action has been taken at all stages of our history.[1]

§ 571. In respect to the legitimacy of those Conventions, as has been observed, it is now too late to raise a question. They have the sanction of long and general approval, and, were there greater doubt than exists as to their regularity or validity, the necessities out of which they sprung, and the evils from which their labors have from time to time rescued our States, would give them strong claims to be recognized as lawful assemblies. More than a century of constitutional history, indeed, has rendered it quite clear that it would have been wise in our earlier Constitutions to forestall doubt by expressly providing, as is very commonly done in those framed in our day, that it should be competent for our legislatures to call Conventions, not only at times definitely fixed, but whenever it should seem to them advisable so to do. In popular governments, it is the part of wisdom to recognize the fact, that what the people strongly desire they are likely in some manner to effect. If the attainment of their purposes by legal means be rendered too difficult, they will probably resort to such as are illegal. Having a right, within the limits imposed by the moral law, and by their Constitutions, State and Federal, to do whatever they please, restrictions should have for their object mainly to make it certain that it is the people who speak, and that the language uttered by them is the expression of their matured opinions.

§ 572. Viewed upon principle, the question discussed in the preceding section is sometimes made to turn upon the applica-

[1] But compare the argument of Mr. Grimke, to the effect that the giving of power to a legislature to propose amendments to the Constitution takes away the power of a Convention to amend, in The State *ex rel.* McCready *v.* Hunt, 2 Hill S. C. Law R., 28, one of the so-called allegiance cases.

bility of the maxim, *expressio unius est exclusio alterius*, to the construction of Constitutions. Were there no authority upon the point, it would be doubtful, perhaps, whether, in dealing with great questions of politics and government, the maxim, if applicable at all, ought to apply with the same strictness as in the construction of contracts between man and man. As a matter of speculation, it might be admitted that the maxim expresses the weight of probability equally in cases of great and of small magnitude. But in practice, where doubt arises, and there is nothing to indicate decisively the intention of those who framed the instrument, perhaps the people, assuming to exercise power under one construction rather than another, should be given the benefit of the doubt. It is questionable policy to attempt, by abstract rules of law, in doubtful cases, to prevent or to control great organic movements of the people. On the other hand, when it is possible to apply the maxim, under the guidance and in aid of an evident intention of the framers of the instrument, sound policy would not disapprove of so doing; though it must be admitted, that to make it applicable only under such a condition would render it practically valueless, since the intention which ought to guide in its application is, without the maxim, a sufficient guide to the proper construction sought.

§ 573. But we are not left, for an answer to the question considered in the last section, to abstract reasoning alone. The applicability of the maxim, *expressio unius*, etc., under various circumstances, has been the subject of frequent discussion in and out of the courts, and it will not be improper to refer briefly to the authorities upon it.

On the one hand, there have been cited, to the effect that the maxim in question is applicable to the construction of Constitutions, opinions delivered by the judges of the Supreme Courts of Massachusetts and Rhode Island, the former in 1833 and the latter in 1883. The Constitutions of those States had provided, in substantially identical terms, that the judges of the Supreme Court should, "upon important questions of law, and upon solemn occasions,"[1] or "whenever requested,"[2] give their opinions to the Governor, or to either branch of the legislature.

The Massachusetts Constitution of 1821 had made provision

[1] Chapter III., Article II., Massachusetts Constitution of 1821.

[2] Article X., Section 3, Rhode Island Constitution of 1842.

for making specific amendments to that instrument through the agency of the legislature, but not for calling a Convention. In 1833, the question being before the legislature of submitting to the people the expediency of calling a Convention to alter or amend the Constitution in some particular parts, a doubt was raised whether it was competent for the legislature to take any steps towards calling a Convention, inasmuch as the Constitution had provided another mode of effecting the same object. The following question was, therefore, submitted to the judges of the Supreme Court: "Can any specific and particular amendment or amendments to the Constitution be made in any other manner than that prescribed in the ninth Article of the amendments adopted in 1820?"

To this question the judges replied, that, "considering that, previous to 1820, no mode was provided by the Constitution for its own amendment, that no other power for that purpose than in the mode alluded to is anywhere given in the Constitution, by implication or otherwise, and that the mode thereby provided appears manifestly to have been carefully considered, and the power of altering the Constitution thereby conferred to have been cautiously restrained and guarded, *we think a strong implication arises against* the existence of any other power, under the Constitution, for the same purposes."[1]

§ 574. In the Rhode Island case, the facts were that the Constitution of 1842 having provided for amendments in the legislative mode only, the Senate of that State, in 1883, asked of the judges of the Supreme Court their opinion, whether, if the General Assembly were "to call upon the electors to elect members to constitute a Convention to frame a new Constitution of the State, and to provide that the new Constitution should be submitted for adoption" to the electors, . . . and if a majority of the electors should vote in favor thereof, "the new Constitution would then become the legally adopted Constitution of the State?" . . . In reply, the judges said: —

"We have to say that we are of opinion that the mode provided in the Constitution for the amendment thereof is the only mode in which it can be constitutionally amended. The ordinary rule is that when power is given to do a thing in a particular way, then the affirmative words, marking out the particular way,

[1] For the whole opinion of the judges, see 6 Cushing's R., p. 573.

prohibit all other ways by implication, so that the particular way is the only way in which the power can be legally executed."[1] They then refer with approbation to authorities holding that the maxim, *expressio unius*, etc., is of very wide application, and cite as a precedent the opinion of the Massachusetts judges.

As to the weight to be accorded this opinion, we will only now observe, that so far as it is based upon that of the Massachusetts judges, it is wholly without force, because the two cases are very dissimilar in their facts, insomuch that, while it is possible to approve the opinion of the Massachusetts judges, it does not follow, according to the principles propounded in it, that that of the Rhode Island judges is to be approved. In the Massachusetts case, where the Constitution had provided a mode in which "specific and particular amendments" might be made through the agency of the legislature, the question put to the judges was whether "any specific and particular amendment or amendments" could be made in any other manner than that provided in the Constitution. To this question the answer ought, according to the principles announced by both courts, to have been in the negative, since it inquired as to the lawfulness of doing the same thing in a different way from that prescribed by the Constitution. But that opinion could not properly be cited as authority in the Rhode Island case, where the question was whether, if a Convention were called "to frame a new Constitution of the State," and it were adopted by the people, it would be valid, the existing Constitution having provided a mode in which amendments thereof might be made, but not having authorized the call of a Convention? Here, as we shall see in a subsequent section, the proposition was to do a different thing, that is, to frame a new Constitution, in a different way, and therefore according to all authorities the maxim could have no application: in other words, because the people could not do *the same* thing in a different way, it does not follow that they could not do a *different* thing in a different way.

§ 574 *a*. In the two preceding sections have been presented opinions by the judges of two very respectable courts bearing, or thought to bear, upon the question we are considering. In respect to the weight and value of these opinions, it may be

[1] 14 R. I. R., 649.

further observed that they were not properly judicial decisions, binding upon either the officers propounding the questions which they purported to answer, or upon the judges themselves.[1] Not only that: the opinion of the Massachusetts judges, so far as it may be supposed to impute illegitimacy to any Convention called "to revise, alter, or amend the Constitution," where that instrument contains a special provision for making particular amendments thereof, in the legislative mode, was repudiated by a subsequent legislature, which called the Convention of 1853, notwithstanding the opinion, and by at least one of the judges who rendered it, the Hon. Marcus Morton, a member of the last named Convention, by whom its entire legality was maintained. But waiving this, we pass to consider opposing authorities affirming the limited applicability of the maxim, and consisting of the opinions of eminent statesmen and lawyers, and of judicial decisions of able tribunals rendered in the actual trial of causes, and after hearing the arguments, *pro* and *contra*, of distinguished legal counsel.[2]

In Broom's Legal Maxims, that author observes in relation to the maxim in question, "that great caution is requisite in dealing with it, for, as Lord Campbell, C., observed, in Saunders *v.* Evans,[3] it is not of universal application, but depends upon the intention of the parties as discoverable upon the face of the instrument or of the transaction." [4]

In the Massachusetts Convention of 1853, upon the question of the constitutionality of that body, the Hon. Joel Parker, formerly chief justice of New Hampshire, then a professor at the Cambridge Law School, said: —

"I believe this Convention to have been lawfully assembled. . . . Is not this mode of amending the Constitution, which is prescribed in the Constitution in express terms, perfectly con-

[1] That opinions delivered by judges under the circumstances stated were merely advisory and binding upon nobody, not even the judges propounding them, see Appendix E, *post*.

[2] How little weight ought, in the judgment of Mr. Justice Story, to be given to opinions rendered by judges upon first impression, without such argument, that eminent jurist himself stated in the Massachusetts Convention of 1820, of which he was a member. See Appendix E, *post*.

[3] 8 H. L. Cas., 729.

[4] Broom, *Legal Maxims*, 7th American, 5th London ed., T. W. Johnson & Co, 1874, p. 653.

sistent with the other mode, by a Convention of delegates? There is no antagonism between the two modes. The people say by their Constitution, 'We will have a convenient mode by which this instrument can be amended without a Convention; and we will therefore embody a provision that the opinion of two successive legislatures that the Constitution ought to be amended, shall be submitted to us for our action without the expense of a Convention.' This is all very well; but does it exclude the idea that a Convention may be holden where there is nothing antagonistic between the two modes? By no means."

Still more explicitly, in the same debate, he said: "I do not understand that there is anything in the terms of this provision of the Constitution which makes it exclusive, — which makes it the sole and only mode in which the provisions of the Constitution are to be amended. I do not understand the principle to be that the mention of one mode excludes all the other modes which would have existed but for the mention of that mode. What is the principle upon this subject? I admit the principle in common law that the designation of one person or one thing in some instances is exclusion of all others; but does that principle apply to this case? That principle applies to all cases where, from the necessity or the nature of the case, it is shown to be the intent that other things should be excluded." [1]

In 1874 Mr. Charles O'Conor, the eminent lawyer, at the instance of the New York Tribune, rendered an opinion touching the validity of certain amendments submitted to the people of New York, in respect to which the regularity of the legislative action had been denied. In the course of his opinion, after stating that concurrent resolutions of the legislative bodies in two different years, and a final approval by the people, constituted the process prescribed by the Constitution, Mr. O'Conor said: —

"This instrument does not prohibit the employment of different means unless such a negative can be implied from its having thus made provision for a method which is undeniably convenient and suitable. I think it is not maintainable by any fair reasoning that a State Constitution which so provides for its own amendment cannot be altered or varied from in any other manner. Certainly such a negative implication is not admissible

[1] *Deb. Mass. Conv.* 1853, Vol. I. p. 153.

in New York, for its present State government came into being on precisely an opposite basis;" that is, was framed by a Convention, for which no provision had been made in the Constitution of 1821.

So in Collier *v.* Frierson, decided by the Supreme Court of Alabama in 1854, under the Constitution of 1819, which authorized amendments thereof by the legislative mode only, the court, per Goldthwaite, J., say: —

"The Constitution can be amended in but two ways: either by the people, who originally framed it, or in the mode prescribed by the instrument itself. If the last mode is pursued, the amendments must be proposed by two-thirds of each house of the General Assembly. . . . We entertain no doubt that, to change the Constitution in any other mode than by a Convention, every requisition which is demanded by the instrument itself must be fulfilled, and the omission of any one is fatal to the amendment."[1] This is cited as the opinion of the judges of the Supreme Court of Alabama, and not as a judicial decision, as it was *obiter dictum*, so far as it relates to the call of a Convention under a Constitution like that then in force in Alabama. The following are not *obiter*, however.

In Eastern Archipelago Co. *v.* The Queen, in the English court of Queen's Bench, in a cause in which it was contended that the maxim applied, for the reason that an express declaration in the proviso, embodied in a charter, to the effect that, in case of non-compliance with certain conditions, the crown might revoke and make void the charter, under the Great Seal or sign manual, excluded every other mode of revocation or annulment, Mr. Justice Williams said: "This maxim of law is by no means of universal or conclusive application. For example, it is a familiar doctrine that, though, where a statute makes unlawful that which was lawful before, and appoints a specific remedy, that remedy must be pursued, and no other, yet, where an officer was antecedently punishable by a common law proceeding, as by indictment, and a statute prescribes a particular remedy in case of disobedience, that such particular remedy is cumulative, and proceedings may be had either at common law or under the statute."[2] Even if it were conceded that authority to make specific

[1] Collier *v.* Frierson, 24 Ala. R., 100, 108.

[2] 2 Ellis & Blackburn R., 878, 879.

and particular amendments was authority to do the same thing as to make a general revision of a Constitution through the agency of a Convention, undoubtedly the mode of doing the thing by a Convention is the common law mode, antecedently well understood and frequently used, and that by the agency of the legislature is a statutory mode, and by analogy the reasoning of the learned judge quoted is perfectly applicable to the question we are considering; in other words, the maxim *expressio unius* cannot be applied to exclude the call of Conventions, though not expressly authorized by the Constitution.

§ 574 *b*. So, in Barto *v*. Himrod,[1] the question was whether a statute of New York establishing free schools, which was to take effect only upon submission to and ratification by the people, was or was not unconstitutional, as delegating the power of legislation to the people. The existing Constitution had authorized the submission to the people only of a law creating a public debt. Upon this point Willard, J., said: —

. . . "I do not mean to lay much stress upon the implication arising from the express provision to submit a law creating a debt to the people, and the silence of the Constitution in relation to submitting to the people any other matters of legislation. The maxim, *expressio unius est exclusio alterius*, is more applicable to deeds and contracts than to a Constitution, and requires great caution in its application in all cases." So, in Wells *v*. Bain,[2] a case to which reference has already been made,[3] where the Constitution of Pennsylvania had expressly authorized amendments only by the legislative mode, but the legislature had called a Convention for the revision of that instrument, the court sustained the constitutionality of the Act calling that body. After quoting the second section of the Declaration of Rights, which affirmed that the people "have at all times an inalienable and indefeasible right to alter, reform, or abolish their government in such manner as they may think proper," the court, per Agnew, Ch. J., say: —

"The words 'in such manner as they may think proper,' in

[1] 4 Seld. N. Y. R., 483, 493. See also Williams *v*. Mayor, etc., of Detroit, 2 Mich. R., 563, 564, where it was held that the maxim is not applicable in the construction of a State Constitution upon the subject of taxation.

[2] 75 Pa. St. R., 40, 46.

[3] See *ante*, §§ 409 *a*, 409 *c*.

the Declaration of Rights, embrace but three known recognized modes by which the whole people — the State — can give their consent to an alteration of an existing lawful form of government, viz.: 1. The mode provided in the existing Constitution; 2. A law, as the instrumental process of raising the body for revision, and conveying to it the powers of the people; 3. A revolution. The first two are peaceful means, through which the consent of the people to alteration is obtained, and by which the existing government consents to be displaced without revolution. The government gives its consent either by pursuing the mode provided in the Constitution, or by passing a law to call a Convention."[1]

§ 574 *c*. The result of the discussion thus far has been, we think, to show that the maxim, *expressio unius*, etc., if applied at all, is in all cases, and especially in that of Constitutions, to be applied with great caution; that it is not of universal application, but depends upon the intention of the parties, as discoverable upon the face of the instrument or of the transaction. But conceding that it may sometimes be applied to Constitutions, let us examine the phraseology employed in those instruments in authorizing the two modes of making amendments, to see if that does not alone set at rest the question of its applicability to those provisions.

Obviously, as we have before remarked,[2] while it may, without absurdity, be claimed that the maxim operates to prohibit the doing of the *same* thing in a different way from that prescribed by law, it cannot be claimed to prohibit the doing of a *different* thing in a different way. Now, it is very clear on the face of the constitutional provisions authorizing amendments through the agency of the legislature, as compared with those authorizing the call of Conventions, that the purpose of the former is different from that of the latter; in other words, the thing authorized to be done by the one class of provisions is a different thing from that authorized to be done by the other. Thus, the purpose of the legislative mode is to bring about amendments which are few and simple and independent; and on the other hand,

[1] Wells *v.* Bain, and Donnelly *v.* Fitler, 75 Pa. St. R., 40, 46. Also, Wood's Appeal, 75 Pa. St. R., 59. As to the proper construction to be given to the constitutional provision quoted by the court, see *ante*, §§ 237–246.

[2] See *ante*, § 574.

that of the mode through Conventions is to revise the entire Constitution, with a view to propose either a new one, or, as the greater includes the less, to propose specific and particular amendments to it. Where a few particular amendments only are desired, if the Constitution provides for both modes, the legislative mode should be employed; but if a revision is or may be desired, the mode by a Convention only is appropriate, or, as we expect to show, permissible. For, note that the phraseology used in authorizing the former mode is in every case, without exception, "any amendment or amendments" may be proposed by the General Assembly; that of the latter is, "if at any time it shall seem necessary to the General Assembly to revise the Constitution," it shall have power to call a Convention, which shall meet "to revise, alter, or amend" the same. Now, in not a single instance is the word "revise," or any of its derivatives, employed with reference to the legislative mode, but only the words "amendment," "amendments," or "alterations."[1] On the other hand, in a large majority of the cases in which authority is given to call Conventions, the purpose of calling them is stated to be "to revise," or "to revise, alter, or amend" the existing Constitution.[2] The language is sometimes still more explicit, the Convention being expressly empowered to make "a revision of the

[1] See the articles relating to amendments in the following Constitutions: Alabama, 1865–1867, and 1875; Arkansas, 1836, 1864, 1868, and 1874; California, 1849 and 1879; Colorado, 1876; Connecticut, 1818; Delaware, 1792 and 1831; Florida, 1838, 1868, and 1885; Georgia, 1798; Illinois, 1848, 1862, and 1870; Indiana, 1851; Iowa, 1846 and 1857; Kansas, 1855, 1858, and 1859; Louisiana, 1845, 1852, and 1864; Maine, 1820: Maryland, 1776, 1864, and 1867; Massachusetts, 1821; Michigan, 1835 and 1850: Minnesota, 1857; Mississippi, 1832 and 1868; Missouri, 1820, 1865, and 1875; Nebraska, 1875; Nevada, 1864: New Jersey, 1776 and 1844; New York, 1846 and 1867; North Carolina, 1835, 1868, and 1876; Oregon, 1857: Ohio, 1851; Pennsylvania, 1838 and 1873; Rhode Island, 1842; South Carolina, 1790 and 1868; Tennessee, 1834 and 1870: Texas, 1845, 1866, 1868, and 1876; Virginia, 1870; Vermont, 1870; West Virginia, 1863 and 1872; Wisconsin, 1848.

[2] The following Constitutions contain the word "revise" or "revision" in stating the purpose of the Convention: California, 1879; Colorado, 1876; Florida, 1885; Illinois, 1818, 1848, 1862, and 1870; Indiana, 1816; Iowa, 1846 and 1857; Kansas, 1855, 1858, and 1859; Maryland, 1864; Massachusetts, 1780 and 1821; Michigan, 1850; Minnesota, 1857; Mississippi, 1817; Missouri, 1865 and 1875; Nebraska, 1867 and 1875; Nevada, 1864; New Hampshire, 1792; New York, 1846; Ohio, 1802 and 1851; South Carolina, 1868; Tennessee, 1796; Virginia, 1870; and Wisconsin, 1848.

entire Constitution."[1] But this is not all. As if to leave no room for doubt that a distinction was intended between the things authorized to be done by the two classes of provisions, in twenty-six of the thirty-four cases in which the word "revise" or "revision" is used in specifying the duty of the Conventions which should be called, the Constitutions contain also an express authorization to make amendments therein in the legislative mode.[2] It seems impossible to escape the conclusion that in these twenty-six cases, the framers of the Constitutions did not suppose they were providing for doing the same thing in both the modes authorized by them. We thus see that the legislative mode is limited to the cases where an amendment or amendments are desired, and the mode by Conventions to those in which a broader purpose is entertained, namely, that of a revision of the whole Constitution, with the purpose of proposing either, first, a new one, or, secondly, the old one, if on the whole satisfactory, but with such amendments as to the Convention should seem desirable. In other words, the legislative mode is confined to a narrow and defined purpose, and that by Conventions to a broader and more general and undefined purpose, embracing within its scope the former, and possibly much more. To say, then, that the purpose of the two modes is the same, is to say that a part is equal to, or the same as, the whole.[3]

[1] See the Constitutions of California, 1849; Florida, 1868; Michigan, 1835; and Nevada, 1864.

[2] See the Constitutions of California, 1849 and 1879; Colorado, 1876; Florida, 1868 and 1885; Illinois, 1848, 1862, and 1870; Iowa, 1846 and 1857; Kansas, 1858 and 1859; Maryland, 1864; Michigan, 1835 and 1850; Minnesota, 1857; Missouri, 1865 and 1875; Nebraska, 1875; Nevada, 1864; New York, 1846 and 1867; Ohio, 1851; South Carolina, 1868; Virginia, 1870; Wisconsin, 1848.

[3] There are a few Constitutions which authorize the call of Conventions either without stating for what purpose, — in which list are those of Delaware, 1792 and 1831; Florida, 1838 and 1865; Georgia, 1868; North Carolina, 1835, 1868, and 1876; and South Carolina, 1790, — or stating it to be, to make alterations or amendments to the Constitution, in which are Maine, 1876; Pennsylvania, 1776; Georgia, 1865; New Hampshire, 1784; and all of the Constitutions of Vermont, except that of 1870, — or stating it to be, to readopt, amend, or change their respective Constitutions, in which are Kentucky, 1792, 1799, and 1850; and Louisiana, 1812. In the West Virginia Constitutions of 1863 and 1873 the phraseology used is, "No Convention shall be called having authority to alter the Constitution," save upon certain conditions stated.

All of these classes of cases, save perhaps the second, substantially accord

§ 574 *d*. Some light is thrown upon the question considered in the last section by recurring to the views, in regard to the purpose for which the legislative mode was intended, of those who were the first to authorize it.[1] Among these, and by far the ablest, was the Massachusetts Convention of 1820. In this body Daniel Webster, as chairman of the committee on the subject of amendments to the Constitution, reported a resolution that it was "proper and expedient to amend the Constitution so as to provide that, if at any time hereafter any specific and particular amendment or amendments to the Constitution be proposed, and be agreed to by two-thirds of the members of each house present and voting thereon, and be afterwards submitted to and approved by a majority of the qualified voters, the same should become a part of the Constitution." Upon a motion to strike out, in relation to the Senate, the words "two-thirds" and insert "a majority," Mr. Webster, explaining to the Convention why the committee had reported in favor of the legislative mode, and had inserted no provision for calling a Convention, said: —

"It occurred to the committee that, with the experience which we had had of the Constitution, there was little probability that, after the amendments which should now be adopted, there would ever be any occasion for great changes. No revision of its general principles would be necessary, and the alterations which should be called for by a change of circumstances would be limited and specific. It was, therefore, the opinion of the committee that no provision for a revision of the whole Constitution was expedient, and the only question was in what manner it should be provided that particular amendments might be obtained. It was a natural course, and conformable to analogy and precedent in some degree, that every proposition for amendment should originate in the legislature, under certain guards,

with those given in the text in making the distinction stated as to the purpose for which they were called.

[1] The order in which this mode was adopted by the earlier Conventions is as follows: By the Conventions of Delaware in September, and Maryland in November, 1776; by the Federal Convention, 1787; Connecticut, 1818; Alabama, August 2, 1819; Maine, October 29, 1819; Missouri, July 19, 1820; Massachusetts, November 15, 1820; and New York, 1821. Of these, the earliest whose debates throw any light upon the subject is the Convention of Massachusetts of 1820, which framed the Constitution of 1821.

and be sent out to the people. The question then arose, what guards should be provided?"[1]

This citation is made simply to show the view entertained by Mr. Webster, and presumably by the rest of the Convention, as to the purpose and function to which the legislative mode was only adapted, and that in their view, on the other hand, the mode by a Convention was alone appropriate when a general revision of the Constitution was desired or anticipated. We may add, that it is not from this remark of Mr. Webster to be inferred that, in his opinion, no Convention could be called unless express authority were given in the Constitution, or that, in leaving out of the new Constitution a provision to that effect, they intended to prevent the call of such a body in the future. He obviously meant only to say that, as it was believed no Convention for a general revision would thereafter be found necessary, it was not thought worth while to encumber the new Constitution with a clause permitting it.

To the same effect, the Convention, in an address published by it to the people, explaining the amendments proposed by it, say: —

"It may be necessary that specific amendments of the Constitution should hereafter be made. The preparatory measures in assembling a Convention, and the necessary expense of such an assembly, are obstacles of some magnitude to obtaining amendments through such means. We propose that whenever two-thirds of the House of Representatives and a majority of the Senate, in two successive legislatures, shall determine that any specific amendment of the Constitution is expedient, such proposed amendment shall be submitted to the people; and if accepted by the people, the Constitution shall be amended accordingly. We believe that the Constitution will be sufficiently guarded from inexpedient alterations, while all those which are found to be necessary will be duly considered, and may be obtained with comparatively small expense."[2]

The force of these quotations may be better apprehended by considering what the Convention meant by a "specific amendment." Undoubtedly it meant an amendment which had been distinctly formulated in its terms in the public mind, and one

[1] *Deb. Mass. Conv.* 1820, pp. 413, 414.

[2] See *Deb. Mass. Conv.* 1820, p. 631.

of which the necessity had been generally acknowledged, in contradistinction from a change, indeterminate in its character and extent, which might be shown to be advisable upon a revision of the whole Constitution. A specific amendment, being a definite proposition, might safely be submitted to the people to pass upon, yes or no; for it required no modification to adjust it to possible changes in other parts of the same instrument. Not so with an indeterminate amendment, to be matured by discussion, and after multiplied adjustments, and which might turn out to be a single proposition, or a few simple propositions, or a completely new Constitution. For such a work only a Convention is adapted.

Recurring, then, to the question whether, where a Constitution contains no provision for amendments save in the legislative mode, a Convention can be called, the answer must be, both upon principle and upon precedent, that a Convention can be called, certainly when a revision of the whole Constitution is desired, to determine what amendments, if any, are needed, or, if deemed advisable, to frame a new Constitution. In general, whenever a Convention is called, the intention is to authorize a revision of the entire Constitution, though, upon its meeting, the result of its labors may be only to recommend specific amendments. But, where the legislative mode is adopted, it is never intended to do more than to formulate certain specific amendments, though, in one or two cases where constitutional commissions have been employed, attempts have been made to adapt the legislative mode to the making of general revisions,— attempts which have not met with such success as to justify their repetition.[1]

§ 574 *e*. As incidental to the questions considered in preceding sections, reference may be here made to certain judicial decisions touching the degree of strictness with which the provisions of Constitutions for amendments in the legislative mode must be pursued. In a previous section it was said, that the power given to a legislature to propose to the people amendments to the Constitution is not an incident to the general grant of legislative power, but, if it exist at all, rests upon some special constitutional provision; in other words, that it is a statutory power. From this it follows that, like all statutory powers, it

[1] See *ante*, §§ 546 *a*–546 *d*.

must be strictly pursued. So far there has been little or no controversy. In several of the States, however, questions have arisen, whether all the steps by the Constitution made requisite to give validity and effect to amendments proposed by the legislature have been taken; that is, whether the provisions of the Constitution have or have not been strictly pursued, within the meaning and intent of the framers of that instrument. The decisions of the courts upon these questions will now be briefly considered.

The earliest case upon the point is that of Collier *v.* Frierson, arising in 1854 under the Alabama Constitution of 1819.[1] This instrument required, for the enactment of amendments in the legislative mode, a two-thirds vote in favor of them of two successive legislatures, and an intervening majority vote of the people. Eight amendments were recommended by the first legislature; but by mistake one was not included among those adopted by the second, although all the other steps were regularly taken. The Supreme Court of the State held, that the omitted amendment did not become a part of the Constitution. So, the Iowa Constitution of 1857 having required, in like manner, the action of two successive General Assemblies, to be followed by a vote of the people, the 18th General Assembly adopted an amendment, but in the course of its transmission to the 19th General Assembly the tenor and effect of the amendment were changed, so that the two General Assemblies had not passed upon the same amendment. It was held by the Supreme Court of the State, in Koehler *v.* Lange, to be invalid.[2] The Kansas Constitution of 1859 had required that amendments proposed by

[1] 24 Ala. R., 100.

[2] 60 Iowa R., 543. See, also, The State *v.* Johnson, 61 Iowa R., 104. Although the decision of the court in this case was clearly right, yet, as the extreme temperance party of the State were dissatisfied with the overthrow of the amendment, which had prohibited the manufacture and sale within the State of spirituous liquors, including wine and beer, a violent agitation was commenced by the friends of the amendment, with a view to punish the court by defeating the reëlection of the judges who had rendered the decision. The good sense and moderation of the people, however, finally prevailed, and the project was quietly abandoned. Constitutional government was thus saved from a most serious calamity, — a decision of an important constitutional question virtually dictated to a court by a mob of excited reformers, in such a State as Iowa; for, it cannot be doubted, that the purpose of the temperance party was to secure such a decision as it desired by packing the court.

the legislature should be entered, with the yeas and nays, upon the journal. In 1879 the legislature, by the requisite vote, submitted to the people a proposition to amend the Constitution. This proposition was not entered at length upon the journal, but was described by its title, scope, and object. Otherwise the submission was regular. The Supreme Court sustained the validity of the amendment, although it conceded that there was an irregularity in respect to its entry upon the journal.[1]

The true rule governing such cases was enunciated by the Supreme Court of Iowa in the case above cited. They say: "While it is not competent for courts to inquire into the validity of the Constitution and form of government under which they themselves exist, and from which they derive their powers, yet, when the existing Constitution prescribes a method for its own amendment, an amendment thereto, to be valid, must be adopted in strict conformity to that method; and it is the duty of courts, in a proper case, when an amendment does not relate to their own powers or functions, to inquire whether, in the adoption of the amendment, the provisions of the existing Constitution have been observed, and, if not, to declare the amendment invalid and of no effect."[2]

§ 574*f*. To determine the degree of strictness with which constitutional provisions authorizing the call of Conventions must be pursued, in the absence of restrictive words, mandatory in their effect, is more difficult. 1. If the position hereinbefore taken be correct, that a legislature, under our constitutional system, has power to call a Convention to amend or revise the Constitution, though not expressly authorized, the case presented by the facts supposed would be this: A legislature having a general power to call a Convention, at its discretion, is expressly given power to do the same thing under certain conditions. What inference is warranted as to the intention of the people in imposing those conditions? Obviously, that they were not content longer to leave so important a power to the unlimited discretion of the legislature, but desired to restrict it by express declarations of their will as to the time when, the purpose for which, and the number and character of the voters by whom, a Convention might be called. If this inference be just, the conditions

[1] *The Constitutional Prohibitory Amendment*, 24 Kans. R., 700.

[2] See to the same effect The State *ex rel.* Hudd *v.* Timme, 54 Wis. R., 318.

laid down for the exercise of the power become, in effect, positive prohibitions upon its exercise in any other way, in conformity to the maxim, good both in the civil and the common law, *expressum cessare facit tacitum.*[1] In this reasoning, the people of the United States have generally, I might say universally, acquiesced, though occasional attempts have been made, under strong temptation, to induce the legislatures of some of the States to discredit it. Thus, the Illinois Constitution of 1848 provided, that whenever two-thirds of all the members elected to each branch of the General Assembly should think it necessary to alter or amend the Constitution, they should recommend to the electors at the next election of members of the General Assembly to vote for or against a Convention; and if it should appear that a majority of all the electors of the State voting for representatives had voted for a Convention, the General Assembly, at their next session, should call a Convention. In 1867, members of the dominant party in the State, desiring an early change of the Constitution, and impatient of the delay necessitated by its strict terms, attempted to carry through an act to call a Convention by what was styled "a short cut," that is, upon a vote of the people alone, omitting a reference of the subject to the next session of the General Assembly to make the call, should that vote favor it, as required by the Constitution. Happily, the scheme was defeated, and the wiser course taken of obeying to the letter the supreme law of the State.

2. On the other hand, suppose the position that a legislature has power to call a Convention, although not expressly authorized by the Constitution, be an erroneous one, then the power expressly given would be a merely statutory power, which, all legal authorities agree, must be strictly pursued.

§ 574 *g.* Where a Constitution authorizes specific amendments thereof by the action of the two successive General Assemblies, and several amendments are proposed by one General Assembly, and one or more of them are rejected by the next General Assembly, those which have received the approval of both are valid as parts of the Constitution, the proceedings being

[1] In Field *v.* The People, 2 Scammon's R., 79, 83, the court laid it down as an established rule, "that, when the means for the exercise of a granted power is given, no other or different means can be implied as being more effectual or convenient."

otherwise regular.[1] Many Constitutions require that, if more than one amendment shall be submitted, they shall be submitted in such manner that the people may vote for or against such amendments separately.[2] The Wisconsin Constitution contains such a provision. In 1882, a question came before the Supreme Court of the State whether the submission to the people, by the legislature, of an amendment consisting of several distinct propositions, to be voted on as one amendment, was a violation of the constitutional provision. The court held, that it was not, declaring it to be within the discretion of the legislature so to submit, "if such propositions relate to the same subject, and are all designed to accomplish one purpose." "The several propositions, submitted in 1881," they say, "all relate to a change from annual to biennial sessions of the legislature, and were intended to effect such a change, and they were properly submitted as a single amendment, and were adopted as such."[3]

In several cases, the question passed upon has been, whether the majority required by the Constitution has been given for the amendment, either in the General Assembly or by the people. Thus, where the Constitution required a vote of two-thirds of each house to propose amendments, it has been held that the meaning of the provision is two-thirds of a quorum of each house.[4] The Indiana Constitution of 1851 required, after an amendment had been approved by a majority of two successive General Assemblies, that, to be valid, it should be submitted to the electors of the State and be ratified by a majority of the same. An amendment submitted to the people in 1880 received less than a majority of all the votes cast at the election, and the Supreme Court of the State held that the amendment had not been ratified.[5] The reasoning of the court seems to have been

[1] Trustees University of North Carolina *v.* McIver, 72 N. C. R., 76; The Constitutional Prohibitory Amendment, 24 Kansas R., 700.

[2] See § 516, note 1, *ante.*

[3] State *ex rel.* Hudd *v.* Timme, 54 Wis. R., 318. See, also, State *v.* McBride, 4 Mo. R., 303.

[4] Green *v.* Weller, 32 Miss. R., 650; The State *v.* McBride, 4 Mo. R., 303

[5] The State *v.* Swift, 69 Ind. R., 505. The court, in this case, remarked that "under a valid statute" the amendment might be again submitted to the people. It also observed, that the General Assembly might provide that the whole number of votes cast at the election at which the amendment was submitted might be taken to be the whole number of electors of the State at that time.

that, no mode having been fixed by law for determining the whole number of the electors of the State, that number might safely be presumed to be greater than the whole number of votes cast.[1]

It has been made a question, when a Constitution has been submitted to the people, what department of the government should determine whether it had been adopted or not; and whether, if the executive of the State be required by law to count the votes and to declare the result, his action therein can be controlled by the judiciary. The act calling the Maryland Convention of 1864 required that body to submit its work to the people, but "in such manner, and subject to such rules and regulations," as the convention might prescribe. Art. XII. sec. 8 of the Constitution, framed by it, directed the returning officers to report the votes on the Constitution to the Governor, who was to make proclamation of the result. A petition was filed in the Superior Court of Baltimore city, asking for a rule upon the Governor to show cause why a writ of *mandamus* should not be issued commanding him to receive and count certain votes rejected by the judges of election, and to exclude others received by them, and which he proposed to count. The court refused to enter the rule, and dismissed the petition, which judgment was, on appeal to the Supreme Court, affirmed. The court held that it was the well-settled law in the United States, that when, as in this case, a discretionary power had been vested in the executive, the judiciary would not interfere with the exercise of that power, and that "the political department has always determined whether the proposed Constitution or amendment was ratified or not by the people," . . . "and the judicial power has followed its decision."[2]

[1] As to the power of a court to look into the proceedings of a General Assembly to see if all the prerequisites to the adoption of an amendment to the Constitution have been complied with, see State *v.* McBride, 4 Mo. R., 303, affirming that power; with which compare Green *v.* Weller, 32 Miss., 650, denying it.

[2] Miles *v.* Bradford, 22 Md. R., 170; Deb. Md. Conv. 1863, Vol. III. Appendix. Before concluding the examination of questions relating to the amending of Constitutions in the legislative mode, it may be useful again to refer to the opinion of Mr. Charles O'Conor, an eminent New York lawyer, before cited, touching certain questions bearing on that subject, not as authority, but as the reasoned view of a trained legal mind touching those questions. Mr. O'Conor gave it as his opinion, —

§ 574 *h.* (*b.*) There remains the question whether, when a Constitution contains no provision for amendments at all, either or both modes we have been considering may be pursued? As to a Convention, if there be no express prohibition, the answer may be unhesitatingly given, that the General Assembly may call a Convention. All our State Constitutions make to the General Assemblies a general grant of legislative power, which is admitted to extend to all subjects of ordinary legislation which are not prohibited by their own or by the Federal Constitution. By a long established usage, in most of the States, and in some of them in repeated instances, those bodies have called Conventions, under the circumstances stated, as a branch of their general legislative power; and, as we have before observed, were there doubt as to the constitutionality of such action, it is too late now to question it. Frequent exercise of the power, and uniform and long acquiescence of the people in it, constitute a fundamental law as binding as though it had been formulated expressly in the Constitution.[1]

1. That when a section of a Constitution contained two independent propositions, and an amendment was proposed by the General Assembly in 1873, which was in effect identical with the first proposition, but was dissented from by the General Assembly in 1874, and so was lost, the section was left thereby as it stood originally, unaffected by the proposed amendment.

2. That when, of a series of amendments referred to the General Assembly by a previous General Assembly, some distinct amendments were disapproved and some approved by the second body, and submitted to and approved by the people, such amendments as were approved were valid; and that to hold, that each set of amendments incorporated at the first session in a single concurrent resolution of approval must be taken up and dealt with as a whole, would be attaching undue importance to a mere mechanical arrangement of subjects, provided the several propositions were, in their nature, contemplated effect, and necessary operation, separable.

3. That when the Constitution required that proposed amendments should be published, the inclusion in the notice published of an item proposed by one house and opposed by the other, and the house proposing it had receded from it, this error did not vitiate the notice as to the other items.

[1] See *ante*, §§ 570, 571.

On the subject of amendments to a Constitution effected by long acquiescence of the people, see Stewart *v.* Laird, 1 Cranch, 299, 309; McCulloch *v.* Maryland, 4 Wheat. R., 316, 401; Briscoe *v.* Bank of Kentucky, 11 Pet. R., 257, 318; Prigg *v.* Pennsylvania, 16 do. 539, 621; New Jersey St. Nav. Co. *v.* Merchants' Bank, 6 How. R., 344; West River Bridge Co. *v.* Dix, Id. 507; Cooley *v.* Wardens, etc., 12 How. R., 299; The Genesee Chief *v.* Fitz Hugh, Id. 443, 458. But compare Sturgess *v.* Crowningshield, 4 Wheat. R., 122, 203.

On the other branch of the question, relating to the legislative mode, the answer may as unhesitatingly be given that, under the conditions stated, that mode could not be pursued. In recommending to the people an amendment or amendments to the Constitution, a General Assembly so far acts merely in a conventional capacity; that is, its act is not one of legislation. For this we have the authority of Mr. Webster, who, in the Massachusetts Convention of 1820, when discussing the provision reported for authorizing amendments in the legislative mode, said: "This was not an exercise of legislative power, — it was only referring to some branch the power of making propositions to the people."[1] Under a general grant of legislative power a legislature could not rightfully exercise a power not legislative. The power to propose amendments, then, not enuring as a part of the general grant, must be authorized by a special provision of the Constitution. And when no such provision can be pointed out the power does not exist.[2]

§ 574 *i*. Allied to the questions discussed in this chapter, which have actually been raised, is one that might be raised, as to the effect upon an old Constitution of the adoption of a new one, where contradictory provisions, but no special repealing clause, have been inserted in the latter. Doubtless, so far as the provisions of the new Constitution are inconsistent with those of the old, the former must be held to repeal the latter. So, when a special power is granted to a department of the government by a Constitution, and the constitutional provision is the only source of the power, a new Constitution merely omitting the grant, without special words of repeal, must be held to annul the power. But, if the power may be derived from some other source than express constitutional grant, or be involved in a grant of power expressly made, as incident to it, then such omission in the new Constitution would not, it would seem, operate as a repeal. The question might arise upon facts not infrequently occurring in the formation of Constitutions. Thus, in some instances, Constitutions providing only for the call of Conventions for the revision

[1] *Deb. Mass. Conv.* 1820, p. 407. See § 549, *ante*.

[2] As to the nature of an amendment to a Constitution and its effect upon existing rights and jurisdiction, see Hollingsworth *v.* Virginia, 3 Dall., 382; Trustees University of N. C. *v.* McIver, 72 N. C. R., 76. But compare *Matter of the Executive Communication*, 15 Fla. R., 739.

or amendment thereof have been followed by new Constitutions making no mention of Conventions, but providing for amendments through the agency of the legislature followed or not by the approval of the people. Thus related to each other were the Constitutions of Georgia, 1789 and 1798; Indiana, 1816 and 1851; Louisiana, 1812 and 1845, etc.; Massachusetts, 1780 and 1822; Mississippi, 1832 and 1865; Tennessee, 1796 and 1834; and Vermont, 1850 and 1870. Now, in all these cases, save those of Indiana and Vermont, the dropping of the provision relating to the call of Conventions was not regarded as a prohibition of the exercise of that power thereafter, because the States have all, except those two, since called conventions, without question or objection: and, doubtless, upon the principles above explained, Vermont and Indiana might at any time have called them. On the other hand, were the facts reversed, the rule would be different. The Constitutions of Maryland, 1776 and 1851, and of Georgia, 1798, 1861, and 1865, present this supposed relation, the first, in each case, having made no provision for amendments save in the legislative mode; and the last of Maryland, and the last two of Georgia, none save by the call of a Convention. As a legislature has no power to act in a conventional capacity, save in pursuance of express constitutional authority, the dropping of that provision in the Maryland Constitution of 1851, and in the Georgia Constitutions of 1861 and 1865, must be held to have withdrawn from their legislature the power to act as authorized by the first Constitutions named.[1]

§ 575. That the principles announced in the foregoing sections, in relation to the amendment of State Constitutions, apply in general to the Federal Constitution, admits of little doubt. The fifth article of that Constitution provides, that "the Congress, whenever two-thirds of both houses shall deem it necessary, shall propose amendments to this Constitution; or, on the application of the legislatures of two-thirds of the several States, shall call a Convention for proposing amendments." The first clause, though in its terms imperative as to the duty of Congress, is yet, in effect, merely permissive, and, like similar provisions of the State Constitutions authorizing amendments in

[1] Compare Sigur *v.* Crenshaw, 8 La. An. R., 401; State *v.* Dubuc, 9 do. 237; *In the matter of the Executive Communication*, 15 Florida R., 739; Penn *v.* Tollison, 26 Ark. R., 545.

the legislative mode, is to be pursued strictly. Doubtless amendments could not be recommended by a less vote than two-thirds, or by other than such a vote of both houses.

The second clause, directing the call of a Convention by Congress, is imperative both in terms and effect, and, it is conceived, should receive a construction similar to that given provisions of the State Constitutions under like conditions. In a previous section,[1] we have seen that when a State legislature is granted express power to call a Convention, in stated circumstances and upon certain conditions, these circumstances and conditions must concur and be fulfilled exactly, or the power cannot be executed. Doubtless, therefore, a Convention of the States could not be called by Congress, upon its own motion merely, by however large a majority of the two houses, or on the application of the legislatures of any number of the States less than two-thirds. That the construction stated is the true one may be inferred from the well-settled rule as to the derivation and extent of the powers of Congress under the Federal Constitution. Congress, the legislature of the Union, possesses only such powers as have been expressly given to it, or as are necessary to the execution of its express powers. In other words, not having received a general power of legislation, as have the State legislatures, such special powers as Congress has received from the people must be strictly pursued, and cannot be enlarged by implication.[2]

§ 576. V. A question of much interest has several times arisen, whether, when a State legislature has once passed upon an amendment to the Federal Constitution proposed by Congress, its action can afterwards be reconsidered by it, or by its successor, and reversed. It may be useful to consider this question in the two cases, 1, where the action of the legislature was negative, rejecting, and 2, where it was affirmative, ratifying, an amendment.

1. The question in its negative form first arose, in 1865, in New Jersey, in relation to the XIII. Amendment.[3]

[1] See § 574 *f*, *ante*.

[2] The question, whether Congress could refuse to call a Convention, when applied to by the legislatures of two-thirds of the States, was considered in the House of Representatives, in discussing the treaty with Great Britain, in 1796. See Speeches of W. Smith, *Benton's Deb.*, Vol. I. p. 653, and of Samuel Lyman, Id. p. 659. The answer was in the negative, and a distinction affirmed between the duty of Congress in this case and in that of ratifying a treaty.

[3] A similar question, it is true, arose in North Carolina at the time of the

The amendment was rejected by the legislature of that State December 1, 1865, and notice thereof was duly given to the Secretary of State at Washington. That officer published his certificate December 18, 1865, declaring that the amendment had been adopted by the votes of twenty-seven States, and had become a part of the Constitution.[1] In this certificate no mention was made of New Jersey. January 23, 1866, the legislature of New Jersey reversed its previous action, and approved the amendment. The same question arose again in North Carolina, South Carolina, and Georgia, in relation to the XIV. Amendment, submitted by Congress to the States on the 16th of June, 1866. The legislatures of those States, together with those of five others, Texas, Virginia, Kentucky, Delaware, and Maryland, rejected the amendment. Afterwards, the governments of ten of the rebel States, including the three first named, were, by the Act of Congress of March 2, 1867, and the acts supplementary thereto,[2] declared to be illegal, and new governments were erected therein under the direction of Congress. By the new legislatures of North Carolina and South Carolina, the former on the 4th and the latter on the 9th of July, 1868, resolutions were passed ratifying the XIV. Amendment. These resolutions were certified to the Secretary of State, and the votes of those States were, in pursuance of a resolution of Congress, counted by that officer as valid votes, and the amendment was on the 20th of July, 1868, in a certificate of that date, proclaimed by him to have been duly ratified. The new legislature of Georgia, in like manner, on the 21st of July, 1868, receded from its vote rejecting the amendment and passed a resolution ratifying it, and that State was included by the Secretary of State amongst the ratifying States in a second certificate, issued July 28, 1868.[3]

§ 577. Were the legislatures in receding thus, and ratifying after having once rejected the amendment, acting within the

adoption of the Federal Constitution. The State Convention at first rejected the Constitution, but afterwards ratified it. So far as we are aware, no objection was ever raised that the State had exhausted its power by its first vote. But, because it was the Constitution itself upon which the Convention was voting, we have not considered the case applicable to the question of adopting amendments under the Constitution.

[1] *U. S. Stat. at Large*, Vol. XIII. p. 774.

[2] *U. S. Stat. at Large*, Vol. XIV. p. 428; Vol. XV. p. 2.

[3] *U. S. Stat. at Large*, Vol. XV. pp. 706, 708.

scope of their powers? The subsequent recognition of the votes by Congress, and by the Secretary of State, as valid, must, we think, settle this question in the affirmative. The Constitution is silent as to the conditions necessary to constitute a valid vote in such a case, and as to the proper authority to pass upon the question when it arises.

The only law relating to the subject is the Act of April 20, 1818, which provides: —

"SECTION 2. That whenever official notice shall have been received at the Department of State, that any amendment, which heretofore has been or hereafter may be, proposed to the Constitution of the United States, has been adopted, according to the provisions of the Constitution, it shall be the duty of the said Secretary of State forthwith to cause the said amendment to be published in the newspapers authorized to promulgate the laws, with his certificate, specifying the States by which the same may have been adopted, and that the same has become valid, to all intents and purposes, as a part of the Constitution of the United States."[1]

Two questions arise upon this act: 1. Is it constitutional? 2. What is its true construction? Does it devolve the duty of deciding upon the validity of votes cast, upon the Secretary of State, or upon some other and what officer or body?

§ 578. That the Act is constitutional, it is conceived, admits of little doubt. Article I., Sec. 8, clause 17 of the Constitution, gives to Congress power "to make all laws which shall be necessary and proper for carrying into effect the powers vested" thereby "in the government of the United States, or in any department or officer thereof." The power to amend the Constitution is a power vested by that instrument conjointly in the State legislatures, or Conventions, and in Congress. It is obvious that some department or officer, either of the general or State governments, must inspect the votes cast by the States, and pass upon their regularity and validity. Of the two, the more proper government to discharge this function is that of the Union; indeed, it would be inconvenient, if not impracticable, for the States to attempt to do so. The necessity of the case, therefore, under the Constitution, authorizes the intervention of Congress to prescribe by law the officer or department who should decide

[1] *U. S. Stat. at Large*, Vol. III. p. 439.

the question. Besides, whether a given amendment has become the law of the land or not, if in some respects a judicial question,[1] is also a high political question, of which Congress, in whose hands the political power is principally vested, ought to assume and retain the control.

But what is the true construction of the Act of 1818? It provides that "whenever *official notice* shall have been received at the Department of State, that any amendment has been adopted according to the provisions of the Constitution," it shall be the duty of the Secretary of State to cause it to be published, etc. "Official notice" received from whom, and how? It may mean, received from the several States, in the shape of certificates that their respective legislatures have ratified the amendment, in number and character sufficient, in the judgment of the Secretary, to make it the law of the land; or it may mean, received from some authority constitutionally declared to be competent to pass upon the votes taken, and to certify to him its decision. Such a discretion has not been given to the Secretary of State, and no such authority, it is believed, exists, unless it be vested in Congress; and, on the principles stated above, it would be difficult to deny to that body the power to act in the matter, if it should choose to do so. But, in the absence of any direction by Congress, it would doubtless be the duty of the Secretary of State, in the first instance, to inspect and pronounce upon the votes cast, provisionally, as a necessary preliminary to the issuance of the certificate required by the act, submitting all doubtful cases to the judgment of Congress. This course has been generally pursued since the foundation of the government. That this is the true view may, perhaps, be inferred from the action of the Secretary of State, Mr. Seward, and of Congress, in the reverse case relating to the XIV. Amendment. When the votes upon that amendment were canvassed, the Secretary

[1] In cases at law or in equity between individuals, doubtless, courts may pass upon the validity of a supposed amendment. See Collier *v.* Frierson, 24 Ala. R., 100; Miles *v.* Bradford, 22 Md. R., 170. The spectacle, however, of a court receiving evidence and presuming to determine, by its judgment, for the executive or legislative department of the same government, whether the Constitution is valid or not, would be a most remarkable one; and, when the political power has spoken upon the question, the judicial department ought, perhaps, in conformity to the general practice of courts in such cases, to follow its decision.

doubted whether those from New Jersey and Ohio, which were necessary to make up the required number, ought to be counted. Those States, as we shall see, had first adopted and afterwards rejected that amendment. Accordingly he issued a certificate, on the 20th of July, 1868, in which he recited the facts and declared the amendment adopted, provided the votes of those States to adopt were to be considered as still valid.[1] On the day following, a concurrent resolution was passed by Congress pronouncing the ratification of the amendment valid and sufficient;[2] whereupon, on the 28th of July, 1868, the Secretary issued a second certificate, reciting the resolution of Congress, and promulgating the amendment as a part of the Constitution.[3]

§ 579. But, whether this decision is authority upon the question now considered or not, the right of a State legislature, after a negative vote has once been passed, to recede from it and ratify an amendment, is, we think, upon principle, unquestionable. The language of the Constitution is, that amendments proposed by Congress, in the mode prescribed, "shall be valid to all intents and purposes, as part of this Constitution, *when ratified by the legislatures of three-fourths of the several States*," &c. By this language is conferred upon the States, by the national Constitution, a special power; it is not a power belonging to them originally by virtue of rights reserved or otherwise.[4] When exercised, as contemplated by the Constitution, by ratifying, it ceases to be a power, and any attempt to exercise it again must be a nullity. But, until so exercised, the power undoubtedly, for a reasonable time at least, remains. Where an amendment has been submitted by Congress four things may follow: 1, the States may not act upon it at all; 2, they may reject it; 3, they may accept it with conditions; and 4, they may ratify it unconditionally. In the first case they must, in effect, be taken to have rejected the amendment, so far as conforming to the constitutional provision is concerned; for that makes no mention either of cases in which no votes are taken, or of those in which the votes are to reject, but only of votes which ratify. The amendment is to be valid *when ratified by three-fourths of the States.*

[1] *U. S. Stat. at Large*, Vol. XV. p. 706.

[2] Id. 708.

[3] Ibid.

[4] Art. V. Const. U. S.

So of the third case, that of conditional ratifications: they do not come within the scope of the Constitution; do not conform to the conditions of the power vested in the States; and such votes must, upon the question of adoption, be accounted as either not cast at all, or as rejecting the amendment. It is only votes of the fourth description that can be counted, and States casting other votes than those are not reckoned at all save to determine the number necessary to complete the ratification.

§ 580. There are, touching conditional ratifications, some precedents from the early days of the republic. When the Constitution was submitted to the States, in 1788, many of them were inclined to append conditions to their ratifications: but, upon full discussion by the best minds of that time, Hamilton, Madison and others, who doubted both the validity and the expediency of such ratifications, the same were made absolute, though with an understanding that amendments should be early adopted to cover the points embraced in the conditions; an understanding which was carried into effect by the first Congress that met under the Constitution in 1789. The result was, that ten of twelve amendments submitted by Congress were adopted by the States, and became a part of the Constitution. All votes, therefore, which do not ratify, or which ratify upon conditions, must stand on the same footing as though they had rejected; and neither they nor the States casting them are to be counted save for the purpose, as we have said, of fixing the proportional number of States necessary to ratify the amendment. Such has been, it is believed, the uniform practice of the State Department in relation to negative votes, or to those cases in which no action has been taken by the States; they have all been ignored, save that in one case, relating as we shall see to the XIV. Amendment, Secretary Seward stated the facts in regard to the votes of Ohio and New Jersey, which had first ratified and then attempted to recede from their ratifications, and of certain lately reconstructed States, in respect to which he had doubts whether they should be counted or not, and therefore brought the subject to the attention of Congress.

§ 581. To the conclusion, that rejection forms no barrier in the way of afterwards ratifying an amendment, it may be objected that it recognizes power in the States to ratify, but no power to reject a proposed amendment. This objection is specious, but it has no real foundation. To say that a State has no power to reject would be untrue; for it is an historical fact that, in point of form, many States have rejected amendments, and it would be puerile to contend that a right to pass upon a proposition does not involve a right either to reject or to ratify it. The real question here is what, under the Constitution, is the consequence of rejection? Does it, or does it not, as to the rejecting State, definitively settle the fate of the amendment? What we insist upon is, that a State has a right at some time to ratify an amendment submitted to it. That is precisely what is asked of it by Congress, and it is that which the Constitution empowers it to do. The authority charged with inspecting such votes, therefore, cannot refuse to receive one, certainly if offered within a reasonable time, until after a ratifying vote shall have been received. This view of the question was well presented by Governor Bramlette, of Kentucky, to whom the resolutions above mentioned rejecting the XIII. Amendment had been communicated for his approval, in a message to the legislature of that State. Declining to return the same with his dissent, on the ground that the action of the legislature was complete without his approval, but yet expressing his dissatisfaction with them, and his regret that the amendment had not been ratified, he undertook, as requested in the second resolution, to forward them to the President and to the presiding officers of the two houses of Congress. In the course of his message he said: —

"Rejection by the present Legislative Assembly only remits the question to the people and the succeeding legislature. Rejection no more precludes future ratification than refusal to adopt any other measure would preclude the action of your successors. When ratified by the legislatures of three-fourths of the several States, the question will be finally withdrawn, and not before. Until ratified it will remain an open question for the ratification of the legislatures of the several States. When ratified by the legislature of a State, it will be final as to such State; and, when ratified by the legislatures of three-fourths of the several States, will be final as to all. Nothing but ratification forecloses the right of action. When ratified all power is expended. Until ratified the right to ratify remains."[1]

§ 582. 2. The question in its affirmative form, whether a

[1] *Acts General Assembly, Ky.*, 1865, p. 157.

State, whose legislature has ratified an amendment, has power to withdraw its ratification or to reject the same, though not free from difficulty, admits, we think, of a satisfactory solution. The question has arisen in several cases, namely, in substance, in those of the slave States, which in 1832–33, and again in 1860 and 1861, by Conventions or legislatures, sought virtually or expressly to repeal the ordinances of the Conventions which, in 1788, ratified the Federal Constitution ; and it arose afterwards, in those of New Jersey, Ohio, and New York, whose legislatures sought to withdraw the assent previously given by those States, the first two to the XIV. and the last to the XV. Amendment. The proceedings of the Southern Conventions in passing nullifying or secession ordinances are so well known that we shall not stop to describe them minutely, particularly as they did not relate to amendments, but to the Constitution itself. In the three Northern States the proceedings were as follows: September 11, 1866, the legislature of New Jersey, by resolution, ratified the XIV. Amendment; a second resolution was passed in April, 1868, by a subsequent legislature, to withdraw that ratification;[1] January 11, 1867, the legislature of Ohio ratified the same amendment, but in January, 1868, in like manner attempted to withdraw its ratification.[2] The legislature of New York, in 1869, ratified the XV. Amendment, but afterwards, in January, 1870, by resolution attempted to withdraw its ratification.[3] These are believed to be the only instances in which the power to withdraw the assent of a State to an amendment has ever been claimed or sought to be exercised. Does that power exist under the Constitution? The question may be considered from the point of view, 1, of the States seeking to withdraw; and, 2, from that of the States which ratify.

§ 583. 1. The power of a State legislature to participate in amending the Federal Constitution exists only by virtue of a special grant in that Constitution. It is a power which it could not assume under any notion of a general right to legislate, for that right is confined within State limits, and to the enactment of ordinary laws. An Act of Congress, even, would not give it the power. The power, moreover, cannot be enlarged by impli-

[1] *U. S. Stat. at Large*, Vol. XV. p. 708.

[2] Ibid.

[3] *U. S. Stat. at Large*, Vol. XVI. p. 1131.

cation, or by reason of any supposed but unexpressed intention of those who granted it, but must be strictly pursued. So, when the State legislature has done the act or thing which the power contemplated and authorized — when the power has been exercised — it, *ipso facto*, ceases to exist, unless it be one of the terms of the grant that it shall continue with a view to its further exercise, which in this case is not pretended. Now, the language of the Constitution is, that an amendment proposed by Congress shall be valid, &c., "*when ratified by the legislatures* of three-fourths of the several States." Suppose, after it has been ratified by three-fourths less one, the legislature of another State notifies the Secretary of State that it has also ratified it, has that amendment not been ratified by the legislatures of three-fourths of the States? If so, it has become valid as a part of the Constitution, and the power of the State legislatures over the subject matter is gone. This no one probably would deny. Is it any more a power exercised, and therefore a power no longer existing, because other States have acted, or enough other States to have made the amendment a part of the Constitution? To hold thus would be to make the constitutional provision read that the amendment should be valid "when ratified by the legislatures of three-fourths of the States, each adhering to its vote until three-fourths of all the legislatures should have voted to ratify." It is enough to say that such is not the language of the Constitution; but that it shall be valid when ratified by the legislatures of three-fourths of the States.

§ 584. 2. The aspect of the question is the same when viewed from the side of the other ratifying States. The first State to ratify an amendment may reasonably be supposed to exert an influence upon the other States. While, doubtless, there is no contract, — for the States have in this matter nothing to make the subject of a contract, — it can never have been intended that a State, having once solemnly assented to a proposition submitted to the States, and thus probably induced like action of other States, should be at liberty at any time thereafter to withdraw such assent. If that were permitted, each State afterwards ratifying would have the same right, and one or more of them would be pretty certain to exercise it. Such a mode of transacting business of so transcendent importance would be puerile.

As the power of withdrawal, if it exist at all, must be implied as conforming to the intention of those who framed the Constitution, it is proper to inquire into the consequences of withdrawal, in order to determine the probability of such an intention. If a State may withdraw its ratification, at what time may it do it? If a change of circumstances should occur such as to make a change of its vote desirable, before three-fourths of the States have ratified, and if the power were conceded then to withdraw, why should not the same power be conceded at any time after a three-fourths vote has been obtained, upon a like change of circumstances? The absurdity of such a rule was made apparent in 1860 and 1861, when the seceding States sought by virtue of it to repeal their several acts of ratification of the Federal Constitution, passed by their Conventions, in some cases, seventy years before. What was then resisted as improper, in relation to the Constitution itself, cannot now be conceded as legal and proper in relation to amendments to the Constitution.

Another consequence is that the power contended for would lead, as it has already done, to inextricable confusion and civil war. It is only those who regard the Constitution as a treaty, basing that instrument upon compact, and finding in it the doctrine of State Sovereignty, who advocate the right to withdraw. They maintained, in 1788, the right of the States to ratify the Federal Constitution conditionally, and then, if the condition were not fulfilled, to recede from their ratifications; also, in 1832–33, maintained with South Carolina the right to nullify the laws of the United States, or virtually to repeal the ratification of the Constitution of 1788, if "the mode and measure of redress" demanded, in relation to the tariff, were not complied with by the United States; and who, in 1861, maintained the same right in relation to slavery.

Waiving the consideration of principles, however, the question may be regarded as settled by authority, if a resolution of Congress upon it is to be taken as decisive. We have seen that when the votes upon the XIV. Amendment were canvassed by the Secretary of State, doubts were entertained by him whether those of New Jersey and Ohio, whose legislatures had first adopted, and then attempted to reject, that amendment, were to be counted as having adopted it. This doubt was settled by Congress, which declared by resolution that they were to be counted among the ratifying States, which was accordingly done.

§ 585. VI. Two further questions may be considered: 1. When Congress has submitted amendments to the States, can it recall them? and 2, How long are amendments thus submitted open to adoption or rejection by the States? 1. The first question must, we think, receive a negative answer. When Congress has submitted amendments, at the time deemed by itself or its constituents to be desirable, to concede to that body the power of afterwards recalling them would be to give to it that of definitively rejecting such amendments; since the recall would withdraw them from the consideration of the States, and thus render their adoption impossible. However this may be, it is enough to justify a negative answer to say that the Federal Constitution, from which alone Congress derives its power to submit amendments to the States, does not provide for recalling them upon any event or condition; and that the power to recall cannot be considered as involved in that to submit, as necessary to its complete execution. It therefore cannot exist.

2. The same consideration will, perhaps, furnish the answer to the second question. The Constitution gives to Congress the power to submit amendments to the States; that is, either to the State legislatures or to Conventions called by the States for this purpose, but there it stops. No power is granted to prescribe conditions as to the time within which the amendments are to be ratified, and hence to do so would be to transcend the power given. The practice of Congress in such cases has always conformed to the implied limitations of the Constitution. It has contented itself with proposing amendments, to become valid as parts of the Constitution, according to the terms of that instrument. It is, therefore, possible, though hardly probable, that an amendment, once proposed, is always open to adoption by the non-acting or non-ratifying States.

The better opinion would seem to be that an alteration of the Constitution proposed to-day has relation to the sentiment and the felt needs of to-day, and that, if not ratified early while that sentiment may fairly be supposed to exist, it ought to be regarded as waived, and not again to be voted upon, unless a second time proposed by Congress.

§ 586. In discussing the question of the right of the States to vote upon proposed amendments at any time after the date of their proposal, it is proper to look into the consequences of such a right. If they have that right, there are now floating about us, as it were, *in nubibus*, several amendments to the Constitution proposed by Congress, which have received the ratification of one or more States, but not of enough to make them valid as parts of that instrument. Congress could not withdraw them, and there is in force in regard to them no recognized statute of limitation. Unless abrogated by amendments subsequently adopted, they are, on the hypothesis stated, still before the American people to be adopted or rejected.

In 1873, the Senate of Ohio acting upon the theory that, once proposed, an amendment to the Constitution is always open to ratification, adopted a joint resolution ratifying the second of the twelve amendments submitted to the States by Congress in 1789, but then rejected, providing that "no law varying the compensation of members of Congress shall take effect until an election for representatives shall have intervened." This resolution, prepared by Madison, was an excellent one; but suppose it had been unjust, proposed perhaps in the interest of a section or of a party, and, failing at the time to receive the requisite majority, it had subsequently, by a concerted rally of those interested in its adoption, been carried without discussion, or a clear expression of the existing public will: is that a true construction of the Constitution which may be followed by so dangerous consequences? And, supposing the right referred to exists, by what majority shall the resurrected amendment be adopted? If proposed in 1789, when the States numbered but thirteen, and when a majority of ten States might have ratified the amendment, how many would have been requisite in 1873, when there were thirty-eight States which would have been called upon to vote? If the answer should be, that twenty-nine States must have voted to ratify, since that number was three-fourths of all the States in 1873, however reasonable such an answer might seem, it would be founded upon no statute or custom of the country, and therefore different opinions as to its reasonableness might well be entertained. Hence the danger of confusion or conflict. We discuss this question here merely to emphasize the dangers involved in the Constitution as it stands, and to show the necessity of legislation to make certain those points upon which doubts may arise in the employment of the constitutional process for amending the fundamental law of the nation. A constitutional statute of limitation, prescribing the time within which proposed amendments shall be adopted or be treated as waived, ought by all means to be passed.

In the foregoing discussion no mention has been made of the powers of State Conventions. If an amendment to the Federal Constitution should be proposed by Congress, and submitted to State Conventions instead of to the legislatures, the powers and disabilities of the two classes of bodies in respect to the amendment would, it is conceived, be precisely the same.

APPENDIX.

A.

EXTRACTS FROM AN ARTICLE PUBLISHED IN THE REVUE DES DEUX MONDES FOR OCTOBER 15, 1871, BY THE FRENCH PUBLICIST, M. ÉD. LABOULAYE, ENTITLED DU POUVOIR CONSTITUANT.

. . . PARMI les principes de 1789, il en est beaucoup qui ont résisté à l'épreuve du temps et dont les bienfaits ont prouvé la solidité. L'égalité civile, la liberté religieuse, la liberté du travail, sont entrées dans nos mœurs et dans nos lois pour n'en plus sortir. Il est toutefois d'autres maximes qui n'ont jamais été appliquées sans traîner après elles le désordre et la ruine. Signaler ces erreurs condamnées par l'expérience, c'est en empêcher le retour, c'est épargner à nos enfans les fléaux que l'ignorance du législateur a déchaînés sur nous.

Au premier rang de ces théories funestes, il faut placer celle du pouvoir constituant telle qu'on l'a conçue en 1789. Établir ou reformer une constitution a été regardé par nos pères comme une œuvre magique qu'on ne peut confier qu'à une assemblée unique, convoquée extraordinairement et maîtresse de refaire à son gré l'état et la société. Et non-seulement on concentre tous les pouvoirs dans les mêmes mains, ce qui est la définition même du despotisme, mais encore on donne aux constituans une autorité telle qu'ils peuvent imposer leur gouvernement à la nation sans lui demander son avis, et lui défendre d'y toucher avant l'époque et par d'autres moyens que ce qu'il leur plait de décider dans leur vanité. En nommant une assemblée de révision, le peuple fait acte de souverain, mais du même coup il abdique au profit de ses représentans, sans se réserver seulement le droit de contrôler et d'accepter ce qu'on fait en son nom. Les constituans ne sont pas les mandataires, ils sont les maîtres du pays.

C'est ainsi que les choses se sont passées en 1789; on peut juger de l'arbre par ses fruits. Une assemblée souveraine, dont rien ne gênait la volonté, la passion ni le caprice, a détruit tout ce qu'elle a touché : monarchie, administration, finances, armée, marine, église ; elle a condamné un peuple trop confiant à traverser toutes les misères de l'anarchie en lui montrant à l'horizon une liberté qui fuyait toujours. C'est à ce prix que la France a été dotée d'une constitution qui n'était même pas viable. Promulguée avec éclat le 14 septembre 1791, l'œuvre de l'assemblée constituante disparaissait le 21 septembre 1792 devant ce jugement dédaigneux et mérité: "la convention déclare qu'il ne peut y avoir de constitution que celle qui est acceptée par le peuple." Ni cet échec, ni cet arrêt significatif, n'ont empêché les législateurs de 1848 de reprendre avec une pieuse ignorance la tradition d'erreur qui datait de 1789; ils ont mené la France au même abîme et par le même chemin. La leçon nous a-t-elle profité? Non, nous en sommes restés au même point; nous n'avons pas perdu une seule de nos illusions. L'expérience n'instruit que ceux qui doutent et qui cherchent, elle n'existe pas pour un peuple que la foi révolutionnaire illumine, et qui se croit naïvement en possession de la vérité absolue.

Étudier la nature et le caractère du pouvoir constituant n'est donc pas une œuvre de pure curiosité; c'est une question qui porte en ses flancs l'avenir de la France. Il est utile, il est nécessaire de montrer comment d'une vérité mal comprise le législateur de 1789 a tiré les conséquences les plus fausses et les plus désastreuses. Il faut voir comment, en partant du principe de la souveraineté nationale, il en est arrivé à confisquer cette souveraineté au profit d'une assemblée que la toute-puissance a enivrée et perdue.

Pour faire toucher du doigt l'erreur de nos pères, je dirai de quelle façon l'Angleterre et les États-Unis s'y prennent pour réformer leurs constitutions. Il y a là deux systèmes différens d'apparence, mais animés d'un même esprit. Si l'Angleterre ne peut nous servir d'exemple, il n'en est pas de même de l'Amérique; elle nous offre d'excellens modèles, et il est inutile de raisonner à l'aventure quand on a sous la main la solution du problème. . . .

Si l'Angleterre ne peut nous servir d'exemple, il en est autrement de l'Amérique, et pour plus d'une raison.

C'est aux États-Unis que nous avons emprunté les constitutions écrites, les déclarations de droits, l'idée du pouvoir constituant et le nom même des conventions, c'est-à-dire des assemblées qui sont spécialement chargées de faire et de réviser les constitutions. On n'a point assez étudié cette influence des États-Unis, quoiqu'elle soit hautement confessée par ceux qu'en 1789 on appelait les Américains, c'est-à-dire les Lameth, les Lafayette, les Noailles et leurs anciens compagnons de la guerre d'indépendance. Il est vrai que l'imitation n'a pas toujours été heureuse, et que plus d'une fois, en exagérant un principe juste, on en a fait une erreur; mais trop souvent aussi l'assemblée constituante a préféré aux idées américaines des chimères inventées par les élèves de Rousseau. C'est ce qui est arrivé dans la question qui nous occupe. Sieyès l'a emporté sur Lafayette, et en confondant le pouvoir constituant et le pouvoir législatif il a tout brouillé et tout perdu.

L'Amérique a encore pour nous ce grand avantage qu'elle est une démocratie. Le fondement de ses institutions, c'est la souveraineté du peuple. C'est à la nation seule qu'il appartient de choisir la constitution qui lui convient, car, ainsi que l'écrivait John Adams dès l'année 1775, le peuple est la source de toute autorité, l'origine de tout pouvoir. C'est là un principe universellement reçu aux États-Unis, principe que personne ne conteste et que chacun s'efforce d'appliquer de son mieux. Quoique les Américains aient gardé l'esprit juridique de leurs ancêtres de la Grande-Bretagne, quoique dans le droit civil ils s'attachent de préférence à la coutume et aux précédens, néanmoins en politique ils n'invoquent que la volonté nationale. Tout leur souci est d'assurer dans sa plénitude la souveraineté du peuple et de ne la laisser confisquer par personne, — et, grâce à une pratique aussi sincère que hardie, ils en sont arrivés, non moins heureusement que les Anglais, à des institutions protectrices de la sécurité, de la liberté, et du bien-être de tous les citoyens.

Enfin l'Amérique est une fédération, aujourd'hui composée de trente-sept états particuliers et d'un gouvernement général. Il ne se passe guère d'années qu'on n'établisse une constitution, qu'on n'en réforme une autre. Depuis moins d'un siècle, on compte plus de cent soixante-dix essais de ce genre; il n'en est pas un seul qui ait jamais inquiété le pays. Ce qui en Europe est une crise, une maladie dangereuse, est aux États-Unis une fonction habituelle de la vie politique, une institution régulière. On conçoit quel est pour nous l'intérêt de ces expériences réitérées; nous ne pouvons pas avoir la prétention d'être plus républicains, plus démocrates que les Américains, et leur exemple nous démontrera combien nous sommes encore entichés d'idées despotiques. Nous exaltons en paroles la souveraineté du peuple, mais en fait les partis ne la respectent guère, tout leur effort consiste à l'éluder ou à l'usurper.

Pour bien comprendre le jeu des constitutions américaines et celui des conventions, il faut donc se faire une idée nette de la façon dont on entend et dont on pratique aux États-Unis la souveraineté du peuple. Sur ce point, nous avons beaucoup à apprendre et beaucoup à oublier.[1]

Le principe dominant, celui qui pénètre et anime toutes les institutions américaines, c'est que l'ensemble des citoyens, hommes, femmes, enfans, a droit de régler son gouvernement comme il l'entend. Aux États-Unis, on ne connait pas l'idée de légitimité qui fait du gouvernement la propriété d'une famille privilégiée; on n'admet pas davantage la maxime doctrinaire qui donne à la raison, à la justice, le droit de commander, car c'est reculer le problème et non le résoudre. Qui décidera ce qui est juste et ce qui est raisonnable? Les Américains prennent les choses de moins haut, et restent sur un terrain plus solide. Pour eux, c'est une loi divine, c'est l'instinct, c'est la sympathie qui fonde et maintient les sociétés humaines. Il y a là un fait naturel qu'il n'appartient pas à l'homme de changer; mais quant au gouvernement, que les Américains réduisent au maniement des intérêts généraux de la communauté, c'est une œuvre tout humaine; son objet est d'assurer le bien-être et la liberté de chacun et de tous par la volonté et le concours de chacun et de tous. Comme le disait l'excellent Lincoln en consacrant le cimetière de Gettysburg, "cette nation, conçue dans la liberté, vouée à l'égalité, veut maintenir sur la terre le gouvernement du peuple par le peuple et pour le peuple." Ces simples paroles contiennent tout le système politique des États-Unis. . . .

Qu'on lise le discours prononcé en 1861 à la convention d'Alabama par M. Williams L. Yancey; on y reconnaîtra des sophismes qui nous sont familiers. "On demande que l'ordonnance de sécession soit soumise au peuple," disait M. Yancey. "Cette proposition repose sur l'idée qu'il y a une différence entre le peuple et ses délégués à la convention. C'est une erreur. Il y a une différence entre le peuple et les députés ordinaires, parce que certains pouvoirs sont réservés au peuple, et que l'assemblée législative ne peut pas les exercer; mais la convention est omnipotente. il n'y a point de pouvoirs réservés. Le peuple

[1] Dans tout ce que je vais dire de l'Amérique, mon autorité est l'excellent ouvrage de John Alexander Jameson, juge à la cour supérieure de Chicago et professeur de droit constitutionnel à l'université de la même ville. Ce livre, intitulé *The Constitutional Convention, its history, powers and modes of proceeding*, a été publié à New-York en 1867. Pour la richesse des documens et la solidité des jugemens, il peut soutenir la comparaison avec le commentaire de Story sur la constitution des États-Unis.

est ici dans la personne de ses députés. Vie, liberté, propriété, tout est dans nos mains. . . . Tous nos décrets sont suprêmes sans ratification, parce que ce sont les décrets du peuple agissant dans sa capacité souveraine." [1]

Cette doctrine, qui a enfanté la guerre de la sécession, les publicistes américains la repoussent avec horreur. Pour eux, c'est un démenti donné à l'expérience et au bon sens; le jurisconsulte Jameson ne craint pas de l'appeler *une des plus impudentes hérésies de notre temps.*[2] En effet c'est la négation de toutes les maximes, de toutes les pratiques constitutionnelles qui ont fait la grandeur et la prospérité des États-Unis. Là-bas, il est passé en axiome que le plus sûr moyen de perdre une république, c'est de confier le pouvoir législatif à une assemblée unique; combien la ruine n'est-elle pas plus prompte et plus certaine, si l'on confie le pouvoir constituant à une seule chambre? N'est-ce pas l'omnipotence d'une assemblée unique qui a toujours fait avorter en France les essais de liberté? D'ailleurs sur quel principe appuyer cette étrange concession d'un pouvoir absolu? Toutes les constitutions proclament que la souveraineté est inhérente à la société politique, et que par conséquent elle est indivisible et inaliénable. La déléguer sans condition à une poignée de législateurs, n'est-ce pas la diviser et l'aliéner? Un peuple n'a pas plus le droit d'abdiquer sa souveraineté qu'un individu n'a le droit de vendre sa liberté. Quelle que soit l'ignorance ou la faiblesse d'une nation, ce transfert, cet abandon de la souveraineté est nul de soi; rien ne peut légitimer l'usurpation de ceux qui ne sauraient être que les mandataires et les serviteurs du pays.

Tels sont les principes reçus aux États-Unis, et, selon moi, ce sont les vrais principes de la démocratie. Si nous ne les avons jamais suivis, c'est que l'école révolutionnaire a faussé toutes nos idées. La souveraineté du peuple n'a été chez nous qu'un cri de guerre exploité par quelques ambitieux: elle n'a jamais servi qu'à détruire; quand nous voudrons en faire un rouage régulier, une force conservatrice, nous prendrons exemple des Américains. . . .

Rentrons en France, voyons comment on y a compris et exercé le pouvoir constituant.

Dans l'ancienne monarchie, il n'y a pas de constitution écrite; le seul souverain et le seul législateur, c'est le roi. Il est donc naturel que l'idée d'un pouvoir constituant ne paraisse qu'à la veille de la révolution; Sieyès s'en déclare l'inventeur. "Une idée saine et utile," nous dit-il, "fut établie en 1788: c'est la division du pouvoir constituant et des pouvoirs constitués. Elle comptera parmi les découvertes qui font faire un pas à la science; elle est due aux Français." [3]

Dans une note sur Sieyès,[4] Lafayette remarque qu'avant 1788 les Américains avaient eu des conventions pour réformer leurs constitutions particulières, et pour rédiger leur constitution fédérale, que par conséquent l'idée du pouvoir constituant n'est pas une invention française. Il ajoute avec raison que les Français, loin de faire sur ce point un pas à la science, l'ont plutôt fait ré-

[1] Jameson, p. 296.

[2] Jameson, p. 3.

[3] Discours sur le projet de constitution et sur *la jurie constitutionnaire.* — *Moniteur* du 7 thermidor an III (25 juillet 1795).

[4] *Mémoires de Lafayette,* t. IV. p. 36.

trograder par le mélange des fonctions constituantes et législatives dans l'assemblée de 1789 et dans la convention nationale, tandis qu'en Amérique ces fonctions ont toujours été distinctes. C'était mettre le doigt sur une des erreurs fondamentales du système français, — mais en 1789 on était infatué de Sieyès et de ses visions politiques; quant à l'ami de Washington, on l'admirait, mais on ne l'écoutait pas. Lorsque l'assemblée, près de se séparer, décréta le chapitre de la constitution qui traite de la révision, toutes les propositions de Lafayette furent écartées. "M. de Lafayette," disait le *Journal de Paris* du 1er septembre 1791, "n'a voté pour aucun de ces décrets: toutes ses vues y étaient trop opposées, il a trop bien étudié les *pouvoirs constituans* pour vouloir confier leur mission aux *pouvoirs constitués;* mais, lorsqu'il a cité l'exemple de l'Amérique, on a dit : *Ah! l'Amérique!*"[1]

J'ai grand peur qu'en parcourant ces pages plus d'un lecteur ne pousse le même cri. Renoncer à un préjugé révolutionnaire n'est pas chose aisée pour un Français. Cependant en l'an III, au sortir des excès de la convention, le législateur, effrayé de son omnipotence, avait introduit dans la constitution un système de révision imité des Américains, et depuis l'an III combien de fois les événemens n'ont-ils pas donné raison au général Lafayette !

Tandis qu'aux États-Unis l'appel d'une convention est un fait aussi simple et aussi pacifique que la convocation d'une législature ordinaire, a-t-on jamais vu en France une assemblée constituante qui n'ait amené une révolution? L'œuvre de ces législateurs tout-puissans a-t-elle jamais été viable? La constitution de 1848 a-t-elle été moins chimérique et moins funeste que celle de 1791? Oserait-on remettre en vigueur cette charte républicaine que la France a laissée tomber avec une complète indifférence? Aujourd'hui même ne sentons-nous pas que le terrain tremble sous nos pieds? Si nous avions trouvé la vérité, en serions-nous réduits à marcher au hasard et à tâtonner dans la nuit?

Toute notre théorie du pouvoir constituant repose sur une erreur et sur un sophisme. L'erreur, c'est la délégation de la souveraineté : la souveraineté ne se délègue pas. Le sophisme, c'est l'identité du peuple et de ses représentans, la confusion du mandataire et du mandant. Nous aurons beau faire des discours pompeux et crier que le monde a les yeux sur nous, cette conception du pouvoir constituant n'en est pas moins la négation même de la souveraineté du peuple. Pour les partis, c'est le moyen infaillible de se jouer de la volonté nationale, et de soumettre le pays au despotisme d'une minorité.

De cette double erreur, comme d'une source empoisonnée, sortent toutes nos fautes et toutes nos misères.

Les constituans étant considérés comme le peuple même en vertu de la délégation qu'ils ont reçu, et le peuple étant l'origine de tout pouvoir, nos politiques en concluent que l'assemblée possède tous les droits de la souveraineté, et suivant eux (ce qui est encore une erreur révolutionnaire) ces droits sont illimités. L'autorité de l'assemblée est donc absolue. Vie, liberté, propriété, religion, tout est entre les mains de cet abrégé de la nation. En d'autres termes, c'est au despotisme que nous nous en remettons du soin de créer la liberté. Il faut toute la force de l'habitude pour nous aveugler sur la fausseté et le danger d'une pareille invention.

1 *Mémoires de Lafayette*, t. III. p. 113.

A cette assemblée, armée déjà d'un pouvoir formidable, on soumet le gouvernement tout entier. La première garantie de la liberté, la séparation des pouvoirs, disparaît. C'est toujours une suite de la même erreur. On suppose qu'en l'absence d'une constitution le peuple gouverne par lui-même, et l'assemblée représente le peuple. C'est la fiction même sur laquelle les césars édifièrent leur tyrannie. Quel est l'effet de cette concentration de pouvoirs? Écoutons Daunou décrivant en 1793 le désordre qu'il avait sous les yeux. "Une assemblée chargée de faire une constitution mutile et paralyse par sa seule existence toutes les autorités qui sont autour d'elle. Elle est trop facilement entraînée à confondre le droit de créer et de modifier chaque pouvoir avec le droit de l'exercer immédiatement. Elle devient une puissance énorme et dictatoriale qui ne peut être longtemps salutaire. C'est une autorité presque nécessairement despotique et tellement contre nature qu'elle opprime ceux même qui l'exercent." [1] N'est-ce pas là l'histoire de la convention?

En vertu du même sophisme, l'assemblée, après avoir achevé son œuvre, ne la soumet pas au vote populaire. Le mandataire s'attribue le droit de lier son commettant sans lui demander son aveu. Pour un Américain, il y a là une usurpation de la souveraineté, un crime de lèse-majesté nationale. Un Français qui appartient à l'école révolutionnaire ne voit dans cet étrange procédé que la conséquence logique de l'hypothèse, plus que téméraire, qui identifie le représentant et le représenté. Pourquoi consulter le peuple? C'est lui qui a parlé par la bouche de ses députés.

Enfin, et ceci ne me paraît justifiable en aucune façon, non-seulement nos assemblées constituantes imposent au pays une constitution qui d'ordinaire lui déplaît, mais elles lui interdisent d'y toucher avant l'époque qu'il leur convient de fixer. Dès par l'architecte qui a construit le nouvel édifice politique, il est défendu au peuple souverain de se trouver mal logé et de choisir un autre abri, — et cela pendant de longues années. Sait-on quand il était permis à la France de modifier la constitution de 1791, cette constitution qui mourut au berceau? En l'an de grâce 1821! A cette date, la France avait traversé six révolutions, et elle en était à son huitième gouvernement.

[1] Daunou, *Essai sur la Constitution.* Paris, 1793, p. 55.

B.

COMPLETE LIST OF CONSTITUTIONAL CONVENTIONS HELD IN THE UNITED STATES.

N. B. In this list are included many Conventions which framed Constitutions or amendments that never took effect, having been rejected by the people, or that took effect only for a short time, and were annulled by superior authority, as those framed by the seceding States during the Rebellion, and in the earliest attempts made by them at reconstruction.

The section marks refer to the sections *ante*, where the Conventions indicated are described or referred to.

NAMES.	DATE OF ASSEMBLING.	DATE OF ADJOURNMENT.	REMARKS.
1. Continental Congress (2d).	May 10, 1775.	March 1, 1781.	This body was not properly a Convention, but for convenience is classed as such, like the Revolutionary Conventions in general. The Constitution framed by it was submitted to the legislatures of the various States. §§ 159–162, 502, 503.
2. South Carolina.	November 1, 1775.	March 26, 1776.	This Convention was the "Provincial Congress" of South Carolina. The Constitution framed by it was not submitted to the people. It was subsequently held by the Supreme Court of the State to be a mere act of the General Assembly, repealable at pleasure. See §§ 133, 134, 136, note 2.
3. South Carolina.	January 5, 1778.	March 19, 1778.	This so-called Convention was the General Assembly sitting as a Convention, without warrant, and the Constitution framed by it was subsequently held by the Supreme Court of the State to be a mere act of the General Assembly, and as such to be repealable at pleasure. See §§ 135, 136, note 2.
4. South Carolina.	May 12, 1788.	May 23, 1788.	Called to ratify the Federal Constitution. § 167.
5. South Carolina.	May, 1790.	June 3, 1790.	The Constitution framed by this Convention was not submitted to the people. § 218.
6. South Carolina.	December 17, 1860.	January 5, 1861.	Secession Convention. The Constitution framed by it was not submitted to the people. §§ 247–250.
7. South Carolina.	September 13, 1865.	September 27, 1865.	Reconstruction Convention. The Constitution framed by it was not submitted to the people, and, together with the government organized under it, was subsequently, by the Acts of Congress of March 2d and 23d, and July 19, 1867, declared not to be a legal government. §§ 250–258.
8. South Carolina.	January 14, 1868.	March 17, 1868.	Reconstruction Convention called under the Acts of Congress of March, 1867. The Constitution framed by it was submitted to the people April 14 and 16, 1868, and adopted by a vote of 70,558 for, to 27,288 against. §§ 258 *a*–258 *d*.

NAMES.	DATE OF ASSEMBLING.	DATE OF ADJOURNMENT.	REMARKS.
9. New Hampshire.	December 21, 1775.	January 5, 1776.	This body was the "Congress" of New Hampshire. The Constitution framed by it was not submitted to the people. § 131.
10. New Hampshire.	June 10, 1778.	June 5, 1779.	The Constitution framed by this Convention was submitted to the people and rejected. § 132.
11. New Hampshire.	2d Tuesday June, 1781.	October 31, 1783.	The Constitution framed by it was submitted to the people in town meetings and adopted. § 132. This Convention submitted three different Constitutions to the people, two of which were rejected and one adopted. It held eight sessions, reconvening from time to time in pursuance of the original Convention Act.
12. New Hampshire.	1788.	June 21, 1788.	Called to ratify the Federal Constitution. § 167.
13. New Hampshire.	September 7, 1791.	September 5, 1792.	The Constitution framed by it was submitted to the people and adopted. §§ 217, 218.
14. New Hampshire.	November 6, 1850.	April 17, 1851.	At its first session, this Convention proposed amendments, which were submitted to the people and rejected. At a second session, in 1851, other amendments were proposed, which were submitted to the people, and three of them adopted. §§ 217, 218.
15. New Hampshire.	December 6, 1876.	December 16, 1876.	The Constitution framed by it was submitted to the people and adopted, March 13, 1877. §§ 217, 218.
16. Virginia.	May 6, 1776.	June 29, 1776.	The Constitution framed by this Convention was not submitted to the people. § 138.
17. Virginia.	June 2, 1788.	June 27, 1788.	Called to ratify the Federal Constitution. § 167.
18. Virginia.	October 5, 1829.	January 15, 1830.	The Constitution framed by this Convention was submitted to the people and adopted by a vote of 26,055 for, to 15,563 against. §§ 217, 219.
19. Virginia.	October 14, 1850.	August 1, 1851.	The Constitution framed by this Convention was submitted to the people, and adopted by a vote of 67,562 for, to 9,938 against. §§ 217, 219.
20. Virginia.	February 13, 1861.	August 1, 1061.	Secession Convention. The ordinance of secession, and the Constitution amended by it, were submitted to the people and ratified by a vote of 128,884 for, to 32,734 against. §§ 178, 247-250.
21. Virginia.	June 11, 1861.	August 21, 1861.	By this Convention the reconstruction of the State was attempted, and proceedings taken for forming the new State of West Virginia. The question of forming such new State only was submitted to the people to be embraced therein, and answered in the affirmative. §§ 178, 247-250.
22. Virginia.	February 13, 1864.	April 11, 1864.	This was the Virginia legislature acting as a Convention, under the authority of the people, for the reconstruction of the State. The Constitution framed by it was not submitted to the people. The government organized under it received a partial rec-

NAMES.	DATE OF ASSEMBLING.	DATE OF ADJOURNMENT.	REMARKS.
			ognition from Congress, but was by the Acts of Congress of March 2d and 23d, and July 19, 1867, declared not to be a legal State government. §§ 179-181, 250-258.
23. Virginia.	December 3, 1867.	April 17, 1868.	Reconstruction Convention, called under the Acts of Congress of March, 1867. The Constitution framed by it was not submitted to the people until April, 1869, when submission was required by Congress. The clauses relating to the test oath and to disfranchisement, which were separately submitted, were rejected, and the remainder of the Constitution was adopted by a vote of 210,585 for, to 9,136 against. §§ 258 *a*-258 *d*.
24. New Jersey.	June 10, 1776.	July 2, 1776.	The Constitution framed by it was not submitted to the people. § 139.
25. New Jersey.	2d Tuesday December, 1787.	December 18, 1787.	Called to ratify the Federal Constitution. § 167.
26. New Jersey.	May 14, 1844.	June 29, 1844.	The Constitution framed by it was submitted to the people. §§ 217, 219.
	June 1, 1881.		At the date here mentioned, met a Constitutional Commission, appointed by the Governor, under an Act of the legislature, to propose to that body amendments to the Constitution; hence, not a Constitutional Convention. §§ 546 *a*-546 *d*.
27. New York.	July 9, 1776.	April 20, 1777.	The Constitution framed by it was not submitted to the people. §§ 150-152.
28. New York.	June 17, 1778.	July 26, 1788.	Called to ratify the Federal Constitution. § 167.
29. New York.	October 13, 1801.	October 27, 1801.	The five amendments framed by this Convention were not submitted to the people. §§ 217, 219.
30. New York.	August 28, 1821.	November 10, 1821.	The Constitution framed by it was submitted to the people in February, 1822, and was adopted by a vote of 74,732 for, to 41,402 against. §§ 217, 219.
31. New York.	June 1, 1846.	October 9, 1846.	The Constitution framed by it was submitted to the people in November, 1846, and adopted by a vote of 221,528 for, to 92,436 against. §§ 217, 219.
32. New York.	June 4, 1867.	February 28, 1868.	The Constitution framed by it was submitted to the people and rejected, save Art. VI., relating to the judiciary, which was adopted. §§ 217, 218.
	December 4, 1872.	March 15, 1873.	Between these dates sat a Constitutional Commission, appointed by the Governor, under an Act of the legislature, to propose to that body amendments to the Constitution; hence not a Constitutional Convention. §§ 546 *a*-546 *d*.
33. Pennsylvania.	July 15, 1776.	September 28, 1776.	The Constitution framed by it was not submitted to the people. §§ 143, 144.
34. Pennsylvania.	November 10, 1783.	September 25, 1784.	Council of Censors. Abortive. § 222.
35. Pennsylvania.	November 20, 1787.	December 12, 1787.	Called to ratify the Federal Constitution. § 167.

NAMES.	DATE OF ASSEMBLING.	DATE OF ADJOURNMENT.	REMARKS.
36. Pennsylvania.	November 24, 1789.	September 2, 1790.	This Convention framed a Constitution, and adjourned February 26, 1790, that the people might examine it. August 9, 1790, the Convention reassembled, and September 2, 1790, proclaimed the Constitution, which was not otherwise submitted to the people. §§ 221, 222.
37. Pennsylvania.	May 2, 1837.	February 22, 1838.	The Constitution framed by it was submitted to the people and adopted by a vote of 113,971 for, to 112,759 against. §§ 217, 219.
38. Pennsylvania.	November 3, 1872.	December 27, 1873.	This Convention framed a Constitution, and November 11, 1873, adjourned to December 27, 1873. In the mean time the Constitution was submitted to the people, and adopted by a vote of 293,564 for, to 109,198 against. §§ 217, 219.
39. Maryland.	August 14, 1776.	November 11, 1776.	The Constitution framed by it was not submitted to the people. § 145.
40. Maryland.	April 21, 1788.	April 28, 1788.	Called to ratify the Federal Constitution. § 167.
41. Maryland.	November 4, 1850.	May 13, 1851.	The Constitution framed by it was submitted to the people June 4, 1851, and adopted. §§ 224, 225.
42. Maryland.	April 27, 1864.	September 6, 1864.	The Constitution framed by it was submitted to the people October 12 and 13, 1864, and adopted by a home vote of 27,541 for, to 29,536 against, and a soldiers' vote of 2,633 for, to 263 against. §§ 217, 218.
43. Maryland.	May 8, 1867.	August 17, 1867.	The Constitution framed by it was submitted to the people, September 18, 1867, and adopted by a vote of 27,152 for, to 23,036 against. §§ 217, 218.
44. Delaware.	August 27, 1776.	September 20, 1776.	The Constitution framed by it was not submitted to the people. §§ 141, 142.
45. Delaware.	1787.	December 7, 1787.	Called to ratify the Federal Constitution. § 167.
46. Delaware.	June, 1792.	June 12, 1792.	The Constitution framed by it was not submitted to the people. §§ 217, 219, 225.
47. Delaware.	November 8, 1831.	December 2, 1831.	The Constitution framed by it was not submitted to the people. §§ 217, 218.
48. Delaware.	1st Tuesday December, 1852.	April 30, 1853.	The Constitution framed by it was submitted to the people and rejected. §§ 217, 218.
49. Georgia.	1st Tuesday October, 1776.	February 5, 1777.	The Constitution framed by it was not submitted to the people. § 147.
50. Georgia.	October 26, 1787.	January 2, 1788.	Called to ratify the Federal Constitution. § 167.
51. Georgia.	November 4, 1788.	November 24, 1788.	The Constitution framed by it was submitted to a Convention called for the purpose of ratifying or rejecting it, which met January 4, 1789. §§ 148, 149.
52. Georgia.	January 4, 1789.	1789.	Called to pass upon the Constitution framed by the next preceding Convention. It proposed amendments, which were submitted to the following Convention. §§ 148, 149, 218.
53. Georgia.	May 4, 1789.	May 6, 1789.	Called to pass upon the Constitution framed and amended by

NAMES.	DATE OF ASSEMBLING.	DATE OF ADJOURNMENT.	REMARKS.
			the preceding two Conventions. §§ 148, 149, 218.
54. Georgia.	May 2, 1795.	May 6, 1789.	This Convention framed amendments to the Constitution of 1789, but did not submit them to the people. §§ 217, 218.
55. Georgia.	May 8, 1798.	May 30, 1798.	The Constitution framed by it was not submitted to the people. §§ 217, 218.
56. Georgia.	May, 1833.	May 15, 1833.	Amendments to the Constitution were proposed and submitted by this Convention, but were rejected by the people. §§ 217, 219.
57. Georgia.	1st Tuesday May, 1839.	May 16, 1839.	The Constitution framed by it was submitted to the people and adopted. §§ 217, 219.
58. Georgia.	January 16, 1861.	March 23, 1861.	Secession Convention. The Constitution framed by it was submitted to the people and adopted. §§ 247-250.
59. Georgia.	October 25, 1865.	November 8, 1865.	Reconstruction Convention. The Constitution framed by it was submitted to and adopted by the people, but the government organized under it was by the Acts of Congress of March 2d and 23d, and July 19, 1868, declared not to be a legal State government. §§ 250-258.
60. Georgia.	December 9, 1867.	March 11, 1868.	Reconstruction Convention, called under the Acts of Congress of March, 1867. The Constitution framed by it was submitted to the people, and adopted by a vote of 89,007 for, to 71,309 against, March 11, 1868. §§ 258 *a*-258 *d*.
61. Georgia.	July 11, 1877.	August 25, 1877.	The Constitution framed by it was submitted to the people and adopted, December 5, 1877. §§ 217, 218.
62. North Carolina.	November 12, 1776.	December 18, 1776.	The Constitution framed by it was not submitted to the people. § 146.
63. North Carolina.	July 21, 1788.	August 4, 1788.	Called to ratify the Federal Constitution. § 167.
64. North Carolina.	1789.	November 21, 1789.	Called to ratify the Federal Constitution. § 167.
65. North Carolina.	June 4, 1835.	July 11, 1835.	The amendments framed by it were submitted to the people and adopted by a vote of 26,771 for, to 21,606 against. §§ 217, 219.
66. North Carolina.	May 20, 1861.	1861.	Secession Convention. The ordinance of secession and the Constitution framed by this Convention were not submitted to the people. §§ 247-250.
67. North Carolina.	October 2, 1865.	October 19, 1865.	Reconstruction Convention. Amendments proposed by it were submitted to the people, and adopted by a vote of 20,506 for, to 2,002 against. May 24, 1866, the Convention reassembled and revised the Constitution, but their work was rejected by the people by a vote of 19,570 for, to 21,552 against. The government organized under this Constitution was, by the Acts of Congress of March 2d and 23d, and July 19, 1867, declared not to be a legal State government. §§ 250-258.

NAMES.	DATE OF ASSEMBLING.	DATE OF ADJOURNMENT.	REMARKS.
68. North Carolina.	January 14, 1868.	March 16, 1868.	Reconstruction Convention, called under the Acts of Congress of March, 1867. The Constitution framed by it was submitted to the people and adopted by a vote of 93,118 for, to 74,009 against. §§ 258 *a*–258 *d*.
69. North Carolina.	September 6, 1875.	October 11, 1875.	The Constitution framed by it was submitted to the people and ratified by a vote of 122,912 for, to 108,829 against. §§ 217, 218.
70. Vermont.	July 2, 1777.	July 8, 1777.	The Constitution framed by it was not submitted to the people. §§ 153, 154.
71. Vermont.	1st Wednesday June, 1785.	1st Thursday February, 1786.	Council of Censors. It submitted the amendments framed by it to the next following Convention. §§ 217, 220.
72. Vermont.	1st Thursday June, 1786.	1786.	Called to ratify the amendments framed by the last Council of Censors. §§ 217, 220.
73. Vermont.	January, 1791.	January 10, 1791.	Called to ratify the Federal Constitution. § 167.
74. Vermont.	1792.	179–.	Council of Censors. It submitted the amendments framed by it to the Convention next following. §§ 217, 220.
75. Vermont.	July 3, 1793.	July 9, 1793.	Called to ratify the amendments framed by the last Council of Censors. §§ 217, 220.
76. Vermont.	1799.		Council of Censors. Abortive. §§ 217, 220.
77. Vermont.	1806.		Council of Censors. Abortive. §§ 217, 220.
78. Vermont.	1813.		Council of Censors. Abortive. §§ 217, 220.
79. Vermont.	June 7, 1820.	March 26, 1821.	Council of Censors. It submitted the amendments framed by it to the next following Convention. §§ 217, 220.
80. Vermont.	February 21, 1822.	February 23, 1822.	Called to ratify five amendments to the Constitution framed by the last Council of Censors. All were rejected. §§ 217, 220.
81. Vermont.	June 6, 1827.	December 1, 1827.	Council of Censors. It submitted amendments to the Constitution framed by it to the next following Convention. §§ 217, 220.
82. Vermont.	June 26, 1828.		Called to ratify the amendments to the Constitution framed by the last Council of Censors, some of which it adopted. §§ 217, 220.
83. Vermont.	1834.	January 15, 1835.	Council of Censors. It submitted amendments to the Constitution framed by it to the next following Convention. §§ 217, 220.
84. Vermont.	January 6, 1836.	January 14, 1836.	Called to ratify the amendments to the Constitution framed by the last Council of Censors, twelve of which it adopted. §§ 217, 220.
85. Vermont.	June 2, 1841.	February 15, 1842.	Council of Censors. It submitted amendments to the Constitution framed by it to the next following Convention. §§ 217, 220.
86. Vermont.	January 4, 1843.	January 12, 1843.	Called to ratify the amendments to the Constitution framed by the last Council of Censors, all of which it rejected. §§ 217, 220.
87. Vermont.	June 7, 1848.	February 28, 1849.	Council of Censors. It submitted

NAMES.	DATE OF ASSEMBLING.	DATE OF ADJOURNMENT.	REMARKS.
			amendments to the Constitution framed by it to the next following Convention. §§ 217, 220.
88. Vermont.	January 2, 1850.	January 14, 1850.	Called to ratify the amendments to the Constitution framed by the last Council of Censors, ten of which it adopted. §§ 217, 220.
89. Vermont.	June 6, 1855.	February 26, 1856.	Council of Censors. It submitted amendments to the Constitution framed by it to the next following Convention. §§ 217, 220.
90. Vermont.	January 7, 1857.	January 12, 1857.	Called to ratify the amendments to the Constitution framed by the last Council of Censors, all of which it rejected. §§ 217, 220.
91. Vermont.	June 4, 1862.	October 25, 1862.	Council of Censors. Abortive. §§ 217, 220.
92. Vermont.	June 2, 1869.	October 22, 1869.	Council of Censors. It submitted amendments to the Constitution framed by it to the next following Convention. §§ 217, 220.
93. Vermont.	June 8, 1870.	June 15, 1870.	Called to ratify amendments to the Constitution framed by the last Council of Censors, three of which, including one abolishing the Council of Censors, were adopted. §§ 217, 220.
94. Massachusetts.	January, 1778.	February 28, 1778.	The Constitution framed by it was submitted to the people and rejected. § 156.
95. Massachusetts.	September 1, 1779.	June 16, 1780.	The Constitution framed by it was submitted to the people and adopted. §§ 157, 158.
96. Massachusetts.	January 9, 1788.	February 7, 1788.	Called to ratify the Federal Constitution. § 167.
97. Massachusetts.	November 15, 1820.	January 9, 1821.	The Constitution framed by it was submitted to the people and adopted. §§ 217, 218.
98. Massachusetts.	May 4, 1853.	August 1, 1853.	The Constitution framed by it was submitted to the people and rejected by a vote of 63,222 for, to 68,150 against. §§ 217, 219.
99. Federal Convention.	May 14, 1787.	September 17, 1787.	The Constitution framed by it was submitted to Conventions in the several States, and adopted. §§ 162–166.
100. Connecticut.	January 4, 1788.	January 9, 1788.	Called to ratify the Federal Constitution. § 167.
101. Connecticut.	August 26, 1818.	September 16, 1818.	The Constitution framed by it was submitted to the people October 5, 1818, and adopted by a vote of 13,918 for, to 12,361 against. §§ 217, 219.
102. Rhode Island.	1790.	May 29, 1790.	Called to ratify the Federal Constitution. §§ 167.
103. Rhode Island.	1824.		The Constitution framed by it was submitted to the people and rejected. §§ 217, 219, 226.
104. Rhode Island.	1834.		Abortive. §§ 217, 219, 226.
105. Rhode Island.	October 4, 1841.	November 18, 1841.	The "People's Convention." The Constitution framed by it was submitted to the people of the State at large, and adopted. §§ 226, 246.
106. Rhode Island.	November, 1841.	February, 1842.	Called by the Charter government. The Convention framed and published a Constitution in November, 1841, and adjourned to February, 1842. March 21st,

NAMES.	DATE OF ASSEMBLING.	DATE OF ADJOURNMENT.	REMARKS.
			22d, and 23d, the Constitution was submitted to the persons under its provisions admitted to vote, and was rejected by a vote of 8,013 for, and 8,689 against. §§ 217, 219.
107. Rhode Island.	September 12, 1842.	November 5, 1842.	Called by the Charter government. The Constitution framed by it was submitted to the people and adopted, November 21-23, 1842, by a vote of 7,032 for, to 59 against. §§ 217, 219.
108. Kentucky.	1st Monday April, 1792.	April 19, 1792.	The Constitution framed by it was not submitted to the people. §§ 173, 174.
109. Kentucky.	July 22, 1799.	August 17, 1799.	The Constitution framed by it was not submitted to the people. §§ 217, 218.
110. Kentucky.	October 1, 1849.	June 11, 1850.	The Constitution framed by it was submitted to the people and adopted, by a vote of 71,563 for, to 20,302 against. §§ 217, 219.
111. Kentucky.	November 18, 1861.	November 20, 1861.	Secession Convention. The work of this Convention was not submitted to the people.
112. Tennessee.	January 11, 1796.	February 6, 1796.	The Constitution framed by it was not submitted to the people. §§ 190-197.
113. Tennessee.	May 19, 1834.	August 30, 1834.	The Constitution framed by it was submitted to the people March 5 and 6, 1835, and adopted by a vote of 42.666 for, to 17,691 against. §§ 217, 218.
114. Tennessee.	1861.	1861.	The State legislature sitting as a Secession Convention. Its work was submitted to the people and adopted. §§ 247-250.
115. Tennessee.	January 9, 1865.	January 26, 1865.	Reconstruction Convention. The amendments framed by it were submitted to the people and adopted, February 22, 1865. The government organized under it was recognized by Congress. §§ 250-258.
116. Tennessee.	January 10, 1870.	February 22, 1870.	The Constitution framed by it was submitted to the people, March 26, 1870, and adopted by a vote of 98,128 for, to 33,872 against. §§ 217, 219.
117. Ohio.	November 1, 1802.	November 29, 1802.	The Constitution framed by it was not submitted to the people. § 187.
118. Ohio.	May 6, 1850.	March 10, 1851.	The Constitution framed by it was submitted to the people, and adopted by a vote of 126.663 for, to 109,699 against. §§ 217, 218.
119. Ohio.	May 13, 1873.	May 14, 1874.	The Constitution framed by it was submitted to the people and rejected. §§ 217, 218.
120. Louisiana.	1st Monday November, 1811.	January 22, 1812.	The Constitution framed by it was not submitted to the people. § 187.
121. Louisiana.	August 5, 1844.	May 16, 1845.	The Constitution framed by it was submitted to the people, November 5, 1845, and adopted. §§ 217, 218.
122. Louisiana.	July 5, 1852.	July 31, 1352.	The Constitution framed by it was submitted to the people, November 1, 1852, and adopted. §§ 217, 219.
123. Louisiana.	January 23, 1861.	March 26, 1861.	Secession Convention. The amendments framed by it were not submitted to the people. §§ 247-250.

NAMES.	DATE OF ASSEMBLING.	DATE OF ADJOURNMENT.	REMARKS.
124. Louisiana.	April 6, 1864.	July 25, 1864.	Reconstruction Convention. The Constitution framed by it was submitted to the people, September, 1864, and adopted by a vote of 6,836 for, to 1,566 against. The government organized under it was, by the Acts of Congress of March 2d and 23d, and July 19, 1867, declared not to be a legal State government. §§ 250–258.
125. Louisiana.	November 23, 1867.	March 9, 1868.	Reconstruction Convention called under the Acts of Congress of March, 1867. The Constitution framed by it was submitted to the people August 17 and 18, 1868, and adopted by a vote of 66,152 for, to 48,739 against. §§ 258 *a*–258 *d*.
126. Louisiana.	April 21, 1879.	July 23, 1879.	The Constitution framed by it was submitted to the people and adopted. §§ 217, 219.
127. Indiana.	June 10, 1816.	June 29, 1816.	The Constitution framed by it was not submitted to the people. § 187.
128. Indiana.	October 7, 1850.	February 10, 1851.	The Constitution framed by it was submitted to the people and adopted. §§ 217, 219.
129. Mississippi.	July 7, 1817.	August 15, 1817.	The Constitution framed by it was submitted to the people and adopted. § 187.
130. Mississippi.	September 10, 1832.	October 24, 1832.	The Constitution framed by it was submitted to the people and adopted. §§ 217, 218.
131. Mississippi.	January 7, 1861.	1861.	Secession Convention. The amendments framed by it were not submitted to the people. §§ 247–250.
132. Mississippi.	August 14, 1865.	August 26, 1865.	Reconstruction Convention. The amendments framed by it were not submitted to the people, and the government organized under them was, by the Acts of Congress of March 2d and 23d, and July 19, 1867, declared not to be a legal State government. §§ 250–258.
133. Mississippi.	January 7, 1868.	May 15, 1868.	Reconstruction Convention called under the Acts of Congress of March, 1867. The Constitution framed by it was submitted to the people, June 28, 1868, and rejected, but when submitted a second time was adopted. §§ 258 *a*–258 *d*.
134. Illinois.	1st Monday August, 1818.	August 26, 1818.	The Constitution framed by it was not submitted to the people. § 187.
135. Illinois.	June 7, 1847.	August 31, 1847.	The Constitution framed by it was submitted to the people, March 5, 1848, and adopted. §§ 217, 218.
136. Illinois.	January 7, 1862.	March 24, 1862.	The Constitution framed by it was submitted to the people and rejected. §§ 217, 218.
137. Illinois.	December 13, 1869.	May 13, 1870.	The Constitution framed by it was submitted to the people and adopted, July 2, 1870, by a vote of 154,227 for, to 35,443 against. §§ 217, 218.
138. Alabama.	July 5, 1819.	August 2, 1819.	The Constitution framed by it was not submitted to the people. §§ 186, 187.
139. Alabama.	January 7, 1861.	March 20, 1861.	Secession Convention. The work

NAMES.	DATE OF ASSEMBLING.	DATE OF ADJOURNMENT.	REMARKS.
			of this Convention was not submitted to the people. §§ 247-250.
140. Alabama.	September 12, 1865.	September 30, 1865.	Reconstruction Convention. The Constitution framed by it was not submitted to the people, and the government organized under it was, by the Acts of Congress of March 2d and 23d, and July 19, 1867, declared to be not a legal State government. §§ 250-258.
141. Alabama.	November 5, 1867.	December 6, 1867.	Reconstruction Convention called under the Acts of Congress of March, 1867. The Constitution framed by it was submitted to the people and adopted. §§ 258 *a*-258 *d*.
142. Alabama.	September 6, 1875.	October 2, 1875.	The Constitution framed by it was submitted to the people, December 6, 1875, and adopted. §§ 217, 218.
143. Maine.	October 11, 1819.	October 29, 1819.	The Constitution framed by it was submitted to the people and adopted. §§ 175, 177.
	January 19, 1875.	February 10, 1875.	Between these dates sat a Constitutional Commission, appointed by the Governor, under a resolution of the legislature, to consider and frame amendments to the Constitution, and report them to that body for final submission to the people in September following. The Commission reported seventeen amendments, of which nine were submitted to the people and adopted. §§ 546 *a*-546 *d*.
144. Missouri.	June 12, 1820.	July 19, 1820.	The Constitution framed by it was not submitted to the people. § 187.
145. Missouri.	November 17, 1845.	January 14, 1846.	The Constitution framed by it was submitted to the people and rejected. §§ 217, 219.
146. Missouri.	February 28, 1861.	July 1, 1863.	The amendments framed by it were not submitted to the people. §§ 217, 219.
147. Missouri.	January 6, 1865.	April 10, 1865.	The Constitution framed by it was submitted to the people and adopted, June 6, 1865, by a vote of 43,670 for, to 41,808 against. §§ 217, 219.
148. Missouri.	May 5, 1875.	August 2, 1875.	The Constitution framed by it was submitted to the people, October 30, 1875, and adopted by a vote of 90,600 for, to 14,362 against. §§ 217, 218.
149. Michigan.	May 11, 1835.	June 29, 1835.	The Constitution framed by it was submitted to the people, November 2, 1835, and adopted by a vote of 6,299 for, to 1,350 against. §§ 188, 198, 201, 209.
150. Michigan.	September 26, 1836.	1836.	Called to assent to a condition of admission imposed by Congress. It refused to assent. §§ 188, 199, 202.
151. Michigan.	December 14, 1836.	December, 1836.	Called to assent to the condition of admission imposed by Congress. It declared its assent. §§ 188, 197, 199-201, 203-209.
152. Michigan.	June 3, 1850.	August 15, 1850.	The Constitution framed by it was submitted to the people, and adopted by a vote of 36,169 for, to 9,433 against. §§ 217, 218.

NAMES.	DATE OF ASSEMBLING.	DATE OF ADJOURNMENT.	REMARKS.
153. Michigan.	May 15, 1867.	August 22, 1867.	The Constitution framed by it was submitted to the people and rejected. §§ 217, 218.
	August 27, 1873.	October 16, 1873.	Between these dates sat a Constitutional Commission, appointed by the Governor under an Act of the legislature, to report to that body at its next session amendments to or a revision of the Constitution. §§ 546 *a*-545 *d*.
154. Arkansas.	January 4, 1836.	January 30, 1836.	The Constitution framed by it was not submitted to the people. §§ 188, 189, 210.
155. Arkansas.	March 4, 1861.	March 21, 1861.	Secession Convention. The work of the Convention was not submitted to the people. §§ 247-250.
156. Arkansas.	January 8, 1864.	1864.	Reconstruction Convention. The Constitution framed by it was submitted to the people and adopted, by a vote of 12,177 for, to 226 against. The government organized under it was, by the Acts of Congress of March 2d and 23d, and July 19, 1867, declared not to be a legal State government. §§ 250-258.
157. Arkansas.	January 7, 1868.	February 11, 1868.	Reconstruction Convention called under the Acts of Congress of March, 1867. The Constitution framed by it was submitted to the people, February 11, 1868, and adopted by a vote of 27,913 for, to 26,597 against. §§ 258 *a*-558 *d*.
158. Arkansas.	July 14, 1874.	1874.	The Constitution framed by it was submitted to the people and adopted. §§ 217, 219.
159. Florida.	December 3, 1838.	January 11, 1839.	The Constitution framed by it was not submitted to the people. §§ 188, 189, 210.
160. Florida.	January 3, 1861.	1861.	Secession Convention. The work of this Convention was not submitted to the people. §§ 247-250.
161. Florida.	October 25, 1865.	November 13, 1865.	Reconstruction Convention. The government organized under the Constitution framed by it was, by the Acts of Congress of March 2d and 23d and July 19, 1867, declared not to be a legal State government. The Constitution framed by it was not submitted to the people. §§ 250-258.
162. Florida.	January 20, 1868.	February 25, 1868.	Reconstruction Convention called under the Acts of Congress of March 2d and 23d, and July 19, 1867. The Constitution framed by it was submitted to the peopeople, May, 1868, and adopted by a vote of 14,520 for, to 9,491 against. §§ 258 *a*-258 *d*.
163. Florida.	1885.	1885.	The Constitution framed by it was submitted to the people in November, 1886. §§ 217, 218.
164. Iowa.	October 7, 1844.	November 1, 1844.	The Constitution framed by it was submitted to the people and rejected. §§ 188, 189, 210.
165. Iowa.	May 4, 1846.	May 19, 1846.	The Constitution framed by it was submitted to the people, August 3, 1846, and adopted by a vote of 9,492 for, to 9,036 against. §§ 188, 189.
166. Iowa.	January 19, 1857.	March 5, 1857.	The Constitution framed by it was

NAMES.	DATE OF ASSEMBLING.	DATE OF ADJOURNMENT.	REMARKS.
			submitted to the people, August 3, 1857, and adopted by a vote of 40,311 for, to 38,681 against. §§ 217, 218.
167. Texas.	July 4, 1845.	August 27, 1845.	The Constitution framed by it was submitted to the people, October 13, 1845, and adopted by a vote of 4,174 for, to 312 against. § 187.
168. Texas.	January 21, 1861.	February 1, 1861.	Secession Convention. The secession ordinance was submitted to the people, and adopted by a vote of 34,794 for, to 11,235 against. Amendments to the Constitution framed by it were not submitted to the people. §§ 247–250.
169. Texas.	February 10, 1866.	April 2, 1866.	Reconstruction Convention. The Constitution framed by it was submitted to the people, June 25, 1866, and adopted by a vote of 34,794 for, to 11,235 against. The government organized under it was, by the Acts of Congress of March 2d and 23d and July 19, 1867, declared not to be a legal State government. §§ 250–258.
170. Texas.	June 1, 1868.	February 6, 1869.	Reconstruction Convention called under the Acts of Congress of March, 1867. The Constitution framed by it was submitted to the people, and adopted by a vote of 72,395 for, to 4,924 against. §§ 258 *a*–258 *d*.
171. Texas.	September 6, 1875.	November 24, 1875.	The Constitution framed by it was submitted to the people, February 17, 1870, and adopted by a large majority. §§ 217, 219.
172. Texas.	1885.	1885.	§§ 217, 219.
173. Wisconsin.	October 5, 1846.	December 16, 1846.	The Constitution framed by it was submitted to the people and rejected. §§ 187, 210.
174. Wisconsin.	December 15, 1847.	February 1, 1848.	The Constitution framed by it was submitted to the people, March, 1848, and adopted by a vote of 16,442 for, to 6,149 against. §§ 188, 210.
175. California.	September 1, 1849.	October 13, 1849.	The Constitution framed by it was submitted to the people, November 13, 1849, and adopted by a vote of 12,061 for, to 811 against. §§ 188, 210.
176. California.	September 28, 1878.	March 3, 1879.	The Constitution framed by it was submitted to the people and adopted. §§ 217, 218.
177. Kansas.	October 23, 1855.	November 2, 1855.	The Topeka Convention. The Constitution framed by it was claimed to have been submitted to the people, and adopted by a vote of 1,731 for, to 46 against. §§ 188, 211, 212.
178. Kansas.	September 5, 1857.	November 7, 1857.	The Lecompton Convention. The Constitution framed by it was submitted to the people. The slave-holding clause was submitted, December 31, 1857, receiving 6,226 votes, against 589 votes. The entire Constitution was submitted by both its advocates and its opponents, the former claiming its adoption by a vote of 6,143 for, to 589 against; and the latter, its re-

NAMES.	DATE OF ASSEMBLING.	DATE OF ADJOURNMENT.	REMARKS.
			jection, by a vote of 10,126 against to 138 votes for it with slavery, and 24 for it without slavery. §§ 188, 213.
179. Kansas.	March 23, 1858.	April 3, 1858.	The Leavenworth Convention. The Constitution framed by it was submitted to the people, and adopted by a vote of 4,346 for, to 1,257 against, but Congress refused to admit the State under it. §§ 187, 216.
180. Kansas.	July 5, 1859.	July 29, 1859.	The Wyandotte Convention. The Constitution framed by it was submitted to the people, October 4, 1859, and adopted by a vote of 10,421 for, to 5,530 against. §§ 188, 216.
181. Minnesota.	July 13, 1857.	August 29, 1857.	The Constitution framed by it was submitted to the people, and adopted by a vote of 36,240 for, to 700 against. § 187.
182. Oregon.	August 17, 1857.	September 18, 1857.	The Constitution framed by it was submitted to the people, and adopted by a vote of 7,195 for, to 3,195 against. §§ 188, 210.
183. West Virginia.	November 26, 1861.	February 19, 1862.	The Constitution framed by it was submitted to the people, and adopted by a vote of 28,321 for, to 572 against. §§ 178–185.
184. West Virginia.	January 16, 1872.	April 9, 1872.	The Constitution framed by it was submitted to the people and adopted. §§ 217, 218.
185. Nevada.	1863.		The Constitution framed by it was submitted to the people and rejected. §§ 188, 210.
186. Nevada.	July 4, 1864.	July 28, 1864.	The Constitution framed by it was submitted to the people, October 11, 1864, and adopted. §§ 187, 210.
187. Nebraska.	July 4, 1864.		Abortive, the Convention failing to frame a Constitution. §§ 187, 210.
188. Nebraska.	February 3, 1866.	February 9, 1866.	The Territorial Legislature. The Constitution framed by it was drawn up by a caucus of private individuals, passed by both branches of the legislature, and approved by the Governor. It was then submitted to the people, June 21, 1866, and approved by a majority of 145. §§ 188, 210.
189. Nebraska.		June 12, 1875.	The Constitution framed by it was submitted to the people, October 12, 1875, and adopted. §§ 217, 218.
190. Colorado.	1864.	1864.	The Constitution framed by it was submitted to the people and rejected. §§ 187, 210.
191. Colorado.	August, 1865.	1865.	The Constitution framed by it was submitted to the people, September 5, 1866, and was adopted by a majority of 105. Congress passed an Act at the ensuing session admitting the State into the Union under it, but the Act was vetoed by President Johnson, as was also a second Act in January, 1867. §§ 188, 210.
192. Colorado.	December 20, 1875.	March 14, 1876.	The Constitution framed by it was submitted to the people, July 1, 1876, and adopted; and under it the State was admitted into the Union, August 1, 1876. §§ 188, 210.

C.

(See § 377, *ante.*)

In 1874, there appeared in Sybel's *Historische Zeitschrift* (vol. xxxii.) the following article by Dr. Von Holst, the learned author of *Verfassung und Demokratie der Vereinigten Staaten*, containing a notice of this work. Although, on the whole, the article will be seen to be commendatory of the purpose, spirit, and execution of the task assumed by the author, it criticised the work upon two points, in respect to which a few observations may here be justified. We refer to these criticisms of the learned historian because, whether just or not, they are pertinent to the issue pending before the nation for decision, as to the true character and relations of the Constitutional Convention. This issue in the foregoing pages we do not pretend to decide — we argue it; and we deem it but fair that all the facts and principles which can be claimed to bear upon it should be laid before the American people, with whom rests the decision. For, while it is important that the novel and interesting institution of which we have attempted to trace the character and history should be developed upon safe constitutional lines, it is not important that the opinions respecting it entertained by either the author or Dr. Von Holst should prevail, unless, after all pertinent tests, they should be decided to be sound. Guided by this principle, we have, in this edition, conceded the justness of the criticism made by Von Holst of the sections of the earlier editions of this work which recognized the existence in the States of a "*quasi*-sovereignty" (§§ 52, 53), although it would be easy to vindicate the substantial consistency of what is there stated, if properly understood, with what we, equally with him, maintain to be the true doctrine of sovereignty, — that which attributes it to the nation alone. Those sections have, however, been rewritten, and the notion of a *quasi*-sovereignty in the States has been abandoned. It costs us nothing thus to surrender the shadowy semblance of sovereignty which in those sections we described as attributed to the States by courtesy merely, and by a figure of speech. Equally then as now we maintained that State sovereignty had no real existence, but that the idea of it sprang from confounding the permissive exercise of sovereign powers by the States with the possession of original sovereignty.

The second criticism, to the effect that, in our discussion of the relations of the Convention to the legislature, we attribute to the latter too great power to bind and control the former, we deem less fortunate. Von Holst complains that, in that discussion, we put upon the Convention, to use what he himself characterizes as a strong expression, "a straight-jacket," and thereby, he says, place ourselves "in hostile opposition to the fundamental character of constitutional law, — that which leaves wide play to what is in process of becoming." More specifically, he says the author "has allowed himself to be led astray in his political thinking by the history of secession," which, in substance, is an intimation that this work is what the Germans call a *tendenz* work, written to maintain a particular thesis, the subordination of the Constitutional Convention to the law of the land. This charge we admit to be true; this is a *tendenz* work, in that sense; and we may ask, what work upon history or constitutional law was ever written which was not a *tendenz* work in the same sense; that is, written from some special point of view to establish truths, of which the author was strongly convinced, and to refute errors deemed dangerous and, if not combated, likely to prevail? This work was written whilst our armies were fighting the rebellion, and to maintain the same thesis for which they fought, — that these States are a nation, that State rights in the Southern sense were a political heresy, and that secession was treason; written, in short, every line of it, literally, to the beating of the Union drums. If, therefore, it leans strongly against that theory of conventional power which had made possible and easy the wicked revolt of the South, it is no more than the exigencies of the time when it was written and of truth demanded, and now demand. History shows that, in many of the seceding States, the people and their General Assemblies were, at first, opposed to secession, and that it was through the agency of Conventions selected for the purpose, through the influence of a few traitorous leaders, and fed with seductive fancies as to their sovereign powers, that the people were misled into rebelling against the Union How could such a danger be met, or guarded against, but by proclaiming the true principle, that a government, once established, represents the sovereign, and that while it lasts no body of men can assemble and assume more perfectly or more rightfully than that government to represent the sovereign; still more, that, while that government survives, no earthly power has a right to shape the policy of the State superior to that of its own legislature, — to shape it either, first, by declaring that a Convention to revise the fundamental law shall meet, if at all, under conditions prescribed by such legislature, and that it shall report the result of its deliberations, for approval, to the body which called it, or to the people; or, secondly, by refusing to call a Convention, when it is plain that the forces of anarchy are clamoring for such an assembly for treasonable purposes; or, finally, by providing a penalty against any citizen who shall assume to sit as a member of a Constitutional Convention not called by lawful authority? Whether, in any case, it is or is not politic to call a Convention, or, if called, to tie its hands by restrictions, or to leave it free to act at its own discretion, is a question for the legislature alone. If the safety of the State be thought, on the one hand, to be not incompatible with such freedom of action, or, on the other, to require stringent limitations, "the fundamental character of constitutional law" demands that the legislature shall act accordingly. Of the two things, perfect freedom of action, or limitation by law to courses of action deemed safe and wise, the latter is always, in the absence of special circumstances, to be preferred. This the learned critic himself substantially concedes. He says: "In contests of this kind, as to their relative powers, between the Constitutional Convention and the legislature, the spirit of constitutional law demands that priority should be given to the claims of the Convention over those of the legislature, where other and weightier considerations do not require a decision in favor of the latter." Who is to determine what are weightier considerations? Under our system, it must be the legislature, else our Constitutions are no better than those of the first French republic, characterized by Burke as "digests of anarchy." With what Von Holst says as to the impolicy of hampering Conventions unnecessarily, and the propriety of leaving "ample play for what is in process of becoming," we heartily concur; and we would deprecate as strongly as he the placing of a "straight-jacket" upon the Convention, if it were true that it would "endanger the development of an institution which has shown itself, on the whole, one of the most imperishable (lebensfähigsten) and beneficent creations of the political life of the United States. But, in politics as in social life, there must be straight-jackets, because, in both, men sometimes go mad. The Convention system, as we know by bitter experience in 1861, at the South, went mad, and came near wrecking our ship of state. While in some respects that institution has proved itself to be all that Von Holst has painted it, in others it has been found to contain the elements of extreme danger. Shall no attempt be made to neutralize or eliminate these, provided those which make it "one of the most imperishable and beneficent creations" of our political life can be retained and strengthened? A theory of the Convention which makes it the minister of the people certainly does this; and a theory which converts it into the master, and the people into its slaves, as certainly robs it of all its beneficent qualities. Were our people, therefore, in relation to the powers of Conventions, to follow the guidance, not of experience, but of theory, as propounded by Von Holst, those bodies would speedily assume, in all our States and in the nation, the rôle of the French Conventions, by which that theory was adopted and carried to its legitimate consequences, the ruin of France.[1] That the views of Professor Von Holst in regard to the powers of Conventions are merely theoretical is clearly apparent. It is true, in the preparation of his work above referred to, he spent some time in the United States, engaged in the study of our institutions and of our constitutional history. But, considering the magnitude of the task he had undertaken, the time was not long, and he never participated in our political life. He, therefore, could have acquired only that insight into our institutions which may be attained by any foreigner of equal capacity from the reading of books, and from conversations with intelligent Americans. That he failed in some respects properly to appreciate those institutions ought not to be deemed remarkable, when it is remembered that, before him, De Tocqueville also failed. That my critic must have failed — that his brief sojourn amongst us could not have fitted him to dogmatize in regard to the practical operation of the constitutional Convention, a perfectly unique institution, seems to be certain, if the judgment pronounced by one of the most learned of English historians, Mr. E. A. Freeman, is to be taken as sound. In a late work that writer says: . . . "A Swiss or a Norwegian may judge of the workings of free institutions, because he, like the Englishman, has daily experience of their working in their own land. But these things are mysteries to German professors, because they are mysteries to German statesmen also. The German scholar simply reads in a book of things which we are always looking at and acting in. He therefore utterly fails to understand many things at Athens or Rome or anywhere else which come to us like our A B C." After referring to Ranke and Curtius as illustrating this general defect, he closes a high eulogium upon Mommsen with this statement of the points in which he fails as a historian: "What is lacking in him" (Mommsen) "is political and moral insight, the moral insight which is born with a man, the political insight which is gained only by living in communities of freemen." *Methods of Historical Study*, pp. 289–291. Where Curtius and

[1] See Appendix A, *ante*.

Ranke and Mommsen failed to estimate correctly the workings of the simple and ordinary machinery of free communities, it can hardly be deemed remarkable as we have said, that Von Holst should have misapprehended the novel and peculiar institution presented him for study amongst us.

THE CONSTITUTIONAL CONVENTION; its history, powers, and modes of proceeding. By JOHN ALEXANDER JAMESON, LL. D., Judge of the Superior Court of Chicago, Illinois. Third edition. Revised and Corrected. xix., 561. Chicago, 1873.

Richter Jameson ist kein glänzender Geist, aber ein gründlicher Forscher und ein ruhiger und gewissenhafter Denker. Mit einer zuweilen fast an Schwerfälligkeit streifenden Bedachtsamkeit prüft er jede Frage, bevor er sein Urtheil fixirt. Ist er aber einmal zu einer festen Ansicht gelangt, so verfolgt er sie mit einer Consequenz, die etwas Enges und Starres hat. Man kann nicht leidenschaftsloser und sorgsamer eine Frage von allen denkbaren Gesichtspunkten erwägen, als er es thut, bevor er an die Feststellung der grundliegenden Sätze seines Argumentes geht: aber es fehlt ihm die Beweglichkeit des Geistes, die zu einer vorurtheilsfreien und allseitigen Würdigung der sich erst im Verfolg des Raisonnements ergebenden Einwände erforderlich ist. Sein Denken trägt das eigenthümliche Gepräge des Rechtsgelehrten, der seine hohe Schule weniger auf der Advocaten- als auf der Richterbank durchgemacht hat. Er verschließt sich nicht staatsmännischen Erwägungen, aber sie liegen unter dem Druck der juristischen Schulung seines Denkens, während andererseits gelegentlich auch gewisse politische Ueberzeugungen sein juristisches Urtheil bestimmen. Es geht ihm die Weite des Blickes eines Marshall ab, dem nicht nur in der Theorie, sondern in jeder concreten Frage der Unterschied in der Natur des öffentlichen und des privaten Rechtes gegenwärtig war, und der in seinem tiefsittlichen Selbstbewußtsein den Muth fand, das *werdende* Staatsrecht der Republik in richtige Entwickelungsbahnen zu lenken. Jameson geht nicht leicht irre, aber wenn er einmal auf einen falschen Weg geräth, so läßt er sich schwer wieder von ihm abbringen.

In dieser Charakteristik des Autors sind alle die großen Vorzüge so wie die Mängel seines Werkes über die Constitutional Convention angedeutet, das 1867 zuerst erschien und von dem 1873 bereits die dritte Auflage nöthig geworden ist. Das sehr umfangreiche und bis dahin ganz zerstreute Material über dieses äußerst wichtige Capitel des amerikanischen Verfassungsrechtes ist nicht nur in großer Vollständigkeit zusammengetragen und mit richtiger Unterscheidung des Wesentlichen und Unwesentlichen verwerthet, sondern auch die ganze Anlage des Werkes und die Behandlung der einzelnen Fragen verdienen im Allgemeinen hohe Anerkennung. Die Quellen sind sorgfältig angegeben, so daß überall eine genaue Controle möglich ist. Der Stil ist einfach, nicht allgemein verständliche Kunstausdrücke werden möglichst vermieden, der Gedankengang ist klar und man ist nie in Zweifel darüber, was eigentlich die Ansicht des Autors ist — ein Vorzug, der keineswegs allen amerikanischen Werken über das Verfassungsrecht nachgerühmt werden kann. Eine eingehendere Uebersicht des Inhaltes zu geben, muß sich Ref. versagen, um Raum für einige kritische Bemerkungen über die *beiden Punkte* zu gewinnen, die dem europäischen Publikum vornehmlich von Interesse sein dürften. Im Uebrigen beschränkt sich Ref. darauf, unten die Ueberschriften der Capitel[1] anzuführen und sein allgemeines Urtheil dahin auszusprechen, daß Richter Jameson's Werk zu den gediegensten und werthvollsten Arbeiten über einzelne Theile des amerikanischen Verfassungsrechtes gehört.

Die eine wesentliche Ausstellung, die Ref. zu machen hat, betrifft des Autors Stellung

[1] Dieselben lauten: Of the various kinds of conventions Of sovereignty. Of constitutions Of the requisites to the legitimacy of conventions, and of their history. Of the organization and modes of proceeding in conventions. Of the powers of conventions. Of the submission of constitutions to the people. Of the amendment of constitutions. Appendix.

zur Frage der Staatensouveränetät. In dieser Grundfrage sieht der Autor allerdings klarer als irgendein amerikanischer Politiker oder Jurist vor dem Bürgerkriege gesehen; aber zu voller Klarheit ist auch er noch nicht gekommen. S. 55 heißt es: "It is true, nevertheless, in the United States, that although the nation is the only real sovereign, the States are often called sovereign. But this use of the word is proper only as a figure of speech employed out of courtesy to numerous and dignified bodies invested with the exercise, for local purposes, of important sovereign powers. The States, at best, are but quasi sovereign; that is, on account of their permissive supremacy in local State affairs they are to be treated, to a certain extent, as if they were sovereign; precisely as an ambassador, despatched to a foreign court and there representing his sovereign, is received and honored, on account of his office, as if he were himself the sovereign." Es bedarf wohl kaum erst des Beweises, daß der Vergleich mit dem Gesandten in keinem Stück zutreffend ist. Doch das ist nicht von großem Belang. Wohl von Wichtigkeit aber ist die „Quasi-Souveränetät", die hier introducirt wird und auf die der Autor später öfters zurückkommt. Der Ausdruck ist zwar schon vor ihm häufig auf die Staaten der Union angewendet worden, aber Jameson hält eben doch noch an ihm fest. Die Folge davon ist, daß er öfters in die Halbheiten verfällt, zu denen der vage Begriff verführt. J. hat sich aber auch dem weiteren Vorwurf ausgesetzt, daß er mit der Annahme dieses vagen Begriffs seinem eigenen Raisonnement untreu wird. Zunächst stimmt es schlecht zusammen, die Souveränetät der Staaten only a figure of speech zu nennen und dann doch Quasi-Souveränetät zuzugestehen. Ferner ist der Ausdruck "at best" in der Entscheidung derjenigen Frage, die den Eckstein des ganzen Verfassungsrechtes bildet, durchaus unzulässig. Die Staaten der Union repräsentiren nicht wie Gesandte den Souverän. Sie aus „Höflichkeit" „zu behandeln, als ob" sie souverän wären, hat keinen Sinn. Entweder hat ihre Quasi-Souveränetät einen staatsrechtlichen Inhalt, oder sie hat ihn nicht, und dann hat sie einfach nicht Statt; ein Drittes gibt es nicht. Die Motivirung des Zugeständnisses der Quasi-Souveränetät fände in noch viel höherem Grade auf die Bundesregierung Anwendung, und doch ist es noch Niemand eingefallen, ihr Quasi-Souveränetät zuzusprechen. Der Grund dafür aber ist lediglich, daß es sich hier um eine „Regierung" handelt, dort aber das Wort „Staat" in die Ohren klingt. Der Souverän in den Ver. Staaten ist „das Volk der Ver. Staaten", und was darunter zu verstehen ist, sagt J. mit großer Schärfe in dem Satz: "Sovereignty resides in the society or body politic; in the corporate unit resulting from the organization of many into one, and not in the individuals constituting such unit, nor in any number of them as such, nor even in all of them, except as organized into a body politic and acting as such" (S. 19, 20). Neben diesem einen Souverän gibt es ebenso wenig eine Quasi-Souveränetät, als es einen anderen Souverän neben ihm gibt.

Die zweite Ausstellung betrifft des Autors Ansicht über die Competenz der Const. Conv., resp. das Competenzverhältniß von der Legislatur und der Const. Conv.′ J. steht hier unter dem Druck der politischen Ereignisse von 1860 und 1861.

Die Theorie, nach der die Const. Conv. alle dem „Volke" selbst zustehenden Befugnisse hat, taucht zum ersten Male in der Const. Conv. von New-York im J. 1821 auf. (Deb. N. Y. Conv. 1821, S. 199.) Die Lehre gewann nach und nach an Boden und wurde gleichzeitig immer schärfer präcisirt. Als der Conflict zwischen Norden und Süden rasch zum Bruch heranreifte, fanden die südstaatlichen „Feuerfresser" es in ihrem Interesse, sie auf die äußerste Spitze zu treiben. In mehreren Staaten konnten sie mit Bestimmtheit darauf rechnen, in einer Convention das Uebergewicht zu erhalten, während es sehr zweifelhaft war, ob die Majorität der Bevölkerung dazu würde bewogen werden können, aus eigener, nicht nur formell sondern auch thatsächlich vollkommen freier Entschließung den Rubico zu überschreiten. Darum ward der Satz aufgestellt: Die Convention ist „souverän", denn sie ist das „Volk". William L. Yancey sagte in der Convention von

Alabama: "This proposition (die Secessionsordinanz dem Volke zur Ratification zu unterbreiten) is based upon the idea, that there is a difference between the people and the delegate. It seems to me that this in an error. There is a difference between the representatives of the people as the law-making body, and the people themselves, because there are powers reserved to the people by the Convention of Alabama, and which the General Assembly cannot exercise. But in this body is all power — no powers are reserved from it. The people are here in the persons of their deputies. Life, Liberty, and Property are in our hands. Look to the Ordinance adopting the Constitution of Alabama. It states, 'We, the people of Alabama,' etc., etc. All our acts are supreme, without ratification, because they are the acts of the people acting in their sovereign capacity." (Hist. and Deb. Alb. Conv. 1861, S. 114.) Die Conventionen mehrerer Staaten (Alabama, Louisiana, Arkansas, Mississippi u. s. w.) handelten dieser Theorie gemäß. In anderen Staaten, wie z. B. in Virginia, wurde die Secessionsordinanz allerdings einer Abstimmung der Bevölkerung unterworfen, aber erst nachdem die Convention, die Legislatur und der Gouverneur die Secession längst zu einer vollendeten Thatsache gemacht hatten.

Daß diese Früchte der Lehre von der „Souveränetät" der Const. Conv. einen tiefen und nachhaltigen Eindruck auf alle conservativen und national gesinnten Amerikaner gemacht haben, läßt sich wohl verstehen. Und noch viel besser begründet erscheint die unbedingte Verdammung der Doctrin als verfassungsrechtliche Ketzerei und politische Ungeheuerlichkeit, wenn man genauer nach ihrer Motivirung forscht. In der Illinois Convention sagte Peters: "We are the sovereignty of the State. We are what the people of the State would be if they were congregated here in one mass-meeting. We are what Louis XIV said he was, 'We are the State.' We can trample the Constitution under our feet as waste paper, and no one can call us to account save the people." Das ist die einzig denkbare Motivirung der Souveränetät der Const. Conv. Verfassungsrechtlich ist es aber absolut keinem Zweifel unterworfen, daß "the people of the State . . . congregated in one mass-meeting" nicht die geringste rechtliche Befugniß über die Verfassung haben würde. Wäre dem nicht so, dann wäre bald jeder Haufe an irgend einer Straßenecke und in irgend einer Schenke „das Volk", das seinen „souveränen" Willen kund thut, d. h. die Anarchie wäre das Grundgesetz des Landes. Nicht in der Bevölkerung, sondern in dem Volk ruht die staatliche Vollgewalt, d. h. in der Bevölkerung in ihrer ganz bestimmten politischen Organisation. Die Const. Conv. hat daher unfraglich nur die Befugniß, die ihr in dieser ganz bestimmten politischen Organisation zugewiesen ist: sie steht nicht außerhalb und über, sondern innerhalb und unter der Constitution. Das Verfassungsrecht weiß überhaupt von keiner rechtlichen politischen Macht außerhalb der Verfassung; auch dem „Volke" erkennt es eine solche nicht zu. Die Verfassung steht nicht über dem Volk, aber das Volk steht in der Verfassung.

Die Klarheit, mit der J. diese fundamentalen Sätze und die sich aus ihnen ergebenden Consequenzen entwickelt, würden allein hinreichen, sein Werk zu einem sehr werthvollen Beitrag zur Literatur des amerikanischen Verfassungsrechtes zu machen. Allein die Ausschreitung der Gegner — in der Theorie wie in der Praxis — treiben ihn in das entgegengesetzte Extrem. Die Const. Conv. schrumpft ihm so zu sagen zu einem Comité zusammen, dessen Competenz ganz auf die Ausarbeitung eines Entwurfes beschränkt ist und nach der Ueberzeugung des Autors auch beschränkt sein sollte. Das ist nach Ansicht des Ref. verfassungsrechtlich unrichtig und politisch verkehrt. The Nation sagt in ihrer Nummer vom 4. December, 1873: "No portion of the American political system is more obscure than the functions of the constitutional covention regarded as a part of the orderly administration of government, as an instrument for the peaceful and legal reconstruction of the fundamental law." Das Werk J.'s ist der beste Beweis für die Richtigkeit dieser Behauptung. Da nun nach der von J. gegebenen Liste von

1775—1873 bereits 175 solcher Conventionen getagt haben, so kann diese Dunkelheit offenbar nur darin ihren Grund haben, daß die Verfassungen meist nur wenige und sehr allgemein gehaltene Bestimmungen über die Conventionen und ihre Befugnisse enthalten. Sowohl in der Bundesverfassung wie in vielen Verfassungen der einzelnen Staaten finden sich auch andere Bestimmungen, die einen ähnlichen Charakter der Allgemeinheit und Vagheit haben, und das hat neben manchem Uebel auch viel Gutes zur Folge gehabt. Die große Freiheit, welche dadurch der staatlichen Entwickelung geboten ist, entspricht der Thatsache, daß es sich um politische Gemeinwesen handelt, die in eminentem Grade werdende sind. Sowohl der Politiker als der Jurist und Richter haben daher das Recht und sogar die Pflicht, in Fragen, die in Folge jener Allgemeinheit und Vagheit der Verfassungsbestimmungen verschieden beantwortet werden können, ihr Urtheil durch die Forderungen der Staatsraison bestimmen zu lassen. Wenn nun die Staatsraison fordert, daß die Const. Conv. nicht nur ein mit der Ausarbeitung eines Verfassungsentwurfes beauftragter Ausschuß des Volkes sei, so darf mithin ihre Competenz auch nicht unbedingt darauf beschränkt werden, wo es nicht in unzweifelhafter Weise durch die Verfassung selbst geschieht. J. thut das jedoch, indem er die Competenz der Convention aus der Legislatur herleitet. Diese Annahme, wo sie sich nicht auf eine positive Bestimmung der Verfassung stützt, scheint dem Ref. in offenbarem und schroffem Widerspruch mit dem Geiste des amerikanischen Verfassungsrechtes zu stehen. Wo die Verfassung die Berufung von Const. Conv. vorsieht, ist das Motiv dazu offenbar die Ueberzeugung, daß die Legislatur nicht geeignet ist, die der Convention zugewiesene Arbeit zu thun. Bestimmt die Verfassung nicht ausdrücklich anders, so darf man demnach nicht annehmen, daß sie der Legislatur die Mittel hat geben wollen, die Erfüllung des Zweckes der Convention thatsächlich unmöglich zu machen, und man muß annehmen, daß sie der Convention die Mittel hat geben wollen, die Erfüllung ihres Zweckes sicher zu stellen. Steht es aber der Legislatur zu, ganz nach ihrem Gutdünken der Convention Regeln vorzuschreiben und Schranken zu setzen, so ist es natürlich auch in ihre Hand gelegt, das Tagen der Convention von Hause aus zu einer Farce zu machen. Das ist nicht ein doctrinärer Einwand, sondern eine praktische Erwägung von der eminentesten Bedeutung. Ein Beispiel aus der jüngsten Vergangenheit wird das zur Genüge zeigen.

Das Getreibe des „Ringes", der Pennsylvania beherrschte, war nach und nach eine so himmelschreiende und so unerträgliche Schandwirthschaft geworden, daß die öffentliche Meinung die Berufung einer Const. Conv. durchsetzte. Die Legislatur bestimmte jedoch in dem betreffenden Gesetz: "The election to decide for or against the adoption of the new constitution shall be conducted as the general elections of this commonwealth are now by law conducted." Diese Bestimmung wahrte dem „Ring" die Möglichkeit, in Philadelphia die seit Jahren üblichen Correcturen des Wahlergebnisses im größten Maßstabe vorzunehmen, und die Annahme des Verfassungsentwurfes wurde dadurch in hohem Grade fraglich, obgleich es nicht dem geringsten Zweifel unterlag, daß eine bedeutende Majorität der stimmberechtigten Bevölkerung für ihn war. Hatte die Convention das Recht, diese Verfügung der Legislatur bei Seite zu setzen, damit die Frage wirklich durch das Votum des Volkes und nicht durch die Correcturen des „Ringes" entschieden würde? Der oberste Gerichtshof des Staates hat in diesem Falle gegen die Convention entschieden. Diese Entscheidung entzieht sich der Beurtheilung des Ref., da sie ihm bis jetzt nur durch eine kurze Zeitungsnotiz bekannt ist. Eine für alle Fälle giltige Regel zur Entscheidung derartiger Competenzconflicte zwischen der Const. Conv. und der Legislatur läßt sich aber nicht aufstellen. Nur wo eine ausdrückliche Bestimmung der Verfassung entweder der Const. Conv. gewisse Rechte vorenthält (resp. ertheilt), oder der Legislatur das Recht zu beschränkenden Bestimmungen verleiht, ist jeder Zweifel ausgeschlossen. In allen anderen Fällen muß es, wenn nicht die allein maßgebende, so doch eine sehr gewichtige Erwägung sein, daß die Befugnisse sowohl der Legislatur wie der Convention nicht Eigenrechte sondern delegirt sind, hinsichtlich der Aenderung des Grundgesetzes die

Convention aber dem eigentlichen Inhaber der politischen Gewalt näher steht als die Legislatur, ihn unmittelbarer vertritt. In Competenzstreitigkeiten dieser Art zwischen der Const. Conv. und der Legislatur fordert daher der Geist des Verfassungsrechtes, daß den Ansprüchen der Convention der Vorrang vor denen der Legislatur gegeben werde, wo nicht andere und gewichtigere Erwägungen eine Entscheidung zu Gunsten dieser verlangen. Bestimmte Regeln, die eine verlässige und leicht anwendbare Norm in den einzelnen concreten Fällen abgeben, können nur sehr langsam durch die Erfahrung gewonnen werden, und nicht rechtliche sondern politische Momente werden dabei in erster Reihe zu berücksichtigen sein.

Jameson -- um einen starken Ausdruck zu gebrauchen — läßt sich durch die Geschichte der Secession und durch das Ueberwiegen seines juristischen Denkens über sein politisches Denken verführen, der Const. Conv. eine Zwangsjacke anzulegen. Damit setzt er sich in Widerspruch mit dem Grundcharakter des Verfassungsrechtes, das dem Werden weiten Spielraum läßt, und er gefährdet die Entwickelung einer Institution, die sich im Großen und Ganzen als eine der lebensfähigsten und segensreichsten Schöpfungen des politischen Lebens der Ver. Staaten erwiesen hat.

Holst.

D.

OPINION OF THE JUDGES OF THE SUPREME COURT OF NEW YORK, TOUCHING THE VALIDITY OF THE ACT OF ASSEMBLY PASSED APRIL 22, 1846, MODIFYING THE CONVENTION ACT OF MAY 13, 1845.[1]

State of New York,
In Assembly, April 10, 1846.

Resolved, That the bill relating to the apportionment of delegates to the Convention be referred to the justices of the Supreme Court, with a respectful message from the Speaker of this House, requesting them to communicate forthwith to this House whether, in their opinion, the delegates to be chosen to the Convention under the law of the last session, be according to the apportionment of the present members of the legislature, and whether this legislature have any power to alter or amend that law. By order of the Assembly.

A. G. CHATFIELD, *Speaker pro tem.*

The justices of the Supreme Court have received the foregoing resolution, with the bill therein mentioned, and have considered the questions on which their opinion is asked by the Assembly.

The first question touches the construction of the Convention Act of 1845; and the point to be considered is, whether the number of delegates to be chosen under the Act in the several counties, is to be regulated by the apportionment of members of Assembly which was made in 1836, or by the apportionment which has been made at the present session of the legislature.

By the Constitution, the apportionment of members of Assembly which was made in the spring of 1836 took effect for the purpose of electing the members in the fall of that year; but it did not take effect for any other purpose until

[1] This opinion I do not find reported in any of the New York Law Reports, probably for the reason stated in the text, (§ 39?, *ante*,) that there was no constitutional provision authorizing such a reference to the Supreme Court, and the opinion was therefore deemed extra-judicial. As given here, it is taken from *Deb. Mass. Conv.* 1853, Vol. I. p. 138.

the 1st day of January, 1837; and it was to remain unaltered for ten years. In other words, the representation of each county in the Assembly, from the commencement of the political and calendar year 1837 to the commencement of the political and calendar year 1847, was to remain the same.

By the Convention Act, the people were to decide upon a "Convention" or "no Convention," at the fall election of 1845. If they decided for a Convention, the delegates were to be chosen in April, 1846; they were to assemble in June following; and the amendments to the Constitution on which the Convention might agree were to be submitted to the people for adoption or rejection, at the fall election of the same year. Every thing in relation to the Convention was to be both begun and concluded, while the apportionment of members of Assembly made in 1836 remained in force and governed the representation from the several counties.

The seventh section of the Convention Act provides that "the number of delegates to be chosen to such Convention shall be the same as the number of members of Assembly from the respective cities and counties in this State." We are of opinion that this means the number of members from the respective counties, under the apportionment which was in force when the Act of 1845 was passed, and which will be in force until after the delegates have been chosen and their labors have been terminated. Although a new apportionment of members of Assembly has already been made, it cannot take effect for any purpose until the fall of the present year. If an election for members of Assembly in any county for the present year were now to be ordered, and it should be held at the same time that the delegates to the Convention are to be chosen, the apportionment of 1836, and not that of the present session, would govern. The legislature would have no power to make a different rule.

It would have been highly proper, as a just and equitable distribution of the delegates among the several counties, and the legislature of 1845 might have so provided, that the new census and apportionment which were then in prospect, should regulate the representation in the Convention. But we think that has not been done.

It will be seen, on referring to the Assembly documents of 1845, No. 211, that the select committee to whom the Convention bill was referred gave a brief exposition of its provisions, in which they said that "each county is entitled to the same representation it now has in the Assembly." And so far as this question is concerned, the bill was passed in the same words in which it was reported to the House by the committee. It is difficult, therefore, to suppose that the legislature, in passing the bill, intended any other rule of representation than that which had been suggested to the committee. As their attention was plainly called to the subject, it can hardly be doubted that they would have changed the language of the seventh section if the bill was passed with any reference to the new census which was about to be taken, or to the apportionment which might be made under that census.

This goes to confirm the construction which we think must be given to the Act, when looking at nothing but the Statute Book.

The next question is, "Whether this legislature has any power to alter or amend that law." As a general rule, the legislature can alter or annul any law which it has power to pass. A proper solution of the question proposed by the

Assembly involves, therefore, an inquiry concerning the source from which the Act of 1845 derives its obligation.

The legislature is not supreme. It is only one of the instruments of that absolute sovereignty which resides in the whole body of the people. Like other departments of the government, it acts under a delegation of powers, and cannot rightfully go beyond the limits which have been assigned to it. This delegation of powers has been made by a fundamental law which no one department of the government nor all the departments united have authority to change. That can only be done by the people themselves. A power has been given to the legislature to propose amendments to the Constitution, which, when approved and ratified by the people, become a part of the fundamental law. But no power has been delegated to the legislature to call a Convention to revise the Constitution. That is a measure which must come from, and be the act of. the people themselves. Neither the calling of a Convention nor the Convention itself is a proceeding under the Constitution. It is above and beyond the Constitution. Instead of acting under the forms and within the limits prescribed by that instrument, the very business of a Convention is to change those forms and boundaries as the public interests may seem to require. A Convention is not a government measure, but a movement of the people, having for its object a change, either in whole or in part, of the existing form of government.

As the people have not only omitted to confer any power on the legislature to call a Convention but have also prescribed another mode of amending the organic law, we are unable to see that the Act of 1845 had any obligatory force at the time of its enactment. It could only operate by way of advice or recommendation, and not as a law. It amounted to nothing more than a proposition or suggestion to the people to decide whether they would or would not have a Convention. That question the people have settled in the affirmative, and the law derives its obligation from that act and not from the power of the legislature to pass it.

The people have not only decided in favor of a Convention, but they have determined that it shall be held in accordance with the provisions of the Act of 1845. No other proposition was before them, and of course their votes could have had reference to nothing else. They have decided on the time and manner of electing delegates and how they shall be apportioned among the several counties.

If the Act of the last session is not a law of the legislature but a law made by the people themselves, the conclusion is obvious that the legislature cannot annul it nor make any substantial change in its provisions. If the legislature can alter the rule of representation it can repeal the law altogether, and thus defeat a measure which has been willed by a higher power.

A change in the fundamental law, when not made in the form which that law has prescribed, must always be a work of the utmost delicacy. Under any other form of government than our own, it could amount to nothing less than a revolution. The greatest care should, therefore, be taken that nothing be done which can give rise to doubts or difficulties in the choice of delegates or the harmonious organization and action of the Convention. A controversy about the number of delegates to which any county is entitled may lead to irregular and disorderly proceedings at the election, and an imperfect expression of the will of the electors in the choice of delegates. It may embarrass the inspectors of elections and the canvassers of votes It may also tend to disorder in the Convention, where the question must finally be settled who are and who are not members of the body. In the strife of parties, if there should be parties in the Convention and they should be nearly balanced, the body may either be broken up or the moral force of its acts be greatly impaired. As a question of expediency, therefore, as well as of power, we think it the safest course to leave the law as it now is.

If, however, the Assembly should think otherwise, it is then proper that we should take some notice of the bill which has been referred for our consideration.

The first section of the bill is in the following words: —

"Sec. 1. The true intent and meaning of so much of the seventh section of an Act, entitled, 'An Act recommending a Convention of the people of this State,' passed May 13, 1845, as relates to the number of delegates to be chosen to the said Convention in and by the respective cities and counties of this State, is, that the number of delegates to be chosen to the said Convention, in and by the said cities and counties respectively, shall be the same as the number of members of the Assembly which the said cities and counties will respectively be entitled to elect according to the census of the inhabitants of this State taken in the year 1845."

We have already expressed the opinion that such is not "the true intent and meaning" of the law. It is proper to add that, as the section merely professes to declare what the law now is, without either proposing to alter it or commanding any thing in particular to be done or omitted, it cannot change the legal effect of the existing statute. The legislature has no judicial power. Although its opinions are entitled to great consideration, they cannot have the force of a law. If, therefore, it is deemed expedient to legislate on the subject, it is submitted that there should be a positive enactment instead of a mere declaration of opinion.

The second section of the bill goes beyond a mere declaration, and provides that the number of delegates to be chosen to the Convention "is hereby declared to be and *shall be* as follows," [specifying the number to be elected in each county.] The words "shall be" give this section the force of a command, and, if the section should be enacted, it will have the effect of altering the Convention law, if the legislature has any power over the subject.

The two remaining sections of the bill call for no remark.

In this discussion we have assumed, without intending to express any opinion on the subject, that the Constitution can be amended in a different way from that which has been prescribed by the people in the instrument itself.

We cannot close this communication without expressing our regret that questions of so much delicacy and importance should be presented under circumstances which have given us but a few hours for conferring together and reducing our opinion to writing. Neither of us had either examined or thought of the questions until after the reference was made; and it was not until this day that we were able to meet and consult together on the subject.

Respectfully submitted,

GREENE C. BRONSON,
SAMUEL BEARDSLEY,
F. G. JEWETT.

ALBANY, *April* 14, 1846.

E.

(See §§ 393, 574, *ante*.)

The weight to be accorded to the opinions of the Massachusetts, New York, and Rhode Island judges, cited in the text (§§ 573, 574), may be determined by observing the esteem in which they have been subsequently held by the same and other courts, and by respectable legal authorities not judicial. Thus, in Massachusetts, it has been ruled in numerous cases, and is believed to be now the settled doctrine of its courts, as well in opinions rendered under similar circumstances as in solemn judgments in litigated cases, that such opinions are merely advisory and have no binding quality.[1]

Thus, in a criminal case, where the judges of the Supreme Court were required to adjudicate upon a point, on which they had previously given an opinion to the Governor, adverting to this opinion, they declared it to be not binding upon them, and that they had sought to free their minds from all prepossessions resulting from their having given it. "The opinion thus given," they observed, "like all others of a similar character, was formed without the aid of counsel learned in the law, or any statement of the reasons on which the regularity or validity of the proceedings had been called in question. It is well understood," they continue, "and has often been declared by this court, that an opinion formed and expressed under such circumstances cannot be considered, in any sense, as conclusive or binding on the rights of parties, but is regarded as being open to reconsideration and revision." Green *v*. The Commonwealth, 12 Allen R. 155. In another and similar case, they said, by Wilde, J.: "We do not consider that opinion" (given to the Governor) "as binding upon us in this action." Adams *v*. Bucklin, 7 Pick. R. 127.

In Taylor *v*. Place, 4 R. I. R. 324, the same question came before the Supreme Court of Rhode Island, in a litigated case, in respect to which the judges had formerly given an opinion to the Governor, under a provision of the Constitution. The court, by Ames, C. J., say: "This is the first time, since the adoption of the Constitution, that this question has been brought judicially to the attention of the court. The advice or opinion given by the judges of this court, when requested, to the Governor or to either House of the Assembly, under the third section of the tenth article of the Constitution, is not a decision of this court; and given, as it must be, without the aid which the court derives

[1] Adams *v*. Bucklin, 7 Pick. R. 125, note at p. 130; Opinions of Supreme Court Judges, 5 Metc. R. 597; Opinions of Supreme Court Judges, 9 Cush. R. 604; Opinions of the Supreme Court Judges, 122 Mass. R. 603; Opinions of Supreme Court Judges, 126 do. 547, 557; Green *v*. The Commonwealth, 12 Allen R. 155, 163. See also cases in which by custom, or in pursuance of statutes, opinions have been given under similar circumstances, and their character, as being merely advisory and not authoritative, has been affirmed. Certificate of the Judges, 2 Edw. Ch. R. (appendix), 371 and 372 and notes; Best on Evidence, sec. 474; McNaughten's case, 10 Cl. & Fin. R. 200; Opinions of the Justices of the Superior Court, 25 N. H. R. 537; Opinions of the Supreme Court Judges, reported in the following volumes, 37 Mo. R. 135, 51 do. 586, 55 do. 497, 58 do. 369; 64 N. C. R. (appendix), 785–796; Taylor *v*. Place, 4 R. I. R. *Memorandum on the legal effect of opinions given by Judges to the Executive and the Legislature under certain American Constitutions.* By J. B. Thayer, Professor of Law at the Law School of Harvard University. Alfred Mudge & Co., Boston. 1885.

in adversary cases from able and experienced counsel, though it may afford much light from the reasonings or research displayed in it, can have no weight as a precedent." See also Sparks's "Life of Washington, Vol. X., p. 359, Marshall's "Life of Washington," p. 441, for a history of the unsuccessful attempt of Washington to draw from the judges of the United States Supreme Court their opinions as to various questions arising under our treaties with France.

So little were the best legal minds in Massachusetts satisfied with the operation of the constitutional provision in question, that efforts were repeatedly made by them to secure its repeal. Thus, in the Convention of 1820, the judiciary committee of that body, through Mr. Justice Story, its chairman, recommended the annulment of the provision, and, in introducing a proposal to that effect to the Convention, thus explained the reasons which induced the committee to propose it. He said: —

"If they" (the judges) "were liable to be called on, there was extreme danger that they would be required to give opinions in cases which should be exclusively of a political character. There were two classes of cases in which the legislature may demand the opinion of the judges, — those of a public and those of a private nature. A question may be proposed in which the whole political rights of the State are involved. It is impossible that there should be an argument, and the individual most interested will be deprived of a right which is secured to every person by the Constitution, — that of being heard. Questions of fact and of law may be decided without argument and without a jury. There was no necessity for such a provision. In cases where it is necessary to attain a judicial decision, the legislature may by resolve order a suit to be brought to try any question of law or fact, and have it regularly argued. Why, then, should the great principle be violated by taking away the right of trial by jury? The power of calling on the judges for their opinion may be resorted to, in times of political excitement, with the very view to make them odious and to effect their removal from office. A better opportunity could not be afforded to an artful demagogue for effecting the purpose of their removal than by drawing from them opinions opposed to the strong popular sentiment, and subjecting them to popular odium. It ought not to be in the power of the other departments to involve the judiciary in this manner. As the Constitution now stands, the judges are bound to give their opinions, if insisted upon, even in a case where private rights are involved, and without the advantage of an argument. However great the talents of the judges, however extensive their learning, they are never safe in deciding without an argument. Some judges of the greatest learning make it a rule that no opinion which they have given without argument shall be binding upon themselves or on others. The greatest judges have sometimes changed their opinions on argument. They ought always to have the aid of the talents of the bar before pronouncing their opinion. The right of being heard, and the practice of arguing all questions, has more than anything else preserved the uniformity of the common law." *Deb. Mass. Conv.* 1820, pp. 489, 490. Accordingly, the Convention proposed the annulment of the article which permitted such interrogation of the judges, and in an address to the people thus stated the reasons for so doing: —

"We think this provision ought not to be a part of the Constitution, because, — *First.* Each department ought to act on its own responsibility. *Second.* Judges may be called on to give opinions on subjects which may afterwards be drawn into judicial examination before them by contending parties. *Third.* No opinion ought to be formed and expressed by any judicial officer affecting the interest of any citizen but upon full hearing according to law. *Fourth.* If the question proposed should be of a public nature it will likely partake of a political character, and it highly concerns the people that judicial officers should not be involved in political or party discussions. We therefore recommend that this second article should be annulled." Ibid. p. 629.

Upon submission to the people the article of amendment embodying this recommendation was lost, by a vote of 12,471 yeas to 14,518 nays. Ibid. p. 633.

In like manner the Convention of 1853 proposed the annulment of the provision, but the entire Constitution framed by that body was rejected by the people. In Massachusetts, therefore, a proposition which received the approval of the leading lawyers and judges of the Convention, of all parties, and which involved simply a legal or constitutional question, was twice voted down by a majority consisting largely of farmers, mechanics, and tradesmen; though it is fair to say that, upon the last occasion, their hostility to the amendments proposed may have been directed partly or wholly to other provisions.

For a statement of the classes of questions, proper and improper to be submitted under provisions of the kind we are considering, see 10 Cl. & Fin. Ch. R. 200; 37 Mo. R. 135; 51 Mo. R. 586; 55 Mo. R. 497; 58 Mo. R. 469; 64 N. C. R. 785–796; 122 Mass. R. 600; 126 Mass. R. 557, 562; 5 Metc. R. 596; 9 Cush. R. 604.

F.

At the extra session of the New York legislature, in November, 1820, a bill passed both houses, by the provisions of which a Convention was to be called, without referring the question to the people in the first instance. Delegates were to be chosen in February, 1821, and the Convention was to assemble in June following. This bill was sent to the Council of Revision, who returned it with the following objections, drawn up by Chancellor Kent, and concurred in by his Excellency Governor Clinton, and Chief Justice Spencer, and dissented from by Justices Yates and Woodworth, — Justices Van Ness and Platt being absent.

In Assembly, November 20, 1820.

Objections of the Council to the bill calling a Convention. In Council of Revision, November 20, 1820, —

Resolved, That it appears improper to the Council that the bill, entitled "An Act recommending a Convention of the people of this State," should become a law of this State.

1. Because the bill recommends to the citizens of this State to choose by bal-

lot, on the second Tuesday of February next, delegates to meet in Convention, for the purpose of making such alterations in the Constitution of this State as they may deem proper, without having first taken the sense of the people whether such a Convention, for such a general and unlimited revisal and alteration of the Constitution, be, in their judgment, necessary and expedient.

There can be no doubt of the great and fundamental truth, that all free governments are founded on the authority of the people; and that they have at all times an indefeasible right to alter or reform the same, as to their wisdom shall seem meet. The Constitution is the will of the people, expressed in their original character and intended for the permanent protection and happiness of them and their posterity; and it is perfectly consonant to the republican theory and to the declared sense and practice of this country that it cannot be altered or changed, in any degree, without the expression of the same original will. It is worthy, therefore, of great consideration, and may well be doubted, whether it belongs to the ordinary legislature, chosen only to make laws in pursuance of the provisions of the existing Constitution, to call a Convention in the first instance, to revise, alter, and perhaps remodel the whole fabric of the government, and before they have received a legitimate and full expression of the will of the people that such changes should be made.

The difficulty of acceding to such a measure of reform, without the previous approbation of the constituents of the government, presses with peculiar force and with painful anxiety upon the Council of Revision, which was instituted for the express purpose of guarding the Constitution against the passage of laws "inconsistent with its spirit."

The Constitution of this State has been in operation upwards of forty years, and we have but one precedent on this subject, and that is the case of the Convention of 1801. But it is to be observed that the Convention in that year was called for two specific objects only, and with no other power or authority whatsoever. One of these objects was merely to determine the true construction of one of its articles, and was not intended to alter or amend it; and the other was to reduce and limit the number of the Senators and Members of Assembly. The last was the single alteration proposed; and perhaps, even with respect to that point, it would have been more advisable that the previous sense of the people should have been taken. But there is no analogy between this single and cautious case and the measure recommended by the present bill, which is not confined to any specific object of alteration or revisal, but submits the whole constitutional charter with all its powers and provisions, however venerable they may have become by time and valuable by experience, to unlimited revisal. The Council have no evidence before them, nor does any legitimate and authentic evidence exist, that the people of this State think it either wise or expedient that the entire Constitution should be revised and probed, and perhaps disturbed to its foundation.

The Council, therefore, think it the most wise and safe course, and most accordant with the performance of the great trust committed to the representative powers under the Constitution, that the question of a general revision of it should be submitted to the people in the first instance, to determine whether a Convention ought to be convened.

The declared sense of the American people throughout the United States on this very point cannot but be received with great respect and reverence; and it appears to be the almost universal will expressed in their constitutional charters that Conventions to alter the Constitution shall not be called at the instance of the legislature without the previous sanction of the people by whom those Constitutions were ordained.

The Constitution of Massachusetts was established in 1780, and contains the earliest provision on this subject. It provided that, in the year 1795, the sense of the people should be taken on the necessity or expediency of revising the Constitution; and that if two-thirds of the votes of the people were in favor of such revision and amendment, the legislature should provide for calling a Convention. The Convention now sitting in that State was called in consequence of a previous submission of such a question to the people. The Constitution of South Carolina was ordained in 1790; and in that it is declared that no Convention shall be called unless by the concurrence of two-thirds of both branches of the legislature. And the Constitution of Georgia, established in 1798, contains the same provision; thus showing, that though the people be not previously consulted on the question, yet a more than ordinary caution and check upon such a measure was indispensable. The Constitution of Delaware, of 1792, declares very emphatically that no Convention shall be called but by the authority of the people, and that their sense shall be taken by a vote for or against a Convention; and that if a majority of all the citizens shall have voted for a Convention, the legislature shall make provision for calling one. The same constitutional provision, that no Convention shall be called to alter or amend the Constitution, until the sense of the people by vote shall have been previously taken, whether, in their opinion, there was a necessity or expediency for a revision of the Constitution, has been successfully adopted, by the Constitution of New Hampshire, in 1792; by the Constitution of Tennessee, in 1796; by the Constitution of Kentucky, in 1799; by the Constitution of Louisiana, in 1812; by the Constitution of Indiana, in 1816; by the Constitution of Mississippi, in 1817; and by the Constitution of Illinois, in 1818.

It would, as the Council apprehend, be impossible to produce higher and more respectable authority in favor of such a provision, and of its value and safety.

2. Because the bill contemplates an amended Constitution, to be submitted to the people to be adopted or rejected, *in toto*, without prescribing any mode by which a discrimination may be made between such provisions as shall be deemed salutary and such as shall be disapproved by the judgments of the people. If the people are competent to pass upon the entire amendments, of which there can be no doubt, they are equally competent to adopt such of them as they approve, and to reject such as they disapprove; and this undoubted right of the people is the more important if the Convention is to be called in the first instance without a previous consultation of the pure and original source of all legitimate authority. And it is worthy of consideration, and gives additional force to the expediency and fitness of a previous reference to the people, that time will be thereby given for more mature deliberation upon questions arising upon the Constitution, which are always momentous in their nature and calculated to affect not the present generation alone but their distant posterity, and when the legislature may probably have it in their power to avail themselves of a more

just and accurate apportionment of the representation in the Convention among the several Counties in this State.

Ordered, That the Secretary deliver the bill, together with a copy of the objections aforesaid to the Honorable Assembly.

J. V. N. YATES,
Secretary.

INDEX.

A.

B.

M.

P.

R.

www.ingramcontent.com/pod-product-compliance
Lightning Source LLC
LaVergne TN
LVHW100022220926
848483LV00001BA/100
* 9 7 8 1 6 1 6 1 9 3 5 1 5 *